M000265872

What's Wrong with Rights?

Praise for *What's Wrong with Rights*

'This scholarly, but nonetheless most readable, book makes an important contribution to the debate about to be had when the UK government takes forward its promised (some would say threatened) new Commission on the Constitution, Democracy and Human Rights. No stranger to controversy, Professor Biggar argues in effect that the assertion of human rights has got out of hand. He pulls no punches and takes no prisoners. This is a penetrating examination of the relationship between rights and responsibilities and reflects many of the concerns expressed in Jonathan Sumption's 2019 Reith Lectures.'

Lord Simon Brown of Eaton-under-Heywood,
former Justice of the Supreme Court of the UK

'*What's Wrong With Rights?* is one of the most remarkable scholarly achievements I know of: it deftly addresses a wide variety of theoretical and practical problems of great normative importance; it engages with a vast and complex legal, philosophical, and theological literature about the morality of rights; it articulates plausible assessments of the most important contributions to that literature; and perhaps most importantly, the topics it addresses are at the very heart of political discourse in contemporary liberal polities. I cannot recommend it more highly.'

Christopher Eberle, Professor of Philosophy
at the United States Naval Academy, Annapolis

'With the noble post-World War II human rights project increasingly imperiled by misunderstanding and manipulation, Nigel Biggar's new book is a major contribution to clear thinking about what we mean when we speak of rights. Whether or not they agree with his conclusions, friends of human rights everywhere should welcome this timely and informative analysis of what's wrong with rights and what needs to be done to put them right.'

Mary Ann Glendon, Learned Hand Professor of
Law at Harvard University and author of *Rights Talk* (1991)

'Despite its eye-catching title, this book is neither a rejection of rights as such nor of natural morality, but a keen-eyed critique of natural rights in particular. In a discussion both dazzlingly wide-ranging and compellingly concrete, Nigel Biggar shows how natural rights talk undermines appropriate acknowledgement of the contingent, circumstantial character of political and ethical judgments. We do well to recognize that rights are paradigmatically legal and enrich ethical discourse by attending to virtues and duties as much as to rights. *What's Wrong with Rights* is the most significant Christian ethical contribution to reflection on rights since Nicholas Wolterstorff's *Justice: Rights and Wrongs*.'

Jennifer Herdt, Gilbert L. Stark Professor
of Christian Ethics at Yale Divinity School

'*What's Wrong With Rights?* is magisterial, combining theology, intellectual history, and detailed attention to particular cases and examples. "Rights" are, in fact, esteemed highly by Biggar, but only when they are allowed to function properly, by being placed within a more capacious framework, not itself limited to the notion of individual and competing rights. Morality properly operates with a plenitude of concepts, where rights emerge as the conclusion, rather than being the premises and first principles. What is needed is attention to the particularity of circumstances, against the widest possible view of human flourishing and its constitutive goods. The writing is clear, passionate, energetic, and vivid. Biggar is not afraid of making controversial judgements and works towards them in a manner that is honest and transparent, always commanding respect. At a deeper level, his book invites the reader to engage in debates about rights, maybe to disagree, but to do so from within a richer moral tradition, which actually gives more opportunity for insight, nuance, and dissent. The possibility arises of not only better judgements, but better disagreements. Both robust and generous, this landmark book represents a leading theological ethicist writing at the height of his powers.'

Christopher Insole, Professor of Philosophical
Theology and Ethics at Durham University

'Rights talk has dominated public discourse for the past seventy years. But our political disagreements are worse than ever. Nigel Biggar not only explains what happened, he also proposes a comprehensive way forward. We need to move beyond "rights fundamentalism", and retrieve a richer public discourse that emphasizes duty, virtue, and the concrete challenges facing a political community. Crossing the boundaries of theology, philosophy, history, and law, Biggar's incisive analysis shows why talking about "natural rights" isn't helpful: defining, defending, and balancing rights always requires well-functioning legal institutions.'

Cathleen Kaveny, Darald and Juliet Libby Professor
of Law and Theology at Boston College

'*What's Wrong with Rights?* is a finely crafted review of the history of rights and an insightful assessment of contemporary discussions across a range of disciplines and contexts. Nigel Biggar raises important basic questions for theology, ethics, and law, and this book will reshape our ways of thinking about rights in all three fields.'

Robin W. Lovin, Cary M. Maguire University Professor
Emeritus of Ethics at Southern Methodist University, Dallas

'This is a critique of one of most fashionable and incoherent notions of our time, the idea that there are enforceable rights, 'natural' or 'human', that exist independently of collective human choice. It is original, thought-provoking, and carefully reasoned. Such rights have many supporters, and always will have. But they should not be taken seriously unless they are willing to engage with the ideas in this impressive book.'

Lord Jonathan Sumption, QC, former Justice
of the Supreme Court of the UK

'*What's Wong With Rights?* is a timely, wide-ranging, and historically informed book that subjects the prevailing human rights culture, in its various manifestations, to a strong dose of Burkean scepticism. Philosophers will be provoked by his thesis that rights are paradigmatically the creatures of law and form no part of natural morality. Lawyers will be challenged by the vigorous criticisms of what Biggar views as the illegitimate employment of rights vocabulary as a mean of enforcing the moral and political views of an "oligarchy of judges". This is an iconoclastic book that deserves to be reckoned with in the serious conversation about the nature and limits of rights that we desperately need.'

John Tasioulas, Yeoh Professor of Politics,
Philosophy, and Law at King's College London

'This is a cleverly titled, crisply written, and largely clear-eyed engagement with the history, concept, and limits of rights and right talk in the Western tradition and beyond. Nigel Biggar brings a big analytical mind and deft pen to the task – and a pair of sharp elbows too. He engages a substantial library of human rights scholarship and case law with critical acuity and philosophical originality, concluding with a cautious and conditional endorsement of rights.'

John Witte, Jr, Robert W. Woodruff Professor of Law and McDonald
Distinguished Professor at Emory University School of Law,
and Director of the Center for the Study of Law
and Religion at Emory University

What's Wrong with Rights?

NIGEL BIGGAR

UNIVERSITY PRESS

OXFORD
UNIVERSITY PRESS

Great Clarendon Street, Oxford, OX2 6DP,
United Kingdom

Oxford University Press is a department of the University of Oxford.
It furthers the University's objective of excellence in research, scholarship,
and education by publishing worldwide. Oxford is a registered trade mark of
Oxford University Press in the UK and in certain other countries

© Nigel Biggar 2020

The moral rights of the author have been asserted

First Edition published in 2020

Impression: 4

All rights reserved. No part of this publication may be reproduced, stored in
a retrieval system, or transmitted, in any form or by any means, without the
prior permission in writing of Oxford University Press, or as expressly permitted
by law, by licence or under terms agreed with the appropriate reprographics
rights organization. Enquiries concerning reproduction outside the scope of the
above should be sent to the Rights Department, Oxford University Press, at the
address above

You must not circulate this work in any other form
and you must impose this same condition on any acquirer

Published in the United States of America by Oxford University Press
198 Madison Avenue, New York, NY 10016, United States of America

British Library Cataloguing in Publication Data
Data available

Library of Congress Control Number: 2019955331

ISBN 978–0–19–886197–3

Printed and bound in Great Britain by
Clays Ltd, Elcograf S.p.A.

Links to third party websites are provided by Oxford in good faith and
for information only. Oxford disclaims any responsibility for the materials
contained in any third party website referenced in this work.

Ad Virginiam, sine qua non

Acknowledgements

In the course of preparing to write this book, and of writing it, I accumulated considerable debts of gratitude to the following: David Bentley, formerly Legal Counsellor in the UK's Foreign Office and Professor of Law at the University of East Anglia, for comments on Chapters 10 and 11; Theo Boer, Professor of Ethics at the Protestant Theological University, Groningen, for advice on recent developments in the Dutch debate on assisted suicide and voluntary euthanasia; John de Bono, QC, for comments on Chapters 10, 11, and 12; Simon Brown, Lord Brown of Eaton-under-Heywood and formerly Justice of the Supreme Court of the UK, for comments on Chapters 10, 11, and 12; Thomas Brudholm, Associate Professor in the Department of Cross-Cultural and Regional Studies at the University of Copenhagen, for helping me gain sight of a report issued by the Danish Institute for Human Rights; Patrick Bury, formerly Captain in the British Army's Royal Irish Regiment, for providing an expert sounding-board for my views on the intention to kill in combat; Roger Crisp, Professor of Moral Philosophy at the University of Oxford, for advice on the influence of Thomas Hobbes; Jeremy Hill, formerly Legal Adviser in the UK Representation in Brussels and HM Ambassador to Bulgaria and Lithuania, for tempering my scepticism about the European Court of Human Rights (albeit not as much as he would have liked); Jonathan Morgan, Senior Lecturer in Law at the University of Cambridge, for comments on Chapter 10; Sarah Mortimer, Associate Professor of Early Modern History at the University of Oxford, for comments on Chapter 6; Onora O'Neill, Baroness O'Neill of Bengarve, for advice on relevant writings of her own; James Orr, University Lecturer in Philosophy of Religion at the University of Cambridge, for enlightenment about 'factualism'; Andrew Shamel, D.Phil. candidate in the Faculty of Theology at the University of Oxford and my research assistant, for conducting a literature search regarding Chapter 8 and for drafting the bibliography; Stevan Veljkovic, also a D.Phil. candidate in the Faculty of Theology and my research assistant, for conducting a literature search on 'closed material procedures', which enabled me to decide not to write a thirteenth chapter; John Witte, Robert Woodruff Professor of Law and Director of the Center for the Study of Law and Religion at Emory University, for advice on the allegedly humanist education of Calvinists; and to Paul Yowell, Associate Professor of Law at the University of Oxford, for comments on Chapters 10, 11, and 12.

Progress on this book was very considerably advanced by the two periods of research leave afforded me by Oxford's Faculty of Theology, one in 2015 and the other in 2018–19. For this, I am very grateful to the Faculty, as well as to my colleague, Professor Joshua Hordern, who assumed many of my academic responsibilities during my absence. Equally, I am grateful to fellow-members of the Chapter of Christ Church Cathedral, who covered my cathedral duties while I was away.

I was privileged to begin my research leave in 2015 as a visiting fellow at the Center for Theological Inquiry in Princeton, where Dr Will Storrar and Professor Robin Lovin hosted me. I thank them, together with the McDonald Agape Foundation, which generously funded my visit there.

A little of what follows has already appeared in print elsewhere: part of Chapter 6 has been published as 'What's Wrong with Subjective Rights?' in *History of European Ideas*, 45 (2019); Chapter 7 was built out of 'Imprudent Jurisprudence? Human Rights and Moral Contingency', *Journal of Law and Religion*, 30/3 (October 2015) and 'Individual Rights versus Common Security? Christian Moral Reasoning about Torture', *Studies in Christian Ethics*, 27/1 (February 2014); and Chapter 9 comprises a reworking and developing of Chapter 5 of *In Defence of War*. Accordingly, I thank Cambridge University Press, Oxford University Press, Sage Publications, and Taylor & Francis for their kind permission to use these materials in the present work.

Finally, I thank my wife, Ginny, for everything. This book is dedicated to her.

Contents

Contents

Introduction

I

I did not know the answers when I began this book, but I did know some of the questions. Over eight years ago, when I was working on what would become *In Defence of War*,[1] I noticed how David Rodin's formidable critique of 'just war' thinking was largely based on a conception of 'a right to life', while the 1,500-year-old Christian tradition of such thinking, which he ignored, operated largely without any concept of rights at all. Did this mean that the Christian tradition was *passé*, having been overtaken by enlightened liberal individualism, as Rodin appeared to think, or did the older tradition contain wisdom that Rodin had neglected? Since I am a Christian and since I was unsympathetic to the pacifist tendency of Rodin's conclusions, I was naturally inclined to suspect the latter. In chapter 5 of *In Defence of War* I attempted to prove my suspicion, not without success, but afterwards I felt that my answer to the question was less than crystal clear. There was more work to be done—and it now appears in Chapter 9.

That was one stimulus to begin work on this book. Another, related one comprised the judgements of the European Court of Human Rights (ECtHR) in a series of cases about the conduct of British troops in Iraq. It seemed to me that the jurisprudence was alarmingly imprudent, partly because the court comprised a majority of judges whose countries had no living tradition of sending troops abroad, whose historical imaginations were accordingly limited, and whose political assumptions were inclined to be unsympathetic. Consequently, I experienced the judgements as those of a *foreign* court, and for the first time I began to take an interest in arguments that the UK should free itself from the ECtHR's jurisdiction. Chapter 10 is devoted to analysing the relevant jurisprudence, testing my hunches, and, as it happens, substantiating them.

A third stimulus was also jurisprudential. In 2004 I published a book on the ethics of suicide and euthanasia, in which I had come to the conclusion that it would be unwise to make physician-assisted suicide or voluntary euthanasia legal.[2] My judgement was an all-things-considered one, and I was aware that reason could be found on both sides of the argument. In the years that followed I noticed

---

[1] Nigel Biggar, *In Defence of War* (Oxford: Oxford University Press, 2013).
[2] Nigel Biggar, *Aiming to Kill: The Ethics of Suicide and Euthanasia* (London: Longman, Darton, and Todd, 2004).

that attempts were being made to get the UK Supreme Court to declare that Parliament's refusal to legalise assisted suicide was incompatible with the European Convention of Human Rights, and that a minority of judges in the Nicklinson case of 2014 had thought that that was exactly what the court should do. The following year, in the Carter case, the Supreme Court of Canada did the equivalent, judging that the legal prohibition of assistance in suicide was in violation of the Canadian Charter of Rights and Freedoms, and directing the Canadian Parliament to revise the law accordingly. Since, in my view, the arguments for and against legalisation were finely balanced on controvertible judgements about social costs and risks, I wondered, doubtfully, how it was that an oligarchy of judges presumed to take to themselves the responsibility for making such a politically controversial decision. Chapter 11 develops my sceptical wondering into an argument.

A further motivation that has propelled this book was rooted in my work both on the ethics of killing and on the ethics of war. As a proponent of the view that it can be justified to kill deliberately, and that the justification is more permissive in war, I believed that it can be morally justified deliberately to cause very serious, very painful, and sometimes even lethal harm. In this light, observing the debates about torture in the wake of the attack on New York's Twin Towers on 11 September 2001, I was led to wonder what was supposed to make water-boarding and its like so morally unacceptable. What exactly is it that makes torture absolutely wrong? I ventured two article-length forays into this question, which appeared in early 2014 and late 2015.[3] Chapter 7 builds on them and achieves, I believe, a more carefully nuanced conclusion.

Fifth, my thinking about political 'reconciliation' after civil conflict (especially in South Africa and Northern Ireland), which began in the late 1990s, had taught me that political peace is a very great good indeed, without which not much human can flourish at all; that achieving it can sometimes warrant the rethinking of justice and even justify its compromise; and that whatever justice is possible for humans within history is haphazard, fragmented, and sometimes merely symbolic. The implication is that what justice is achievable will vary according to circumstances. What applies to justice applies also to rights. That is one theme in Chapter 8.

But there is another, balancing theme, too. My first visit to Hong Kong in 2013 introduced me to the Confucian tradition of 'just war' thinking, and revealed that two civilisations, which had developed quite independently of each other for millennia, have produced ethics of war that share many of the same principles.[4]

[3] Nigel Biggar, 'Individual Rights versus Common Security? Christian Moral Reasoning about Torture', *Studies in Christian Ethics*, 27/1 (January 2014); 'Imprudent Jurisprudence? Human Rights and Moral Contingency', *Journal of Law and Religion*, 30/3 (October 2015).
[4] One result of the conference that I attended was the publication of Ping-cheung Lo and Sumner B. Twiss, eds, *Chinese Just War Ethics: Origin, Development, and Dissent* (London: Routledge, 2015).

What this means is that, notwithstanding the variety of local, circumstantial instantiations, the basic principles of justice can still be universal.

Finally, ever since the 1980s I have been aware that some Christian ethicists believe that the very notion of a 'subjective' right—that is, a right as the property of an individual—is morally suspect. I began to examine that thesis at the inaugural conference of the McDonald Centre for Theology, Ethics, and Public Life in May 2009, which was devoted to discussing Nicholas Wolterstorff's book *Justice: Rights and Wrongs*.[5] In my paper I argued against some of the sceptics and in defence of Wolterstorff's view that the concept of subjective rights lies deep in biblical tradition and deserves a place in Christian thought.[6] Here, in Chapter 5, I offer a more wide-ranging—and critical—assessment of Wolterstorff's theory, and in Chapter 6 I undertake a more comprehensive treatment of the issue.

II

When, in April 2015, I began work on *What's Wrong with Rights?*, I fondly imagined that I would push out a small volume of four or five efficient chapters by Christmas of the same year. But writing, like war, has a habit of postponing conclusion. So here I am on the cusp of completion, four years and twelve chapters later. I soon discovered, of course, that the literature on rights is vast and straddles a range of academic disciplines. Consequently, I had to conduct some painstaking reconnaissance to discern where I, as a Christian ethicist, could add value to the myriad discussions already under way, and where I had an interest in doing so. The result is a book that addresses a selection of questions. All the questions are, I think, important ones, but there are other important questions that go unanswered, indeed, unasked. Seven chapters each treat a discrete question or problem, but five are devoted to the same one: the issue of natural rights. Once I had decided to tackle that basic, conceptual issue, the requirements of a sufficiently thorough answer demanded either a single chapter the length of a small book or a series of chapters of more normal size. I opted for the latter, mainly for the sake of clarity of organisation and of argumentative control, but partly to give the reader pause for breath along the way.

In what follows, the reader will not find the systematic presentation of a fully worked out theory of rights, with circumspect defence against all likely critics. My thinking is organised as a response to a variety of questions. It is not oriented

---

[5] Nicholas Wolterstorff, *Justice: Rights and Wrongs* (Princeton: Princeton University Press, 2008).
[6] Nigel Biggar, 'Nicholas Wolterstorff, *Justice: Rights and Wrongs*', *Studies in Christian Ethics*, 23/2 (April 2010).

toward answering a single, focal question or articulating a theory from Olympian first principles. Nevertheless, as I have worked out what I think, I have sought to make sure that the emergent view of rights is coherent across the chapters. I have no doubt that the answers I have given here will themselves raise further questions, to which no answers are offered. That means that the answers I have given are not yet known to be ultimately secure. However, since ultimate security is generally in short supply in this world, I am content to offer answers that I think are strong enough as far as they go.

Although I do not offer a systematic theory of rights here, I do endeavour to think out of a coherent ethical point of view. I am both a Christian believer and a professional Christian ethicist. Whenever I think, I try to think as I believe a Christian should, and I have sought to do that here, too. This is not the place to give either a full account or a full defence of my Christian ethic, but it is the place to make plain to the reader certain assumptions that the arguments in this book will make. One basic assumption is that there is such a thing as 'natural morality'. By this I mean simply a body of ethical principles that are objective or real, in the sense that, rather than being the whimsical creatures of human desire or choice, they precede and structure them. In other words, belief in natural morality is a form of moral realism (as in moral 'reality'). The objective or real principles of morality are the various elements or 'goods' of human flourishing, together with the norms of conduct—whether dispositional virtues or rules of action—that their protection and promotion generate. That is, these principles stem from the flourishing that is specific to all beings who share human nature. Hence: 'natural morality'.

I am a moral realist, because I am a Christian. Christians are monotheists, believing that a single, internally coherent, benevolent, divine intelligence is the ground and source of all that is. From this theological belief follows a belief about the world that God has created: that it is, at base, rationally ordered, both physically and morally. Human moral agents choose and act in a world that is already objectively morally structured. In no small part, that is what belief in God means. Christians, of course, are not the only ones who believe this. Among religious believers, other monotheists—at least—believe it too. It is true that such moral realism was very unfashionable in Western, non-religious philosophical circles for decades after the Second World War, when logical positivism first taught that moral statements, being empirically unverifiable, were meaningless, and emotivism followed by teaching that they were merely the expressions of subjective feeling. Nevertheless, moral subjectivism did not reign supreme, partly since many lawyers, troubled by the fact that recent Nazi atrocities had been entirely legal according to Nazi law, recognised the need to invoke a higher, supra-positive, trans-cultural moral authority. And in recent decades, moral realism has enjoyed something of a resurgence in philosophy—as was signalled by Peter Singer's admission in 2011 that Derek Parfit's argument in favour of objectively real values had persuaded him to modify his preference utilitarianism.[7] We shall find further evidence when we come to consider James Griffin's work in Chapter 5.

Again, this is not the place to develop a full-scale defence of moral realism. However, should any readers be inclined to doubt it, my opening response would be to invite them to contemplate the following two implications. The first is that, if there is no objective moral reality, then rights lack moral justification and have only the same amoral, conventional status as, say, racist law that denies rights to Jews or blacks. The second is that if there is no universal moral reality, the phenomenon of moral principles and insights shared by different human cultures that have developed entirely independently of each other is difficult to account for. A reader might be provoked to retort that the explanation lies in the universal, amoral, evolutionary drive to survive, of which 'morality' world-wide is nothing but the conventional instrument. If so, I would point out the irony that such a Hobbesian, materialist, naturalist reading of evolution in fact denies that humans have evolved morally at all, for it tells us that, at base, we are all still driven by the primordial fear of pain and death. I would then observe that such a reading is empirically unrealistic and implausible, for humans have evidently evolved to the point, not only where we care about a wide range of goods (or values), including rational integrity and justice, but also where we are willing to risk pain and death for their sake. Human evolution may be natural, but nature is manifestly capable of generating non-material values. Nature, it seems, is not naturalistic.[8]

In addition to belief in natural morality, my Christian point of view disposes me to be sensitive to the limited power of human creatures. We humans do not have the power to avoid or relieve or rectify every instance of human suffering and injustice; and if we do not recognise our creaturely limits, then we risk compounding the problem. Sometimes, it is better to accept tragedy and learn to live with it, than to deny it desperately, ruthlessly. I acknowledge that this acceptance could amount to complacent acquiescence, but as a Christian I am forbidden to indulge in it. On the contrary, believing in the God who raised Jesus bodily from the dead, I am obliged to hope for a radically better world and to be alert to whatever fresh opportunities to adumbrate it the constraints of tragedy afford me. Therefore, I must stand between pessimism and optimism, uneasily. Whatever the grounds of my Christian faith and hope, at least it enables me to look tragedy

---

[7] See Peter Singer, 'The Most Significant Work in Ethics since 1873', *Times Literary Supplement* (20 May 2011); and Charles C. Camosy, *Peter Singer and Christian Ethics: Beyond Polarization* (Cambridge: Cambridge University Press, 2012), pp. 217–18.

[8] See Nigel Biggar, 'Evolutionary Biology, "Enlightened" Anthropological Narratives, and Social Morality: A View from Christian Ethics', *Studies in Christian Ethics*, 26/2 (2013). At least one eminent, and still atheist, philosopher now argues that mind and value are quite as basic to our cosmos as matter: Thomas Nagel, in *Mind and Cosmos: Why the Materialist Neo-Darwinian Conception of Nature is Almost Certainly False* (New York: Oxford University Press, 2012).

honestly in the eye, and not to wish it away. And I am inclined to think that whatever enables honest perception must itself be close to reality.

A further feature of my Christian viewpoint that will find implicit expression in my consideration of rights is the notion of 'sin'—the idea that all human beings are predisposed to love the wrong things or to love the right things wrongly, and as a result to do both themselves harm and others injustice. What this means is that the idea of the possibility of abusing rights is entirely familiar to me, and that the questions of how to exercise them well or badly, and of how to form citizens in the virtues that dispose to the former, are obvious ones. So is the idea of the possibility that, sometimes, we should not exercise our rights at all. After all, the founder of Christianity himself waived his moral right to just self-defence, and its developer, St Paul, urged Christians not to exploit their rightful freedom from Jewish law to the full, out of love for less liberated brethren and for the sake of peace within the Christian community. In brief, to a Christian it is obvious that there is much more to right than rights.

I do not claim that all the views I have just described are distinctively Christian. Whether or not they are distinctive depends entirely on what they are being compared with. I have no doubt that they are very distinctive in relation to some alternatives (e.g. moral relativism, libertarianism, Nazism), but less so in relation to others (non-theistic moral realism, Kantianism, secular humanism). Probably, as a total package, they are unique. But I do not much care whether these views are distinctive or even unique. All that really matters is whether they are true and supportive of human dignity. I believe that they are, and so I have striven in this book to think within their terms.

III

Before I release the reader into what follows, let me make two comments on my method and offer one set of conceptual and terminological clarifications. To begin with, in the first six chapters readers will find themselves faced with a lot of intellectual history, and at times they might wonder quite where my argument is going—perhaps, where it is at all. The rationale for discussing intellectual history in Chapter 6 is that the question of when subjective rights-talk first came onto the scene, and in what intellectual context, *is* the main issue. In Chapters 1 to 5, the point of showing the history of natural rights-talk is immediately to bring to the surface the variety of concepts and rhetoric, and the purposes they have served. But the ultimate aim is to enable us to get behind familiar, contemporary rights-talk, in order to unearth earlier, alternative forms, and thereby enable critical comparisons that raise questions about what passes for common sense among us, which we would not otherwise think to ask. In other words, visiting the past helps us acquire critical leverage on the present. Doing this is second nature to theologians, who are generally inclined to think that the past might still have something to teach the present, populated as it is by finite, sinful minds. It is not second nature, however, to many philosophers, who tend to see the present as the latest stage in the inexorable, upward intellectual progress of human reason, and for whom the past contains only that which has been sifted, found wanting, and discarded.

My second methodological comment is on the fact that, at many points, readers will find themselves confronted with sizeable blocks of exposition, where I describe what X, Y, and Z have to say. Some might find this pedestrian and, again, wonder where the argument is. If so, my response would be this. In order for analysis and criticism to be accurate and fair, the object of analysis and criticism has first to be well understood. Therefore, before I set about analysing and criticising, I strive to represent as succinctly and clearly as I can what the object actually is in its own terms. In the first place, this enables me to keep a close eye on the accuracy and fairness of my own responses; but in the second place it enables the reader to measure what I think about the object against the object itself. Besides, if the reader does not much like what I have to say, at least she might benefit from my careful exposition of what others have to say.

In fact, readers will find strong hints of what I myself think in the course of my construing intellectual history and expounding other bodies of thought. However, if they just cannot stand the tension and have to peek at the denouement—or at least if they think that it would help them enjoy the journey more, if they knew the destination better—the concluding section of every chapter will tell them directly what I am thinking, and the Conclusion of the whole book will tell them what, in the end, I have decided.

IV

In the course of what follows a variety of concepts of 'right', and a variety of terms that denote them, will appear. In the hope of sparing the reader some of the bewilderment that the author originally suffered when he first met them, let me explain the variety here.

First of all, there is 'moral right', without the indefinite article. This is 'what is morally right', and will often depend upon circumstances. Whereas the act of killing another human being, for example, is morally wrong when done just for fun, it can be morally right when done to defend innocent others against lethal harm.

Insofar as 'moral right' is understood to be rooted in the constant nature of reality, or more specifically in the constant nature of the reality of human being, it is 'natural (moral) right'—again, without the indefinite article.[9]

---

[9] Sometimes this natural moral right is referred to as 'natural law', and stands in contrast to 'positive law', that is, law posited by a particular human community.

With the indefinite article, 'a right' is the property of an individual or corporate body. It is a claim to some freedom or benefit that lies, more or less securely, in their possession and is available to be asserted against threats.

What is meant by 'a right' is exactly the same as what is meant by 'a subjective right', a term that we will meet often in Chapter 6. 'A subjective right' is the property of a human subject or individual; it stands in contrast to 'objective right', which is objectively real 'moral right'.

My view is that a right or a subjective right is paradigmatically 'a legal right'. This is a right that is granted by a particular legal system, which acquires its security through the social authority of law and the prospect of enforcement by the police and the courts. I regard a legal right as paradigmatic, partly because it seems that the concept of a right first entered the bloodstream of Western culture through the thinking of thirteenth-century canon (or church) lawyers, but mainly because the context of supportive social attitudes and institutions explains its distinctive authority as a claim.

Crucial to my argument is the view that 'a right', being paradigmatically legal, is stricter, more stable, and more secure than 'moral right'. It is stricter in the sense that the conditions under which one person may interfere with another are more tightly drawn. It is more stable in the sense that its claim is more precisely defined, so as to be justiciable. And it is more secure in the sense that the claim is backed by the authority of social institutions.

In contrast to a legal right, 'a natural right' is supposed to exist entirely outside of civil society and apart from supportive social institutions. It is sometimes said to exist in 'a state of nature', which can refer to a state of Edenic or Rousseauvian innocence, but usually refers to a condition of anarchy—either before the construction of social institutions or after their collapse. An obvious instance of this would be war between parties who share no commonly recognised conventions.

In Chapters 2 and 6, the reader will encounter two significantly different conceptions of such a state of nature. One is that propounded by Thomas Hobbes, where in the absence of social conventions or contracts, there is no natural, moral law or right at all. For Hobbes moral right arises out of social contracts; it does not precede them. If follows that Hobbes's talk of 'a natural right' misleads, since it connotes a claim that carries moral authority, where there is no such authority to carry.

The alternative conception is that held by Hugo Grotius and John Locke, for whom, in the absence of social institutions the natural, moral law still reigns. Therefore, for example, even where the parties to a war are not constrained by the terms of any common convention, they still remain bound by natural moral norms. Here talk of 'a natural right' is an appeal to moral right that is natural in the sense of preceding social conventions.

The reader should beware, however, that sometimes 'a natural right' does not refer to a state of nature at all. Sometimes it is merely shorthand for 'an actual legal right that is justified by natural, moral right' or 'a claim that, since it is morally justified, *should become* actually legal'.

'A human right' is a kind of natural right, since it is a moral claim that is supposed to be grounded in human nature or, more exactly, in the constant dignity that is the possession of every human being. Talk of human rights became increasingly common after the Second World War in reaction against the idea that the only rights that exist are those posited by a particular legal system—and that where, say, Nazi law in Germany denies legal rights to German Jews, the latter simply have no rights. Gainsaying this, the idea of human rights asserts that German Jews, alongside African Americans and Chinese Uighurs, possess certain moral claims even where positive legal systems deny them.

When human rights are said by advocates to be 'universal', what is meant is that they should find the same or similar legal expression in every political society. Such an assertion is contested by Asian and African critics who regard human rights as more Western than human. I shall argue that rights are universal in the more limited sense that the phenomenon of a more or less legal right (probably) appears in every society, though which rights are granted, and how securely, will vary according to cultural and political circumstance.

Finally, 'an absolute right' can be one that is unconditional, subject to no qualifications. In particular, the Hobbesian natural right, existing in a state of nature where there is no moral law, is absolute in the sense of being immune to any qualification by moral duties. More generally, any right whose definition incorporates conditions is absolute in the sense of pre-empting further qualification. What is usually meant by 'an absolute right', however, is different and more interesting: namely, a right against a kind of action supposed to be intrinsically wrong, which, therefore, must always be granted and may never be suspended. The paradigm of an absolute right is that against torture.

The historical variety of different concepts of 'right', often closely related and sometimes overlapping, and the use of the same terms to refer to different things, is undoubtedly confusing and will tend to confuse. I hope, however, that this preliminary explanation will at least save the reader avoidable grief.

1

Are there Natural Rights?

1: The Sceptical Tradition

I

A right is natural when it is not legal. A legal right is one that is granted by the law of a particular society, whether national or international. A natural right is one that is not granted by law, but that is supposed to exist anyway. If it lacks legal authority, it carries moral authority instead. Its importance, therefore, is that it can be appealed to in the absence of a legal right and in criticism of the legal status quo. In jurisdictions where assistance in suicide is illegal, for example, some people claim that there is a natural, moral right to assisted suicide and that, therefore, there should be a legal one, too.

Nowadays, we tend to talk less of natural rights and more of human ones. They do not always mean quite the same thing, but they can do. Insofar as 'human rights' refer to those rights affirmed in international declarations or conventions subscribed to by states, especially since 1948, they have a kind of legal status. However, when the phrase is used less strictly to refer to rights that any human being—anyone participating in human nature—is supposed to possess, regardless of whether they are recognised by law, then 'a human right' means the same thing as 'a natural right'.

The claim that there are natural rights, which exist before or outside of any ordered civil society and apart from any positively legal expression, has long been controversial. As we are about to see, there is a tradition of scepticism about such rights, stretching at least from the late eighteenth century to the present day. My purpose in this opening chapter is to expound four eminent expressions of this Sceptical Tradition, with a view to distilling it into a set of objections. The subsequent four chapters will then test these objections against natural rights-talk, first, in the pre-modern period (Chapter 2), second in the modern period (Chapter 3), then in modern Roman Catholic thought (Chapter 4), and finally as it comes from the pens of a selection of contemporary defenders (Chapter 5).

II

A classic early critique is the one mounted by Edmund Burke (1729–97) against the French Declaration of the Rights of Man and of the Citizen in 1789. Burke complains that natural rights are too abstract to have a determinate meaning susceptible of evaluation. We cannot evaluate anything related to human actions, he tells us, 'on a simple view of the object as it stands stripped of every relation, in all the nakedness and solitude of metaphysical abstraction. Circumstances... give in reality to every political principle its distinguishing colour, and discriminating effect. The circumstances are what render every civil and political scheme bene-ficial or noxious to mankind.'[1] So, for example, we cannot approve of liberty as such, unless we wish to license madmen and murderers. We cannot tell whether or not liberty is a blessing, until we see how it is combined with government, public force, and property.[2]

Implicit in the problem of abstraction is that of absoluteness. The alleged natural rights of men 'admit no temperament, and no compromise'.[3] 'The pre-tended rights of these [French] theorists are all extremes', he writes, whereas 'the *real* rights of men... are in a sort of *middle*, incapable of definition, but not impossible to be discerned... often in balances between differences of good; in compromises sometimes between good and evil, and sometimes, between evil and evil'.[4] Hence the importance of creating rights, not by philosophers' fiat, but by 'the science of jurisprudence, the pride of the human intellect... [which] is the collected reason of ages, combining the principles of original justice with the infinite variety of human concerns'.[5]

The asserted absoluteness of natural rights is a recipe for the dissolution of society. When entering into civil society, 'the first fundamental right of uncoven-anted man, that is, to judge for himself, and to assert his own cause', and 'the right to self-defence, the first law of nature', must be abandoned: 'Men cannot enjoy the rights of an uncivil and of a civil state together'. Burke continues:

> Government is a contrivance of human wisdom to provide for human *wants*. Men have a right that these wants should be provided for by this wisdom. Among these wants is to be reckoned the want, out of civil society, of a sufficient restraint upon their passions... the restraints on men, as well as their liberties, are to be reckoned among their rights. But as the liberties and the restrictions vary with times and circumstances, and admit of infinite modifications, they cannot be settled upon any abstract rule...[6]

In effect, according to Burke, talk about natural rights is political rhetoric that legitimates indiscriminate and imprudent revolution. '[T]hat vague speculative right' exposes 'their sure [political] inheritance to be scrambled for and torn to

---

[1] Edmund Burke, 'Reflections on the Revolution in France (1790)', in *The Writings and Speeches of Edmund Burke*, ed. Paul Langford, 9 vols, Vol. VIII: 'The French Revolution, 1790–1794', ed. L. G. Mitchell and William B. Todd (Oxford: Clarendon Press, 1989), p. 58.
[2] Ibid., p. 58.   [3] Ibid., p. 109.   [4] Ibid., pp. 109, 112. The emphases are Burke's.
[5] Ibid., pp. 145–6.   [6] Ibid., pp. 110–11. The emphasis is Burke's.

pieces by every wild litigious spirit.'[7] 'The worst of these politics of revolution is this; they temper and harden the breast . . . This sort of people are so taken up with their theories about the rights of man, that they have totally forgot his nature.'[8] The merits of inherited laws and political constitutions are 'confirmed by the solid test of long experience, and an increasing public strength and national prosperity'.[9] 'Nor is it a short experience that can instruct us in that practical science [of reforming a commonwealth]; because the real effects of moral causes are not always immediate.'[10] Therefore, rather than embark on the revolutionary 'fabrication of a new government', reform should be 'carefully formed upon analogical precedent'.[11] For 'by preserving the method of nature in the conduct of the state, in what we improve, we are never wholly new; in what we retain we are never wholly obsolete'.[12]

Burke's critique of the Rights of Man, however, is not the whole story. As Michael Freeman has shown, Burke often appealed to 'real', 'essential', 'true', 'genuine' natural rights in defending subjects against tyrannical government: to 'the real essential rights of mankind' and 'the common rights of men' in defence of American colonists (1774, 1777), 'the rights of human nature' in defence of Irish Catholics (1782), and 'the natural rights of mankind' and 'the rights of humanity and the laws of nature' in defence of the Indian people (1783).[13] How can we best explain these affirmations of natural rights in the light of the critique that we have just analysed? One possibility is simply that Burke changed his mind after the French Revolution. Telling against that, however, is his appeal to 'the true and genuine rights of men' in praise of revolution in Poland, which he made in 1791 *after* the publication of his *Reflections on the Revolution in France* in November 1790.[14] We need to reflect further.

First of all, what was Burke thinking of when he invoked 'natural rights' affirmatively? Sometimes he means liberties or powers that obtain in a state of nature—as in the quotation above: 'the first fundamental right of uncovenanted man, that is, to judge for himself, and to assert his own cause' and 'the right to self-defence, the first law of nature'.[15] It is not immediately clear here whether Burke's concept of the state of nature is Hobbesian or Grotian—that is, whether it is a morality-free zone where atomic individuals are engaged in a constant,

---

[7] Ibid., p. 83.   [8] Ibid., p. 115.   [9] Ibid., p. 108.   [10] Ibid., p. 111.
[11] Ibid., p. 81.   [12] Ibid., p. 84.
[13] Michael Freeman, *Edmund Burke and the Critique of Political Radicalism* (Oxford: Basil Blackwell, 1980), p. 86. With regard to the oppression of Indians in 1783, Burke said that 'the natural rights of mankind are indeed sacred things; and if any public measure is proved mischievously to affect them, the objection ought to be fatal' ('Speech on Fox's East India Bill [1 December 1783]', in *Writings and Speeches*, Vol. V: *India: Madras and Bengal, 1774–1785*, ed. Peter James Marshall and William B. Todd (Oxford: Clarendon Press, 1981), pp. 383–4). Freeman comments that 'sacred' 'is not a term he ever used lightly' (*Burke*, p. 87).
[14] Freeman, *Burke*, p. 86. Freeman observes that Burke felt the need to distinguish 'real' rights (presumably from false ones) as early as 1774, long before the French Revolution (ibid.).
[15] Burke, 'Reflections', p. 110.

no-holds-barred struggle to survive, or whether it is a zone where individuals are constrained by common responsibility to the natural law. However, since Burke did sometimes appeal to a culturally transcendent moral law, we should assume the latter.[16] When he refers to natural 'right', therefore, he means a liberty or power that is morally justified outside of civil society. Nevertheless, it is clear that Burke regards with horror any actual state of nature as a condition where the power of natural law to restrain wicked human behaviour is negligible, and which therefore amounts in practice to violent anarchy. His searing experience of the Gordon Riots of 1780 had impressed deeply upon him the irrationality of mob violence and the fragility of civilised life.[17] Accordingly, he viewed the vision of a state of nature unburdened by social institutions such as law and property, which was propagated by Rousseau (1712–78), as a dangerous fantasy.[18] We may fairly say that Burke's view is Grotian in principle, but Hobbesian in practice. Accordingly, civil society is *much* to be preferred:

> Abstract principles of natural right had been long since given up for the advantages of having, what was much better, society, which substituted wisdom and justice, in the room of original right. It annihilated all those natural rights and drew to its mass all the component parts of which those rights were made up ... [19]

This brings us to a second sense in which Burke sometimes speaks of 'natural rights', namely, as those positive, legal rights that a civil society either does or should grant and uphold, in order to secure natural goods, the constituents of flourishing proper to human nature. Thus, in *Reflections* he writes:

---

[16] For a general account of Burke's relation to the traditions of natural law thinking, which is characteristically astute and nuanced, see Christopher J. Insole, 'Burke and Natural Law', in David Dwan and Christopher J. Insole, eds, *The Cambridge Companion to Edmund Burke* (Cambridge: Cambridge University Press, 2012). Insole judges that Burke drew his ideas of natural law from Cicero rather than Aquinas (ibid., pp. 120–1)—*pace* Russell Kirk ('Burke and Natural Rights', *The Review of Politics*, 13/4 (October 1951), p. 442). Referring to Burke's 1762 'Fragments of a Tract on the Popery Laws', F. P. Lock comments that, in criticising the anti-popery laws in Ireland for exceeding what the public interest required and intending humiliation, 'Burke's use of natural-law arguments supplies some of the strongest evidence of the "natural-law interpretation" of his thought' (*Edmund Burke*, 2 vols, Vol. I: *1730–1784* (Oxford: Clarendon Press, 1998), p. 194; Vol. II: *1784–1797* (Oxford: Clarendon Press, 2006), p. 320). Lock also reports that Burke criticised the rapacious manner of Admiral Sir George Rodney's capture of the Dutch island of St Eustacius in 1781, arguing that the admiral had violated the unwritten 'law of nations' that is to be found 'in the heart', and which governs war, even though there is 'no positive law of nations, no general established laws framed and settled by acts in which every nation had a voice' (Vol. II, pp. 494–5). David Bromwich comments that Burke probably had in mind here authorities such as Grotius, Pufendorf, and Vattel (*The Intellectual Life of Edmund Burke: From the Sublime and Beautiful to American Independence* (Cambridge, Mass.: Harvard University Press, 2014), p. 489 n. 42).

[17] Lock, *Burke*, I, p. 469.   [18] Kirk, 'Burke and Natural Rights', pp. 442–3.

[19] Edmund Burke, 'Speech on Repeal of Test and Corporation Acts (2 March 1790)', in *Writings and Speeches*, Vol. IV: *Party, Parliament, and the Dividing of the Whigs, 1780–1794*, ed. Peter James Marshall and Donald Bryant (Oxford: Clarendon Press, 2015), p. 310.

In denying their false claims of right, I do not mean to injure those which are real, and are such as their pretended rights would totally destroy. If civil society be made of the *advantage* of man, all the *advantages* for which it is made become his right...Men have a right to live by that rule [of law];...a right to justice...a right to the fruits of their industry, and to the means of making their industry fruitful...a right to the acquisitions of their parents; to the nourishment and improvement of their offspring; to instruction in life, and to consolation in death.[20]

An advantage is an element of human flourishing, that is, a good. Therefore, 'natural rights' are those civil rights that are or would be justified by natural moral law, because they secure natural goods. Insofar as a civil society's laws fail to grant such rights, the latter are 'natural' in the sense that, according to natural law, they *should* be (but have not yet been) granted or posited; insofar as society's laws do grant them, the resultant positive rights are 'natural' in the sense of being morally justified by natural law:

The rights of men, that is to say, the natural rights of mankind, are indeed sacred things; and if any public measure is proved mischievously to affect them, the objection ought to be fatal to that measure, even if no charter at all could be set up against it. If these natural rights are clearly defined and secured against chicane, against power, and authority, by written instruments and positive engagements, they are in a still better condition.[21]

Given the actual, anarchic state of nature, as opposed to Rousseau's dangerously alluring fantasy, natural rights have little hope of being secured outside of civil society and its institutions. And since, according to natural law, they *should* be secured, and since civil society is required to secure them, there is a sense in which '[t]he state of civil society...is a state of nature...For man is by nature reasonable; and he is never perfectly in his natural state, but when he is placed where reason may be best cultivated, and most predominates. Art is man's nature.'[22]

However, the exact legal form in which a given civil society should seek to secure natural goods will vary according to that society's circumstances. Therefore, paradoxically, those civil rights are most natural, in the sense of being justified by natural law, which are most prudently artificial—that is, those which have been most aptly formulated by practical reason to secure natural goods in the circumstances that prevail. Morally justified rights are those that mediate prudently between natural goods and historical conditions. 'All

[20] Burke, 'Reflections', pp. 109–10. The emphases are mine.
[21] Burke, 'Speech on Fox's East India Bill', pp. 383–4.
[22] Edmund Burke, 'Appeal from the New to the Old Whigs', in *Writings and Speeches*, IV, p. 449.

government . . . is founded on compromise and barter', Burke tells us. 'We balance inconveniences; we give and take; we remit some rights, that we may enjoy others.'[23] '[T]he decisions of prudence (contrary to the system of the insane reasoners) . . . are determined on the more or the less, the earlier or the later, and on a balance of advantage and inconvenience, of good and evil.'[24] Therefore, as we have already seen above,

> [t]he rights of men are in a sort of *middle*, incapable of definition, but not impossible to be discerned. The rights of men in government are their advantages; and these are often in balances between differences of good; in compromises between good and evil, and sometimes between evil and evil . . .[25]

Accordingly, natural rights—that is, civil rights that secure natural goods—will vary in their exact shape from society to society:

> These metaphysic rights entering into common life, like rays of light which pierce in to a dense medium, are, by the laws of nature, refracted from their straight line. Indeed in the gross and complicated mass of human passions and concerns, the primitive rights of men undergo such a variety of refractions and reflections, that it becomes absurd to talk of them as if they continued in the simplicity of their original direction. The nature of man is intricate; the objects of society are of the greatest possible complexity . . .[26]

Natural rights, according to Burke, are always rights that either do find lodgement, or aspire to find it, in a well-functioning civil society. Otherwise, they cannot achieve their purpose—the effective securing of natural goods. It follows, therefore, that real, genuine natural rights are not the false, abstract, inapt, imprudent ones invoked by revolutionaries to upend civil society, license anarchy, and then install themselves as tyrants:

> Massacre, torture, hanging! These are your [false] rights of men! These are the fruits of metaphysic declarations wantonly made, and shamefully retracted! . . . . The leaders [of the French Revolution] tell [the people] of their rights, as men, to take fortresses, to murder guards, to seize on kings . . . and yet these leaders

---

[23] Edmund Burke, 'Speech on Conciliation with America (22 March 1775)', in *Writings and Speeches*, Vol. III: *Party, Parliament, and the American War, 1774–1780*, ed. Warren M. Elofson, John A. Woods, and William B. Todd (Oxford: Clarendon Press, 1996), p. 157.
[24] Edmund Burke, 'Letter to Sir Hercules Langrishe (1782)', in *Writings and Speeches*, Vol. IX: *I. The Revolutionary War, 1794–1797; II. Ireland*, ed. R. B. McDowell and William B. Todd (Oxford: Clarendon Press, 1991), p. 600.
[25] Burke, 'Reflections', p. 112. The emphasis is Burke's.   [26] Ibid.

presume to order out the troops...to coerce those who shall judge on the principles, and follow the examples, which have been guaranteed by their own approbation.[27]

III

Famously, Jeremy Bentham (1748–1832) exclaimed that '*Natural rights* is simple nonsense; natural and imprescriptable rights, rhetorical nonsense—nonsense upon stilts.'[28] He, too, was responding specifically to the French Declaration of the Rights of Man; and his several objections are very similar to Burke's.

The first was that natural rights are too indefinite and absolute to be either clearly true or prudent. They are the products of 'hasty generalisation, the bane of prudence', comprising 'words and propositions of the most unbounded signification, turned loose without any of those exceptions or modifications which are so necessary on every occasion to reduce their import within compass, not only of right reason, but even of the design in hand'.[29] In the Declaration could be found '[s]carcely an article, which in rummaging it, will not be found a true Pandora's box'.[30] Take, for example, Article X, according to which, 'No one ought to be molested [meaning, probably, by government] for his opinions, even in matters of religion, provided that the manifestation of them does not disturb [better expressed perhaps by saying, except in as far as the manifestation of them disturb, or rather tends to the disturbance of] the public order established by the law.'[31] Bentham comments: 'Observe how nice, and incapable of being described beforehand by any particular marks, are the lines which mark the limits of right and wrong in this behalf—which separate the useful from the pernicious—the prudent course from the imprudent!—how dependent upon the temper of the times— upon the events and circumstances of the day!'[32]

The second element in Bentham's complaint is that talk of natural rights (and behind them, of government based on social contract) is meant to function primarily as rhetoric legitimating revolutionary subversion and tyranny. Take Article I, which claims that '[m]en [all men] are born and remain free, and

---

[27] Ibid., pp. 268–9.
[28] Jeremy Bentham, 'Anarchical Fallacies; being an Examination of the Declaration of Rights Issued during the French Revolution', in Jeremy Waldron, introd. and ed., *Nonsense on Stilts: Bentham, Burke, and Marx on the Rights of Man* (London: Methuen, 1987), p. 53. The emphasis is Bentham's.
[29] Ibid., p. 48.   [30] Ibid., p. 49.
[31] Ibid. The qualifications in square brackets are Bentham's.
[32] Ibid., p. 64. Jeremy Waldron qualifies Bentham's claim, before agreeing with it. He observes that the Declaration does in fact subject the natural rights to exceptions and limitations, but only in the latter parts of the document 'where they would not detract too much from the appearance of absolutism so far as the particular rights were concerned' (ibid., p. 39). Further, where the qualifications are revealed 'they are inevitably cast in language so vague as to undermine *any* force (let alone any *absolute*) force that the initial claims may have had' (ibid.). The emphasis is Waldron's.

equal in respect of rights...'.[33] '*All men are born free? All men remain free?*', queries Bentham, testily. 'All men, on the contrary, are born in subjection.'[34] 'All governments that we have any account of [have] been gradually established by habit, after having been formed by force.' 'The origination of governments from contract is pure fiction...'[35] The aim of the Declaration, he asserts, was 'to excite and keep up a spirit of resistance to all laws—a spirit of insurrection against all governments'. It assumes a posture of domineering self-righteousness, asserting that '[i]n us [the framers of the Declaration] is the perfection of virtue and wisdom: in all mankind besides, the extremity of wickedness and folly. Our will shall consequently reign without control...' 'What is the real source of these imprescriptible rights—these unrepealable laws?', asks Bentham, rhetorically. His answer: 'Power turned blind by looking from its own height: self-conceit and tyranny exalted into insanity.'[36] Natural rights are 'the spawn of despotism... When a man is bent upon having things his own way and gives no reason for it, he says: I have a right to have them so.'[37]

A further element is bound up with the second: the Declaration's affirmation of natural rights serves to reinforce 'the selfish and dissocial passions... [which are] already but too strong'.[38] Consequently, it fosters anarchy. Positive, legal rights to property restrain liberty; without the specification of proprietary rights, 'every man has a right to everything', and 'what is every man's right is no man's right'.[39]

Fourth, Bentham holds that the moral rightness of rights depends on social utility and so upon social circumstances. Properly, rights presuppose political society and law. Article II claims that '[t]he end in view of every political association is the preservation of the natural and imprescriptible rights of man. These rights are liberty, property, security, and resistance to oppression.' However, for Bentham, there *are* no natural rights prior to legal rights in a particular polity.[40] Without government, there are no laws; without laws, no rights; and without rights, no security or property or liberty from stronger individuals. If there are no natural rights, there are no absolute ones: talk of absolute natural rights that no government can abrogate at all is 'terrorist language'. Only 'in proportion as it is *right* or *proper*, i.e., advantageous to the society in question, that this or that right—a right to this or that effect—should be established and maintained, in that same proportion... is [it] *wrong* that it should

---

[33] Ibid., p. 49.   [34] Ibid. The emphasis is Bentham's.   [35] Ibid., p. 55.

[36] Ibid., p. 54.

[37] Jeremy Bentham, 'Supply Without Burthen or Escheat *Vice* Taxation: being a proposal for a saving of taxes by an extension of the law of escheat: including strictures on the taxes on collateral succession, comprised in the budget on 7th December, 1795', in Waldron, *Nonsense on Stilts*, p. 73. Waldron comments: Bentham's legal positivism was 'grounded firmly in a sense of the human advantages of determinate, posited forms of social organisation', and his complaint was that the proponents of natural rights were responding over-dramatically to bad law by calling for the revolutionary overthrow of the entire system of government (ibid., p. 41).

[38] Bentham, 'Anarchical Fallacies', p. 48.   [39] Ibid., pp. 57, 58.   [40] Ibid., p. 52.

be abrogated'.[41] A sensible legal right needs to be specified in terms of the time and circumstances in which it holds: 'the right itself must be specifically described, not jumbled with an indistinguishable heap of others, under any such vague general terms as property, liberty, and the like'.[42] Article IV fails to meet this requirement, when it claims that '[l]iberty consists in being able to do that which is not hurtful to another, and therefore the exercise of the natural rights of each man has no other bounds than those which insure to the other members of society the enjoyment of the same rights. These bounds cannot be determined but by the law'. Bentham comments:

> What liberty?—as against what power? as against coercion from what source? . . . this liberty, this right, which is one of the four rights that existed before laws, owes all the boundaries it has, all the extent it has, to the laws. Till you know what the laws say to it, you do not know what there is of it, nor what account to give of it: and yet it existed, and that in full force and vigour, before there were any such things as laws . . .[43]

Along the same lines he writes elsewhere: 'What a legal right is I know. I know how it was made. I know what it means when made. To me a right and a legal right are the same thing, for I know of no other . . . Right is with me the child of law . . . A natural right is a son that never had a father.'[44] And further:

> The dictates of reason and utility are the result of circumstances which require genius to discover, strength of mind to weigh, and patience to investigate: the language of natural rights require nothing but a hard front, a hard heart, and an unblushing countenance . . . question it, or so much as ask for a proof of it, you are whatever is most odious, sinning equally against truth and against conscience. The strength of this argument is in proportion to the strength of the lungs in those who use it . . . ultimately it depends upon the sharpness of the daggers which he who uses it has in his pocket.[45]

IV

David Ritchie (1853–1903), a moral philosopher in Oxford and St Andrews at the end of the nineteenth century, is now as little known as Burke and Bentham are famous.[46] Nevertheless, his substantial—and sometimes deliciously ironic—

---

[41] Ibid., p. 53. The emphases are Bentham's.   [42] Ibid., p. 54.   [43] Ibid., p. 60.
[44] Bentham, 'Supply Without Burthen', p. 73.   [45] Ibid., p. 74.
[46] In all my reading of contemporary literature on rights, I came across only one reference to Ritchie—in Margaret MacDonald, 'Natural Rights', in Jeremy Waldron, ed., *Theories of Rights*, Oxford Readings in Philosophy (Oxford: Oxford University Press, 1984), p. 33.

critique, *Natural Rights: A Criticism of Some Political and Ethical Conceptions*,[47] continues to be cited (and republished), as it deserves to be.[48]

Ritchie shares with his more famous predecessors a concern about the abstract nature of natural rights, although in his case inspiration came from Hegel (1770–1831). 'Abstract thinking', Ritchie comments, is 'the habit of taking up a formula which may be true enough in its context, isolating it from the surroundings that made it valuable, and carrying it out regardless of consequences.'[49] So instead of 'vague and rhetorical appeals to the Law of Nature', '[w]e can only allow natural rights to be talked about in the sense in which natural rights mean those legal or customary rights which we have come to think or may come to think it most advantageous to recognise'.[50] In other words, natural rights as absolute, lacking information by social exigency and qualification by social circumstance, and so obtaining universally, always and everywhere, do not exist.

For example, there is no general, unconditional natural right to life. '[W]hether preservation of life is to be guaranteed or not must surely depend on whether the life is valuable to the society or injurious to it, or whether, though not valuable, or even to some extent injurious, other considerations of general security, etc., make it expedient to give the preservation of such life the support of the organised force of the community.'[51] To sharpen his point, he adds the ironic observation that '[t]he principle that there is an inalienable and imprescriptible right in all men to preserve their lives, however much social utility may demand the sacrifice of some lives . . . would lead to a rapid disappearance of the civilised men who adopted such a principle before barbarians who did not . . . '[52]

As with life, so with liberty: there is no unconditional natural right to it. '[I]f [anyone] supposes that for liberty *as such* . . . there is any a priori justification as against the claims of "restraint" *as such*, or "interference" *as such*, he has become prey to the old fallacy which consists in taking relative terms as absolute.'[53] Whether the negative liberty of being let alone is good or bad depends on what occasions, in what places, and by whom.[54] And whether the positive liberty to do something is good or bad depends on the goodness or badness of what is to be done.[55] Such positive liberty depends 'upon the existence of elaborate social arrangements, and on a strong and stable government':[56] 'The intermediate meanings, which *seem* to make the principle of equal freedom a plausible account of what justice is, all presuppose an orderly fabric of society in which the rights of individuals are settled for them by a fixed system of law.'[57] 'The principle that the

---

[47] David G. Ritchie, *Natural Rights: A Criticism of Some Political and Ethical Conceptions* (London: Swan Sonnenschein, 1895).

[48] E.g., Stanley I. Benn, 'Rights', in Paul Edwards, ed., *The Encyclopedia of Philosophy* (New York and London: MacMillan, 1967), p. 199. In 2002 Routledge saw fit to republish Ritchie's *Natural Rights* for the fifth time since 1894.

[49] Ritchie, *Natural Rights*, p. 66.   [50] Ibid., p. 270.   [51] Ibid., p. 119.

[52] Ibid., p. 120.   [53] Ibid., p. 136. The emphases are Ritchie's.   [54] Ibid., p. 138.

[55] Ibid., p. 139.   [56] Ibid.   [57] Ibid., p. 147. The emphasis is Ritchie's.

liberty of every one should be limited only by the equal liberty of every one else ... is a principle which is either absurd or anarchical, or both.'[58]

Take, for example, the right to equal free speech. Outside of a particular society or association and its particular social rules, it does not exist.[59] 'Any absolute claim of equal freedom on the part of every individual could only mean the break up of the society.' For that reason, there are no 'natural rights of bores and buffoons'.[60] To avoid anarchy, therefore, the liberty of free expression of opinion has to be restricted. In determining what those restrictions should be, however, appeal to the principle of natural rights is no help at all.[61] Rather, we must look to the requirements of social order. Accordingly, a strong despotism might be able to afford a right to freedom of thought, which a 'free government' could not, since the 'necessity of homogeneity , , , may compel or seem to compel a degree of intolerance which is not necessary under a strong despotism'.[62]

What is true of life and liberty, is also true of equality *as such*.[63] Against both Thomas Hobbes (1588–1679) and John Locke (1632–1704), Ritchie writes that '[h]ow far equality should practically be applied in determining the rights of citizens is a matter that cannot be decided a priori by any reference to Nature, but must be settled in every case by some compromise, based on a consideration of what is safe, when the maintenance of security against external enemies and the avoidance of discontent at home are both considered'.[64]

Take the case of the right to vote: '[o]n whom the suffrage should be conferred is a matter not to be settled a priori, but by reference to the particular circumstances of the country. In this, as before, we have to consider what is safe, regard being had both to external and internal dangers—the latter including the discontent that is apt to arise from the refusal of political rights that are enjoyed by others.'[65] Ritchie seems sympathetic to the argument that a high property qualification is a necessary safeguard against the political instability that would follow from political power falling into the hands of the ignorant and reckless.[66] Nevertheless, he concedes that '[t]he partisan use which can always, unfortunately, be made of the grievance of an excluded class, is indeed one argument for universal suffrage'.[67]

However, it is regarding property that '[t]he confusions which permeate the theory of natural rights come out most conspicuously of all'.[68] What appears to be

---

[58] Ibid., p. 148.   [59] Ibid., pp. 143, 144, 145.   [60] Ibid., p. 145.   [61] Ibid., p. 152.
[62] Ibid., p. 149.
[63] Here Ritchie refers to American, rather than French, declarations of rights: the US Declaration of Independence ('all men created equal'), the Mississippi Declaration of Rights (1817), and the Alabama Declaration (1819: 'all freemen, when they form a social compact, are equal in rights') (ibid., pp. 244, 245).
[64] Ibid., p. 248. Observing Locke's argument that, in the state of nature, all 'creatures of the same species and rank' are born 'to [cf. "with"] the same advantages of Nature and the use of the same faculties' (*Treatise* II, s. 4), Ritchie wonders what determines sameness of natural rank (Ritchie, *Natural Rights*, p. 256).
[65] Ritchie, *Natural Rights*, p. 255.   [66] Ibid., p. 255.   [67] Ibid., p. 257.
[68] Ibid., p. 263.

a natural right to property, according to Locke, is actually the first occupier's natural right to own the best, leaving what remains to those who follow. It cannot mean the equal right of everybody to ownership of the best, for that, Ritchie wryly observes, would result in 'a vast amount of natural litigation, i.e., fighting'. The justification of the property right of the first occupier, therefore, lies in its social convenience: it avoids anarchy. It is 'natural' only in the sense of being, all social things considered, morally justified.[69]

The truth is that we cannot know what a natural right to property means, or whether it exists, without knowing what it implies and under what circumstances. What objects may be held as property? Can we hold slaves, for example? And how far does the right over these objects extend? Is it a right merely to use, or a right to use up? Is it a right to destroy or to alienate? Or is it a right to bequeath, and, if so, with or without limitation?[70] To answer these questions is to specify the right in terms of certain conditions. The 1858 Kansas Bill of Rights claimed, in unqualified terms, that each individual's right of property in—and control of—his person is natural and inalienable. Presumably, however, this was not supposed to apply to a convicted felon.[71] Further, notwithstanding the appearance of absoluteness in its initial affirmation of a natural right to property, the 1793 version of the French Declaration of the Rights of Man in fact makes it subject to 'public necessity'. Similarly, the US Constitution's up-front affirmation is later qualified by the 5th Amendment, which allows that private property may be taken for public use, albeit not 'without just compensation'. What this last qualification amounts to, comments Ritchie, will depend upon the state of public opinion at any given time.[72] In both the French and US cases, in other words, the opening rhetoric of unconditional, natural rights is effectively undermined by subsequent—and inevitable—qualifications.[73]

Of all the purported natural rights, that of obtaining happiness is the most absurd in its utopian detachment from practical contingency. As Ritchie puts it, eyebrows arched, 'The right, not merely of pursuing but of obtaining happiness, which is named as one of the natural rights of man in most American State Constitutions, may seem, in this world of ours, to be a very large order on the bank of Providence.'[74] In other words, one person's right implies another person's obligation; and since 'ought' implies 'can', another's obligation implies his capability. So if everyone has a natural right to *obtain* happiness, someone must be capable of supplying everyone's happiness, and obliged to do so. But who could that possibly be, short of God Almighty himself?

Ritchie shares with Burke and Bentham a suspicion of the abstract and so absolute character of talk about natural rights. He also shares with them a concern about the tendency of such abstract talk to feed revolutionary anarchy. Early in his

---

[69] Ibid., pp. 266–7.   [70] Ibid., p. 263.   [71] Ibid., p. 264.   [72] Ibid., p. 265.
[73] Ritchie's criticism is the same as Jeremy Waldron's above (see note 32).   [74] Ibid., p. 272.

book he quotes with sympathy the comment made by General Ireton (1611–51) on the Levellers: 'When I do hear men speak of laying aside all engagements to consider only that wild or vast notion of what in every man's conception is just or unjust, I am afraid and do tremble at the boundless and endless consequences of it.'[75] As an alternative, Ritchie, like Burke, strongly commends 'customary law ... which admits of proof by means of precedents ... respect for ... which has contributed so largely to the stability and quiet growth of legal and social institutions ... '.[76] 'The only "law of nature" to which we can listen', he writes,

> must be such as will commend itself to our reason as a statement of the principles of a coherent and orderly society which will not throw away the hard-won achievements of man in his struggle with nature and with barbarism, and which will at the same time be progressive, in the sense of being capable of correcting its own faults. Any 'natural rights' which are incompatible with such a society are only another name for anarchy. 'Nonsense upon stilts' Bentham called them in his *Anarchical Fallacies* ... whoever says, '*Fiat justitia, ruat respublica*', whoever appeals to an abstract justice that is incompatible with the continuance of orderly social organisation is ... talking nonsense—and mischievous nonsense, too.[77]

It will be clear by now that Ritchie has no quarrel with positive, legal rights, which are framed and granted in the light of social exigencies and circumstances. He is even content to let them go by the name 'natural rights', if they are deemed to be necessary for social utility:

> In the chaos of conflicting individual impulses, instincts, desires, and interests, we can find no stable criterion. We must go beyond them to the essential nature of things. But what part of the nature of things is here relevant? Is it not simply— human society? If there are certain mutual claims which cannot be ignored without detriment to the well-being and, in the last resort, to the very being of a community, these claims may in an intelligible sense be called fundamental or natural rights. They represent the minimum of security and advantage which a community must guarantee to its members at the risk of going to pieces, if it does not with some degree of efficiency maintain them ... [78]

In Ritchie's eyes, the main drawback of theories of natural rights is that they assume that we can formulate rights 'irrespective of, and prior to, any

[75] Ibid., p. 11.   [76] Ibid., pp. 31, 37.   [77] Ibid., p. 106.
[78] Ibid., p. 88. Cf. p, 94: 'The person who ... appeals to Nature, finds that *her* doctors disagree: and between them who shall decide? The moment the question comes to be really discussed, considerations of *utility* must come in.' The emphases are Ritchie's.

consideration of society'.[79] Therefore, he writes, 'it has been my chief endeavour to show that particular practical solutions cannot be given a priori, but must depend on time, place, and circumstances'.[80]

What rights there *should be* depends on circumstances, one of which is time. While the idea of moral-political evolution is not absent from Burke's thinking, it is much more explicit in Ritchie's. In part, this is attributable to Darwin's influence: 'The evolution theory compels those who accept it to regard social cohesion and durability as the proof of some degree at least of ethical value and truth.'[81] However, it also owes something to the role that Ritchie gives social utility in determining rights: 'social utility...', he writes 'can be tested...by experience. History is the laboratory of politics.'[82] It bears the impression of Hegel, too, as when he says that in practical affairs progress is made dialectically, from one part truth to another opposing part truth.[83] Thus, the individualism of natural rights, which was justified in reaction against the political conditions of overbearing external authority, is no longer justified in different circumstances: 'The creed becomes something very different when it stiffens into a traditional dogma, isolated from any relation to the opinions to which it was opposed.'[84]

In contrast, recognition of the historical evolution of institutions 'gives us...a much more hopeful outlook than if we felt bound to apply to every age the same unvarying "natural" code of right and wrong'.[85] Slavery, for example, was

> a necessary step in the progress of humanity...[since] [i]t mitigated the horrors of primitive warfare, and thus gave some scope for the growth, however feeble, of kindlier sentiments towards the alien and the weak.... Thus slavery made possible the growth of the very ideas which in course of time came to make slavery appear wrong.[86]

There was a stage in history when slavery, 'being useful to the progress of mankind, was not contrary to what could then have been considered "Natural rights", although when slavery is no longer an institution of progressive societies, it becomes contrary to what people now consider "Natural rights"'.[87] It follows that it is not reference to abstract 'natural rights' that tells us what social improvement should amount to: 'visions of a better society are not suggested by vague, irresponsible oracles of Nature; they are inferences from experience.... The oracles of Nature are dumb, save to those who will compel her to speak by torture,

---

[79] Ibid., p. 115. In relation to this point, he observes presciently that in the USA 'a conflict between modern needs and the theories of the eighteenth century about individual rights may prove harsher and more terrible because of the barriers placed in the way of change' (ibid., p. 115).
[80] Ibid., p. 275.   [81] Ibid., pp. 16–17.   [82] Ibid., p. 103.   [83] Ibid., p. 17.
[84] Ibid., pp. 18–19.   [85] Ibid., p. 103.   [86] Ibid., p. 104.   [87] Ibid., p. 104.

i.e., by experiment; and, where experiment is inapplicable, by rational interpretation of experience.'[88]

In Ritchie's eyes, the most serious flaw in natural rights discourse is its tendency to conflate morality with legality: 'the gravest objection to the whole theory of natural rights is, that it is always tending to confuse the two sets of notions, by representing what may on occasion be moral duties as legal or quasi-legal rights, and by concealing under such ambiguous terms as "can" and "cannot" the difference between "ought" and "is", or between "wish" and "power"'.[89] So, for example, talk about a constitutional right to insurrection is 'anarchical and contradictory':[90] 'When allegiance to the Pope is thrown off... although morally resistance may seem perfectly justifiable and necessary, the appearance of legality... has altogether disappeared.'[91] Consequently, '[d]isobedience to the law of the land... can never be a legal or constitutional right; it may be morally excused, or it may be a moral duty'.[92]

Perhaps because he was not reacting to the immediate threat of revolution, Ritchie is better able than either Burke or Bentham to concede that natural rights-talk does have certain commendable functions. First of all, he appreciates that appeals to the law of nature or to natural rights are best understood as criticisms of existing conventions or authorities: 'The real significance of the appeal to nature is, in the first place, the *negative* element in the appeal; it is an appeal *against* authorities that had lost their sacredness, against institutions that had outlived their usefulness...'[93] It is 'a convenient form of criticism, rather than a good basis for construction'.[94]

Ritchie's second concession is his recognition that natural rights-talk has useful political functions in mollifying popular discontent and raising aspirations. So 'it may very well be argued that the existence of... a formal declaration [of the liberty of the press or of opinion], even if it cannot, without risk of anarchy, be made constitutionally or legally binding, has a very important moral effect in restraining the prejudices or the passions of the multitude. And that is really the chief use which such Declarations [of Rights] serve.'[95] Further, notwithstanding all the problems attending an affirmation of equal rights in the abstract, 'the existence of the ideal of equality in the minds of a people is, of course, an important factor in determining what can be done, what ought to be done, and what is likely to be done'.[96]

Ritchie's affirmation of natural rights discourse is not confined to its critical and politically expedient functions. He goes on to concede that the negative, critical function of natural rights-talk necessarily implies positive, substantive claims: its critical force requires the imagination of 'an ideal code, not merely as the common

---

[88] Ibid., p. 105.   [89] Ibid., pp. 242–3.   [90] Ibid., pp. 239, 240.   [91] Ibid., pp. 240–1.
[92] Ibid., p. 243.   [93] Ibid., p. 13. The emphasis is Ritchie's.   [94] Ibid., pp. 20–1.
[95] Ibid., p. 156. Cf. p. 265.   [96] Ibid., p. 248.

or universal element amid the varieties of human usage [i.e. the *ius gentium*], but distinct from positive human laws, which might very often conflict with this code':[97]

> The truth in the theory of Natural Rights—what gave the theory its practical value—was the belief in 'Nature' as an ideal, the belief in a Divine purpose determining the ends which man should set before him, and the belief that this ideal, this Divine purpose, could be discovered by the use of human reason. The defect of the theory lay, as we have seen, in the tendency to set this ideal in abstract antithesis over against the actual and the historical. In the light of the conception of evolution applied to human society . . . we must think of this ideal, this Divine purpose, as something not existing definitely formed in the mind of any one man however inspired, of any set of legislators however honest and however enthusiastic, but as something gradually revealing itself in the education of the human race.[98]

Here Ritchie endorses a vision of human history as a process of the evolution of human understanding of divinely given purposes or ends, which, through the practical outworking of that evolving understanding, are progressively realised in the world. While his emphasis lies firmly on the historical, changing, circumstantially contingent character of human moral and political understanding, it is quite clear that evolutionary change, as he sees it, is not random and merely subjective; rather, it is objectively and teleologically ordered. What evolves is human understanding (and practical realisation) of the ends that the 'Divine purpose' has 'determined', and in this historical process of human education these ends are progressively revealed. Implicit in this account is the affirmation of human ends that always exist (presumably in the mind of God) and towards which human rationality is always ordered. These ends are given in and with the constant nature of human rationality, and are in that sense 'natural'. Thus, it seems, Ritchie presents us with the rudiments of a kind of natural law theory.

This impression gathers strength when we find Ritchie suggesting, in a manner that does not obviously square with his emphasis on social utility, that natural rights can be generated by the requirements of respect for the rational nature of human individuals. He implicitly endorses a Kantian–Hegelian conception of the particular self as 'the imperfect realisation of a universal reason, one and indivisible throughout the universe, though manifested in countless forms and revealed most clearly to us . . . in the work of the human spirit, that is to say in social institutions, in art, in religion, and where thought seeks to be at home with

---

[97] Ibid., p. 41.   [98] Ibid., p. 286.

itself—in the meditations of the philosopher'.[99] Thus, 'because he *potentially* shares in this consciousness of the universal reason; he may claim the opportunity of developing this potentiality as far as possible'.[100] 'Such a metaphysical conception of the self will not indeed justify an abstract claim to equality in anything and everything, but only to such equality as is required for, and is compatible with, the highest conceivable form of social existence.'[101] Quite how one adjudicates between the good of the individual and the good of society, when they conflict, Ritchie does not say. The most he can manage is to affirm that the good of a community is the criterion of what is right for individuals, but that good is identical with the good of its members: 'A healthy body is a body the parts of which are healthy, but none of which is developed at the expense of the others .... The good for man is always a common good.'[102]

In the end, then, it seems that Ritchie is willing to admit that there might be some rights that are genuinely natural in the sense of being grounded in the rational nature of human beings. But the only natural right he explicitly endorses is a moral right of military intervention for humanitarian purposes. A 'right of aggression', as he terms it, to impose order on a disordered neighbouring state, is analogous to a police-measure and a legitimate form of self-defence. It requires 'the superiority in civilisation of the conquering power'[103] and involves 'the use of force by civilised over barbarous or savage peoples':[104]

A savage or barbarous people, misgoverned by some ferocious or incapable tyrant, cannot be regarded, except conventionally, for some special purpose of international convenience, as an independent nation in the same sense as one of the great powers of Europe. In the interests of humanity we can recognise no absolute right in all governments, however bad, never to be interfered with. We laugh at the Divine Right of Kings, claimed by Stuarts or Bourbons; but the natural right of a king of Dahomey, or of every robber chief or murderous pasha, to be left undisturbed by all civilised nations, is at least quite as absurd .... it is good government that alone legitimises conquest; but it does legitimise it in the minds of those who are prepared to think out questions of right and wrong in the light of actual human experience and not of arbitrary and a priori principles or prejudices.[105]

---

[99] Ibid., p. 96. Cf. p. 252, where Ritchie claims that human equality is better grounded on Kant's rationality than on Bentham's sentience. Shortly afterwards, he claims that the equality of human beings as such consists in their potential membership of common society, of which conception 'the idea of *one* God, as the God of all races of mankind, is an essential element' (ibid., pp. 253–4).
[100] Ibid., pp. 96–7. The emphasis is Ritchie's.   [101] Ibid., p. 97.   [102] Ibid., p. 99.
[103] Ibid., p. 233.   [104] Ibid., p. 235.
[105] Ibid. Nevertheless, Ritchie recognises that this right of interference or (intervention) is not unconditional. It holds only where we can 'reasonably hope to leave things in a better condition that that in which we found them—a better condition for the *individuals* whose national or tribal independence has been interfered with' (ibid.). The emphasis is Ritchie's.

V

Our fourth critic of natural rights discourse belongs, not to the eighteenth or nineteenth centuries, but to the twenty-first. Nevertheless, Onora O'Neill opens one expression of her critique by quoting Burke:

> What is the use of discussing a man's abstract right to food or medicine? The question is upon the method of procuring and administering them. In that deliberation I shall always advise to call in the aid of the farmer and the physician rather than the professor of metaphysics.[106]

O'Neill agrees: abstract (natural) rights to goods and services are pointless without the means to secure them.[107] She develops the thought by extending it to positive and justiciable 'welfare' rights: these, too, are pointless, unless those persons or institutions obliged to provide are specified.[108] 'Liberty' rights—such as those of the French Declaration of 1789 to security of tenure of property, the rule of law, habeas corpus, accountable public administration—are different, since they imply universal first-order duties that need no allocation: they oblige everyone. Yet, first-order duties need second-order duties to enforce them, by punishing breaches or failures of liberty rights, and these second-order duties do need allocation.[109]

A major problem with international universal human rights discourse, O'Neill finds, is that it is 'often muddled or vague, or both' about the allocation of the obligations. So, for example, Article 11 of the 1966 International Covenant on Economic, Social, and Cultural Rights (ICESCR) asserts 'the right of everyone to an adequate standard of living for himself and his family, including adequate food, clothing and housing, and to the continuous improvement of living conditions'; and Article 12 asserts 'the right of everyone to the enjoyment of the highest attainable standard of physical and mental health'. Neither specifies who is responsible for providing the goods.[110] The 1948 Universal Declaration of

---

[106] Edmund Burke, *Reflections on the Revolution in France*, ed. Conor Cruise O'Brien (London: Penguin, 1984), pp. 151–2; quoted by Onora O'Neill in 'The Dark Side of Human Rights', *International Affairs*, 81/2 (2005), p. 427.

[107] An abstract right is one that is very vaguely defined. It need not be merely natural and moral, and can be positive and legal—as we shall discover in Chapter 11 in the case of the right to liberty in the Canadian Charter of Rights and Freedoms. Here, however, Burke is referring to the French Declaration of the Rights *of Man*, and O'Neill to post-1945 international *human* rights. Although both of these sets of rights have been affirmed by political documents that have some legal force, they purport to consist of rights that belong to any and every being that is human, that is, every being that enjoys specifically human dignity because it partakes of constant, universal human *nature*. Therefore, these human rights are natural rights.

[108] O'Neill, 'The Dark Side', pp. 427–8.

[109] Ibid., p. 428; 'Pluralism, Positivism, and the Justification of Human Rights' (2014), in Onora O'Neill, *Justice Across Boundaries: Whose Obligations?* (Cambridge: Cambridge University Press, 2016), p. 131.

[110] O'Neill, 'The Dark Side', p. 429.

Human Rights 'gestures to the thought' that certain obligations lie with states, but confusingly it assigns them indifferently to nations, countries, and peoples as well as states, not all of which 'have the integrated capacities for action and decision-making needed for agency, and so for carrying obligations'. Later documents such as the ICESCR assign obligations to signatory states. This implies, however, that non-signatory states are under no obligation to respect or meet the requirement of the rights, and that the obligations created by signing and ratifying covenants are special, and not in fact universal. It follows that neither are the corresponding rights.[111]

The problem is not simply the failure to allocate duties to capable states. More deeply, it is that states are sometimes incapable: weak or failed states sometimes lack the necessary capacity to enforce the performance of duties and so respect for and realisation of rights.[112] It follows that 'weak states cannot coherently be required to carry tasks for which they are not competent. Nor can weak international institutions. Yet we are constantly tempted to assume that weak states and weak international bodies can carry obligations that exceed their capabilities.'[113]

Like Ritchie, O'Neill entertains the possibility that we should view human rights declarations and covenants as merely rhetorical, setting out 'noble aspirations' and trying to mobilise political support for establishing positive justiciable rights.[114] Unlike Ritchie, however, she thinks such an interpretation problematic, since it would be 'wholly at odds' with ordinary understandings of rights, which are usually seen as claim-rights or entitlements that are valid against those obliged:

> There cannot be a claim to rights that are rights against nobody, or nobody in particular: universal rights will be rights against all comers; special rights will be rights against specifiable others.... If we take rights seriously and see them as normative rather than aspirational, we must take obligations seriously. If on the other hand we opt for a merely aspirational view, the costs are high. For then we would also have to accept that where human rights are unmet there is no breach of obligation, nobody at fault, nobody who can be held to account, nobody to

---

[111] Ibid., p. 431.

[112] O'Neill, 'Pluralism', p. 131; 'From Edmund Burke to Twenty-First Century Human Rights: Abstraction, Circumstances and Globalisation' (2014), in O'Neill, *Justice Across Boundaries*, pp. 146–7.

[113] O'Neill, 'Global Justice: Whose Obligations?' (2004), in O'Neill, *Justice Across Boundaries*, p. 169. For this reason, O'Neill rejects the 'statist' focus of the Universal Declaration of Human Rights (ibid., p. 161), arguing that sometimes non-state actors—religious bodies, non-governmental organisations, or trans-national corporations—are better placed to meet the obligations required to realise rights (ibid., pp. 170–2).

[114] O'Neill, 'The Dark Side', pp. 429–30.

blame and nobody who owes redress. We would in effect have to accept that human rights claims are not real claims.[115]

She concludes that there is in fact 'an awkward gap between rhetoric and reality, since human rights are not pre-conventional and universal, but rather grounded in the special obligations assumed by states'.[116] In other words, the gap is between purported universal, natural, moral rights and positive, legal rights whose correspondent duties signatory states have assumed. We might add that the gap is obscured because the documents blur the distinction.

O'Neill's discussion manifests a thought-provoking equivocation about these natural, human rights. On the one hand, she declares that 'rights shorn of counterpart duties are no more than rhetoric and gesture',[117] and that '[r]ights without counterpart duties are illusory'.[118] This provokes the radical thought that, where no state or any other body is capable of performing the duty necessary to realise a right, *there is no right*. That is to say, the natural right does not exist. Yet, elsewhere O'Neill rows back from this, distinguishing between the (natural) right itself and its effective, institutional realisation.[119] She does not mean, she tells us,

> that those whose lives are led in weak states that cannot secure their rights have fewer rights *in the abstract* than those in strong states. They have exactly and only those rights for which sound arguments can be given, as do those in strong states.... What those in strong states have, and those in weak states lack, is *justiciable* rights; where obligations to respect and enforce are allocated to agents with the necessary capabilities.[120]

This is puzzling. Citizens of a weak state lack justiciable rights, because their state is incapable of performing the duties necessary to realise them. If 'sound arguments' nevertheless assign these 'weak' citizens the same rights *in the abstract* as citizens of a strong and capable state, that can only be because *some agent or group of agents other than their own weak state* is both capable of performing the necessary duties to realise their rights and is not prohibited from realising them by other, more stringent responsibilities, and yet is failing to do what it can, may,

---

[115] Ibid., p. 430. O'Neill's criticism here echoes Maurice Cranston: 'The effect of a Universal Declaration which is overloaded with affirmations of so-called human rights which are not human rights at all is to push *all* talk of human rights out of the clear realm of the morally compelling into the twilight world of utopian aspiration' (*What Are Human Rights?* (London: Bodley Head, 1973), p. 68).

[116] O'Neill, 'The Dark Side', p. 436.   [117] O'Neill, 'Pluralism', p. 130.

[118] O'Neill, 'From Edmund Burke to Twenty-First Century Human Rights', p. 145.

[119] O'Neill: 'the fact that rights cannot be respected or realised unless there are others...who are required to discharge the counterpart duties that can *realise* the right' ('Pluralism', p. 130); 'Unless duties are allocated to individuals and institutions that can discharge them, there can be no *effective* rights' ('From Edmund Burke to Twenty-First Century Human Rights', p. 145). The emphases are mine.

[120] O'Neill, 'Global Justice', p. 176. The emphases are O'Neill's.

and therefore should. The abstract right, then, amounts to a morally justified claim against this other agent that it should do its perfect duty, even in the absence of any conventional or legal obligation. However, to say that 'weak' citizens possess the same rights as 'strong' citizens, albeit 'in the abstract', implies that there *are* in fact always some agents, somewhere, who are capable of meeting the need of the 'weak' citizens and not prohibited by other responsibilities from doing so, and therefore that they *ought* to meet it. It implies that there is always someone who carries a perfect duty. But can we assume that? Can we assume that all human suffering is caused by culpable human action or inaction—and that therefore there is only ever injustice, never tragedy? I doubt it. But if we do not assume it, then the situation might be this: 'weak' citizens have their urgent basic human need, which their own weak state cannot meet; others can only be morally obliged to do what they are able and morally free to do; in a particular set of circumstances, no other agent is, in fact, able and free to meet the 'weak' citizens' need; so, therefore, while other agents bear an imperfect duty to do whatever they can and may, none has a perfect duty to do whatever it takes to meet the need. From this it follows that, in such tragic circumstances, the 'weak' citizens have no right at all. Their natural right 'in the abstract' is indeed illusory. It does not exist.

O'Neill's attachment to abstract, natural rights is stiffened by her critique of the scepticism toward them shown by Burke—and subsequently by Hegel, communitarian philosophers, and many feminists.[121] She doubts that the problem with the French Rights of Man is their abstraction, which she thinks 'unavoidable in all uses of language, since we cannot make every feature or aspect of matters we discuss explicit'.[122] Judging that Burke's concern is that abstract rights obscure the importance of material circumstances such as 'the existing constitutions, conventions, traditions, habits, duties, virtues and sentiments of actual human societies and cultures',[123] she observes, wryly, that '[c]ircumstances, such as the fact that some of our rights have an ancient pedigree, indeed were inherited from our forefathers, seem to me unlikely to be useful'.[124] 'So', she writes,

> if we are to consider how rights are to be realised it is not enough to criticise abstraction. We need to work out *which* circumstances we face at a given time or place, *which* to preserve or protect, *which* to ignore, and *which* to (seek to) change... Taking realistic account of circumstances does not damage rights: ignoring them is likely to undermine attempts to respect or to realise rights... Circumstances indeed matter, and changes in circumstances can create reasons for rethinking human rights and their counterpart duties... Working toward schemes for respecting and realising human rights is a political and practical task, and no evaluation of such schemes can be convincing unless it

---

[121] O'Neill, 'From Edmund Burke to Twenty-First Century Human Rights', p. 142 n. 15.
[122] Ibid., p. 142.   [123] Ibid., p. 143.   [124] Ibid., p. 144.

considers the *full* task, and the ways in which rights and duties have been adjusted to one another, to the available financial and human resources, and to actual cultural and social capacities—and readjusted to changes in these circumstances.[125]

In her appreciation of the circumstantial contingency of rights, not least their *political* contingency, O'Neill is thoroughly Burkean, and self-consciously so: 'In arguing that circumstances may render specific ways of institutionalising rights either beneficial or noxious, Burke may have something useful to tell us.'[126] Nevertheless, she overlooks an important part of Burke's concern about abstract rights. It was not simply that they obscure the importance of prudent implementation. Nor just that they challenge moral, legal, and constitutional tradition. It was also that they give the mantle of moral authority to a reckless, utopian political idealism, which licenses anarchy and thereby creates the conditions for tyranny. In fact, Burke's concern about the political effects of the unconditional rhetoric of abstract rights finds an echo in O'Neill's concern with the aspirational rhetoric of human rights. For this not only undermines the seriousness of rights-claims, but also comprises 'a bitter mockery to the poor and needy', giving rise to expectations whose impossibility generates frustration—and, I would add, inappropriate blame and political cynicism.[127]

VI

From the eighteenth to the twenty-first centuries criticism either of the very concept of natural rights, or at least of some discourse about them, has been persistent and also remarkably consistent. Bentham, Burke, and Ritchie all complain about their abstract character, and O'Neill joins them in lamenting their tendency to inspire an inflated, absolutist rhetoric, which is negligent of the moral importance of circumstances, not least feasibility. According to the first three, the lack of definition—or, better, specification—makes them impossible to evaluate. It also gives them an absolute, unqualified character that encourages the recklessly imprudent throwing off of social and political authorities and restraints, which causes anarchy and, ironically, gives rein to arrogant tyranny. Properly, they tend to say, rights are not (simply) natural, but positive and legal. They presuppose a particular political society and legal framework, incorporate considerations of social utility or good, comprise compromise, and are subject to certain conditions.

---

[125] Ibid., pp. 143, 148, 149. The emphases are O'Neill's.   [126] Ibid., p. 142.
[127] Onora O'Neill, *Toward Justice and Virtue: A Constructive Account of Practical Reasoning* (Cambridge: Cambridge University Press, 1996), p. 133.

To this common critique, David Ritchie adds the important observation that talk about 'natural rights' often unhelpfully confuses natural morality and legality—as we shall see in Chapter 6, where a number of theologians have difficulty distinguishing natural, moral rights from legal ones. And Onora O'Neill contributes clarifying distinctions between liberty rights and welfare rights, and between first- and second-order obligations. She then observes that the assertion of universal welfare rights, without the allocation of obligations to identifiable bodies that are actually capable of meeting them, are pointless—except, perhaps, as aspirational and politically mobilising rhetoric. The problem with such rhetoric, however, is that it makes universal normative claims that, obliging no one in particular, oblige no one at all; and rights that oblige no one are not rights.

Nevertheless, when all is said and done, three of our four critics do affirm natural rights in some sense or other, and with more or less confidence. Appealing to culturally transcendent natural moral law, Burke acknowledges that this grounds moral rights (e.g. of self-defence and punishment) in a state of nature. However, since the state of nature that he has in mind is not the one of Edenic or Rousseauvian innocence, but rather the violent, anarchical one of sinful passions, he seriously doubts the efficacy of such rights apart from social institutions to uphold them. Therefore, Burke's overwhelming emphasis falls on positive, legal rights that are natural in the sense of being justified by natural law, since they secure natural goods prudently, that is, in a manner apt to the particular social, economic, cultural, and political circumstances of a given society.

Ritchie agrees: natural rights-talk makes (some) sense when it means positive, legal rights that, being necessary for social utility, are justified, all moral things considered. Further, he acknowledges that natural rights-talk has the useful function of enabling moral criticism, and he recognises that this implies an affirmation of ideal, natural ends. Indeed, he goes so far as to concede that the rational nature of all human individuals should oblige respect, and that this obligatory respect might be a basic ground of 'natural rights'.

Finally, while she recognises the self-subversive effect of asserting rights in abstraction from consideration of the allocation of duties, and while she sometimes infers from this that such rights are illusory, on other occasions O'Neill is still inclined to affirm natural rights 'in the abstract'.

2

Are there Natural Rights?

2: The Sceptical Critique and Rights before 1776

I

Now that I have distilled four of the most notable expressions of the 200-year-old British tradition of scepticism about natural rights into a set of main objections, I shall proceed to test them.[1] In this chapter, I shall consider how well they tell against the concept of natural rights as it was first articulated and developed in the late medieval and early modern periods—before the US and French Declarations in the late eighteenth century.

II

A seminal moment in the articulation of a concept of a natural right was the fourteenth-century 'Franciscan Controversy' about the status of private property. In 1321 Pope John XXII (1244–1334) launched an attack on the Franciscan doctrine of apostolic poverty, which held that the renunciation of all property rights was essential to the teaching of Christ and his apostles, and so to evangelical perfection.[2] Exactly what caused the Pope to do this is not clear.[3] Concern about the doctrine's institutionally subversive implications for church property and authority seems a likely motive.[4] Beyond this, it is plausible to speculate that the Pope felt the need to counter the more broadly revolutionary, even anarchical, implications of the views of Franciscan apologists like Bonagratia of Bergamo (1265–1340), who held that the prelapsarian, property-free State of Innocence is a

---

[1] I describe the tradition of scepticism about natural rights as 'British', because Bentham was English, Ritchie was Scottish, Burke was Irish when the whole of Ireland was subject to the British Crown, and O'Neill was born and raised in Northern Ireland.

[2] See Thomas Turley, 'John XXII and the Franciscans: A Reappraisal', in James Ross Sweeney and Stanley Chodorow, eds, *Popes, Teachers, and Canon Law in the Middle Ages* (Ithaca, NY, and London: Cornell University Press, 1989).

[3] Brian Tierney, *The Idea of Natural Rights* (Grand Rapids, Mich.: Eerdmans, 1997), p. 95: the 'reasons...remain obscure'. See also Turley, 'John XXII and the Franciscans'.

[4] Turley, 'John XXII and the Franciscans', *passim*, but esp. pp. 79, 83–4.

normative condition, to which humans could and should return.[5] Whatever the cause of the Pope's reaction, the effect was his development of an argument that private property is natural. Pope John argued that a right to use something does not confer the right to destroy or consume it; only a right of ownership confers that. Therefore, insofar as the Franciscans consume food justly, they own property and have a right to it. As with the Franciscans, so with Adam in the State of Original Innocence: he had *dominium* or ownership over temporal things, and so the right to consume them—and he had this right, even when there was no one else to exchange commodities with. Therefore, the right to private property is natural.

At first glance, it might seem that the Pope was merely confirming a view already articulated by the likes of Godfrey of Fontaines (1250–1306/9), namely, that since 'each one is bound by the law of nature to sustain his life, which cannot be done without exterior goods, therefore also by the law of nature each has a dominion and a certain right in the common exterior goods of this world...'.[6] That is to say, the duty of self-preservation implies the right to use and consume what that preservation needs, and this is a kind of property-right. A certain kind of ownership is inseparable from simple use: for if it is morally right that I should use a certain consumable, and if that consumable is sufficient only for one, then it is morally wrong that others should consume it. Yet note that this view of a natural right to property assumes a social situation, where there is the possibility of competition or friction: the right marks out what is mine *against* possible rivals or aggressors. It assumes a condition of conflict, perhaps sin, not one of harmony and innocence. As the Pope conceived it, however, Adam had a property-right even when he was entirely alone. That is to say, property is 'natural' in the sense of being primordial and ideal, not merely in the sense of being a reasonable, morally justified, pacifying way of responding to the conflict engendered by sin after the Fall.[7]

In asserting the natural right to property as primordial, ideal, and absolute, observes Brian Tierney, Pope John 'went counter to the whole tenor of the canonistic tradition that he had inherited'.[8] Inspired by the common ownership of goods in the early Church as recorded in the Acts of the Apostles, this tradition shared with some early Fathers a suspicion of, even hostility towards, the very notion of private property. Thus, St Ambrose: 'No one may call his own what is common, of which if a man takes more than he needs, it is obtained by violence.'[9]

---

[5] Tierney, *The Idea of Natural Rights*, p. 153. 'Prelapsarian' refers to the original state of innocence before the biblical Fall of Adam and Eve and their expulsion from the Garden of Eden; 'postlapsarian' refers to the subsequent condition of sin.

[6] Ibid., p. 38.

[7] Jean Gerson later expressed the same view, when he not only asserted that every creature has a natural *dominium* as a gift of God that confers a *ius* to use inferior things for its own preservation, but then likened this to Adam's primordial *dominium* over the fowls of the air (*De Vita Spirituali Animae*, *Oeuvres*, III, p. 145; cited in Tierney, *The Idea of Natural Rights*, p. 27).

[8] Tierney, *The Idea of Natural Rights*, pp. 22, 154–6.   [9] Ibid., pp. 138, 140.

According to this view, private property is not natural, in the sense of primordial and ideal. Rather—as Huguccio (1140?–1210) put it—it is a social convention justified '*propter iniquitatem*', that is, as a prophylactic against the sins of covetousness and avarice.[10] Thomas Aquinas (1225–74) assumed a more nuanced, moderate position, holding that, quite apart from sin, private property is a reasonable, positive convention for encouraging attentive management and avoiding social confusion and discord over the division of responsibility. Nevertheless, he distinguished between the rightness of individuals acquiring and administering property privately, and the subjection of their using it to a social obligation to succour those in need.[11] In other words, while private property is natural as a reasonable convention for ordering human society, it is not natural in the sense of being absolute, conferring complete freedom of disposal on the owner.

This tradition of a morally conditional affirmation of a positive legal right to private property was represented against Pope John in the 1320s by William of Ockham (c. 1287–1347), who argued that Adam's original *dominium* ('dominion') was granted, not just for himself, but for the sake of Eve and their progeny, too.[12] This *dominium commune*[13] was a natural, inalienable right (*ius*) of using commodities as necessary to meet the common needs of the whole human race; it was not a natural right to own private property.[14] After the Fall and in the condition of sin, however, reason dictated that it was expedient for individuals to be granted the power to appropriate things (*potestas appropriandi*) to themselves. Only then, therefore, did a positive, legal right to private property (*dominium proprium*) arise, through social contracts enforceable by judicial institutions.[15] Ockham's account is designed to make clear the moral conditionality of the right to private property by asserting that in the Beginning things were distributed according to the needs of everyone, that at the End of History they

[10] Ibid., p. 141.   [11] Ibid., p. 146.   [12] Ibid., p. 159.

[13] William of Ockham, *Breviloquium*, III.7, in Richard Scholz, *Wilhelm von Ockham als politischer Denker und sein Breviloquium de principatu tyrannico*, Schriften des Reichinstituts für ältere deutsche Geschichtskunde [Monumenta Germaniae historica] 8 (Stuttgart: Hiersemann Verlag, 1944), pp. 125, 126.

[14] William of Ockham, *Opus Nonaginta Dierum*, in *Opera Politica*, ed. H. S. Offler, 4 vols, Vol. II (Manchester, 1963), p. 562: 'iuri utendi naturali nulli renuntiare licet'. Elsewhere Ockham writes of the 'power' (*potestas*), rather than the 'right', of disposing and using temporal things (e.g. *Breviloquium*, III.7, p. 126). However, since this power 'was introduced by divine law' (*Breviloquium*, III.7, p. 126: 'introductum ex iure divino'), it is clearly rightful and so is indistinguishable from a 'right' (*ius*). Indeed, in the *Opus Nonaginta Dierum* he writes that 'the right [*ius*] of heaven is nothing other than a power [*potestas*] conformed to right reason apart from any compact' (*Opus Nonaginta Dierum*, p. 579: 'Ius autem poli est aliud quam potestas conformis rationi rectae absque pactione'). Like Ockham, Grotius distinguished between the common 'use of fact' at the beginning of the human race and *dominium* in the sense of private property (*Freedom of the Seas* (1916), pp. 22–4; cited in Tierney, *The Idea of Natural Rights*, p. 167).

[15] Ockham, *Breviloquium*, III.7, pp. 126, 127. Tierney, *The Idea of Natural Rights*, pp. 163–6. A. S. McGrade and John Kilcullen helpfully observe that all Latin words with the root '*propr*-'—such as *appropriandi*, *proprium*, and *proprietas*—imply the exclusion of other persons (William of Ockham, *A Short Discourse on Tyrannical Government*, Cambridge Texts in the History of Political Thought, ed. A. S. McGrade, trans. John Kilcullen (Cambridge: Cambridge University Press, 1992), p. 88 n.27).

shall be, and that in the secular interim they should be. It is true that in the condition of sin, where access is subject to competition and threat, the distribution of goods needs to be susceptible of defence by law and public authority. Nevertheless, the legal right to private property remains subject to the moral obligation to use all things according to need.

This dispute over the alleged natural right to property exposes the importance of different conceptions of nature. If the state of nature is one of Adamic solitariness, abundance, and innocence, where there is neither scarcity nor greed, then talk of a natural *right* sounds odd. Why? Because in the absence of competition for limited resources, and of sinful motives that infect competition, injustice cannot arise. And where there can be no injustice, there is no need for individuals to possess moral claims or rights for assertion in self-defence. Certainly, Adam had the *power* to use goods, and since that power was morally unobjectionable, we *could* say that he 'had a natural right' to them. However, such talk connotes that there might be a challenge to Adam's power, where there cannot be. Since there is no rival to 'mine', there is no need to define it by means of a right.

However, if the state of nature is one of innocence and abundance, but comprising more than one saint, then some clear allocation of things would be necessary as a precaution, not against injustice, but against mere confusion over the allocation of responsibility. My right to property would be designed, not to fend off your greed, but rather to make clear who is responsible for managing it. But this right would be moral, not legal, since the state of nature by definition lacks judicial institutions.

Suppose, however, that the state of nature is one of scarcity and competition. The portion of goods that I deserve will depend on the circumstances of the quantity available, my need relative to others', and the order of priority of my social obligations. These circumstances will shift over time, perhaps quite rapidly. At one moment it will be morally right or just that I have portion X, but at the next moment it will be right that I have portion Y. I *could* say at each moment that I have 'a right to X' or 'a right to Y'. But that, too, would sound odd. Why? Because to talk of 'a right' is to talk of 'a possession', and such talk implies a thing or substance that endures through time and has some stability. In the state of nature, however, there is no such stability.

What should we conclude about natural rights from this analysis of the Franciscan Controversy? First, talk of a natural right to private property that implies an absolute imperviousness to any overriding moral claims should be rejected by anyone who believes (as I do) in an objective or natural morality. Second, where 'natural' means 'reasonable or justified according to natural morality', we could say that the legal right to private property is 'natural', in that it serves the good of social order by clarifying the distribution of responsibilities or by raising a bulwark against avarice. However, we had better not, since such talk tends to confuse. The word 'natural' connotes what is pre-conventional, whereas the institution of private property (for whatever purpose) belongs to civil society. Further, a 'right' to private property connotes a possession that, thanks to the institutions of civil society, is relatively stable, whereas the conditions of uncivilised state of nature, before or outside of settled society, are not.

The medieval debate about whether or not private property is 'natural' gave rise, not only to the claim that an owner has a natural, absolute right to it, but also to the opposite claim that the indigent have a natural right to help themselves to such private property as is surplus to the needs of its legal owner. Aquinas famously wrote that such indigents would not be committing theft by helping themselves, but he refrained from ascribing to them possession of 'a right' to do so.[16] As to why he refrained, we can only speculate. One plausible possibility is that he was aware of the politically anarchic implications of his assertion that theft in the eyes of human law can be justified in the eyes of natural law. Consequently, he was keen to stress the objective contingency of the occasion—the need must be manifest and urgent—and to discourage subjective presumption, and he recognised that this was best achieved by the cautious statement that 'it can be permissible for someone' than by the more confident 'someone has a right'.[17] Others were less cautious. Hostiensis (c.1200–1271), for example, wrote that

---

[16] Aquinas, *Summa Theologiae*, 2a2ae, q. 66, a.7. What he says is that 'it can be permissible' (*licite potest*) for someone to meet his own need by means of another's superabundant property, where that need is urgent. The permission is given, of course, not by positive law (*iure humano*), but by natural law or right (*iuri naturali*). Dominic Legge has argued ('Do Thomists Have Rights?', in *Nova et Vetera*, 17/1 (2019)), *pace* Tierney and Fortin, that Aquinas can be found to talk of natural rights—for example, 'liberis... habent ius et facultatem repugnandi quantum ad aliqua praecepta regis vel principis' (*De Virtutibus*, q.1, a.4: 'free men... have the right and capacity in some cases to resist the precepts of a king or prince') and 'liberis... habent ius in aliquo contradicendi' (*Summa Theologiae*, 1a2ae, q. 58, a.2: 'free men... have the right of contradiction'). The reference to 'free men', however, suggests that Aquinas is referring to a specific legal status, with attendant rights and liberties, conferred by a positive system of law, not by nature. Therefore, I do not think that Legge has succeeded in dislodging Ernest Fortin's claim that '[i]n all cases' where Aquinas uses the word *iura* ('rights'), 'the reference is to canonical or civil rights' ('"Sacred and Inviolable": *Rerum Novarum* and Natural Rights', *Theological Studies*, 53 (1992), p. 220).

[17] Consonant with this is Michael Zuckert's explanation of the general absence of natural rights-talk in Aquinas. While it would have been possible to restate natural law in terms of natural rights, Aquinas preferred not to, because '[a] rights version focuses on self-assertion of agents; the genuine natural law version focuses on the moral command or address to each. The rights version misrepresents, or at least encourages a misunderstanding, of the nature of morality: conscientiousness, not self-assertion, is the proper moral attitude'. What is more, '[r]ights are both specific and conclusory in a way that natural law is not' ('Do Natural Rights Derive from Natural Law?', *Harvard Journal of Law and Public Policy*, 20/3 (Summer 1997), pp. 716, 717). Jean Porter observes that, while scholastics in the twelfth and thirteenth centuries—including Aquinas—generally did not develop a doctrine of subjective natural rights, they 'did have the linguistic and conceptual resources' to do so, on occasions came close to adopting natural rights-talk, and in a few cases actually did so ('From Natural Law to Human Rights: Or, Why Rights Talk Matters', *Journal of Law and Religion*, 14/1 (1999–2000), pp. 81, 84, 85). She then uses this to argue that 'an incipient doctrine of natural subjective rights can already be found in this period' and that 'there is no sharp break between the high middle ages and early modernity on this issue' (ibid., p. 89). Unlike Zuckert, she does not consider whether most scholastics, including Aquinas, had good reasons to hold back from endorsing such a doctrine.

'[o]ne who suffers the need of hunger seems to use his right [*iure suo*] [in taking from another's surplus] rather than to plan a theft'.[18] Three centuries later Hugo Grotius (1583-1645) expressed himself in similar terms that, in cases of extreme necessity, 'that antient [*sic*] right of using things, as if they remained in common, must revive, and be in full force'.[19] The problem with such talk is twofold. First, 'a right' here connotes a legal entity, whereas what is being talked about is not: it is moral. What is more, it is *il*legal, since taking what is needed from someone else's surplus property without their permission is, in the eyes of positive law, theft. Second, 'a right' connotes something stable and enduring that can normally be presumed upon, whereas what is being talked about here comes and goes according to the happenstance of indigence and surplus. The justifying conditions are exceptional, not normal, and should not be casually presumed upon. Therefore, rather than talking of the indigent 'possessing a natural right' to surplus private property, it would be less misleading and politically dangerous to say that, 'in certain circumstances, it would be morally right or just' for the indigent to avail themselves of private property-owners' surpluses. In this respect, Aquinas was wiser than Hostiensis and Grotius in avoiding natural rights-talk.

III

The radical Franciscan challenge to the institution of private property was not the only stimulus for debate about a natural right to *dominium* in the late medieval and early modern periods. Another was the challenge posed to the legitimacy of established institutions of property and self-government by the assertion of papal authority. In the thirteenth and early fourteenth centuries some, like Hostiensis and Giles of Rome (*c*.1243-1316), argued that all rightful *dominium* is ultimately derived from the Pope and that there is therefore no rightful property or government outside of the Christian Church.[20] Against this, and following the earlier natural law reasoning of Pope Innocent IV (*c*.1195-1254),[21] Ockham asserted that 'true lordship [*dominium*] of temporal things and true temporal jurisdiction' can exist even among unbelievers, since the power (*potestas*) to appropriate temporal things exclusively to particular persons and collectivities, and the power (*potestas*) to institute government, were conferred on the whole human race in God's grant to Adam and Eve after the Fall.[22] Although the word *potestas*—rather than *ius*—is

---

[18] Tierney, *The Idea of Natural Rights*, p. 73.

[19] Hugo Grotius, *The Rights of War and Peace*, 3 vols., ed. Richard Tuck (Indianapolis: Liberty Fund, 2005), II.II.VI.1, 2, p. 434; *Hugonis Grotii De Iure Belli ac Pacis Libri Tres*, edition secunda (Amsterdam: Guilielmum Blaeuw, 1631), II.II.VI, p. 107: 'ius illud pristinum'.

[20] Tierney, *The Idea of Natural Rights*, pp. 144, 147.   [21] Ibid., pp. 143, 144.

[22] Ockham, *Breviloquium*, III.4, 7, pp. 118, 128. Tierney misleads slightly when he reports that Ockham argued that 'the right to acquire property and the right to institute government were both conferred on the whole human race (including infidels) in God's original grant to Adam' (*The Idea of*

used here, it is clear enough that 'morally rightful power' is intended. At this point, therefore, we find Ockham arguing *for* what we might call (even if he did not) 'a natural right', rather than against it, as in the Franciscan Controversy. However, the meaning of the right has changed. When defending the Franciscans, Ockham was arguing against any absolute, morally unqualified natural right to private property. Here he is contending for existing positive, customary rights to property and self-government that are justified by the norms of natural law.

The same line of argument appears in the sixteenth century, when Francisco de Vitoria (1492–1546) held that 'all forms of dominion [*dominia*] derive from natural or human law';[23] that 'the foundation of dominion is the fact that we are formed in the image of God';[24] and that the American Indian, though a sinner and unbeliever—and even if a child, in terms of cultural development—is nevertheless a human being and so 'an image of God by nature, that is by natural powers',[25] having 'the use of reason in his own way'.[26] The American Indians are therefore genuine or rightful masters (*veri domini*).[27] Unlike Ockham, Vitoria talks here explicitly in terms of the Indians having a natural, moral right to private property and self-government (*habent ius rerum*).[28] Nevertheless, this right is conditional, not absolute. If, for example, its exercise involves tyrannical oppression such as human sacrifice and cannibalism, then the right fades, and other people—such as the Spanish—acquire the right to intervene on behalf of the innocent victims, whether or not they request it.[29]

In these two discussions of the rightful security of property and political autonomy, the word 'natural' plays two distinct roles. First, it stands in contrast to 'Christian'. The assertion of a natural right is a claim to a measure of autonomy that appeals to the rational nature of all human beings. The implicit argument is that, while sin may have weakened and distorted human rationality, it has not destroyed it. Therefore, provided that unbelievers do not degenerate into very

Natural Rights, p. 172). The relevant divine grant was not 'original', in that it was made both to Adam and to Eve *after the Fall*, in order to restrain avarice, cupidity, and managerial neglect (*Breviloquium*, III.7, pp. 125–7; Ockham, *Short Discourse*, pp. 87–90).

[23] Francisco de Vitoria, 'On the American Indians', in *Political Writings*, ed. Anthony Pagden and Jeremy Lawrence (Cambridge: Cambridge University Press, 1991), q.1, a.3, p. 244.

[24] Vitoria, 'On the American Indians', q.1, a.5, p. 249.

[25] Francisco de Vitoria, *Relectio de Indis*, ed. L. Pereña and J. M. Perez Prendes, Corpus Hispanorum de Pace (Madrid: Consejo Superior de Investigaciones Científicas, 1967), I.1.3: 'sed homo est imago Dei per naturam, scilicet per potentias naturales'; I.1.13: 'Pueri ante usum rationis possunt esse domini. Hoc patet, quia possunt pati iniuriam; ergo habent ius rerum; ergo illis dominium, quod nihil aliud est quam ius' ('Children before the age of reason can be masters. This is self-evident, first, because a child can be the victim of an injustice; therefore a child can have legal rights; therefore it can have a right of ownership [*dominium rerum*], which is a legal right' (Vitoria, 'On the American Indians', q. 1, a. 5, p. 249)).

[26] Vitoria, *Relectio de Indis*, I.1.15, p. 29: 'habent pro suo modo usum rationis'.

[27] Ibid., I.1.16, p. 30.   [28] See note 25.

[29] Vitoria, 'On the American Indians', q. 3, a. 5, p. 288.

grave forms of injustice, Christians ought not to interfere with them. This implies a second, objective role for 'natural' in the argument: namely, that the entitlement to property and autonomy is based on the moral law, which is given in and with the created nature of things, and not on the exercise of papal authority.

As Vitoria handles it, the argument proceeds in terms of the Indians having a conditional, natural, moral right, but Ockham shows that it need not do so. For he pursues essentially the same line of reasoning in terms of possessing, not exactly a right, but rather a power that is rightful, according to the universal, natural law of God.

IV

Among the other powers or liberties that attracted natural rights-talk in the early modern period was that of self-defence. As with the putative natural right to private property in the eyes of Godfrey of Fontaines, the rightful natural liberty— or natural right—to self-defence was held to derive from the duty, under natural law, of self-preservation. It is not natural in the Hobbesian sense of being absolute or unconditional, since, according to Vitoria, there are circumstances where it would be laudable for someone to surrender 'the right that he has over his own body' and suffer death.[30] However, according to Grotius in the following century, it is natural in another sense. In civil society an individual's liberty of self-defence is severely restricted by transferring responsibility for the maintenance of law and order to the civil authorities, in order to prevent anarchy.[31] Nevertheless, in a situation of extreme necessity—say, where the civil powers have become 'excessively cruel'—the natural liberty to resist injury revives.[32] Grotius applies exactly the same reasoning to the liberty to punish: in the absence of properly functioning judicial institutions, the individual's 'antient Liberty [to punish], which the Law of Nature at first gave us' revives.[33] To speak in these cases of the revival of a rightful natural liberty (Grotius) or of a natural right (Vitoria) is to say that, outside of civil order, the individual's recourse to less restricted self-defence and punishment is justified according to natural morality. But only less restricted, not absolutely unrestricted, for self-defence is morally justified, not against any aggression whatever, but only against that which is unjust; and punishment is morally justified only when meted out proportionately against wrongdoers.

[30] Francisco de Vitoria, On Homicide, trans. and introd. John P. Doyle (Milwaukee, Wis.: Marquette University Press, 1997), section 24, pp. 92–5: 'ius quod homo habet in proprium corpus'.
[31] Grotius, Rights of War and Peace, I.IV.II, pp. 338–9.
[32] Ibid., I.IV.VII, p. 358: 'I dare not condemn indifferently all private persons, or a small part of the people, who finding themselves reduced to the last extremity, have made use of the only remedy left them, in such a manner as they have not neglected in the mean time to take care, as far as they are able, of the publick good.
[33] Ibid., II.XX.VIII.5, p. 970; see also II.XX.IX.5, p. 975.

In addition to a natural right to self-defence, and regarding the Spanish presence in the Americas, Vitoria also asserted that the Spanish 'have the right to travel and dwell in those countries, so long as they do no harm to the barbarians'.[34] This is because, first, since 'friendliness toward all men is part of the natural law [de iure naturali] . . . it is against nature [contra naturam] to avoid the company of harmless men'[35] and it is 'inherently evil' to refuse to welcome strangers and foreigners.[36] Therefore, according to the law of nations, which either is or derives from natural law,[37] it is considered inhuman to treat strangers and travellers badly without some special cause. Second, in the beginning of the world all things were held in common and everyone was allowed to visit and travel through any land he wished, and this permission was not taken away by the (post-lapsarian) division of property.[38] What applies to travel and residence applies also to trade and citizenship: according to the ius gentium, travellers may trade so long as they do no harm to native citizens;[39] and anyone born in a political community is a citizen de iure gentium, otherwise he, a civil animal (animal civile), would not be a citizen of any community at all.[40] Should the barbarians refuse the Spanish their right (ius suum) in these matters, then it is permissible for the latter to go to war to obtain it.[41]

These natural rights of travel, residence, trade, and citizenship are not unconditional, since they are qualified by the duty not to harm the natives. Nevertheless, they are supposed to be presumptive: in the absence of harm these trans-national rights stand, and the burden of proof lies with those who would restrict them.

V

Behind talk of rightful natural liberties or natural rights in the thought of Ockham, Vitoria, and Grotius lies a concept of the state of nature, a condition of human existence where the social institutions of law, police, courts, and prisons are absent. This could be the mythical condition of Adam, or the historical conditions of the original habitation of terra nova, or anarchy, or lawless war. Whichever it is, the principles of God-given natural morality still obtain. Even if no positive law

---

[34] Vitoria, 'On the American Indians', q. 3, a. 1, p. 278 ('habent ius peregrinandi in illas provincias et illic degendi' (Vitoria, Relectio de Indis, I.3.1, p. 78)).

[35] Vitoria, Relectio de Indis, I.3.1, p. 79.

[36] Vitoria, 'On the American Indians', q. 3, a. 1.5, p. 281; Vitoria, Relectio de Indis, I.3.4, p. 83: 'de se malum'.

[37] Vitoria, Relectio de Indis, I.3.1, p. 78: 'ex iure gentium, quod vel est ius naturale vel derivatur ex iure naturali'.

[38] Ibid., I.3.1, p. 78: 'Non autem videtur hoc demptum per rerum divisionem.'

[39] Vitoria, 'On the American Indians', q. 3, a. 1.3, p. 279.

[40] Ibid., q. 3, a. 1.5, p. 281; Vitoria, Relectio de Indis, I.3.4, p. 83.

[41] Vitoria, 'On the American Indians', q. 3, a. 1.5, p. 282; Vitoria, Relectio de Indis, I.3.5, p. 84.

tells us that 'I have a right' to a certain something, natural law nevertheless tells us that 'it is morally right' that I should have a certain something.

There is, however, another, amoral conception of the state of nature. Here all morality arises from social contracts. Before such contracts there is no morality; instead, there is absolutely untrammelled liberty. This was Hobbes's view, which stands in a long tradition of thought that reaches back to the Roman concept of pre-legal *dominium* or absolute 'mastery'[42] that is implied in Cicero's version of the state of nature: 'There was a time when men wandered at large in the fields like animals ... they did nothing by the guidance of reason ... '.[43] This Roman tradition was adopted by Renaissance humanists in the sixteenth century, such as Andrea Alciato (1492–1550), who wrote that 'ancient authors relate that in the first infancy of humankind men were unsociable ... unconscious of religion or of human duties ... '[44] Accordingly, Richard Tuck writes, 'there was no place in [the] thinking [of humanist lawyers] for natural rights of any kind'.[45]

It does seem that the idea of an original absolute liberty can be found in some reaches of late medieval and early modern scholastic thought, as well as in Renaissance humanism. Tuck detected the identification of *ius* with *dominium* in the thought of Gersonians such as Luis de Molina (1535–1600), for whom man is *dominus* of his own liberty and can enslave himself at will.[46] Annabel Brett qualifies Tuck's argument by insisting that this identification is 'far from being the universal outlook in the moral theology of the later middle ages', that William of Ockham's understanding of *ius* as *potestas* need not amount to liberty or *dominium* 'in the strong sense', and that Jean Gerson's own theory is 'very clearly distinguished' from those who identify *ius* with *dominium*.[47] Nonetheless, when all is said and done, she concedes that some of those who followed Gerson (1363–1429)—for example, Konrad Summenhart (c.1450–1502)—did read him as assimilating *ius* to *dominium*.[48]

The concept of an original liberty that is absolute, suffering no constraint, logically displaces any notion of natural moral law. Therefore it should also displace any notion of natural *right*, insofar as 'right' connotes *moral* authority

---

[42] Tierney, *The Idea of Natural Rights*, pp. 16–17.

[43] Cicero, *De Inventione*, 1.2; cited in Richard Tuck, *Natural Rights Theories: Their Origin and Development* (Cambridge: Cambridge University Press, 1979), p. 33.

[44] Tuck, *Natural Rights Theories*, p. 36.   [45] Ibid., p. 40.   [46] Ibid., pp. 49, 53.

[47] Annabel S. Brett, *Liberty, Right, and Nature: Individual Rights in Later Scholastic Thought* (Cambridge: Cambridge University Press, 2003), pp. 11, 51, 86.

[48] Ibid., pp. 119–20. If one strand of scholastic thought adopted the classical idea of an original, absolute liberty, another strand did not. The latter remained true to Thomas Aquinas, for whom, according to Tuck, 'men do not have a *prima facie* natural right to liberty any more than they have a *prima facie* natural right to dominate other men' (Tuck, *Natural Rights Theories*, p. 20). One faithful disciple of Aquinas in this respect was Francisco de Vitoria, who saw human liberty as constrained by the law of God (ibid., p. 49). Another, in effect, was Hugo Grotius, for whom liberty in disposing one's life is limited by the duty not to commit suicide or surrender oneself to servitude (ibid., p. 70). A third, as we shall see in Chapter 6, was John Locke.

or force. In Hobbes's case, however, it did not. Notwithstanding his conception of natural law as subsequent to social contracts, Hobbes persisted in asserting a single, original, natural 'right' of self-preservation. By 'right' here, he does not mean merely liberty; he seems to mean something closer to 'duty', since it is something that one can not (may not?) renounce.[49] However, Hobbes's natural 'right' is not really a moral right or duty at all, but rather a psychic drive: it is not a moral norm, but a brute fact.[50] As such, it may compel, but it cannot oblige.

<h1 style="text-align:center">VI</h1>

Although most Christian scholastics dissented from humanist thinking about the amoral liberty of the state of nature, they did develop a concept of a natural right to liberty in specifically political terms. Indeed, reporting that Ockham's 'persistent emphasis on natural rights as setting limits to a ruler's power has no clear precedent in earlier writings',[51] Brian Tierney judges that his *Breviloquium* has a plausible claim to be regarded 'as the first essentially rights-based treatise on political theory'.[52] Here Ockham argues that the tyrannical abuse of power by the Pope is 'opposed to the rights and liberties granted ... by God and nature'.[53]

In fact, however, Ockham tends to argue in terms, not of natural law, but of the evangelical, Christian 'law' of freedom—as befits a case against papal tyranny within Christendom. This evangelical law, which lightens the burden imposed by the law of Moses, militates against the claim that the Pope has the power to do (and command) by right (*de iure*) whatever is not opposed to divine or natural law. Were this not so, Christians would be 'in the strictest sense of the term the pope's slaves'.[54] In *De Imperatorum et Pontificum Potestate*, Ockham appeals to the Gospels against any use of power to serve the ruler's interests rather than common utility (*communem utilitatem*): 'The kings of the gentiles lord it over them, Not so you ...' (Luke 22:25–6).[55] In *An Princeps* his focus lies on temporal

---

[49] Tuck, *Natural Rights Theories*, p. 129.

[50] It seems that my perception here is not original. The Spanish Jesuit theologian Gabriel Vazquez (1549–1604), the jurist Samuel Pufendorf (1632–94), and the moral philosopher David Ritchie all anticipated it. Vazquez called 'natural liberty' what Hobbes later called 'natural right' (Annabel S. Brett, *Liberty, Right, and Nature: Individual Rights in Later Scholastic Thought* (Cambridge: Cambridge University Press, 1997), p. 205). According to Brett, 'Vázquez refuses to call the liberty of the state of nature a right at all: it is rather a fact' (ibid., p. 235). Similarly, Pufendorf argued that only those natural powers are rights, which have 'some moral Effect, with regard to others, who are partners ... in the same Nature'; that every man has a natural power or licence to use anything destitute of sense or reason; and that, since such things lack any obligation to yield themselves, such power is no right. In short, a Hobbesian right is no right, since it lacks a corresponding obligation (Tuck, *Natural Rights Theories*, pp. 159–61). And Ritchie succinctly remarked that, with Hobbes, 'natural rights are equivalent to natural mights' (*Natural Rights*, p. 83).

[51] Tierney, *The Idea of Natural Rights*, p. 193.   [52] Ibid., p. 185.

[53] Ockham, *Short Discourse*, 'Prologue', p. 3.   [54] Ibid., p. 23.

[55] Tierney, *The Idea of Natural Rights*, p. 190.

rights: 'the supreme pontiff does not have power from Christ to despoil others of their liberties, rights [*iuribus*] and goods by his arbitrary will', except in case of extreme necessity or great utility.[56] Elsewhere—for example in the *Breviloquium*—his concern extends to the defence of spiritual freedom against the Pope's imposition of works of supererogation such as the vow of virginity or the renunciation of property, 'without some fault on the part of those subject to him and without urgent necessity or clear utility'.[57] Tierney comments that, when discussing works of supererogation, Ockham had in mind a concept of liberty as 'a core of spiritual autonomy inherent in the human person, granted "by God and nature", a freedom of choice in responding to divine love and divine demands'.[58] This is not quite right, for, strictly speaking, the spiritual autonomy in question is the property only of the redeemed, *Christian* person. It is granted by the Holy Spirit of God-in-Christ, not by fallen nature.

It seems that Tierney is only expressing a conflation present in some of the medieval material itself, since it can be found both before Ockham and after. In the 1180s the English author of the *Summa, In Nomine* wrote of *ius naturale* that one of its meanings is 'licit and approved, neither commanded nor forbidden by the Lord or any statute... whence, upon the words of the Apostle [Paul in 1 Corinthians 6:12], "All things are licit for me"'.[59] However, the freedom of which St Paul writes is that proper to the Christian, especially vis-à-vis Jewish law. If it is a *ius*, it is not straightforwardly *naturale*. We find the same thing a generation after Ockham in the thought of Jean Gerson. From the 1250s disputes arose about the claim of mendicant friars who, relying on papal privileges, were entering dioceses and parishes without permission of the local secular clergy (bishop or priest). In response, Gerson argued that the usurpation of the rights and dignities of others (to preach, to hear confession) is an act of theft. And, appealing to St Paul's image of the Church as one body, he wrote that it was wrong for the Pope as head of the Church to 'usurp against the nature of a single member the duties of all the other members... if all were an eye or head, where is the foot, where the hand?'[60] Again, the conflation: the usurpation of rights is described as being both 'against nature' and contrary to the body of Christ.

The liberty of the Christian is that of one, who, obedient to God-in-Christ, is infused by his Spirit and so endowed with a virtuous character, and who can therefore be relied upon to use freedom well, and, above all, charitably. It is the liberty of one whose nature has been saved from sin and renewed. For that reason

---

[56] Ibid., pp. 190–1.
[57] Ockham, *Breviloquium*, II.17, p. 91; Ockham, *Short Discourse*, II.17, p. 54.
[58] Tierney, *The Idea of Natural Rights*, p. 189.   [59] Ibid., p. 67.
[60] Jean Gerson, 'De Potestate Ecclesiastica', in *Oeuvres complètes*, ed. P. Glorieux, Vol. VI: *L'Oeuvre ecclésiologique* (Paris: Desclée, 1965), p. 239: 'Addamus ita Summum Pontificem... neque velit usurpare contra naturam singularis membri omnia officia membrorum, quibus singulis, ut ait Apostolus, proprium datum est officium; nam si omnia oculus vel caput, ubi pes, ubi manus?'

she need not—and should not—be excessively trammelled by external authority and law, and each member of the Church should be given freedom to follow his or her individual vocation by God. However, what applies within the Church does not apply straightforwardly outside it, since those not infused with the renewing Spirit of Christ are, presumably, less truly virtuous and so less capable of handling freedom well. In the context of medieval Christendom, of course, all members of society were also members of the Church: there was no 'outside'. Therefore, appeals to Christian freedom could be deployed to defend already posited, local, legal rights against incursions by papal (or royal) authority, or to argue that such rights *should* be granted.

Latent in these Christian arguments for political freedom, however, was the germ of another, 'natural' one, which came to the fore in the sixteenth century, when scholastic thinkers turned to consider the case of non-Christian infidels, namely, the American Indians. Since an appeal to Christian freedom would not be an apt ground for non-Christian rights to freedom, the scholastics—as we have already seen in the case of Vitoria—turned instead to the rational, morally responsible nature of all human creatures, insofar as this has not been eradicated by sin. Thus Bartolomeo de las Casas (1484–1566): 'As regards humans, ... from the beginning of their rational nature, they were born free ... For liberty is a right [*ius*] necessarily instilled in man from the beginning of rational nature and so from natural law [*iure*].'[61] Ultimately, the two forms of argument—from Christian freedom and from natural law—can be made to cohere: the freedom that the Spirit of Christ bestows *is* the recovery and renewal of the freedom to which all human beings are called by nature, but from which sin prevents them.

VII

Where Ockham approximated natural rights-talk ('rightful natural power') to justify constraints on papal power within the Church, Vitoria resorted to it explicitly to justify constraints on Spanish civil power vis-á-vis the American Indians. During the second half of the sixteenth century Lutherans and Calvinists sometimes, but not always, deployed the language, of subjective natural rights when arguing for limits to the power of the Holy Roman Emperor or Catholic monarchs to suppress Protestant communities or states.[62] Thus in its

---

[61] Tierney, *The Idea of Natural Rights*, p. 278.

[62] Tuck argues that since many Calvinists, including Beza, were trained in law schools presided over by humanists such as Alciato, their theories of resistance focus more on compacts than natural law, and operate more in terms of social utility than natural rights (*Natural Rights Theories*, pp. 42, 44, 45). John Witte shows that this is not so (*The Reformation of Rights: Law, Religion, and Human Rights in Early Modern Calvinism* (Cambridge: Cambridge University Press, 2007)). In personal correspondence with the author, he has commented: 'There were scores of Calvinist resistance writers in England, Scotland, the Netherlands, France, Geneva, Germany, Hungary, who had all kinds of training, sometimes with

opening summary, the Lutheran Magdeburg Confession (1550)[63] asserted that, if the emperor should dare to harass, not only his (Protestant) subjects, but in them 'divine or natural right, true doctrine and worship', then the inferior magistrate 'is responsible to oppose him by the power of God's command'.[64] While this does not speak in terms of 'rights', it does imply that, according to divine and natural law or right, the people should be allowed to have certain freedoms—especially of religious exercise—and that should these freedoms be gravely interfered with, then the natural rightness of them should be asserted against the invader. This approximates talk of 'natural rights'. The approximation becomes an identity when the Confession expands on this point in the body of its text. There the reference to divinely created rights becomes explicit, where we are told that the gravest kind of tyranny, which deserves opposition by armed force, is that which not only harasses the persons of the lower magistracy and their subjects, but in their persons 'the highest and most necessary right, and with that our Lord God himself, who is a giver of the same rights [*desselbigen Rechten*]'.[65] That said, we should note that the document does not in fact talk of the lower magistrate's *right* to resist, but rather of his being responsible or obliged to do so under God (*schuldig aus Krafft Gottlichs befehls*).[66] It prefers duty-talk to rights-talk.

humanists, sometimes not. Calvinists were themselves often humanists, and had widely variant ideas about resistance, rights, compacts, covenants, etc. Alciato's own views changed quite dramatically in his life-time, and for a time, he, too, was quite strong on natural law theory.' I have depended heavily on Witte's work to guide me through the literature that I discuss in this section.

[63] Witte describes the Confession as 'a forceful distillation and extension of the most radical Lutheran teachings on resistance to political tyranny' (*Reformation of Rights*, p. 113). According to David Whitford, 'To date neither a critical edition nor the original texts of the Magdeburg *Bekenntnis* exist. The earliest extant German edition is contained in a collection of writings associated with the German Wars of Charles V, published in 1615' (David Mark Whitford, *Tyranny and Resistance: The Magdeburg Confession and the Lutheran Tradition* (St Louis: Concordia, 2001), p. 13).

[64] *Bekentnis und unterricht und vermanung der pfarrhern und prediger der christlichen kirchen zu Magdeburgk* (Magdeburg, 1550), 'Kurzer begriff oder inhalt dieses buchs': 'Wenn die hohe Obrigkeit sich unterstehet/mit gewalt und unrecht zu verfolgen/nicht so fast sie Personen ihrer unterthanen/als in ihnen das Göttliche oder naturliche Recht/rechte Lere und Gottesdienst ausszuheben und auszureuten/ So ist die unter Oberigkeit schuldig/aus Krafft Gottlichs befehls/wider solch der Obern fuernehmen/ sich kampt den ihren/wie sie kan ausszuhalten'; *Confessio et Apologia Pastorum et reliquorum ministrorum Ecclesiae Magdeburgensis* (Magdeburg, 1550), 'Syllogismus continens argumentum libri': 'Quando superior magistratus vi persequitur in subditis, ipsum ius vel naturale, vel divinum, vel veram religionem et cultum Dei, tunc inferior magistratus debet ei resistere ex mandato Dei'. The 'Kurzer begriff' is a single page in length and is not paginated.

[65] *Bekentnis*, 'Der Ander teil dieses Buchs von der Nothwere', 'Der vierde Grad [unrechtes Gewalts]', p. K.iii, plus 1: 'das höchste unnd nötigste Recht/und gleich unsern Herrn Gott selbst/der ein stiffter ist desselbigen Rechten'. The plural 'Rechten' in the German text is reduced to the singular 'iuris' in the Latin version: '. . . Deum quem authorem iuris' (*Confessio*, p. F.iv.v). Each main part of the Confession is paginated by letter in alphabetical order (A, B, C, etc.), and between the letters by Roman numeral (i, ii,.iii, etc.). However, between each paginated page and the next (e.g. between K.iii and L) fall several pages with no pagination. Thus 'K.iii., plus 1' means 'the first page after the one identified as "K.iii"'.

[66] *Bekentnis*, 'Kurzer begriff': 'So ist die unter Oberigkeit schuldig/aus Krafft Gottlichs befehls/wider solch der Obern fuernehmen/sich kampt den ihren/wie sie kan ausszuhalten'; *Confessio*, 'Syllogismus': 'tunc inferior magistratus debet ei resistere ex mandato Dei'. The 'Kurzer begriff' is not paginated.

Another important expression of Protestant thought about political resistance appears in *How Superior Powers Ought to be Obey'd* (1558) by Christopher Goodman (1520–1603), a Marian exile in Geneva.[67] Goodman went further than his predecessors in attributing the authority or duty to resist, not only to lower magistrates, but also to the common people. Well known in the sixteenth and seventeenth centuries, his thought influenced John Knox (1513–72), John Locke, and Thomas Jefferson (1743–1826).[68] Goodman ascribes a certain freedom to human beings on the dual grounds of rational nature and Christian equality:

> the people ... oght not to suffer all power and libertie to be taken from them, and therby to become brute beastes, with out iudgemente and reason, thinking all thinges lawfull, which their Rulers do without exceptiō, commād them, be they never so farre from reason or godlynesse: as thoghe they were not reasonable creatures, but brute beastes: as thoghe there were no difference betwixt bonde slaves, and free subiectes ... [T]he people may be assured by Gods worde that this libertie apparteyneth to them, which becometh members of one bodie and brethren, because the Lorde God him self (from whom kinges have their auctoritie and power) calleth their subiectes and people their brethren, charging them in no case to lift them selves above them, but as brethren to rule in all humbleness and love over them: evenso the people, *if they suffer this right to be taken from them*, which God of his singular favour hath graunted, then are they an occasiō that their kiges and Rulers are turned to tyrants ... [69]

A right that ought not to be taken from the people is a right that they ought to have, according to natural and divine law; and if they do not already have it in positive law, then it must be a natural right. Should any doubt remain that Goodman is affirming such a right as the property of an individual, then it should evaporate upon reading his reference, a little later, to the 'libertie [that] belongeth unto them [the people], by the worde of God, whiche they maye lawfullie clayme, *as their owne possessiō*, and are likewise bounde at all tymes to practice'.[70] And what is this liberty? The freedom not to be forced to do anything that God forbids, or to be forcibly prevented from doing anything that he commands—first and foremost in the Decalogue.[71]

---

[67] Christopher Goodman, *How Superior Powers Ought to be Obey'd* (Geneva: John Crispin, 1558; Amsterdam: Theatrum Orbis Terrarum, 1972).

[68] Whitford, *Tyranny and Resistance*, p. 59.

[69] Goodman, *How Superior Powers Ought to be Obey'd*, pp. 148–9, 149–50. John Witte presents as a quotation of Goodman, that 'God will "not suffer" that "the rights and liberties that he has given to all his people ... be taken from them"' (*Reformation of Rights*, p. 121). Unable to locate this quotation, I have concluded that it is in fact an inadvertent paraphrase of the latter part of the passage here quoted. The emphasis is mine.

[70] Goodman, *How Superior Powers Ought to be Obey'd*, p. 160. The emphasis is mine.

[71] Ibid., pp. 161, 171, 173.

Seminal in the development of Calvinist thought about political responsibilities and resistance to tyranny was the concept of covenant, which was a leading feature of the thought of Theodore Beza (1519–1605).[72] In *Du Droit des magistrats sur leur sujets* (*On the Right of Rulers over their Subjects*) (1574),[73] Beza argued for a three-way covenant (*convention, contract*)[74] between God, the ruler, and the people. The presence of the first party, God, signals a crucial difference between the Bezan covenant and the Hobbesian social contract. Rather than originating the moral law, the covenant binds both ruler and ruled to abide by the *prior* 'right of God and nature'.[75] This right or law, spoken plainly in the Decalogue, is never-theless echoed in natural law, whose 'common principles still dwell in man, however corrupted by sin he be'.[76] It outlaws any ruler's commands that are 'irreligious' (against the First Table of the Decalogue) or 'iniquitous' (against charity to one's neighbour).[77] Therefore, should a ruler command his subjects to attend 'the execrable service of mass', the duty of all faithful people is to disobey him and attend true, Protestant worship instead. The same applies to the duties that we owe to other people, according to 'the right of God and nature':[78] if a ruler would deter his subjects from them, they must disobey.[79] In extremis, where a ruler has manifestly become a tyrant—especially where he persecutes true reli-gion[80]—and where subordinate magistrates, who are oath-bound to defend the laws, are therefore reduced to such necessity, 'they are bound' to protect those in their charge, if possible by force of arms.[81]

The logic of Beza's thinking is that divine and natural right or law prescribe certain negative and positive duties, imply the rightful need of freedom to perform them, and so ground the natural duty to resist rulers who would restrict that freedom unjustly. We could say that, by implication, he justifies the natural right to resist—since the performance of a duty requires the freedom to perform it, and a freedom that is challenged must be asserted as a right. Nevertheless, before we do that, we should pause and reflect upon the fact that Beza does not actually say

---

[72] Witte, *Reformation of Rights*, p. 137. According to Whitford, '[p]erhaps more than any other thinker in the Reformed Tradition,... Beza... was most responsible for Calvinist understandings of resistance' (*Tyranny and Resistance*, p. 60).

[73] *On the Right of Magistrates over their Subjects* was probably written first in Latin. However, the earliest extant editions were published in French in 1574 (Théodore de Bèze, *Du droit des magistrats*, introd. and ed. Robert M. Kingdon, Les Classiques de la Pensée Politique 7 (Geneva: Librairie Droz, 1971), p. xxviii).

[74] Bèze, *Du droit des magistrats*, VI, *Conclusion de la puissance des estats*, p. 44; *De Iure Magistratum* (1580), ed. Klaus Sturm, Texte zur Geschichte der Evangelischen Theologie (Neukirchen-Vluyn: Neukirchener Verlag des Erziehungsvereins, 1965), VI, *Epilogus ac Conclusio de Authoritate Ordinum*, p. 66: 'conventio', 'pactum'.

[75] Bèze, *Du droit des magistrats*, III, p. 6: 'le droit de Dieu et de nature'; *De Iure Magistratum* (1580), III, p. 32: 'tam iure divino quam naturae'.

[76] Bèze, *Du droit des magistrats*, 'Conclusion', p. 45.   [77] Ibid., I, p. 3.

[78] Ibid., III, p. 6: 'le droit de Dieu et de nature'.   [79] Ibid., III, p. 6.   [80] Ibid., X, p. 63.

[81] Ibid., VI, p. 20: 'ils sont tenus... de pourvoir contre une Tyrannie toute manifeste, à la salvation de ceux qu'ils ont encharge'; *De Iure Magistratum*, VI, p. 44: 'teneri ipsos omnino adversus manifestam tyrannidem salutem eorum procurare... qui ipsorum fidei et curae sunt traditi'.

that—and, indeed, that he does not often talk explicitly about rights (in the plural) at all. This is somewhat obscured by the only English translation (of the 1595 Latin edition), which renders the title 'De Iure Magistratum' as 'The *Rights* of Rulers' rather than 'The *Right* of Rulers'. John Witte has the effect of confirming the misleading appearance by tending to read more explicit rights-talk into Beza's political thought than is actually there. So, for example, he reports that Beza affirms a private person's 'rights to free speech and political petition',[82] whereas what the text actually says is that the offended subject 'can have recourse to his sovereign, as the laws entitle him'[83]—which, at best, is an oblique endorsement of a positive, legal right. What is more, Beza immediately goes on to warn that private subjects should consider, not only what is permissible, but 'what is expedient',[84] observing that St Paul chose not to assert his legal right (*son droit*) against the magistrate at Philippi, who had had him flogged 'in violation of the laws [*les loix*] of Roman citizenship'.[85]

Beza's choice of words is significant in three respects. First, his concept of the 'right' of rulers is first and foremost about duties, and only secondarily about liberties and their assertion as rights. Indeed, strictly speaking, he does not affirm a right to resist at all. What he says is that, faced with a tyrannical sovereign, lesser magistrates have a duty to resist in defence of the people's legal liberties—that is, they have a duty to assert the people's legal rights. What this signifies, at least, is that, for Beza, 'rights-talk' is not the only moral talk in town, nor even the most important. Second, Beza's affirmation of the duty to disobey or resist (in defence of legal rights) is cautious and heavily qualified, lest it be mistaken to license the kind of anarchy that revolutionary Anabaptists had wrought at Münster—whom he called 'these rabid [*enragez*] Anabaptists . . . or other rebels and mutineers'.[86] Therefore, before he concedes the duties to disobey and resist, he takes care to laud, out of all the other virtues, Christian patience.[87] What this suggests is that the doctrine of Christian patience in the face of oppression, together with sensitivity to the evils of anarchy, militates against rights-talk. Third, to have a right is not yet to have moral permission to assert it: the requirements of the social good might make it expedient (and so prudent) not to assert it. All that said, it is true that there are occasions when Beza engages in rights-talk—that is, talk about rights as liberties that are the rightful property of subjects—as, for example, when

[82] Witte, *Reformation of Rights*, p. 129.
[83] Bèze, *Du droit des magistrats*, IV, p. 7: 'peut avoir recours à son souverain, comme les loix le portent'; *De Iure Magistratum*, IV, p. 32: 'licebit per leges iniuriam passo ad supremam magistratum recurrere'.
[84] Bèze, *Du droit des magistrats*, IV, p. 7: 'à ce qui est expedient'.
[85] Ibid., IV, p. 7: 'contre les loix de la bourgeoisie de Rome'; *De Iure Magistratum*, IV, p. 32: 'contra ius civium Romanorum'.
[86] Bèze, *Du droit des magistrats*, IV, p. 8: 'ces enragez Anabaptistes ou . . . autres seditieux et mutins'.
[87] Ibid., V, p. 11: 'Je louë doncques la patience chrestienne comme tres-recommendable entre toutes autres vertus.'

he speaks of the sovereign abusing his superior authority 'against all divine and human rights [*droits, iura*]'.[88] Yet the contrast between divine and human indicates that he is referring here to positive, legal rights, not natural ones.

Johannes Althusius (1557–1638), 'the clearest and most profound' Calvinist political thinker,[89] is only slightly less cautious. He does sometimes speak explicitly of a subjective natural right, as when he refers in his *Dicaeologicae libri tres* to '*ius libertatis*'.[90] Yet, when he could have written of 'a people's God-given right to constitute their own form of government', he wrote instead that God has given to all peoples, 'by the very law of nature [*ab ipso naturae iure*]', the free power of creating rulers for themselves.[91] And when he could have written of qualified 'natural rights' to various kinds of freedom', he wrote instead that all human beings have been granted by natural law (*iure naturali*) certain liberties, within the bounds of what is generally permissible: the freedom to use one's own body (*libertas corporis*) but also 'freedom of soul or mind [*libertas animi*]' or a free power (*libera potestas*) to want, evaluate, and make choices, which is not impeded by anyone's command, order, threat, or coercion.[92]

VIII

Before we bring the British Sceptical Tradition to bear, let us first stand back and take critical stock of our analysis of late medieval and early modern discussions of natural rights and their approximations. One obvious feature that it has revealed is a diversity of meanings, which requires a diversity of evaluations. Talk about a natural right to private property makes sense, insofar as it means to say that the civil institution of private property has grounding and justification in natural law or morality, whether as a prophylactic against simple confusion and friction or against sinful covetousness or greed. It also makes sense insofar as it means that, in certain circumstances outside of civil society, it would be morally right that a

---

[88] Ibid., IV, p. 8: 'abusant de sa domination contre touts droits divins et humains'; *De Iure Magistratum*, IV, p. 32: 'contra omnia iura tum divina tum humana'.

[89] Carl Joachim Friedrich, 'Introductory Remarks', in Johannes Althusius, *Politica Methodice Digesta*, introd. Carl Joachim Friedrich, Harvard Political Classics II (Cambridge, Mass.: Harvard University Press, 1932), p. xviii.

[90] Johannes Althusius, *Dicaeologicae libri tres, totum et universum ius, quo utimur, methodice complectentes* (Herborn, 1617), 1.25.9, 10.

[91] Althusius, *Politica Methodice Digesta*, XVIII.20, p. 139: 'Omnibus igitur gentibus Deum ab ipso naturae iure liberam fecisse potestatem sibi principes, reges, magistratusque constituendi, hinc colligi potest...'

[92] Althusius, *Dicaeologicae libri tres*, I.25.7, 8. It has not been my intention in this section to contradict John Witte's claim, in *The Reformation of Rights*, that explicit rights-talk, and even natural rights-talk, was widespread among early modern Calvinists. I do think, however, that he sometimes sees rights-talk where it does not quite exist; that it was somewhat less widespread than he thinks; and that the reasons why the likes of Beza chose other terms to express their meaning are worth reflecting on.

certain individual should be at liberty to use or consume some good or other. However, in both cases natural rights-talk tends to mislead. In the first case, it obscures the fact that the right under discussion assumes a civil context and is in fact positive and legal, albeit sanctioned by natural moral law. In the second case, talk about an individual 'having a right' connotes that such a natural right has the same kind of stability as a positive, legal one. Since this is not so, it would be wiser to take the trouble of speaking in long-hand terms, and to say that it 'is morally right' that an individual should have ownership of this good in these (ephemeral) circumstances. Finally, insofar as talk about a natural right to private property suggests that it is absolute, in the sense of being immune from qualification by natural moral obligations, the case for avoiding it strengthens.

Many of the other implicit approximations or explicit references to 'natural rights' that we have encountered are ways of appealing to natural morality beyond—and sometimes against—positive, conventional law: for example, the natural liberty or right of the indigent to take what he needs from the surplus of another's legally established property; the natural liberty or right of anybody, outside of civil society and its judicial institutions, to defend himself against injustice or to punish wrongdoing proportionately; and the natural power or right of an individual or community to defend their autonomy (illegally) against unjust, but constitutional, interference by their own sovereign, or (non-legally) against interference by a foreign one, where their relationship is ungoverned by international law in its black-letter, treaty form. In all these cases, the natural liberty or power or right is highly contingent upon circumstances, including moral considerations such as justice, proportion, and harm to the social good. The danger of natural *rights*-talk here, as above, is that it inclines us to overlook the contingencies, and to think of the relevant moral rightness as the fixed, stable, and even absolute property of the holder. I have speculated that that is the reason why Aquinas declined to assert 'a natural right' of the indigent to the surplus of the superabundant—lest the contingency of its rightness upon extraordinary conditions be overlooked, the moral rightness of breaking positive law presumed upon, and the perils of anarchy imprudently risked. In Beza's case there is less need to speculate about why he preferred to speak of the lesser magistrates' 'duty', rather than their 'natural right', to resist tyranny. He himself tells us that enraged, revolutionary Anabaptists were on his mind. He also cautions against too ready a resort to protest or resistance. What is morally or legally permissible—a 'right'— is not sufficient moral justification for action, for within the sphere of the permissible a judgement about what is expedient in the circumstances should also be made, and in making that judgement the virtue of patience or self-restraint should be exercised (as St Paul exercised it at Philippi). The danger of rights-talk here is that it misleads the holder into supposing that his possession is far more secure and unconditional than it really is. It suggests that what is right is ready-made and can be presumed upon, whereas, in fact, *the* right—whether or not one has *a* right *here and now*—is contingent upon a judgement about expediency and upon the exercise of virtue. One can use a liberty or make a claim well or badly, virtuously or viciously—as Ockham's appeal to *redeemed, Christian* liberty implied. Whether or not we have a right, then, depends partly on whether or not we also have the relevant virtue. The right should not be taken as already granted, lying just *there* and awaiting our pleasure.

Whereas in these cases quasi- or explicit natural rights-talk usually functions to ground morally legitimate exceptions to civil norms of self-restraint regarding another's private property, self-defence, punishment of wrongdoing, and interference by the civil power, in other cases it has the opposite function. Vitoria's talk of natural rights to travel, trade, reside, and acquire citizenship is designed to affirm certain liberties as morally normal, not exceptional. The ground of these rights is the prima facie friendliness and original community of goods prescribed by natural moral law. These rights can be infringed or suspended, but only for special reason of harm. Apart from such reason, they stand: they are normal and can be presumed upon. It is well to remember the context in which Vitoria was thinking these thoughts: the Spanish encounter with the natives of the Americas. It is also well to remember his conclusion: that should the natives refuse the Spanish their natural rights of travel, trade, and residence, it would be a just cause for war. What Vitoria's argument implies is that the natives should adopt a policy of open borders, until harm is proven. This assumes that strangers, traders, and immigrants are normally benevolent and trustworthy, and that their numbers normally pose no threat of harm to the social cohesion and political stability of the receiving society. Sadly, that is not a reasonable assumption. Sometimes it will be true, but, except in an Edenic state of nature, it will not be normally true and to presuppose otherwise would be naive. Indeed, it would have been naive of the native Americans to presuppose it of the Spanish in the 1500s—and it would have been even more naive of the native Americans to presuppose it of European immigrants to the Wild West in the 1870s. Whether strangers are trustworthy and threaten no harm depends entirely on the circumstances and cannot be presumed, prudently. Vitoria himself implicitly argues against such a presumption when he asserts a settled people's right to autonomy, except in case of atrocious injustice—that is, when he asserts a rival presumption in favour of a settled people's freedom to govern themselves. There cannot be *both* a presumption in favour of the freedom to travel and settle *and* a presumption in favour of a settled people's political freedom from foreign interference. There cannot be natural rights to both of them at the same time. Therefore, rather than trying to capture the issues in the too-unsupple terms of natural rights, it would be better to say that travelling, trading, and settling are in themselves morally indifferent and can be either right or wrong, according to circumstances; that travellers etc. *have a duty* to respect their hosts' ways and need for social cohesion and political stability, except in case of egregious injustice; that natives *have a duty* to be hospitable to foreigners, perhaps even to take some charitable risks in trusting them, except where they pose a threat to cohesion and stability; and that whether travellers or natives are failing in their duties can only be determined by considering a variety of moral factors in the circumstances and at the conclusion of an all-things-considered process of moral deliberation. It cannot be determined by invoking this or that natural right, and if we try to, we shall simply shut down thought with the noise of rhetoric.

Implicit in the conceptual hinterland of the alleged natural rights to travel and trade lies the deep, Christian anthropological tenet that Vitoria and Las Casas made explicit in their defence of the rights of 'barbarians' to own property and govern themselves, and that Goodman, Beza, and Althusius made explicit in their defence of the rights to freedom of conscience, bodily action, and religious exercise: namely, the presumptively right natural liberty (or 'natural right') of all rational, human beings as *imagines Dei* to a certain discretionary liberty or autonomy in the management of their lives. Such a rightful liberty or right is not absolute, however. Rather, it is responsible to the natural law (made manifest in the Decalogue), and so obliged by the basic requirements of social life. This Christian natural law is not reducible to the Hobbesian drive for self-preservation, but comprises a wider range of basic goods, including friendship or society. What is more, its exercise is liable to restraint by the virtues of prudence and patience. This Christian view is basically at odds with the Renaissance's humanly degrading concept of the primordial, pre-conventional, natural right to absolute liberty, secure against any moral constraints while bound to the tyranny of monomaniacal self-preservation. Such a 'right' is less an obliging moral claim or duty than a brute compulsion or psychic drive. Truly, it is not a moral right at all.

IX

Now that we have laid out, analysed, and reflected upon late medieval and early modern discussions of natural rights and their approximations, we are in a position to assess how cogently the criticisms of Burke, Bentham, Ritchie, and O'Neill tell against them.

There is one respect in which the pre-modern tradition corrects modern scepticism. Burke and Bentham both accuse natural rights of being recklessly anarchical in their abstract lack of specification. Yet we have observed that Pope John XXII's assertion of a natural right to property was probably intended to *defend* positive, legal rights to private property *against* the anarchical implications of socially radical Franciscan doctrine. At least this shows that not all talk of natural rights need be socially subversive, and, indeed, that some can be socially conservative.

Otherwise, the pre-modern discussions tend to confirm the views of the sceptics. In their critiques, Burke, Bentham, and Ritchie were reacting mainly against late eighteenth- and early nineteenth-century American and French declarations of human or natural rights, and O'Neill was reacting against post-1945 universal human rights discourse. None of them was responding to a Hobbesian natural right to original, amoral, absolute liberty. Implicitly, however, they all align themselves with the majority of late medieval and early modern scholastics in ruling against such a right, and affirming an objective, humanly dignifying, moral reality that is not, at base, simply the instrument of the individual's amoral drive to survive.

Because they are not reacting against the revolutionary assertion of natural rights, as the British critics were (and are), the pre-moderns cannot be sceptical of it. Nonetheless, they do anticipate post-revolutionary doubt with pre-revolutionary caution. Often they talk about liberties that are rightful according to natural moral law, without quite talking about natural rights. Why this is so, is important to consider. I have proposed that they did it, sometimes at least, in order to avoid encouraging an imprudent presumption in favour of politically dangerous liberties, which obscures the extent to which the liberties' rightfulness is actually contingent upon circumstances. In so doing the pre-moderns implicitly align themselves with the sceptics against abstract rights that pretend to an absoluteness, or at least a presumptiveness, which short-circuits moral deliberation by asserting a conclusion before all the relevant factors have been considered—goods, duties, virtues, and consequences.

Sometimes, the pre-moderns do explicitly resort to natural rights-talk. Often, however, this functions as shorthand for talk of natural morality: a 'natural right' is in fact a positive, legal right that natural morality sanctions, and so deserves to be either defended or created. However, this is problematic, because it is liable to the fault that Ritchie identified: namely, the conflation of the legal and the moral. The fault consists in one of two things. One is the misleading implication that *what is right* according to natural morality in a state of nature enjoys the stability and security characteristic of *a right* according to civil law. The other fault is the need constantly to take back with one hand what has just been given by the other. As Ritchie himself put it: 'What is the good of declaring rights one moment and revoking them the next? But this is what has to be constantly done by the theorists of natural rights, when they are not anarchists.'[93]

On other occasions, pre-moderns such as Vitoria assert natural rights that are not morally justified legal rights, but rather presumptive moral claims to certain liberties (of travel, etc.), which are supposed to hold outside of civil society and even in the absence of international law. The problems with such natural rights

---

[93] Ritchie, *Natural Rights*, p. 128 n. 1.

are, first, that their presumptions are unreasonable; and, second, that they are liable to clash with each other, since their presumptions are inconsistent. Once again, whether a liberty is rightful or not depends on the circumstances, and cannot prudently be determined in advance by asserting a right. Moreover, when two rights conflict, the issues involved can only be resolved by breaking out of rights-talk altogether and deploying a wider range of ethical vocabulary.

3

Are there Natural Rights?

3: The Sceptical Critique and Rights after 1776

I

We move now to extend our testing of the critiques of natural rights from the pre-modern and early modern periods to classic modern affirmations. Here in this chapter we begin with the American and French declarations of the late eighteenth century, before proceeding to two famous treatises of the same period, Thomas Paine's *Rights of Man* and Mary Wollstonecraft's *A Vindication of the Rights of Woman*, and then concluding with the Universal Declaration of Human Rights and the International covenants of the mid-twentieth century. Consideration of the modern Roman Catholic tradition of rights has been reserved for Chapter 4.

II

First of all, we can confirm that the eighteenth-century declarations do indeed purport to talk about *natural* rights, since they attribute them to all beings created in a certain (human) fashion by God or possessed of human nature. The 'rights of man' are, therefore, natural rights. Thus the Virginia Declaration of Rights (12 June 1776) asserts '[t]hat all men are by nature equally free and independent, and have certain inherent rights....';[1] the Declaration of Independence of the United States of America (4 July 1776) asserts 'that all men are created equal, that they are endowed by their Creator with certain inalienable Rights';[2] and the French Declaration of the Rights of Man and the Citizen (1789) asserts 'the natural, inalienable, and sacred rights of man'.[3]

Some of the articles of these declarations assert very general political rights. Thus the French Declaration affirms the right of all citizens to participate in shaping the general will as expressed in legislation, and the right to equality under the law and so to the universal rule of law.[4] This simply articulates the political implications of the conviction that all human beings share a certain basic equality. To those who share that conviction (but not to others) the inference of such a

---

[1] Ritchie, *Natural Rights*, p. 287.   [2] Ibid., p. 289.   [3] Waldron, *Nonsense on Stilts*, p. 26.
[4] French Declaration, 6, 7 (Waldron, *Nonsense on Stilts*, p. 27).

natural right will be unobjectionable. However, it is unobjectionable only because it operates at a very high level of generality, which makes its claim to absoluteness plausible.

Another general political right asserted, this time by the US Declaration of Independence, is 'the Right of the People' to reform any form of government that has become destructive of its proper, natural ends, and even to 'throw [it] off' 'when a long train of abuses and usurpations... evinces a design to reduce them under absolute Despotism'.[5] If we accept the assumption that government is always and everywhere subject to certain natural moral obligations, then this general assertion of a natural right is also unobjectionable.

Some other rights asserted by the French Declaration escape objection by being made explicitly conditional. Thus a right is affirmed against persecution for opinions, including religious ones, but only 'provided that the manifestation of these does not disturb the public order established by legislation'.[6] And the 'inviolable and sacred right' to own property is made subject to the qualification, 'unless some public necessity... clearly requires it'.[7] These assertions are made plausible only because they do not claim to be absolute—although in the case of a right to property its contingency is rhetorically disguised by clothing it in epithets such as 'inviolable' and 'sacred'. The effect of the assertions is to establish a presumption in favour of expressed opinion and of property. A presumption, however, can be overcome. It follows that the rights are not in fact inviolable, if we are talking about positive rights. And if we are talking about natural rights, then it follows that they fade in and out of existence as circumstances dictate, altogether lacking the stability and security that possession of a right connotes.

The tendency to confuse natural rights that are absolute, obtaining always and everywhere, with natural rights that exist only sometimes or with corresponding positive rights that may sometimes be violated—with the result that contingent rights are mistaken for absolute ones—surfaces in the French Declaration's description of the contingent right to property as 'inviolable' and 'sacred'. But the same confusion is sometimes evident beneath the surface, especially in the American Declarations. Thus the Virginia Declaration insists that there is a right of suffrage (conditional on a property qualification), denies that there is a right to suspend or execute laws without popular consent,[8] and attributes the right to reform or abolish delinquent government not just to 'the People' (as does the US Declaration), but more specifically to 'a majority of the community'.[9] These claims go well beyond the general principles that the people should (somehow) participate in shaping the laws, public policies, and forms of government to which they

---

[5] US Declaration of Independence, preamble (Ritchie, *Natural Rights*, p. 289).
[6] French Declaration, 10 (Waldron, *Nonsense on Stilts*, p. 27).
[7] French Declaration, 17 (Waldron, *Nonsense on Stilts*, p. 28).
[8] Virginia Declaration, VII (Ritchie, *Natural Rights*, p. 288).
[9] Virginia Declaration, III (Ritchie, *Natural Rights*, p. 287).

are subject, and specifies democratic mechanisms. Such mechanisms might have been the best way to realise the general principles in late-eighteenth-century Virginia; whether they are always and everywhere the best way is a moot point. Recent Western experience in Iraq and Afghanistan has rightly given ideological democrats pause for considerable thought. The Virginia Declaration, however, makes no explicit distinction between the 'inherent rights' of 'all men' in Article 1 and the rights that follow. As a consequence, all of the rights asserted appear to be graced with the moral authority of absolute natural rights that obtain always and everywhere, whereas in fact many of them are rights justified at best by natural morality in certain contingent circumstances. Insofar as the US Bill of Rights is read in the light of the Declaration of Independence, and its rights share in the moral authority of the 'inalienable rights' with which 'all men' are endowed, the same problem arises. In circumstances where there is no standing police force or army to enforce the law and defend borders, or where there is reason to think it politically dangerous to permit them, it could make sense to grant every citizen a right 'to keep and bear arms', with a view to serving in an ad hoc militia.[10] However, that would be a natural right only in the sense that, in those circumstances, natural morality justifies a positive right; it would not be a natural right in the sense that it is always and everywhere appropriate, and so 'inalienable'. In the French Declaration, the tendency to mistake all the rights listed as absolute is sometimes checked by the explicit addition of conditions—as shown above. There is no such check in the American declarations, which assert the freedom of the exercise of religion, of speech, and of the press without any qualifications at all.[11]

Some of the articles in the modern declarations affirm very general, universal, absolute political rights that are unobjectionable, if one accepts the premises that all human beings are, in some basic sense, equal, and that a government is obliged to intend to serve the interests of all its citizens. Some articles affirm very general, universal rights that are plausible, because they are explicitly made conditional upon certain circumstances. Some assert rights that might well be justified by natural morality in certain circumstances, but fail to distinguish these clearly from absolute, inalienable natural rights. Most problematic of all, however, are those that assert rights to objects that are so indefinite as to lie open to a wild variety of interpretations, some of them lunatic. For example, the Virginia Declaration asserts the inherent, inalienable right to 'the enjoyment of life and liberty', and the US Declaration of Independence, inalienable rights to life and liberty.[12] While

---

[10] United States Bill of Rights, Amendment II (<http://www.archives.gov/founding-docs/bill-of-rights-transcript>, as at 26 September 2017).

[11] Virginia Declaration, XII, XVI (Ritchie, *Natural Rights*, pp. 288–9); United States Bill of Rights, Amendment I (<http://www.archives.gov/founding-docs/bill-of-rights-transcript>, as at 26 September 2017).

[12] Virginia Declaration, I (Ritchie, *Natural Rights*, pp. 287); US Declaration of Independence, preamble (Ritchie, *Natural Rights*, p. 289).

it is, of course, possible to construe these in sensible ways (e.g. as rights not to be killed or otherwise interfered with, except under certain circumstances), as they actually stand they are capable of licensing absurd expectations (e.g. rights to immortality against God Almighty; to absolute immunity from all killing, whether intended or unintended; to entirely untrammelled liberty; and to escape from prison, no matter the reasons for being put there).

Further, even if the Virginia Declaration only affirms an 'inherent' right '*to the means* of ... obtaining happiness and safety', rather than to happiness and security themselves, it remains, as David Ritchie dryly observed, 'in this world of ours ... a very large order on the bank of Providence'.[13] On the one hand, rights to freedom from external interference are invariably possible, since other people always have the power to refrain either from interfering or from forcing others to interfere. On the other hand, rights to benefits, *and even to the means of acquiring benefits*, are not invariably possible. They depend on the availability of resources—and of resources of which one may, morally, avail oneself. Quite possibly the framers of the first article of the Virginia Declaration were thinking of the apparently infinite resources of uncultivated land stretching as far as the eye could see west of the Appalachians. And maybe, when they asserted the right to 'the means of acquiring and possessing property, and pursuing and obtaining happiness', they did so against the 'tyrannical' constraint of colonists from settling the western lands imposed by the 10,000 redcoats stationed along the mountains by King George III.[14] If so, the Virginian framers were oblivious of the natural moral claims of aboriginal Americans to those same lands, claims that the British had in effect resolved to bolster thirteen years before in the Royal Proclamation of 1763, which followed the end of the French and Indian Wars. Besides, even if the western lands had been entirely empty of rival claimants, not everyone everywhere has such prospects on their doorstep. There is, therefore, no natural, inherent, universal, inalienable, absolute right to the means of obtaining happiness. And if there is no absolute right to the means, there cannot be such a right *even to the pursuit* of happiness—with all due respect to the (slightly) more modest US Declaration of Independence.

---

[13] Ritchie, *Natural Rights*, p. 272. The emphasis is mine. Ritchie claims that most American state constitutions assert a natural human right 'not merely of pursuing but of obtaining happiness'. This is not true of the Virginia Declaration, which affirms, a little more modestly, only a right *to the means* of such pursuit and achievement.

[14] Certainly, James Madison (1751–1836), who had been involved in composing the Virginia Declaration, explicitly asserted the natural right of American colonists to the western lands nine years later. Corresponding with the Marquis de Lafayette in 1785, he wrote: 'Nature has given the use of the Mississippi to those who may settle on its waters, as she gave the United States their independence.... Nature seems on all sides to be reasserting those rights which have so long been trampled on by tyranny and bigotry ... If the United States were to become parties to the occlusion of the Mississippi they would be guilty of treason against the very laws under which they obtained and hold their national existence' (Ralph Ketcham, *James Madison: A Biography* (Charlottesville: University of Virginia, 1990), p. 177; see also pp. 96–7).

While the American and French declarations are primarily concerned to assert natural rights, they are not entirely oblivious of other elements of moral life. Thus the Virginia Declaration's third article asserts the right to reform, alter, or abolish a form of government 'in such manner as shall be judged most conducive to the common weal'.[15] Expressions of awareness of the claims of the common good—sometimes overriding—also appear in the French Declaration, as we have seen, where it makes the rights against persecution for opinions or to property conditional upon the requirements of 'public order' or some other 'public necessity'.[16]

Further, the declarations sometimes acknowledge duties. In the French case the acknowledgement is largely a perfunctory recognition of the logical implication of rights, as when the Declaration of the Rights of Man describes itself as 'a constant reminder to [all members of the body social] ... of their rights and duties'.[17] Nevertheless, in Article 11 it also states that citizens are accountable 'for any abuse of ... freedom [of communication of thoughts and opinions] according to the cases established by legislation'.[18] This might show some awareness that within the sphere of freedom protected by a right there nevertheless remains the burden of responsibility about whether and how to exercise it—a responsibility that can find itself subject to moral duties. If there is such awareness, however, it is rather obscured by the qualification of accountability as 'according to the cases established by law'. This implies that accountability is merely legal, not moral, and that the only obligations that govern the exercise of a right are ones prescribed by positive law—say, laws proscribing such things as defamation or hate-speech. Article XVI of the Virginia Declaration is more whole-hearted in its assertion of the importance of moral duty, when, after affirming that 'all men are equally *entitled* to the free exercise of religion', it adds that 'it is the *duty* of all to practice Christian forbearance, love and charity towards each other'.[19] What this implies is that the rights of some citizens will not be respected unless other citizens recognise, and feel the obliging force of, moral obligations.

It is notable that the duty specified here is a duty of virtue. In the previous article (XV), the Virginia Declaration also makes a strong statement about the political necessity of citizens accepting the obligations of virtue: 'no free

---

[15] Virginia Declaration, III (Ritchie, *Natural Rights*, pp. 287).
[16] French Declaration, 10, 17 (Waldron, *Nonsense on Stilts*, pp. 27–8).
[17] French Declaration, preamble (Waldron, *Nonsense on Stilts*, p. 26). During the summer of 1789 concern that an assertion of equal rights would encourage widespread socially destructive egoism led to the proposal of a motion in the National Constituent Assembly that a declaration of the duties of the citizen accompany that of his rights. On 4 August 1789 the motion was defeated by 570 votes to 433. However, after the Jacobins were removed from power, the Convention approved another declaration of rights on 22 August 1795, which included a set of nine duties designed to encourage the individual citizen to obey the law, respect property, and serve the *patrie* (Jeremy Jennings, *Revolution and the Republic: A History of Political Thought in France since the Eighteenth Century* (Oxford: Oxford University Press, 2011), pp. 37–8, 40).
[18] French Declaration, 11 (Waldron, *Nonsense on Stilts*, p. 27).
[19] Virginia Declaration, XVI (Ritchie, *Natural Rights*, pp. 288–9). The emphases are mine.

government, or the blessing of liberty, can be preserved to any people, but by a firm adherence to justice, moderation, temperance, frugality and virtue.'[20] And the US Declaration also recognises the need for the exercise of rights to be tempered by virtue when, after asserting the right of the people to change the form of its government, it immediately qualifies it thus:

> Prudence, indeed, will dictate that Governments long established should not be changed for light and transient causes; and accordingly all experience hath shown, that mankind are more disposed to suffer, while evils are sufferable . . . But when a long train of abuses and usurpations . . . evinces a design to reduce them under absolute Despotism, it is their right, it is their duty, to throw off such Government . . . [21]

In sum, I find that the sceptical critics of these classic modern declarations of natural rights are both fair and unfair. On the one hand, they are quite correct to complain about the ludicrous possibilities and expectations licensed by assertions that are too indefinite. They are also correct to complain about the failure to distinguish between absolute natural rights, which obtain always and everywhere, and conditional positive rights that natural morality justifies in a particular set of circumstances. And they are correct to object to rights whose lack of explicit qualifications renders them implausible. On the other hand, the declarations do sometimes assert natural rights of a very general political kind, which seem unobjectionable on certain (Christian, humanist) anthropological assumptions. Further, they do sometimes assert rights and then make them plausible by adding conditions. Further still, they do sometimes recognise that rights-talk is not sufficient either for overall political well-being or for maintenance of rights simply: they can be found to acknowledge the claims of the common good and of moral duty, and the need for virtue.

With regard to this last point, it is remarkable that the Virginia Declaration goes beyond the recognition of the need for virtue to recognise also the need for a cultural matrix of virtue. Thus, its assertion of rights assumes a generally Christian society, and takes for granted a citizenry that is morally formed by Christian traditions through Christian churches. Hence, the unembarrassed reference to 'Christian forbearance, love and charity'. That is to say, the Virginia Declaration recognises the importance for the maintenance of political and other rights of civil social bodies that form their members in the requisite virtues. That there is none of this in the US Bill of Rights should be forgiven, since the bill's sole intention was to prevent the federal Congress's 'misconstruction or abuse' of its powers. Not so forgivable is the lack of any such recognition in the French Declaration, whose

---

[20] Virginia Declaration, XV (Ritchie, *Natural Rights*, pp. 288).
[21] US Declaration of Independence, Preamble (Ritchie, *Natural Rights*, p. 289).

ambitions were altogether broader, namely, to educate all citizens about their rights.[22] The Declaration's relentless focus is to assert the individual's natural rights and the rule of law, and to insist that the former be limited only by the latter in terms of the equal rights of others and public necessity. This leads to the statement that '[n]othing not forbidden by legislation may be prohibited nor may any individual be compelled to do anything that legislation has not prescribed'.[23] The concern here with defending the individual citizen's freedom from undue interference by the state has entirely eclipsed any concern with how the individual behaves within his sphere of legally defined freedom, how the individual's exercise of his freedom might affect the common good and the practice of respect for the rights of others, and how the individual might be educated and formed to use that freedom well rather than badly.[24]

It can also be argued that, while the qualification of rights—for example, the subjection of the right against persecution for opinions and the right to own property to the requirements of public order and necessity—succeeds in rendering them plausible, at the same time it also renders them indeterminate. We cannot tell what they amount to without reference to a particular set of prevailing circumstances, in particular an estimation of the present requirements of the social good and their urgency—and on this crucial question the declarations are

---

[22]   According to Jeremy Jennings, the view that a declaration of rights was needed to educate citizens was widespread in the summer of 1789 (*Revolution and the Republic*, p. 32).

[23]   French Declaration, 5 (Waldron, *Nonsense on Stilts*, p. 27).

[24]   Christian doubts about the Declaration's fixation on law as the means of bolstering respect for rights, and its consequent neglect of the deeper, unruly, sinful springs of disrespect, found early expression in the brusque dismissal by the Comte de Montlosier (1755–1838) of the Declaration's naive (Enlightenment) notion that ignorance, forgetfulness, and contempt for rights are 'the sole causes of public misfortune'. 'Are we to believe', he asks, 'that fear ... the desire to dominate, all the vehement lusts of pride, ... laziness ... have no influence on public misfortune or on the corruption of governments ... ?' ('la peur, ... le désir de la domination, toutes les affections véhémentes de l'orgueil, ... l'indigence ... croit-on que toutes ces causes n'aient influé en rien sur les malheurs publics, ou sur la corruption des gouvernements ... ?') (*Essai sur l'art de constituer les peuples; ou Examen des opérations constitutionnelles de l'Assemblée nationale de France*, 2nd edn (Paris: Gattey, 1791), p. 41). Agreeing, Louis de Bonald (1754–1840) wrote: 'I concur with theology, which makes an uncontrolled will, a disordered self-love, and depraved or criminal action the source of all our disorders and the origin of all our ills' (*Theorie du pouvoir politique et religieux dans la société civile, démontrée par le raisonnement et par l'histoire* (1796), in *Oeuvres de M. de Bonald* (Paris: Librairie d'Adrien le Clere, 1854), 2 vols, Vol. I, p. 131: 'Je suis d'accord avec la théologie, qui fait d'une volonté déréglée, d'un amour de soi désordonné, d'une action dépravée ou criminelle la source de tous nos désordres, et l'origine de tous nos maux'). Later, when concern had shifted from fending off the threat of tyranny to preserving the stability of democracy, French Republicans openly recognised the need for the cultivation of virtue and exhortation to duty. Thus Jules Barni (1818–78), one of the most widely respected political philosophers in late nineteenth-century France, asserted that '[t]here is no republic worthy of its name and that will last without the proper habits of liberty'—habits such as hard work, sobriety, chastity, recognition of the sanctity of the family, and respect for the law (*Morale dans la démocratie* (1868)). The good citizen, he claimed, must display 'the virtue of abnegation' (*La Manuel Républicain* (1872)). And in *Solidarité* (1896, 1904) Léon Bourgeois (1851–1925) wrote that 'this liberty [conferred by the Revolution] would not be assured to all if everyone, not recognising a limit to their own liberty and profiting from the personal strength and advantages given to them by chance, made use of liberty in a selfish fashion'; and that it is therefore necessary 'to complete the declaration of the rights of man by adding a declaration of duties'. For references, see Jennings, *Revolution and the Republic*, pp. 61–2, 63, 65.

silent.[25] David Ritchie is therefore correct: a sheer appeal to 'nature' cannot answer the question of what *kind* of individual freedom should be protected *here and now*. Recourse must be had to considerations of common good.

III

An early, popular, spirited, and now classic riposte to Burke's critique of the rights asserted by the French Declaration was Thomas Paine's *Rights of Man*, which was published in two parts, the first in March 1791 and the second in February 1792.[26] Against Burke's defence of the pre-revolutionary, monarchical government of France, Paine (1737–1809) comments bitterly: 'Not one glance of compassion, not one commiserating reflection...has he bestowed on those who lingered out the most wretched of lives, a life without hope, in the most miserable of prisons.... He pities the plumage, but forgets the dying bird'.[27] Where Burke opposes abstract, revolutionary rights with those bequeathed by constitutional tradition, Paine dismisses his appeal to 'musty records and mouldy parchments' in favour of the invocation by the Marquis de Lafayette (1757–1834) of 'the sentiments which Nature has engraved in the heart of every citizen'.[28] Foremost among these is the 'divine principle of the equal rights of man... [the sentiment that] all men are born equal, and with equal natural right'.[29] These natural rights are the foundation of all civil rights. Those that that are better secured by entering civil society—most notably, the rights to security and the redress of injury—are exchanged for civil rights.[30] Other natural rights, however, are retained. These include the nation's 'inherent indefeasible right to abolish any form of Government it finds inconvenient, and establish such as accords with its interest, disposition, and happiness'.[31] A government's right to exist depends entirely upon the social contract into which individuals entered to create it.[32] Government established and conducted in the interest of the public is 'republican', and while it need not be representative, that is its most natural form.[33] A hereditary,

[25] As Jennings writes of the composition of the several French declarations of rights during the Revolutionary period, '[l]ittle attention was given to the need to assess the competing demands of natural rights and social utility' (*Revolution and the Republic*, p. 30).

[26] Mark Philp observes that Paine's *Rights of Man* 'was without doubt the single most successful response to Burke (Thomas Paine, *Rights of Man, Common Sense, and Other Political Writings*, ed. and introd. Mark Philp (Oxford: Oxford University Press, 1995), p. xii). Indeed, 'in Britain, the *Rights of Man* outsold Burke three times over within two years; in ten years it probably did so thirtyfold' (ibid., p. xxiii).

[27] Thomas Paine, 'Rights of Man: being an answer to Mr Burke's attack on the French Revolution' (March 1791), in Paine, *Rights of Man*, p. 102.

[28] Paine, 'Rights of Man (1791)', pp. 95–6.   [29] Ibid., p. 117.   [30] Ibid., pp. 119–20.

[31] Ibid., p. 193.   [32] Ibid., p. 122.

[33] Thomas Paine, 'Rights of Man: Part the Second, combining principle and practice' (February 1792), in Paine, *Rights of Man*, p. 230.

monarchical regime such as England's, however, arises out of conquest, not contract, and is naturally tyrannical.[34] Instead of being 'ingrafted on the principles of [society], [it] assumes to exist for itself, and acts by partialities of favour and oppression, [and] becomes the cause of the mischiefs it ought to prevent'.[35] Whereas '[a]ll delegated power is trust, ... all assumed power is usurpation'.[36] Those rights bequeathed by Magna Carta, the English Civil War, and the 'Glorious Revolution' of 1688, which Burke praises so extravagantly, are merely 'restrictions on assumed power', bargains that 'the parts of the government made with each other to divide powers, profits, and privileges'.[37] As for Burke's hysterical depictions of bloody anarchy—his 'horrid paintings'—Paine claims that, whereas '[t]he revolutions that have taken place in other European countries, have been excited by personal hatred.... in the instance of France, we see a revolution generated in the rational contemplation of the rights of man, and distinguishing from the beginning between persons and principles', and that 'when the French Revolution is compared with the revolutions of other countries, the astonishment will be, that it is marked with so few sacrifices'.[38]

Paine's appeal to natural rights in order to ground criticism of positively legal arrangements or policies would have been entirely familiar to scholastics of the late medieval and early modern periods. Indeed, Burke himself was not above appealing to them for that reason, as we have seen.[39] Less familiar and more radical would have been the identification of the fundamental natural right as one to political equality, and therefore freedom from oppressive social and political hierarchy. From this Paine derives a people's natural right to throw off tyrannical government, asserting it in an unqualified—one might say, abstract—manner that would have alarmed Beza. Nowhere does Paine address concerns about the political dangers of such a licentious abstract right. Nowhere does he consider who has the right to speak in the name of 'the people', and whether their self-styled representatives might become tyrants whose tyranny is made all the grosser by ideological zeal. No doubt Paine can be forgiven for not asking these questions in *Rights of Man*, since he wrote it in 1791–2 when the French Revolution was still in its conservative phase, and before the execution of King Louis XVI in January 1793, followed by the dictatorship of Robespierre and the Jacobins with their Reign of Terror from June 1793 to July 1794.[40] However, it seems that his own personal experience of revolutionary terror—in which only a stroke of good

---

[34] Paine, 'Rights of Man (1791)', p. 123; 'Rights of Man (1792)', p. 224.
[35] Paine, 'Rights of Man (1792)', p. 216.   [36] Ibid., p. 238.   [37] Ibid., p. 246.
[38] Paine, 'Rights of Man (1791)', pp. 99, 100–1.   [39] See Chapter 1, p. 12.
[40] In September 1792 Paine was elected to the French National Convention, where he argued against the execution of the king and made an enemy of Robespierre. He was arrested and imprisoned in December 1793, but released a year later, thanks to the diplomatic efforts of James Monroe, future President of the USA.

fortune saved him from the guillotine—did not move him subsequently to revise his earlier sanguine view of the natural popular right to effect regime-change.[41]

IV

The year 1792 saw the publication of *two* classic treatises on natural rights: not only Paine's *Rights of Man*, but also Mary Wollstonecraft's *A Vindication of the Rights of Woman*. Like Paine, Wollstonecraft (1759–97) appeals to a fundamental natural right to human equality against artificial social distinctions, although the ones that concern her are those dividing the sexes. The general problem, as she sees it, lies in

> [t]he preposterous distinctions of rank, which render civilization a curse, by dividing the world between voluptuous tyrants, and cunning envious dependents, [and so] corrupt, almost equally, every class of people, because respectability is not attached to the discharge of the relative duties of life, but to the station, and when the duties are not fulfilled the affections cannot gain sufficient strength to fortify the virtue of which they are the natural reward.[42]

Against Rousseau, Wollstonecraft does not ascribe the cause of this social evil to civilisation as such, and so she does not follow him in recommending retreat to 'a brutal state of nature'. After all, God in his benevolent wisdom has created humankind 'to have a capacity to rise above the state in which sensation produced brutal ease'. No, the cause of the problem lies in 'arbitrary power' and 'hereditary distinctions', and the solution in advance to the establishment of 'true civilization'.[43]

The specific form of the problem that preoccupies Wollstonecraft is the denial to women of their natural human right to participate in government, by withholding from them equal civil and political rights.[44] She articulates her objection to this in terms, however, not primarily of its sheer unfairness, but rather of its socially corrupting effects. Because women are excluded from roles that carry responsibility for the public good, and from the education that would fit them to carry it, they 'attempt to do themselves justice by retaliation'.[45] This they achieve by cunningly exploiting their sexual power to exercise a certain tyranny, becoming 'alluring mistresses [rather] than affectionate wives and rational mothers'.[46] The social consequence is that women, men, and the relations between them are made

---

[41] According to Mark Philip, editor of the Oxford University Press edition of *Rights of Man*, in personal correspondence with the author.

[42] Mary Wollstonecraft, *A Vindication of the Rights of Woman* (Mineola, NY: Dover Publications, 1996), p. 149.

[43] Ibid., pp. 13–14, 17.   [44] Ibid., pp. 2–3.   [45] Ibid., p. 4.   [46] Ibid., pp. 6, 10.

vicious, and the institution of marriage accordingly weakened.[47] 'The box of mischief thus opened in society,' Wollstonecraft asks, 'what is to preserve private virtue, the only security of public freedom and universal happiness?'[48]

The answer lies in granting women equal civil and political rights, which would liberate them both from dependence 'on their senses for employment and amusement, when no noble pursuit sets them above the little vanities of the day',[49] and from economic dependence on their men:

> There must be more equality established in society, or morality will never gain ground... It is vain to expect virtue from women till they are, in some degree, independent of men; nay, it is vain to expect that strength of natural affection, which would make them good wives and mothers. Whilst they are absolutely dependent on their husbands they will be cunning, mean, and selfish, and the men who can be gratified by the fawning fondness of spaniel-like affection, have not much delicacy, for love is not to be bought, in any sense of the words, its silken wings are instantly shrivelled up when any thing beside a return in kind is sought.[50]

In this way with 'more equitable laws forming... citizens, marriage may become more sacred:... young men may choose wives from motives of affection',[51] wives may become more faithful, and mothers more reasonable.[52]

Wollstonecraft's *Vindication* is strong evidence that advocacy for rights, natural or legal, need not occlude concern for the promotion of virtue and the common good. For in her case, the ultimate reason for recognising the natural right to human equality by granting women equal civil and political rights was not the sheer justice of it, but through that the virtues of women, men, and their relationships, and the flourishing of the basic social institution of marriage. In Wollstonecraft the liberal promotion of rights serves communitarian ends.

V

The Universal Declaration of Human Rights (UDHR, 1948), and the subsequent International Covenants on Economic, Social and Cultural Rights (ICESCR, 1966) and on Civil and Political Rights (ICCPR, 1966), are not simply affirmations of natural rights. Insofar as states have signed and ratified them, they have acquired a measure of positive legal force. Nevertheless, in its opening sentence, the Universal Declaration ascribes 'equal and inalienable rights' to 'all members of the human

---

[47] Ibid., p. 4.   [48] Ibid., p. 4.   [49] Ibid., p. 28.   [50] Ibid., pp. 145–6.
[51] Ibid., p. 4.   [52] Ibid., p. 154.

family', suggesting that these derive from their 'inherent dignity'.[53] Then, in their opening sentences, the two International Covenants quote the Universal Declaration's ascription verbatim and state expressly that 'these rights derive from the inherent dignity of the human person'.[54] These declarations, therefore, have the status of the 'law of nations' (*ius gentium*)—that is, the widespread, transcultural recognition of the principles, and more or less specific implications, of natural morality.

As in the early modern declarations, so here some assertions of rights are so indefinite as to license absurd interpretations. For one example, take the UDHR's unqualified assertion of rights to 'life, liberty, and security'.[55]

Sometimes the asserted rights are merely truisms—for example, the UDHR's rights to 'just' conditions of work, to 'just' remuneration ensuring for the individual and his family an existence 'worthy of human dignity', and to 'reasonable' limitation of working hours;[56] and the ICESCR's right of workers to 'fair' wages.[57] No one can quarrel with what is 'just', 'fair', 'reasonable', and 'worthy of human dignity', of course, but so long as their content remains unspecified their claims on conduct are empty and rights to them are idle.

In other instances, rights do have substance and therefore normative force, but appear to claim an absoluteness that strains credibility. Thus the UDHR asserts unqualified rights to freedom to manifest one's religion or belief, and to freedom of opinion and expression[58]—although the ICCPR is more prudent and subjects them to limiting conditions.[59]

Sometimes a right equivocates between being absolute but absurdly indeterminate, and being determinate but not absolute. So, the ICCPR asserts 'the inherent right to life'.[60] Echoing the reference to the 'inherent dignity... of all members of the human family' in the covenant's opening sentence, this seems to be a right that is grounded in a distinctive characteristic of human being, rather than dependent on contingent circumstances. In that sense, therefore, it seems to be absolute. Quite what it amounts to, however, is uncertain. As it stands, without any further specification, it gives licence to all manner of absurd or doubtful claims—for example, to immortality against God Almighty. One way to achieve a credible interpretation would be to read it in the light of the second sentence following its assertion: 'No one shall be arbitrarily deprived of his life.' In other words, we should take the 'right to life' to amount to a right against illegal killing. Obstructing this interpretation, however, is the intervening sentence, 'This right

---

[53] Universal Declaration of Human Rights (UDHR), Preamble. The derivation is suggested by the verbal priority of 'inherent dignity' to 'equal and inalienable rights of all members of the human family'.

[54] International Covenant on Economic, Social, and Cultural Rights (adopted by the General Assembly of the United Nations, 16 December 1966), Preamble; International Covenant on Civil and Political Rights (adopted by the General Assembly of the United Nations, 19 December 1966), Preamble.

[55] UDHR, Article (Art.) 3.   [56] UDHR, Art. 23.1,3, 24.   [57] ICESCR, Art. 7 (a) i.
[58] UDHR, Art. 13.1, 13.2, 18, 19.   [59] ICCPR, Art. 18.3, 19.3.   [60] ICCPR, Art. 6.1.

shall be protected by law,' which implies a distinction between a prior natural ('inherent') right and its subsequent protection by positive law. The former is not reducible to the latter. Alternatively, perhaps, we should understand the 'right to life' in terms of subsequent clauses in the article, so that it means a right against the death penalty for anyone below eighteen years of age and for pregnant women, and for all others except 'for the most serious crimes in accordance with the law in force at the time of the commission of the crime etc.', together with a right of those sentenced to death to seek pardon or commutation.[61] The problem with this reading is that there is nothing *inherent* about a right to immunity at the age of 18, rather than at 16 or 20. Moreover, the seriousness of a crime does not lie simply in the inherent nature of the agent, but in circumstantial contingencies such as the effects of his act on other people. So: insofar as the 'right to life' is inherent or absolute, it is implausibly indeterminate; insofar as it is plausibly determinate, it is not inherent or absolute.

What about rights that assert the rule of law against arbitrary arrest, detention, or exile; against arbitrary interference with privacy, family, home, or correspondence; against arbitrary deprivation of property; in favour of a presumption of innocence until proven guilty; and in favour of 'a fair and public hearing by an independent and impartial tribunal' in the case of a criminal trial?[62] What is their claim to the status of 'natural'? If by 'arbitrary', 'unfair', and 'partial' what is meant is simply 'morally unjustified', then, of course, we could talk confidently of natural rights against things of such immoral quality. However, in the absence of any further information about what makes them unjustified, the concepts would be practically useless. Moreover, what the international covenants almost certainly mean by 'arbitrary' is any action by the state that infringes upon the liberty of individual citizens in a manner unconstrained by the rule of law. And their references to the presumption of innocence, to a fair and public hearing, and to an independent and impartial tribunal clearly envisage judicial institutions. The rights against arbitrariness and to fairness and impartiality, therefore, presuppose a political context, not a natural one. They are therefore not natural rights in the sense of existing outside of political society and positive law.[63] We could, nevertheless, call them 'natural' in the sense that they are positive, legal rights, which are justified by natural morality. But the danger in so doing is that we wrongly

---

[61] ICCPR, Art. 6.2, 3, 4, 5.   [62] UDHR, Art. 9, 10, 11, 12, 17.2.

[63] The fact that many of the reservations declared by States Parties upon subscribing to the ICCPR bear upon rights that concern judicial or penal practice, is evidence, if evidence were needed, that these are positive, contextually-dependent rights. Thus the UK reserved the right not to apply the guarantee of free legal assistance in Art. 14(d) 'in so far as the shortage of legal practitioners and other considerations render the application of this guarantee in British Honduras, Fiji and St Helena impossible' (p. 287); and not to apply Art. 25(c) insofar as it applies to jury service in the Isle of Man (pp. 287–8). Thus, too, with regard to Art. 10.3 Denmark reserved the right 'to maintain possibilities of flexible arrangements' concerning the segregation of juvenile offenders from adults (p. 290: also Sweden, p. 299), and with regard to Art. 14.1 it claimed a more permissive right to exclude the press and the public from trials (p. 290).

suppose that such rights are morally justified always and everywhere, or at least that their content remains the same in all circumstances. In fact, however, in time of emergency or war, prudence might require that constraints on the action of the state be relaxed; and in a case involving counter-terrorism, prudence might require that the optimally open and public nature of a trial be compromised for the sake of protecting secret sources of intelligence. The right against state arbitrariness would remain, but the state's room for discretion would be enlarged and a greater correlative risk of state arbitrariness would be accepted; and the right to a fair hearing by an independent and impartial tribunal would remain, but it would no longer be entirely and optimally public. The danger attaching to natural rights-talk here is that the circumstantial contingency of their natural moral justification is lost from sight.

Other rights asserted by the post-war documents are obviously not natural, in the sense of inhering in the dignity of human nature and so applying always and everywhere. Most notorious among them is the ICESCR's right to 'periodic holidays with pay'.[64] Less notorious, but no less imprudent, is the UDHR and ICCPR's treatment of political rights. On the one hand, their assertion of the right of everyone 'to take part in the government of his country, directly or through freely chosen representatives'[65] is unobjectionable, if too vague to have much practical grip. On the reasonable assumption that any government should serve the legitimate interests of all its people, not just some of them, it follows that all the people must have the means of representing their interests and views to the government. On the other hand, however, both the UDHR and the ICCPR— like their eighteenth-century predecessors—go beyond this generic right to political representation by specifying elections by universal suffrage as *the* form that it must take.[66] For reasons explained in section II of this chapter, I consider this to be democratic overreach.

Rights that are over-specified, so that they are too closely tied to the particular economic and political structures and histories of the West, have no good claim to be natural, universal, applicable always and everywhere. Nor do welfare rights that are explicitly made contingent on a state's available resources. For one example, take the UDHR's affirmation of everyone's entitlement to the realisation of 'the economic, social and cultural rights indispensable for his dignity and the free development of his personality' '*in accordance with the organisation and resources of each State*'.[67] For another example, take the ICESCR's commitment of each State Party 'to take steps ... *to the maximum of its available resources*, with a view to achieving progressively the full realization of the rights recognised in the present Covenant by all appropriate means'.[68]

---

[64] ICESCR, Art. 7 (d).   [65] UDHR, Art. 21.1; ICCPR, Art. 25(a).
[66] UDHR, Art. 21.3; ICCPR, Art. 25(b).   [67] UDHR, Art. 22. The emphasis is mine.
[68] ICESCR, Art. 2.1. The emphasis is mine.

As for welfare rights that are not made contingent on a state's available resources, they buy their claim to natural, universal, absolute status only at the expense of practical plausibility. The idea that everyone has the right to enjoy in foreign countries asylum from persecution on account of political crimes assumes that there will always be some countries that can afford to provide asylum and that the number of asylum-seekers will never be overwhelming.[69] Such an assumption may seem safe enough in current circumstances, but both reflection on history and not implausible speculation about the future call it into some doubt. Vulnerable to greater doubt is the assertion of a 'fundamental right of everyone to be free from hunger'.[70] This makes sense only on the assumption either that every state has the resources to preserve its people from hunger or that other states or non-governmental bodies have the resources, together with the obligation, to do so instead. Circumstances could arise, however, where no state or other body has the requisite means. But even where they do have the means, states and other bodies normally carry multiple responsibilities and are subject to multiple obligations. No state is subject to a single, overriding obligation in all circumstances. Presumably, preserving its people from starvation should be a high priority for any state, but so should preserving them from violent crime and invasion. It is not obvious that the former should always trump the latter—and that, for example, the Soviets should have surrendered to the Nazis rather than see Leningrad starve in the Second World War. However, if for the sake of argument, we were to agree that every state has an overriding obligation to keep its own people free from hunger, it would follow that no state can have an *overriding* obligation to secure such freedom for another people. Other states have prior obligations to provide sufficient prosperity and security to *their own* peoples. Once those obligations have been met, obligations to other peoples do arise. But no one state, having satisfied its domestic obligations, has the resources to save *all* other peoples from famine (or invasion or tyranny). So while a state, having met its domestic obligations, is indeed subject to an obligation to aid foreign peoples, it nevertheless retains the discretion to decide which foreign peoples it can best aid, and how. It is quite conceivable, therefore, that circumstances may arise where a state is not able to keep its own people free of hunger, and where other states or bodies are not obliged to aid it (rather than other ailing states). Since someone's right implies someone else's obligation, where no one is obliged, there cannot be a right. It follows that there is no fundamental, natural, universal, absolute, applying-always-and-everywhere right to be free from hunger.

To some extent the rights asserted by the post-war documents are not freedoms and benefits that the subscribing states bind themselves to uphold and provide, but rather goals that they commit themselves to try to realise. In other words, the

---

[69] UDHR, Art. 14.   [70] ICESCR, Art. 11.2.

'rights' are aspirational. Thus the UDHR describes itself as 'a common standard of *achievement* for all peoples and nations', which is proclaimed 'to the end that every individual and every organ of society . . . shall *strive* by teaching and education to promote respect for these rights and freedoms and by *progressive* measures, national and international, to secure their universal and effective recognition and observance'.[71] The aspirational quality of some of the asserted rights is most evident (if not explicit) in the ICESCR, whose welfare right to work liberally includes 'technical and vocational guidance and training programmes, policies and techniques to achieve steady economic, social and cultural development and full and productive employment under conditions safeguarding fundamental political and economic freedoms to the individual', and which grants the ambitious right to 'the enjoyment of the highest attainable standard of physical and mental health'.[72] These are indeed tall orders on the Bank of Providence.

It seems, then, that the tradition of scepticism about natural rights does score several hits against classic post-war affirmations of universal rights. Some of these purported rights are too indefinite or too absolute to be plausible or useful; others are too specific to be natural (in the sense of universal or absolute, applying always and everywhere); and yet others are truistic or merely aspirational.

It is true that some rights in the post-war documents are rendered plausible by being made conditional. Thus the ICCPR declares that the freedom to manifest religion or beliefs 'may be subject . . . to such limitations as are prescribed by law and are necessary to protect public safety, order, health or morals or the fundamental rights and freedoms of others'; that the exercise of rights to hold opinions without interference and to freedom of expression 'may . . . be subject to certain restrictions, . . . these shall . . . be such as are provided by law and are necessary: (a) For respect of the rights and reputations of others; (b) For the protection of national security or of public order . . . or of public health or morals'; and that the rights of peaceful assembly and of association are subject to restrictions 'imposed in conformity with the law and which are necessary in a democratic society in the interests of national security or public safety, public order . . . the protection of public health or morals or the protection of the rights and freedoms of others'.[73] Similarly, the ICESCR subjects the right to form and join trade unions to restrictions 'prescribed by law and . . . necessary in a democratic society in the interests of national security or public order or for the protection of the rights and freedoms of others'.[74] More generally, the ICESCR tells us that the States Parties may subject its asserted rights 'to such limitations as are determined by law . . . in so far as this may be compatible with the nature of these rights and . . . for the purpose of promoting the general welfare in a democratic society'.[75] Further still, both of the covenants include articles that permit the States Parties, in extremis, to

---

[71] UDHR, Preamble. The emphases are mine.   [72] ICESCR, Art. 6.2, 12.1.
[73] ICCPR, Art. 18.3, 19.3, 21, 22.2.   [74] ICESCR, Art. 8.1(a).   [75] ICESCR, Art. 4.

derogate from all of their obligations to uphold rights—with certain stated exceptions.[76] Thus, the ICCPR declares that

> [i]n time of public emergency which threatens the life of the nation and the existence of which is officially proclaimed, the States Parties to the present Covenant may take measures derogating from their obligations under the present Covenant to the extent strictly required by the exigencies of the situation, provided that such measures are not inconsistent with their other obligations under international law and do not involve discrimination solely on the ground of race, colour, sex, language, religion or social origin.[77]

All that is true. However, insofar as a right is subject to legally prescribed social conditions or susceptible to derogation by a State Party, it does not obtain in a state of nature, nor is it absolute, applying always and everywhere. It is a legal right, not a natural one.

It is also true that, while the UDHR and the two covenants are primarily concerned to assert rights, they are not entirely deaf to the call of duty. In its penultimate article, for example, the UDHR acknowledges that 'everyone has duties to the community in which alone the free and full development of his personality is possible';[78] in its Preamble, the ICESCR recognises that 'the individual ... [has] duties to other individuals and to the community';[79] and, more specifically, the ICCPR recognizes that the exercise of the right to freedom of expression 'carries with it special duties and responsibilities'.[80] Again, however, the duties that the covenants recognise (like the French Declaration) are *legal*, not simply moral ones; they may restrict the exercise of rights only in a manner 'determined [or provided] by law'.[81]

VI

Our scrutiny of modern natural rights-talk has found ample evidence to substantiate many of the sceptics' charges: some of the rights asserted are truistic or merely aspirational; others are ludicrously or dangerously abstract, licensing unrealistic hopes and political recklessness; yet others conflate conditional positive rights justified by natural morality with natural rights, misleadingly endowing the

---

[76] This general permission is withheld only from the rights to life; against torture and cruel, inhuman, or degrading treatment or punishment; against slavery and servitude; against imprisonment merely on the ground of inability to fulfil a contractual obligation; against being held guilty of any criminal offence that was not an offence at the time it was committed; to equal status as 'a person before the law'; and to freedom of thought, conscience and religion (ICCPR, Art. 6, 7, 8.1, 8.2, 11, 15, 16, 18).

[77] ICCPR, Art. 4.1.   [78] UDHR, Art. 29.1.   [79] ICESC.R, Preamble.

[80] ICCPR, Art. 19.3.   [81] UDHR, 29.2; ICCPR, 19.3.

former with the universality and inviolability of the latter. Further, David Ritchie's claim has been substantiated: the content of certain rights cannot be determined by a sheer appeal to 'nature', and apart from consideration of the common good in the relevant circumstances.

On the other hand, we have learned that it is possible for rights-talk to acknowledge the insufficiency of rights for overall political well-being; to talk also of duties; and to recognise the need for virtue and a cultural matrix that generates it. Indeed, it is possible to talk up rights *for the sake of* promoting virtue and the common good.

In addition, our survey has brought to light some rights that have strong prima facie claim to be natural in the sense of 'universal', and are not merely tautologous but sufficiently concrete to guide judgement. These comprise political rights of a very general kind—to political equality and political participation—as well as rights against slavery and servitude, and against torture or cruel, inhuman, or degrading treatment or punishment. We shall defer discussion of these candidates to the end of Chapter 5.

4

Are there Natural Rights?

4: The Sceptical Critique and the Modern Roman Catholic Tradition

I

Unlike the French Declaration of the Rights of Man, the post-1945 documents bear the impression of Roman Catholic thought, not only in their acknowledgement of duty but more specifically in their assertion of the right of the family—a social body, not an individual—to protection by society and the state. As the Universal Declaration puts it, 'The family is the natural and fundamental group unit of society and is entitled to protection by society and the State.'[1] How such an impression came about—and more broadly, how the Roman Catholic Church came to be a leading advocate of human rights in the decades after the end of the Second World War—bears reflection. This is because, throughout the nineteenth century, Catholicism had set its face against the idea of the rights of man for reasons that often echo the objections raised by the British tradition of natural-rights scepticism. Understanding why the Church changed its mind, therefore, might help us discern how far a certain conception of natural rights is able to overcome those objections.

In the wake of the French Revolution, the Roman Catholic Church refused natural or human rights-talk because of its association with Rousseau's doctrine of popular sovereignty, whereby the national general will is the final moral and political authority, unconstrained by natural law. Thus in 1864 the Syllabus of Errors, which was authorised by Pope Pius IX (1792–1878), included the following:

> 3. Human reason, without any reference whatsoever to God, is the sole arbiter of truth and falsehood, and of good and evil; it is a law to itself.... 39. The State, as being the origin and source of all rights, is endowed with a certain right not circumscribed by any limits...56.... [I]t is not at all necessary that human laws should be made conformable to the laws of nature and receive their binding power from God.[2]

---

[1] UDHR, Art. 16.3; see also the ICESCR, Art. 10.1.

[2] Pius IX, 'The Syllabus of Errors' (1864), Arts 3, 39, and 56. The Pope's concern here is the same as that of the contemporary Anglican theologians, who are discussed in Chapter 6, for objectively 'right order'.

It is commonly—and rightly—supposed that it was through the famous 1891 encyclical, *Rerum Novarum*, which was authorised by Pope Leo XIII (1810–1903), that human rights first entered the Church's social teaching.[3] Thus Leo affirms that 'every man has by nature the right to possess property of his own', since human being is distinguished primarily by the rational ability to make provision for the future.[4] It is significant, however, that this affirmation of an individual's right to property is quickly associated with a social duty. The very next rights to be mentioned are 'the natural and primitive right of marriage' and the rights (and duties) of the pre-political family, which are asserted against any socialist state that would abolish them. Then we are told that 'it is a most sacred law of nature that a father must provide food and all necessaries for those whom he has begotten'.[5] Other individual rights are also qualified by moral obligations. '[I]t is one thing to have a right to the possession of money,' Leo tells us, 'and another to have a right to use money as one pleases'.[6] Appealing to Aquinas, he proceeds to argue that where private property is surplus to the needs of the owner and his family, the right to it is subject to the duty of charity to give to the indigent.[7] Later on, Leo reinforces the authority of objective obligation by asserting the 'most sacred and inviolable' rights *of God*, which constrain the liberty of individuals by obliging them not to outrage 'that human dignity which God Himself treats with reverence' by giving themselves up to servitude.[8] Finally, he supplements and qualifies rights-talk by invoking, not only duties, but virtues. So while the encyclical affirms that 'to enter into a [working men's] "society" . . . is the natural right of man', except where such association is for purposes 'evidently bad, unjust, or dangerous to the State',[9] it then goes on to urge Catholic workers to join Catholic associations, since these keep before the eyes of their members 'the precepts of duty and the laws of the Gospel', inculcating moderation, modesty, honesty, dutifulness, and, above all, charity, 'the mistress and queen of virtues'.[10]

Building on the work of Mary Ann Glendon and John Nurser, Samuel Moyn has recently tracked and highlighted the major influence of Roman Catholic thinking upon the rights-talk of the Universal Declaration and the immediate

---

[3] See, for example, David Hollenbach, *Claims in Conflict: Retrieving and Renewing the Catholic Human Rights Tradition* (New York: Paulist Press, 1979), pp. 43–9; and Martin Shupack, 'The Church and Human Rights: Catholic and Protestant Human Rights Views as Reflected in Church Statements', *Harvard Human Rights Journal*, 6 (1993), pp. 127, 139, 146. Zachary Calo dissents: 'The language of rights is sufficiently muted, and the encyclical sufficiently shrouded in antimodernist overtones, that it might be overly generous to characterise Leo's writing as having introduced into Catholic social thought the concept of human rights' ('Catholic Social Thought, Political Liberalism and the Idea of Human Rights', *Journal of Christian Legal Thought* (Fall 2011), p. 5). I disagree: while *Rerum Novarum*'s rights-talk is strongly qualified by other moral considerations, and therefore diverges from the anti-Christian French Revolutionary tradition, its affirmation of natural rights is unequivocal.

[4] Pope Leo XIII, *Rerum Novarum*, in *Seven Great Encyclicals*, introd. William J. Gibbons, SJ (New York: Paulist Press, 1963), sections 5–6, pp. 3–4.

[5] Ibid., sections 9, 11, pp. 5–7.   [6] Ibid., section 19, p. 11.   [7] Ibid.

[8] Ibid., section 32, p. 19.   [9] Ibid., section 38, p. 24.

[10] Ibid., sections 40, 41, 44, 45, pp. 25–30.

post-war period.[11] While Moyn has been correctly castigated for dating the Catholic endorsement of rights only from the 1940s, and for dismissing its rootage in the medieval period, his thesis that 'human rights [at the time of the Declaration was] a project of the Christian right, not the secular left', is plausible.[12] By attributing this project to the 'Christian right', Moyn means (disapprovingly) that it involved the assertion, not simply of the rights of individuals, but also of the rights of social institutions and considerations of the common good.[13] This socially qualified kind of rights-talk, which (*pace* Moyn) had already come to expression in *Rerum Novarum*, spoke (again) in the famously anti-totalitarian encyclical of 1937, *Mit brennender Sorge*, which was authorised by Pope Pius XI (1857–1939):

> Man, as a person, possesses rights that he holds from God and which must remain, with regard to the collectivity, beyond the reach of anything that would tend to deny them, to abolish them, or to neglect them. To disregard this truth is

[11] Samuel Moyn, *Christian Human Rights* (Philadelphia: University of Pennsylvania Press, 2015), p. 12.

[12] Moyn, *Christian Human Rights*, p. 8. For two very critical reviews of Moyn's genealogy of rights, see David Little, 'Critical Reflections on *The Last Utopia: Human Rights in History* by Samuel Moyn', in David Little, *Essays on Religion and Human Rights: Ground to Stand on* (Cambridge: Cambridge University Press, 2016), esp. pp. 58, 67–72; and John Witte, 'Review of Samuel Moyn, *Christian Human Rights* (2015)', *Books and Culture*, 22/2 (March/April 2016).

Moyn argues that Pius XII's affirmation of 'fundamental personal rights' in his Christmas message of 1942 was 'a critical turning point... that has defined history since' (*Christian Human Rights*, p. 2) and that '[t]he ideological association of Christianity and human rights depended on contingent and time-bound circumstance no later than the 1940s and shortly before' (ibid., p. 4). He is confidently, even superciliously, dismissive of claims that human rights have deep roots in Christian tradition: 'No one could plausibly claim... that the history of human rights is one of wholly discontinuous novelty, whether in the 1940s or after. But radical departures nonetheless occurred very late in Christian history, even if they were unfailingly represented as consistent with what came before... Christian human rights were injected into tradition by pretending they had always been there, and on the basis of minor antecedents now treated as fonts of enduring commitments' (ibid., p. 5). Of Jacques Maritain's attempt to ground human rights in natural law (*The Rights of Man and Natural Law*, 1942), Moyn tells us that he finds it curious because 'nearly all histories of the political language [of rights] concur that the rise of rights in political theory occurred after and because of the destruction of the Thomistic natural law tradition'. And then he comments: 'In either a stroke of a master, or a sleight of hand, or both, Maritain—as if the Thomistic movement had not long and unanimously rejected modern rights—claimed that the one implied the other' (ibid., p. 83). '[C]ontrary to the overwhelming weight of his own tradition', he argued that Catholic natural law was the best framework for modern human rights (ibid., p. 122).

While it is certainly true that the papal endorsement of human rights in the twentieth century marked an important shift away from the unqualified opposition that the Roman Catholic Church had mounted through most of the nineteenth century, it is also true that that shift actually began half a century earlier than Moyn recognises. What is more, in the light of what Brian Tierney and Annabel Brett have shown in exhaustive detail, the medieval antecedents of papal endorsement from 1891 onwards were hardly 'minor', which implies that the twentieth-century shift was less than 'radical'. In his discussion of the rootage of human rights in Christian tradition, Moyn sides with Leo Strauss, Richard Tuck, Michel Villey against John Witte and Nicholas Wolterstorff (ibid., pp. 5, 204 n. 42). He does so, however, without reckoning at all with the work of Tierney and Brett, of whom he makes no mention. As will be clear from Chapter 2 and Chapter 6, I think that the main theses of Strauss and Villey have been discredited by Tierney and Brett.

[13] Moyn, *Christian Human Rights*, pp. 38, 44.

to forget that the true general good is determined and recognised, in the final analysis, by the nature of man, which harmoniously balances personal rights and social obligations, and by the good of society, which is also determined by this same human nature.[14]

Pope Pius XII (1876–1958) continued in the same vein, when he argued in 1941 that safeguarding 'the inviolable sphere of the rights of the human person ... flow [s] from that genuine concept of the common good which the State is called upon to promote'.[15]

II

The influence of Roman Catholic thought upon the Universal Declaration and post-war rights-talk is most obviously visible in the work of the theologian Jacques Maritain (1882–1973), who was, according to Moyn, 'the most prominent expositor' of human rights during the Second World War and 'the most prominent thinker of any kind across the world to champion rights in the postwar moment'.[16] In his seminal work *The Rights of Man and Natural Law* (1944) Maritain reveals how the historical context of the war against Nazi tyranny—'a war wherein the destiny of civilisation is at stake'[17]—had made it imperative to assert 'the liberty ... the dignity ... the rights' of the human person.[18] His conception of these things is, naturally, theological. Thus, the 'absolute dignity' of the individual person consists, not merely in his 'hold[ing] himself in hand by his intelligence and his will', but also in his being 'in direct relationship with the absolute'.[19] '[B]y reason of other relationships ... to things more important than common life,' he writes, 'there are in me gifts, rights, and values which exist neither by the State nor for the State and which are outside the sphere of the State'—there are 'absolute goods' of the person.[20] 'The tap-root of human personality is not society, but God.'[21] This 'intrinsic constitution of human nature',[22] whereby the individual person is called 'to the order of absolute values and to a destiny superior to time',[23] gives rise to

[14] Pope Pius XI, 'Mit brennender Sorge', 14 March 1937, in Georges Passelecq and Bernard Suchecky, *The Hidden Encyclical of Pius XI*, trans. Steven Randall (New York: Harcourt Brace, 1997), pp. 105–6.
[15] Pope Pius XII, 'The Anniversary of *Rerum Novarum*' (1 June 1941), *Logos*, 5.4 (Fall 2002), p. 163; cited by Moyn, *Christian Human Rights*, p. 77.
[16] Moyn, *Christian Human Rights*, pp. 16, 72–3.
[17] Jacques Maritain, *The Rights of Man and Natural Law* (London: Geoffrey Bles, 1944), p. 5.
[18] Ibid., pp. 5–6.   [19] Ibid., p. 6.   [20] Ibid., pp. 12, 13.   [21] Ibid., p. 14.
[22] Ibid., p. 40.   [23] Ibid., p. 45.

fundamental rights ... to existence and life; ... to personal freedom or to conduct one's own life as master of oneself and of one's acts, responsible for them before God and the law of the community; ... to the pursuit of the perfection of moral and rational human life; ... to the pursuit of the eternal good; ... to keep one's body whole; ... to private ownership of material goods; ... to marry according to one's choice and to raise a family which will be assured of the liberties due to it; ... of association.[24]

These 'fundamental rights' are expressly distinguished from the 'rights of the civic person' and the 'rights of the working person' that spring directly from positive law and only indirectly from natural law,[25] which they express 'in a contingent manner'.[26] This appears to imply that 'fundamental rights' are absolute.

Militating against such a reading, however, is the contrast that Maritain draws between the French Declaration's 'rationalist' conception of rights and the Christian one. The former finds its inspiration in Rousseau's anthropology and is characterised by egoism and a correspondingly rigid absoluteness.[27] Since the human being is thought to be subject only to the law of his own sovereign will and freedom, Maritain tells us, his rights appear 'as themselves divine, hence infinite, escaping every objective measure, denying every limitation imposed upon the claims of ego, and ultimately expressing the absolute independence of the human subject and a so-called absolute right ... to unfold one's cherished possibilities at the expense of all other beings'.[28] Against this 'code of absolute and universal justice' he posits the 'creative wisdom' of the Christian conception of rights.[29] The clear implication here is that 'Christian' rights are more malleable, more context-sensitive, more conditional upon the claims of social duty than atheist, rationalist ones. The implication is confirmed, first, by Maritain's general claim that love should qualify justice, transforming it into civic friendship or fraternity;[30] and, second, by his more specific claim that the fundamental rights of individual persons may sometimes be suspended by the legitimate demands of the common good. So, for example, '[i]n the case of extreme peril and for the safety of the community, the State can forcibly requisition the services of each of us and demand that each of us risk his life in a just war; it can also deprive criminals of certain of their rights.'[31]

Therefore, while Maritain affirms that the common good 'implies and demands the recognition of the fundamental rights of the person', he also affirms that a society's common good is more than the aggregate of the individual goods of its

---

[24] Ibid., pp. 44–5.   [25] Ibid., p. 46.   [26] Ibid., p. 40.

[27] Note that for Maritain the source of modern, atheistic, egoistic rights-talk is Rousseau, and not, as for the Anglican theologians treated in Chapter 6, Hobbes. In this respect Maritain's view is typical of Roman Catholic thought, whose *bête noire* is the French Revolution.

[28] Ibid., p. 38.   [29] Ibid., p. 45.   [30] Ibid., pp. 22, 29.   [31] Ibid., p. 44.

constituent members.[32] Quite how conflict between personal rights and the common good is to be negotiated and resolved, and whether or not some rights should be impervious to the latter's claims, remains unclear to the reader. And it seems that it remained unclear to Maritain, too, since he wrote that 'the mutual relationship between the individual and society is complex and difficult to perceive and to describe in its complete truth'.[33]

The same tension appeared five years later in Maritain's two contributions to a set of essays sponsored by UNESCO in 1949 with a view to bolstering the philosophical credentials of the Universal Declaration.[34] On the one hand, against 'the absolutist concept of human rights held by the philosophy—or better the rhetoric—of the eighteenth century', which attributes unlimited rights to the deified individual, he asserts that human rights are subject to modification and limitation.[35] The specification of natural law, in terms of rights and obligation, proceeds 'according to the needs of time and circumstance, by the contingent dispositions of human law'.[36] Indeed, echoing one of David Ritchie's themes, he writes that 'the human group's awareness of the obligations and rights implicit in the natural law evolves slowly and painfully in step with the evolution of the group'.[37] Therefore, '[n]o declaration of human rights will ever be exhaustive and final. It will ever go hand-in-hand with the state of moral consciousness and civilisation at a given moment in history.'[38]

On the other hand, Maritain remains wedded to the notion that (some) rights are 'inalienable', implying that they are absolute in the sense that they are always and everywhere possessed. Here, however, he seeks to resolve the tension by way of a distinction: 'Even where rights are "inalienable", a distinction must be made between the possession and exercise, the latter being subject to modifications and limitations dictated in each instance by justice.' Thus, for example, a criminal may be condemned to lose his life because he has, by his crime, 'deprived himself, not of his right to existence, but rather of the possibility of demanding that right with justice'. Thus, too, the 'fundamental right' to have the heritage of human culture imparted by teaching and upbringing is

> subject to the physical capacity of a given society, and justice may forbid its enjoyment by all being demanded *hic et nunc*, if such enjoyment is only conceivable through the dissolution of the social body, as in the case of the slave-owning society of ancient Rome, or the feudal society of the Middle Ages; the claim nevertheless remains a legitimate goal to be achieved over time.[39]

---

[32] Ibid., pp. 8–9.   [33] Ibid., p. 10.
[34] Jacques Maritain, 'Introduction' and 'On the Philosophy of Human Rights', in *Human Rights: Comments and Interpretations*, ed. UNESCO (London and New York: Allan Wingate, 1949).
[35] Maritain, 'Introduction', pp. 14–15; 'On the Philosophy', p. 73.
[36] Maritain, 'On the Philosophy', p. 73.   [37] Ibid., p. 73.   [38] Ibid., p. 74.
[39] Maritain, 'Introduction', p. 15.

The notion that a right can still be possessed, when it may not be exercised, is a curious one (and one that we will encounter again in Chapter 5 in the thought of Onora O'Neill and James Griffin). Surely it sounds odd to say that a criminal, even as he suffers execution, still possesses a fundamental right to existence. Perhaps it would help to recall that we are talking about natural rights here, rather than positive ones. In a positive system, either an unqualified 'right to existence (or life)' would not be granted at all (according to common law tradition), or if it were granted (according to civil law tradition), it would be subject to qualifying conditions such as not being found guilty of a capital crime. In other words, positive law would either not recognise such a right or say that, under certain conditions, it would not obtain or could be lost. It would be most unlikely to say that the right is still possessed even when it lacks all effective legal force. Might it, however, make better sense to say that of a natural right? To some extent, perhaps it might. We could say that one continues to possess a fundamental right, even when it may not be exercised, in that its effective exercise remains a goal to be striven for. That is, the right is inalienable in the sense that we ought always and everywhere to strive to create the conditions where it can be exercised. It retains absolute normative force as a moral goal or aspiration. Such an aspirational meaning makes sense, but it does so at a high cost. For, as we have seen Onora O'Neill argue, it undermines the ordinary understanding of rights as valid claims against those they oblige.[40]

Whatever the wisdom of talking about fundamental, natural rights as absolute moral aspirations, one thing is clear: Maritain does affirm that some rights are absolute in a different sense, namely, that they should be exercised always and everywhere, regardless of circumstance. There are, he says, 'rights inhering by nature in the human being' that the civil community is required to 'recognise and enforce as universally valid, and *whose abolition or infringement no consideration of social utility can even for a moment authorise*'.[41] However, while the affirmation is clear, the content of what is affirmed is not. For among the rights that 'meet an absolute requirement of natural law', he lists only those to existence and to liberty of conscience and religion.[42] And, as we have just seen, the right to existence is sometimes absolute only as an obligatory moral aspiration, not as an effective moral claim.

III

The affirmation of absolute rights that, 'flowing directly and simultaneously from [man's] very nature, . . . are therefore universal, inviolable and inalienable' is much

---

[40] See Chapter 1, pp. 28–9   [41] Maritain, 'On the Philosophy', pp. 75–6. The emphasis is mine.
[42] Ibid., p. 74.

more pronounced in the famous papal encyclical of 1963 *Pacem in Terris*, in which Pope John XXIII (1881–1963) placed rights-talk at the heart of the Roman Catholic Church.[43] Most of the encyclical's assertions of liberty and welfare rights are entirely unencumbered with qualifications—whether to life, bodily integrity, the means necessary and suitable for 'the proper development of life', security, worship, work, a just wage, private property, assembly, and association.[44] The importance of the common good is affirmed ('every civil authority must take pains to promote the common good of all'),[45] but it is understood to consist of the upholding of rights rather than conflict with them: 'the common good is chiefly guaranteed when personal rights and duties are maintained'.[46]

On one occasion, however, there is recognition of the possibility of conflict, as when we are told that 'by the natural law every human being has ... the right to freedom in searching for truth and in expressing and communicating his opinions ... *within the limits laid down by ... the common good*'.[47] And there are a handful of other occasions, when different kinds of qualification are admitted—e.g. the right to emigrate to other countries and take up residence there, '*when there are just reasons for it*';[48] and the right to private property, in which '*a social duty [is] essentially inherent*'.[49] Indeed, the suggestion is made that other rights are qualified by duties, too—for example, the right to a decent manner of living by the duty of living it becomingly, and the right to investigate freely by the duty of seeking the truth and of possessing it ever more completely and profoundly.[50]

When all is said and done, we are left uncertain by *Pacem in Terris* about which, if any, rights are 'universal, inviolable, and inalienable' in the sense of being cogent moral claims obtaining always and everywhere, as distinct from being obligatory moral aspirations that civil authorities should strive to realise.[51] And while the possibility of conflict between the common good and the rights of individual persons is acknowledged—just—we are given no guidance about how such conflict should be negotiated rationally.

---

[43] Pope John XXIII, *Pacem in Terris* (1963) in *Seven Great Encyclicals*, introd. William J. Gibbons, SJ (New York: Paulist Press, 1963), section 9, p. 291. In 2010 J. Bryan Hehir described *Pacem in Terris* as the most systematic statement of Roman Catholic teaching on rights to come from the papacy ('The Modern Catholic Church and Human Rights: The Impact of the Second Vatican Council', in John Witte and Frank Alexander, eds, *Christianity and Human Rights: An Introduction* (Cambridge: Cambridge University Press, 2010), p. 120).

[44] John XXIII, *Pacem in Terris*, sections 11, 13, 14, 18, 19, 20, 21, 23, pp. 291–3.

[45] Ibid., section 56, p. 301.   [46] Ibid., section 60, p. 302.

[47] Ibid., section 12, pp. 291–2. The emphasis is mine.

[48] Ibid., section 25, p. 294.

[49] Ibid., sections 21, 22, p. 293. The emphasis is mine.   [50] Ibid., section 29, p. 295.

[51] Ibid., section 63, p. 303: the common good demands that civil authorities 'should make earnest efforts' to create a situation where individual citizens can easily exercise their rights and fulfil their duties.

IV

An unusually sophisticated account of the relationship between rights and the common good was developed seventeen years after the publication of *Pacem in Terris* by John Finnis, the eminent Roman Catholic philosopher of law. In his seminal *Natural Law and Natural Rights* (1980) he reprises the constant Christian refrain that the concept of rights is not sufficient to settle questions of justice. He does so against modern rights-talk, which 'often...though not inevitably or irremediably' hinders 'the rational process of investigating and determining what justice requires in a given context', because the ascription of a right expresses the conclusion of such a process and so has 'conclusory force'.[52] That is to say, the modern tendency to invoke rights at the beginning of a course of deliberation about justice, rather than declare them at its end, has the effect of short-circuiting the process of rational reflection: 'Human rights...can certainly be threatened by uses of rights-talk which...prematurely ascribe a conclusory or absolute status to this or that human right (e.g., property, contract, assembly, speech)'.[53] In fact, both the explanation of claims of right and the resolution of many conflicts between such claims require reference to *other* principles, among them, ultimately, the 'basic aspects of human flourishing' (otherwise known as 'basic human goods').[54] 'The aspects of human well-being', however, 'are many':

> the commitments, projects, and actions that are apt for realizing that well-being are innumerable even for an individual contemplating his own life-plan; when we contemplate the complexities of collaboration, coordination, and mutual restraint involved in pursuit of the common good, we are faced with inescapable choices between rationally eligible but competing possible institutions, policies, programmes, laws, and decisions.[55]

In order to make a rational, just choice between competing options, therefore, we need to admit the requirements of practical reasonableness, a basic aspect of human flourishing that generates duties (as well as correlative rights).

The determination of what is just requires more than rights-talk. It also requires reference to basic aspects of human flourishing (or basic human goods), duties, and 'the common good'. One thing Finnis does *not* mean by this last term is the 'aggregate collective good'; for, since the basic human goods are incommensurable, 'the common good...cannot be measured as an aggregate, as utilitarians suppose'.[56] What, then, does it mean? At its most elementary 'the common good' means that the flourishing of any individual is social in the sense that it depends on the conduct of other people: it requires their 'collaboration, coordination, and

---

[52] John Finnis, *Natural Law and Natural Rights* (Oxford: Clarendon Press, 1980), pp. 210–11.
[53] Ibid., p. 221.   [54] Ibid., pp. 198, 205, 208.   [55] Ibid., p. 210.   [56] Ibid., p. 213.

mutual restraint'. This could be read in a Hobbesian direction to imply that the cannily prudent pursuit of egoistic self-interest issues in mutually beneficial social contracts. But it means much more than that for Finnis. For one thing, being practically reasonable is part and parcel of any individual's flourishing, not merely instrumental to it. Moreover, it involves much more than just choosing efficient servants of the desire to avoid pain and death. It also involves recognising a principle of fundamental human equality: the term 'common good' implies 'that each and everyone's well-being, in each of its basic aspects, must be considered and favoured at all times by those responsible for coordinating the common life'.[57]

Further, the common good comprises the assignation of rights and duties: it is 'precisely the good of individuals whose benefit, from fulfilment of duty by others, is their right because required of those others in justice'.[58] What Finnis does not spell out here is that, in order to be truly common, the common good must benefit those who fulfil their duty as well as those who receive their right. This it does, insofar as duty issues from the requirements of practical reasonableness, which is an aspect of the dutiful individual's own flourishing.

Further still, 'common good' can also refer to 'a diffuse common benefit in which all participate in indistinguishable and unassignable shares' (D. N. MacCormick)—such as public morality and public order. Without such common benefits—which comprise 'a context or framework of mutual respect and trust and common understanding, an environment which is physically healthy and in which the weak can go about without fear of the whims of the strong'—the enjoyment of human rights cannot be secured.[59] Take, for example, public morality in respect of sexual conduct:

Now if it is the case that sexuality is a powerful force which only with some difficulty, and always precariously, can be integrated with other aspects of human personality and well-being—so that it enhances rather than destroys friendship and the care of children, for example—and if it is further the case that human sexual psychology has a bias towards regarding other persons as bodily objects of desire and potential sexual release and gratification, and as mere items in an erotically flavoured classification (e.g., women), rather than as full persons with personal and individual sensitivities, restraints, and life-plans, then there is reason for fostering a milieu in which children can be brought up (and parents assisted rather than hindered in bringing them up) so that they are relatively free from inward subjection to an egoistic, impulsive, or depersonalized

[57] Ibid., p. 214. The emphases are Finnis's. Cf. ibid., p. 221: 'the modern usage of rights-talk rightly emphasizes equality, the truth that every human being is a locus of human flourishing which is to be considered with favour in him as much as in anybody else. In other words, rights talk keeps justice in the foreground of our considerations.'
[58] Ibid., p. 210. The emphases are Finnis's.   [59] Ibid., p. 216.

sexuality...[T]his is an aspect of the common good and fit matter for laws that limit the boundless exercise of certain rights...[60]

According to Finnis's sophisticated understanding, then, the common good is not the simple competitor of individual rights, involved in a zero-sum game where it gains only at the latter's expense. Rather, the common good is constituted by a social ethos and by public policy that regards the flourishing of every member as of equal worth; by the consequent doing of duty by one member that *both* enables the right of another to flourish in certain ways *and* fulfils the dutiful member's own participation in the good of practical reasonableness; and by a public order and morality that limit certain freedoms, so as to restrain egoistic human tendencies to have the self's desires obscure the equality of others, in order to render members capable of doing their duty in respecting rights. Therefore,

> [o]n the one hand, we should not say that human rights, or their exercise, are subject to the common good; for the maintenance of human rights is a fundamental component of the common good. On the other hand, we can appropriately say that most human rights are subject to or limited by each other and by other *aspects* of the common good...which are fittingly indicated...by expressions such as 'public morality', 'public health', 'public order'.[61]

It follows that the determination of rights should not be attempted, and the resolution of conflict between them cannot be achieved, by 'prematurely ascrib-[ing] a conclusory or absolute status to this or that human right'.[62] Rather, what is needed is free public deliberation about what forms of communal life best foster the flourishing of individuals (in a given society), concluding in political compromises that are susceptible of reconsideration.[63]

So far, so flexible and provisional. But that is not the whole story, for Finnis goes on to assert the absoluteness of certain *basic* rights. His seventh requirement of the good of practical reasonableness is that one should perform no act that 'directly and immediately' or 'intentionally' damages a basic good.[64] On this, we are told, rests 'the strict inviolability of basic human rights':[65]

> it is always unreasonable to choose directly against any basic value...[which] are aspects of the real well-being of flesh-and-blood individuals. Correlative to the

---

[60] Ibid., p. 217.   [61] Ibid., p. 218. The emphasis is Finnis's.   [62] Ibid., pp. 220–1.
[63] Ibid., pp. 219–20. It is noteworthy that, in the light of his understanding of rights and their relation to the common good, Finnis views the Universal Declaration of Human Rights as embodying 'the modern "manifesto" conception of human rights', which is 'simply a way of sketching the *outlines of the common good*, the various aspects of individual well-being in community' (ibid., p. 214. The emphasis is Finnis's.).
[64] Ibid., pp. 120, 123.   [65] Ibid., p. 121.

exceptionless duties entailed by this requirement are, therefore, exceptionless or absolute human claim-rights—most obviously, the right not to have one's life taken directly as a means to any further end; but also the right not to be positively lied to in any situation (e.g., teaching, preaching, research publication, news broadcasting) in which factual communication ... is reasonably expected; and the related right not to be condemned on knowingly false charges; and the right not to be deprived, or required to deprive oneself, of one's procreative capacity; and the right to be taken into respectful consideration in any assessment of what the common good requires.[66]

These absolute, basic rights are, presumably, distinct from those provisional ones formulated through a process of public deliberation and political compromise, and granted through legislation in positive law. In that sense they are 'natural', applying always and everywhere and enjoying immunity from any qualifying claims by other aspects of the common good.

What should we make of such rights? Should we agree, for example, that there is an absolute right 'not to have one's life taken directly as a means to any further end'? The word 'directly' is best understood to refer, not to physical causation, but to the agent's intention. Much then depends on what is meant by 'intention'. It cannot mean 'choice', insofar as one endorses some version of double-effect reasoning, as Finnis does (and as I do).[67] According to any version of that

---

[66] Ibid., p. 225.

[67] According to Finnis, the morality of an act is determined by the proposal for action that the agent chooses and the act realises. The proposal comprises both the ultimate end and its means or proximate end (*Moral Absolutes: Tradition, Revision, and Truth* (Washington, DC: Catholic University of America Press, 1991), p. 40). The goodness of the ultimate end cannot justify the choice of evil means (ibid., p. 66). What makes those means evil is that they involve a 'choice to destroy, damage, or impede a basic human good' (ibid., p. 54). Since goods cannot be commensurated, one cannot *rationally* choose to harm one good for the sake of another (ibid., pp. 54–5). The evil in the act is both subjective (or reflexive) and objective. It is primarily subjective in that an irrational choice has the reflexive effect of hindering the agent's participation in the good of practical reasonableness and so of disturbing the peace of his rational integrity. What causes the irrational choice are feelings such as those of egoism, partiality, hatred and vengeance (ibid., pp. 43–4, 46). Insofar as these subjective feelings find expression, they cause the objective evil of injustice.

Finnis admits that 'one can never avoid *harming* some instances of human goods' (his emphasis), but holds that one should not *intend* harm, either as an end or a means. Here he develops a version of the principle of double effect. States of affairs connected perhaps very closely with the carrying out and outcome of one's action, but 'which are neither needed nor wanted as part of one's way of bringing about what one proposes to do and bring about' are unintended or side-effects; 'they are not chosen, that is, are not intended, even if they are foreseen (even foreseen as certain)'; rather they are permitted or 'accepted'. Since one is responsible for whatever one knowingly brings about, one is responsible for the foreseen side-effect that one accepts, but not in the same way as for what one 'chooses (intends) as part (whether as end or means) of one's proposal' (ibid., pp. 70–1). The form of voluntariness involved in knowingly causing side-effects does not have the same 'self-constituting effect' as that form which we call 'intending (choosing)': 'For choosing is adopting a proposal, and what one thus adopts is ... synthesized with one's will .... One *becomes* what ... one chose: what one intended' (ibid., p. 72; his emphasis). '[E]very choice, once made, lasts in one's character' (ibid., p. 73). Nevertheless, the voluntary acceptance of a side-effect can be culpable, if it is unfair or involves the breaking of a commitment (ibid., p. 82).

reasoning, an agent may choose to perform an act that he foresees will cause an evil effect—possibly, probably, or even certainly—provided that he 'intends' another, good effect and merely accepts, with proportionate reluctance, the evil one. 'Intend' here cannot mean 'choose', since the agent's decision to perform the act is a deliberate one, and part of the deliberation involves foreseeing its causing the evil effect. In that sense, therefore, the agent chooses to accept—possibly, probably, or certainly—the evil affect, even though he does not intend it. What, then, is it to 'intend' something? I have proposed that we should take 'intend' to

It seems, then, that an act can be morally wrong and culpable in two ways. Either it can intend (choose) to harm a basic human good as the proximate or ultimate end of a proposal, or it can accept such harm unfairly or in violation of a binding commitment. In the first case, through his will, the agent identifies himself with the evil of harm; in the second case, he is negligent of the obligations of fairness and commitments. Both involve a reflexive malformation of character, but the latter less seriously than the former.

Most relevant to our concerns, Finnis wants to argue that any act that involves the intention to harm a good as a means or proximate end is morally wrong *in itself*, regardless of its ultimate end, motive, or proportionality. Thus however loving one's motive, however noble one's ultimate end, or however necessary the means, it is always and everywhere wrong to intend to kill the innocent, torture the guilty, or prevent conception. It is so, simply because it involves a voluntary choice to do the evil of harming or impeding the good of life. This account cannot be squared, however, with the principle of double effect. For that permits the deliberate *choice* to accept an evil side-effect. For sure, in accepting the evil rather than intending it, the agent's will relates differently to its object. It does not want the evil; it would rather avoid it; and if it happens to achieve its ultimate end without incurring the evil, it would be entirely satisfied. But what distinguishes intention from acceptance is not the agent's *choice*: as Finnis himself admits, one 'chooses to cause' side-effects that one 'does *not* choose (whether as end or as means' (ibid., p. 81; his emphasis). Rather, what distinguishes them is the *manner* of choice. The choosing involved in acceptance is reluctant: the agent really does not *want* to cause the evil. The choosing involved in intention is eager: the agent really does want to cause the evil. Note, then, that what makes an act wrong, after all, is not the mere 'choice to destroy, damage, or impede a basic human good' (ibid., p. 54). The source of the wrongness lies in the malevolent disposition of the agent's choosing will: its motive of hatred or vengeance. The choice to harm a good is not wrong in itself; whether or not it is wrong depends, at least, on the circumstance of motive.

Finnis himself inadvertently implies this in his consideration of contraception. He argues that, by intending that 'a prospective new human life not begin', an act of contraception is 'simply contralife' (ibid., p. 86). The word 'contralife' is ambiguous. It can be taken in a purely descriptive sense, meaning that an act of contraception intends to avoid conceiving new human life at a certain time. But it cannot mean just that, because Finnis deploys the word in order to explain why such an intention is morally wrong. What he considers wrong about it is that it expresses the view 'that regular sexual satisfaction is a natural right' (ibid., p. 86), because 'sexual release and expression by orgasm are simply necessary for personal well-being' (ibid., p. 88), and so involves a failure in 'respect' for human life (ibid., p. 87). The implication here seems to be that those intending contraception are motivated by an introverted, egoistic, hedonistic desire for sexual satisfaction, which involves a rejection of the extroverted social responsibility of parenthood. Consequently, Finnis tries to argue that 'Natural Family Planning' (NFP), the system of identifying fertile times and avoiding intercourse during them, need not involve an intention to impede the coming-to-be of a new child, but rather one 'only to avoid the bad side effects which having a baby would bring about' (ibid., p. 86). This is implausible. For sure, avoiding bad side effects is the ultimate end of NFP, but preventing conception is surely its necessary proximate end. It can hardly be said that the impeding of conception is 'neither needed nor wanted as part of one's way of bringing about what one proposes to do'; it cannot be described as a side-effect. Those who use NFP intend contraception, too. What this shows is that sheer intention here is not the morally decisive factor. One can intend to contracept temporarily, to avoid certain undesirable effects of conceiving a child; or one can intend it constantly, to avoid one's selfish, frivolous pursuit of sexual pleasure being disturbed by the onerous responsibilities of parenthood. What makes the latter morally wrong is not the intention, but the egoism.

mean 'want'.[68] Thus the agent chooses to perform an act that might or will cause an evil effect, which he does not want (and merely 'accepts'), for the sake of a good effect, which he does want (that is, 'intends').

One possible objection to this is that sometimes we intend what we do not want: I can intend to go to the dentist, even when I really do not want to. What this shows, however, is not that 'intending' cannot mean 'wanting', but that there are different kinds of wanting. On the one hand, I do *not* want to go to the dentist, because I fear the physical pain or the monetary cost that my visit will involve. On the other hand, I *do* want to go to the dentist, because I want healthy, trouble-free teeth. So in choosing to go, I resolve to pursue one desire rather than another—I do not intend something that I *simply* do not want.

How, then, should we understand intention? First of all, intending cannot be quite the same as merely wanting. This is because there are many things that we want—many desires that we have—which we do not move to realise. 'Intention' therefore connotes *a commitment to realise* what we want. But second, since it can involve a commitment to realise one desire *in spite of* another, intention is best understood as the commitment to realise a *predominant* desire.

Is it, then, always morally wrong to intend to take another's life as a means to a further end? And, correspondingly, is there an absolute natural right against having one's life so taken? My view is that it is always wrong to want or desire the death of anybody *for its own sake or as an ulterior end in itself*, since that would involve at least subjective malicious hatred, and probably also objective dispro-portion. (If I am unjustly threatening an innocent person with lethal injury, justice might permit or even oblige you, *ceteris paribus*, to use such force against me as is necessary to stop my assault. But if you hate me, and *want me dead*, you will be inclined to use more force than is necessary to do justice. That is, your use of force will probably be disproportionate.) It follows, perhaps counter-intuitively, that it is always wrong even for combat soldiers to intend the death of the enemy in this way.[69] Soldiers may want to overcome and disable the enemy, and commit themselves to doing so; and in practice, what is necessary to achieve that—what is proportionate—will often be lethal. But it is important that the death of the enemy is not what is intended, for otherwise soldiers, having overcome the enemy and rendered them harmless, will have a motive to kill them anyway. That would be immoral and also, as it happens, a crime according to current laws of war.

So: I consider it always and everywhere morally wrong to intend someone's death in the sense of wanting it *for its own sake*—that is, out of a motive of sheer

---

[68] I made this proposal originally in *Aiming to Kill: The Ethics of Suicide and Euthanasia* (London: Darton, Longman, and Todd, 2004), Chapter 3, and repeated it in *In Defence of War* (Oxford: Oxford University Press, 2013), Chapter 3 and in 'In Response', *Soundings*, 97/2 (2014). However, under the pressure of Tom Simpson's criticism, I acknowledged the need to reconsider the matter in 'In Response', *Studies in Christian Ethics*, 28/3 (August 2015), pp. 332–3. 'Chapter 3'.

[69] Biggar, *In Defence of War*, pp. 103–6; 'In Response', in *Studies in Christian Ethics*, pp. 332–3.

hatred—and to commit oneself to realising such a desire. I consider such an intention always and everywhere wrong. What, then, about an intention to take someone's life for the sake of some other, good end? Is this also absolutely wrong? I do not think so. For example, I am not of the opinion that capital punishment is absolutely wrong. It is certainly imaginable, and I think it also possible, that a situation could arise where a state is not able to incarcerate—either at all or in humane conditions—a criminal who continues to pose a lethal threat to other citizens. In such a situation, the choice to intend to take the life of the criminal would not necessarily be motivated by vindictive hatred or sadism, and could be marked by appropriate regret.[70] Nor would it be necessarily unjust, involving an arbitrary preference for some lives over others: since the criminal is himself posing an unjust threat to the lives of innocents—and all the more so because he is culpable for so doing—the choice to kill him would not be arbitrary. Nor would the execution be disproportionate, since no other effective means of protecting the innocent are available. Because the criminal cannot be contained, due care of innocents requires that he be killed. I do not think, therefore, that there is an absolute right 'not to have one's life taken directly as a means to any further end'.[71]

What about the alleged 'right not to be deprived, or required to deprive oneself, of one's procreative capacity'? Is it always and everywhere wrong that others should 'deprive' us of the capacity to procreate? The answer depends upon what is meant. If Finnis has in mind state-sponsored policies of coercive sterilisation, then we might well look sympathetically upon rights against state intrusion into

---

[70] To 'intend' a death, according to Finnis, is to 'turn against' the good of life, whether through active hostility or passive negligence, and is therefore always morally wrong. Nevertheless, endorsing a version of the doctrine of double-effect, Finnis argues that to choose to perform an act that will possibly, probably, or certainly have the effect of causing someone's death need not be immoral, provided that one merely accepts the death reluctantly as a side-effect, and does not intend it. However, to choose to perform an act that one knows will cause death is to choose an act that will destroy life. Therefore, it, too, is surely an act of objectively 'turning against' the good of life. And yet, as Finnis himself admits, such a turning against need not be subjectively motivated by 'hostility' (in the sense of vindictive hatred) or careless negligence, and therefore can be morally permissible. The same applies to cases of intentional killing: the choice of an intention to destroy a life need not be rendered immoral by vindictive hostility or culpable negligence. Nor need it be unjust or disproportionate.

[71] I think that it tells in favour of my argument here that, eleven years after the publication of *Natural Law and Natural Rights*, Finnis equivocated over the morality of capital punishment. At one point in *Moral Absolutes* he reports that Aquinas held that capital punishment need not involve a choice to destroy a human good either as an end or means, but can instead intend to restore the order of justice violated by the one killed who, by his violation, had removed himself from the dignity of the human. Then he comments: 'Here, I believe, Aquinas's explanation may be challenged' (ibid., p. 56)— although on what grounds he does not say. Then, later on, he tells us that, on the question of whether the infliction of capital punishment entails a choice to destroy the basic good of human bodily life, '[t]here is room . . . for debate and further reflection'. And he adds, gingerly: 'It seems possible to hold that, insofar as the action chosen immediately and of itself instantiates the good of retributive justice, the death of the one punished is not being chosen either as an end in itself or as a means to an ulterior end' (ibid., p. 80). This really does not work. While capital punishment may intend the good of retributive justice as its ultimate end, it necessarily also intends the death of the criminal as its means or proximate end. We know this because, should an attempt at capital punishment fail, further attempts will be made until the death of the criminal is achieved.

this most intimate realm of personal and marital responsibility. But are we quite sure that a state should *never, ever* adopt policies to limit population growth? Are we sure that such rights are natural and absolute, and not merely positive, conditional, and revisable? If forced sterilisation seems too brutal ever to be just, what about proportionate legal penalties for having more than a certain number of children? That would certainly be intended to deprive us of use of our procreative capacity, when it becomes, arguably, anti-social. Although we might well raise prudential doubts about the wisdom of such a policy, are we entirely sure that it would be always and everywhere morally wrong, and that therefore there is an absolute natural right against it? I, for one, doubt it.

Nevertheless, there are three of Finnis's purported absolute natural rights that are incontrovertible, if not useful. One is the right 'not to be positively lied to in any situation (e.g., teaching, preaching, research publication, news broadcasting) in which factual communication . . . is reasonably expected'. This is absolute, but only because it is tautologous.[72] *Of course*, where accurate factual communication is reasonably expected, it would always be unreasonable (and therefore morally wrong) to communicate falsehoods intentionally ('positively'). Yet this would be absolutely true only as a matter of logic: for its truth would be built into it by the inclusion of the word 'reasonable'. In order for this to be at all practically illuminating, we would need to think about what expectations are reasonable, and once we have started to do that, we would discover that what is reasonable is conditional, varying according to circumstance. Thus, it would surely be unreasonable to communicate falsehoods intentionally in the context of a school or university in peacetime. But what about treatment of the enemy in wartime? Are we always obliged to speak the truth when they expect it? Would it be reasonable for them to expect it of us? Presumably, if we were to identify ourselves as their opponent, they would not expect it—and our lying would be futile. But are we always obliged to reveal our true identity to the enemy? Would it be reasonable for them to expect that of us? I do not think so. In that case, therefore, while the enemy would reasonably expect someone on their own side to tell the truth, they could not reasonably expect an enemy either to tell the truth or not to pretend to be on their side. It follows that, in time of war, it would be reasonable and so morally permissible for us to pretend to be on the enemy's side and intentionally to tell them falsehoods, when the enemy, misperceiving us to be in their side, expect the truth from us. Therefore, while it might be true to say there is an absolute right 'not to be positively lied to in any situation . . . in which factual communication . . . is reasonably expected', this truth cannot guide action until

---

[72] Insofar as what is 'reasonable' to expect involves morally normative assumptions (as I think it does), Finnis's reasoning here falls foul of the stipulation that he made eleven years later, namely, that absolute moral norms identify specific types of action 'without any reliance on any evaluative term which presupposes a moral judgment on the action' (*Moral Absolutes*, p. 2).

'reasonable expectations' have been analysed, and, when they are, it becomes clear that they vary according to different circumstances.

The same applies to the putative right 'to be taken into respectful consideration in any assessment of what the common good requires'. Every member of a society deserves to have their legitimate interests 'taken into account' in deliberation about law and public policy. But since some ways of being taken into account can be merely nominal, that is not sufficient. Members deserve to have their legitimate interests considered seriously or 'respectfully'. What 'respect' amounts to, however, will vary according to time and circumstance. 'Respectful consideration' need not require universal adult suffrage, for example. So, while this absolute natural, moral right is plausible, it is so only because it operates at a very high level of generality, one that is too abstract to be practically illuminating. What is more, a right to respectful consideration with regard to the requirements of the common good is one that presupposes political institutions. It cannot, therefore, be a natural right in the strict sense of a moral right that exists before and apart from any positive legal system.

Also plausible is the right 'not to be condemned on knowingly false charges'. While it is always unjust to be condemned on false charges, one could not have a natural, moral right against non-culpable mistakes: sometimes false charges are not known to be so, and no one can be blamed for honest ignorance. In such a case the injustice is tragic, but not immoral. One could, however, have a natural, moral right against being condemned on false charges, where the falsity is intended and therefore culpable. Note, however, that the absolute moral wrongness, upon which the absolute right is founded, is built into the statement: as soon as we hear that the charges are 'knowingly false' we know that the condemnation is culpably unjust. And since everyone, always and everywhere, deserves to be free from culpable injustice, we could say, with impeccable logic, that there is an absolute natural, moral right against condemnation on intentionally false charges. Again, however, we probably should not say it, because 'condemnation on charges' implies the social institution of judicial process, and in a state of nature there is no such institution. What we should say, instead, is that natural morality prescribes that there should be, always and everywhere, a legal right against condemnation on false charges, be they made knowingly or not.

V

We embarked on the study of the Roman Catholic appropriation of rights-talk since *Rerum Novarum*, in order to see whether or not Catholic tradition has proven better able than other 'modern' traditions to meet the sceptics' objections to natural rights. Certainly, through its affirmation of a larger moral order ('natural law'), Catholic thinking about rights has shown itself more ready to talk in terms of moral categories other than 'rights'. Thus, *Rerum Novarum* justified the natural right to property as a precondition of a father's fulfilment of his *duty* to provide for his family, and then qualified it by the duty of charity to apply any surplus to the needs of the indigent. It also asserted the duty to exercise the *virtues* of moderation, honesty, charity while exercising the right (of workers) to associate.

Catholic rights-talk is also unusual in the prominence it gives to the *common good*. Sometimes this finds expression in the specific and distinctive assertion of the right of a social body such as the family to state protection. On other occasions it finds voice in the general assertion of an interdependence between the rights of individuals and the common good. This raises, of course, the important and intriguing question of how exactly individual rights and the common good relate to one another. Popes Pius XI and XII are not much help in finding an answer: the former merely asserts 'harmony' between them; the latter merely claims that the former 'flow' from the latter. *Pacem in Terris* makes the useful point that the common good actually consists of upholding the rights of individuals. That is surely part of the truth: the health of a society is constituted by the respect that members show one another's rights. But if that were the whole truth, then the common good would disappear into rights without remainder. John Finnis shows why this is not so by referring to the important concept of diffuse common benefits (e.g. social ethos, public policy), whose limitation of the freedom of individuals is necessary to enable them to do their duty and respect others' rights.

Finnis also identifies a common problem with much other 'modern' rights-talk: that, since the very concept of a right has an absolute, 'conclusory' force, rights-talk has the logical tendency to shut down wider deliberation about justice. Instead, Finnis argues, rights themselves require explanation—and conflict between them requires resolution—by reference to human goods, especially practical reasonableness. Rights, then, should emerge at the end of deliberation about a range of factors—moral, social, and political—rather than be invoked at the beginning. This appears to affirm socially contingent positive rights rather than absolute natural ones. Maritain's opposing the 'creative wisdom' of Christian rights-talk to the rights absolutism of the French Revolution points in the same direction.

But that is not the whole story, because the Catholic rights tradition also asserts some absolute natural rights. Maritain affirms 'inalienable' or 'fundamental' rights that issue from human nature; *Pacem in Terris* affirms 'unconditional' rights; and Finnis affirms 'exceptionless or absolute human claim-rights'. However, as we have seen, Maritain's inalienable rights end up being aspirational, thus falling prey to Onora O'Neill's objection. *Pacem in Terris* leaves us entirely uncertain about *which* rights are 'universal, inviolable, and inalienable', as distinct from goals that civil authorities are obliged to aspire to. And Finnis, while clearer in proposing particular examples of absolute rights, fails to establish either their absoluteness, their status as natural, or their practical usefulness.

All things considered, then, the modern Catholic tradition of rights does display a superior ability to recognise the larger, multi-faceted moral order of which 'rights' are only a part; and it does recognise that morally justified positive rights are the socially contingent products of political deliberation about the common good. What it has not yet succeeded in establishing, however, are non-tautologous, practically illuminating, natural rights that, transcending variable social circumstances, are absolute, applying always and everywhere.

5

Are there Natural Rights?

5: The Sceptical Critique and
Contemporary Theories

I

In Chapter 4 we considered one contemporary theory of natural rights, that offered by John Finnis. Here we shall examine a selection of others, before, at last, proceeding to make a final judgement. Our selection comprises the rebuttals of Onora O'Neill's critique by John Tasioulas and Elizabeth Ashford, both of whom invoke Henry Shue's work; the Christian theistic defence by Nicholas Wolterstorff; and the non-theistic philosophical account of James Griffin.

II

The two rebuttals of O'Neill were provoked by the desire to defend a universal human right to be free from severe poverty. Tasioulas reports O'Neill's view that proclaiming such a right, without first establishing institutions that identify the corresponding duty-bearers, risks seeming 'bitter mockery to the poor and needy'.[1] Her argument, as he summarises it, is as follows. A genuine right must be claimable, and in order to be claimable, the correspondent duty-bearer must be specified.[2] Negative duties—for instance not to be tortured—easily meet this condition, because the duty is universal; but positive duties to provide

---

[1] O'Neill, *Toward Justice and Virtue*, p. 133; quoted by Tasioulas in 'The Moral Reality of Human Rights', in Thomas Pogge, ed., *Freedom from Poverty as a Human Right: Who Owes What to the Very Poor?* (New York: UNESCO and Oxford University Press, 2007), p. 79.

[2] In addition to addressing O'Neill's argument about claimability, Tasioulas also seeks to rebut Raymond Geuss's argument that a condition of the existence of a right is that it is actually enforceable, and that to assert a right against severe poverty is to confuse the existence of a right with a moral belief about what would be a valuable state of affairs (Raymond Geuss, *History and Illusion in Politics* (Cambridge: Cambridge University Press, 2001), pp. 143, 146, 156; cited by Tasioulas in 'Moral Reality', pp. 79–80). Against Geuss, Tasioulas appeals to 'ordinary discourse', according to which '[w]e often speak of rights in indicative terms as being exercised or violated even before they have become law'—for example, slaves in the USA's pre-abolitionist era were often thought to possess rights that were in fact violated, even when those rights were not enshrined in law. What is more, there may be prudential reasons (say, the avoidance of grave social unrest) not to enshrine a human right in law, or a human right might be better secured by non-legal means, or a legal system itself (say, Nazi) might deny a right ('Moral Reality', pp. 85–6).

opportunities and resources—for example, food—cannot be universal. Therefore a human right to be free from severe poverty needs an institutional structure to allocate duties and define their content. Until then, there remains only an imperfect duty of charity to give aid and help construct institutional systems of welfare rights, with no corresponding moral rights; and appeals to such rights are 'mainly rhetoric, which proclaim "manifesto" rights against unspecified others'.[3] When institutions have been built, which allocate perfect duties of justice, corresponding welfare rights come into being—but not as universal *human* rights, only as special, institutional ones.[4]

Tasioulas aligns himself with O'Neill in her complaint that imperfect duties of charity, mercy, gratitude, etc. get squeezed out of our picture of ethical life by those who treat rights as 'the fundamental ethical category'.[5] He also affirms that she 'is perfectly justified in rebuking those human rights activists who proclaim all manner of rights without giving any apparent consideration to the justifiability, distribution or coherence of associated duties. This shows that rights discourse is vulnerable to abuse.'[6] And he agrees that an assertion of a right against severe poverty—or, indeed, of any human right—has to satisfy the condition of feasibility: 'the existence of human rights is to be determined with respect to a specified historical context, given that any such context will enable suitably determinate

---

Moral philosophers do have a tendency to appeal to 'ordinary discourse', as if it were some kind of moral authority. Thus Joel Feinberg argues in favour of moral rights on the ground that they 'are common parts of the conceptual apparatus of most, if not all, people when they make moral and political judgments'—notwithstanding his acknowledgement that 'some fifty years ago... in moral philosophy... moral rights were suspect' ('In Defense of Moral Rights', in Joel Feinberg, *Problems at the Roots of Law: Essays in Legal and Political Theory* (New York: Oxford University Press, 2002), pp. 37, 41). Lacking an awareness of historical alternatives, the philosopher is bound to become captive to current convention. So, *pace* Feinberg and Tasioulas, I find myself unmoved by the appeal to what 'we are inclined to say' (ibid., p. 37), since what 'we' often say now is not what 'we' said *much at all* before the seventeenth century, nor what we said *often* before 1945, and since much of the burden of this and Chapters 2–4 has been to scrutinise that difference for its significance—and in particular to consider what, if anything, is gained or lost by speaking of somone 'having a right', rather than saying that 'it is right that someone...'. Moreover, I think that any claim has to command the backing of some social authority in order to be sufficiently secure to deserve the title of 'a right'. Such an authority need not take the form of statutory law, and might comprise only custom or social norms. However, it must comprise more than prevalent public opinion and individual conscience, since these are too unreliable to provide the claim with any assurance of security. The importance of the backing of social authority is that it supports the right-holder by confronting a would-be violator with the prospect of some kind of unwelcome retribution. However, since the level of security enjoyed by a right will be variable and might amount to deterrence of violation rather than enforcement after violation, I think that 'enforceability' is too stringent a condition of the existence of a right. The support of social authority is a better candidate.

[3] O'Neill, *Toward Justice and Virtue*, p. 132; quoted by Tasioulas in 'Moral Reality', p. 90.

[4] Tasioulas, 'Moral Reality', p. 80.

[5] O'Neill, *Toward Justice and Virtue*, p. 143; quoted by Tasioulas in 'Moral Reality', p. 99. Tasioulas agrees with O'Neill that rights are not conceptually fundamental. For him, if not for her, rights are derivative from certain basic human interests ('Moral Reality', p. 88).

[6] Tasioulas, 'Moral Reality', p. 99.

judgments of feasibility to be reached'. Feasibility, however, is distinct from claimability, which, he will argue, is not an existence-condition.[7]

Tasioulas opens his argument by appealing to Henry Shue's 'classic discussion' in *Basic Rights* (1980, 1996), which, he says, has taught us to regard the distinction between 'negative' liberty rights and 'positive' welfare rights with suspicion.[8] The reasons that Shue gave for this suspicion were, first, that, while liberty or security rights can be respected simply by omitting to violate them (that is, through 'negative' action), they cannot be protected without positive action; second, that a welfare right such as that to subsistence need not be more expensive of resources than the effective protection of security rights—a food stamp programme, for example, could be cheaper than an anti-drugs programme; and third, that a right to subsistence can sometimes be satisfied, not by providing commodities, but by protecting people from interference by others that harms their growing, making, and buying those commodities. A welfare right to subsistence, then, corresponds to three kinds of duty: to avoid depriving, to protect from deprivation, and to aid the deprived. Therefore, rights cannot be distinguished simply into negative liberty rights and positive welfare ones.[9]

Endorsing Shue's argument, Tasioulas seeks to bring it to bear on O'Neill. He argues that she takes an epistemological difference of degree—relating to how much we can typically know about counterpart obligations independently of the establishment of institutional structures—and exaggerates it into an ontological difference of kind, so as to conclude that that welfare rights are institutionally dependent for their very existence, while liberty rights are not.[10] But, counters Tasioulas, it is central to the 'fulfilment' of the supposedly negative right not to be tortured that institutions allocating positive duties be established, because in their absence the right's claimability has only 'limited importance'. So, regarding the matter of the existence of human rights,

> why should we be so impressed by the negative duty which is pre-institutionally allocated, as opposed to the set of no less important positive duties to implement and enforce that right, which are not? Admittedly, violators of liberty rights will be in principle knowable, and this is no trivial matter. Reflection on it may even lead us to conclude that claimability is ordinarily a precondition for speaking in a meaningful way of *violations* of duties entailed by human rights... But why should the conditions for determinate assessments of human rights *violations* be criterial for the seemingly prior and independent question of whether a human right *exists* or, for that matter, goes *unfulfilled*? ... a human right will

---

[7] Ibid., p. 81.   [8] Ibid., pp. 89–90.

[9] Henry Shue, *Basic Rights: Subsistence, Affluence, and U.S. Foreign Policy*, 2nd edn (Princeton: Princeton University Press, 1980, 1996), pp. 37, 39, 45, 52–3.

[10] Tasioulas, 'Moral Reality', pp. 89–90.

exist if universal individual interest is sufficient to generate duties to advance and protect that interest in various ways.[11]

Further, we often have enough information to know that there are duties corresponding to welfare rights, without the performance of those duties being *claimable* against specifiable others. Thus,

> I can know... that everyone has a right not to live in extreme poverty and that, therefore, the imposition of duties on others to secure that condition is justified ... [T]he interest is important enough to generate the counterpart duties given the constraints set by human capacities, available resources and general features of social life. But *who* should best be assigned those duties will be a separate question requiring further deliberation.[12]

Again, Tasioulas is at pains to make clear that the issue is not that of feasibility. The bracketing of further questions about the allocation and specification of duties does not originate in uncertainty about whether it is feasible to secure the right through the imposition of duties. 'If that were the case,' he says, 'then the very existence of the relevant rights would be doubtful, since rights ground duties and duties must satisfy the maxim "ought" implies "can" ... '.[13] Since that is unthinkable, he implies, the indeterminacy must arise from the fact that there are multiple ways of allocating and rendering more precise the duties corresponding to the right, and which ways command normative authority will vary according to social circumstances. But this should not be understood to undermine the very existence of the right. 'Why', he asks rhetorically,

> is not the person's interest and the fact that it is sufficient to generate duties to respect, protect, and further it, etc. enough to warrant the existence of the right? ... What is crucial to the existence of rights is the duty-grounding character of the underlying interests they protect, not whether a particular distribution or specification of duties has been fixed.[14]

One basic question raised by Tasioulas's attempted rebuttal of O'Neill is how well he understands his target, and whether he hits it rather than some other one. First of all, as we have already observed, O'Neill is equivocal about whether unallocated welfare rights exist or not: sometimes she says that they are 'illusory', at other times she says that they exist 'in the abstract'.[15] On these latter occasions, she takes a

---

[11] Ibid., p. 91. The emphases are Tasioulas's.   [12] Ibid., p. 92.   [13] Ibid., p. 93.
[14] Ibid., pp. 94–5.
[15] Earlier Joseph Raz had also asserted the existence of abstract rights. In 1986 he argued that 'one may know of the existence of a right and of the reasons for it without knowing who is bound by duties based on it or what precisely are those duties' (*The Morality of Freedom* (Oxford: Clarendon Press, 1986), p. 184). The example he gives is that of a child's right to education. Ignorance of the duties entailed by this right,

position not dissimilar to Tasioulas's. Still, since she does express doubt about the existence of such unallocated rights, let us proceed on the assumption that that is her view.

However, even given that, whether and how far O'Neill differs from Tasioulas still remains uncertain. This is because it is clear that O'Neill's objection to the assertions of alleged welfare rights, which do not specify whose duty it is to do what, *is* based, at least to a large extent, on doubt about feasibility. As we saw in Chapter 1, not only after Tasioulas's 2007 article in her 2014 Isaiah Berlin and Edmund Burke Lectures, but also before it in a contribution to a 2004 multi-author collection, O'Neill objected to the failure to allocate duties, because that failure is attributable to an assumption that states and international bodies have the requisite capacities, whereas in fact they often lack them.[16] What is more, the common sense distinction between negative and positive duties and rights, which O'Neill deploys, is also based on a distinction in feasibility. Negative duties to refrain from interfering action are generally feasible, since everyone generally has the power not to act. And since everyone is generally a competent negative duty-bearer, negative rights against interference can exist without the need to specify whom they are held against. In contrast, positive duties to do or provide something are not generally feasible, since not everyone has the power to do or provide. Since not everyone is a competent positive duty-bearer, therefore, positive rights cannot exist without specifying a competent duty-bearer.

Shue seeks to muddy the waters of this clear distinction by observing that liberty rights also need protection and enforcement, which require positive action and the expenditure of resources. Are we to say, then, that liberty rights do not exist until

and of the right-bearer's identity, 'shows that the person's knowledge of the precise content of the right to education is incomplete. But this merely means that he does not know all the implications of the right to education...' (ibid., p. 185). The problems with this are several. First, while it is true to say that parents have a duty to educate their children, it would be odd to say that children have a right to an education, which they can hold against their parents. Besides, in the case of feral children in an anarchical, wartime state of nature, there will be no parents to hold the right against. And it would be even odder to say that children have a right that they can hold against each other or even themselves. Second, until we know what kind of education a child has a right to, and who is obliged to provide it, we cannot know whether it is feasible. If we mean only that a child has a right to be taught basic skills of survival, then presumably parents, if they exist, can be obliged to do that. Usually, however, a right to education is held against the state and is a right to some level of formal schooling. But that presupposes a functioning state with sufficient resources to perform the duty entailed by the right—and such a state cannot be presumed always to exist. From this I conclude that no universal, natural, moral right to education exists.

[16] 'Unless the primary duties to provide food or health care are *allocated*, moreover allocated effectively to specific individuals and institutions *with competence and capacity to discharge them...*' (O'Neill, 'Pluralism', p. 131 (2014 Isaiah Berlin Lecture); the first emphasis is O'Neill's, the second is mine); 'states can only discharge the second-order duties to ensure that rights are respected and realised if they have the *necessary capacities* to enforce the performance of duties and thereby respect for an realisation of rights. Yet many states...lack...these capacities' ('From Edmund Burke to Twenty-First Century Rights', pp. 146–7 (2014 Edmund Burke Lecture); the emphasis is mine); 'weak states cannot coherently be required to *carry tasks for which they are not competent.* Nor can weak international institutions. Yet we are constantly tempted to assume that weak states and weak international bodies can *carry obligations that exceed their capabilities*' ('Global Justice', p. 169; originally published in Deen K. Chatterjee, ed., *The Ethics of Assistance: Morality and the Distant Needy* (Cambridge: Cambridge University Press, 2004); the emphases are mine).

the duties of protection and enforcement have been allocated? Assuming a negative answer to this question, and that liberty rights should be supposed to exist before the allocation of correspondent duties, Shue argues that it follows that welfare rights, too, may be thought to exist before such allocation. To test this argument, let us take an actual case, which we shall consider more fully in Chapter 8, where a state lacked the resources to provide those accused of criminal acts with professional legal counsel. Would it make sense to say that the liberty right to a fair trial did not exist in those circumstances? It would certainly make sense to say that a natural, moral right to a fair trial as conceived in the contemporary West, and embodied in international human rights standards, did not exist, since there cannot be a right to something that is impossible. Nonetheless, we could sensibly say that a right to a fair trial of some kind did exist, because, in those circumstances alternative, less costly, although less secure safeguards of fairness were provided, those obliged to provide them having been identified. That, however, would only be a legal right, not a simply natural, moral one. So let us suppose circumstances where public, formal, procedural safeguards of any kind are entirely lacking: should we still say that a natural right to a fair trial exists? Insofar as it always remains possible for *any* persons accusing, witnessing, and judging to treat the accused with scrupulous honesty—that is, insofar as there always remains the safeguard of individual's conscience—we *could* say that the natural right to a fair trial exists, insofar as the accused would have a moral claim upon the consciences of others. However, in the real world of human passion and corruption this safeguard is not very reliable, and relying on it entails a high risk of unfairness—as Edmund Burke was acutely aware. So to say that a natural *right* exists in these circumstances would misleadingly imply a degree of publicly supported control and security that is, in fact, entirely absent. Henry Shue, therefore, is half right and half wrong. He is right to say that liberty rights depend, like welfare rights, on social institutions and the resources that support them. But he is wrong to say that, since liberty rights exist in the absence of such institutions, so do welfare ones. He is wrong, because in such an absence liberty *rights* do *not* exist—only insecure liberty claims to conscience do.

Nevertheless, a distinction between negative liberty duties and positive welfare duties still stands. For, while the absence of social institutions would so reduce the security of fairness in a trial as to make talk of a right misleading, it would not abolish the possibility of fairness. In the most primitive, resource-poor, and insecure circumstances, it would still remain possible for parties *not* to make false accusation or witness, and *not* to stint on the scrupulous scrutiny of the case for the prosecution and on the giving of reasonable benefit of doubt. The exercise of personal virtue could deliver fairness.[17] In contrast, if one lacks the requisite

---

[17] Shue himself inadvertently admits this when he writes that one can avoid violating liberty rights by refraining to act, even before they are protected by positive action (*Basic Rights*, pp. 37, 53). The point here is that refraining from right-violating action is the fruit of virtue, which is itself a kind of protection.

resources, one simply cannot give aid. It is not possible; no amount of humanitarian virtue can conjure food out of thin air. So a distinction between negative and positive *duties* still stands, the former always being feasible, the latter not. Yet, while an appeal by the accused to the authority of the consciences of witnesses and judges need not be in vain, its power is too uncertain to warrant talk of his possessing a natural right to fairness.

So far, the existence of a natural right has been considered in relation to the feasibility of performing the corresponding duties by identified agents. We need to know who the appropriate duty-bearers are supposed to be, in order to confirm that they are capable of bearing it. Where there are capable duty-bearers, there is a right; otherwise, not. Insofar as Onora O'Neill's argument against the existence of unallocated welfare rights is an argument about feasibility, Tasioulas makes clear—twice—that he has no quarrel with it. Evidently, however, he thinks that her argument is sometimes based on other considerations. While I am not at all confident that he has shown this, let us assume it for the sake of argument. How telling, then, are his criticisms?

One criticism is that O'Neill exaggerates the difference between liberty and welfare rights in terms of whether we can identify the corresponding duty-bearer without an allocating institution. She thinks that we can in the case of liberty rights, but not of welfare ones. In response, Tasioulas argues that the 'fulfilment' of a supposedly negative, liberty right—say, against torture—needs institutions to allocate positive duties. That is true, insofar as the right is made much more secure when it has the backing, say, of legal institutions and professional training. However, there can be some less secure realisation that falls short of the fulfilment of maximal security—as Tasioulas himself concedes when he writes that, short of institutional backing, the right's claimability has 'limited importance'. By 'importance' I take him to mean something like power or effect. Limited effect, however, is still effect. It is still generally possible for the right to claim the dutiful restraint of any person. Even a right with only limited effect still exists. Note, however, that the argument comes down to the question of feasibility: the right exists so long as there are agents who are capable of performing the correspondent duty—for whom the duty is feasible. That is why the negative duties entailed by liberty rights should impress us so much when considering the existence of rights: we can be confident that everyone is generally capable of withholding themselves from right-violating action, which self-restraint is a real effect of the right's moral claim upon the individual's conscience. The issue does not turn at all on identifying the violators of rights; it turns on identifying capable duty-bearers.

Tasioulas appears to disagree. He claims that we can often know that there are duties corresponding to welfare rights, without the performance of those duties being *claimable* against specifiable others. There are moments when he appears to think that the very urgency of a universal human interest alone is sufficient to generate duties that bring rights into existence: '[I]s not the person's interest and the fact that it is sufficient to generate duties to respect, protect, and further it, etc. enough to warrant the existence of the right?', he asks rhetorically.[18] But then he reminds us that he takes the feasibility of those duties for granted: '[T]he interest is important enough to generate the counterpart duties *given the constraints set by human capacities, available resources and general features of social life.*'[19]

Tasioulas's view seems to be this. Given that we know that the duties entailed by a right to meet its claim are feasible, that right exists, even before we have allocated its correspondent duties—or, to be more exact, even before we have selected from the many practical options the best allocation and definition of duties in the circumstances. This implies that not only is the issue of a right's existence separate from that of the allocation of its correspondent duties, but so is the issue of the feasibility of those duties. I doubt that allocation can be so cleanly separated from feasibility. For how can we be sure of a duty's feasibility without knowing who is to bear it, what capacities they have, and what other responsibilities constrain them? Perhaps at the back of Tasioulas's mind rests the assumption that the resources of affluent countries are so considerable that the cost to them of eliminating severe poverty across the globe would be relatively slight.[20] Note, however, that this assumes not only that the duty is feasible, but that we have identified a group of duty-bearers *for whom* it is feasible—that is, the states of affluent societies (or other bodies coordinating the activities of their populations). It also assumes that we have worked out that these states could meet all of their other obligations and still afford to do, collectively, what it would take to eliminate global poverty—and that it is clear that our calculation has greater claim to moral authority than those of the governments concerned. All that remains to be done, therefore, is merely to create institutions to distribute the burden of aid across these states, coordinate their various efforts, and so implement what we already know can be done.

I doubt, however, that anybody who does not bear responsibility for making hard decisions about government priorities and the allocation of limited resources, especially decisions for which account must be given to morally and politically divided democratic electorates, should *presume* to know better than those who are responsible. Further, until international institutions have been created, where national capacities for giving aid can be determined and compared, taking into account rival duties, and burdens allocated accordingly, we really cannot know whether the total result of coordinated effort will in fact be sufficient to meet the need. Until then, therefore, the only right that the severely impoverished possess is that each affluent state should perform its imperfect duty to do what it thinks it can, given all its other responsibilities, to relieve global poverty,

---

[18] Tasioulas, 'Moral Reality', pp. 94–5.   [19] Ibid., p. 92. The emphasis is mine.

[20] Elizabeth Ashford makes this claim in the same volume where Tasioulas's chapter appears ('The Duties Imposed by the Human Right to Basic Necessities', in Pogge, *Freedom from Poverty as a Human Right*, p. 208).

while working toward the creation of international institutions of distribution and coordination. The impoverished cannot yet have a right to subsistence, because, in the absence of distributing and coordinating institutions, sufficient aid to eliminate poverty is not possible by any one state's efforts. Each state has an imperfect duty only to do what it thinks it can do, not to do whatever is sufficient to abolish poverty. The right to subsistence does not exist, because the collective duty to provide it is not yet feasible. Feasibility, therefore, remains the crucial issue, and where the duty correspondent to a supposed right is not feasible—perhaps because of the absence of necessary institutional coordination—the right does not exist. Just as O'Neill has (sometimes) claimed, it is illusory.

III

O'Neill's 'influential argument' is also the subject of critical attention from Elizabeth Ashford.[21] Like Tasioulas, she objects to the claims, first, that the existence of a welfare right remains doubtful until the duties it entails have been rendered feasible by institutions, which determine their content, distribute them to capable agents, and make them perfectly binding; and second, that, because of its contingency upon institutions, such a welfare right is only ever a special right, not a universal human one.[22] Like Tasioulas, too, there are moments when she seems to subscribe to rights-fundamentalism, supposing that the urgency of the human interest alone is sufficient to generate a right: 'Human rights are a set of urgent and rock-bottom moral claims against others that every human being has simply in virtue of their humanity';[23] 'There is a compelling case for the claim that there is a human right to basic necessities, given the devastating impact the lack of them has on persons' interests and the threat it poses to their lives.'[24] But also like Tasioulas, she does concede (in a footnote) that whether the lack of basic necessities amounts to the deprivation of a human right 'depends on whether agents have causal responsibility for this situation and *on the ease with which persons' access to basic necessities could be secured*'.[25] That is to say, she concedes that the deprivation of the right depends on the feasibility of its correspondent duty. Whether she thinks that a right whose correspondent duty is not feasible still *exists*, is not clear, but she does not say that it does not.

Developing Henry Shue's critique of the sharp distinction between negative liberty and positive welfare rights, one of Ashford's arguments is that, in certain economic conditions where the right against severe poverty is not met, the

---

[21] Elizabeth Ashford, 'The Alleged Dichotomy between Positive and Negative Rights and Duties', in Charles R. Beitz and Robert F. Goodin, eds, *Global Basic Rights* (New York: Oxford University Press, 2011), p. 102.

[22] Ibid., pp. 99, 102.   [23] Ashford, 'Duties Imposed', p. 84.   [24] Ibid., p. 83.

[25] Ibid., p. 83.n. 2. The emphasis is mine.

fundamental human interest in subsisting can undermine the perfect nature of duties not to violate certain liberty rights.[26] Her first, admittedly bizarre and controversial example, is taken from Shue: where the normal means of subsistence are lacking, the poor 'could not be said to actually enjoy security against torture, because they would be vulnerable to being drawn into a bargain (with, say, a sadistic millionaire) of undergoing torture in exchange for subsistence'.[27] Her second example is less outlandish: where a family is destitute, the parents should not be thought subject to a perfect duty not to violate the right against child labour and send their children to work, nor employers to a perfect duty not to employ them.[28] What this implies is that the feasibility of the duty to respect this liberty right is contingent upon the creation of institutions to eliminate severe poverty.[29] Until then, the duty the right imposes is only the imperfect one to seek institutional reform, which obliges a multiplicity of agents, among whom the burdens have not been distributed and determined, and who must therefore use their own discretion in determining them.[30] From these two examples it follows that 'it is not an essential feature of rights that they impose perfect duties',[31] for

> [i]f the duties imposed by genuine liberty-rights can be imperfect, then the imperfect nature of duties of aid that correspond to welfare rights, prior to the institutionalisation of such rights, is no reason to deny that these are duties of justice that correspond to [universal] human rights.[32]

However, Ashford's analysis of the torture case is confused. The putative right against torture imposes a perfect negative duty on sadistic millionaires not to torture the vulnerable poor for fun; it does not obviously impose a perfect duty on the vulnerable poor never to volunteer to be tortured. So while the condition of severe poverty renders the poor vulnerable to the millionaire's exploitation, it does not compromise the millionaire's perfect duty. His performance of the negative duty remains perfectly feasible.[33] As for the right against child labour, the case she

---

[26] Ashford, 'The Alleged Dichotomy', pp. 92, 97, 99–100.

[27] Shue, *Basic Rights*, pp. 184–7 n. 13; cited by Ashford in 'The Alleged Dichotomy', pp. 94–5. I say that this 'torture' example is controversial, because it has attracted criticism from Mark Wicclair (reported by Shue ibid.) and from Andrew Cohen ('Must Rights Impose Enforceable Positive Duties?', *Journal of Social Philosophy*, 35 (2004)).

[28] Ashford, 'The Alleged Dichotomy', pp. 104, 106–7, 110.   [29] Ibid., p. 109.

[30] Ashford, 'Duties Imposed', p. 201.   [31] Ashford, 'The Alleged Dichotomy', pp. 110–11.

[32] Ibid., p. 112.

[33] Ashford's discussion, following that of Shue, Wiccair, and Cohen, becomes sidetracked onto the issue of the security of the right against torture, which is undoubtedly weakened by conditions of severe poverty by making it rational for the poor to enter into nefarious contracts. While admitting that there are other ways of bolstering the right's security, Ashford argues that securing the welfare right to subsistence is necessary for the *full* security and enjoyment of the liberty right against torture: 'I am not denying that important and genuine steps can be taken towards protecting other rights such as the right not to be tortured independently of securing the right to subsistence. My claim is that *full* enjoyment of such rights—enjoyment to a reasonable degree of security—cannot be said to have been achieved, in the

presents raises doubts about whether this should be regarded as a universal human right, imposing a perfect duty never in any circumstances to send children to work or to employ them. The rationale for such a right is dependent on economic conditions in a way that the right against torture is not. However ideal it is that children should be free to devote their childhood to play and education, it is an ideal that has not been feasible for most of history and still is not feasible in many societies, not least predominantly agricultural ones. So while we have an imperfect duty to do what we can to create economic conditions that do not necessitate child labour, arguably, there is neither a perfect duty never to employ children, nor a correspondent universal human right of children never to be employed. Or to be exact, there might be a 'manifesto' right, but not a real one.

There is a second line of argument that Ashford pursues, in order to blur the distinction between negative liberty rights and positive welfare rights. It focuses on O'Neill's claim that '... when a liberty right is violated, then, whether or not specific institutions have been established, there are determinate others to whom the violation might be imputed'.[34] What this implies is that the duty correspondent to a negative liberty right is perfect, because we know the content of the duty (some kind of inaction), we know that it is generally feasible by anyone, and so we know that everyone is a bearer of the duty. In contrast, the duty correspondent to a positive welfare right is imperfect, because we cannot assume that it is feasible by everyone, and until allocating institutions are created, we cannot know who bears responsibility for doing what. Against this, Ashford argues that, pre-institutionally, we do know that a large number of agents are responsible, directly or indirectly, through negligence more than malice, for depriving the poor of access to subsistence,[35] even though we cannot identify any particular agent 'as solely or primarily responsible'[36] or 'specifically responsible'.[37] It is not quite clear how this is supposed to undermine O'Neill's critique of rights to assistance, but it is clear that Ashford thinks it does.[38] Her point seems to be that we do not need institutions to tell us in general terms who bears the duty correspondent to the right to subsistence and so who is responsible for violating it; and that therefore the distinction between liberty and welfare rights is shown to be void.

However, this does not show that the duty of aid falls on everyone; it only shows that it falls on a group of agents, whose members we have had to identify by some means. Maybe we do not need allocating institutions to do that, but, even so, the duty of aid remains special, not universal (and 'human'). Moreover, to identify the members of a group collectively responsible for violating the right to subsistence

---

substantive sense of enjoyment in which such security is worth having, until subsistence has been secured' (ibid., p. 97). My view is that this entire discussion is beside the point.

[34] O'Neill, *Toward Justice and Virtue*, p. 132; quoted by Ashford in 'Duties Imposed', p. 205.

[35] Ashford, 'Duties Imposed', pp. 193–4.   [36] Ibid., p. 192.   [37] Ibid., p. 205.

[38] Ibid., p. 206.

might tell us to whom falls the duty to cease from harmful economic interference, but only if we assume that such ceasing does not involve acts of dismantling that are unfeasibly expensive for particular agents. Further, it does not tell us which members of the group are capable of offering positive aid, taking into account their manifold other responsibilities. Further still, it does not tell us whether, when all the capable members of the group have given their positive aid, it will be sufficient to enable the severely poor to subsist and so to meet the claim that their supposed right makes. For the duties, negative and positive, to be allocated to particular agents in the light of their capabilities, some international or global institutional coordination will be necessary; and until such institutions have been built and have completed their allocating, the members of the responsible group have only imperfect duties to do what they can to refrain from harmful interference and to provide aid, while doing what they can to build coordinating institutions. Ashford agrees: 'The task of reforming the system is a shared one that has not been allocated among agents... Agents therefore have considerable latitude in how they fulfil this duty. Nevertheless, the claim that can be made against them by victims of the system is not empty.'[39] Indeed, it is not empty, but nor is it perfect. The class of agents sharing the responsibility do not have a perfect duty to enable all of the world's poor to escape severe poverty; they only have an imperfect duty to do what they can, all things considered, to relieve the problem. There is, therefore, no universal, human right to subsist.

Ashford resists this conclusion, asserting that

> people possess the human right to secure access to basic necessities before the positive duty to guarantee this right has been institutionally defined and allocated. In the absence of just institutions, again, the onus is on individual agents to take the initiative in deciding how to implement their share of this duty and to seek to institutionalise the task. And again, the right-holders' claim is a claim against every agent who is not doing enough to implement their share of the shared duty. The right exists independently of the institutions that define and allocate the duty of aid.[40]

This is true, but the right and its correspondent duty are imperfect. Each duty-bearer must use its discretion in determining *what its share is*. This determination is, of course, open to criticism by the severely poor or their advocates, and, no doubt, the duty-bearer should consider carefully what they say. However, if the duty-bearer is a state, as is most likely, then it will carry a multitude of responsibilities and be subject to a multitude of demands from all quarters, the sum total of which it cannot possibly satisfy. So it falls to the government of that state to decide

[39] Ibid., p. 216.   [40] Ibid., p. 217.

which demands to meet and how far. The poor might disagree with its determination of what is its fair share of the collective duty of aid, but the government is not
obliged to yield. And even if the poor are right to claim that a government's fair
share is larger than it reckons, and that it should do more, they still cannot claim
that it should do enough to enable all the world's poor to subsist. They cannot yet
claim a universal, human right to subsistence. Why does Ashford resist this
conclusion? The answer is that she simply cannot accept its practical implication:

> If the duty to protect persons' access to basic necessities were taken to be a[n
> imperfect] duty of benevolence, each affluent agent would have a duty to help
> some chronically poor individuals some of the time... [Affluent agents] could
> permissibly choose to help others in need instead. Any particular destitute
> individual would not be entitled to be helped and could not justifiably demand
> this. Therefore if the duty of aid is taken to be a duty of benevolence it is highly
> probable that some individuals will continue to lack access to certain basic
> necessities...[41]

Ashford states the tragic truth, but she cannot abide it.

This brings an end to my examination of the rebuttals made by John Tasioulas
and Elizabeth Ashford of Onora O'Neill's critique of human rights. My conclusion
is that the critique survives wholly intact.

IV

In *Justice: Rights and Wrongs* (2008), Nicholas Wolterstorff does not respond to
any of the members of the Sceptical Tradition, as I have presented it: none of
Burke, Bentham, Ritchie, or O'Neill appears in the index to his book. Early in his
text he does refer once to Bentham's dismissal of rights as nonsense and of natural
rights as nonsense on stilts, but only to reply briskly, 'The way to respond to this
charge is obvious: develop an account of rights that makes sense.' As to why
Bentham thought as he did, Wolterstorff shows no curiosity.[42] That is because his
concern is to mount a defence of natural rights that faces in a very different
direction: toward the many Protestant Christians who think that love should
entirely supplant justice, but more particularly toward several of the theological
proponents of 'right order', whom we shall meet directly in Chapter 6, especially
Oliver O'Donovan.[43]

---

[41] Ibid., p. 210.
[42] Nicholas Wolterstorff, *Justice: Rights and Wrongs* (Princeton: Princeton University Press, 2008),
p. 4.
[43] Ibid., pp. 1, 3. That Wolterstorff is addressing Protestants in general is revealed in an essay
published two years later, where he observes that rights-talk is either marginal or non-existent in

Wolterstorff observes, with evident frustration, that those making the right order 'polemic' spend most of their time telling a story about the conceptual history of natural rights, and offer 'surprisingly little' systematic argumentation.[44] Consequently, he feels the need to supply what they have not, and sets about bringing to clear light the view they dimly imply. 'Right order', he infers, is a socially transcendent standard of rightness or 'natural law', which comprises 'a matrix of objective obligations'.[45] In a nutshell the 'right order' position, quoting Oliver O'Donovan's alleged apophthegm, is *Natural right but no natural rights*.[46]

However, argues Wolterstorff, objective natural obligations entail subjective natural rights. Yet, '[c]ontemporary right order theorists regularly talk as if there could be natural subjective duties without there being natural subjective rights. That cannot be.'[47] The theorists, he thinks, mistake themselves: they are not in fact hostile to natural rights as such. They are not hostile to natural rights that are divinely conferred; only to natural rights that are inherent.[48] '[T]he fundamental issue under dispute', he writes, '... [is] whether natural rights are inherent in the worth of the bearer or conferred on the bearer by some objective norm or standard.'[49] Wolterstorff concurs with the theologians' desire to accord a fundamental role for God in their account of morality, but he denies that this should be done at the expense of inherent natural rights. He argues that rights do inhere in the worth of human beings, but that this worth is not essential or intrinsic to humans—nor, more specifically, is it tied precariously to variable human capacities. Rather, it is conferred by the love of God.[50]

I think that Wolterstorff misconstrues the 'right order' theorists. It is not possible to be sure about the content of their order, since they do not explain it. It could comprise goods and virtues as well as obligations, however, and Wolterstorff does not *show* us that it consists only of the latter. But even if he is

the thought of every one of the great Protestant theologians of the twentieth century—Karl Barth (1886–1968), Emil Brunner (1889–1966), Dietrich Bonhoeffer (1906–44), Anders Nygren (1890–1978), and Reinhold Niebuhr (1892–1971) ('Protestant developments in human rights', in Witte and Alexander, *Christianity and Human Rights*, pp. 156, 157, 158, 162, 165).

[44] Wolterstorff, *Justice*, p. 12.   [45] Ibid., pp. 29–30, 265.

[46] Oliver O'Donovan, *The Desire of the Nations: Rediscovering the Roots of Political Theology* (Cambridge: Cambridge University Press, 1996), p. 262; cited by Wolterstorff in *Justice*, p. 31. The emphasis is Wolterstorff's. In fact, no such saying appears on the page cited. Still, it is a fair summary of O'Donovan's view.

[47] Wolterstorff, *Justice*, pp. 33–4, 35.   [48] Ibid., p. 317.   [49] Ibid., p. 63.

[50] Ibid., pp. 36, 352–60. Wolterstorff makes this argument, not only to accord God a fundamental role, but also to avoid the menacing implications for hindered human beings of an account of human worth that runs in terms of capacities such as 'rationality' or 'autonomy' (ibid., pp. 323–34, 349). I entirely sympathise with the concern, but, regrettably, I do not think that the argument works. This is because it does not explain *why* God loves *human* beings in a special way that he does not love other species—and, taking his cue from the biblical metaphor of human creatures being made 'in the image of God', Wolterstorff is quite clear that the worth of human beings is special (ibid., pp. 342–7). The requisite explanation has to come in terms of some characteristic of humans other than the fact that God loves them.

correct, the exact content of the envisaged 'right order' is beside the point. Oliver O'Donovan's main objection is not a narrow one to the priority of (moral) rights to obligations, but a broader one to the concept of multiple rights as radical or fundamental.[51] This is because if multiple rights are fundamental, then when they conflict, there is no prior, overarching moral framework in terms of which that conflict can be resolved rationally (rather than politically): their fundamental multiplicity militates against 'a conception of order, which demands *a* resolution of each controversy, *a* right thing to be done'.[52] Instead, a right should be considered, 'not an atomic unit that can be multiplied and added up, but a *moment* emerging out of a larger whole, *Ius* as an undivided garment'.[53] That is to say, a right should be the *conclusion* of a process of moral deliberation that operates in terms of a coherent moral order, which involves a wider range of moral concepts—rather than a *basic premise*. Therefore, so long as multiple rights are regarded as only prima facie, representing '*claims* that have to be balanced out in concrete deliberation', there is no problem.[54] If O'Donovan does conceive of the objectively right order basically in terms of obligation, I would join Wolterstorff in objecting that rights and obligations can only be ultimately intelligible in terms of prior goods.[55] However, that is beside the main point, which is that rights are not ethically basic, but contingent on a process of wider ethical deliberation. On whether there are any moral rights at which ethical deliberation always and everywhere concludes—that is, whether there are any natural rights— O'Donovan is silent. However, since, if there were any, they would presumably become basic premises, the logic of his thought militates against it.

Given his theoretical approval of the concept of inherent natural rights, it comes as no surprise that Wolterstorff's judgement on the right order theorists' 'declinist' story is uncompromising: 'The narrative told by [them] , . . to the effect that the idea of natural rights was born of philosophical nominalism and indi-vidualism, is indisputably false, as is their ancillary claim that the idea loses intelligibility outside such contexts'.[56] I agree—as Chapter 6 will explain. Addressing American Christians more broadly, Wolterstorff goes on the offensive to argue that the concept of natural rights, which only came to unequivocal expression in the thirteenth century, is nevertheless implicit in both the Old and New Testaments of the Christian Bible and in the thought of the Early Fathers of

---

[51] O'Donovan never actually refers to 'natural rights', only to 'rights'. Nonetheless, when he refers to legal rights, he says so, which implies that the rest of the time he is speaking about socially transcendent moral rights.

[52] O'Donovan, *Desire of the Nations*, p. 194. The emphases are O'Donovan's.

[53] Oliver O'Donovan, 'The Justice of Assignment and Subjective Rights in Grotius', in Oliver O'Donovan and Joan Lockwood O'Donovan, *Bonds of Imperfection: Christian Politics, Past and Present* (Grand Rapids, Mich.: Eerdmans, 2004), p. 195. The emphases are mine.

[54] Oliver O'Donovan, 'The Language of Rights and Conceptual History', *Journal of Religious Ethics*, 37/2 (June 2009), p. 195. The emphasis is O'Donovan's.

[55] Wolterstorff, *Justice*, p. 4.   [56] Ibid., p. 62.

the Church. He shows that we find there a concept of being wronged, and a special concern for the wrong done to vulnerable persons, which, he thinks, implies the violation of rights that inhere in their human worth:

> The writers of the Hebrew and Christian Scriptures did not explicitly conceptualize natural rights; explicit conceptualization had to await the canon lawyers of the twelfth century. They did, however, recognize what you and I call 'natural rights'.[57]
>
> Perhaps the Church Fathers did not yet have the concept of a natural right, perhaps their lexicon did not have a phrase that can be translated as 'natural right'; nonetheless, ... they recognised and assumed the existence of what we would call *natural rights* in things they said.[58]

I am not convinced. Wolterstorff's argument assumes that any case of being wronged may be translated, without loss, into a case of a right being violated. Certainly, we could make this translation without talking nonsense, and, indeed, we are increasingly making it. We could say, for example, that when a child lies to its parent, he violates the parent's right to the truth. We could say that when a confidante betrays a confidence, she violates her friend's right to privacy. We could say that when a shopkeeper speaks rudely to a customer, he violates her right to civility. We could say all these things and make ourselves readily understood. But we tend not to speak that way, and before the modern period we spoke even less in that way than we do now. This raises the question as to *why* we tend not to. One possible answer is that our historic tendency lacks justification, and what is more, that using more rights-talk has the advantage of drawing our attention to the plight of the wronged. This is Wolterstorff's view: talk about duty or virtue brings into focus the agent-dimension of the moral order, and in the case of wrongdoing, the agent's guilt, whereas rights-talk brings to speech (and consciousness) the recipient-dimension of the moral order, and in the case of wrongdoing, the victim's injury.[59] However, it is not clear to me that talking of someone being wronged attracts any less attention than talking of someone having their right violated. Moreover, one reason why we tend not to translate everyday wrongdoing into rights-violations is that the latter introduces an inappropriate whiff of the courtroom: legal rights are paradigmatic. The whiff is inappropriate because it carries connotations of institutional formality and fixity that do not fit the informal and supple quality of domestic relations or ordinary social encounters.[60] Further, rights-talk does tend to overlook the contingency of rights, and in the case of rights in the state of nature, their ephemerality—their status, as O'Donovan nicely puts it, as moments rather than atoms.

---

[57] Ibid., p. 388.   [58] Ibid., p. 60. The emphasis is Wolterstorff's.   [59] Ibid., p. 7.
[60] See n. 110 in this chapter.

Wolterstorff inadvertently confirms this point in his discussion of St John Chrysostom's sermons on the New Testament's parable of Lazarus and the rich man in AD 388 or 389. Repeatedly Chrysostom (347–407) asserts that the failure of the wealthy to share with the destitute is theft, because the 'means of sustenance *belong* to the poor'—not on account of the laws and practices of Antioch, but on the ground of their needs as human beings. 'It is true', Wolterstorff writes, 'that there is no word in the passage that is a synonym of our word "a right". But the recognition of natural rights is unmistakeably there: the poor are *wronged* because they do not have what is theirs by natural right, what they have a natural right to.'[61] Firmly rooted in the human needs of the poor, the right to sustenance appears to lie securely in their hands. Over 200 pages later, however, when Wolterstorff comes to reflect on 'the situated character of rights', he returns to Chrysostom's rights of the poor: 'In most situations, people have a right to fair access to adequate means of sustenance; they have this right, so Chrysostom argued, just by virtue of being human. But when extreme widespread drought occurs and no food is available, nobody any longer has that right against anyone.'[62] The natural right is real in one context, but illusory in another: Wolterstorff ends up standing alongside the radical Onora O'Neill. Ironically, he also ends up standing next to O'Donovan, for his natural right enjoys only a momentary existence, coming and going, fading in and out, according to the full range of moral considerations that each new concrete situation, within the framework of objectively right order, brings into play.

V

James Griffin's 2008 book *On Human Rights* has been described by one friendly critic as 'arguably the most significant philosophical meditation on human rights to emerge in the human rights-intoxicated era inaugurated by the *Universal Declaration of Human Rights*'.[63] In it resounds an appreciative echo of Wolterstorff's main reason for promoting rights—namely, that they bring to centre stage the recipient-dimension of wrongdoing. For rights-talk, Griffin tells us,

> highlights a certain consideration, attracts our attention to it, marks its import-
> ance in our culture, makes its discussion easier, increases the chances of its

---

[61] Wolterstorff, *Justice*, pp. 61–2. The emphasis is Wolterstorff's.   [62] Ibid., p. 287.
[63] John Tasioulas, 'Taking Rights out of Human Rights', in Roger Crisp, ed., *Griffin on Human Rights* (Oxford: Oxford University Press, 2014), p. 10. Noel Malcolm, a less friendly critic, nevertheless agrees, describing Griffin's work as 'one of the best modern books on the whole subject' and 'one of the most impressive theories of its kind' (*Human Rights and Political Wrongs: A New Approach to Human Rights Law* (London: Policy Exchange, 2017), pp. 110, 115).

having certain social effects such as ease of transmission and potency in political action. It can facilitate deep moral shifts, such as the emergence of individualism at the end of the Middle Ages. It lends itself to political slogans and provides the centrepiece of popular movements. It allows lists of 'human rights', and so checklists for the sort of monitoring done by Amnesty International and Human Rights Watch. It can empower individuals...

And getting something accepted as a human right transforms one's case. One is transformed from beggar ('you ought to help me') to chooser ('it is mine by right'). If one can claim by right, one is not dependent upon the grace and kindness or charity of others.[64]

Yet Griffin's concern is not at all Wolterstorff's: he wants to restrain rights, not promote them. The problem that bothers him is not the view that love is an adequate substitute for justice, but what he calls '[t]he runaway growth of the extension of the term ["human right"] in our time'.[65] Whereas in the seventeenth and eighteenth centuries the focus was on civil and political rights as the answer to the problem of arbitrary government, 'by the twentieth century... [c]onstitutions and international instruments began including hotly resisted welfare rights, as well as suspect items such as rights to peace, to inherit, and to freedom of residence within the borders of one's own country'.[66] Not only have novel rights proliferated, so has the meaning of old ones. In the US Constitution, for example, the right

---

[64] James Griffin, *On Human Rights* (Oxford: Oxford University Press, 2008), pp. 19, 92.

[65] Ibid., p. 17. In contrast, committed to making the international human rights regime the starting-point of his thinking, Allen Buchanan is initially reluctant to admit that it suffers from undesirable inflationary expansion. 'If one adopts my approach', he writes, 'the supposed truism that there is human rights inflation looks less obviously true.' For example, the basis of well-worn criticism of the right to periodic holidays with pay 'must be that there is no corresponding moral human right'; but since there need be no such corresponding moral right, this is not an instance of inflation (*The Heart of Human Rights* (Oxford: Oxford University Press, 2015), p. 75). 'Instead of complaining that the international legal human rights system is bloated, we should conclude that a theory of moral human rights is too slender a basis for developing a satisfactory justification for the system of international human rights' (ibid., p. 77). There is truth here. The cultural inappropriateness or simple unfeasibility of such a legal right to holidays does indeed call into question the existence of any correspondent moral right: as we have seen already in this chapter, there cannot be a universal moral right to the performance of a duty that is unfeasible. However, that does not save the right to holidays from inflationary status, since there cannot be a moral *or a legal right* that demands what cannot be done.

In fact, Buchanan later abandons his scepticism: 'I suspect that there are some cases of rights inflation', he tells us, partly because the international system lacks the doctrinal and institutional resources to do much to specify the state's performance of basic welfare functions, and partly because drafters of human rights treaties are tempted to include rights that aspire to ensure maximal human flourishing (ibid., p. 158). Toward the end of his book, he repeats and elaborates the point. One of the limitations of the international legal regime, he says, is that it lacks the resources for achieving appropriate constraints on the proliferation of rights, especially welfare ones: 'The worry is that unbridled proliferation damages the very idea of international human rights by abandoning the notion of extraordinarily high priority norms in favour of an ever-expanding list of protected interests, and that the political effectiveness of the enterprise is likely to be compromised by dispersing energies in the pursuit of the realization of so many norms' (ibid., p. 286). Griffin would applaud.

[66] Griffin, *On Human Rights*, p. 17.

to life was conceived in a largely negative fashion as a right not to be deprived of life without due process (i.e. not to be murdered). But 'the scope of the right seems irresistibly to expand': 'The putative right has grown from a right against the arbitrary termination of the normal life of someone already living (murder), to a right against other forms of termination of life (abortion, suicide, euthanasia), to a right against the prevention of the formation of life (contraception, sterilization), to a right to basic welfare, to a right to a fully flourishing life.'[67] As a consequence of this ballooning of content, '[t]here is cynicism about the whole discourse, which, being so fatally malleable, is exploited as a weapon in power politics'.[68] There are '[w]idespread doubts about certain reputed civil rights, objections to the lavishness of some welfare rights, scepticism about the whole class of group rights...'.[69] The cause of this problem of runaway inflation Griffin attributes to the gradual abandonment of the original theological, metaphysical content of a natural right in the course of the seventeenth and eighteenth centuries, and the failure to replace it with anything else.[70] 'There has been no theoretical development of the idea itself since then', he writes, with the result that '[t]he term "human right" is nearly criterionless'.[71]

So what solution does Griffin offer the problem? He rejects any proposal that tries to avoid 'broad ethical commitment', including that which simply stipulates that the international consensus on human rights is bedrock.[72] Mere agreement on

---

[67] Ibid., pp. 97, 213.   [68] Ibid., p. 203.   [69] Ibid., p. 204.   [70] Ibid., p. 2.

[71] Ibid., pp. 13–14. According to Buchanan, Griffin's complaint that the idea of human rights has remained indeterminate for hundreds of years only applies to moral rights. International legal human rights have become more determinate through jurisprudence and specification by international treaty bodies (*The Heart of Human Rights*, p. 19): 'Griffin says far too little about why he thinks that the indeterminacy of the idea of "human rights" is such a big problem' (ibid., p. 20). So, let us speak where Griffin is reticent. The reason that this indeterminacy is a problem is that international treaties and national charters often affirm highly abstract, capacious rights, which give their judicial interpreters ample, and politically dangerous, room for creative elaboration—as was adumbrated in Chapter 3, and as we shall see most clearly in Chapter 11. In fact, Buchanan himself acknowledges this, when he proposes judicial restraint as one solution to the problem of 'overly expansive interpretations' of rights-law. In ironic tension with his prevailing confidence in the authority of International Human Rights Law (IHRL), he admits that, since the most excessive expansion has tended to occur at the international (not least European) level, an increasing acknowledgement of the supremacy of the international legal regime 'may exacerbate the problem of inflation' (ibid., pp. 290–1).

[72] Griffin, *On Human Rights*, pp. 27, 280 n. 19. Griffin refers here to Charles R. Beitz, a leading advocate of the 'practical' view, which 'takes the doctrine and practice of human rights as we find them in international political practice as basic' ('Human Rights and the Law of Peoples', in Chatterjee, *The Ethics of Assistance*, p. 197). Allen Buchanan 'whole-heartedly concurs' with Beitz that philosophical consideration of human rights should begin with its current practice, especially its legal core, which is the international human rights regime (*The Heart of Human Rights*, p. 22). According to Beitz, this 'Practice' is a response to the Second World War and the Holocaust, which aims to curb the sovereignty of states and thereby the mistreatment of their own people (ibid., p. 39). IHRL is 'widely thought to be morally obligatory', and commands a moral authority that no pre-theoretical or philosophical theory approaches (ibid., p. 7). What is more and consequently, it is better able to influence the behaviour of signatory states, whether because legality is taken seriously by powerful domestic constituencies or because it is understood to be important reputationally. Further, 'once a state acknowledges that it has obligations under human rights law, it is not necessary to argue the moral issues from the ground up. The fact of legality narrows the space for debates about what morality requires' (ibid., p. 9). Further still,

a list of such rights will struggle to generate wholehearted promotion, will contain disagreement over content and priorities, and cannot sustain deeply rational and uniform resolutions.[73] What is more, it cannot dispel scepticism about the international rights regime itself.[74] Instead, therefore, Griffin proceeds to offer an ethically substantive theory of the ground of genuinely, strictly human rights, which provides criteria for narrowing the content of some already acknowledged and rejecting the candidacy of others altogether. In doing this, he disowns both a stance of general scepticism toward values and the particular view that moral judgements are mere expressions of personal preferences.[75] In effect, if not in name, he endorses moral realism, insofar as that affirms that human values or interests are not merely the creatures of human desires:[76] 'merely caring about

'because of its saliency, its relative determinateness, and the prestige it enjoys, international human rights law serves as a moral standard that can be employed for political mobilization to change the behaviour of states, corporations, and other agents, even in cases where it does not impose clear duties on them' (ibid., p. 26). Besides, the basic idea of a system of international legal human rights is considerably independent of philosophical notions of moral rights, and many international legal rights have a 'scope' (in terms of correlative duties) that far exceeds that of corresponding moral rights (ibid., p. 4 n. 1).

All these things may be true. It is also true, however, that *inter*national human rights are not the only ones; how IHRL is able to command intercultural consensus requires an explanation; and international legality does *not* confine morality. Regarding this last point, international law, as it now stands, can sometimes *shield* a massively murderous regime from outside interference, should the UN Security Council fail to authorise intervention. As a result states, and even international lawyers, have been compelled to appeal to supra-legal moral authority. So, with regard to military intervention in defence of the Kurds of northern Iraq in 1991, the French argued that '[t]he law is one thing, but the safeguard [sic] of a population is another, quite as precious, to which humanity cannot be indifferent' (Mary Ellen O'Connell, *The Power and Purpose of International Law: Insights from the Theory and Practice of Enforcement* (New York: Oxford University Press, 2008), p. 206). And of NATO's intervention in Kosovo in 1999, the eminent international lawyer Martti Koskenniemi has written that 'most lawyers— including myself—have taken the ambivalent position that it was both formally illegal and morally necessary' ('"The Lady Doth Protest Too Much": Kosovo and the Turn to Ethics in International Law', *The Modern Law Review*, 65/2 (March 2002),p. 162). See further Nigel Biggar, *In Defence of War* (Oxford: Oxford University Press, 2013), chapter 6. Many years ago, John Tasioulas observed that Griffin was more '[s]ensitive to the disorder of the human rights culture in a way that [Richard] Rorty is not...' ('Human Rights, Universality, and the Values of Personhood: Retracing Griffin's Steps', *European Journal of Philosophy*, 10/1 (2002), p. 82). What then applied to Rorty, now applies to Buchanan.

[73] Griffin, *On Human Rights*, p. 26.   [74] Ibid., p. 204.   [75] Ibid., pp. 111–16.

[76] It is true that Griffin explicitly distances himself from 'realism', which he associates with the affirmation of 'belief-independent reality' (ibid., p. 122). However, such an association seems to me unnecessary. If there are interests, values, or goods that all human beings recognise—as I think there are, and as Griffin seems to—then we may say that these goods are constant features of the practical rationality of human beings, that they belong to the rational dimension of human nature. They are values that are at once facts about the world—they are moral facets of reality. In effect, this is Griffin's position when he rejects the 'sharp separation of fact and value' characteristic of 'the usual kind of reductive naturalism' (ibid., pp. 123, 124), and espouses instead 'an expansive naturalism', in which the boundaries of the 'natural' and 'factual' are pushed out to encompass human interests (ibid., p. 124). These interests, he tells us emphatically, 'are part of *human* nature, and not just human nature as seen by society' (ibid., p. 119).

Griffin's moral realism reduces the distance between his 'secular' ethic and the Christian natural law one that originally generated natural rights. Of the secularisation of ethics he writes, 'Our moral role changed from obedience to God-given law to compliance with self-given law' (ibid., p. 150). And yet, according to Griffin's concept of autonomy, the law is not simply self-given, since autonomous

something does not make it valuable. For anyone to see anything as valuable, from any point of view, requires being able to see it as worth wanting.' Desires that are part of normal intentional action, rather than afflictions, 'aim at the good'.[77] Sometime persons affirm value-notions that they have never been taught and that are alien to the ethos of their society: 'In the end the best explanation... is that the person has hit upon, has become sensitive to, something valuable, and that its being valuable is to some extent independent of the process of coming to regard it as such.'[78] Griffin's moral realism entails his rejection of universal ethical relativism:[79] while human rights are historically a Western product, and while different societies might prioritise them differently, the values on which they are based are not just Western.[80] It is true that what is culturally alien can be baffling, but bafflement can be overcome—as Westerners have adopted Eastern religions, so Easterners may embrace Western human rights. Besides, Westerners exaggerate the cultural differences by exaggerating the strictness of their own conception of rights.[81]

At the core of the largely Western-inspired discourse of human rights is the idea 'that human beings are unique, that we are made in God's image (Genesis 1.27), that we too are creators—creators of ourselves, and by our actions, of part of the world around us, on which we shall be judged'.[82] This responsibility requires autonomy, which in turn requires the exercise of the individual's conscience; and it is this moral agency that accords human being the elevated status or dignity that is 'personhood'.[83] Moral agency can be analysed into three components: first, 'autonomy', whereby we choose our own path toward a worthwhile life, rather than being dominated or controlled by someone else; second, minimum education and information, so that our choice is real, and minimum provision of the

wrongdoing is possible (ibid., pp. 153, 156). The individual's autonomy operates within the framework of objective goods—a framework given in and with human nature, not conjured up by any individual subject. Thus far, Griffin's view is identical to that of Christian proponents of natural law. The remaining difference between them lies in their answers to the question of whether it makes best sense to explain this givenness in terms of God or biology (ibid., pp. 116–17).

[77] Ibid., p. 115.   [78] Ibid., p. 119.   [79] Ibid., p. 129: 'universal ethical relativism is ... false.'
[80] Ibid., p. 133.   [81] Ibid., pp. 137–8.
[82] Ibid., p. 26. Since Griffin is deliberately trying to offer a 'secular' account of human rights, it is slightly odd to be told here that the idea that we are made in God's image lies 'at the core' of Western rights-talk. It is even odder to find the value protected by human rights described, deep into the book, as that of being 'a normative agent, a self-creator, made in God's image' (ibid., p. 181). Perhaps Griffin thinks that this theological concept is equivalent to 'moral agency' and can be translated without loss into it. If so, he is more optimistic than Jürgen Habermas, as I interpret him in 'Not Translation, but Conversation: Theology in Public Debate about Euthanasia', in Nigel Biggar and Linda Hogan, eds, *Religious Voices in Public Places* (Oxford: Oxford University Press, 2000), pp. 163–5.
[83] Griffin, *On Human Rights*, p. 26. Despite his several reservations about Griffin's project, Allen Buchanan's view of the special moral significance of the human individual is not so very different from Griffin's. He adopts a 'Kantian understanding of equal basic moral status' (*The Heart of Human Rights*, p. 138), the qualification for which is 'the capacity for responsiveness to reasons ... for participating in practices involving rational accountability' (ibid., p. 138).

resources and capabilities necessary for acting; and third, 'liberty' from having one's pursuit of the a worthwhile life hindered or stopped by other people.[84] These three values of personhood are the ground of human rights,[85] which should be understood specifically (and strictly) as protections of them.[86]

The three values of personhood are the primary ground of most of the conventional list of human rights—to life, to security, to a voice in political decision, to free expression, and to worship. They are also the ground of a right against torture. That ground cannot be the mere fact that torture gratuitously inflicts great pain, since many such cases—e.g. one married partner's psychological abuse of the other—do not attract the protection of a right. Torture is distinctive:

> It is used to make someone recant a belief, reveal a secret, 'confess' a crime whether guilty or not, abandon a cause or do someone else's bidding. All of these characteristic purposes involve undermining someone else's will, getting them to do what they do not want to do, or are even resolved not to do. In one way or another, they involve an attack on normative agency.[87]

Of all these rights it is important to note that they are moral claims, not to whatever promotes human *good or flourishing*, but merely to what is needed for human *status:* they are protections of 'a characteristically human life'.[88]

Sometimes personhood alone is sufficient to determine the content of a right— for example, against torture. However, sometimes it is not sufficient—for example, in the case of a putative right against being forced to donate a kidney.[89] In these cases 'practical considerations' must be brought into play—that is, empirical information about human *nature* and the *nature* of society. Prominent among these will be awareness of the natural limits of human understanding and motivation. Thus a right should incorporate consideration of the limited human ability to predict consequences and provide benefits, and what it would take for a right to be 'an effective, socially manageable claim'.[90]

Such practicalities, Griffin tells us, 'are not relative to particular times or places. They are universal, as any existence condition for rights that one has simply in virtue of being human must be.'[91] That cannot be the whole truth, however, for

---

[84] Griffin, *On Human Rights*, p. 26. Since 'autonomy' might be thought to privilege those who are articulate, educated, and possessed of fully able mental faculties, it is important to point out that Griffin makes clear that it does not require 'rational deliberation', that some people 'simply have a good nose' for distinguishing true values from false, and that '[a]nyone who has the capacity to identify the good, whatever the extent of the capacity and whatever its source, has what I mean by "a conception of a worthwhile life"' (ibid., p. 46). Nevertheless, this generosity has its limits: 'My belief is that we have a better chance of improving the discourse of human rights if we stipulate that only normative agents bear human rights—*no exceptions*: not infants, not the seriously mentally disabled, not those in permanent vegetative state' (ibid., p. 92. The emphasis is Griffin's).

[85] Ibid., p. 51.   [86] Ibid., p. 26.   [87] Ibid., p. 52.   [88] Ibid., p. 34.
[89] Ibid., p. 37.   [90] Ibid., pp. 38, 70–1, 127.   [91] Ibid., p. 38.

practicalities are determined, not only by the generic limitations of universal human nature, but also by the contingent circumstantial particularities that determine what those limitations actually are at any one time and place.[92] That is why, though resistant to trade-offs with other elements of a good life, no 'human right is absolute',[93] since circumstances may conspire to justify its compromise or violation for the sake of other elements of a good life. Thus, it is widely accepted that if there is a sufficiently great threat to the survival of the nation and its ability to protect the life and liberty of its citizens, a government may set aside certain rights.[94]

At this point emerges an unresolved tension, one we have already encountered in the thinking of John Tasioulas and Elizabeth Ashford. On the one hand, Griffin wants certain rights to be securely grounded in the requirements of personhood: they are possessed *simply in virtue of being a human person*. However, if no right is absolute against circumstantially justified compromise or suspension, then how secure can its grounding be? One symptom of the problem appears in Griffin's discussion of just imprisonment. Where someone convicted of a crime is fairly sentenced to imprisonment, he tells us, his (natural, moral) right to liberty has been 'outweighed' by the demands of justice. What he refuses to say is that his right 'disappears': 'the personhood account leaves no space for forfeits; an offender is still a person.'[95] So the imprisoned offender supposedly retains his right, though quite how is not clear. One possibility hinted at is that punishment usually comes

---

[92] John Tasioulas anticipated this point in 2001, when he discerned in Griffin's conception of 'practicalities' a submerged distinction between universal and non-universal, 'local' elements. This occasioned his suspicion 'that non-universal practicalities, rather than rendering human rights norms more determinate, may instead undermine their universality' ('Human Rights, Universality, and the Values of Personhood', p. 86). Tasioulas contends more boldly than Griffin for a certain historical relativisation of those rights possessed simply in virtue of being human persons: 'Perhaps we can intelligibly conceive of cavemen as possessing a right not to be tortured, but how can we reasonably ascribe to them rights that refer to activities that are simply not conceivable, let alone feasible, in their historical epoch, such as rights to a fair trial, to an adequate standard of living, or to political participation?' ('Taking Rights out of Human Rights', p. 33). How, indeed? From this, Tasioulas concludes that human rights cannot (all) be 'natural rights' possessed in a state of nature, and consequently opts for a 'temporally relativized interpretation' of the human rights emanating from the requirements of personhood. Yet he insists that '[t]he formal feature of universality is still retained, since human rights apply to all those properly designated "human" within the specified historical period' (ibid., pp. 35–6). While I approve of the direction of travel, I am sceptical that universality can always be maintained plausibly across widely differing empirical conditions and historical contexts. After all, we have seen Tasioulas—alongside Ashford and Griffin—attempt to do that by dogmatically affirming their faith in universal human rights in situations where the duties of the asserted right to subsistence are not known to be feasible, and the substance of the right to liberty has been lost absolutely and irrevocably.

[93] Griffin, *On Human Rights*, p. 138. When Griffin writes that no human right is absolute, it is not entirely clear whether he is referring to those rights enshrined in classic documents such as the Universal Declaration, International Covenants, and European Convention, which sometimes come with explicit qualifications, or whether he is referring more broadly to natural, moral rights. Since he is discussing the cultural controversy about the universal status of international human rights, I take it that his reference is to trans-cultural, natural, moral rights.

[94] Ibid., p. 59.   [95] Ibid., p. 65.

in degrees, and so the prisoner forfeits only part of his right, retaining the rest. That would make sense, but, since that *does* give space to forfeits, it cannot be the answer. Besides, in the cases of morally justified execution and killing in war, the *whole* right is surely lost. In the end, Griffin merely leaves us with the unsatisfying conclusion that this might be one of those conflicts that is 'neither dissoluble nor resolvable'.[96]

The same unresolved tension appears when Griffin discusses welfare rights. On the one hand, acknowledging the principle that 'ought' implies 'can',[97] he does not hide his incredulity at the 'uncritical generosity' of the Universal Declaration and subsequent rights documents.[98] Thus he judges that ICESCR's right to 'the highest attainable standard of physical and mental health' (Art. 12.1) is 'not even a reasonable social aim'.[99] And on the subsequent interpretation of the right by the UN Committee on Economic, Social, and Cultural Rights, so as to mean that each state party should attain the level it can 'to the maximum of its available resources', he comments: 'But no current state, no matter how rich, spends "the maximum of its available resources on health. Nor should it."'[100] Nevertheless, Griffin resists the implication that the inability to perform a corresponding obligation actually undermines a fundamental right of personhood. Normative agency requires autonomy and liberty, autonomy and liberty require life, and life requires a minimum provision of supporting material goods.[101] This generates a requirement to protect another person from losing agency and, if lost, to restore it—'at least if one can do this without great cost to oneself'. 'All of this', he tells us, 'is involved simply in *having* a right to autonomy or welfare'.[102] But observe: on the one hand, he recognises that the capacity to protect is conditional, contingent upon circumstances ('if...'); on the other hand, he asserts that such protection is the subject of a moral right-claim and so, presumably, obligatory. Therefore, it seems, 'ought' does not require 'can'. Let us suppose circumstances where it is not possible for protection to be offered, or at least not without excessive cost. Does the right still exist there? Is it still possessed? If so, how? We are not told.

Given this, it is predictable that Griffin would clash with the radical version of Onora O'Neill, and, indeed, he does. He opposes O'Neill's view that we have no right unless the correlative duty-bearer is identifiable, that identifiability requires institutions, and that therefore international welfare rights cannot therefore be *human* rights, only civil ones.[103] Instead, he argues that social institutions are not necessary for claimability in the case of most international rights that imply positive duties. For example, AIDS sufferers in Africa have a right both to help and to the deliberation necessary to identify the extent of the duty and its bearers. This needs no special institutions; all it needs is deliberation about ability,

---

[96] Ibid., p. 66.   [97] Ibid., p. 98.   [98] Ibid., p. 186.   [99] Ibid., p. 99.
[100] Ibid., p. 100.   [101] Ibid., pp. 179–80.   [102] Ibid., p. 181. The emphasis is Griffin's.
[103] Ibid., p. 107.

responsibility, fairness of burden etc., and organisation by various bodies.[104] He agrees that a right with no identifiable duty-bearer would be 'at best, an admirable aspiration', but the duty-bearers need only be 'identifiable in thought', not 'confrontable in flesh and blood'.[105] He sees no problem with a supply-side shortfall, which is due, say, to permissible partiality, because it is sufficient for claimability that the specifiable duty-bearers might come to exist, not that they do so already.[106]

This returns us to territory familiar from the first section of this chapter. So long as it is not certain that there are duty-bearers capable of meeting a given need, individually or collectively, there cannot be a right to have that need met. Until the duty-bearers have been identified, we cannot know that they are sufficiently capable, all their other responsibilities considered. The identification of duty-bearers, deliberation about their relative capabilities, coordination of their efforts, and the distribution of burdens will require more than ad hoc cooperation. Therefore, before international institutions have been created, the needy can only urge others to do their imperfect duty to give as much direct aid as they can, and to work with other imperfect duty-bearers to create the conditions under which their efforts will be sufficient to meet the need. Whether their aid will be sufficient to meet the need, and whether their efforts to create need-meeting conditions will succeed, we cannot be certain. So until international institutions have been established, the needy have no right to have their need met; and, if their need is the minimum required by moral agency, then the right they lack is one that protects personhood. Yet Griffin cannot recognise this: 'What seems to me undeniable', he writes, 'is that there is a human right to the minimum resources needed to live as a normative agent.'[107] He will not countenance the possibility of circumstances where the rights of personhood *cannot* be met. Those rights *must* be absolute.[108]

Griffin seeks to rein in the runaway proliferation of rights partly by restricting their purpose to the protection of moral agency and its requirements, partly by requiring them to take limiting 'practicalities' into account, and partly by (sometimes) applying the principle that 'ought' implies 'can'. A fourth restraint is his salutary refrain that rights are not the whole of morality. 'We have constantly to remind ourselves', he writes,

of the destructive modern tendency to turn all important moral matters into matters of rights, especially of human rights. We have to recover our sense of the

[104] Ibid., p. 108.   [105] Ibid., p. 109.   [106] Ibid., p. 110.   [107] Ibid., p. 206.
[108] John Tasioulas agrees with Griffin about this, of course, and commends his resistance to O'Neill, commenting: 'there are good reasons to resist this...step [taken by O'Neill], one being its deeply revisionary implications for human rights, which include demoting so-called "welfare rights" from the ranks of *bona fide* human rights' ('Taking Rights out of Human Rights', p. 19). Griffin could hardly endorse this reason, however, since he himself is intent upon some radical revisions of his own. Besides, since when did the disturbing implications of a line of thought become a sufficient reason to doubt its cogency?

power of the rest of our moral vocabulary—for example, the language of justice and fairness . . . Once we recover a sense of the full range of our moral vocabulary, we shall no longer feel the need to turn all important moral claims into claims of rights.[109]

This view would not please Wolterstorff, who wants to regard every wrong as the violation of a right.[110] But it is one at which representatives of the medieval and early modern Christian tradition of conceiving natural rights within the wider, qualifying terms of natural law would rejoice—as should their contemporary 'right order' descendants.[111]

However, Griffin's salutary view that there is more to morality than rights also serves as a basis for undermining his insistence that certain, properly human rights are *securely* lodged in personhood and its requirements *alone*. Against Griffin, I have argued that whether or not the destitute person's need of those resources requisite for moral agency amounts to a right cannot depend entirely on the personhood of the destitute; it must depend also on the feasibility of providing (all) the necessary resources. Similarly, the cases of just execution or killing in war show, surely, that the right of a convicted prisoner or unjust warrior to liberty cannot depend entirely on their personhood. Rather, it depends on a wider array of morally significant factors: the guilt (at least objective) of the prisoner or warrior, the motive and intention of those who would kill them, the goodness of their ends, and the proportionality to those ends of lethal means.

---

[109] Griffin, *On Human Rights*, p. 95. See also ibid., p. 41: 'Human rights do not exhaust the whole moral domain; they do not exhaust even the whole domain of justice and fairness'; and ibid, p. 43: 'My proposal . . . goes against a not uncommon current belief that the domains of human rights and of justice are identical . . . . It is a great, but now common, mistake to think that, because we see rights as especially important in morality, we must make everything especially important in morality into a right.'

[110] Ibid., p. 201: 'It is deeply counter-intuitive to regard all serious moral wrongs, even all substantial injustices, as infringements of human rights.'

[111] On this point Griffin makes a confusing comment about Grotius. After noting that Aquinas regarded natural laws as equivalent to 'basic moral principles governing this large sense of duties', he writes: 'If we derive natural rights from natural laws, do these rights then also exhaust this range of morality? Grotius and Pufendorf seem to have thought so. Most of us today do not; we believe that they exclude the claims of charity and perhaps more' (ibid., p. 281 n. 21). If the contemporary problem is our tendency to reduce the whole of morality to rights, and so to exclude and neglect the claims of charity, then that is not a problem that attends Grotius. For him, for example, the natural right of liberty from bodily interference or harm is subject to the overriding claims of the social good: 'if one subject, tho' altogether innocent, be demanded by the enemy to be put to death, he may, no doubt of it, be abandoned, and left to their discretion, if it is manifest, that the state is not able to stand the shock of that enemy' (*Rights of War and Peace*, II.XXV.III.1, p. 1152) Yet the reasoning here is not simply that the urgent requirements of the social good trump an individual's right, but also that virtues other than justice can sometimes encourage, even oblige, us to 'a greater piece of goodness' and 'to abate somewhat of our right', than rigorously to pursue it' (ibid., II.XXIV.I.1, p. 1133). Thus in general the virtue of charity often advises and sometimes commands us 'to prefer the advantage of many persons to my own single interest' (ibid., II.I.IX.3, p. 405), and in this particular case it obliges the subject to surrender himself to the enemy (ibid., II.XXV.III.2, p. 1153).

It is at this point, therefore, that Allen Buchanan's critique of Griffin strikes home. Buchanan observes that highly plausible international legal rights have a much broader scope than putative moral rights, which are grounded 'solely in the moral importance of features of the individual right-holder'.[112] Thus the legal right to health commands a plural justification, namely, that it can 'promote social utility, contribute to social solidarity, help to realise the ideal of a decent or a humane society, increase productivity and to that extent contribute to the general welfare, and provide an efficient and coordinated way for individuals to fulfil their obligations of beneficence'.[113] Similarly, the legal rights that promote physical security—say, against arbitrary killing and torture—'serve several important values, including individual autonomy, peaceful and productive social cooperation, social utility, the protection of minority groups, and the protection of property rights (by shielding individuals from coercive expropriation of their property)'.[114] '[L]aw', he rightly says, 'is an instrument capable of serving quite diverse purposes, including the realization of a diversity of moral concerns.'[115] A plural justification of rights, which bears this in mind, can still keep in centre-view that idea that every individual is of moral significance on his own account, while at the same time appealing to a wider range of moral arguments.[116] What this implies for the solution to the problem of rights-inflation is that it needs to take a variety of forms: not just distinguishing a set of primary goods, but also, for example, admitting the decisiveness of the feasibility of duties, allowing other moral considerations full room to operate, and arguing for restraint upon judicial creativity.

VI

Before we move to draw general conclusions from our testing of natural rights-talk from the medieval period to the present against the sceptics' critique, let us

---

[112] Buchanan, *Heart of Human Rights*, p. 276.   [113] Ibid., p. 53.   [114] Ibid., p. 54.
[115] Ibid., p. 55.
[116] Ibid., p. 276. John Tasioulas has also argued that human rights should be grounded on a plurality of human goods, not just those centred on personhood. Among other advantages, such a 'pluralist' account would enhance the authority of human rights in cultures that do not attach the special value to autonomy and liberty that the heirs of the Enlightenment do ('Human Rights, Universality, and the Values of Personhood', pp. 88, 93, 94). Similarly, Roger Crisp argues that Griffin 'should be prepared to extend the ground of human rights beyond normative agency' ('Human Rights: Form and Substance', in Crisp, *Griffin on Human Rights*, p. 148). John Gardner implicitly sides with the 'pluralists', too: 'many rights on the conventional list seem to go beyond what reliance on our humanity alone could justify' ('Simply in Virtue of Being Human: the Whos and Whys of Human Rights', *Journal of Ethics and Social Philosophy*, 2/2 (February 2008), p. 18). Noel Malcolm points out that Griffin himself is an inadvertent pluralist, when he concedes that freedom of (artistic) expression is protected by human rights, because 'it may be a part, not just of deliberating about, but also simply of having a good life' (*On Human Rights*, p. 193). This implies, argues Malcolm, that such things as art are the subject of a right because of their intrinsic value, and not just because of their relation to normative agency (*Human Rights and Political Wrongs*, p. 114).

first take stock of the fate of contemporary defences. In one respect James Griffin's defence agrees with the critique, namely, in objecting to the inflationary rhetoric of natural or human rights-talk. However, whereas Burke and Bentham worried about the rhetoric's legitimation of political anarchy, Griffin joins O'Neill in worrying about its generation of political disappointment, disillusionment, and cynicism.

Otherwise, the arguments made by Shue, Tasioulas, Ashford, and Griffin fail to dislodge the critique of human rights made by O'Neill in her radical moments: namely, that where capable holders of feasible correspondent duties have not been identified, universal human rights are not merely abstract, but illusory; they do not exist. No amount of humanitarian, compassionate magic can conjure a human right out of urgent need or the basic requirements of moral agency alone.[117] In spite of her own defence of abstraction against Burke's scepticism, O'Neill's argument has the effect of confirming his insistence that rights are contingent on the circumstances of feasibility and capability. It also has the effect of confirming Allen Buchanan's rejection of the 'Mirroring View', according to which, behind every human right that commands a measure of international consensus, stands a corresponding natural moral right.[118] Such international legal rights might be justified by natural morality, according to circumstance, but while the principles of natural morality are constant, the conclusion that they justify a legal right is not—circumstances being changeable. Therefore, it seems, there is no constant, natural right.[119]

But what about rights to such things as a fair trial? Surely they are constant, universal, and (in that sense) natural? Yes, they are, but only in the same sense that a right against unjust killing or unjust lying is natural: they are universally true, because they are tautologous. Of course, it is always true that it is wrong to suffer unfairness or injustice: logic requires it. However, until the meanings of abstract unfairness and injustice are specified, and until those specifications are publicly endorsed in law, custom, or social norms, those who stand at risk of being unfairly

---

[117] As Jeremy Bentham put it: 'a reason for wishing that a certain right were established is not that right; a want is not supply; hunger is not bread' (*Jeremy Bentham's Economic Writings*, 3 vols, ed. W. Stark (London: Allen and Unwin, 1952), Vol. I, p. 333). Kieran Cronin agrees: 'the obsessive desire to rid humanity of all pain and deprivation is not a good basis for developing a set of realistic rights-claims' (*Right and Christian Ethics* (Cambridge: Cambridge University Press, 1992), p. 114).

[118] Buchanan, *Heart of Human Rights*, p. 14.

[119] The danger of rights-talk becomes evident in the case of the *ius sustentationis* (the 'right to subsistence'), which medieval canon lawyers asserted, and according to which the poor could take from the available stock of property in times of dearth (R. R. Helmholz, 'Human Rights in the Canon Law', in Witte and Alexander, *Christianity and Human Rights*, p. 106). Such a right presupposes not only a condition of dearth, but also a society where rich people own more than enough to subsist, their surplus is accessible to the poor, and that surplus is sufficient to meet the needs of all the poor. For only then could there be a right of the poor that imposes a perfect duty on the rich to meet their claim. To talk of there being 'a right to subsistence' rather than to say that, 'in these circumstances, it is right that the poor should take what they need from the rich', encourages us to overlook the right's high contingency upon variable conditions—as do Tasioulas and Ashford.

or unjustly treated have nothing to appeal to beyond fickle public opinion or the unreliable consciences of other agents. And should that opinion or those consciences happen to diverge from their own, their appeal would lack all force. In these circumstances, it would be quite misleading to talk of possessing a right, since that would imply a degree of security that does not actually obtain.

VII

Now that my testing of the sceptical critique against the history of natural rights-talk is complete, I am in a position to draw some general conclusions. One seminal conclusion I have reached is that the paradigm of a right is positively legal, granted by law-makers in a particular society and commanding the support of social institutions. This is partly because the concept of a right first crystallised in the thought of medieval canon lawyers, and partly because lawyers in general regard legal rights as paradigmatic.[120] The main reason, however, is that it is the institutional support that explains the heightened authority that distinguishes a right from other kinds of claim. Therefore, I consider a right to be paradigmatically a liberty or a benefit that is the property of an individual or a social body, which designated others are bound by law (broadly conceived) to respect or provide, and in failing to respect or provide it they become liable to some kind of legal penalty.

From this it follows that when 'a natural right' refers to something distinct from a positive legal right, it is only analogous to it—both similar and different, but not identical. Such a natural right might not be granted by a particular legal system— or by any legal system at all. It is supposed to exist in some state of nature or realm of abstract principle, which precedes and transcends all actual legal systems and their positive law. The authority of such a natural right, therefore, is fundamentally moral, rather than legal. For that reason, moral criticism of positive law can be made by appeal over its head to a supposed natural right.

To call a right 'natural', however, need not claim for it a moral authority that trumps positive law. It can also be to claim a moral authority that operates in the complete absence of positive law and its social institutions—in a state of nature. A state of nature is usually conceived as a set of historical conditions either where social institutions have not yet come into existence or where they have failed— virgin territory, civil anarchy, or international war governed by no agreed norms. Such a state can be conceived in amoral, Hobbesian terms, in which case 'a right' is

---

[120] Naturally, lawyers take legal rights as paradigmatic, tending to regard 'moral rights' as lacking key features of real (legal) rights—such as enforceability (Michael J. Perry, *Towards a Theory of Human Rights: Religion, Law, and Courts* (Cambridge: Cambridge University Press, 2007), p. xii). Jeremy Waldron claims that it is widely believed that talk about individual rights 'is most at home in the context of positive law' ('Introduction', in Waldron, ed., *Theories of Rights*, Oxford Readings in Philosophy (Oxford: Oxford University Press, 1984), p. 4).

really a misnomer. Alternatively, it can be conceived in Christian—or other morally realist—terms as a condition where natural law or morality obtains.

Talk of natural rights in a moral state of nature implies a certain kind of universality, insofar as 'nature' is not merely the alternative to 'society', but refers to a set of features that are constant through time. The constancy could be thought to characterise the principles of moral law, which command every moral agent in all places and at all times. More specifically, this moral law could be conceived as generated by the 'dignity' that attaches to every being of *human* nature—that is, to every 'image of God', or moral agent, or person. Here, a natural right would be the same as a human right. We should note, however, that where the moral law is understood to flow from the dignity of human nature—as is often the case in the wake of Kant (1724–1804)—such dignity tends to generate rights first and cor-respondent duties only subsequently. While that need not be so—since in the ancient or medieval past, 'a right' was sometimes thought to subject the right-holder to obligations as well as enabling him to assert rightful claims—it is so among us now.

Sometimes a putative natural right is both universal and absolute, possessed by every person and holding everywhere and always. So, for example, we might say that there is a natural right not to be physically harmed out of malice or disproportionately. This applies to all persons universally and in all circumstances. However, a natural, universal right need not be absolute. For example, it may belong to all persons to have the natural right to punish wrongdoing in a state of nature. Yet there can be good moral reasons of prudence to surrender this right for the greater impartiality and security of a positive right in civil society, which is backed by the courts. Should the courts seriously fail or civil society collapse altogether, the natural right would revive, but otherwise it remains suspended. Despite its lodgement in constant human nature, it does not apply universally, under all conditions.

One thing that our study of natural rights-talk has taught us, therefore, is that 'a natural right' can mean a bewildering variety of different things, and that any evaluation must be careful to distinguish them. Bearing that caveat in mind, I proceed now to conclude that my critical analysis of both concepts and rhetoric from the medieval period to the modern has revealed a number of different problems from which natural rights-talk can suffer. Not at all prominent among these, however, is its foundation upon Hobbes's alleged natural right to an original, amoral, absolute liberty. Almost invariably those who talk about natural rights acknowledge that they are qualified by other, equally original moral claims, whether of the common good or of virtue.[121]

---

[121] One notable exception is H. L. A. Hart: 'If there are any moral rights at all, it follows that there is at least one natural right, the equal right of all to be free' ('Are There Any Natural Rights?', in Waldron, *Theories of Rights*, p. 77).

The basic problem that afflicts talk about natural rights is that it attributes to them the same stability and security that are possessed by positive rights. As I have said, I take positive legal rights—rights posited by human law or custom—to be paradigmatic of rights in general. Accordingly, the very concept of *a right*, as distinct from *what is right*, is the concept of the property of an individual, an office-holder, or a social body. As their property, it is in their possession. What is possessed, and under what conditions it may be forfeit, will be defined with some precision by legal text or customary memory, and refined by precedent. In that sense, its content is stable. But its possession is also made more or less secure by the social institutions of law, police, courts, and prisons, which support the threat of legal sanction against right-violators. Thus, within limits, the individual's positively legal right is under his or her control. It is usually *there* to be used by the right-holder; it lies to hand.

The concept of a natural right is significantly different. It might not be expressed or defined in human, positive law at all. Indeed, one of its main functions is to provide a metaphysical basis for criticism of positive law or for moral appeals in its absence. Nevertheless, it is supposed to obtain in states of nature, where there are no positive law or courts—on virgin territory before the development of society, or on civilised territory that has collapsed into anarchy, or in war ungoverned by agreed rules. Even there it is always wrong to harm or kill a person malevolently or disproportionately, and it is usually wrong to harm or kill them intentionally. We could say, therefore, that there is a natural right not to be harmed or killed under these conditions. That is, we could move, with untortured logic, from a statement of natural morality or 'right' to a statement of 'a natural right'. The problem with such a move, however, is not with the logic, but with the connotation. For if positive legal rights are paradigmatic, then, unless we are more careful than we usually are, we will easily forget that natural rights are not the same, but only analogous. They do not share the same degree of stability or security as positive rights. As circumstances change, the natural right comes and goes: there and then, when my would-be assailant wanted me dead out of sheer vindictiveness, I possessed a natural right against harm; but here and now, when my just enemy wants me dead, because I continue to pose a lethal threat to innocent people and it is not possible to incarcerate me, I possess no such right.

In a civilised context, where law backed by effective policing and courts cause just relations and social peace to prevail, the individual's possession of a right against harm and killing enjoys some measure of security and can be presumed. That is, the presumption in favour of the right will be high. In rare cases, where an individual is harmed or killed, the courts will deliberate over whether or not the harm or death was justified. If they judge that it was justified, they might say that the positive, legal right was justifiably violated—which is a jarring expression, suggesting that it was right to do wrong. But what they will mean morally, rather than legally, is that, under the circumstances, the *natural, moral* right had ceased to exist. Outside of a civilised context, however, where, in the absence of law, police, and courts, peace does not prevail and life is generally insecure, the presumption in favour of a right against harm and killing weakens. The onus of deciding whether or not to use harmful or lethal force to defend the innocent falls entirely on the consciences of individuals. The judgements of conscience will be more urgent and agile than those of courts, but, given human ignorance and vice, also more prone to error. If there is to be justice at all, it will be rougher and more haphazard, and the prospect of justice in any form will not be secure. This is one of Edmund Burke's main points, and it is correct. So the danger that lies in importing the concept of 'a right' into states of nature—of importing natural rights-talk—is that we mistakenly suppose that the same presumption in its favour obtains as in civil society, and that the judgement about whether or not it obtains in the circumstances can be deferred to a court. In principle, therefore, talk about natural rights could be perfectly appropriate, provided that we are scrupulously careful to remember that analogues are not quite the same as paradigms. In practice, however, we are seldom so careful and natural rights-talk misleads.

The inapt attribution of the stability and security of rights in civil society to rights in states of nature is one problem attendant upon natural rights-talk. A second is the assertion of natural rights to liberties or benefits whose lack of definition permits ludicrous or recklessly licentious construals—such as natural rights to 'life' and 'liberty', without specification.

Natural rights-talk also errs when it gets carried away with its own high-flying rhetoric, claiming, for example, that the right to own property is 'sacred' and 'inviolable', whereas in fact it is liable to suspension in extreme circumstances. The same problem arises more frequently when natural rights are simply asserted as if they were unconditional, when they are not—such as the right to freedom of expression.

Further, sometimes a specific, historical form of what is arguably a natural right is confused with the right itself. Thus, democracy with universal suffrage becomes the *only* acceptable way to satisfy the natural right to political participation; and the positive right of every citizen to keep and bear arms becomes the *only* way to satisfy the natural right to security against gravely unjust interference by other people and the state.

Yet another kind of problem occurs when natural rights are asserted to benefits either that no particular body has an assigned duty to supply, or that might be owed to others instead, or that might not be available for supply at all. These include putative natural rights to the means of obtaining happiness, to be free from hunger, and to asylum. They do not exist.

Sixth, natural rights-talk is deficient when it fails to recognise that, after the assertion of a right to some kind of freedom, there arises the question of how to exercise it well or morally. In other words, natural rights-talk misleads when it does not proceed to talk about the duties of virtue that oblige *the right-holder*. We know that rights-talk need not mislead in this way, for we have seen it make space for talk about duties and recognise the need for virtue and a cultural matrix that generates it. Indeed, Mary Wollstonecraft has shown that it is possible to talk up natural and civil rights *for the sake of* promoting virtue and the common good. However, once rights have opened the door to wider considerations of duty, virtue, and the common good, they can no longer claim to be fundamental. Whether they exist and what shape they take will depend on other moral factors.

Finally, as John Finnis says, a right has a 'conclusory' force and the rhetoric of natural rights is often deployed to short-circuit moral deliberation by forcefully asserting at the beginning what really remains to be argued and proven. That, too, is a problem.

VIII

Given these various problems that often attend natural rights-talk, should we conclude that it is best avoided altogether? Or are there some ways of talking about natural rights that we should retain? One prominent candidate is the set of rights that are supposed to be generated by the nature of 'images of God' or moral agents or persons—rights that have been asserted at least since Francisco de Vitoria and most recently by James Griffin, and whose possibility even the sceptical David Ritchie entertained. There is no doubt that, according to Christian tradition and its secular humanist part-offshoots, human being has a special value, higher than that of other forms of physical being. Ever since the Book of Genesis, this value has been associated with the distinctive ability of humans to exercise a certain freedom of judgement in managing the world around them. Such power of discretion, however, is not absolute: it does not consist of cunning practical reason serving the will to survive with a morally untrammelled, Hobbesian liberty. Rather, its exercise is responsible to God and His created moral law.[122] Thus in subsequent Christian thought, conscience is understood to operate within the terms set by natural law. Even Kant's semi-Christian autonomy is not as autonomous as it seems, since, while persons legislate for themselves, they do so as beings who

---

[122] Genesis 1:26–8: 'Then God said, "Let us make humankind *in our image*, according to our likeness; and let them *have dominion* over the fish of the sea, and over the birds of the air, and over the cattle, and over all the wild animals of the earth, and over every creeping thing that creeps upon the earth." So God created humankind *in his image, in the image of God* he created them; male and female he created them. God blessed them, and God said to them, "Be fruitful and multiply, and fill the earth and subdue it; and *have dominion* over the fish of the sea and over the birds of the air and over every living thing that moves upon the earth."' The emphases are mine. The biblical concept of 'the image of God' is often understood as a metaphor that takes its cue from actual images of a king or emperor in the form of public statuary set up in distant provinces, or impressed upon coinage used throughout the realm, which represents royal or imperial authority. A human being made 'in the image of God', therefore, has and exercises dominion, but properly as a representative of God, his authority, and his law. Human dominion is subordinate and accountable.

participate in *universal* Reason and are subject to its consistent demands. And, as we have seen, Griffin's free moral agency plays out in a field defined by goods that are objective or real in the sense that they are not merely the whimsical creatures of individual desire, but given—*there*—before human choosing.

If humans or moral agents or persons are regarded are having a special value, it follows that they deserve especially careful treatment, since what is more valuable generally deserves greater care. Therefore, we ought not to hinder their flourishing, except in unusual circumstances. For example, as a rule we ought not to harm or kill them, unless they are posing a threat to innocents; and, as a rule, we ought not to gainsay their freedom to think, express themselves, and shape the world around them, unless they are abusing their freedom to perpetrate injustice. Clearly, therefore, natural morality prescribes certain duties of self-restraint. Presumably, it also prescribes duties of aid, requiring us to help persons to flourish as much as we can.

But does it follow that the special value of personhood generates rights? Straightforwardly, we can say that it justifies many positive legal rights. For example, it justifies rights against physical harm or interference with freedom of speech or expression, except in extraordinary circumstances; and it justifies as much security of protection as possible. It also justifies rights to the fulfilment of as many of the conditions of human flourishing—say, subsistence and minimal education—as is feasible. But note the qualifications: 'as possible' and 'as is feasible'. That is to say, exactly what legal rights, and what degree of security, are morally justified depend upon what is possible and prudent in the prevailing circumstances.

If the positive, legal rights justified by the value of personhood are often contingent upon the obligatory requirements of prudence, then the natural, moral rights that some think it justifies are more highly contingent upon a wider range of moral factors than they tend to suppose. Remember: the value of personhood is not simply a matter of its freedom; it is a matter of its *morally responsible* freedom. So whereas legally, at least in a liberal society, a citizen has the simple right to believe all manner of things that are untrue and unjust, morally, she is permitted to believe them only on condition that she has exercised the virtues of humility and courage in striving to discern what is true and just, thereby exposing her views to criticism and correction.[123] And whereas legally the right to freedom of expression allows all manner of gratuitous insult, unfair distortion, and malicious provocation, morally that freedom is subject to the duties of justice and charity. Therefore, insofar as it is now common to understand personhood in abstraction from a situation of responsibility to principles of morality that are created, given, natural, or real—that is to say, insofar as it is common to

---

[123] The implication is that avoidable error, for which one is culpable, has no *moral* rights. The mistake of Pope Pius IX in his 1864 Syllabus of Errors was to infer from this that there should be no *legal* right of religious freedom.

understand 'rights' apart from any order of moral 'right'—to speak of personhood as generating natural, moral rights to liberties is to risk obscuring their contingency upon the dutiful exercise of virtues. Safely, we can say that the morally responsible, virtuous exercise of freedom of thought and expression are especially important parts of human flourishing—that is, they are especially important goods. But there is no simple, straightforward moral right to such liberties, since their moral rightness is contingent upon the performance of duties of virtue. The bare right itself is not rock-bottom; it is not fundamental or natural. It only waxes into existence when other moral factors have come into play.

IX

The alleged rights of personhood are the most prominent candidates for the status of natural rights. Closely related to these are those political rights supposed to stem from the view of human beings as free and equal persons—rights such as those to political equality and participation. Since these assume a settled, political context and are therefore positively legal, what talk of 'natural rights' refers to here is not rights in a state of nature, but legal rights justified by the goods of human nature. I myself accept that all persons are equally dignified by responsibility for defending and promoting what is good in the world under created or given moral law. That was not a view held by Aristotle, Nietzsche, or the Nazis, but it is one generally shared by Christians with other humanists. From this equality-in-responsibility, certain principles of political justice follow: for example, that any polity should be so arranged as to defend and promote the human flourishing of all of its members, as far as fairness and prudence allow; and that therefore any just polity will provide means for the perceived interests of all citizens to be taken into account in the making of law and policy. If that is what we mean by it, we could say that all citizens have a natural right to 'political participation'. However, 'political participation' is highly indeterminate and raises a host of controversial questions, to which a quarrelling variety of answers could be given, each more or less reasonable in terms of a different set of historical and cultural circumstances. Just political participation cannot be equated to mass electoral democracy, since that would imply, implausibly, that sufficient political justice never graced the earth until the late eighteenth century at the very earliest. Since we lack a firm grip on what the supposed right is a claim *to*, since there is no broad agreement about its content, it cannot be asserted with any cogency and so lacks the distinctive authority of a claim that is a *right*. Therefore, rather than restate the principle of natural justice as a natural right, we would do better to stick with all-things-considered justice-talk.

Another putative political natural right to which the history of natural rights-talk has introduced us is the right to remove by force a legally established government that is unjust. If this exists, it can only be as a natural right, since no positive set of constitutional laws could recognise it. Moreover, it derives indirectly from the equal dignity of those with a personal nature, insofar as an unjust regime is one that serves the private interests of the rulers at the expense of the common good of the ruled. However, whether or not it is justified to undertake forcible regime-change depends on a host of contingent conditions: given the costs and hazards of the undertaking, the injustice should be grave, persistent, and systemic; the use of force should be a last resort; regime-change should be sustainable by commanding sufficient popular support; the rebels should be capable of substituting an alternative and more just government; and only those in a position to make the substitution should launch the rebellion.[124] Provided that we remember to hedge it about with the appropriate host of conditions—not least the duty of exercising the virtues of patience and prudence—we could talk of a natural right to armed rebellion. However, there are three reasons why this would be unwise: the contemporary cultural tendency of rights-talk to occlude talk about duty and virtue altogether; the cultural tendency to romanticise the 'rebel'; and the fact that a right to rebel is not the universal property of every citizen, but only *becomes* the property of those capable of providing a government-in-waiting and of commanding sufficient popular support.

Joel Feinberg confirms this last reservation, albeit inadvertently. He argues in favour of moral rights as more than merely morally justified legal rights and as existing in the absence of any corresponding legal right. One example he gives is the 'moral right to *rebel* against a tyrannical government', 'which we all have *now*'.[125] Such a right must be moral, because it cannot be legal, and it cannot be legal, 'because it would be difficult to formulate such a right-conferring rule so as not to encourage misguided violence or to increase political instability generally ... [T]his is what Bentham hated, and with good reason: the idea that moral grievances automatically ground revolutionary violence.'[126] However, what Feinberg does not seem to notice is that the difficulty in qualifying a legal right applies equally to a moral one, and that *that* was the reason why Bentham (and Burke) objected to the very idea of a natural, moral right. Consequently, notwithstanding his sympathy for Bentham's objection to revolutionary licence, Feinberg actually promotes it, when he tells us that 'we all' have a moral right to rebel. But 'we' do not. Only those who have good claim to represent the public good, and as a mark of that can command sufficient popular support, may initiate rebellion. And if they intend

---

[124] Protestant Christian thinking about justified rebellion tends to prescribe that it be conducted by 'lesser magistrates', that is, those who already have some constitutional authority to govern (Quentin Skinner, *Foundations of Modern Political Thought*, 2 vols, Vol. II: *The Age of Reformation* (Cambridge: Cambridge University Press, 1978), chapters 7–9). Accordingly, Helmuth Thielicke (1908–86), the mid-twentieth-century Lutheran theologian, made the 'availability of a successor government' the first condition of an ethically legitimate revolution (*Theological Ethics*, 2 vols, ed. William H. Lazareth, Vol. II: *Politics* (Grand Rapids, Mich.: Eerdmans, 1979), pp. 343–5).

[125] Feinberg, 'In Defense of Moral Rights', p. 45. The emphases are Feinberg's.   [126] Ibid., p. 47.

regime-change, they must also be in a position to supply an alternative government. Ironically, Feinberg's own defence illustrates the tendency of talk about 'a moral right' to obscure its own contingency upon conditions.

For similar reasons we should eschew talk of 'a natural right' to military intervention for humanitarian purposes—with all due respect to Francisco de Vitoria and David Ritchie. I do not doubt that there are circumstances when such intervention is morally justified—indeed, I have argued that it can be morally justified, even when it is strictly illegal.[127] Nevertheless, its morality is highly contingent on a wide range of conditions, and because of its great costs and hazards, it is not something that should be presumed upon. Therefore, it would be prudent to talk cumbersomely of 'circumstances where intervention becomes morally right', rather than efficiently of 'a natural right to intervene'.

X

So far, we have not found a satisfactory candidate for the status of a natural right, which is distinct from a morally justified legal right. Sometimes, there is insufficient clarity about what a supposed natural right is a claim *to*. More often, its moral justification is contingent on a range of conditions, including the performance of duties of virtue and practical feasibility, which makes it too unstable to warrant the title of 'a right'. Nevertheless, there remain at least two further candidates, whose content is sufficiently specific and whose claim seems unconditional: the putative rights against slavery and torture. Should we not consider these—and others like them—to be natural rights?

There are three reasons why natural rights-talk might be appropriate in such cases as these, but not in others. First of all, we can be sure when the putative rights apply, because what they are against is unjust by definition (i.e. the exercise of dominance or the infliction of pain that is sadistic, cruel, gratuitously humiliating, disproportionate, etc.).[128] Therefore, since we always deserve to be free from what

---

[127] Biggar, *In Defence of War*, chapters 6 and 7; 'After Iraq: When to Go to War?' (London: Policy Exchange, 2017).

[128] Militating against my assumption here that 'slavery' is always and everywhere morally wrong, is David Ritchie's observation that practices that we—members of the Christianised, liberal West in the early twenty-first century—regard as beyond the moral pale have *not* always been so regarded and, in some cases, were originally instances of moral progress. So, he tells us, slavery was 'a necessary step in the progress of humanity... [since] [i]t mitigated the horrors of primitive warfare, and thus gave some scope for the growth, however feeble, of kindlier sentiments towards the alien and the weak...Thus slavery made possible the growth of the very ideas which in course of time came to make slavery appear wrong' (*Natural Rights*, p. 104). My response to this is as follows. First, as I have defined it, 'slavery' is a morally loaded term: it has the qualities of sadism, cruelty, and gratuitous humiliation built into it. It is certainly true, therefore, that not every historical institution that goes by the name of 'slavery' is a member of my morally pejorative species. It is possible, for example, that, in the late first century AD, the slave-owner Philemon did in fact heed St Paul's injunction to receive back his runaway slave, Onesimus, as 'a beloved brother' (Epistle to Philemon, 1.6). If so, in that case slavery as a legally defined

is unjust, we can be confident that the rights obtain always and everywhere, regardless of circumstances. They are not contingent upon any further moral conditions.

Second, although these rights are tautologous—*of course*, there is a moral right against what is unjust—they are not merely formal and empty of content. The meanings of 'slavery' and 'torture' are informed by paradigmatic instances that embody their wrong-making features. For example, our understanding of 'slavery' is informed by infamous historical instances such as the savage practices on plantations in the ante-bellum South of the United States, or captives chained to their oars in Ottoman galleys, or forced labourers being worked to death under the Nazis. These paradigms make clear enough the kind of things that are prohibited, which everyone is duty-bound not to do, and which everyone has rights against, even if room remains for further deliberation and controversy about whether a given instance is, in fact, a member of the moral species and, therefore, about the precise meanings of 'sadism', 'cruelty', and 'disproportionality'. It remains open to Marxists, for example, to argue that the condition of the industrial working class is equivalent to that of American slavery. Still, the paradigms provide a basis for analogical deliberation: when we meet a novel case and must ask whether *this* is the kind of thing against which we have a right, the paradigms give us models against which to measure and compare it. So, while the rights are tautologous, they are sufficiently definite to ground a claim and sufficiently specified to guide judgement and enable it to develop.

Third, not only can we be confident that we know sufficiently the kinds of thing that should not be done, and that we should never do them; we can also be confident that it is always possible not to do them. That is to say, the duties corresponding to the rights against slavery and torture are always feasible—since it is always within anyone's power to choose *not* to enslave or torture.

In these three respects, therefore, the putative natural rights against slavery and torture do not suffer from the flaws that attend other candidates. Should we, therefore, recognise at least these two natural rights? I think not, for a reason that will be familiar. Insofar as these would be genuinely *natural* rights, obtaining in a simple state of nature such as civil or international anarchy, the power to secure the liberty they seek to protect would be very weak indeed, since the only supportive authority that could be invoked would be the fickle consciences of

---

social institution continued to define his relationship with Onesimus, but without the damning characteristics of humiliation, carelessness, and cruelty. (Although I suspect that the logic of fraternal love would have grated against the logic of the law.) Second, we can recognise slavery as a moral improvement upon the wholesale slaughter of prisoners-of-war, and yet still condemn it *insofar* as it involved forms of domination that were gratuitously cruel and sadistically humiliating. We can distinguish between such cruelty and humiliation on the one hand, and the serious deprivation of liberty on the other, and we can judge that the former has *always* been morally wrong. The fact that ancient peoples sometimes also recognised wanton cruelty and humiliation for the injustices they are, serves to confirm our judgement.

other people. Insofar as rights are paradigmatically legal, they assume a set of supportive social institutions and connote a considerable degree of consequent security. Therefore, to talk of *rights* against slavery and torture in such anarchic conditions would be misleading.

Nowadays, however, the world is not in fact quite so anarchic. Slavery and torture are now prohibited by international law, which is policed by international human rights bodies and ultimately backed by the International Criminal Court, which means that the morally rightful claim to be free from such things can appeal to an international authority that transcends the unreliable consciences of individuals. It is true that this authority is a lot less powerful than those of states, since its power depends on their compliance and support, which is often not forthcoming.[129] Therefore, any morally rightful claim that invokes the authority of international law and institutions will usually be weaker and more insecure than one that appeals to national law and institutions. Still, such a claim has the form of law and a measure of institutional backing, and is therefore powerful enough to merit the title of 'a right'. For that very reason, however, rights against slavery and torture cannot be *natural* rights, since, by definition, a state of nature lacks supportive institutions. Rather, they should be considered *human* rights, since such rights presuppose the post-1945 international order, with its international law and institutions; and unlike some current human rights, these ones do have a morally justified claim to universal application.

XI

In a nutshell, therefore, my answer to the question, 'Are there natural rights?', is this. There is natural right or law or morality, that is, a set of moral principles that are given in and with the nature of reality, specifically the nature of human flourishing. There are also positively legal rights that are, or would be, justified by natural morality. But there are no natural rights.

---

[129] According to Manfred Nowak, Professor of International Human Rights at the University of Vienna and former UN Special Rapporteur on Torture, torture is still practised in more than 90 per cent of all countries and constitutes a widespread practice in more than 50 per cent ('What's in a Name? The Prohibitions on Torture and Ill Treatment Today', in Conor Gearty and Costas Douzinas, *Cambridge Companion to Human Rights Law* (Cambridge: Cambridge University Press, 2012), p. 307). Eric Posner, Professor of Law at the University of Chicago, argues that the amount of torture actually *increased* in the average country after ratifying the ICCPR (*The Twilight of Human Rights Law* (New York: Oxford University Press, 2014), pp. 74–5).

6

What's Wrong with Subjective Rights?

I

Whether a right is natural or legal, it is a kind of property. It is something that one possesses. It is a liberty or a claim that belongs to a subject (usually an individual person, though sometimes a corporate body), by means of which he acquires the power, through appeal to moral or legal authority, to require others either to refrain from acting or to act.

Some people consider that the very idea of a right as an individual's property is morally dubious. Broadly pursuing an intellectual trajectory set by Leo Strauss (1899–1973) and C. B. Macpherson (1911–87),[1] certain Christian thinkers believe that such a modern concept is tied—certainly historically but perhaps also logically—to Hobbesian social contract theory or Ockhamist nominalism, and therefore to radical individualism and moral subjectivism. As a consequence, they think that to affirm individuals' subjective *rights* is necessarily to exclude a larger, qualifying, objective order of moral *right*. Subjective rights exclude moral law that transcends individuals, subjects them to duties, and resolves conflicting claims. They function as vehicles for atomistic egos to assert their selfish desires, and they exclude consideration of the common good. Prominent among those who think this are Alasdair MacIntyre, Joan Lockwood O'Donovan, Oliver O'Donovan, John Milbank, and Ernest Fortin.

II

MacIntyre was the first to tell the story of modern cultural disintegration. In the thirteenth century Thomas Aquinas could take for granted a shared cultural allegiance to a conception of the ultimate human good. This allowed him to conceive of *ius* ('right' or 'justice') basically in terms of service of the common good, of *ius naturale* ('natural law or right') as an invariant set of just rules of conduct, and of *iura* ('rights') as just assignations of recognition and reward according to variant social circumstances.[2] However, during the 'Franciscan

---

[1] Leo Strauss, *Natural Right and History* (Chicago: University of Chicago, 1953); C. B. Macpherson, *The Political Theory of Possessive Individualism: Hobbes to Locke* (Oxford: Clarendon Press, 1962).

[2] Alasdair MacIntyre, 'Community, Law, and the Idiom and Rhetoric of Rights', *Listening: Journal of Religion and Culture*, 5 (1991), pp. 99, 100, 102.

Controversy' over property rights in the early fourteenth century, MacIntyre argues ('closely' following Richard Tuck), William of Ockham developed a new meaning for *ius*, which was the root of 'the distinctively modern concept of "a right"'. This was 'a conception of a right attached to individuals as such, independent of the place and status of such individuals in a community, let alone their contribution to the common good'.[3] It also denoted 'a *dominium* of exclusive control and disposal'.[4]

The subsequent, modern erosion of a common conception of the ultimate good dismantled any shared form of rational justification and fostered the view that appeals to principle are 'nothing more than disguised expressions of desire, preference, and will'.[5] As a result, rights have come to be understood as means of defending each person against becoming merely an instrument for the achievement of someone else's desires, and they have multiplied.[6] Moreover, MacIntyre writes, '[g]enerally and characteristically they are used to present continually renewed challenges to what is taken by those who present them to be the institutional *status quo*, challenges designed to dissolve the bonds, and undermine the authority, of all institutions intermediate between the individual on the one hand and government and the justice system on the other: such institutions as families, schools, and churches'.[7] Therefore, he concludes, with at least half an eye on the US National Conference of Catholic Bishops, that it is 'seriously imprudent... to adopt the contemporary idiom and rhetoric of rights'.[8]

Macintyre's description of contemporary rights-talk rings several bells of truth, and right at the end of this chapter we shall return to his account of the disintegration of the moral culture of the West, as he details it in *After Virtue*.[9] Before then, however, I shall argue that Richard Tuck's account of Ockham's role in the development of 'modern rights' is doubtful—and if Tuck's, then also MacIntyre's.

III

As MacIntyre admonishes the US Catholic bishops for adopting modern rights-talk, so Joan Lockwood O'Donovan observes, disapprovingly, that the concept of human rights has become 'a virtually unassailable datum of Christian social conscience'.[10] She wonders why Christian thinkers have been willing 'to adopt a child of such questionable parentage'[11] and judges their appropriation of the language of rights to be 'naïve and facile'.[12] Whence her scepticism?

---

[3] Ibid., p. 103.   [4] Ibid., p. 102.   [5] Ibid., p. 101.   [6] Ibid., pp. 101, 104.
[7] Ibid., p. 105.   [8] Ibid., pp. 96, 106.
[9] Alasdair MacIntyre, *After Virtue* (Notre Dame, Ind.: University of Notre Dame Press, 1981).
[10] Joan Lockwood O'Donovan, 'Historical Prolegomena to a Theological Review of "Human Rights"', *Studies in Christian Ethics*, 9/2 (1996), p. 65.
[11] Ibid., p. 53.   [12] Ibid., p. 65.

Until the fourteenth century, Lockwood O'Donovan tells us, Christian political thought 'functioned virtually without any concept of subjective natural rights'.[13] Such a concept 'has entered contemporary political and legal currency primarily through the liberal contractarian tradition bequeathed by Hobbes and Locke, Rousseau and Kant, and the theoretical exponents of the American and French Revolutions'.[14] This tradition has roots in the 'voluntarist, individualist and subjectivist orientations' of fourteenth- and fifteenth-century Christian theology.[15]

In this period, a subjective right—a right attaching to an individual subject—was first conceived in terms of a right to property, and this early conception 'decisively shaped' subsequent theoretical developments.[16] The generative occasion was the dispute in the 1320s, which we encountered in Chapter 2, over whether the Franciscan Order's vow of absolute poverty entailed a repudiation of all rights to the ownership of property. On the one hand, arguing against such an entailment, Pope John XXII asserted that all lawful consumption of material goods necessarily involves 'a full property right'[17]—'a legal right'[18]—in them or *dominium* over them; and that such dominion over earthly goods belonged to Adam in his created state, reflecting the divine dominion over the earth.[19] On the other hand, William of Ockham held that, in the Adamic state of created innocence and before the Fall, all external things were held in common, without possession and its claims of 'mine' and 'thine'.[20] There was a natural, subjective 'right of use' according to individual need, but this was non-proprietorial.[21]

Lockwood O'Donovan sides with Ockham on this point, since she finds in his view the 'profound truth' that 'the most perfect love of God and neighbour leaves no room for claiming earthly goods for oneself and against one's neighbour. Because property-right creates the possibility of defending one's claim to something in court, it is disruptive of the human response to divine love'. Property as such, she thinks, tempts the proprietor to assert ownership and in so doing he 'approaches selfishness and covetousness'.[22]

However, where Ockham defines an individual natural right as a subjective 'power', Lockwood O'Donovan begins to step away from him. This is because the idea of *ius* as a power belonging to a subject was subsequently interpreted by Jean Gerson (1363–1429) to mean, first, the natural right of every creature to 'take inferior things into its own use for its own preservation'; and second, the

---

[13] Lockwood O'Donovan, 'Rights, Law, and Political Community: A Theological and Historical Perspective', *Transformation*, 20/1 (January 2003), p. 31. The title of *subjektives Recht* or 'subjective right' comes from German jurisprudence, and stands in contrast to *objektives Recht* or 'objective right' (H. L. A. Hart, 'Are There Any Natural |Rights?', in Waldron, *Theories of Rights*, p. 83).
[14] Lockwood O'Donovan, 'Historical Prolegomena', pp. 52–3.   [15] Ibid., p. 54.
[16] Ibid., p. 55.   [17] Ibid., p. 56 n. 6.
[18] Lockwood O'Donovan, 'Rights, Law, and Political Community', p. 32.
[19] Lockwood O'Donovan, 'Historical Prolegomena', p. 56 n. 6.   [20] Ibid., p. 56 n. 6.
[21] Lockwood O'Donovan, 'Rights, Law, and Political Community', p. 33.   [22] Ibid., p. 32.

WHAT'S WRONG WITH SUBJECTIVE RIGHTS? 135

individual's *dominium* or *facultas* of liberty over his own body and actions. This latter notion later led the Salamancan Jesuits Luis de Molina (1535–1600) and Francisco Suárez (1548–1617) to argue that individuals can lawfully contract to enter into slavery.[23]

'The full flowering' of the proprietary paradigm of subjective right arrived, Lockwood O'Donovan claims, in the seventeenth century with Thomas Hobbes, John Locke, and the Levellers.[24] What all these share in common is an understanding of the individual as 'free in as much as he is the proprietor of his person and capacities', his freedom being conceived as both independence of the wills of others and 'a function of possession'.[25] Hobbes redefined the 'right of nature' as each individual's unrestrained liberty to use his own power and to act for his own self-preservation.[26] Richard Overton (1599–1664), the Leveller, assimilated subjective right to property as an 'exclusive power of self-disposal effective against the whole world' (the classical Roman-law sense of *dominium*).[27] And Locke attributed to the individual an exclusive proprietary right over the objects created by his work.[28]

Lockwood O'Donovan's reservations about the concept of a subjective right are several and various. First of all, she objects to its proprietorial paradigm. One reason for her objection is that it tempts rights-holders to selfishness and fosters a competitive, adversarial relationship between them, which is contrary to Christian love. In a world governed by the law of God, she implies, there would be no property, only a right of use according to need.

However, the distinction that Lockwood O'Donovan draws here is too stark. Property would appear even in the kingdom of God, where everyone loves their neighbours as they love themselves. Take a set of circumstances where several individuals have need of a certain quantity of a resource, and where that quantity is either sufficient to satisfy all needs, or where principles of justice distribute a scarce resource justly. In such circumstances, we can certainly say that *it is right* that a certain individual should have a certain quantity of the resource. But we could also say that a certain individual *has a right* to such a quantity.[29] In these

---

[23] Lockwood O'Donovan, 'Historical Prolegomena', pp. 56–7. Whereas in 'Historical Prolegomena' Lockwood O'Donovan appears to locate the onset of the conceptual rot directly in Gerson's thought, in 'Rights, Law, and Political Community' she changes tack and traces it rather to 'some of Gerson's followers', who carried the faculty concept of right further in a 'voluntaristic, subjectivist, and proprietary' direction (p. 33).

[24] Lockwood O'Donovan, 'Rights, Law, and Political Community', p. 35.

[25] Macpherson, *The Political Theory of Possessive Individualism*, p. 3, quoted in Lockwood O'Donovan, 'Historical Prolegomena', p. 57.

[26] Thomas Hobbes, *Leviathan*, ed. M. Oakeshott (1962), p. 103, quoted in Lockwood O'Donovan, 'Historical Prolegomena', p. 58.

[27] Lockwood O'Donovan, 'Historical Prolegomena', pp. 58–9.

[28] Lockwood O'Donovan, 'Rights, Law, and Political Community', p. 36.

[29] As did Godfrey of Fontaines in the thirteenth century, when he wrote that 'by the law of nature each one has a certain right [*ius*] in the common exterior goods of the world, which cannot be licitly renounced' (quoted by Tierney, *The Idea of Natural Rights*, p. 75).

circumstances, *this* is what is due to him; this is *his* due.[30] To speak in terms of a right that is possessed by—that is the property of—an individual is merely to define what rightly belongs to him and what he is morally at liberty to take and dispose of, and to distinguish this from what rightly belongs to others. In so doing, rather than pitting one neighbour against another, it serves to prevent friction and conflict between them. Here a right conceived as property is the expression of a just social ordering, not necessarily of social antagonism.

Yet what is right in one set of circumstances might not be right in another set. Whether or not one *has* a right is often a contingent matter. One's right is not absolute. It depends on our need, on the availability of resources to meet it, and on other people's rightful claims to it. It depends also on our social obligations. So, if we do speak of *having* or *possessing* a right here, we must recognise that our possession is not fixed or stable.

Talking thus, it becomes clear that the kind of proprietary right under discussion is not the kind granted by an established system of law, be it statutory or customary. Positive legal rights are fixed and stable. They need not be absolute, in that they might be explicitly qualified, but they do not change according to fleeting circumstance. In positive law my right to a resource might exceed my need, in fact, while yours falls short of it. Nevertheless, whatever moral obligations have to say about how I should exercise my legal freedom of disposal, the law is unyielding: that freedom is *mine* legally, even if I abuse it morally. The reason for such legal inflexibility is to prevent both the social anarchy that would arise, were the boundaries of jurisdiction unclear, and the tyranny that might arise, were the state permitted to micro-manage or supplant individuals' exercise of conscience and discretion.

The proprietorial rights with which Lockwood O'Donovan is concerned here are not positively legal, but natural. They exist in a state of nature, that is, either before the establishment of political society, whether at the beginning of prehistory or on virgin territory—or following its breakdown, as in war between or within states. These putative natural rights fade in and out of existence according to circumstances, including social obligations. They cannot assert their claims in a public court of law, but they can in the private court of conscience. Since, by definition they express what is right, they cannot become the vehicles of selfishness nor the weapons of forensic combat. So if there is something objectionable about the very concept of a subjective right, it is not its proprietary nature *as such*.

A further reason for Lockwood O'Donovan's objection to the 'proprietary paradigm' is that it issues in a concept of a right of freedom as a power of acting

---

[30] Ulpian's famous third-century definition—*suum ius cuique tribuere*—implies that justice *(ius)* involves giving to each individual what belongs to him—that is to say, in a certain, conditional sense, his 'property'. However, what belongs to him could be an obligation or punishment, as much as a liberty or claim.

possessed by a subject that entails an obligation of non-interference on the part of others, especially government.[31] Here the subject of discussion cannot be a right in the state of nature, since by definition government does not exist there. It must be a positive legal right. There are, of course, good prudential reasons for granting to the members of a political society rights of freedom against arbitrary or excessive interference by the state. Such rights need not be absolute, of course, and usually are not. When a political society is under grave threat, for example, the rights of *habeas corpus* or of freedom of speech could be—and have been—suspended for the sake of the public interest in common security. Positive rights to freedom possessed by individual citizens are usually qualified, not unconditional.[32] *Pace* Lockwood O'Donovan, therefore, the 'proprietary paradigm' need not, and usually does not, generate rights that are absolutely impervious to the demands of the social good or public interest. Nor need it exclude an understanding that positive rights to freedom from interference by the state (or other people) are nonetheless subject to demands by the moral law regarding the deployment of that freedom— and indeed regarding whether to assert or to waive the right. Therefore, again, if something is awry with the concept of subjective rights, it is not its proprietary nature as such.

Where else might the fault lie? A second objection that Lockwood O'Donovan suggests is the concept of an individual's natural right to 'take inferior things into its own use for its own preservation'. Again, note that this concerns a natural right, not a positive legal one. Positive law upholds the rights of property-owners to possess more than they need for self-preservation, even to hoard it, while others have less than they need. It is true that Thomas Aquinas argued that, where one neighbour possesses a surplus of material goods, while another neighbour is destitute, and where the former fails to give freely to the latter what he needs, the latter may take it without committing theft.[33] However, in any ordered society such a taking would undoubtedly be regarded as theft in the eyes of positive law. What Aquinas must have meant, therefore, was that it would not constitute theft in the eyes of *moral* law. So, in circumstances where some have more than they need (and hoard it), and others have less, we might say that the indigent have a natural, moral right to take what they need to preserve themselves. However, this is circumstantially contingent. It depends on others having a surplus. Where no one has a surplus, a natural right to self-preservation does not exist, either because all lives are morally equal and no one has the right to prefer his own self-preservation to another's and so to seize his property, or because some are morally

[31] Lockwood O'Donovan, 'Historical Prolegomena', pp. 60–1.
[32] For example, rights to freedom of speech and expression of religion are regularly subject to the requirements of public order. Thus Article 18.3 of the 1966 ICCPR states that the '[f]reedom to manifest one's religion or beliefs may be subject ... to such limitations as ... are necessary to protect public safety, order, health, or morals or the fundamental rights and freedoms of others'.
[33] Thomas Aquinas, *Summa Theologiae*, 2a2ae, q. 66, a.7.

obliged to sacrifice themselves for others. Therefore, to think of an individual's subjective right as taking the basic form of an absolute, natural right of self-preservation is indeed unacceptable.

The same should be said of the conception of an individual's basic natural right as comprising an absolute liberty over his own body and actions. It is true that there are good reasons why a political society should choose to grant its members certain positive, legal rights, which can be defended by the threat of judicial sanction against violators—rights to freedom of speech, for example, or from the arbitrary seizure of property, or from arbitrary arrest. Such positive rights prevent the general anarchy that would arise where everyone presumes to act as judge in his own case or the tyranny that would arise where the state can do with individuals whatever it thinks fit. Nevertheless, within the sphere of freedom that the law grants, the individual is still accountable to the moral law. In that sense, he is not simply sovereign. While the positive law might permit him to exercise his free speech in spewing out gratuitous insults to Muslims, for example, the moral law still forbids him. So whereas a positive legal right might grant to individuals a sphere of liberty, in which they may do exactly as they please (in the eyes of the law), no equivalent natural right exists. Even in political society the exercise of positive, legal rights is subject to the requirements of natural, moral law. In a state of nature, however, there is no basic right to a general freedom of self-disposal. The state of nature is not a moral desert. The moral law stands there, too. And even where it permits individuals to choose freely, even arbitrarily, between a plurality of morally permissible options, the moral law still constrains, limits, channels—structures—free human choices.

In the case neither of a putative natural right to self-preservation, nor of such a right to a general freedom of self-disposal, does the problem lie in its conception in proprietary terms. Rather, it lies partly in the extension to a state of nature of a right that is only at home in a political society. Mostly, however, it lies in what Lockwood O'Donovan calls 'the denial of a common moral universe'.[34] What is this, exactly? It is the Hobbesian denial that there is any basic natural right other than that of self-preservation or of the absolute freedom of self-disposal, and that social obligations arise only where sovereign individuals contract them in the prudent service of their own self-preservation or arbitrary will.

Lockwood O'Donovan is quite right to say that, under this Hobbesian conception, natural right is not coordinate with natural obligation.[35] There is an asymmetry, a priority: the right to self-preservation is natural and primary; social obligation is artificial and secondary. If everyone has only one fundamental natural right, and if that is a right to self-preservation, then no one is obliged to prefer another's preservation to his own. Here it becomes evident that the

---

[34] Lockwood O'Donovan, 'Rights, Law, and Political Community', p. 37.
[35] Lockwood O'Donovan, 'Historical Prolegomena', p. 64. See also p. 58.

language of 'right' is actually out of place—as I have already explained.[36] There cannot be a right that fails to oblige someone. To talk of my having a 'right' to self-preservation, where there is no one in the world against whom I can claim my right, is meaningless. What is being talked about is not a claim with moral authority, but merely a force, a strong desire, a psychic drive. In the state of nature everyone has a natural drive to self-preservation. Morality, right, and obligation are nowhere to be found. Where everyone's appetitive force is a 'right', 'right' is nothing at all. Rights and obligations only come into being when individuals, advised by prudence in the service of their natural drive, make social contracts with each other. They are the creatures and instruments of each individual's natural drive to self-preservation, and they retain authority only so long as they prove useful to that end.

Lockwood O'Donovan is also correct to identify the basic error in this conception of natural right as its reduction of the range of basic goods, to which human beings are naturally inclined, to one only.[37] Where Thomas Aquinas and his scholastic followers observed a plurality of basic human goods—not only self-preservation, but society or friendship, and knowledge of the truth about God[38]— Hobbes reduced it to one: self-preservation or, more exactly, the preservation of the self from pain and death. One might suppose that he could be forgiven such cynicism, because of his own political experience. After all, he wrote *Leviathan* in the light of the fierce political conflict and then terrible Civil War that had afflicted England in the 1640s. So perhaps it was not unreasonable for him to conclude that in the state of nature, either before the construction of political society or after its collapse into anarchical violence, human life is famously 'solitary, poore, nasty, brutish, and short', and social relations comprise a war of 'every man against every man'.[39] However, there is empirical, historical reason not to extend charity quite so far. For Hobbes articulated his disillusioned view of human being from the armchair safety of Paris. A few years before, his friend Lucius Carey (1609/10–43), 2nd Viscount Falkland, lord of the Oxfordshire manor of Great Tew and amateur theologian, had demonstrated that not even England's internecine bloodbath always lived down to Hobbes's dismal state of nature.[40] Toward the end of the battle of Edgehill on 23 October 1642, Falkland interposed himself between his

---

[36] See p. 43n.50.

[37] Lockwood O'Donovan, 'Historical Prolegomena', p. 63: 'The secularisation of liberalism in the 18th and 19th centuries has entailed the self-positioning, personal creative will acknowledging fewer and fewer external obligations and objective goods.'

[38] The contemporary Thomists John Finnis and Germain Grisez have expanded the list of basic goods to include life, knowledge, friendship and sociability, play, aesthetic experience, practical reasonableness, and religion (see Finnis, *Natural Law and Natural Rights*, Part I.IV).

[39] Thomas Hobbes, *Leviathan*, ed. and introd. C. B. MacPherson (Harmondsworth: Penguin, 1968), I.XIII, pp. 185, 186.

[40] Hobbes's relations with Falkland and his circle of friends at Great Tew were 'evidently close' (Hugh Trevor Roper, *Catholics, Anglicans, and Puritans: Seventeenth Century Essays* (London: Fontana, 1989), pp. 182–3).

own victorious royalist comrades on the one hand, and a sorry group of surrendered parliamentarians on the other, in order to stop the latter being slaughtered
by the former.[41] Out of a strong and steadfast love of social peace, he transcended
his own drive for self-preservation from pain and death, in order to save others.
And these others were not his kin; they were not even members of his political
faction; and they were not just strangers. They were the very enemy.[42]

According to Lockwood O'Donovan, the Hobbesian view of natural 'right' and
the prudential-contractual basis of social obligation occasions a further objection
to the very concept of subjective rights. This is that it makes basic the untrammelled competitive operation of market forces, subordinates public welfare and
law to its logic,[43] and makes citizens behave like consumers in relation to the state:

> On the basis of their ever more explicit contractual relations with the state, as
> formalized in bills and charters of rights, citizens have growing incentives and
> opportunities to demand legal redress of the failures of governmental and public
> agencies to furnish the expected goods and services. Such political contractualism
> spells the reduction of public law and the common good it enforces to private law
> and private good.[44]

This seems a cogent complaint against the egoism of Hobbes's account of human
motivation, and the materialism of his account of the goods that motivate. What is
doubtful is that it tells against 'the proprietary conceptual framework'[45] of subjective rights, since property rights need not be conceived as absolute or as
impervious to the external claims of natural moral law. And how far it tells against
the very concept of subjective rights in general depends on how culturally
influential one thinks the influence of Hobbes's philosophy really is. It may be
influential—it may possibly be 'majoritarian'[46]—but it is certainly not the only
player on the field.

Lockwood O'Donovan, however, writes as if it is. '[T]he meanings attached to
the term "rights" in both popular and scholarly usage', she tells us, 'cannot

[41] Edward Hyde, Earl of Clarendon, *The History of the Rebellion*, ed. and introd. Paul Seaward, Oxford World's Classics (Oxford: Oxford University Press, 2009), p. 188: 'at Edgehill, when the enemy was routed, [Falkland] was like to have incurred great peril by interposing to save those who had thrown away their arms, and against whom it may be others were more fierce for their having thrown them away: insomuch as a man might think he came into the field only out of... charity to prevent the shedding of blood'.
[42] Although virtually unknown now, Falkland was a hero of the English tradition of rational religion and liberal politics for Victorians. A statue of him was erected in St Stephen's Hall in the Palace of Westminster between 1848 and 1852, and Matthew Arnold devoted an essay to him (Matthew Arnold, *Mixed Essays* (London: Smith, Elder & Co., 1880), pp. 205–36).
[43] Lockwood O'Donovan, 'Historical Prolegomena', pp. 62–3; 'Rights, Law, and Political Community', pp. 30, 37.
[44] Lockwood O'Donovan, 'Rights, Law, and Political Community', p. 37.
[45] Lockwood O'Donovan, 'Historical Prolegomena', pp. 60–1.
[46] Lockwood O'Donovan, 'Rights, Law, and Political Community', p. 30.

properly be ascertained in detachment from this theoretical context [the liberal contractarian tradition] ... '.[47] This is because the theoretical elaborations of the concept of rights from the fifteenth to the eighteenth centuries 'have invested it with *lasting* intellectual content', which is 'in varying degrees *inescapable*, being woven into the civilisational fabric of politics in this century'.[48] Non-complacent Christian political thought 'recognises the need to divest the concept of rights of its offensive theoretical fabric, but when it attempts to rescue conceptual threads from the fabric the result *inevitably* falls short: either too much of the fabric adheres to the threads or they lose their coherent texture'.[49]

Lockwood O'Donovan's view contains three distinct, and not entirely consistent, historical-cultural judgements. This first, which I have just presented, is that the modern liberal contractarian conception of subjective rights is now culturally predominant, radical, and irreversible. This implies a second judgement, namely, that the pre-modern, late medieval conception of subjective rights, which continued to acknowledge the claims of 'objective right, of natural and divine law',[50] has been irrecoverably supplanted and marginalised. The same applies to the late scholastic conception of the contractual transition from the state of nature to political society, which was 'for the most part set within a solid matrix of more traditional theo-political premises concerning man's natural sociality'.[51] Indeed, at one point Lockwood O'Donovan goes so far as to suggest that the very concept of a subjective right as an individual's property carried within itself the seeds of conceptual degeneration, and that the subsequent, increasing attenuation of the authority of objective moral law was not an unhappy accident, but somehow logically natural or necessary, when she claims that, with Hobbes, Locke, and the Levellers, arrived '*the full flowering* of the proprietary paradigm of subjective right'.[52]

Such a diagnosis of the problem, combined with cultural pessimism, leads Lockwood O'Donovan to the conclusion that Christian theological ethics must jettison subjective rights-talk. The theological tradition, she tells us, understands that the work of civil justice exists in dependence on 'the communion of self-giving love that is the body of Christ; and that the true relationship between Christological love and civil justice is spoken in the language of goodness and right

---

[47] Lockwood O'Donovan, 'Historical Prolegomena', pp. 52–3.
[48] Lockwood O'Donovan, 'Historical Prolegomena', p. 55. The emphases are mine.
[49] Ibid., p. 55. The emphasis is mine.
[50] Lockwood O'Donovan, 'Rights, Law, and Political Community', p. 32. See also 'Historical Prolegomena', p. 55. Lockwood O'Donovan acknowledges that even in the thought of Jean Gerson and his followers subjectively possessed rights and contracts were not 'severed from objective right as determined by divine and natural law', although the relation of those rights to objective law was left unclear ('Rights, Law, and Political Community', p. 33).
[51] Lockwood O'Donovan, 'Historical Prolegomena', pp. 61–2.
[52] Lockwood O'Donovan, 'Rights, Law, and Political Community', p. 35. The emphasis is mine.

and law, of obligation and obedience, *rather than in the language of subjective rights*.[53]

However, the diagnosis and pessimism here does not square with a third view that she expresses. On one occasion Lockwood O'Donovan describes Roman Catholic social teaching, stemming from *Rerum Novarum*, about the rights of the labourer to property and of the family to fulfil its natural purpose of mutual love and provision, as 'more astute' than other contemporary Christian appropriations of rights-thinking.[54] While she does not pause to explain what she means by this, she nevertheless implies the possibility of a Christian concept of subjective rights that does not naively adopt a way of thinking that is radically alien to Christian theological tradition, but actually succeeds in rescuing congenial conceptual threads from the hostile fabric.

On another occasion she comments that the secular liberal-democratic rights culture of today is only prevented by the remnants of Christian political thought and practice from collapsing into legal and political incoherence, and that '[i]f liberal democratic polities are to retain any semblance of legal coherence, they will have to ensure that the concepts of rights is *a secondary language* of justice, subordinate to and continuous with that of law, in the sense of objective right and duty....'.[55] This clearly implies that the pre-modern, late medieval, Christian thinking *together* of subjective rights and objective right need not disappear into modern libertarianism and contractarianism, that it has in fact survived to contest the field, and that it continues to shape contemporary legal and political thinking to this day. If that is so, then the task is actually not to *jettison* talk about subjective rights, but rather to *save* it by re-setting it in a larger framework of objective right.

IV

To some extent, Oliver O'Donovan displays a more positive regard for subjective rights than Joan Lockwood O'Donovan. 'The language of subjective rights (i.e., rights which adhere to a particular subject)', he told us in 1996, 'has...a perfectly appropriate and necessary place within a discourse founded on law. One's "right" is the claim on which the law entitles one to demand performance...'[56] And thirteen years later he admitted—albeit more gingerly—that there is 'no very great problem' with a concept of specific, multiple rights so long as they are prima facie, representing '*claims* that have to be balanced out in concrete deliberation'.[57]

---

[53] Ibid., p. 38. The emphasis is mine.   [54] Ibid., p. 31.

[55] Ibid., p. 38. The emphasis is mine.

[56] O'Donovan, *Desire of the Nations*, p. 248; see also Oliver O'Donovan, *The Ways of Judgment* (Grand Rapids, Mich.: Eerdmans, 2005), pp. 198–9.

[57] O'Donovan, 'The Language of Rights', p. 195. The emphasis is O'Donovan's.

O'Donovan judiciously distinguishes the concept of rights as such from Hobbesian anthropology and political theory: 'individualism, partly as a legacy of 17th century contract theory, has impressed itself on the discussion of "rights"; but not all appeals to original subjective rights have been concerned with "individual rights"'.[58] (By 'individual' here, I take him to mean 'individualist'.[59]) Indeed, '[t]he idea of original subjective rights, though especially prominent in the modern era, has an instructive pre-history. It arose from the social conceptions of feudalism.'[60] Still, O'Donovan follows Richard Tuck (who himself follows Leo Strauss) in denying that the medieval use of subjective right is the source of the modern liberal tradition, and in claiming 'with plausibility' to discern 'a radical new development' of the concept of subjective right in the seventeenth century,[61] of which Hobbes was 'surely ... the high June'.[62] This was when the conceptual Fall occurred, and when subjective rights, instead of remaining a humble subdivision of justice, 'made totalitarian claims to colonise and reorganize the whole sphere'.[63]

Confusingly, at one point O'Donovan dissents from 'the theory of an Enlightenment innovation', when he argues against Tuck's attribution of the decisive change to Hugo Grotius in the seventeenth century and points instead to the Salamancan incorporation of a notion of right as a form of dominion or property in the previous century.[64] Ambiguity attends his subsequent claim that this proprietary concept 'made a decisive landfall'[65] on English philosophical soil through Hobbes. On the one hand, this could mean that the Salamancans made the decisive conceptual move and that Hobbes merely picked it up and gave it Anglo-Saxon wings; on the other hand, it could mean that Hobbes picked it up and deployed it in a decisively novel way. Charity obliges us to save O'Donovan's consistency and prefer the second option.

A similar ambiguity threatens to open up when (in 1996) he identified Jean Gerson as the one who, in the fifteenth century, 'initiated the tradition of conceiving freedom as a property in one's own body and its powers', and then comments, 'All this explains why the concept of rights cannot be invoked without some care.'[66] Later (in 2009), however, he recognised that, for Gerson, subjective rights are derived from, and subordinate to, 'primary justice', and that they therefore withhold themselves from any totalitarian claim.

[58] O'Donovan, Desire of the Nations, p. 248.
[59] O'Donovan's choice of language here is unhelpfully ambiguous and imprecise. 'Individual rights' could refer to rights that attach to individual subjects. However, he has just asserted that he sees nothing wrong with such a notion. Alternatively, 'individual rights' could refer to rights that attach to individual subjects, which are conceived individualistically. I take it that he means the latter.
[60] Ibid., p. 248.   [61] O'Donovan, 'The Justice of Assignment', p. 171.
[62] Ibid., p. 171. O'Donovan does not follow Tuck, however, in regarding Grotius as 'the spring swallow' that announced the radical novelty.
[63] O'Donovan, 'The Language of Rights', p. 201.   [64] Ibid., pp. 201–2.   [65] Ibid., p. 202.
[66] O'Donovan, Desire of the Nations, p. 248.

All things considered, and notwithstanding these elements of ambiguity, it seems fair to say that O'Donovan consistently holds that the conceptual serpent did not slither into intellectual history until Hobbes, *after* the late medieval period.[67]

So what was the 'radical new development' that came to full form in Hobbes? 'The founding element in the modern idea of [natural] right', O'Donovan tells us, 'is "that liberty which each man hath to use his own power as he will himself for the preservation of his own nature" (Hobbes, *Leviathan*)'.[68] Since the individual's self-preservation is the *only* basic good—and here I interpret O'Donovan rather than expound him—it follows that all other goods are strictly secondary and instrumental to it. Social goods have no independent worth. Thus the good of 'friendship', which is usually held to involve bonds of benevolent—even self-sacrificial—commitment, is really nothing but an expedient social contract struck in the interest of each individual party's pursuit of self-preservation. And the social good of 'justice', which is usually held to involve treating persons as they deserve, meeting obligations, and respecting rights, is really nothing but a social convention, whose authority survives only so long as it serves the basic interest of its participants. Or rather, since the basic interest of all persons cannot always be served equally, and since all 'right' ultimately reduces to sheer might, 'justice' is really a moral delusion conjured up by the more powerful to convince the less powerful to accept their own exploitation as nothing more than their due. (Thus Hobbes leads straight to Marx [1818–83], notwithstanding the latter's inconsistent moral indignation at the delusion.) Where the individual's liberty or power of self-preservation alone is basic, where it is unqualified and uninformed by other goods, including irreducibly social ones, there really is no moral order—there is no objective 'right'—at all. There is only war or political negotiation and manipulation.

This, I take it, is what O'Donovan means when he writes of 'the fissiparation ... of a singular notion of "right" into a plurality of subjective "rights"'.[69] To be quite clear, the rights under discussion here are natural, not positively legal. They are not the contingent creatures of a particular social system of law (to which O'Donovan has no objection in principle), but, supposedly, an essential feature of human nature. Moreover, the plurality of the rights does not

---

[67] Notably, O'Donovan does not locate the root of the problem in late medieval nominalist metaphysics or voluntarist theology. Instead, he is careful to report that, according to Michel Villey, the shift in the concept of right in the fourteenth century was merely 'synchronous with'—*not 'caused by'*—'the scholastic development of nominalism and voluntarism' ('The Language of Rights', pp. 196–7).

[68] O'Donovan, *Desire of the Nations*, p. 276. The quotation is from Thomas Hobbes, *Leviathan*, ed. Richard Tuck (Cambridge: Cambridge University Press, 1991), p. 14. See also O'Donovan, 'The Language of Rights', pp. 202–3, where he identifies the target of his criticism as the 'rights project', which shares with 'the modern tradition prevailing in the liberal West since the seventeenth century' an affinity for 'grounding political community in the wills of the individuals who compose it'.

[69] O'Donovan, *Desire of the Nations*, p. 276.

refer to their kinds, but to their owners. There is only one basic, natural kind: the 'right' or, better, the liberty or power of self-preservation; yet there are multiple proprietors of this kind of right. And since the lives of all individuals cannot always be equally preserved, and since the preservation of one life sometimes threatens others, these liberties or powers are in radical competition with each other.[70]

Accordingly, O'Donovan objects that the Hobbesian view sees individuals as 'rights-bearers prior to their communal existence'.[71] It sets rights apart from social right, and makes them destructive of society.[72] Since they derive from 'the radical ontological distinctness and multiplicity of human persons', rights are themselves 'radically multiple'.[73] As such it is doubtful that they are 'sufficient to ground the social and moral phenomenon we call *obligation* or *duty*'.[74] Indeed, they render unintelligible the idea of one individual choosing to suffer for the sake of another.[75]

For O'Donovan the root of the problem lies in the Hobbesian conception of human flourishing, namely, as consisting of the original, natural, radical, and *entirely untrammelled* liberty or power of each individual to preserve the self and assert it as he pleases. This results in a radical multiplicity of individual rights, which sets 'what is due to each above every idea of moral order'[76] and so militates against 'a conception of order, which demands *a* resolution of each controversy, *a* right thing to be done'.[77] On the contrary, according to O'Donovan's own Christian view, human beings flourish when they respond freely to the created, objective moral obligations of sociability.[78] This morally realist affirmation of an objective moral order makes it possible to conceive of justice in terms other than that of meeting an individual's rights. As O'Donovan observes in his study of Grotius:

> There is...a surplus in the notion of right that goes beyond proprietorial exchange...We have a duty of responsibility which outruns subjective rights. The qualified candidate [for a job] who has no right to assert...nevertheless constitutes a positive obligation. The right that confronts us, we may say, is not *his* right, but the right of *his situation*.[79]

---

[70] Ibid., pp. 247–8: 'What is distinctive about the modern conception of rights...is that subjective rights are taken to be original, not derived. The fundamental reality is a plurality of competing, unreconciled rights...The right is a primitive endowment of power with which the subject first engages in society; not an enhancement which accrues to the subject from an ordered and politically formed society.'

[71] O'Donovan, 'The Language of Rights', p. 198.   [72] Ibid., p. 194.   [73] Ibid., p. 195.

[74] Ibid., p. 195. The emphasis is O'Donovan's.   [75] O'Donovan, *Desire of the Nations*, p. 276.

[76] Ibid., p. 202.   [77] Ibid., p. 194. The emphases are O'Donovan's.

[78] Ibid., p. 254; *Ways of Judgment*, p. 221.

[79] O'Donovan, 'The Justice of Assignment', pp. 181, 202. The emphases are O'Donovan's.

146 WHAT'S WRONG WITH RIGHTS?

Here O'Donovan presents the affirmation of the conceptual primacy of objective right over subjective rights as requiring the rejection of the paradigm of individual entitlement and ownership.[80] In other words, he implies that the proprietary paradigm *is* indeed part of the problem. Elsewhere, however, he writes approvingly of a conception of a particular (natural) right that a subject *may possess* as 'not an atomic unit that can be multiplied and added up, but a *moment* emerging out of a larger whole, *Ius* as an undivided garment'.[81] That is to say, what is problematic is not the conception of a natural right as property, but rather its conception as *permanent* property, immune to moral contingency.

If O'Donovan differs from Lockwood O'Donovan in his equivocation over the problematic nature of the proprietary paradigm of subjective rights, he nonetheless shares her cultural pessimism. He considers the radically individualist conception of rights as key to 'modernity as a civilizational totality'.[82] He argues that 'the use of rights language in the revolutionary era to gain a critical advantage over existing systems of justice', which was self-consciously revived by the decision to base post-war reconstruction on a Universal Declaration of Human Rights, has 'put paid' to flexibility in the use of such language to refer to unitary right as well as multiple rights.[83] 'The logical necessity', he tells us, 'of our present discussions springs from that moment of resolute new beginning.'[84]

But O'Donovan cannot really mean 'logical necessity' here. He cannot be saying that history determines logical necessity. He must be saying that the predominant intellectual and political climate makes impossible—puts paid to—the recovery of pre-modern right-order rights-talk. But why should such a recovery be any more impossible than that of Christian, pre-modern liberalism, which is no small part of O'Donovan's own project? We are not told.

Besides, while 'modernity' might comprise a comprehensive, total *theory* of civilisation—although at best it surely comprises several rival theories—it does not yet comprise a totalitarian cultural reality anywhere, not even in the contemporary West. The actual culture of the West today is an unstable mixture of plural elements, where 'modernity' vies with 'pre-modernity' and different 'modernities' and 'pre-modernities' vie with each other. The empirical truth is much closer to Alasdair MacIntyre's reading than to O'Donovan's—more fragmentary and confused.[85] But by the same token it is less determined and more open.

---

[80] Ibid., pp. 200–3. O'Donovan does tend to share Lockwood O'Donovan's suspicion of the proprietary conception of subjective rights: 'To the Franciscans and their defenders belongs the doubtful credit of launching the concept of subjective right on a trajectory independent of property, *though still parallel to it*' (*Desire of the Nations*, p. 248. The emphasis is mine).

[81] O'Donovan, 'The Justice of Assignment', p. 195. The emphases are mine.

[82] O'Donovan, 'The Language of Rights', pp. 195–6.   [83] Ibid., p. 202.   [84] Ibid.

[85] Alasdair MacIntyre, *After Virtue* (Notre Dame, Ind.: University of Notre Dame Press, 1981).

V

In his 2014 essay 'Against Human Rights', John Milbank in effect reprises Oliver O'Donovan's position, adding an observation about political absolutism and making one historical qualification, and develops it against Nicholas Wolterstorff's genealogical defence of subjective rights.[86] He argues that a modern, morally subjectivist concept of subjective rights now prevails. These rights are subjective because they adhere to individual subjects as absolute properties.[87] They are subjectiv*ist* (or voluntarist) because they are grounded simply in the individual's will. This will is 'arbitrary' or 'nihilistic'[88] and 'egotistic'.[89] It is untrammelled by any larger moral order—any order of objective, unitary 'right'[90]—especially any given, natural, created ends or goods, and most especially any common goods and social obligations.[91] Hence, the 'logical slide of liberalism into a nihilism of the enthroned will'.[92]

These subjectivist subjective rights are also logically connected, Milbank argues, with 'an absolutist account of the sovereignty of the centralised state'.[93] They undermine intermediate or civic 'bonds of trust' and associations,[94] and so tend to political absolutism.[95] There are three reasons for this. First, if rights depend ultimately on the individual's sheer will, then they are alienable: nothing stands in the way of their alienation, except the individual's consent.[96] Second, the reduction of an individual to an inscrutable abstract interiority of negative will renders her a replaceable and disposable atom.[97] And third, 'where no shared implicit agreements guarantee personal security, no tacit and embedded horizons, then it can only be guaranteed by a centralist *surveillance*... perverted solipsistic freedom will always require alien and draconian enforcement'.[98]

Milbank's historical qualification of O'Donovan's thesis is that he traces the modern, subjectivist concept of rights back beyond Hobbes to William of Ockham in the fourteenth century.[99] In giving birth to 'the modern notion of absolute ownership', where one can do whatever one likes with one's own property,[100] Ockham was part of a 'longer-term Franciscan... drift towards voluntarism... and individualism',[101] which foreshadows 'a fully modern sense of subjective right'.[102]

---

[86] John Milbank, 'Against Human Rights: Liberty in the Western Tradition', in Costas Douzinas and Conor Gearty, eds, *The Meanings of Rights: The Philosophy and Social Theory of Human Rights* (Cambridge: Cambridge University Press, 2014). Wolterstorff makes his defence of subjective rights in *Justice*.

[87] Milbank, 'Against Human Rights', p. 62.   [88] Ibid., p. 47.   [89] Ibid. , p. 39.

[90] Ibid., p. 46.   [91] Ibid., p. 39.   [92] Ibid., p. 47.   [93] Ibid., pp. 39–40.

[94] Ibid., p. 43.   [95] Ibid., p. 40.

[96] Ibid., pp. 40–1. See also p. 43: 'the subject's fundamental moral standing is defined in formal, voluntarist terms that sidestep any questions of normative goals or substance and therefore imply the performative contradiction that the true test of freedom's exercise is one's right to abandon it altogether'.

[97] Ibid., pp. 43–4.   [98] Ibid. The emphasis is Milbank's.   [99] Ibid., p. 47.

[100] Ibid., p. 62.   [101] Ibid., p. 60.   [102] Ibid., p. 62.

Because of their source in Ockham, therefore, modern human rights have 'their buried foundation in a questionable theological voluntarism and a questionably atomising metaphysic'.[103]

Against this genealogy, however, Wolterstorff, while endorsing Brian Tierney's demonstration of the concept of subjective rights as early as the twelfth century in the thought of the canonists, has gone beyond him to discover it in biblical and patristic tradition.[104] Since, along with others in the 'American Christian liberal camp' such as Tierney and John Witte,[105] Wolterstorff—according to Milbank—'oppose[s] the idea that justice is grounded in cosmic "right order"',[106] he understands subjective rights in subjectivist terms. Therefore he concludes that *modern subjectivist* rights are compatible with a Christian vision of things.

But Wolterstorff, argues Milbank, is wrong. In fact, what we find before Ockham is a non-voluntarist, non-nominalist, non-subjectivist, realist tradition of thinking about subjective rights, which operated with reference to an objective 'right order' and issued in political constitutionalism.[107] These rights carried duties as well as liberties. They comprised an objectively right share in the distribution of things, according to justice:[108] 'the foundation of the right of one party and the duty of another lies in objective *ius* and not in the sheerly subjective right of the claimant'.[109] And unlike modern subjective rights, which are absolute and unconditional, these realist rights were contingent on the performance of prior duties and so forfeitable.[110] Accordingly, law 'was a branch of practical philosophy, a matter of exercising *iuris-prudentia* [that is, discernment according to circumstance and a sense of the transcendent good], and not a matter of deduction from foundational principles or of applying positive prescriptions in the light of a rigid attachment to precedent'.[111] *Ius* was conceived 'as dialectically arrived-at equity'.[112] Therefore, the fact that Wolterstorff finds *a* concept of subjective rights operative before Hobbes and Ockham in biblical, patristic, and medieval tradition does not mean that modern liberal subjecti*vist* rights are Christian.[113]

Quite what part this interpretation of intellectual history plays in Milbank's argument is not clear. He appears to say that, when Tierney and Wolterstorff find subjective rights before Hobbes and Ockham, they do not find a more properly Christian, realist *alternative* to modern, subjectivist rights, but merely an embryonic form of them. Yet Milbank himself admits that a realist alternative was in fact

---

[103] Ibid., p. 68.   [104] Wolterstorff, *Justice*, Part I: 'The Archeology of Rights'.
[105] Milbank, 'Against Human Rights', p. 46 and n. 17. Milbank accuses Brian Tierney of the same 'common Christian-American doublethink', in arguing that human rights as understood in the United States today are compatible with Catholic Natural Law thinking (ibid., p. 58).
[106] Ibid., p. 46.   [107] Ibid., pp. 49–50.   [108] Ibid., pp. 49–54.   [109] Ibid., p. 52.
[110] Ibid., p. 53.   [111] Ibid., p. 54.   [112] Ibid., p. 58.
[113] Ibid., p. 50: it does not mean that the Middle Ages 'usually possessed precisely our modern liberal notion of a subjective civil right, never mind of a subjective natural right. Subjectivisation does not necessarily mean subjective grounding.'

there to be found. So why does he assume that Wolterstorff seeks grounding in Christian medieval, patristic, and biblical tradition for subjectivist, rather than realist, rights? As a Christian theist Wolterstorff would be behaving very oddly indeed, if he were to reject altogether some notion of an objective 'right order' created by God and setting the terms of human moral responsibility. One prima facie reason for doubting that he does this lies in the very title of his book *Justice: Rights and Wrongs*, where the concept of justice logically precedes that of rights. This reason is then confirmed when we find Wolterstorff affirming that 'the good is prior to the right' and that 'sociality is built into the essence of rights'.[114] And it is further confirmed when we read that subjective rights derive from the worth of human beings, whose objectivity is anchored in God's love for them.[115] So while it is true that Wolterstorff is explicitly critical of 'right order theorists' like the O'Donovans on account of their hostility towards subjective rights, and while it is true that he does not explicitly own an alternative, rights-friendly concept of objective right order, it remains true that he does espouse one implicitly. Milbank has misunderstood his target.

Nevertheless, there is an ambiguity in the thought of at least one of the Christian defenders of subjective rights, John Witte. In his introduction to a *Journal of Law and Religion* symposium on Christianity and human rights, Witte argues that medieval canon lawyers and Protestant reformers 'anticipat [ed] most of the rights formulation of modern liberals'.[116] In other words, he is at pains to emphasise the *continuity* between Christian and Enlightenment views. What is more, Witte happily sweeps up into the Christian tradition that he endorses both Ockham and the Salamancan Scholastics,[117] whom Milbank and O'Donovan, respectively, finger as Christian roots of modern, individualist, subjectivism. So Witte does give Milbank some reason to suspect him of simply baptising modern subjectivist rights. It is doubtful that this is what he really intends to do, since in his essay 'A Dickensian Era of Human Rights' Witte refers critically to 'the libertarian accents that still too often dominate our rights talk today';[118] and in his *Law and Religion* introduction he sets himself against 'the dominant liberalism of much contemporary rights talk'.[119] Indeed, in *The Reformation of Rights* he quotes with approval Don Browning's lament:

---

[114] Wolterstorff, *Justice*, pp. 4–5.   [115] Ibid., chapters 13 and 16.

[116] John Witte, 'Christianity and Human Rights: Past Contributions and Future Challenges', *Journal of Law and Religion*, 30/3 (October 2015), Abstract, p. 353.

[117] Ibid., p. 368.

[118] John Witte, 'A Dickensian Era of Religious Rights', in *God's Joust, God's Justice: Law and Religion in the Western Tradition* (Grand Rapids, Mich.: Eerdmans, 2006), p. 111. See also Witte, *The Reformation of Rights*, p. 341: 'It is beyond doubt that many current formulations of human rights are suffused with fundamental libertarian beliefs and values ... But libertarianism does not and should not have a monopoly on the nurture of human rights'; and his 'Introduction', in Witte and Alexander, *Christianity and Human Rights*, p. 13, where he laments 'the pronounced libertarian tone of many recent human rights formulations'.

[119] Witte, 'Christianity and Human Rights', p. 379.

What remains [of modern human rights thought] is a list of subjective natural rights that are asserted more or less independently of any theory of objective natural rights. They function as an unchecked wish-list, in which these rights increasingly seem to contradict each other, sow seeds of distrust and disregard among the nations of the world, and get used as tools of manipulation by various interest groups around the world to accomplish their own particular political and legal ends. A new critical grounding for human rights is required if the entire tradition is not to explode into scores of conflicting subjective wants that have no real authority and, in reality, can never be implemented.[120]

But how can Witte endorse such a view and still be *for* 'the rights formulation of modern liberals'? What is needed here is a clear distinction between different kinds of liberalism.

To his credit Milbank makes such a distinction—and more unequivocally than either of the O'Donovans—when he endorses the quest for 'an alternative modernity that can retrieve, and repeat differently, the authentic legacy of the west which is Christian and equitably egalitarian rather than simply "emancipatory"'.[121]

VI

Lockwood O'Donovan and Milbank both trace the root of modern subjective rights back to the nominalist and voluntarist theology of the fourteenth and fifteenth centuries. While Lockwood O'Donovan accuses Jean Gerson, Milbank accuses William of Ockham. Again, quite what role these claims about intellectual history play in their arguments against 'modern rights' is not clear. Their complaints could still stand, if the genealogy were to find its beginnings in a later date—say, with Hobbes. In Lockwood O'Donovan's case, however, the medieval rootage does serve to support her suggestion that the very notion of subjective rights is corrupt—that there is no distinction to be made between an unacceptable 'modern' concept and an acceptable 'pre-modern' one.[122]

Whatever the argumentative significance of these historical claims, there are good reasons to think them mistaken. Against those who hold that subjective right

---

[120] Don Browning, 'The United Nations Convention on the Rights of the Child: Should it be Ratified and Why?', *Emory International Law Review*, 20 (2006), pp. 157, 172–3; quoted by Witte in *Reformation of Rights*, p. 334.

[121] Milbank, 'Against Human Rights', p. 70.

[122] Lockwood O'Donovan is equivocal about this. Her statement that Christian political thought 'functioned *virtually* without any concept of subjective natural rights' ('Historical Prolegomena', p. 31, my emphasis) until the fourteenth century, when nominalist and voluntarist theology emerged, does imply that *pre*-nominalist and *pre*-voluntarist political thought did function with *some* such concept. She does not think this significant enough to pay it much attention, however, presumably because she thinks that the very notion of a subjective right as an individual's property is suspect.

is the corollary of a voluntarist theology running from Gerson to Hobbes, Annabel Brett observes that the language of *ius* as *facultas* or *potestas* or *dominium*, signifying a sphere of indifferent liberty or sovereignty, 'does not fit the texts to which it is supposed to apply'.[123] One of the clearest signs of this is that for almost all of the voluntarist authors usually cited, *ius* is predicable of animals, to which the same authors consistently deny liberty.[124] Brett also observes that the equivalence of *ius* and *dominium*, which is supposed to mark the beginning of the modern concept of a subjective right, was far from being the universal outlook in the moral theology of the later Middle Ages.[125]

In his painstaking study of the medieval origins and development of the concept of subjective rights, Brian Tierney argues against Georges de Lagarde, Michel Villey, and Michel Bastit that Ockham's view of natural rights was not derived from his nominalist and voluntarist philosophical theology, and that it was therefore not morally anti-realist, individualist, and socially atomistic.[126] He observes that basically similar ideas about rights were propounded by Thomists, Scotists, and Ockhamists, who held very different views on universals and essences.[127] In particular, against Bastit's claim that Ockham's view of the absolute power of the will of God issued in an analogous concept of 'individualistic' natural rights, Tierney argues that '[f]or [Ockham] the divine will and human wills were incommensurable. In God there was no distinction between will and intellect; all that God willed was just and right. A human will, on the other hand, could choose good or evil, and so needed to be guided by reason.'[128] And against Bastit's claim that Ockham made no real distinction between reason and will in general, he quotes Ockham's own statement that reason directs the will 'as something other than itself',[129] and argues that he emphasised right reason as the basis of both natural law and natural rights:[130] 'For Ockham a natural right was not an assertion

---

[123] Brett, *Liberty, Right, and Nature*, p. 6.   [124] Ibid., p. 6.   [125] Ibid., p. 11.

[126] Tierney, *The Idea of Natural Rights*, pp. 8, 97.

[127] Ibid., p. 5. Tierney cites Charles Zuckerman as 'certainly' showing that there is no correlation between metaphysics and political theory in the thought of many medieval thinkers: 'We can find Thomists and realists and nominalists at every point on the political spectrum' (ibid., pp. 31–2). He also cites J. B. Morrall and W. Kölmel as arguing that Ockham's political ideas have no necessary connection with his early speculative philosophy and are drawn from more traditional sources (ibid., p. 97). Francis Oakley, who is sympathetic to the idea of subtle and indirect continuities between Ockham's fundamental philosophical and theological commitments and his later political writings, nevertheless finds Villey's argument 'really quite loose-limbed, grounded, in effect ... on little more than reiterated assertion' (*Natural Rights, Laws of Nature, Natural Rights: Continuity and Discontinuity in the History of Ideas* (New York: Continuum, 2005), pp. 98–9).

[128] Tierney, *The Idea of Natural Rights*, p. 197. Brett agrees: Ockham's theological voluntarism does not affect his understanding of subjective right (Brett, *Liberty, Right, and Nature*, pp. 51–2).

[129] Tierney, *The Idea of Natural Rights*, p, 198 n. 6.

[130] Ibid., pp. 127, 181. Oakley agrees: the fact that Ockham used the language of subjective rights and helped to shape the notion of natural rights did not mean that he 'was led to abandon a commitment to the idea that there exists a natural law accessible to the right reason of all men and prescribing for their living objective moral norms' (*Natural Rights*, p. 99).

of naked will but a power conformed to reason.'[131] Tierney also makes clear that Ockham's emphasis on individual rights in his political works was always balanced by a concern for the common good or utility—indeed, that the two concepts are mutually implicated, insofar as common utility requires rulers to respect the natural rights of their subjects, except in cases of extreme necessity.[132]

Similarly, Tierney contradicts Richard Tuck's claim that Gerson innovated a concept of an individual subject's right to the power of liberty, whose sovereignty is like God's, and which is paradigmatic of 'the modern concept'.[133] Tierney objects that Tuck gives 'an impossible account of Gerson's theological ideas', which 'is not ... sustainable'.[134] This is because Gerson does not think of the relationship between divine and human sovereignty as 'a reciprocal one between equals';[135] and while he does think of a subjective right as the power to act freely, without constraint by external law, he nevertheless considers it accountable to (internal) reason and conscience.[136] Tierney also observes that Gerson's thinking assumed a church-political context, in which he was concerned to limit the power of the Pope to usurp the freedom and power of subordinate individuals.[137] Appealing to St Paul's image of the Church as one body, he wrote that it was wrong for the Pope as head of the Church to usurp 'the duties [*officia*] of all the other members ... if all is eye or head, where is the foot, where is the hand?'[138] What this implies is that the subjective rights that Gerson asserted were positively legal, rather than natural.[139]

Tierney denies that the source of the modern, subjectivist concept of subjective rights can be fairly traced to either Ockham or Gerson. He does not contradict Oliver O'Donovan's perception that the Salamancan Scholastics endorsed a concept of right as a subject's property or dominion. However, Tierney makes clear that this had to do with asserting the natural right of the natives of the Caribbean

---

[131] Tierney, *The Idea of Natural Rights*, p. 199. Brett agrees. While she defends Ockham's originality in assimilating *ius* to *dominium*, she argues that he did not mean that latter 'in the strong sense' and that he developed 'a notion of subjective natural right connected with the objectively rational order or law of nature' (Brett, *Liberty, Right, and Nature*, p. 51).

[132] Tierney, *The Idea of Natural Rights*, pp. 189, 191. From his recognition of an exceptional case of extreme necessity, it follows that Ockham did not regard individual or corporate rights against arbitrary political interference as absolute. This implies that Michel Villey is mistaken to attribute a 'modern' concept of subjective natural right to Ockham on the ground that he first combined the idea of *ius* ('right') with that of *potestas* ('power'), insofar as the 'modern' concept thinks of the relevant power as absolute *dominium* ('dominion') (Tierney, *The Idea of Natural Rights*, pp. 28–30). In fact, according to Oakley, research subsequent to Villey has 'made it increasingly clear' that there was 'nothing particularly novel' about Ockham's speaking of *ius* as a licit *potestas*, such a concept being common as early as the twelfth century (*Natural Rights*, pp. 100, 102).

[133] Tierney, *The Idea of Natural Rights*, pp. 217–18.   [134] Ibid., p. 218.   [135] Ibid., p. 217.

[136] Ibid., p. 53. Brett agrees (Brett, *Liberty, Right, and Nature*, pp. 86–7).

[137] Tierney, *The Idea of Natural Rights*, pp. 207, 223–4.   [138] Ibid., p. 224.

[139] The significance of the political context is confirmed by Tierney's observation that, around 1500, a widespread reaction against recent disorders in Church and state replaced concern with the rights of individuals and corporations with alarm at 'the overmighty subject' and 'lack of governance'. Neither Machiavelli's *The Prince* (1513) nor Thomas More's *Utopia* (1516) raise the topic of rights (ibid., p. 253).

to 'brotherly kindness and Christian love', and to self-rule and property against unjustified Spanish incursion.[140] This conception of original freedom is not the same as Hobbes's. It is not freedom from the requirements of objective right order and natural justice.[141] Rather, it is freedom *under these* from unjust coercion.

And while he agrees with both of the O'Donovans and with Milbank that Hobbes proposed a concept of the subjective right of the individual as a power subject to no objective moral constraints,[142] Tierney denies that this was seminal for subsequent, 'modern' thought. Later thinkers continued to think of subjective rights in the context of an objective right order. Indeed, 'Hobbes's work is best seen', Tierney argues, 'as an aberration from the mainstream of natural rights thinking that flowed from the medieval jurists through Ockham, Gerson, and Grotius to Pufendorf and Locke and writers of the Enlightenment like Burlamqui and Wolff...'.[143]

In confirmation of Tierney's reading of early modern intellectual history, we can invoke the work of Samuel Mintz, Jon Parkin, and Richard Tuck. Mintz recognises that Hobbes did succeed in imposing his own 'strict, rational standards of argument' upon his critics.[144] Beyond that, however, '[t]he truth is that Hobbes's influence on his countrymen during his own lifetime and for almost a century after was negative. He left no disciples. He founded no school. He made no such impact on English thought as did...Locke, whose influence was felt throughout the eighteenth century.'[145] Forty-five years later Parkin qualified Mintz's conclusion, arguing that Hobbes's critics often absorbed some of his ideas, and that the wider cultural imagination was often haunted by the metaphor of his description of the state of nature. Nevertheless, this absorption was critical, taming what was appropriated.[146] In the end, Parkin confirms Mintz's main conclusion:

> By 1700 the cumulative effect of five decades of critical engagement with Hobbes's writings had produced the image of the philosopher with which

---

[140] Ibid., pp. 265, 277–8. See also p. 297 on de Vitoria and p. 305 on Suárez.

[141] Richard Tuck agrees. He observes that the Spanish Dominicans generally put the objective sense of *ius* (what is just) at the centre of their concerns (*Natural Rights Theories*, p. 47), and that, accordingly, Vitoria denies that individuals are generally free to enslave themselves, since their liberty is subject to the law of God (ibid., p. 49).

[142] Tierney, *The Idea of Natural Rights*, pp. 50–1.

[143] Ibid., pp. 340–1. In support of this reading of the history of political theory after Hobbes, Tierney cites Brett, *Liberty, Right, and Nature*, Knud Haakonssen, *Natural Law and Moral Philosophy: From Grotius to the Scottish Enlightenment* (Cambridge: Cambridge University Press, 1996), and J. Tully, *A Discourse on Property. John Locke and his Adversaries* (Cambridge: Cambridge University Press, 1980) (*The Idea of Natural Rights*, pp. 48, 233 n. 80).

[144] Samuel Mintz, *The Hunting of Leviathan: Seventeenth-Century Reactions to the Materialism and Moral Philosophy of Thomas Hobbes* (Cambridge: Cambridge University Press, 1962), pp. 149–51.

[145] Mintz, *The Hunting of Leviathan*, p. 147.

[146] Jon Parkin, *Taming the Leviathan: The Reception of the Political and Religious Ideas of Thomas Hobbes in England 1640–1700* (Cambridge: Cambridge University Press, 2007), pp. 412–15.

I began this book... He had become a household name, but one associated with atheism, immorality, selfish behaviour, a poor view of human nature and unacceptable political views. Taken together these views constituted 'Hobbism', a well documented creed to be detested by all God-fearing people and a set of view associated with a minority of 'Hobbists'.[147]

In effect, Richard Tuck concurs. According to his story of the development of natural rights theories in the early modern period, Grotius triumphed over Hobbes. Standing in the late medieval scholastic tradition, Grotius affirmed natural rights under a natural order and rejected Hobbes's vision of the state of nature as an amoral *bellum omnium contra omnes*.[148] The 'radical' political tradition in the seventeenth century generally followed Grotius,[149] as did his 'true heirs' Pufendorf and Locke.[150] According to the latter, the law of nature limits the right to property, so that what is surplus to beneficial use belongs to others who need it.[151]

<h1 style="text-align:center">VII</h1>

Ernest Fortin, however, disputes this reading of intellectual history. A Roman Catholic disciple of Strauss, Fortin is convinced that 'no ultimate synthesis between a consistent natural law theory and a consistent natural rights theory is possible',[152] and, like MacIntyre, he criticises the Roman Catholic Church for trying to marry the 'pre-modern' Aristotelian, teleological tradition, which affirms a supreme good and stresses duties, with the 'modern', non-teleological tradition, which denies such a good and stresses rights.[153] '[N]atural rights', he tell us, 'are totally foreign to the literature of the premodern period.'[154] The medievals speak only of legal rights qualified by antecedent law, contingent upon the performance of prior duties, and so forfeitable—not of 'rights in the modern sense, which are variously described as absolute, inviolable, imprescriptible, unconditional, inalienable, or sacred'.[155]

Therefore, against both Tuck and Tierney, Fortin seeks to bolster the Straussian view that Locke's view of natural right was Hobbesian, in effect defending the line taken by the O'Donovans that Hobbes determined the

[147] Ibid., p. 410.   [148] Tuck, *Natural Rights Theories*, pp. 61–2, 68, 81.
[149] Ibid., pp. 154–5, 164.   [150] Ibid., pp. 159–60, 175.   [151] Ibid., p. 172.
[152] Ernest L. Fortin, 'On the Presumed Medieval Origin of Individual Rights', *Communio*, 26 (Spring 1999), p. 78. Fortin's view is at one with those of Leo Strauss and Michel Villey who 'shared a marked hostility to the modern notion of individual subjective rights' and 'the firm conviction' that it was wholly incompatible with the traditional notion of natural law (Oakley, *Natural Law*, p. 95).
[153] Ernest L. Fortin, '"Sacred and Inviolable": *Rerum Novarum* and Natural Rights', *Theological Studies*, 53 (1992), pp. 203–4, 227.
[154] Ibid., p. 219.   [155] Ibid., p. 221.

'modern', egoistic concept of subjective rights.[156] He contends that 'the characteristic Enlightenment view of rights' is not the 'basically classical and medieval'
one of Grotius[157] or of Christian Wolff (1679–1754), where '*ius* provides the
means for what *lex* provides as an end'.[158] The crucial question, he claims, is the
ranking of rights and duties, and what distinguishes the specifically modern
notion of rights that comes to the fore with Hobbes is less its definition of
right as power, than 'its proclamation of rights rather than duties as the primary
moral counter'. The classic expression of this view lies in the fourteenth chapter
of *Leviathan*, where Hobbes asserts the unrivalled primacy of the natural right of
self-preservation.[159] 'This', Fortin tells us 'is precisely the teaching that was taken
over by subsequent theorists, including Locke', according to whom, 'in the state
of nature everyone has the executive power of the law of nature'.[160] Such teaching
is 'clearly of a piece' with the Hobbesian notion of the state of nature, 'that
prepolitical state in which one is not bound by any law whatsoever and is free to
deal with others as one sees fit'.[161]

   In prosecution of his claim that Locke is basically a disciple of Hobbes, Fortin
assimilates their views of a prisoner's right to resist execution and of suicide, and
contrasts them with Aquinas's. On the one hand, according to Aquinas, while a
prisoner is not morally forbidden to escape from prison while awaiting execution,
he is forbidden to use physical force to defend himself against the executioner.[162]
On the other hand, according to Hobbes, the prisoner suffers no such moral
constraint, since

> no man is supposed bound by covenant not to resist violence. In the making of a
> commonwealth, every man gives away the right of defending another, but not of
> defending himself... before the institution of commonwealth every man had a
> right to everything and to do whatever he thought necessary to his own preser-
> vation, *subduing, hurting,* or *killing* any man in order thereunto...[163]

Locke, claims Fortin, follows Hobbes, not Aquinas. In his *Second Treatise of Civil
Government* Locke argues that, because of 'this fundamental, sacred, and inalienable law of self-preservation', none has the power to surrender their preservation
'to the absolute will and arbitrary dominion of another'.[164] Everyone is bound to

---

[156] Fortin, 'On the Presumed Medieval Origin', p. 56. Cf. Strauss, *Natural Right and History*,
pp. 165–6. Fortin describes Locke's concept of the state of nature as a 'polite reformulation' of
Hobbes's ('"Sacred and Inviolable"', p. 225).
[157] Fortin, 'On the Presumed Medieval Origin', p. 76.   [158] Ibid., p. 65.
[159] Ibid., pp. 65–6. See also Fortin, '"Sacred and Inviolable"', p. 223.
[160] Fortin, 'On the Presumed Medieval Origin', p. 66. In substantiation of this reading, Fortin cites
John Locke's *Second Treatise of Civil Government*, II.6, 7, 8, 13.
[161] Fortin, 'On the Presumed Medieval Origin', p. 66.   [162] Ibid., p. 67.
[163] Ibid., p. 68, quoting Hobbes, *Leviathan*, XXVIII. The emphases are Fortin's.
[164] Locke, *Second Treatise*, XIII.149; cited by Fortin, 'On the Presumed Medieval Origin', p. 69.

preserve the rest of mankind as well as himself, but only so long as his own self-preservation does not 'come into competition' with anyone else's.[165] In other words, Fortin tells us, in the final analysis, for Locke as for Hobbes, 'rights take precedence over duties'.[166]

Locke's assimilation to Hobbes is also apparent in his view of suicide. While the medieval scholastics, viewing self-preservation as foremost a duty, forbade suicide, Hobbes and Locke, viewing self-preservation as a right, permitted suicide.[167] 'If self-preservation is an unconditional right and if, as Hobbes and Locke contend, such rights are to be defined in terms of freedom, that is to say, if human beings are free to exercise or not exercise them,' Fortin argues, 'one fails to see why it would be forbidden to commit suicide or allow oneself to be enslaved by other human beings'.[168] In support, he quotes Locke's assertion that the state that 'all men are naturally in...is a state of perfect freedom to order their actions and dispose of their possessions and persons as they think fit, within the bounds of the law of nature, without asking leave or depending upon the will of any other man'.[169] Since, according to Locke, man is the 'executor of the law of nature', there are no restrictions other than the ones that an individual may decide to impose on himself. This appears to be contradicted by Locke's statement that 'everyone is bound to preserve himself and not to quit his station wilfully', inasmuch as all human beings are 'the workmanship of an omnipotent and wise Maker...made to last during his, not one another's pleasure'.[170] But the contradiction is merely apparent, for Locke nowhere says that God has commanded human beings to preserve themselves, only that God directs them to preserve themselves by means of their 'senses and reason', as he directs animals to do so by 'sense and instinct'.[171] That is, both men and animals have implanted in them a 'desire' for survival.[172] From this Fortin confidently concludes:

> Clearly, the 'law of nature' of which Locke speaks is his own natural law. It is strictly a matter of calculation and has nothing to do with the self-evident principles on which the moral life is said to rest by the medieval theorists. In short, it is not at all certain that in Locke's mind there were any compelling moral arguments against suicide.[173]

Fortin's reading of Locke is perverse. It is true that, according to Locke, in the state of nature human beings enjoy 'perfect freedom' of action 'without asking leave or depending upon the will of any other *man*'. However, they do so 'within

[165] Locke, *Second Treatise*, II.6; cited by Fortin, 'On the Presumed Medieval Origin', p. 69.
[166] Fortin, 'On the Presumed Medieval Origin', p. 69.   [167] Ibid., p. 70.   [168] Ibid., p. 71.
[169] Locke, *Second Treatise*, II.4; cited by Fortin, 'On the Presumed Medieval Origin', p. 71.
[170] Locke, *Second Treatise*, II.6; cited by Fortin, 'On the Presumed Medieval Origin', p. 71.
[171] Locke, *First Treatise*, IX.86; cited by Fortin, 'On the Presumed Medieval Origin', p. 71.
[172] Fortin, 'On the Presumed Medieval Origin', p. 71.   [173] Ibid., p. 72

the bounds of the Law of Nature'.[174] The crucial questions are, What does Locke understand by this law? Does it precede and govern natural right, or does natural right precede and govern it?

For Hobbes, the answer is clearly the latter:

> THE RIGHT OF NATURE, which Writers commonly call *Jus Naturale*, is the Liberty each man hath, to use his own power, as he will himselfe, for the preservation of his own Nature; that is to say, of his own Life; and consequently, of doing any thing, which in his own judgement, and Reason, hee shall conceive to be the aptest means thereunto... A LAW OF NATURE, (*Lex Naturalis,*) is a Precept, or generall Rule, found out by Reason, by which a man is forbidden to do, that, which is destructive of his life, or to take away the mans of preserving the same; and to omit, that, by which he thinketh it may be best preserved.[175]

In other words, the law of nature is the rational servant of the 'right' of nature, which consists of the liberty of self-preservation. Since that right suffers absolutely no constraint, but extends 'even to one anothers body', the state of nature is 'a condition of Warre of every one against every one'.[176] Moved by the desire for self-preservation in such a situation of general insecurity, instrumental reason gives birth to a series of laws of nature. The first and fundamental of these is the obligation to seek peace for the sake of better self-defence; and the second, to enter into a contract or covenant with others to surrender the natural 'right to all things' and suffer reciprocal constraints upon original liberty.[177] This voluntary surrender creates an obligation or duty (of consistency) not to hinder those to whom the right has been transferred—an obligation whose force derives 'from Feare of some evill consequences upon the rupture'.[178] This comprises the third law of nature, 'that Men performe their Covenants made', in which 'consisteth the Fountain and Originall of Justice. For where no Covenant hath preceded, there hath no Right been transferred, and every man has right to everything; and consequently, no action can be Unjust'.[179] However, covenants of mere mutual trust, where fear remains of non-performance, are invalid; and until the cause of such fear is removed, there can be no injustice: 'Therefore before the names Just and Unjust can have place, there must be some coercive Power, to compel men

---

[174] John Locke, 'An Essay Concerning the True Original, Extent, and End of Civil Government' ('Second Treatise'), in *Two Treatises of Civil Government*, introd. W. S. Carpenter (London: J. M. Dent, 1924), II.4, p. 118. The emphasis is mine.

[175] Hobbes, *Leviathan*, I.XIV, p. 189.

[176] Ibid., pp. 189–90. Cf. I.XIV, p. 191: 'there is nothing to which every man had not Right by Nature.'

[177] Ibid., p. 190. A covenant is a species of contract, where one party fulfils his side of the bargain, but trusts the other to perform his part at a later time (I.XIV, p. 193).

[178] Ibid., pp. 191–2.

[179] Ibid., pp. 201–2. As he puts it succinctly elsewhere: 'where law ceaseth, sin ceaseth' (II.XXVII, p. 337).

equally to the performance of their Covenants, by the terrour of some punishment, greater than the benefit they expect by the breach of their Covenant.'[180]

Locke's view is quite different. Aligning himself with the scholastic tradition by quoting at length 'the judicious Hooker', Locke asserts that the law of nature precedes and governs and limits the 'perfect freedom' enjoyed in the state of nature: since '[t]he state of Nature has a law of Nature to govern it, which obliges everyone', the 'state of liberty... is not a state of licence'.[181] This law of nature is generated by the equal and independent status or dignity of all human beings as called by God to his service: they are

> the workmanship of one omnipotent and infinitely wise Maker; all the servants of one sovereign Master, sent into the world by His order and about His business; they are His property, whose workmanship they are made to last during His, not one another's pleasure.

This basic human equality obliges us not to destroy one another, 'as if we were made for one another's uses'. We may not take away or impair another's life, 'unless it be to do justice on an offender'.[182] In very striking contrast with Hobbes, Locke explicates the practical meaning of the law of nature almost invariably in terms of obligations, and on the one occasion that he does refer to subjective rights, it is to others' rights, not the self's.[183]

It is true, as Fortin reports, that Locke writes that man is the 'executor of the law of nature'. But he does not mean to say that the individual invents the law of nature to suit himself. The textual context is a discussion of how to restrain some from 'invading others' rights' under the law of nature in the state of nature. In such conditions 'the execution of the law of Nature is... put into every man's hands, whereby every one has a right to punish the transgressors of that law to such a degree as may hinder its violation'.[184] Clearly this is not a Hobbesian matter of using the several laws of nature as rational tools of self-preservation. Rather, it is a matter of doing justice in the absence of judicial institutions, of discriminating between the innocent and the guilty, to preserve the one and restrain the other: 'everyman in the state of Nature has a power to kill a murderer, both to deter others from doing the like injury... and also to secure men from the attempts of a criminal who, having renounced reason, the common rule and measure God hath given to mankind, hath, by the unjust violence and slaughter he hath committed upon one, declared war against all mankind'.[185] Locke makes it perfectly clear that this executive power is not absolute and arbitrary, but constrained by the prior law of Nature:

[180] Ibid., p. 202.   [181] Locke, *Second Treatise*, II.6, p. 119.   [182] Ibid., II.6, p. 120.
[183] Ibid., II.7, p. 120.   [184] Ibid., II.7, p. 120.   [185] Ibid., II.7, 11, pp. 120, 122.

in the state of Nature, one man comes by a power over another, but yet no absolute or arbitrary power to use a criminal, when he has got him in his hands, according to the passionate heats or boundless extravagancy of his own will, but only to retribute to him so far as calm reason and conscience dictate, what is proportionate to his transgression, which is so much as may serve for reparation and restraint.[186]

For Locke the individual's power in the state of nature to execute the law of nature is the power to do justice. For Hobbes justice only comes into being with social contracts and property and a sovereign to back them. In the state of nature, therefore, there is none:

Where there is no Own, that is, no Propriety, there is no Injustice; and where there is no coercive Power erected, that is, where there is no Common-wealth, there is no Propriety; all men having the Right to all things: Therefore, where there is no Common-wealth, there is nothing Unjust.[187]

Fortin is also correct to report that when Locke writes that everyone ought to do whatever he can to preserve the rest of mankind, he adds the qualification, 'when his own preservation comes not in competition'.[188] However, given Locke's assertion in the immediately preceding sentence and in subsequent clauses of the very same sentence that we may not destroy one another 'as if we were made for one another's uses', and 'unless it be to do justice on an offender', this cannot mean that, in the state of nature, one may take another's life whenever he threatens one's own. It cannot mean that one's right to self-preservation always trumps one's duty to preserve the lives of others. Rather, it must mean that there is no general duty to prefer another's life to one's own. Whether there is such a duty at all depends on the circumstances.

It is also true that Locke writes of a 'fundamental, sacred, and inalienable law of self-preservation'.[189] But this takes its specific meaning from its textual context: namely, a discussion of civil government and the relative powers of the community and their legislators. What is being asserted is that the equal dignity of human beings, which generates the law of nature, forbids them to surrender themselves into the 'slavish condition' of being subject 'to the absolute will and arbitrary dominion of another'.[190] In that sense, humans have an inalienable natural right to self-preservation. But we may not infer from this a right to do with others whatever is necessary to preserve oneself from death and pain.

---

[186] Ibid., II.8, 120.   [187] Hobbes, *Leviathan*, I.XIV, p. 202.
[188] Locke, *Second Treatise*, II.6, p. 120.   [189] Ibid., XIII.149, p. 193.
[190] Ibid., XIII.149, p. 193.

Nor may we infer, as Fortin does, a liberty right to commit suicide. Crucially, Locke never speaks of a 'right' to self-preservation, only of a 'law'. As such, it *obliges* an individual 'to preserve himself, and not to quit his station wilfully',[191] just as it *obliges* him not to surrender himself to slavery. Fortin argues that Locke claims only that God has implanted in humans a desire for survival, not that He commands humans to preserve themselves. However, this reading is strangely negligent of the familiar scholastic assertion, going back at least to Thomas Aquinas, that the natural inclination to self-preservation is (somehow) normative. It also violates the clear logic of Locke's own text, which moves from the assertion of the status of the human being as a child and servant of God, to the implication that he is God's property 'made to last during His [God's] ... pleasure', and then to the normative claim that '[e]very one ... is bound to preserve himself'.

A reading of Locke that cares to do justice to his written text reveals that he is far more akin to Grotius and Kant than he is to Hobbes. Unlike Hobbes, and like Grotius, Locke believes that there is such a thing as justice in the state of nature, because that state is ruled by the primordial, God-given law of nature.[192] And unlike Hobbes, and like Kant, he believes that the status or dignity of the human individual generates a natural law comprising duties both to others and to the self.

The upshot of this critique of Fortin, therefore, is that his thesis—which is also Lockwood O'Donovan's—falls: Hobbes did not come to dominate modern rights-talk through Locke.[193] Accordingly, Tuck and Tierney's theses stand: Hobbes's radically individualist and subjectivist conception of an original and sole natural 'right' to self-preservation remained marginal for at least a generation after his death, perhaps longer; and the intellectual tradition stemming from scholastic

---

[191] Ibid., II.6, p. 120.

[192] I observe that this is also David Ritchie's view: 'the idea of a law of nature, which passed from Locke to Rousseau to the fathers of the American republic, came to Locke mainly from Grotius, Pufendorf, and Hooker ... [W]hereas Hobbes makes the laws of nature all simply consequences of the natural instinct of self-preservation, Locke, thinking of his state of nature as a social state, although not yet a political state, includes in his conception of law of nature very much what Thomas Aquinas includes in it' (*Natural Rights*, pp. 39, 42).

[193] What applies to Fortin also applies to Strauss, whose interpretation Fortin follows. As long ago as 1958 John Yolton referred to Strauss's reading of Locke as 'violently distorted', commenting that '[i]t is an odd kind of perversity on Strauss's part which keeps him from finishing Locke's sentence and prevents his readers from seeing the correct meaning of Locke's statements ... There is no ground at all for equating Locke's concept of the state of nature with that in Hobbes' ('Locke on the Law of Nature', *The Philosophical Review*, 64/4 (October 1958), in Paul Sigmund, ed., *The Selected Political Writings of John Locke* (New York: W. W. Norton, 2005), pp. 281, 284, 285). More recently (in 2005) Francis Oakley has written that Strauss's assimilation of Locke to Hobbes defies 'overwhelming textual evidence' and can be sustained only by 'reading between the lines of the texts themselves' (*Natural Law*, pp. 92, 93). Oakley had offered substantiation of his view many years before (Francis Oakley and Elliot Urdang, 'Locke, Natural Law, and God', *Natural Law Forum*, 11 (1966) and Francis Oakley, 'Locke, Natural Law, and God: Again', *History of Political Thought*, 17 (1997)). Fortin's 1999 article offers no rebuttal of Oakley's claim. To the authority of Yolton and Oakley we can add that of Nicholas Wolterstorff, author of *John Locke and the Ethics of Belief* (Cambridge: Cambridge University Press, 1996), who has written: 'I think there is reason to believe that this was ... Locke's view: subjective natural rights are grounded in objective divine law ... Leo Strauss is completely oblivious to the possibility that Locke was in this way carrying on a tradition rather than subverting it' (*Justice*, p. 64 n. 30).

thought, which happily combined the idea of subjective rights with that of an objective moral order, advanced into the modern era through the advocacy of figures as seminal as Grotius and Locke.[194]

It is nevertheless possible, of course, that Hobbes's concept of subjective rights did come to dominate Western culture at a later date. Knud Haakonssen holds that David Hume (1711–76) and Adam Smith (1723–90) 'brought to fruition' Hobbes's morally 'conventionalist' idea of rights.[195] However, even if that is true, Hume and Smith contributed to the development of a Utilitarian tradition that was fiercely critical of natural rights. Besides, Haakonssen makes no claim that Hume and Smith swept all before them. On the contrary, he argues that the early seventeenth-century founder and a mid-eighteenth-century conveyor of 'the modern theory of rights', respectively Grotius and Jean-Jacques Burlamaqui (1694–1748), remained faithful to the scholastic tradition with its concept of 'an objective, metaphysically or religiously based moral order'.[196] Samuel Mintz observes that Hobbes attracted admiration from Utilitarians and legal positivists in the nineteenth century and 'a host of sympathetic commentators' in the twentieth. Nevertheless, he notes that, far from dominating the field, Hobbes continues to be a source of controversy.[197]

It is true that Mary Ann Glendon claims that the malign influence of Hobbes lives on specifically in US law, when she attributes to Hobbes and Locke the tendency of the Anglo-American legal tradition to assert the individual's absolute right to autonomy, contrasting it with the Romano-German legal tradition, which, influenced by Rousseau, is more inclined to let the claims of public good qualify the individual's right to liberty.[198] However, her diagnosis is doubtful for two reasons. First, as we have seen, Locke should not be equated with Hobbes; and second, she later transfers her accusation to J. S. Mill (1806–73).[199]

---

[194] By the same token, Robert P. Kraynack's criticism of Tierney and Tuck fails. He understands them as arguing, wrongly, that the canonists' conception of subjective rights was 'a forerunner of . . . modern natural rights' (*Christian Faith and Modern Democracy: God and Politics in a Fallen World* (Notre Dame, Ind.: University of Notre Dame, 2001), pp. 111–12). His first mistake is to join Fortin in reading Locke as a medium of Hobbes; his second, to identify 'modern natural rights' with Hobbes's conception of them; and his third, to suppose that Tierney and Tuck agree with him on those two points.

[195] Knud Haakonssen, 'The Moral Conservatism of Natural Rights', in Ian Hunter and David Saunders, eds, *Natural Law and Civil Sovereignty: Moral Right and State Authority in Early Modern Political Thought* (Basingstoke and New York: Palgrave, 2002), p. 28. By moral conventionalism Haakonssen means 'the idea that morality is entirely a contingent product of the interaction between individuals' (ibid.).

[196] Haakonssen, 'The Moral Conservatism of Natural Rights', pp. 28, 39.

[197] Mintz, *Hunting of Leviathan*, p. 155. I have been told that, while David Gauthier (1932–) is an example of a contemporary neo-Hobbesian philosopher, his is a rare species and his influence has quickly waned.

[198] Mary Ann Glendon, *Rights Talk: The Impoverishment of Political Discourse* (New York: Free Press, 1991), pp. 13, 34, 40–1, 68, 69, 70.

[199] Ibid., pp. 72–3.

The truth about contemporary culture appears to be that its discussion of rights actually employs a variety of rival concepts and theories—as Ernest Fortin inadvertently acknowledged when he noted that twentieth-century discourse contains the 'pre-modern' ideas of Jacques Maritain and John Finnis, as well as the 'modern' ones of John Rawls and Ronald Dworkin.[200] The mistake of the theological critics of subjective rights—expressing a habit of resentful, uncharitable alienation that is too common among theologians[201]—is to essentialise contemporary rights-talk, prejudging it in the abstract terms of a pejorative ideal-type, instead of actually looking at the phenomenon—or rather, the phenomen*a*. Thus Joan Lockwood O'Donovan refers to '*the* liberal contractarian tradition', bundling together the views of Hobbes, Locke, and Kant as if they were all essentially the same.[202] Thus, too, Oliver O'Donovan writes of modernity as 'a civilizational totality', to which the radically individualist conception of rights is key.[203] But why does he assume that modernity is a totality rather than a somewhat incoherent plurality? Perhaps he means 'modernity' merely as an intellectual system, in which case it would be a coherent whole—a 'totality'—by definition. However, he cannot mean that, since the adjective 'civilisational' denotes an historical, cultural reality and not merely a theoretical construct. No, O'Donovan claims that contemporary Western discourse about rights is predominantly 'modern', and that 'modernity' stems essentially from Hobbes. Sensitive empirical observation and careful intellectual history indicate that neither claim is true: contemporary rights-talk, like contemporary culture as a whole, contains both modern and unmodern elements.[204]

VIII

If there is something problematic about contemporary rights-talk, then, it is not its determination, or even its domination, by Hobbes. There is no such thing as *the* 'modern' concept or theory of subjective rights. Contemporary discussion of rights certainly does not universally assume that, at bottom, positively legal rights are simply the expedient tools of radically individual egos, which are untrammelled by any primordial moral constraints in their natural drive to preserve

---

[200] Fortin, 'On the Presumed Origin', p. 65.
[201] See Nigel Biggar, *Behaving in Public: How to do Christian Ethics* (Grand Rapids, Mich.: Eerdmans, 2011), pp. 95–100.
[202] Lockwood O'Donovan, 'Historical Prolegomena', pp. 52–3. The emphasis is mine.
[203] O'Donovan, 'The Language of Rights', pp. 195–6.
[204] I have deliberately resisted the temptation to join Fortin in saying that contemporary culture contains both 'modern' and '*pre*-modern' elements, for that would be to imply that the latter have been displaced by the former, whereas the claim is precisely that modern and *un*modern elements coexist and vie with one another.

themselves from pain and death. It might well be that some do think this, but it is not self-evident that most do, and no one has demonstrated that that is the case.

Nor does the problem lie with the proprietary paradigm—the concept of a right as the property of an individual. The theological critics are generally not careful to distinguish the proprietary concept as such from Hobbes's specific version of it. Yet it is perfectly coherent to think of a right as an individual's property without supposing that that confers an absolute liberty to do just as he pleases. It may be that in Roman thinking *dominium* denoted a pre-legal sphere of absolute liberty and control,[205] described by Cicero as 'a time when men wandered at large in the fields like animals...[and] did nothing by the guidance of reason...'.[206] Nevertheless, one might expect that, when they adopted the language of *dominium*, medieval Christian thinkers modified its meaning; and there is evidence that they did. Thus Brett observes that, while Ockham did assimilate *ius* to *dominium*, he did not mean the latter 'in the strong sense' (of being unconstrained by natural moral law); rather, he developed 'a notion of subjective natural right connected with the objectively rational order or law of nature'.[207] So if there is such a thing as a natural right, one need not conceive of it amorally, as Cicero (and Hobbes) did.

And as for legal rights, few, if any, are completely impervious to social obligations, and none need be impervious to the demands of natural morality. In statute or customary law, rights are usually specified and often conditional. In time of severe public disturbance, for example, it is common that rights to free speech and expression of religion may be legally suspended. Further, there is nothing about the very concept of a statutory or customary right that makes it absolute or unconditional in the sense that its exercise is immune to the claims of moral law. The idea that one might be morally obliged to constrain or waive one's legal right (e.g. to free speech), or to exercise it in one way rather than another (e.g. by giving one's legal property to the indigent), is perfectly coherent and not entirely unfamiliar.

Their preoccupation with radical individualism, their tendency to identify the very notion of a subjective right with Hobbes (or radically individualist readings of Gerson or Ockham), and their failure clearly and consistently to distinguish natural from legal rights, seem to have prevented the theological critics from duly appreciating the extent to which the medieval development of the concept of subjective rights was specifically designed to give individuals—and civil

---

[205] Tierney, *The Idea of Natural Rights*, p. 17; Tuck, *Natural Rights Theories*, p. 11.

[206] Tuck, *Natural Rights Theories*, p. 33. According to Andrea Alciato (1492–1550), Cicero's vision was typical of 'ancient authors', who 'relate that in the first infancy of humankind men were unsociable...unconscious of religion or of human duties...' (Tuck, *Natural Rights Theories*, p. 36). Alciato's student, the jurist Francois Connan (1508–51), seems to have made it his own, when he wrote that 'the *ius naturale*...relates to man as an animal, prudent and cunning admittedly, but when at home not much different from the beasts' (Tuck, *Natural Rights Theories*, p. 38). This is essentially Hobbes's view.

[207] Brett, *Liberty, Right, and Nature*, p. 51.

associations—legal protection from abuse by other persons, social bodies, and political authorities, not least papal ones. As such the development of subjective rights was a natural expression of the high Christian esteem of the human individual as a subject of God's calling.[208] It is most doubtful that any of the theological critics object to this, and yet it hardly tempers their deep and abiding suspicion of the very concept.

All that said, while most of their criticism shoots wide of the mark, some of it does reach the target. No doubt there is some contemporary rights-talk that is infected with the dismal, Hobbesian view that human motivation is basically egoistic and materialist. Certainly, game-theory, which is popular in some reaches of moral philosophy and social science, assumes it. For those (like me) who think that this view of human being is empirically false, corrosive of individual and social well-being, and politically dangerous, this is a problem.

More generally, there does appear to be a tendency for today's rights-talk to suck the oxygen out of any other kind of moral discourse. Of course, rights imply obligations, but the obligations of rights-*holders* are seldom talked up. And the notion that the exercise of the liberty given by a legal right remains subject to the constraints and demands of moral law, while not entirely unrecognised, is nevertheless uncommon. Whereas we have no trouble at all in confidently asserting our own legal rights or those of others, we become diffident and tongue-tied in talking about duties and virtues and moral law. Rights-talk does not embarrass us, while talk about what is morally right does.[209] It is not that we do not know that there is more to morality than rights. We do, and we show it in many ways. But we do so shyly and obliquely, not directly. That is very curious; it is also very troubling. For a liberal society needs more than legal rights to freedom; it also needs citizens who are capable of using their own freedom well and of respecting that of others. A sustainable liberal society needs citizens who have been so formed in the virtues of humility, forbearance, forgiveness, justice, and charity as to withhold themselves from provoking others and to tolerate their exercise of legal freedom in uncongenial ways. Liberal society cannot live on rights alone.[210]

---

[208] See Maurice de Wulf, 'L'Individu et le groupe dans la scolastique du XIIIe siècle', *Review néo-scolastique de philosophie*, 22/88 (1920): in scholastic social thought, and *pace* Aristotle, 'L'État est pour le bien du citoyen, et ce n'est pas inversement le citoyen qui est pour l'Etat' (pp. 343, 347: 'The state exists for the citizens' good, not, conversely, the citizen for the state's'). For a more nuanced account, see Antony Black, 'Chapter 18: The Individual and Society', *Cambridge History of Medieval Political Thought, c.350–c.1450*, ed. J. H. Burns (Cambridge: Cambridge University Press, 1988). See also Larry Siedentop, *Inventing the Individual: The Origins of Western Liberalism* (London: Allen Lane, 2014).

[209] Onora O'Neill agrees: 'Today duty and virtue remain familiar ethical terms, but both are often seen as old-fashioned, and sometimes as suspect or obsolete' ('Ethical and Political Justification in the Twentieth Century', section 2, p. 3, unpublished paper, delivered at the meeting of the American Philosophical Association in San Diego, March 2018).

[210] O'Neill appears to share this view: 'it is far from clear that human rights standards can be implemented without also relying on and cultivating ethical duties' ('Justice without Ethics: A Twentieth Century Innovation?', unpublished paper, p. 11, due to appear in John Tasioulas, ed., *Cambridge Companion to the Philosophy of Law* (Cambridge: Cambridge University Press, 2020)).

What is more, our public inarticulacy about human goods, moral virtues, and social obligations or duties makes it very difficult for us to recognise the contingency of rights upon other moral considerations, and so upon justice, all things considered in the circumstances. Consequently, notwithstanding the qualifying conditions frequently written into the international covenants or national legislation, we tend to talk about rights as if they were fundamental, absolute, and inalienable, even when we half-acknowledge that their maintenance is financially impossible or subversive of the very political order upon which the whole apparatus of legal rights depends.[211] The poverty of our public ethics makes our rights-talk rigidly imprudent, and so jeopardises its credibility.

Quite why we have become so dangerously tongued-tied about ethical discourse other than rights-talk is not clear. Since the river of culture is usually fed by many different streams, we should not look for a single source—certainly not in William of Ockham or Thomas Hobbes, nor just in political philosophy. More likely, our current diffidence is the product of a confluence of factors. Onora O'Neill observes a 'turn to subjectivity' in the thought of Matthew Arnold in 1867 and the privatised ethics of G. E. Moore's 1903 *Principia Ethica*. She then traces a correlative hostility to external duty from Nietzsche's 1895 *The Antichrist*, through the British 'War Poets' of 1914–18 and W. B. Yeats's 'An Irishman Foresees his Death' (1918), to E. M. Forster's famous 1938 aphorism, 'If I had to choose between betraying my country and betraying my friend, I hope I should have the guts to betray my country' ('What I Believe').[212] This cultural trend toward ethical subjectivism was then confirmed and given philosophical respectability by '[t]he startling success of logical positivism' before and after the Second World War, with its rejection of both duties of justice and ethical duties as 'literally meaningless'.[213]

In *After Virtue* Alasdair MacIntyre concurs (roughly) with O'Neill in seeing 'emotivism' as a proximate cause of contemporary ethical confusion. This non-cognitivist theory of ethical statements was elaborated by C. L. Stevenson in 1944, but had found earlier expression in the work of the logical positivist A. J. Ayer (*Language, Truth, and Logic*, 1936).[214] However, Macintyre regards emotivism as a very late symptom of a much earlier problem reaching, through Nietzsche (1844–1900) and Kierkegaard (1813–55), back beyond the nineteenth century. The original culprit, he discovers, is the flawed ambition of the 'Enlightenment project' to replace the Aristotelian-Christian teleological tradition with a shared, rationally justifiable, secular basis for morality. Yet, according to MacIntyre's

---

[211] As we have seen in Chapter 5, and shall see again in Chapters 8 and 10.
[212] O'Neill, 'Justice without Ethics', pp. 4–7.   [213] O'Neill, 'Justice without Ethics', p. 7.
[214] Alasdair MacIntyre, *After Virtue* (Notre Dame, Ind.: University of Notre Dame Press: Duckworth, 1981), chapters 2 and 3.

story, the project's prime movers are not Hobbes and Locke in the seventeenth century, but David Hume and Denis Diderot in the eighteenth.[215]

To these philosophical sources of our contemporary diffidence about ethics we should surely add two further, and more recent factors: first, the cultural rejection of traditional mores in favour of personal fulfilment, which became widespread in the West in the 1960s, partly in protest against the Vietnam War; and second, the mushrooming of rights-activism in the 1970s, with its exclusive focus on changing the behaviour of states.[216]

The good news is that, precisely because the culture of the West is not a single, impregnable, monolithic 'totality', but rather an unstable plurality of vying alternatives, change is possible. Indeed, in moral philosophy O'Neill already spies the stirrings of something fresh, when she writes that 'now, deeper justifications of the principles of justice are no longer taken to be impossible'.[217]

---

[215] Hobbes attracts only three incidental references in *After Virtue*, according to its index.
[216] See Jan Eckel, 'The Rebirth of Politics from the Spirit of Morality: Explaining the Human Rights Revolution of the 1970s', in Jan Eckel and Samuel Moyn, eds, *The Breakthrough: Human Rights in the 1970s* (Philadelphia: University of Pennsylvania Press, 2014).
[217] O'Neill, 'Justice without Ethics', p. 12.

7

Are there Absolute Rights?

I

In the course of my discussion of natural rights in the first five chapters of this book, I observed that the rhetoric often claims for them an absolute, 'sacred', 'inviolable' status that does not survive scrutiny. Moreover, one of the main objections I formulated against natural rights-talk is that the legally paradigmatic connotation of a certain stability tends to obscure the fact that the existence of a putative natural right is actually contingent upon a range of moral considerations. In other words, it obscures the natural right's conditional status. Further still, where I did recognise some absolute rights (in John Finnis's thinking), I judged that they were either not natural, or too abstract and unspecified to be practically illuminating, or both. Here in this chapter I return to the topic, to consider whether, and how, it can make good sense to talk of absolute rights.

In one sense, any right that is carefully specified is absolute. Once all the appropriate conditions are built into it, it applies always and everywhere. Its application is not dependent on any further conditions. It is absolute—albeit only trivially. That, however, is not what is usually meant by 'an absolute right'. What is usually meant is a right against a kind of action that is wrong 'in itself', which must therefore be always granted and never suspended, no matter what the circumstances—and in particular, no matter what the consequences. It is commonly supposed that the paradigm is the right against torture, and that is what I shall focus on here.[1]

II

Something that is morally wrong in itself is something that no one should ever do, and no one should ever suffer. Torture is commonly assumed to be such a thing. Commonly, then, the word 'torture' is morally loaded, carrying morally pejorative connotations. It refers, not just to a bare, physical action, but also to wrong-making qualities that are supposed to be bound up with it, and which render it, necessarily, immoral.[2] What might these qualities be?

---

[1] For example, see Henry Shue, John Tasioulas, Elizabeth Ashford, and James Griffin in Chapter 5.
[2] In what follows, the reader should be aware that, while the word 'torture' usually carries morally pejorative connotations, sometimes it does not. As we shall see, Matthew Kramer sometimes uses it to denote deliberate pain-infliction that is or might be morally permissible.

For a pacifist, what makes torture wrong is simply that it deliberately inflicts physical or psychological harm on another human being. But for those of us who are not pacifists, the answer has to be more complicated. For proponents (such as me) of Christian 'just war' reasoning, under certain conditions—such as objective injustice, right motive and intention, last resort, and proportionality—it is permissible for someone deliberately to perform harmful acts that he knows will have the effect of punching bloody holes through others' bodies, tearing limbs off them, wrenching their heads from their shoulders, making them vanish altogether in a 'pink mist', and of causing severe psychological distress to those who survive. Therefore, when 'just war' proponents come to the issue of torture, what is immediately striking is that the kinds of physical and psychological damage that torture involves are not necessarily and obviously graver than those permissibly inflicted on the battlefield. This raises the question: If it can be morally right to wound or dismember or kill an enemy soldier, why can it not be right to subject a terrorist prisoner to verbal threats, sleep deprivation, or waterboarding? If torture is immoral, then it does not seem to be because of the objective harm that it does to the tortured.

Here I disagree with views of Jeremy Waldron and Jean Porter, for whom torture is intrinsically evil, mainly because of what it does to the victim. Waldron writes of torture that 'it involves the deliberate, studied, and sustained imposition of pain to the point of agony on a person who is utterly vulnerable, prostrate before his interrogator, and it aims to use that agony to shatter and mutilate the subject's will, twisting it against itself and using it for the purposes of the torturer'.[3] And elsewhere he tells us that it involves 'the savage breaking of the will... inducing a regression of the subject into an infantile state, where the elementary demands of the body supplant almost all adult thought'.[4] Responding to Waldron, Porter elaborates the same view, albeit in Thomistic terms. According to Aquinas, she tells us, a person is the image of God 'insofar he... is the principle of his works, as it were possessing free judgment and power over himself'.[5] This image is present in every human person without exception, including those who exercise their rational freedom in sinful and destructive ways. Nevertheless, it is possible to destroy someone's abilities to express her capacities as an image of God and to experience herself as such. This is what torture does: it 'subverts the will itself by assaulting or undermining the delicate psychic forces that sustain the individual's integrity, sense of well-being and self-command'.[6] Thus it is 'intrinsically cruel', regardless of what motivates it.[7]

---

[3] Jeremy Waldron, *Torture, Terror, and Trade-Offs: Philosophy for the White House* (Oxford: Oxford University Press, 2010), p. 5.

[4] Ibid., p. 233.

[5] Aquinas, *Summa Theologiae*, Ia IIae, introduction; quoted by Porter in 'Torture and the Christian Conscience: A Response to Jeremy Waldron', *Scottish Journal of Theology*, 61/3 (2008), p. 349.

[6] Porter, 'Torture and the Christian Conscience', p. 349.

[7] Ibid., p. 347 n. 16. James Griffin's view is basically the same as Waldron's and Porter's: '[Torture] is used to make someone recant a belief, reveal a secret, "confess" a crime whether guilty or not, abandon

It is important to be aware of what Waldron and Porter have in mind as instances of torture. For Waldron these are 'brutal and degrading techniques... ranging from psychological attacks on the subjects' religious practices and sense of sexual modesty, through techniques such as sleep deprivation, solitary confinement in darkness with rodents and insects, stress positions, the use of heat and cold, and auditory assault by constant noise, all the way to direct physical assaults like severe beatings... repeated waterboardings, and assaults using animals'.[8] For Porter, they range from paradigmatic cases such as stretching on a rack to induce admission of heresy or pulling out fingernails to induce betrayal of names of fellow spies, to the terrors of drowning through waterboarding and humiliation by defacing the victim's sacred scriptures.[9] Sometimes they aim 'to terrorise others by a display of ruthless power'.[10] She explicitly quotes from the testimony of two victims of torture. One is Diana Ortiz, who, at the hands of Guatamalan security forces in 1989, suffered being burned with cigarettes, gang-raped, lowered into a pit filled with human bodies (some grotesquely dead, some still living), and being forced to participate in the torture of another person. Ortiz comments: 'This is the world I lived in: No one cared. No law, no God, no justice, no peace, no hope.'[11] Porter's second witness is Jean Améry, a survivor of the Nazi death camps, who wrote that '[a]nyone who has suffered torture will never again be at ease in the world... Faith in humanity, already cracked with the first slap in the face, then demolished by torture, is never acquired again.'[12]

There are two notable features of this hinterland of assumptions about torture. The first is its refusal to make any moral distinction between stress positions and waterboarding on the one hand, and Nazi death camps on the other. All these methods of coercion are regarded as abominably (if not equally) degrading; all destroy what should be inviolable.[13] The second feature is that the objection to torture is composed of a variety of elements, which are not clearly distinguished. While it concentrates predominantly on the objective harm suffered by the victim, it sometimes diversifies into the torturer's motives and intentions. The talk of mutilation, savagery, brutality, and cruelty necessarily connotes something

a cause or do someone else's bidding. All of these characteristic purposes involve undermining someone else's will, getting them to do what they do not want to do, or are even resolved not to do. In one way or another, they involve an attack on normative agency' (Griffin, *On Human Rights*, p. 52).

[8] Waldron, *Torture*, p. 7.   [9] Porter, 'Torture and the Christian Conscience', p. 346.
[10] Ibid., p. 346.
[11] Diana Ortiz, 'Theology, International Law, and Torture: A Survivor's View', *Theology Today*, 63/3 (October 2006), p. 346); quoted by Porter, 'Torture and the Christian Conscience', p. 350.
[12] Quoted by Ortiz, 'Theology, International law, and Torture', pp. 346–7; quoted by Porter, 'Torture and the Christian Conscience', p. 350.
[13] I agree with Sir Gerald Fitzmaurice in doubting that sleep deprivation, hooding, white noise, stress postures, and severe limitations on food and water need be the same, morally speaking, as having one's finger nails torn out, being slowly impaled on a stake through the rectum, or roasted over an electric grid (Sir Gerald Fitzmaurice, 'Separate Opinion', in *Ireland v. United Kingdom* [Application 5310/71], 18 January 1978, at para. 35; quoted by Waldron, *Torture*, p. 199 n. 39).

malicious about the torturer's motives; and where Waldron mentions the torturer's general aim or intention to elicit and use the victim's pain, Porter refers to his specific aim to use the victim's pain in order to terrorise others.

I am not convinced by these arguments. I am not persuaded that the use of these extreme forms of coercion need be motivated by malice. On the contrary, it seems to me quite plausible that the deliberate infliction of pain on a criminal or terrorist, in order to elicit information, could be impelled by a governing motive of genuine concern for the well-being of innocent fellow-citizens. For sure, to be psychically capable of deliberately inflicting pain on another human being one has to callous oneself against his distress, but not all callousness is vicious. Surgeons have to exercise it, when they cut into the living flesh of patients, where anaesthetics are unavailable; military officers have to exercise it, when they order their comrades to their probable or certain deaths; and indeed, even senior managers have to exercise it, when they resolve to deliver severely disappointing news to failed candidates or sacked colleagues.[14]

Nor am I persuaded that any act that deliberately chooses to inflict pain for some ulterior purpose is intrinsically immoral. That, for example, is exactly what I am doing when, having rugby-tackled the mugger and brought him to the ground, I twist his arm up his back, in order to force him to release my wallet. What is more, one of the proper aims of punishment in general is the communication to the wrongdoer of the wrongness of his action, and toward this end it deliberately causes the wrongdoer to suffer. It *uses* his suffering to press him—to coerce him—to reconsider what he has done. And sometimes this punitive coercion can be very considerable, even taking the form of the destructive force of war.[15] I cannot see anything wicked *as such* about the deliberate infliction of pain.[16]

Nonetheless, both Waldron's and Porter's objections to torture have their centre of gravity in the objective harm done to the tortured, rather than in the motives and intentions of the torturer. Indeed, Porter is explicit in describing torture as 'intrinsically cruel', regardless of its motives. The objective harm, as they see it, is something more radical and devastating than the mere coercion of the will. Waldron speaks of the will being shattered and mutilated; Porter, of its being subverted. In the light of the cases of Ortiz and Améry, to which Porter refers,

---

[14] See Nigel Biggar, *In Defence of War* (Oxford: Oxford University Press, 2013), pp. 117–18.

[15] Let me be quite clear here. While punishment may deliberately aim to cause the wrongdoer to suffer some kind of pain or other, it may not do so for the sake of the wrongdoer's suffering *as such*. Therefore, in that sense, it may not be 'retributivist'. It may, however, deliberately aim to cause suffering as a means of communicating a salutary social rebuke. See *In Defence of War*, pp. 67–9; and 'In Defence of Just War: Christian Tradition, Controversies, and Cases', *De Ethica: A Journal of Philosophical, Theological, and Applied Ethics*, 2/1 (2015), pp. 7–8: <http://www.de-ethica.com/archive/articles/v2/i1/a03/de_ethica_15v2i1a03.pdf>.

[16] Matthew Kramer proposes other morally permissible kinds of the deliberate infliction of pain: aversion therapy, military resistance-training, and rare medical treatment to stop a patient falling into a permanent coma (*Torture and Moral Integrity: A Philosophical Enquiry* (Oxford: Oxford University Press, 2014), pp. 46, 47, 101–3).

I can certainly appreciate how someone's sense of himself as a morally responsible agent in a morally structured world could be crushed, were he to become the helpless object of torture motivated by sadistic malice, which uses the suffering of others to revel in its own absolute power. But I do not yet see that that must happen, were he to be subjected to sleep deprivation or white noise with the aim of eliciting particular information.[17]

Further still, it is not clear to me exactly what kind of rational freedom *remains* in the likes of a Hitler or Pol Pot or fanatical agent of 'Islamic State', which ought not to be compelled. This is a doubt that even finds expression in Thomas Aquinas. It is true that he wrote that 'every man, even the sinner, has a nature which God made, and which as such we are bound to love, whereas we violate it by killing him';[18] and that to kill someone 'who retains his natural dignity is intrinsically evil'.[19] Nevertheless, while Aquinas does attribute to human life a certain objective goodness, he does not consistently think it inalienable. For in another passage in the same *quaestio* he tells us that a sinner may lose his 'human dignity' and lapse into bestial servitude, so as to serve the purposes of others.[20] As with Aquinas, so even with the contemporary liberal philosopher Henry Shue, who, in his classic 1978 article, found himself compelled to ask, '[W]hat sort of integrity could one have violated by torturing Hitler?'[21]

The word 'integrity', however, can mean several different things. It can mean either rational coherence, or personal consistency, or moral uprightness. Clearly in this case we are not talking about the last: in the case of a Hitler there is no moral integrity to violate. That leaves the first two: very delusional world-views and perverse value-systems can have a certain internal intellectual coherence, and they can be the objects of consistent personal commitment. Since the deliberate infliction of pain is not apt to demonstrate the rational incoherence of a world-view, we cannot be talking about the former. That leaves us with the latter: consistent personal commitment.[22] It seems, then, that Shue is incorrect: in

---

[17] Kramer correctly cautions against hyperbole in discussing torture (*Torture and Moral Integrity*, p. 169). *Pace* Elaine Scarry, he holds that, while torture can cause its victim to suffer 'the complete dissolution of their epistemic access to the world' through all-consuming agony, in many cases this is either partial or temporary (ibid., p. 167). And *pace* Jeremy Wisnewski, he denies that torture always aims to destroy the agent and 'demolish the victim's mental faculties' (ibid., pp. 170, 171). On the contrary, sometimes it aims to compel the victim to exercise his agency, say, in divulging information (ibid., p. 172).

[18] Aquinas, *Summa Theologiae*, Blackfriars edn, vol. 38, 'Injustice' (2a2ae, 63–79), ed., trans., and introd. Marcus Lefébre, OP (London: Eyre & Spottiswoode, 1975), 2a2ae, q. 64, a. 6, resp., pp. 36, 37.

[19] Ibid., 2a2ae, q. 64, a. 2, ad 3, pp. 24, 25. The Latin is less proprietorial: 'someone remaining in his dignity'.

[20] Ibid., 2a2ae, q. 64, a. 2, ad 3, p. 25.

[21] Henry Shue, 'Torture', in Sanford Levinson, ed., *Torture: A Collection* (Oxford: Oxford University Press, 2004), p. 60 n. 11. We might well suppose that, even if no such rational or moral dignity in fact remains in the likes of a Hitler, it would nevertheless be morally dangerous for us to presume to *know* so. Still, I strain to understand what kind of dignity might remain.

[22] This is more clearly the conception of integrity operative in Shue's later thinking, where he describes what torture seeks to overcome as 'a person's identity, self, or personality, embodying her

torturing a Hitler (to get him to betray his cause) we would certainly be *assaulting* his consistent personal commitment and seeking to break it. But would we be *violating* it—that is, would we be doing anything wrong in assaulting it? Shue's quizzical question suggests that he doubts it. So do I. Surely there are malicious commitments of the will that deserve to be broken or shattered or subverted—if they can be?[23]

Shue's case against torture does not operate simply in terms of the duty to respect the victim's integrity. It also holds that what distinguishes torture from morally justified killing in war, and specifies its moral wrongness, is its objective unfairness, which consists in the torturer enjoying total dominance over his completely defenceless victim.[24] This argument fails for several reasons. One is that, to be justified, belligerency must have some prospect of winning a war; and in order to win a war, one side must achieve overwhelming dominance over the other. Therefore, for example, there is nothing morally wrong with knocking the enemy's air force out of the skies, and then proceeding to bombard his troops on the ground, when they lack anti-aircraft guns. Nor is there anything wrong with

---

commitments and values [whatever they are]. One's identity as a person is the "resistance" that must be broken!' ('Torture (2015)', in Henry Shue, *Fighting Hurt: Rule and Exception in Torture and War* (Oxford: Oxford University Press, 2016), p. 133; also p. 142).

[23] Matthew Kramer agrees: 'As a moral matter, the repudiation of a hideous aspect of oneself is exactly what is permissible and obligatory. Psychologically wrenching though it might be—at least initially—the shedding of one's viciously immoral detachments is not ethically untoward in any way' (*Torture and Moral Integrity*, p. 131). Quite how he squares this with his endorsement of David Sussman's view, however, is not obvious. Sussman argues that the distinctive wrongness of torture lies in its inducing 'a kind of forced self-betrayal', in which the victim is made to experience himself 'not just as a passive victim, but as an active accomplice in his own debasement' (Sussman, 'What's Wrong with Torture?', *Philosophy and Public Affairs*, 33 (2005), pp. 4, 23; quoted by Kramer in *Torture and Moral Integrity*, pp. 155, 157). The 'debasement' appears to consist in the victim being forced, through his own body, to comply with the torturer's demands and to betray his cause. In other words, what is wrong with torture is that it sets the victim's body at war with his intellectual and moral commitments—it assaults his psychosomatic integrity. In the quotation above, however, Kramer sees nothing at all wrong with this in the case of someone whose commitments are 'viciously immoral'. Nor does Jeff McMahan: 'If a person has made it the case through his own autonomous choices that the only way to prevent his previous action from killing innocent people is to exploit his vulnerability in order to turn his will against himself, then that may be precisely what his exercise of his autonomous agency has made him liable to have done to him' ('Torture in Principle and Practice', *Public Affairs Quarterly*, 22/2 (April 2008), p. 119); 'Justice requires that what is, for us, an unavoidable harm be distributed to [the terrorist] rather than being allowed to be inflicted by him upon the innocent' (ibid., p. 118).

Kramer also offers two further criticisms of 'Kantian' objections to torture such as Jeremy Waldron's, which appear to be based on a view of the inviolable value of consistent personal commitment—that is, of 'integrity' as personal autonomy. This makes torture wrong because it fails to respect a person's dignity by destroying her 'ability to control and regulate her actions in accordance with her own apprehension of norms and reasons that apply to her' and the capability 'of giving... an account of herself' ('How Law Protects Dignity', *Cambridge Law Journal*, 71 (2012), p. 202). Kramer's telling criticisms of this view are first, that it cannot account for the wrongness of the torture of animals or of humans who lack the capability for reflective agency (*Torture and Moral Integrity*, pp. 150, 152, 162); and second, that it cannot account for torture that aims to use the victim's suffering to intimidate other people, rather than to break his will (ibid., p. 49).

[24] Shue, 'Torture', pp. 49–51.

using long-range artillery to shell enemy troops, when they have none of their own with which to reply in kind. In war, if one can render oneself invulnerable and the enemy defenceless, then one should; that is how victory is won. Justice here does not require the equal distribution of power; if it did, war would be interminable.[25]

In war, of course, once an enemy has become incapable of threatening harm and has surrendered, no moral justification for harming him remains. He might still be party to a threat, insofar as he has knowledge of plans for further attacks by his comrades; but he poses no direct threat himself. According to the Law of Armed Conflict, he may not be coerced into telling what he knows, even if the cause that he serves is gravely unjust. Morally, he ought to betray such a cause; legally, he may not be compelled to. The reason for this is to establish an unambiguous, practicable norm, and to erect a clear barrier against abuse: once an enemy has surrendered, one may not compel him to reveal anything beyond his name, rank, and number. In the case of war, where civil laws governing the infliction of physical harm have been relaxed, and where the passions of fear and hatred are unusually high and widespread, the need for such a norm is unusually strong.

However, proposals for the morally justified infliction of pain typically refer to a significantly different kind of case: namely, a civil situation where a captured terrorist knows of plans that intend the imminent slaughter of civilians on a massive scale. This is the so-called 'ticking bomb' scenario. Here the terrorist's knowledge concerns, not a legitimate military operation, but a gravely immoral and criminal act. He might be defenceless, but he is still complicit in a developing act of aggression that is seriously wicked.[26] What is more, the context is one where the institutions of civil society are functioning effectively, stringent laws against

[25] David Decosimo also seeks to distinguish torture from just belligerency in terms of the former's kind of 'domination', understood paradigmatically as the power exercised by masters over slaves and conquerors over conquered ('Killing and the Wrongness of Torture', *Journal of the Society of Christian Ethics*, 36/1 (Spring/Summer 2016)). Such power is 'arbitrary', since it is non-reciprocal, lacking in mutual respect, unaccountable to the dominated, and irrational (ibid., pp. 188–9). The tortured is 'utterly vulnerable, entirely at the torturer's mercy' (ibid., p. 189). The torturer is 'malevolent' (ibid., p. 191), aiming proximately 'to so co-opt [the] victim's agency as to reach into his soul and essentially make him [the torturer's] puppet' (ibid., pp. 184–5). Torture is therefore 'soul-violating' or 'soul-terrorizing' (ibid., p. 185) and quite distinct from just belligerency (ibid., p. 193). Decosimo is correct, of course, that the tortured lies helplessly at the mercy of the torturer. He is wrong, however, to think that such dominance distinguishes the torturer from the just warrior. He is also wrong to assume that anyone in such a position of dominance must be malevolent and must use his dominant power arbitrarily. It is quite possible that the torturer will have no interest in messing with the 'soul' of the tortured, as distinct from eliciting salutary information from him. Moreover, if Decosimo's 'soul' is the same as Shue's personal 'integrity' or 'identity', then his argument falls prey to the same objections.

[26] Manfred Nowak locates the specific wrongness of torture in 'the use of force and coercion against a *powerless* human being': 'As soon as the person is arrested, handcuffed and, therefore, *powerless*, i.e., under the direct control of the police officer, no further use of force is permitted' ('What's in a Name? The Prohibitions on Torture and Ill Treatment Today', in Gearty and Douzinas, *Cambridge Companion to Human Rights Law*, pp. 316, 319; the emphases are mine). Normally, this would be true: where someone no longer poses a threat, because he has been disarmed—because he is 'innocent' in the technical sense of 'non-harming' (*in-nocens*)—the use of force against him would be disproportionate. However, the captured terrorist continues to pose a threat, insofar as he is complicit in an ongoing operation to commit a terrorist atrocity; and unlike the captured soldier who is complicit in an

causing physical harms are generally authoritative, the level of social security and its perception is consequently high, and the passions of anxiety and hatred are largely contained. In such a situation, therefore, to permit the coercive extraction of life-saving information would incur fewer risks of precipitating widespread abuse.

Nevertheless, it might be argued that, whereas the soldier can always end the violent coercion to which he is subject by surrendering, the victim of torture cannot.[27] That would certainly be true of someone subject to sadistic torture, whose purpose is to excite and prolong the torturer's pleasure, but it would not be true of a subject of aggressive interrogation, where the victim knows the information that is sought. For here, the victim is free at any time to bring an end to his own suffering by telling the truth. Shue concedes this in the case of someone not very fervently committed to her cause, but denies it in the case of one who is very dedicated and so cannot collaborate without denying her 'highest values'.[28] He deems it morally unacceptable to make the 'denial of one's self' a condition of release.[29] However, as we have already seen, Shue undermines his own position, when he admits that 'there are probably rare individuals so wicked as...to lack any integrity worthy of respect'.[30]

III

Objections to torture that proceed in terms of the objective harm done to the victim are not, it seems to me, cogent. Matthew Kramer agrees, which is why he shifts the weight of his own critique from the objective foot onto the subjective one. What he finds decisively objectionable lies in the disposition of the torturer.[31]

It follows that sometimes there is nothing morally wrong with the deliberate infliction of pain, since there is nothing objectionable about the agent's disposition. Sometimes that disposition can be benevolent and use the infliction of pain with the intention of promoting the well-being of the one inflicted—as in aversion

---

ongoing military operation, the informed terrorist is complicit in a criminal act of mass murder, which he retains the power to stop.

[27] Shue does argue this, when he (with David Luban) writes: '[P]art of the special wrongfulness of torture lies...in the limitlessness of the extent to which the victim is at the mercy of the torturer...Unlike even war, torture has no natural end. It ends when the torturer chooses to end it' (David Luban and Henry Shue, 'Mental Torture: A Critique of Erasures in U.S. Law', *Georgetown Law Journal*, 100 (2012), p. 859; quoted by Shue in 'Torture (2015)', pp. 138–9).

[28] Shue, 'Torture', p. 55.   [29] Ibid., p. 55.   [30] Ibid., p. 136 n. 14.

[31] Kramer uses the word 'torture' in a morally indeterminate fashion, to refer at different times to morally wrong acts and morally right or permissible ones. Since 'torture' usually carries morally pejorative connotations, I think that Kramer's usage risks confusion. Therefore, in my discussion of his thinking, I use 'intentional pain-infliction' to refer to a morally neutral action, and I reserve 'torture', 'torturer', and 'tortured' to refer to an immoral action, its agent, and its victim.

therapy, military resistance-training, and rare medical treatment to stop a patient falling into a permanent coma.[32] If that intention is genuine, then the pain-infliction will be minimally invasive, causing no more than is necessary—that is, it will be proportionate to its end.[33]

It also follows that where the primary intention is 'inherently illegitimate'—as in the sadistic pleasure of the torturer or the gratuitous humiliation of the tortured—we can know sufficiently that the deliberate infliction of pain is morally impermissible.[34] At one point Kramer moves to broaden the wrong-making subjective disposition of the torturer to include any hostility or indifference toward the bodily and psychological well-being of the victim.[35] But then he recognises that such attitudes can also find expression in morally legitimate instances of 'ephemerally incapacitative torture',[36] thereby implying—as he should—that there are morally good and bad kinds of hostility and indifference.[37]

Instead, Kramer proceeds to locate the subjective factor that makes most torture morally impermissible in a version of St Augustine's *libido dominandi*—the lustful will to dominate. This sullies the moral integrity of the torturer by using the victim's pain 'as an instrument and an expression of his ascendance over her' and by elevating himself to 'a position of overweening dominance . . . a godlike position'.[38] This is particularly true of calamity-averting interrogational torture, which is 'minutely controlling' and reduces the victim to an 'instrument or marionette' or 'a mere plaything'.[39] Every instance of such torture is characterised

---

[32] Kramer, *Torture and Moral Integrity*, pp. 46, 47, 101–3. Aversion therapy and military resistance-training also show that 'veritable torture' can be consensual: 'the open-ended infliction of severe pain for the purpose of . . . overcoming a harmful addiction or toughening one's resistance to future hardships is outright torture even when the person who undergoes the pain has readily consented to the ordeal' (ibid., p. 112). Therefore, even if lack of consent were always a wrong-making feature, it is not necessarily a characteristic of torture (ibid., p. 113). But 'the absence of genuine control' is not always a wrong-making feature, since some deliberately agony-inducing conduct that intends to avert a patient's lapse into a coma can be morally permissible, even though the patient lacks genuine control over the termination of the conduct (ibid., p. 113 n. 31). While Kramer usually deploys 'torture' in a morally indeterminate way, he is half-aware of the word's usual, morally pejorative connotations. Thus, at one point, he describes the intentional infliction of agony as 'non-torturous', in order to make clear that he means 'not the morally impermissible kind'.

[33] Kramer stipulates the 'Minimal Invasion Principle', although he does not explicitly recognise its role as a test of the genuinely benevolent character of intention (ibid., pp. 177–8).

[34] Ibid., p. 176.   [35] Ibid., p. 185.

[36] Ibid., p. 192. 'Ephemerally incapacitative torture' deliberately inflicts severe pain in order to stop someone performing an action, but intends no permanent ill-effects. When the action to be stopped is seriously wrongful, such pain-infliction can be morally permissible (ibid., p. 77).

[37] Someone who does serious wrong, whether intentionally or through culpable negligence, deserves to be met with hostility out of due love for the good he has damaged. Such hostility can be governed by love and need not be vindictive or disproportionate. As regards indifference, I have already argued in favour of a virtuous kind of professional callousness. And in referring to certain morally objectionable dispositions as 'heartlessly indifferent' and 'stonily indifferent' (ibid., p. 77), Kramer himself signals by his qualifications that indifference is not by definition stone-hearted.

[38] Ibid., p. 192.

[39] Ibid., pp. 181, 194. Kramer deploys Jonathan Bennett's distinction between omissions and acts to find a moral difference between 'ephemerally incapacitative torture' and 'calamity-averting interroga-tional torture'. Whereas the former aims to prevent or stop the performance of a wrongful action, the

by 'hubris',[40] where the torturers depart from 'the elementary modesty that is required of them as agents interacting with another sentient creature' and so render their conduct wrongful as a mode of 'overweening self-aggrandizement'.[41]

Kramer's account appears plausible only by conflating two distinct elements: the objective asymmetry of power in the relationship between torturer and tortured, and the subjective attitude of the torturer. The fact that one human being—whether a soldier or a torturer—stands in a position of invulnerable dominance over another certainly presents him with a grave temptation to use his untrammelled power abusively. Sinful humans enjoy power. Sometimes they become addicted to it. And sometimes their lust becomes sadistic or murderous. Nevertheless, it is not true that everyone who finds another person at their mercy becomes merciless, casting off all moral constraints, and glorying in his own godlike freedom for capricious power. My own reflection on human behaviour and my study of military experience indicates that the connection between objective dominance and subjective hubris is not psychologically necessary. Kramer thinks otherwise, telling us of the 'hubris that is characteristic of every instance of calamity-averting interrogational torture'.[42] This is an empirical claim, however, for which he offers no evidence at all; and until I find such evidence, I shall continue to doubt the claim.[43]

IV

I do not think that the attempts by Waldron, Porter, and Shue to locate the wrong-making feature of all torture in what is done objectively to the victim—whether it be kinds of physical or psychic damage or injustice-as-unfairness—succeed. I agree with Kramer that the intentional infliction of severe pain on another person can be analysed into morally different kinds, and I sometimes agree—more or less—with his evaluation of them.[44] On the one hand, 'edifying' pain-

---

latter aims to impel the performance of a calamity-averting act of disclosure. Therefore, Kramer asserts, the former is morally permissible, but the latter is not. Why does he diverge from Bennett in regarding this (alleged) instance of the act/omission distinction as morally significant? Because thwarting an action is 'much less minutely directive . . . less fine-grained in its controllingness' than forcing the performance of one (ibid., pp. 194–6, 198). And what, we might ask, is wrong with fine-grained control? It puts the torturer in a position of godlike dominance and so makes what he does 'a mode of overweening self-aggrandizement' (ibid., p. 196). I doubt that this is necessarily so, however, as I am about to argue in the text.

[40] Ibid., p. 198.   [41] Ibid., p. 196.   [42] Ibid., p. 198.

[43] Kramer tells us that he is not conducting a psychological or sociological study of torturers, but a moral and philosophical assessment, asking, 'What are the moral bearings of the general outlooks that are credibly ascribable to people who inflict the agony of torture on others?' (ibid., p. 190). But how can we know what is 'credibly ascribable' without reference to what we (think we) know about the experience of being a torturer? Such reference is, by definition, empirical.

[44] Ibid., pp. 56–104.

infliction such as aversion therapy, military resistance-training, or medical treatment to avert a coma is morally permissible because it is benevolent, intending to
benefit the inflicted, and insofar as it commands their explicit or presumed
consent. What Kramer refers to as 'ephemerally incapacitative torture', which
intends to prevent a grave wrong by disabling a wrongdoer whose wrongdoing has
forfeited his right not to be harmed,[45] and which proportions its means to that
end, is also permissible. (Clarity would have been better served here by talking of
morally permissible 'ephemerally incapacitative *intentional pain-infliction*'.) On
the other hand, torture that is sadistic is ruled out by its motive. That which aims
to humiliate or to assert ethnic or racial dominance is ruled out by both motive
and intention. That which aims to terrorise or extort other people is ruled out by
its intention, and, if the tortured is innocent, also by justice. And that which is
'extravagantly [or demonically] reckless'[46] is ruled out because it is disproportionate, exceeding what is necessary to realise a legitimate intention (and thus casting
doubt on the genuineness of such a declared intention).

But what about 'punitive' torture? As I see it, punishment is properly retributive
in form, but not retributivist in aim. That is to say, it is always a hostile response to
wrongdoing, meting out deserved contradiction and opposition, offering due pay-
back. As such, it is retributive. However, the ends of its pay-back remain an open
question. Its proper ends include defence, deterrence, communication, and ultimately repentance and reconciliation. They do not include the suffering of the
wrongdoer *for the sake of creating an equality of misery between victim and
perpetrator*, for such a state confers no worthwhile benefit.[47] In that sense, then,
punishment should not be retributivist.

Still, all retributive punishment involves intentional pain-infliction. Does it
follow that torture may be a specific form of punishment to which a convicted
criminal is sentenced by a court? No, insofar as torture is by definition malevolent,
since either it would exceed what is necessary for any of the proper ends of

---

[45] Ibid., p. 186. According to Kramer, whereas the victim of ephemerally incapacitative torture can
forfeit his right (against intentional subjection to severe pain), the victim of interrogational torture
cannot (ibid., p. 186). Since it is conceivable that the latter is guilty of graver wrong-doing than the
former, the forfeiture seems not to depend on the victim's wrongdoing at all. Accordingly, Kramer tells
us that the interests of a mass-murdering terrorist in being free from excruciating pain 'are of no
positive ethical weight' (ibid., p. 187), and yet he still insists that such a terrorist retains his right against
interrogational torture. What distinguishes the cases morally, in Kramer's eyes, is that interrogational
torture is always an expression of the torturer's self-aggrandising desire for godlike dominance, whereas
ephemerally incapacitative torture need not be. The forfeiture of the right against such torture,
therefore, is made to depend on the subjective disposition of the torturer (ibid., p. 187). However,
the coherence of Kramer's account is not aided by his statement on the next page that every person is
endowed with 'weakly absolute inviolability' by dint of her status as a reflective agent (ibid., p. 188).
This implies that the wrongness of all torture lies in the *objective harm* done to the victim. It also
implies that *all* kinds of 'torture' (or, as I would put it, 'deliberate pain-infliction') involve such
wrongful harm—even when it is morally correct that it should be done (hence the inviolability is
only 'weakly absolute').
[46] Ibid., p. 75.
[47] The obvious unworthwhile benefit is the (temporary) slaking of the victim's thirst for revenge.

punishment (and so be disproportionate) or it would not be able to serve them at all. Incarceration is sufficient for defence, and incarceration's loss of liberty is sufficient for deterrence. Since the imposition of severe pain is coercive, not communicative—since it is apt to force rather than persuade—it conduces to mere compliance rather than repentance and genuine reconciliation with society. And torture that aims to even up the score between a wrongdoer and his victim by balancing the latter's suffering with the former's is a retributivist form of retribution, and therefore lacks moral justification.[48]

<h1 style="text-align:center">V</h1>

One further species remains to be considered: interrogational pain-infliction, designed to elicit information. If this is to be morally permissible at all, it must be retributive—that is, directed against someone guilty of grave wrongdoing. Might it be designed to elicit information about historic wrongs, with a view to initiating criminal proceedings against other wrongdoers? Arguably not, since the need is not urgent enough to warrant measures so drastic. What, then, about a case of a very grave crime that is in process and is not yet complete? Could pain-infliction be morally permissible then, to obtain information necessary and sufficient to cut off the crime? Kramer's answer is, at first sight, very odd indeed. He tells us that, all other things being equal, it would be at once morally impermissible *and* morally obligatory. I will return to that paradox later. Here, let me recall that the reason Kramer thinks that calamity-averting interrogational pain-infliction is always impermissible is that he believes that it is always vitiated by the self-aggrandising will-to-godlike-dominance. (In other words, he thinks that such pain-infliction must always be 'torture'.) I have already explained above why I doubt that. So, if the moral wrongness of interrogational torture does not lie there, where else might it lie?

One possibility that lies neither in the objective wrong done to the victim, nor in the subjective vice of the torturer, is interrogational pain-infliction's inefficacy: the fact that it does not work, since it does not produce information that can be relied upon. If the deliberate infliction of pain upon another human being is to be morally justified, it has at least to produce a good effect that can be reckoned proportionate. So, if interrogational pain-infliction is ineffective, then it cannot possibly be moral. This is a highly controversial issue. On the one hand, Michael Gross reports that there is 'emerging, although relatively scant, evidence' that

---

[48] Since he is a legal philosopher, it is understandable that Kramer considers 'punitive torture' only in the narrow sense of a judicial sentence upon a convicted criminal (ibid., pp. 39–40, 69–72). As such he considers it morally impermissible (ibid., p. 186)—as do I. What he does not consider is torture as punitive and retributive in a broader, moral sense.

aggressive interrogation techniques do not work (because they produce false or stale information) and that other methods such as cultivating trust or using informants work better—although he concedes that the evidence falls short of proof.[49] Yuval Ginbar, on the other hand, is less equivocal. Invoking the experience of both Israel and the United States,[50] he asserts that '[i]t would be futile to argue that interrogational torture is never effective in the immediate sense'.[51] David Omand, formerly Intelligence and Security Coordinator in the British government's Cabinet Office 2002–5, seems to confirm Ginbar's assertion, when he writes that '[a]lthough some of the methods used by the US on those captured were not accepted as legitimate by the UK, the intervention in Afghanistan did provide valuable intelligence that, in the words of the UK parliamentary oversight committee "saved lives"'.[52] Since Omand knows whereof he speaks, I am disposed to believe his testimony and to conclude that interrogational pain-infliction can sometimes work.[53]

If that is so, then to refrain from it—all other considerations apart—is to weaken society's defences. It is to forgo one effective means of gaining advantage over a menacing enemy. It is to incur a social cost. I once asked a serving officer if the British security and intelligence services used interrogational pain-infliction. Without hesitating, he said, 'No.' But then he added, referring to terrorist prisoners: 'We can't touch them. We can't even threaten them. And they know it. And they laugh at us.' Now, while the officer was expressing frustration, I did not get the impression that he was yearning to have his interrogating hands untied. It is one thing to suffer being laughed at, when you know that you are impotent. It is another to suffer it, when you know that you are playing the long game, and that the last laugh may yet be yours. And to forswear aggressive interrogation in order to retain the moral high ground is to play the long game.

---

[49] Michael L. Gross, *Moral Dilemmas of Modern War: Torture, Assassination, and Blackmail in an Age of Asymmetric Conflict* (Cambridge: Cambridge University Press, 2010), p. 123. Reflecting on his experience as the Senior Psychologist involved in gathering intelligence from prisoners of war for the British government during and after the Second World War, Cyril Cunningham observed: 'The best interrogator I ever met, the one who trained me, had the demeanour of an unctuous parson' (Cyril Cunningham, Letter to *The Times*, 25 November 1971; quoted by Yuval Ginbar, *Why Not Torture Terrorists? Moral, Practical, and Legal Aspects of the 'Ticking Bomb' Justification for Torture* (Oxford: Oxford University Press, 2008), p. 126).

[50] Ginbar, *Why Not Torture Terrorists?*, p. 265.   [51] Ibid., p. 125.

[52] David Omand, *Securing the State* (London: Hurst, 2010), p. 175.

[53] Henry Shue has recently argued that 'we have no empirical basis on which to believe that interrogational torture is the most effective form of interrogation' ('Torture (2015)', p. 143), citing in support the testimony of one US Air Force interrogator, 'Matthew Alexander', who 'personally has conducted three hundred interrogations and supervised more than a thousand, and who... believes that alternatives to torture are more effective' (ibid., p. 145). This, of course, does not support the claim that interrogational pain-infliction can never be effective. Indeed, since Shue would have made that claim, had he been able to, the fact that he does not implies that it can indeed be effective in certain circumstances. Further, while I have no reason to doubt that in many or most cases psychologically astute interrogation is more fruitful than pain-infliction, I do doubt that all cases would permit sufficient time and patience for the former.

A concern to retain the moral high ground might look like a rather precious, fastidious preoccupation—a narcissistic obsession with keeping one's hands clean. But it need not be that at all. There might be strong prudential reasons for retaining the high ground and bearing the short-term costs of doing so. For example, crucial to winning a counter-terrorist campaign is the business of 'draining the swamp', of robbing terrorists of popular support, of winning hearts and minds. That is certainly a major consideration in present British counter-terrorist efforts to suppress home-grown Islamic jihadism, given the showing of a 2006 survey that 13 per cent of British Muslims regarded the London suicide bombers of 7 July 2005 as martyrs.[54] That 13 per cent amounted to over 200,000 people—which is a much, much larger pool of supporters and potential recruits than that ever enjoyed by the IRA in the recent 'Troubles' in Northern Ireland. If the British government were known to subject terrorist complotters to interrogational torture, however proportionate, its efforts to woo British Muslims would be severely damaged. This fact, therefore, gives the government a strong political, prudential reason to eschew such interrogation and to grant all British citizens a positive legal right against it.

What is morally wrong with interrogational pain-infliction, then, is not the objective harm it does to the inflicted, nor the necessary vitiation of the inflicter, nor the ineffectiveness of the infliction. What is wrong with it is its political counter-productiveness—and in that sense its disproportion, the means not being apt to the end. That wrongful feature would be sufficient to rule it out in some cases. Proportionality, however, is a prudential feature, not a deontological one; and prudential features do wax and wane according to circumstances. So, we cannot be sure that interrogational pain-infliction would *always* be politically counterproductive and so disproportionate. Therefore, it cannot ground an absolute moral prohibition of it.

VI

Perhaps what could ground such things is the moral damage it does to the interrogator and to the institutions that support him. Certainly, Jean Porter thinks so. Making no distinctions, she writes that '[t]orture is cruel, and it inevitably renders its practitioners cruel'.[55] This is because our good intentions cannot keep our dispositions toward others detached 'from the immediate effects of our actions ... from what it is that we are actually doing, from the immediate relation between ourselves and the world that this act, here and now, establishes'.[56] Torture is intrinsically cruel, she tells us, because it 'requires the torturer to override the

---

[54] See <http://www.populus.co.uk/the-times-itv-news-muslim-77-poll-050706.html>.
[55] Porter, 'Torture and the Christian Conscience', p. 351.   [56] Ibid., p. 352.

natural aversion to hurting' and may make it enjoyable: 'the practice of torture initially requires, and then fosters, a willingness to hurt another, which can readily lead to positive pleasure in the infliction of pain and humiliation'.[57] This in turn makes it impossible to proportion the infliction of pain to what is strictly necessary.[58]

This is not true, however. For sure, in order deliberately to inflict suffering on another human being, an aggressive interrogator has to callous himself. But, as I have already pointed out, that is what surgeons operating without anaesthetic have to do, as well as commanding generals, when they order units to sustain 100 per cent casualties. Such professional callousness need not make a monster out of a man. As Winston Churchill wrote of General Douglas Haig (1861–1928), who presided over the slaughter that was the Battle of the Somme in 1916: '[h]e presents to me in those red years the same mental picture as a great surgeon before the days of anaesthetics:... intent upon the operation, entirely removed in his professional capacity from the agony of the patient... He would operate without excitement... and if the patient died, he would not reproach himself'. But then Churchill adds: 'It must be understood that I speak only of his professional actions. Once out of the theatre, his heart was a warm as any man's.'[59]

There is one important difference, however, between the surgeon and the battlefield general on the one hand, and the interrogational pain-inflicter on the other: the former have no interest in causing pain as such, whereas the latter deliberately seeks it. Some might argue that to intend pain as a means is to intend an intrinsic evil, which is always immoral. But if it is an evil, it is a non-moral one. Pain is obviously not good, but whether its infliction involves *moral wrong* depends on motive, intention, and proportion. As I have already indicated, I cannot see anything morally wrong *as such* with deliberately causing pain to a mugger by pushing his arm up his back, in order to get him to release a stolen wallet, or with deliberately causing suffering to a wrongdoer, in order to communicate to him the wrongness of what he has done.

Of course, it is possible that an interrogator who starts off wanting to cause pain strictly as a proportionate means toward obtaining life-saving information will end up wanting to cause it for the sake of his own sadistic pleasure. This is certainly possible, but is it necessary? Porter herself suggests not, when she writes that torture 'may' make hurting other people enjoyable, and that an initial willingness to hurt 'can' become a positive pleasure. 'May' and 'can' do not add up to 'does' or 'must'. Nevertheless, given human sinfulness, given our *libido dominandi*, given the fact that we often find the sheer domination of other people to be deeply satisfying, the psychological forces tending to corruption are indeed great. Jeremy Waldron makes the point well:

---

[57] Ibid., p. 352.   [58] Ibid., p. 353.
[59] Winston Churchill, *Great Contemporaries* (London: Thornton Butterworth, 1937), p. 227.

the use of torture is not an area in which human motives are trustworthy. Sadism, sexual sadism, the pleasure of indulging brutality, the love of power, and the enjoyment of the humiliation of others—these all-too-human characteristics need to be kept very tightly under control, especially in the context of war and terror, where many of the usual restraints on human action are already loosened. If ever there was a case for an Augustinian suspicion of the idea that basic human depravity can be channeled to social advantage, this is it. Remember too that we are not asking whether these motives can be judicially regulated in the abstract. We are asking whether they can be regulated in the kind of circumstances of fear, anger, stress, danger, panic, and terror in which, realistically, the hypothetical case must be posed.[60]

Therefore, given the high risk of the moral corruption of the interrogators, we might reasonably decide against making a normal practice of interrogational pain-infliction, lest it become torture.

VII

What is more, the risk of corrupting individual interrogators is not the only one. There is also the risk of corrupting social institutions. This plays an important, if secondary, role in Waldron's argument. 'Torture metastasizes', he tells us; 'it infects all aspects of a state's operation'—not least its legal system.[61] He warns of a slippery slope: once the prohibition on torture is removed, it will become more difficult to defend the prohibition of lesser evils. Against those who argue that a slide can always be halted by the making of rational distinctions, he retorts that the fate of legal systems hangs less on philosophical precision than on social acceptability; and that, while we cannot be sure about the effects on the rest of a legal system of relaxing the prohibition on torture, the gravity of the risks make caution reasonable.[62] In empirical corroboration of his worries, he cites Hannah Arendt's observation that the tradition of racist administration in African

---

[60] Waldron, *Torture*, p. 221.

[61] Ibid., p. 5. Waldron acknowledges that the best account of this point is Henry Shue's: 'Any judgment that torture could be sanctioned in an isolated case without seriously weakening existing inhibitions against the moral general use of torture rests on empirical hypotheses about the psychology and politics of torture. There is considerable evidence of torture's metastatic tendency' ('Torture', *Philosophy and Public Affairs*, 7 (1978), reprinted in Levinson, *Torture*, p. 58).

[62] Waldron, *Torture*, pp. 243–6. Yuval Ginbar makes a similar slippery-slope argument, holding that 'it is impossible in practice to erect an efficient wedge which would allow the production of [torture's] justified results while barring the unjustified ones' (*Why Not Torture Terrorists?*, p. 113), and that the result would be, not just the suffering of innocents, but the corrupting of the judicial and medical professions and the weakening of international mechanisms for the protection of human rights (ibid., p. 115).

colonies eased the acceptance of atrocious oppression in mid-twentieth-century Europe.[63]

The empirical evidence, however, appears indecisive. Arendt (1906-75) does not argue that colonial racism made the perpetration of genocide in Europe more socially acceptable to *all* the colonisers. She does not establish a *necessary causal connection* such as would corroborate Waldron's slippery slope speculation. Moreover, the claim that torture naturally tends to metastasise has not gone unchallenged. Richard Posner asserts baldly that history does not support the claim that recourse to torture causes a society to sink into barbarism—torture in Algeria did not barbarise France; nor torture in Northern Ireland, the UK; nor torture against the Intifada in the West Bank, Israel.[64] Similarly, Michael Gross has written:

> There is little evidence to suggest that torture in Britain, Israel, or the United States leached into the local criminal justice system and affected the prosecution of ordinary criminals... Interrogational torture has yet to prove the cancer some feared... democracies have kept enhanced interrogation in check by confining it to a specific and well-defined group of individuals: unlawful combatants.[65]

In effect, Matthew Kramer adds his voice to this chorus, when he comments that worries about a slippery slope in liberal democratic regimes 'are not well substantiated' empirically, although he admits that the hypothesis of a 'metastasizing tendency' is well founded in the case of authoritarian ones.[66] On Henry Shue's argument that torture is bound to spread and become institutionalised, he observes a 'dearth of evidence offered in support of his empirical contentions'.[67] Where Shue argues that '[t]orture is not for amateurs', since it requires professional skill,[68] Kramer counters with the actual case of *Leon v. Wainwright*, where policemen used, to good effect, the 'decidedly unsophisticated' method of twisting the arm and throttling the neck of a kidnapper,[69] and he comments that 'many of the ordinary and legitimate techniques of policing and soldiering are not very sharply distinct from some of the sinister techniques of torturing'.[70]

Notwithstanding all this, we know that human beings are susceptible of a lust, sometimes sadistic, for domination; we know that social norms can change for the

---

[63] Hannah Arendt, *Origins of Totalitarianism* (New York: Harcourt, Brace, Jovanovich, 1973), pp. 185-6, 215-16, 221; quoted by Waldron, *Torture*, p. 249.

[64] Richard A. Posner, 'Torture, Terrorism, and Interrogation', in Levinson, *Torture*, p. 294.

[65] Gross, *Moral Dilemmas*, pp. 138, 146.

[66] Kramer, *Torture and Moral Integrity*, p. 123. Where there is empirical evidence it refers to torture used for purposes other than the prevention of imminent calamities—for example, by American soldiers and intelligence officers in Iraq and Afghanistan and at Guantanamo Bay (ibid., pp. 146-7).

[67] Ibid., p. 133-4, citing Henry Shue, 'Torture in Dreamland: Disposing of the Ticking Bomb', *Case Western Journal of International Law*, 37 (2006) and now also in Shue, *Fighting Hurt*.

[68] Shue, 'Torture in Dreamland', in *Fighting Hurt*, p. 63.

[69] Kramer, *Torture and Moral Integrity*, pp. 60, 135.   [70] Ibid., p. 136.

worse; we know that institutions can become gravely corrupt; we know that legal
and judicial institutions can become vindictive and cruel; and we know that police
and soldiers can abuse their power brutally and sadistically. At very least, therefore, we cannot be confident that what begins as a well-intentioned, reluctant
choice to cause pain that is proportioned to the end of obtaining life-saving
information will not grow into a glad wanting for the sheer pleasure of it. Nor
can we be confident that this libidinous growth will be confined to isolated
individuals and not infect their institutions.

Further, even if there is a real, practicable distinction between well-intentioned
and strictly proportionate interrogational pain-infliction and other, vicious, tor-
turous kinds, we can be sure that our enemies will not acknowledge it. In that case,
even if our practice of interrogational pain-infliction is morally scrupulous, it will
still be politically counterproductive. Further still, the scrupulous eschewal of
anything that approximates torture can be positively productive in terms of
winning hearts and minds and therefore in terms of intelligence-gathering.

In the light of all these considerations, therefore, it would be prudent to
conclude that *any* intentional infliction of pain, physical or mental, for the
purpose of gaining information should be outlawed; and that anyone within the
relevant jurisdiction should have a positively legal right to be free from it.[71]

VIII

However, this would not be to say that an act of interrogational pain-infliction
could never be morally right. Situations could arise where an interrogator judges
that the stakes are so very high as to warrant the intentional subjection of a
complotter to severe pain, so as to elicit information that would avert a murderous
calamity; and, morally speaking, he might be quite correct. The victim could in
fact be complicit in murderous plans and the interrogator could have very good
reason for thinking that.[72] Moreover, the interrogator could be motivated primarily by concern for the innocent under threat, his intention could be strictly to save
them, and his use of pain-infliction could be proportioned to that end. Such
situations might be rare, but they are not fanciful.[73]

[71] This, of course, is what the Convention Against Torture, Article 1(1) does: 'torture means any act
by which severe pain or suffering, whether physical or mental, is intentionally inflicted on a person for
such purposes as obtaining from him or a third person information or a confession...'.
[72] As Kramer says, sometimes a stringent epistemic standard can be met (*Torture and Moral
Integrity*, pp. 126, 60–1).
[73] Henry Shue disagrees, arguing that the high stakes involved are the only realistic feature of the
'ticking bomb hypothetical': 'Its other features are all too good to be true, especially to be true in
conjunction: the right man and the prompt result and the judicious decision to refrain from all further
torture until the next catastrophe almost certainly looms. This happy conjunction is not rare—it is
virtually impossible given the kind of people who rise to the top in politics... The ticking bomb
hypothetical is too good to be true—it is torture conducted by wise, self-restrained angels' ('Torture in

One way or another, a legal system should be made able to recognise this. The issue of what would be the optimal—that is, fairest and safest, all things considered—set of legal arrangements is one best settled by lawyers and legislators. There are several possibilities. One, famously proposed by Alan Dershowitz, would be to place the onus of responsibility on judges by having them decide on applications for interrogational torture warrants in the full glare of public scrutiny.[74] This would require judicial assessment of the evidence of the guilt of the one to be interrogated, which would be vitally important, since such deliberate pain-infliction could only ever be justified in the case of someone presumed to be guilty, and since that presumption should only be made on the basis of very strong grounds. Against this some have raised the practical objection that it would be unfeasible to obtain warrants in an emergency.[75]

Another possibility would be to let the courts acquit on the ground of a successful defence of tragic 'necessity', articulated in terms of proportion, effectiveness, and last resort.[76] Objections to this include the excessive elasticity of the

Dreamland', pp. 61–2). Note how the passionate rhetorical force is effectively punctured by the qualification 'virtually'. Note also how its authority is tarnished by the academic's sanctimonious scorn for 'the kind of people who rise to the top of politics'.

Besides, there are cases other than the 'ticking bomb' scenario. There was the real von Metzler case in 2002. On 27 September 2002 the 11-year-old son of a well-known banking family in Frankfurt, Jakob von Metzler, was kidnapped by a law student, Magnus Gäfgen. Having watched the boy suffocate to death, Gäfgen sent an extortion demand for €1m to Jacob's parents. After receiving the money, he was arrested, whereupon he refused to say whether or not the boy was alive and misled the police about his location. The vice-president of Frankfurt's police-force, Wolfgang Daschner, threatened to hurt him, unless he revealed the boy's whereabouts. This Gäfgen then did. The von Metzler case provoked sustained discussion in Germany about the rights and wrongs of police torture. I observe that philosophers of law Michael Pawlik and Winfried Brugger, and Christian social ethicist Clemens Breuer, all arrived at the same conclusion that I have reached: that, while there should be a general legal prohibition of torture, lest 'the mere knowledge of the possibility of the use of torture ruin public trust in the integrity of a state governed by law' ('" bereits das Wissen um die Möglichkeit ihres [der Folter] Einsatzes das allgemeine Vertrauen in die Integrität des Rechtsstaates" ruinieren würde'), nevertheless, there can be 'justification on moral grounds for a criminal to be threatened with coercive measures in narrowly defined cases' ('scheint es aus moralischen Überlegungen gerechtfertigt zu sein, dass in eng umgrenzten Fällen...ein Verbrecher mit Zwangsmaßnahmen bedroht werden darf') (Clemens Breuer, 'Das Foltern von Menschen: Die Differenz zwischen dem Anspruch eines weltweiten Verbots und dessen praktischer Missachtung und die Frage der möglichen Zulassung der "Rettungsfolter"', in Gerhard Beestermöller and Hauke Brunkhorst, eds, *Rückkehr der Folter: Der Rechtstaat im Zwielicht?* (Munich: C. H. Beck, 2006), pp. 17, 19, 20, 21).

[74] See Dershowitz,*Why Terrorism Works* (New Haven: Yale University Press, 2002); 'The Torture Warrant: A Response to Professor Strauss', *New York Law School Law Review*, 48 (2003); and 'Tortured Reasoning'.

[75] For example, Kramer, *Torture and Moral Integrity*, p. 259. Kramer's main objection, however, is that torture warrants would incorporate into law the 'countenancing of seriously wrongful actions that involve major violence' (ibid., p. 265). This only has force, of course, if one accepts his argument that all forms of interrogational pain-infliction are always and everywhere morally wrong.

[76] This is the position of Israel's legal system, since the judgement of her Supreme Court in 1999 (Gross, *Moral Dilemmas*, p. 137). It is also supported by Eric Posner and Adrian Vermeule in 'Should Coercive Interrogation be Legal?', *Michigan Law Review*, 104 (2006); and *Terror in the Balance* (Oxford: Oxford University Press, 2007).

defence of necessity,[77] and the unfairness of leaving the interrogator unsure how the courts will judge.[78]

The safest course would be for the law to treat any deliberate act of interrogational pain-infliction as a criminal violation of a positive legal right against 'torture', for which the interrogator must answer in a court. That way the law would remain absolute, and the taboo maintain maximal strength. Should the particular features of the case persuade the court that what had been done was, while illegal, nevertheless morally justified, the jury could decide to prefer justice to the letter of the law and acquit. Alternatively, in the case of conviction, the judge could suspend the sentence.[79] The problem with both of these is that they leave morality and legality at odds with one another; and, in addition, the latter brands a moral hero as a convicted criminal. Nevertheless, it might be considered a reasonable, if tragic, price to pay.[80]

It seems that, whatever the legal arrangement, there will be risks and costs. On which arrangement prudently involves the least risk and cost and distributes them most justly, I am agnostic. However, one solution that seems to me quite unacceptable is Matthew Kramer's. Kramer regards all interrogational pain-infliction as morally impermissible, because it always sullies the moral integrity of the interrogator with the self-aggrandising desire for godlike dominance. Nonetheless, he holds that on 'a prodigiously rare occasion' the absolute duty of public officers to refrain from torture (i.e. deliberate pain-infliction) is 'over-topped' by their duty to protect citizens against extraordinary perils. In such a case, interrogational torture is at once morally impermissible and 'morally optimal', by which he means 'more stringently obligatory'.[81] That the absolute duty to refrain from torture is 'overtopped' rather than 'overridden' signals that the duty still retains all its normative force: it remains absolute.[82] Therefore, in such a case the public officer is morally correct—indeed, morally obliged—to do what he is absolutely forbidden to do (even if the absoluteness here is only weak or

---

[77] Alan Dershowitz, 'Tortured Reasoning', in Levinson, *Torture*, pp. 260–1. Michael Gross agrees, observing that interrogators have rarely stood trial in Israel, and that in 2002 the state prosecutor declared that they would not be tried for their actions, even where jurists regard these as unjustified, as long as they act 'in a reasonable manner' (*Moral Dilemmas*, p. 137). Gross comments: 'What began as a carefully controlled exception gradually morphed into an acceptable rule of conduct demanding little in the way of accountability or defence' (ibid.).

[78] Dershowitz, 'Tortured Reasoning', p. 263.

[79] This is Shue's position in 'Torture', in Levinson, *Torture*, p. 59.

[80] This is similar to the UK's current legal arrangement with regard to assisted suicide, which I prefer: that it remain illegal, but that the Director of Public Prosecutions has the authority to use his discretion to decide against prosecution, according to the circumstances of the case.

[81] Kramer, *Torture and Moral Integrity*, p. 13. Moral optimality, he tells us, is a function of *deontic* stringency (ibid., p. 8 n. 6. The emphasis is mine). But then he muddies the waters when he says that an overtopped deontological obligation retains all its normative force despite being surpassed in stringency 'by a formidably weighty *consequentialist* requirement' (ibid., p. 27; cf. p. 240. The emphasis is mine).

[82] Ibid., p. 10.

susceptible of being 'overtopped' by a more stringent obligation). Merely to state such a position, I suggest, is to expose its baffling incoherence.

The reason that Kramer takes this position is that he believes in the possibility of radical moral conflict, where doing what is morally obligatory is not exonerative of breaches of less stringent duties: 'Any such breach is indeed a breach—that is, a moral wrong—and it will thus trigger remedial obligations.'[83] The moral optimality of the breach serves only to extenuate the gravity of its wrongness.[84] In the case of morally optimal interrogational torture, the remedial obligations should include legal sanctions.[85]

The one example Kramer gives us—outside of the exotic realm of torture—is that of promise-breaking. Someone who breaks a promise (say, to meet for lunch) in order to perform a morally optimal act (say, of emergency charity) nevertheless does wrong, according to Kramer, and is therefore obliged to apologise to the promisee and undertake suitable remedial measures.[86] I consider this view basically mistaken. It is quite true that, having broken my promise, I owe my would-be lunch partner an apology. But if my act really was optimal, if I correctly allowed a more stringent duty to take priority, then my apology should not take the form of a confession of wrongdoing, since I have committed none. Rather it should take the form of an expression of regret and an explanation. I should express regret, in order to show that I take responsibility for the disappointment that I have caused, and to show my disappointed friend that I am sorry for his disappointment and do not treat it lightly. I should also offer an explanation, in order to persuade my friend that, under the circumstances, I did the morally right thing, that he suffered a tragic disappointment rather than a moral wrong, and that he can continue to trust me in the future to keep my promises, except in rare cases where, we agree, moral obligation requires their breach. In short, the remedial action that I should take is not confession of wrongdoing, repentance of it, and penance for it. Rather, it is an exercise in showing due respect, reassuring doubt, and maintaining trust.

By analogy, if a case of interrogational pain-infliction could ever be morally obligatory, all things considered—as both Kramer and I think it could be—then the one who does it commits no moral wrong. The victim's legal right against torture may have been 'overtopped', but he has not been morally wronged, since he has not suffered a morally vicious kind of deliberate pain-infliction. The

---

[83] Ibid., pp. 9, 116.   [84] Ibid., p. 20.

[85] It is true that Kramer argues that only where an individual official has performed non-optimal torture (e.g. where the threat was not imminent or where other means of averting it were available) should criminal sanctions be imposed (ibid., p. 293); and that in cases of optimal calamity-averting interrogational torture, sanctions should be borne collectively by the relevant institution (e.g. police force or intelligence service) (ibid., pp. 293–4, 296). Nevertheless, he goes on to say that even in the latter case, where individual officials have done their optimal duty, they should be subject to institutional sanctions (ranging from outright dismissal, through suspension and demotion, to fines), which 'can aptly serve as a means of authoritatively recognising the wrongness of the acts of torture which they have performed' (ibid., pp. 295–6).

[86] Ibid., p. 233.

interrogator does owe a remedial apology in the sense of an *apologia*—a justifying account of what he did. And he also owes an expression of deep regret at the pain he was morally obliged to cause, thus showing the victim due respect and demonstrating that his own integrity was not sullied by a lustful delight in sadistic dominance—as, I have argued, it need not be. He owes these things as remedies, not of wrongdoing, but of social doubt and nascent mistrust. Therefore, although he is subject to remedial obligations, he does not deserve to be punished. To think otherwise, as Kramer does, is to put the public officer in an impossible position: for on the one hand, if he fails to do what is morally optimal, he deserves moral opprobrium; but if he does it, he deserves punishment. Why on earth would anyone volunteer for such an office?

IX

Insofar as 'torture' is defined in morally pejorative terms, and refers to deliberate pain-infliction that is vitiated by sadism, etc., it is morally wrong by definition. It is absolutely wrong, always and everywhere. One could say, therefore, that there is an absolute natural, moral right against it. That would be misleading, however, since, as I explained at the end of Chapter 5, it would connote a degree of security that does not exist naturally, apart from social institutions.

Nevertheless, where there are social or international institutions of law and law-enforcement, there should be a legal right against torture. Insofar as its wrongness is informed and specified by paradigmatic examples, which provide standards against which candidates for membership of the class can be measured, such a legal right would be practicable.

Further, there is good reason why this legal right should be absolute in the sense that it may not be suspended in any circumstances. There is also good reason why it should be absolute in the sense of prohibiting *all* forms of non-consensual pain-infliction, including the interrogational kind. That is to say, the legal definition of 'torture' should include all non-consensual pain-infliction.

The reason for this second kind of absoluteness, however, is prudential, and as such it waxes and wanes according to circumstances: even if it holds in the vast majority of cases, it will not hold in all. It follows that it will not always be the case that interrogational pain-infliction is politically counter-productive or corrupting, any more than it will always be the fruit of self-aggrandising lust for godlike domination or of sadism. It will not always be morally wrong. Accordingly, there might arise an extraordinary case where a conscientious interrogator judges that the stakes are so very high as to warrant the use of methods of deliberate pain-infliction and so the violation of a positively legal right against them; and, morally speaking, he might be quite correct. In support, I observe that even a liberal philosopher such as Henry Shue concedes such a possibility—and so, implicitly, does Jeremy Waldron.[87] In such a rare case, the interrogator should follow his conscience, render himself accountable to the courts, make a moral case for his conscientious law-breaking, and entrust his fate to the discretion of the judge and jury. For, while it is prudent to draw a bright legal line against all non-consensual pain-infliction, including the interrogational kind, by granting an absolute, exceptionless legal right against it, there is no correspondingly absolute moral prohibition.

In sum, then, there are kinds of action that are absolutely wrong by definition, and one of these is torture. It follows that there is a natural moral duty never to perform such an action. However, since there are no natural moral rights at all, there is no natural right against this. Nonetheless, there are good moral reasons of prudence why there should always be an absolute *legal* right against 'torture', so defined as to encompass all instances of non-consensual pain infliction, even though rare cases might be morally permissible. There is, therefore, at least one absolute legal right—and there might well be others like it.

---

[87] Henry Shue concedes the possibility of rare cases of morally justified torture (i.e. deliberate interrogational pain-infliction): 'I can see no way to deny the permissibility of torture in a case *just like this* [where a fanatic has set a hidden nuclear device to explode in the heart of Paris]' ('Torture', p. 57. The emphasis is Shue's). So, implicitly, does Jeremy Waldron when he comments on Shue, 'But few cases are *just like this*'—few being more than none (*Torture*, pp. 41–2. The emphasis is Waldron's). And so, implicitly, did Jean Porter once upon a time: 'I am very reluctant to say that torture could ever be justified, and yet one can imagine situations in which an absolute prohibition would be difficult to sustain, situations of genuine emergency in which the consequences of such a prohibition would be not only tragic, but catastrophic (say, triggering a nuclear war)' ('From Natural Law to Human Rights: Or, Why Rights Talk Matters', *Journal of Law and Religion*, 14/1 (1999–2000), p. 92). Jeff McMahan is more robust: 'I believe that absolute prohibitions of act-types such as torture and killing are unacceptable ... torture can be morally permissible in principle ... [However,] the moral justifiability of torture in principle is virtually irrelevant in practice and that it is morally necessary that the law, both domestic and international, should prohibit the practice of torture absolutely—that is, without exceptions' ('Torture in Principle and Practice', p. 111). I would differ only in emphasising the word 'virtually', and pointing out that the all-things-considered moral justification for an absolute legal right against torture must somehow accommodate the rare case where what is legally prohibited is nevertheless morally right. It is no accident, I think, that McMahan and I have both reached this position by approaching the issue of torture from the 'just war' tradition of reasoning about the ethics of killing.

8
Are Human Rights Universal?

I

Since 1945 the volume of rights-talk has risen to unprecedented levels, but the topic has changed from 'natural' to 'human'. A human right is one that is supposed to belong to individuals just because they are human, rather than citizens of a state whose law happens to grant it. That is to say, human rights transcend the frontiers of sovereign states, qualifying their sovereignty. The assertion of such rights after the Second World War was a reaction against recent abuses by Germany's Nazi regime, which, sanctioned by Nazi law, were perfectly legal. A human right, therefore, carries moral force, even where no actual legal system acknowledges it; and insofar as states agree to acknowledge it by international treaty, it acquires trans-national legal force, too.

To a large extent, therefore, a human right is the same as a natural right, in that it is supposed to be the property of anyone participating in human nature. There is, however, one difference. 'Human rights' usually refers to those bodies of rights that have attracted international (if not yet universal) recognition by states since the end of the Second World War. Rights subscribed to by states acquire legal status, a status that is all the stronger where institutions of enforcement have been put in place—for example, the European Court of Human Rights in Strasbourg. Consequently, the authority of human rights derives from the fact of national recognition, confirmed by a measure of international consensus, and reinforced further by international courts. Such authority endows a natural, moral claim with the characteristic force of 'a right'.

II

From the early 1970s onwards, the advancing tide of international human rights began to provoke increasingly vocal resistance from non-Western parts of the world, especially Asia and Africa, and most especially those countries newly independent of colonial rule. The most general complaint was that 'human rights' were more Western than they pretended to be and that they carried with them 'neo-imperialist' assumptions about the intellectual and moral superiority of Western culture. The Japanese Tatsuo Inoue represents the critique thus:

Asia, as the [Western] Orientalists see it, is essentially different from the West...they assume that only the West...has the intellectual competence and resources to understand and conceptualize this essence of Asia and thereby to lead it. The West is the knowing agent and Asia is the object to be known, which cannot have a clear self-perception without having its own meaning determined through the Orientalist matrix of the West.... The West represents Modernity, and Asia must ipso facto represent Counter-modernity.[1]

Along the same lines, but more angrily, the Kenyan-born Makau (wa) Mutua describes the Universal Declaration of Human Rights as 'Eurocentric...sanctimonious', decries its 'arrogance', and views it as testament to the 'domination of the European West over non-European peoples and traditions' of the moral universe'.[2] 'International human rights', he continues,

> fall within the historical continuum of the European colonial project in which whites pose as the saviors of a benighted and savage non-European world. The white human rights zealot joins the unbroken chain that connects him to the colonial administrator, the Bible-wielding missionary, and the merchant of free enterprise...This view of human rights re-entrenches and revitalizes the international hierarchy of race and color in which whites, who are privileged globally as a race, are the models and saviors of nonwhites, who are victims and savages.[3]

Beyond a general resentment of what they perceive as Western arrogance and presumptuousness, some non-Western critics have argued that civil and political 'human rights' are not appropriate in the early stages of nation-building, when the overriding concern of government should be economic development. The most famous advocate of this view was Lee Kuan Yew, the first Prime Minister of Singapore, who began to talk up the so-called 'Lee hypothesis' in the early 1990s.[4] According to this hypothesis, the primary task of governments is to guarantee their peoples' right to the means of subsistence through economic development by providing strong political leadership and efficient management, and the civil and political rights of liberal democracy are luxuries that only developed countries can afford.[5] While the philosopher Robert Goodin resists this line of thinking in favour of a presumption *against* the claim that curtailing civil rights advances economic development, he nevertheless concedes (in a

---

[1] Tatsuo Inoue, 'Liberal Democracy and Asian Orientalism', in Joanne R. Bauer and Daniel A. Bell, *The East Asian Challenge for Human Rights* (Cambridge: Cambridge University Press, 1999), pp. 38–9.
[2] Makau Mutua, *Human Rights: A Political and Cultural Critique* (Philadelphia: University of Pennsylvania Press, 2008), p. 154. Sometimes, his name appears as 'Makau wa Mutua'.
[3] Ibid., p. 155.
[4] Lee Kwan Yew, 'Democracy, Human Rights and the Realities', speech in Tokyo, 10 November 1992.
[5] Inoue, 'Liberal Democracy and Asian Orientalism', p. 34.

footnote) that, where a certain level of wealth—for instance subsistence—is in fact
a prerequisite for respecting rights, a short-term sacrifice of rights '*might* be
morally permissible'.[6] Telling against the actualisation of such a possibility, however, is the authority of the Indian economist and Nobel Prize-winner Amartya
Sen. Sen argues that systematic statistical studies give no real support to the claim
that there is a general conflict between political rights and economic performance.
Indeed, Botswana, one of the fastest growing countries in the world, with the best
consistent record of economic growth in Africa, has been an oasis of democracy.[7]
Moreover, civil and political rights enable people to draw their government's
attention to major economic disasters: 'no substantial famine has ever occurred
in any country with a democratic form of government and a relatively free press.'[8]
India, for example, had famines right up to independence in 1947, after which they
stopped abruptly: 'No government can afford to face elections after a major social
calamity, nor can it deal easily with criticism from the media and opposition
parties while still in office.'[9] The Nigerian-born Bonny Ibhawoh pushes back
somewhat in favour of the 'Lee hypothesis', when he argues that a basic level of
subsistence is a prerequisite for civil and political rights. 'In some African countries,' he writes, 'it has become common for poverty stricken rural voters to sell
their votes for as little as a handful of salt or rice. For this category of Africa's
poorest, the need for immediate survival surpasses any other long-term political or
civil rights considerations.'[10] Ibhawoh's defence, however, is not effective. All it
shows is that economic destitution sometimes increases the risk of the abuse of the
right to vote; it does not show that the rights of the destitute to vote, to associate, or
to air their views in public hinder their economic liberation and must be traded off
against it.

III

A much broader objection to 'Western human rights' is cultural, rather than
economic. Here the argument is that Asian and African values differ in important
ways from Western ones in that non-Western cultures are communal, whereas

---

[6] Robert Goodin, 'The Development–Rights Trade-off: Some Unwarranted Economic and Political
Assumptions', *Universal Human Rights*, 1/2 (April–June 1979), p. 32 n. 2. The emphasis is Goodin's.

[7] Amartya Sen, 'Human Rights and Economic Achievements', in Bauer and Bell, *The East Asian
Challenge for Human Rights*, p. 91.

[8] Ibid., p. 92.

[9] Ibid., p. 93. Jack Donnelly makes essentially the same point when he observes that the denial of
civil and political rights brings economic costs by allowing officials to be corrupt, indifferent, and ill
informed ('Human Rights and Asian Values: A Defense of "Western" Universalism', in Bauer and Bell,
The East Asian Challenge for Human Rights, p. 73).

[10] Bonny Ibhawoh, 'Cultural Relativism and Human Rights: Reconsidering the Africanist
Discourse', *Netherlands Quarterly of Human Rights*, 19/1 (2001), p. 60.

Western culture is individualistic.[11] As Lee Kuan Yew put it, Asians have 'little doubt that a society with communitarian values where the interests of society take precedence over that of the individual suits them better than the individualism of America'.[12] The African version of the same argument, as represented by Ibwahoh, is that 'the dominant African conception of human rights combines a system of rights and obligations which gives the community cohesion and viability', and this puts it at odds with 'the Western conception of rights which conceives rights in terms of abstract individualism without corresponding duties'.[13]

It seems, then, that some critics conflate 'Western human rights' with radical, amoral, Hobbesian individualism, for only there, where the original, natural right is not a moral claim at all but rather a psychological drive, is there no corresponding duty. However, as I argued in Chapter 6, it is an error to suppose that modern human rights owe their basic form to Hobbes. Such an error is perhaps forgivable in the light of a statement such as that of the eminent American moral philosopher Joel Feinberg, that personal sovereignty is 'an all or nothing concept; one is entitled to absolute control of whatever is within one's domain however trivial it may be'. Joseph Chan quotes this in his exposition of a Confucian view of rights, in the course of which he observes that some scholars of Confucianism suppose that human rights are necessarily associated with a (Hobbesian) view of human beings as 'fundamentally asocial'.[14] However, even Feinberg admits that sovereign individuals should rule their own lives only so long as they do no harm to others—that is to say, that the right to personal sovereignty is limited by the duty to do no harm. What is more, insofar as Feinberg is talking here about a moral or legal claim to personal sovereignty—and he is—it entails a duty: my right to sovereignty entails your duty to respect it. The general association of human rights with radically asocial individualism is a mistake, which unnecessarily poisons the waters of inter-cultural dialogue.[15]

---

[11] It is true that the thesis that non-Western 'communal' values differ from 'individualistic' Western ones, so as to establish an importantly different view of human rights, rose to prominence over thirty years ago and has since been subject to widespread criticism and refinement. Nevertheless, in the opening decades of the twenty-first century it remains an intellectual force. In 2008, for example, Makau Mutua made a vigorous argument in favour of African cultural difference in *Human Rights: A Political and Cultural Critique*; and in 2012 Yvonne Tew reported that the 'Asian values' approach continues to influence the political and judicial elites of South-East Asian countries such as Malaysia and Singapore ('Beyond "Asian Values": Rethinking Rights', Centre of Governance and Human Rights Working Paper 5 (Cambridge: University of Cambridge, 2012), pp. 3, 9, 10–11).

[12] Lee Kuan Yew, *International Herald Tribune*, 9–10 November 1991; quoted by Bauer and Bell in 'Introduction', *The East Asian Challenge for Human Rights*, p. 6.

[13] Ibhawoh, 'Cultural Relativism and Human Rights', p. 54.

[14] Joel Feinberg, *Harm to Self* (Oxford: Oxford University Press, 1986), p. 55; quoted by Joseph Chan in 'A Confucian Perspective on Human Rights for Contemporary China', in Bauer and Bell, *The East Asian Challenge for Human Rights*, p. 231. See also ibid., p. 216.

[15] Charles Taylor gestures toward the same point, I think, when he writes that ecumenical dialogue would be aided by distinguishing a legal culture of rights enforcement from the Western philosophical conception of human life that foregrounds the autonomous individual ('Conditions of an Unforced

In the mistaken identification of 'Western' human rights with Hobbesian anthropology we observe a first sign that the depiction of a stark opposition between Western and non-Western cultures is overdrawn, since it is an error that some Asian and African critics share with the theologians whom we met in Chapter 6. A second sign appears when we remember that a communitarian critique of individualism is not unfamiliar to Western culture, Since the 1980s 'communitarianism' has named a school of (mainly) American social and political philosophers, including eminent figures such as Robert Bellah, Charles Taylor, Alasdair MacIntyre, and Michael Sandel; and it is arguable that Western social and political thought has contained communitarian streams for very much longer—among them, Burkean conservatism and Roman Catholic social thought. As we have seen, Burke was allergic to abstract rights, and Roman Catholic thinking sought to integrate the rights of individuals with the claims of the common good. That East and West might overlap rather more than some critics assume is implied by Robert Ames's observation that Sandel's critique of the 'runaway liberalism' of American democracy suggests that the latter might benefit from a greater appreciation of Confucian values.[16]

IV

If non-Western critics of human rights have underestimated the communitarian features of the Western cultural hinterland, they have also, some claim, under-estimated the individualistic features of traditional Asian and African cultures. Thus, for example, Inoue notes the importance of self-development in neo-Confucianism and how, in the seventeenth century, Huang Tsung-hsi emphasised the need for institutional and legal reforms to enable free critical discussion that would act as a check upon rulers.[17] Margaret Ng emboldens the point when she reports Wang Gungwu's argument that the reciprocal entitlements of ruler and ruled, according to 'prototypical Confucianism', amounted implicitly to rights.[18] Along the same lines, El-Obaid Ahmed El-Obaid and Kwadwo Appiagyei-Atua argue that the pre-installation oath for newly elected chiefs among the Ashanti in western Africa was 'a reflection of typical civil and political rights'. 'We do not

Consensus on Human Rights', in Bauer and Bell, *The East Asian Challenge for Human Rights*, pp. 128, 129).

[16] Roger T. Ames, 'Continuing the Conversation on Chinese Human Rights', *Ethics and International Affairs*, 11 (1997), pp. 181, 192.

[17] Inoue, 'Liberal Democracy and Asian Orientalism', p. 51, reporting the views of William Theodore de Bary in *The Liberal Tradition in China* (New York: Columbia University Press, 1983).

[18] Margaret Ng, 'Are Rights Culture-bound?', in Michael C. Davis, ed., *Human Rights and Chinese Values: Legal, Philosophical, and Political Perspectives* (Hong Kong: Oxford University Press, 1995), pp. 64–5.

want you to abuse us', the oath ran. 'We do not want you to be miserly; we do not want one who disregards advice; we do not want you to regard us as fools; we do not want autocratic ways; we do not want bullying; we do not like beating.'[19] It has to be said, however, that the values of individual self-development or of freedom of speech or of responsible government do not, by themselves, amount to legal rights.[20] Nor exactly do customary entitlements *as such*, since they leave unanswered the question of what should happen when the ruler decides that he is at liberty to break the custom.[21] Indeed, it was when English monarchs in the early thirteenth and the seventeenth centuries decided that they had divine authorisation to dispense with customary constraints that the clamour for establishment of formally legal rights went up.[22]

Be that all as it may, it is surely true, as Mahmood Mamdani has observed, that '[w]herever oppression [or abuse] occurs—and no continent has had a monopoly over this phenomenon in history—there must come into being a conception of rights'.[23] At very least every human society must hold the value of the lives of its members in some high esteem, otherwise it would not long survive. Accordingly, it will restrict the conditions under which such life may be taken and discourage its being taken outside them. One important form of discouragement is liability to judicial scrutiny and legal punishment. It should come as no surprise, then, when Makau Mutua reports that in pre-colonial Akan and Akamba societies in Africa human life was so highly valued that the authority to take it was reserved for a few elders and exercised only after an elaborate judicial procedure with appeals from one court to another.[24] Where human life is protected by the (conditional) threat

---

[19] El-Obaid Ahmed El-Obaid and Kwadwo Appiagyei-Atua, 'Human Rights in Africa—a New Perspective on Linking the Past to the Present', *McGill Law Journal*, 41 (1996), p. 829.

[20] As Stephen Angle comments on the claim that a concern for rights can be found in classical Confucianism: '[t]he humanistic ideals found in the populist chapters of the *Analects* certainly resonate with some of the ideals expressed in the more general assertions of the UDHR, but this is very different from finding "rights" in the *Analects*' (*Human Rights and Chinese Thought: A Cross-Cultural Inquiry* (Cambridge: Cambridge University Press, 2002), p. 21).

[21] Anthony C. Yu agrees, when he observes that, notwithstanding assertions by late medieval Confucians of the subject's duty of fearless remonstrance, rights have not come into existence until subjects are secure from exile, imprisonment, or execution, should a ruler not appreciate their loyal remonstrance ('Enduring Change: Confucianism and the Prospect of Human Rights', in Elizabeth Bucar and Barbra Barnett, eds, *Does Human Rights Need God* (Grand Rapids, Mich.: Eerdmans, 2005), pp. 120, 122, 123–4).

[22] Margaret Ng acknowledges that Confucian entitlements of the ruled never developed into a check on the government's absolute power over the individual ('Are Rights Culture-Bound?', p. 63); and Joseph Chan, while arguing that Confucianism would 'not reject...outright' a case for a right to freedom of speech, admits that neither Confucius nor Mencius ever advocated such a thing ('A Confucian Perspective', pp. 228–9).

[23] Mahmood Mamdani, 'The Social Basis of Constitutionalism in Africa', *The Journal of Modern African Studies*, 28/3 (1990), p. 359.

[24] Makau Mutua, 'The Banjul Charter and the African Cultural Fingerprint: An Evaluation of the Language of Rights and Duties', *Virginia Journal of International Law*, 35/1 (1995), pp. 350–1, quoting Timothy Fernyhough, 'Human Rights and Precolonial Africa', in Ronald Cohen, Goran Hyden, and Winston P. Nagan, eds, *Human Rights and Governance in Africa* (Gainesville: University of Florida Press, 1993), p. 56.

of legal sanction against its taking, there we certainly have a legal right to personal security.

But do we yet have a *human* right to personal security? In other words, is this right extended to every human being, even foreigners to one's own community? Rhoda Howard thinks not. She holds that 'traditional Africa protected a system of obligations and privileges based on ascribed statuses, not a system of right to which one was entitled merely by virtue of being human', and she offers as evidence the system of indigenous slavery among the Ashanti, which, by the late nineteenth century, had become brutally exploitative.[25] Against this reading, however, El-Obaid and Appiagyei-Atua point out that the Ashanti did grant property rights to slaves.[26] At least we may conclude, therefore, that the idea that some rights belong to human non-members was not entirely foreign to all pre-colonial African societies. No doubt these societies granted far fewer such rights than 'Western human rights' do today. But, if so, it is only fair to point out that so did Western societies in the not-so-distant past: 200 years ago, even European societies were implicated in slavery and granted slaves few rights, if any at all. The issues of who is a full member of a society, and which non-members deserve what rights, are ones that every society has had to tackle and continues to wrestle with. Even in the contemporary West, where the bounds of the human community have been dramatically expanded, these issues have still not been settled. The political peace of many Western countries today remains somewhat disturbed by the fact that embryonic human beings have no rights at all and may be killed upon the request of their mothers. .

V

It seems clear that the concept of a right as the legal property of an individual is not entirely foreign to non-Western, traditional cultures. Nor is the concept of a human right that transcends the bounds of political communities. It is also clear, as we should expect, that not every Asian and African holds the same values and shares the same view of human rights. Thus, on the one hand, we find Lee Kuan Yew downplaying the importance of 'Western' political rights in Singapore, and Chinese businessmen resisting attempts to enhance representative democracy in Hong Kong, in the early 1990s.[27] On the other hand, during the same period and fuelled by the Tiananmen Square massacre of 1989, the Hong Kong Legislative

---

[25] Rhoda E. Howard, 'Group Identity versus Individual Identity in the African Debate on Human Rights', in Abdullahi Ahmed An-Naim and Francis M. Deng, eds, *Human Rights in Africa: Cross-Cultural Perspectives* (Washington, DC: Brookings Institution, 1990), pp. 166–7.

[26] El-Obaid and Appiagyei-Atua, 'Human Rights in Africa', pp. 830–1.

[27] Jonathan Dimbleby, *The Last Governor: Chris Patten and the Handover of Hong Kong*, reprint (London: Pen & Sword, 2017), pp. 107, 119, 159, 397–8.

Council enacted a bill of rights in 1991 and, in the run-up to the Bangkok Declaration of 1993, Chinese dissidents and Asian NGOs poured scorn on the Chinese government's appeals to national sovereignty and cultural relativism to shield itself from criticism in terms of human rights.[28] Thus, too, within the Muslim world (at least according to Fred Halliday in the mid-1990s),

> [t]here is... a world of difference between the positions of the government of Saudi Arabia, on the one hand, with its promotion of a conservative 'Islamic' code of rights, and that of Tunisia, which has been in the forefront of the battle *for* universal rights, and which even proposed to the pre-Vienna 'African' conference a denunciation of the threat to human rights posed by religious fundamentalism.[29]

Further, if non-Westerners, who presided over authoritarian, post-colonial regimes, invoked cultural relativism to fend off 'neo-colonial' interference in the name of 'Western human rights' from the late 1960s onwards, other non-Westerners (or maybe even the same ones) had invoked those very rights against the relativist apologias of colonial regimes during the preceding fifteen years.[30]

Not all non-Westerners share the same, negative view of human rights, especially their civil and political items. Some have found reason to embrace such rights, notwithstanding their Western provenance, whether because of traditional culture, or despite it, or a bit of both. One such reason is that societies outside of Europe and the Anglosphere are no longer as traditional as they used to be. In particular, they have developed large, bureaucratic, centralised modern states, which wield unprecedented power. In the face of this novel political development, it is arguable that traditional informal, moral, and customary constraints upon the exercise of executive power are no longer sufficient. Instead, the apparatus of human rights, involving judicial support from courts at home and abroad, and political support from foreign states and global NGOs, is needed as a stronger substitute for 'medieval safeguards against state tyranny'.[31]

---

[28] Michael C. Davis, 'Adopting International Standards of Human Rights in Hong Kong', in Michael C. Davis, ed., *Human Rights and Chinese Values: Legal, Philosophical, and Political Perspectives* (Hong Kong: Oxford University Press, 1995), pp. 169–70, 175; Michael C. Davis, 'Chinese Perspectives on Human Rights', in Davis, *Human Rights and Chinese Values*, p. 17; Roland Burke, *Decolonization and the Evolution of International Human Rights* (Philadelphia: University of Pennsylvania Press, 2010), p. 142.

[29] Fred Halliday, 'Relativism and Universalism in Human Rights: The Case of the Islamic Middle East', *Political Studies*, 43 (1995), pp. 155–6. The emphasis is Halliday's.

[30] Roland Burke, *Decolonization and the Evolution of International Human Rights* (Philadelphia: University of Pennsylvania Press, 2010), pp. 114–22, 126–9, 131–42.

[31] Inoue, 'Liberal Democracy and Asian Orientalism', p. 32. See also Edward Kannyo, *Human Rights in Africa: Problems and Prospects*, a report prepared for the International League for Human Rights, May 1980).

VI

Claims of a stark contrast between non-Western values and 'Western human rights' are exaggerated. Rights, even human rights, are not unknown to traditional societies outside the West, and some of their members have seen fit to embrace post-war formulations of civil and political rights and invoke them against powerful, authoritarian states. Nevertheless, it might still be the case that there ought to be room for further inter-cultural dialogue about which items should compose a truly international corpus of human rights, and about what specific form these should take in different cultural and political contexts.

An especially forceful expression of this view may be found in the writings of Makau Mutua. Mutua objects to 'the imposition of the current dogma of human rights on non-European societies', which 'rejects the contributions of other cultures in efforts to create a universal corpus of human rights...a truly universal platform', and he pleads for 'a genuine cross-contamination of cultures to create a new multicultural human rights corpus'.[32] As we observed earlier in this chapter, Mutua regards current rights dogma as a continuation of the racism of European missionary colonialism, whose ignorant prejudice does arrogant violence to traditional African cultures. Instead of 'the zealotry of the current rhetoric', which simply assumes that a certain African practice offends against human rights, we need to become more open, inquisitive, and dialogical, considering its important social function and the controversy about it within traditional society, with a view to finding a way of modifying or discarding it 'without making its practitioners hateful of their culture and themselves'.[33] Contrary to Western 'stereotypes of barbaric natives in the "dark" continent', the 'savagery' of the one-party state or of female genital mutilation (FGM) inheres, he argues, not in the things themselves but 'in the theory and practice'.[34]

Mutua's resentment of attacks on traditional African culture leads him, in particular, to question the right to religious freedom. As he sees it, the 'messianic faiths' or 'imperial religions' that are Christianity and Islam are guilty of something approaching 'cultural genocide' through their destruction of traditional African religion. Because that religion is closely bound up with social norms and cultural identities, its destruction has 'robbed Africans of essential elements

---

[32] Mutua, *Human Rights*, pp. 8, 11.

[33] Ibid., pp. 8, 84, 155–6. It might discomfit Mutua—or it might not—to know that his defence of a practice on the ground of its important social function is one that Ottoman authorities used to deflect British pressure to abolish slavery. In 1840 Lord Ponsonby (1809–80), British ambassador to Istanbul, wrote to Lord Palmerston, the British Foreign Secretary, that his urging the Ottomans to act against slavery and the slave trade had been greeted 'with *extreme astonishment and a smile* at the proposition of destroying an institution closely interwoven with the frame of society' (Ponsonby to Palmerston, 27.12.1840, PRO, FO/195/108, quoted by Ehud R. Toledano in *Slavery and Abolition in the Ottoman Middle East* (Seattle: University of Washington, 1998), pp. 116–17. The emphasis is Ponsonby's.)

[34] Mutua, *Human Rights*, p. 11.

of their humanity'.[35] To illustrate his point, Mutua refers to Chinua Achebe's famous novel *Things Fall Apart*, which tells a story about the encounter between, on the one hand, Okonkwo, guardian of Igbo culture and religion, and on the other, colonial administrators and missionaries. The story is propelled to its tragic climax when Okonkwo's son is converted to Christianity by an Igbo Christian, who congratulates him with the words, 'Blessed is he who forsakes his mother and father for my sake.' Beholding the train of events, a tribal elder laments that the white man 'has put a knife on the things that held us together and we have fallen apart'. Mutua comments that the encounter between Christianity and the Igbo religion involved 'the recruitment of converts, usually from among the social "rejects"', and that missionary schools 'usually preyed on the youth, capturing them and tearing them from their cultural moorings'.[36]

Against this Western assault on traditional African culture, Mutua argues that the right to religious freedom includes 'the right to be left alone—to choose freely whether and what to believe'. The current human rights regime, however, privileges the free competition of ideas over 'the right against cultural invasion ... the right [of indigenous beliefs] to be respected and left alone by more dominant external traditions'.[37] He doubts, however, 'that there is inherent benefit in cross-fertilisation or contact with "otherness"'—'an assumption that is still being tested ... without final proof'.[38] Accordingly, the right to religious freedom should not contain a right to proselytise:

On religious freedom, it is wrongheaded to simply protect the right of missionary Christianity to proselytize and decimate non-Western spiritual traditions and cultures at will. Western knee-jerk reactions to restrictions on Christians in non-Western countries such as China and India must be balanced against the duty of those societies to protect their spiritual heritages from the swarming, imperial faiths bent on the total domination of the spiritual universe.[39]

Mutua's fierce critique of 'Western human rights' is motivated by a deeply felt sense of dismay and anger at the destruction of traditional African values and customs: 'It is this loss that I mourn', he confesses, 'and for which I blame Christianity and Islam.'[40] While his grief deserves sympathy, his reasoning deserves critical scrutiny. First of all, notice how he operates with a very loose concept of coercion and violence, which, however common it may now be among post-colonialists, is dubious. He tells us that Christianity's entry into Africa was just as 'violent' as Islam's, 'coming as it did in partnership with the colonial

[35] Makau wa Mutua, 'Limitations in Religious Rights: Problematizing Religious Freedom in the African Context', *Buffalo Human Rights Law Review*, 5 (1999), p. 75.
[36] Mutua, *Human Rights*, pp. 115–16.   [37] Mutua, 'Limitations in Religious Rights', pp. 75–6.
[38] Ibid., p. 100.   [39] Mutua, *Human Rights*, p. 156.
[40] Mutua, 'Limitations in Religious Rights', p. 105.

imperial powers'.[41] This is historically misleading, however. British colonial involvement in east Africa was initially inspired in the 1890s to suppress the slave-trade, which was no doubt regarded as unwarranted interference, sometimes violent, by the African sellers and the Arab buyers, but presumably not by the slaves. And often British colonial administrators—for example, in northern Nigeria—actively discouraged Christian missionary activity, precisely because they wanted to avoid the political unrest that cultural interference tended to cause.[42] Africans were not, in fact, forced to convert to Christianity at the point of a British colonial gun. Indeed, Mutua himself admits as much, when he contends that there should be a right against 'coerced conversion', even when that occurs indirectly 'through the manipulation and destruction of other cultures', and that the most fundamental right of self-determination should disallow 'imposition by external agencies through acculturation'.[43] The 'coercion' he is talking about is not, in fact, physical violence at all, but the power of cultural attraction. In Chinua Achebe's story no one literally compels Okonkwo's son to convert; and Mutua does not claim that missionary schools literally took African youth captive. And while Mutua appears to disdain the missionaries' recruitment of 'social rejects'—rather as Indian Brahmins disdained the Christian recruitment of Untouchables, or Jewish pharisees Jesus' recruitment of sinners—presumably the rejects themselves would have a different story to tell. To talk, as Mutua does, of the conversion of Africans to Christianity as a form of 'violence', 'coercion', or even 'imposition' is simplistic and misleading. It also betrays a rather low view of the agency of (non-conformist) Africans. Mutua reports Elisabeth Isichei's observation that '[t]oday most Igbo have been baptized, and traditional religion is the preserve of a small aging minority'.[44] To suppose that 'most Igbo' are merely gullible sheep would not only show a lack of curiosity; it would also patronise.

Deep down, Makau Mutua's complaint against the destruction of traditional African religion is part of a larger complaint against 'modernisation'—against the 'process of de-Africanization . . . and the wholesale subversion of traditional values

---

[41] Ibid., p. 86.

[42] It is an irony that would probably not amuse Professor Mutua that his views overlap those of the colonial powers in the early 1950s, when they resisted the extension of 'human rights' to their colonies in the name of protecting traditional culture and the deeply rooted customs of the natives against catastrophe (Burke, *Decolonisation*, pp. 115, 121). Thus in the debate over the Special Colonial Application clause of the 1950 draft covenant on human rights, the Belgian delegate, M. Soudan, argued that to force human rights abruptly on less civilised peoples would be socially destructive (ibid., pp. 116–17). Roland Burke is cynical about the motives of the colonial delegations to the UN Third (Social, Humanitarian, and Cultural Affairs) Committee, telling us that they 'feigned' reverence for traditional culture, because, '[e]ver anxious about stability and the limits of their policing power', they were disinclined to alienate traditional elites (ibid., pp. 114, 127). Since, as Burke himself tells us, the colonial powers usually regarded traditional culture as inferior, it is doubtful that they revered it much (ibid., pp. 114, 116–17). But they were certainly worried about political stability, and since instability often meant bloodshed, since anarchy threatens all forms of human good, and since it is the special moral responsibility of ruling authorities to prevent anarchy, their worry was well founded.

[43] Mutua, 'Limitations in Religious Rights', pp. 101–2.   [44] Mutua, *Human Rights*, p. 116.

and structures', which has been fuelled by industrialisation and urbanisation.[45] This may be a process that Western colonialism started, but, as Mutua himself laments, it is also one that post-colonial African rulers have often been very happy to adopt.[46] Indeed, in the 1950s and 1960s nationalist movements were frequently hostile to the 'feudal' customs and traditions of their own peoples, and post-colonial states were at the forefront of UN activity to eradicate cultural practices considered harmful to women.[47] Again, while it is possible that African elites were slavishly going with the flow of what appeared to be 'progress', it is also possible that they had perceived in modern, Western ideas such as human rights values that seemed to them good and worthy of embrace. Maybe, on first encounter, those ideas seemed absolutely novel and alien; more likely, they resonated with elements already present in traditional culture, while giving them a novel articulation, emphasis, and force. More likely, they were at once somewhat familiar and somewhat novel: familiar enough to grasp, novel enough to propel fresh, critical lines of thought. Cultures are seldom entirely separate and are normally in the process of negotiating with each other. Even if it were right to preserve them in a state of quarantine, it is usually not possible. But while we might agree that there should be a right of individuals against being forced against their will to adopt foreign beliefs and practices, we might doubt, *pace* Mutua, that there should be a right of communities to prevent their members from choosing to adopt them. If so, we would share that doubt with plenty of Africans. For while Mutua might retain a fondness for FGM, because of its function in promoting social solidarity, the Association of African Women for Research and Development have opposed it, and the likes of El-Obaid Ahmed El-Obaid and Kwadwo Appiagyei-Atua regard it as 'unacceptable, even repulsive'.[48]

That said, Mutua is not wrong to feel that important things—such as social cohesion and responsibility—are lost, or weakened, or threatened in the process of modernisation. Nor is he alone: proponents of 'Asian values' behold the symptoms of *anomie* in contemporary American culture and find them deeply unattractive.[49] Again, however, the line between modernity and its critics does not run between the West and the Rest; it runs right through each of them. Different aspects of modernity have provoked criticism from Westerners for centuries: as we have seen, Edmund Burke and Jeremy Bentham were decrying abstract rights over 200 years ago; Roman Catholics have been trying to achieve a happier marriage between individual rights and the common good since the 1890s; American communitarians have been attacking liberal individualism since the 1980s; and some British Anglican theologians have been calling into

[45] Mutua, 'Limitations in Religious Rights', p. 103.   [46] Ibid., pp. 96–7.
[47] Burke, *Decolonisation*, p. 126.
[48] Mutua, *Human Rights*, pp. 26–7; El-Obaid and Appiagyei-Atua, 'Human Rights in Africa', p. 850.
[49] See, for example, Lee Kuan Yew's comments in Fareed Zakaria and Lee Kuan Yew, 'Culture is Destiny: A Conversation with Lee Kuan Yew', *Foreign Affairs*, 73/1 (March–April 1994).

202 WHAT'S WRONG WITH RIGHTS?

question the very idea of subjective rights since the 1990s. 'Modernity' can mean all manner of thing and the West is still engaged, as it has long been engaged, in a contest over what modernity *should* mean. Indeed, this book is part of that contest.

VII

Even if it is doubtful that there should be a right of traditional cultures to immunity against foreign influence and the threat of modernising change, there remain grounds to suppose that there should be room for further negotiation between Western and non-Western cultures over what items should appear in the standard list of human rights, how they should be formulated, what conditions should qualify them, and how quickly they should be established. For example, some Confucian scholars, according to Joseph Chan, deny that there should be a right to publish pornography, because of the threat it poses to the cultivation of the ethical life.[50] In the late 1970s and 1980s eminent liberal philosophers in the West, such as Bernard Williams, Ronald Dworkin, and Joel Feinberg, argued that it is doubtful that pornography causes harm, but that if it does, it either affects only the individual using it and no one else or such harm is insufficiently grave to warrant state interference (except perhaps in the form of a public education campaign).[51] Since then, and notwithstanding feminist criticism, their views have largely prevailed in the West. Yet, note that their case rested on an estimation of social harm, namely, that it is either non-existent or insufficiently grave. Over thirty years later, however, with the development of widely accessible online pornography, and anecdotal evidence of its harmful effect on the socio-sexual development of children, not least upon the attitude of male children toward women, doubts are being expressed in public about the wisdom of the current liberal regimen. So even in the liberal West, the *extent* of legal freedom remains a contested matter, and arguments about it continue to turn upon varying estimations of harm to social welfare. Nowadays, even liberal Westerners are being provoked to wonder whether the bounds of freedom have not been drawn too liberally with regard to pornography. The possibility that more socially conservative cultures—whether Confucian or Christian—might have something important to say on the matter is no longer as breezily dismissed as it once was.

[50] Chan, 'A Confucian Perspective', p. 231.
[51] See, for example, the *Report of the Committee on Obscenity and Film Censorship*, Cmnd. 7772 (London: HMSO. 1979), which was chaired by Bernard Williams; Ronald Dworkin, 'Do We Have a Right to Pornography?' in *A Matter of Principle* (Cambridge, Mass.: Harvard University Press, 1985), chapter 17, esp. pp. 335–47; Joel Feinberg, 'Pornography and the Criminal Law' in D. Copp and S. Wendell, eds, *Pornography and Censorship* (Buffalo, NY: Prometheus, 1983), pp. 105–37; and Joel Feinberg, *Offense to Others* (Oxford: Oxford University Press, 1985), chapters 11 and 12.

More conservative East and more liberal West share a common concern here, and there is further scope for reasoning together about it.

In addition to inter-cultural dialogue about the wise determination of the limits of certain liberties, there should also be room for dialogue about the possibility that some 'human rights' ought not to be implemented at all in certain cultural and political conditions. It is true that regimes often appeal to political stability as the justification for refusing to recognise human rights, when they simply want a pretext to shield their malicious or rapacious conduct from inconvenient criticism and constraint. However, it is also true that occasions do arise when the stability of a tolerably just regime is genuinely under serious threat. When the loss of stability would amount to anarchy, in which nothing human can flourish, a government could be justified in suspending certain destabilising rights or in refusing to assert them in the first place. Sometimes, a trade-off between stability and rights can be morally justified.[52] For example, Roland Burke reports the fate of a bill to grant equal political rights to women, which was introduced into the Iranian *majlis* (parliament) in 1952. After more than 100,000 signatures in its support had been presented to the government, intense pressure from influential clerics forced its withdrawal: 'Struggling with domestic unrest and foreign policy problems, the Iranian government, then ruling by decree, had little interest in raising the issue again.'[53] Burke does not say what he thinks should have happened, but since he is generally cynical about the political authorities' concern for stability, it is reasonable to presume that he thinks that the government should have persevered. However, whether or not he is correct depends on political judgements about the effect upon domestic unrest of defying the clerics, and about the level of the threat posed by that unrest to the regime. It also depends on a moral judgement about whether the regime deserved to fall, which itself depends on a political judgement about whether a better alternative was actually available. If it was reasonable to suppose that the effect of defying the clerics would have been to exacerbate widespread unrest, if that unrest would have issued in bloodshed, if it would have brought down the government or even undermined the state, and if the subsequent regime would have been significantly more illiberal and despotic, then a prudent concern for human rights in general would have justified a decision not to push this set in particular—at least for the time being.

The same considerations arose in a more recent case. In Malaysia a Malay-Muslim woman, Lina Joy, wanted to have her conversion from Islam legally recognised, so that she could marry her Christian fiancé. In 2007 the majority of

---

[52] Michael Ignatieff agrees: 'Stability... may count more than justice' (*Human Rights as Politics and Idolatry* (Princeton: Princeton University Press, 2001), p. 25); 'the problem in Western human rights policy is that by promoting ethnic self-determination, we may actually endanger the stability that is a precondition for protecting human rights' (ibid., p. 29); and 'the chief threat to human rights comes not from tyranny alone, but from civil war and anarchy' (ibid., p. 35).

[53] Burke, *Decolonization*, p. 123.

the Federal Court, Malaysia's highest appellate court, ruled that Muslims wishing to convert from Islam must obtain a certificate of apostasy from the Sharia Court—knowing, presumably, that the latter had never issued such a certificate to any living Malay-Muslim in Malaysia. Yvonne Tew observes that '[t]he majority were clearly concerned about community stability and religious harmony. In the leading judgement, the Chief Justice reasoned that the effects of allowing apostates to convert out of Islam would be to cause "chaos among Muslims".'[54] Malaysia is not yet a State Party to the International Covenant on Civil and Political Rights (ICCPR), and so, while it does affirm the right of every person to profess and practise his or her religion, it does not recognise a person's 'right... to adopt a religion or belief of his choice'.[55] Whether or not it should recognise such a right depends on an empirical, political judgement about the readiness of Malaysian society to accept such an innovation without violence, and about the ability of the state to suppress such violence, should it arise.

In case such a 'trade-off' be thought morally insupportable, we should remember that the ICCPR itself recognises that it may be justified to qualify or suspend certain rights for reasons of political stability: 'In time of emergency which threatens the life of the nation and the existence of which is officially proclaimed, the States Parties to the present Covenant may take measures derogating from their obligations under the Present Covenant to the extent strictly required by the exigencies of the situation...'[56] It is true that such derogation may not apply to Article 18, which asserts the right to freedom of religion, including the freedom to adopt a religion.[57] However, Article 18 itself states that the '[f]reedom to manifest one's religion or beliefs' may be subject to legally prescribed limitations, which are 'necessary to protect public safety, order, health, or morals, or the fundamental rights and freedom of others'.[58]

While compromise should be uncomfortable to live with, it may still be morally justified. One justifying feature is that the active intention to promote human rights is not simply abandoned; rather, the means of achieving it are made more politically tactful and patient.[59] Thus in the 1820s Sir John Malcolm counselled that the British in India should express their disapproval of such indigenous practices as *sati* (the self-immolation of widows on the funeral pyres of their late husbands) and female infanticide, but that they should not interfere with

[54] Tew, 'Beyond "Asian Values"', pp. 3–4.   [55] ICCPR, Art. 18.1.   [56] ICCPR, Art. 4.1.
[57] ICCPR, Art. 4.2.
[58] ICCPR, Art. 18.3. It is not entirely clear from the wording of the article whether the qualified freedom to manifest one's religion includes the freedom to adopt a new one—that is, whether clause 3 of Article 18 covers everything in clause 1. It is difficult to see, however, why the freedom to adopt a new religion should not be subject to the same conditions as the freedom to manifest one's religion, unless the thought is that anyone is free to change their beliefs, so long as they do not give public expression to the change.
[59] See Nigel Biggar, 'Compromise: When is it Morally Wrong?', *Studies in Christian Ethics*, 31/1 (February 2018), pp. 34–47.

them, since they lacked the power to manage the consequent political unrest. Addressing officers of the East India Company, he wrote:

> You are called upon to perform no easy task; to possess power, but seldom to exercise it; to witness abuses which you think you could correct; to see the errors if not crimes, of superstitious bigotry, and the miseries of misrule, and yet forbear, lest you injure interests far greater than any within the sphere of your limited duties, and impede or embarrass, by a rash change and innovation that may bring local benefit, the slow but certain march of general improvement.[60]

Instead of unilaterally mounting a direct assault on practices that he found personally abhorrent—and that might be described as violations of human rights—Malcolm sought out a native ally in the Hindu holy man Sahajanand Swami, and together they agreed in 1830 upon a campaign to abolish *sati* and female infanticide by *moral persuasion*.[61]

Another case of morally justified compromise over human rights is the Peace of Vereeniging in 1902. This was the final settlement of the Second Anglo-Boer War of 1899–1902, fought in South Africa between the British and the two Afrikaner or Boer republics of the Transvaal and the Orange Free State. One reason for the war was Boer resentment at British criticism of their mistreatment of black Africans and correlative interference by the imperial authorities to secure African rights. Cape Colony had granted black Africans the vote, under certain conditions, as early as 1853; and in the 1881 Convention of Pretoria, which ended the First Anglo-Boer War, the British had insisted on the suzerainty of their Empire, partly to secure the right of imperial authorities to intervene in defence of black Africans. However, at the Peace of Vereeniging in 1902, the victorious British agreed to let the question of African rights be decided by the Boer republics *after* they had been removed from post-war imperial supervision and granted confederal autonomy. That is, they agreed that the republics should decide the matter for themselves, even though this made the prospect of African rights in the short term most insecure. The reason that the British compromised was that they feared, with good reason, that to insist on African rights would be to pour salt into the wounds of a bitter war, and could even result in its resumption. They also perceived that for the imperial authorities to try and enforce such rights in the republics would require a level of military and financial commitment that could not sustain domestic political support. Therefore, they compromised. But they did not simply surrender the cause of African well-being. Rather, they compromised in the hope that, long

---

[60] John Malcolm, *Malcolm: Soldier, Diplomat, Ideologue of British India* (Edinburgh: John Donald, 2014), p. 455.

[61] Ibid., p. 506. As it happened, when the government in Calcutta outlawed *sati* in 1829, Malcolm followed suit, and the social and political repercussions were minimal (ibid., p. 507).

term, once the Boer republics had settled down in the British Empire and discovered the benefits of its administration, and once immigration had increased the British proportion of their populations, the issue of the rights of black Africans could be successfully addressed by political means.[62] Such compromise was indeed an instance of *Realpolitik*, but in its original, rather than its received, sense—that is, not the cynical, ruthless pursuit of power at all costs, but rather the canny pursuit of liberal, humane goals by politically realistic, patient, gradual means.[63]

VIII

The necessity—and moral propriety—of compromise between human rights and political reality is made starkly visible in the Rwandan government's resort to *gacaca* courts after the genocide of 1994. By 1998 Rwanda's gaols incarcerated 130,000 suspected *génocidaires* in space designed for 12,000 prisoners. The living conditions of the inmates were accordingly awful, and thousands died.[64] Between December 1996 and 1998 conventional courts had tried only 1,292 suspects, not least because the genocide had killed a large number of judges and other judicial staff and destroyed much of the judicial infrastructure. 'At that rate,' comments an NGO report, 'genocide trials would have continued for more than a century, leaving many suspects behind bars awaiting trial for years and even decades.'[65] Moreover in 1998 President Paul Kagame announced that the annual cost of maintaining such a large number of prisoners—US$20 million—was unsustainable.[66] Subsequently, he convened a broad array of national leaders in a series of

---

[62] See G. B. Pyrah, *Imperial Policy in South Africa, 1902-10* (Oxford: Clarendon Press, 1955), chapter IV: 'The Non-European Majority', esp. pp. 92–6; John Marlowe, *Milner, Apostle of Empire* (London: Hamish Hamilton, 1976), pp. 121–2, 132, 140; Terence H. O'Brien, *Milner: Viscount Milner of St James's and Cape Town, 1854–1925* (London: Constable, 1979), p. 220; G. H. L. Le May, *British Supremacy in South Africa, 1899–1907* (Oxford: Clarendon Press, 1965), p. 203.

[63] Nowadays *Realpolitik* denotes nothing but the ruthless pursuit of power—as represented classically by Macchiavelli. Originally, however, it meant something quite different. It was coined in 1853 by Ludwig August von Rochau (1810–73), a liberal who had been disillusioned by the crushing of the various attempts in Europe to establish liberal constitutions in 1848, which had invariably failed. (Europe's 1848 was rather like the Arab Spring, except that it expired within twelve months.) Von Rochau invented the word 'Realpolitik' to describe and recommend the pursuit of liberal constitutional goals by politically realistic—gradual and patient—means. Originally, it meant the pursuit of liberal ends by politically canny, rather than politically stupid, means. Only later under Bismarck did its meaning degenerate into the ruthless pursuit of power in a social Darwinist struggle for survival. See John Bew, 'The Real Origins of Realpolitik', *The National Interest*, 130 (March/April 2014) and *Realpolitik: A History* (New York: Oxford University Press, 2016).

[64] Human Rights Watch [HRW], *Justice Compromised: The Legacy of Rwanda's Community-based Gacaca Courts* (New York: Human Rights Watch, 2011), p. 14.

[65] HRW, *Justice Compromised*, p. 2. Notwithstanding the launch of a major judicial overhaul in 1996–7, including a campaign to train new judges and lawyers, by 2000 the courts had still only heard 2,500 cases, less than 3 per cent of the backlog (Phil Clark, *The Gacaca Courts, Post-Genocide Justice and Reconciliation in Rwanda: Justice without Lawyers*, Cambridge Studies in Law and Society (Cambridge: Cambridge University Press, 2010), pp. 55–6).

[66] Clark, *The Gacaca Courts*, p. 51.

conferences at Urigwiro in 1998–9, to decide how to resolve the problem of national reconstruction. The main result was the decision to use a modified version of traditional community *gacaca* ('grass') courts to try lower-level suspects, leaving higher-level ones to the national courts and the International Criminal Tribunal for Rwanda.[67] The intention of this decision was twofold: first, to speed up the hearing of cases and so reduce the prison population more quickly;[68] and second, to engage the Rwandan people in the process of reconstruction, helping them to discover the truth of what had happened, to own the process of coming to terms with the past, to learn the virtues of conflict-resolution, and to move toward reconciliation.[69] With a view to promoting this latter end, judges were to be elected by the people, subject to certain conditions of eligibility, and professional lawyers were to be forbidden to assist suspects or witnesses, lest their participation jeopardise an 'open, non-adversarial' approach.[70] The use of *gacaca* courts, declared President Kagame, would be '[a]n African solution to African problems'.[71]

That may be so, but it is a solution that Western human rights advocates have found seriously wanting. Take, for example, the 2011 report published by the New York-based body, Human Rights Watch (HRW)—*Justice Compromised*. The report was not unappreciative of the achievements of the *gacaca* courts. It acknowledged that their experiment in mass community-based justice had shed light on the truth of what happened, helped families to locate murdered relatives' bodies, ensured that tens of thousands of perpetrators were brought to justice, and set in motion reconciliation.[72] Nevertheless, the *gacaca* system had also involved violations of 'due process', many of which can be traced back to 'the single most significant compromise', namely, 'the curtailment of the fair trial rights of the accused'.[73] While the *gacaca* laws had protected some rights (e.g. to be presumed innocent until proven guilty) and modified others (e.g. to have adequate time to prepare a defence), it had 'entirely sacrificed' some rights altogether (e.g. to legal counsel).[74] The government justified this sacrifice on three grounds: that it was impossible to provide legal counsel to all of the very high number of accused without significantly delaying the trials; that the participation of local communities would serve to guard against false testimony; and that the involvement of adversarial lawyers would hinder community ownership.[75] Nevertheless, HRW

[67] Ibid., pp. 63–4. The International Criminal Tribunal for Rwanda had been authorised by the UN in November 1994 to prosecute the primary orchestrators of the genocide and the most serious perpetrators (Ibid., p. 20). As an example of the expensive cumbersomeness of this court, and the enormous task of sustaining it, the two-year budget for the Tribunal in 2012 and 2013 was $174,320,000 (down from $257,080,000 in 2010 and 2011). By February 2013, it had indicted 93 people and completed 75 cases, of which 47 were convicted. See Posner, *The Twilight of Human Rights Law*, p. 54.
[68] Clark, *The Gacaca Courts*, pp. 32, 51, 57.   [69] Ibid., pp. 5, 28, 237, 256.
[70] Ibid., pp. 75, 77.   [71] HRW, *Justice Compromised*, p. 1.   [72] Ibid., p. 3.
[73] Ibid., p. 4.   [74] Ibid., pp. 4, 27.   [75] Ibid., p. 28.

observed that compliance with its international obligations 'was not [the government's] top priority',[76] and judged that its 'substantial compromises' had not 'adequately protect[ed] the rights of the parties and [had] led in many instances to unfair trials'.[77] It reported instances where the fundamental right to the presumption of innocence, and the right to be informed of the case for the prosecution and have time to prepare a defence, had 'not always been respected'.[78] It also reported that the communal check against false testimony had not always worked, because of the fear of social ostracism.[79] Moreover, HRW claimed that the Rwandan government could have put in place alternative measures that would have both accelerated the process and guaranteed the right to legal counsel, had it not turned down two proposals: one by the UN, EU, and non-governmental bodies early in 1995, for foreign judges and legal personnel to work alongside Rwandan judicial officials; and another by the Danish Centre for Human Rights in 2002, for national and international 'judicial defenders' (legal professionals, not lawyers), funded by foreign donors, to provide the accused with pre-trial legal advice and speed up the judicial process by encouraging the guilty to confess in exchange for reduced sentences under the system's plea-bargaining scheme.[80] In conclusion, the HRW report recommended that the Rwandan government announce a definitive deadline for ending *gacaca* trials and that it confirm that all outstanding and new genocide-related cases would be decided by conventional courts.[81] It also recommended that any other country considering the adoption of a process analogous to the *gacaca* system should ensure the guarantee of fair trial rights, including access to pre-trial legal advice.[82]

From the foregoing it would be reasonable to think that HRW believed that the Rwandan government could have squared the circle: that it could have accelerated the hearing of the backlog of cases and reduced the prison population *without compromising* fundamental rights of accused individuals to due process. In fact, however, HRW's report is much more equivocal than that. It concedes that the scale and complexity of the genocide 'would have overwhelmed even the best-equipped judicial system'.[83] It would have been impossible to staff the more than 12,000 *gacaca* courts with 'legally trained professionals', for while the number of judges had more than tripled by 1996, it was still insufficient.[84] Therefore, '[t]he government's need to complete all genocide trials in years rather than decades made the usual type of legal representation for each and every accused impossible',[85] and its decision to adopt the *gacaca* system 'was not an unreasonable way to offer some form of justice for the genocide'.[86] The report even concedes that '[a] number of compromises may have been inevitable in the context of *gacaca*', just

---

[76] Ibid., p. 28.   [77] Ibid., p. 27.   [78] Ibid., pp. 31, 34, 46.   [79] Ibid., p. 4.

[80] Ibid., p. 29. HRW attributes the proposal to the Danish *Institute* for Human Rights. In fact, the proposal was made by the Danish *Centre* for Human Rights, before it became the Institute in June 2002.

[81] Ibid., p. 7.   [82] Ibid., p. 10.   [83] Ibid., p. 13.   [84] Ibid., p. 65.   [85] Ibid., p. 29.

[86] Ibid., p. 130.

after stating that compromises had led to 'significant due process violations'. Nevertheless, it still insists that 'certain fundamental rights—such as... the right to be informed of the charges with enough specificity and adequate time to prepare and present a defense (including through defense witnesses)—should have been better protected'.[87]

It is unclear whether HRW actually accepted that the 'inevitable' compromises were the same ones that led to due process violations, or whether it believed that the violations resulted from other compromises that could have been avoided. Here lies the crucial equivocation—between insisting that the government uphold standard rights to due process, while half-admitting that the resources for doing so were unavailable. The invocation of alternative proposals that the Rwandan government turned down leave the reader with the impression that additional resources of legal counsel could have been made available, had the government accepted what was proposed. Yet the report does not actually tell us whether the proposals carried with them guarantees of sufficient external funding, or how far the additional resources would have sufficed to solve the problem. In fact, there are strong reasons for doubt on the first and more fundamental of these points. The very article cited by the report to substantiate its reference to the 1995 proposal tells us that 'by late 1995, very little of the promised bilateral or multilateral aid for the judicial system had been delivered'.[88] Regarding the Danish Centre for Human Rights' 2002 proposal, its report of that year, *Partners in Progress*, merely tells us that the 'DCHR is now proposing a form of pre-trial and appeal counselling for victims and the accused... this activity will be a part of DCHR's funding submissions for 2002'.[89] However, in its 2004 report on the legal assistance available in Rwanda the Centre, which had become the Danish *Institute* for Human Rights, describes a situation where the funding of providers was not only insufficient, but where donations were short term and uncoordinated and donors were becoming increasingly weary: donor funding, it reported, had been 'drying up... as the years pass after the genocide'.[90] The previous year

[87] Ibid., p. 130.

[88] William A. Schabas, 'Justice, Democracy, and Impunity in Post-genocide Rwanda: Searching for Solutions to Impossible Problems', *Criminal Law Forum*, 7/3 (1996), p. 528.

[89] Birgit Lindsnaes, Tomas Martin, and Lisbeth Arne Pedersen, *Partners in Progress: Human Rights Reform and Implementation*, 2nd edn (Copenhagen: Danish Institute [formerly, Centre] for Human Rights, 2007), p. 42. The second edition is 'basically a reprint of the original version from 2002' (ibid., 'Notes on 2nd edition'). Thomas Brudholm helped me obtain a copy of this report.

[90] Danish Institute for Human Rights, *Legal Aid in Rwanda: A Report on the Legal Assistance Available in Rwanda* (Kigali: Danish Institute for Human Rights, April 2004), p. 52. See also p. 26, where we are told that fundraising for the Association des Veuves du Génocide Agahozo (Avega) 'has become more difficult as the years have passed after the genocide'. HRW's 1996 report on Rwanda makes clear that, from the beginning, international funding of the judicial system had been slow in coming: 'In July 1995, about a third of a promised [in late 1994] $13 million had actually been delivered' (HRW/Africa, *World Report 1996: Rwanda* (New York: HRW, 1996), p. 599).

Amnesty International's report *Rwanda: Gacaca—a Question of Justice* had observed the same thing: 'Donor fatigue has set in'.[91]

A similar refusal to grasp the nettle attends this statement in the Conclusion of *Justice Compromised*: 'The SNJG's [National Service of *Gacaca* Jurisdictions] *inability* or unwillingness to effectively monitor and remedy problems in the *gacaca* system as a whole stemmed from *inadequate resources*, a lack of political will, and a failure to proactively monitor cases and listen to local communities and outside observers about worrying trends that developed countrywide'.[92] But was the SNJG actually *unable*? Did it in fact *lack sufficient resources*? If so, then, arguably, its lack of political will, its practical failures, and its ceasing to listen to unrealistic external critics stemmed from its lack of power and should be forgiven. HRW gives no clear answer to these questions. The fact that its recommendations do not forgive implies that the necessary resources were available, yet HRW's report does not show that they were available and other sources suggest that they were not.[93]

Besides, the report nowhere addresses the issue of the 'restorative' dimension of the *gacaca* system—that is, the fact that it was designed to promote 'reconciliation', at least in the minimal sense of restoring social coexistence, by bringing to public light the local truth of what had happened in 1994, having perpetrators face victims (or their relatives), and having victims (or their relatives) come to sustainable terms with their injuries. Unlike the form of transitional justice embodied in South Africa's Truth and Reconciliation Commission, Rwanda's *gacaca* process involved, not only confession, but judgement and punishment. Nevertheless, this retributive element was ordered toward the larger restorative end, by taking the form, for example, of community service.[94] The Rwandan government's argument was that to involve adversarial lawyers in this process would have hindered popular ownership and interpersonal reconciliation. Whether or not this argument is cogent, nowhere does HRW's report take care to rebut it.[95]

---

[91] Amnesty International, *Rwanda: Gacaca—A Question of Justice*, AI Index: AFR 47/007/2002 (London: Amnesty International, December 2002), p. 42.

[92] HRW, *Justice Compromised*, p. 131. The emphases are mine.

[93] To its credit the HRW did edge closer to nettle-grasping than Amnesty International (AI). In *Rwanda: Gacaca*, AI reports several times over the Rwandan government's argument that the paucity of resources had compelled it to compromise international human rights standards governing due process (p. 42). It also acknowledges donor fatigue (ibid.). But then it merely asserts, without any argument whatsoever, that the government had used that argument 'too readily' to derogate from human rights standards (ibid.). Two pages later it proceeds to lay down its long list of demands for legal safeguards.

[94] Those found guilty by *gacaca* courts could commute half of their sentences by taking part in community service projects designed to improve the lives of victims and the community as a whole (Amnesty International, *Rwanda: Gacaca*, p. 43).

[95] In this respect HRW's 2011 report conforms to the dominant type of *gacaca*-criticism, of which Phil Clark complains: it concentrates on the retributive element of justice to the neglect of the restorative end; and it therefore fails to take seriously the importance of popular ownership (*The Gacaca Courts*, pp. 4, 28). Regarding this point, Clark quotes the pointed comment of Tharcisse Karugarama, then Rwandan Minister of Justice, that 'lawyers are arrogant people and unfortunately

In the first book-length account of the *gacaca* process and its critics, Phil Clark objects that, in general, human rights organisations have complained about the rights violations incurred by the lengthy detainment of suspects in harsh conditions, while insisting that the acceleration of trials should not be achieved at the expense of due process.[96] In other words, they *assume* that the circle *can* be squared, without showing so. But suppose that the restorative orientation of transitional justice is appropriate after civil bloodletting on a society-wide scale. Suppose that this, as well as the absence of resources, requires and justifies the compromise of certain legal rights that are standard in stable, liberal societies. Suppose that this compromise involves, not exactly the denial to the accused of the right to defend himself, but only the refusal of the right to standard means (e.g. legal counsel) and the substitution of other means (e.g. the opportunity for the community to challenge false testimony).[97] This does not amount to the abandonment of the right to a fair trial, but rather only to the taking of *greater risks* with the fairness. The fact that the *gacaca* process did involve abuses and miscarriages of justice is no small matter, but nor is it extraordinary. All human judicial systems are vulnerable; none is foolproof. And in certain circumstances, it may be justifiable to take greater risks. Indeed, it may be politically irresponsible not to. The standard rights to due process are maximally safe means of ensuring fairness. But in certain social, economic, and political contexts, the adoption of less safe means may be morally justified. Judging by HRW's equivocal report, which is more nuanced than others, some human rights advocates find that impossible to swallow.[98]

I belong to that clan . . . they think that justice is their exclusive right. They think their exclusive right is the law without realising the justice is the domain of all the people. Law and justice are separate entities' (*The Gacaca Courts*, pp. 59, 241).

[96] Clark, *The Gacaca Courts*, p. 174.

[97] Anuradha Chakravarty conducted field-research on the tribunals of the pilot phase of the *gacaca* process. This, he claims, 'shows that several factors considerably mitigate the risk of unfair trials. The accused have a chance to present their case in front of the community during the pre-trial phase. At this time, and even later on in the information-gathering period, witnesses are able to testify for or against defendants. When the actual trial is underway, defendants are informed of the charges against them and are given the right to speak and present their cases. As a matter of procedure, judges give defendants the opportunity to add testimony if they think the record is incomplete in any way. Defendants are even able to contest judges' categorisation of the crimes they are accused of, in which case judges retire to a private room to deliberate on the merits of the claims. The trial reconvenes only after the nine judges arrive at a decision by majority vote on how to proceed. Finally, the sentence is subject to appeal. Defendants are asked whether they are satisfied that the sentence is fair, and if not, they can file papers for appeal on the spot' ('Gacaca Courts in Rwanda: Explaining Divisions within the Human Rights Community', *Yale Journal of International Affairs* (Winter/Spring 2006), p. 135.

[98] Chakravarty observes a difference among human rights NGOs in Rwanda. Some—such as Avocats sans Frontiéres, Réseau de Citoyens, and Penal Reform International—assumed a supportive posture of 'critical partnership' with the Rwandan government, which enabled them to appreciate the practical constraints to which it was subject, and to see that these rendered 'the absolute application of human rights principles virtually impossible' ('Gacaca Courts in Rwanda', pp. 139, 142). In contrast, others—such as Amnesty International and HRW—view human rights as essentially freedoms from abuse, oppression, cruelty, and interference *by the state*: 'The state is perpetually an object of critique as human rights advocates exercise eternal vigilance against the state's expanding sphere of control' (ibid.,

IX

Western advocates of human rights should learn from their encounter with non-Western cultures that there is room for reasonable discussion and disagreement about the extent of certain freedoms. They should also learn that, in some political contexts, it would be imprudent and counterproductive to assert certain rights, but that this need not amount to the simple surrender that amounts to a bad compromise. Sometimes it is justified to expose to greater risk the liberties that legal rights seek to secure.

Something else that human rights advocates should learn is that rights are not ethically sufficient. Indeed, for Confucians, they are secondary to the exercise of virtue in the management of healthy relationships, and only come into play as a litigious last resort in case of conflict.[99] Even then, however, the issue arises of how to exercise rights virtuously, and the ability to do so requires the 'inner freedom' that issues from the self-cultivation that consists in the ordering of conflicting desires and the mastery of lower ones.[100]

Take, for example, the right to freedom of speech. The staunch apologist for 'Western human rights', Jack Donnelly, is uncompromising:

> Essential to any plausible conception of human rights…is the claim that all human beings have certain rights prior to and irrespective of their discharge of social duties…A right to free speech has no logical connection to an obligation not to disseminate lies. Society and the state may legitimately punish me for spreading vicious lies that harm others. The penalties, however, rest on the rights or interests of those who I harm, not my right to free speech. If I slander someone, I do not lose my right to freedom of speech—if we conceive of it as a human right. Incitement to communal or religious hatred may be legitimately prohibited and punished, but even the most vocal hate monger still has a right to express his views on other subjects—if free speech is a human right. Defensible limits on the exercise of a right should not be confused with duties inherent in the possession of a right.[101]

Donnelly is correct, of course, to say that the legal right to free speech does not itself logically entail any duty on the part of the right-holder; and that it is *other*

---

p. 141). As a consequence, these NGOs, generally 'unburdened by the need to build working relationships with governments', displayed 'a reluctance to understand [the Rwandan government's] dilemmas', and offered only 'escalating criticism' (ibid., pp. 139, 141).

[99] Chan, 'A Confucian Perspective', pp. 220–1, 226, 227, 228: 'the Confucian perspective would take rights as a fallback auxiliary apparatus that serves to protect basic human interests in case virtues do not obtain or human relationships clearly break down'.

[100] Seung-hwan Lee, 'Liberal Rights or/and Confucian Virtues?', *Philosophy East and West*, 46/3 (July 1996), pp. 369–70, 372.

[101] Donnelly, 'Human Rights and Asian Values', pp. 78–9.

legal rights against libel or slander or hate-speech that impose legal duties and constrain the lawful exercise of freedom of speech. What Donnelly misses, however, is that, even *within* the space remaining for free speech, after all the constraints by relevant legal rights have been taken into account, *moral* obligations arise. Within certain bounds the law will not prohibit gratuitous insult or needling provocation or wilful misrepresentation or uncharitable interpretation, but morality, arguably, does.[102] These moral duties then raise the question of what it takes to be the kind of person who is in sufficient control of himself as to be *capable* of not insulting, provoking, misrepresenting, and being uncharitable. That is to say, it raises the question of the formation of moral virtue. This is what Confucian eyes see—but Donnelly's 'human rights' eyes miss—when they contemplate 'American-style' or libertarian free speech.[103]

However, it is not only traditionally 'Eastern' eyes that are alert to the ethical insufficiency of rights-talk. Western Christians, who are in touch with their moral tradition and their Sacred Scriptures, will be alert to it, too. One of the matters that St Paul treats on several occasions in his epistles to the early Christian communities in Corinth and Rome is the Christian's proper attitude toward Jewish law or regulations structuring the religious life, especially the eating of 'pure' or 'impure' food. Paul himself came to the view that religious faith in Christ permits the Christian to dispense with the law. This is the negative dimension of Christian liberty or freedom—freedom *from* Jewish law. There is, however, also a much more important positive dimension—freedom *for* love. When considering the treatment of unnecessarily scrupulous Christians (those with a 'weak conscience'), who do not feel free to dispense with Jewish law, Paul counsels their more enlightened and liberated brethren (those with 'knowledge') to restrain their own exploitation of negative freedom for the sake of exercising the positive freedom of love. As he writes to the Corinthian Christians:

> Now about food sacrificed to idols: We know that 'We all possess knowledge.' But knowledge puffs up while love builds up. Those who think they know something do not yet know as they ought to know. But whoever loves God is known by God.
>
> So then, about eating food sacrificed to idols: We know that 'An idol is nothing at all in the world' and that 'There is no God but one' ... for us there is but one God, the Father, from whom all things came and for whom we live; and there is but

[102] I argued this with regard to the *Charlie Hebdo* murders in January 2015. See Nigel Biggar, '*Charlie Hebdo* took Offensiveness too Far', *The Times*, 9 January 2016: <https://www.mcdonaldcentre.org.uk/sites/default/files/content/charlie_hebdo_took_offensiveness_too_far_the_times.pdf> (as at 8 January 2019).
[103] Bauer and Bell, 'Introduction', in *The East Asian Challenge for Human Rights*, pp. 14, 17; Chan, 'A Confucian Perspective', p. 234.

one Lord, Jesus Christ, through whom all things came and through whom we live.

But not everyone possesses this knowledge. Some people are still so accustomed to idols that when they eat sacrificial food they think of it as having been sacrificed to a god, and since their conscience is weak, it is defiled. But food does not bring us near to God; we are no worse if we do not eat, and no better if we do.

Be careful, however, that the exercise of your rights [ἐξουσία][104] does not become a stumbling block to the weak. For if someone with a weak conscience sees you, with all your knowledge, eating in an idol's temple, won't that person be emboldened to eat what is sacrificed to idols? So this weak brother or sister, for whom Christ died, is destroyed by your knowledge. When you sin against them in this way and wound their weak conscience, you sin against Christ. Therefore, if what I eat causes my brother or sister to fall into sin, I will never eat meat again, so that I will not cause them to fall.[105]

Along the same lines Paul addresses the Christian community in Rome:

I am convinced, being fully persuaded in the Lord Jesus, that nothing is unclean in itself. But if anyone regards something as unclean, then for that person it is unclean. If your brother or sister is distressed because of what you eat, you are no longer acting in love...

Let us therefore make every effort to do what leads to peace and to mutual edification. Do not destroy the work of God for the sake of food. All food is clean, but it is wrong for a person to eat anything that causes someone else to stumble. It is better not to eat meat or drink wine or to do anything else that will cause your brother or sister to fall.

So whatever you believe about these things keep between yourself and God...

We who are strong ought to bear with the failings of the weak and not to please ourselves.[106]

Whatever our liberty rights—be they legal or moral—our exercise of them is subject to moral duties. One of these is the duty not to alienate other people by slaughtering their sacred cows for trivial or unnecessary reasons. Eastern Confucians recognise this as a duty of *ren* or benevolence; Western (and Eastern) Christians, as a duty of love. Both recognise that not everyone is

---

[104] The Greek word ἐξουσία can mean 'authority', 'power', or freedom of choice'. In this context it means, not exactly 'a right' or 'rights', but rather 'a rightful freedom' from Jewish law. Not for the first time a modern translator has found rights-talk in a pre-modern text, where it does not exist.

[105] St Paul, First Epistle to the Corinthians, 8:1–13 (New International Version).

[106] St Paul, Epistle to the Romans, 14:14–15a, 19–22a; 15:1 (New International Version).

characteristically disposed to be able to perform such duty, and that the virtue of benevolence or love needs to be cultivated. Those whose ethics are confined to rights-talk cannot see this.

X

So, are human rights universal? Certainly, there is plenty of evidence that some of the goods or values or, more specifically, liberties that Western human rights aim to secure have long been recognised in traditional social and political systems outside of the West. The protection of innocent life from physical harm, or individual freedom from arbitrary curtailment, or of fairness in trying a criminal case, for example, is, quite unsurprisingly, not unique to the West. However, even though the moral rightness of such protection has been widely recognised, the chosen means of protection have often not taken the form of strictly *legal* rights backed by the threat of judicial sanctions against their violation. Sometimes the virtue of the ruler, or the authority of customary law or of prevalent social opinion, has been thought sufficiently reliable. As Kwasi Wiredu writes of the Akan-speaking peoples of West Africa, the individual's 'rights' to aid from other members of the community 'did not have the backing of state sanctions', but instead 'enjoyed the strong backing of public opinion'.[107]

Still, if custom prescribes that violations should be met with communal sanctions, then we do have a form of legal right.[108] Therefore, we can conclude that some legal rights have long been recognised outside of modern, Western culture, even if not the whole panoply of post-war human rights.[109] While I strongly suspect that certain such rights have been recognised by every human society, since they seem necessary for social survival, only a comprehensive global survey of human societies, past and present, could prove it. Since I know of no such conclusive study, I will not claim here that some customary legal rights are universal.

However, even if some rights are universal in the sense of being present in every society, their scope of application will often be limited; that is, they will apply only to insiders, and not to outsiders. There is plenty of historical evidence to substantiate doubt that every human society has always recognised that members of other

[107] Kwasi Wiredu, 'An Akan Perspective on Human Rights', in An-Naim and Deng, *Human Rights in Africa*, p. 247.
[108] As explained in Chapter 5 (p. 94n.2), I doubt that the authority of public opinion, backed by the threat of social opprobrium against transgressors, is sufficient to warrant talk of 'a right'. This is both because prevalent public opinion is seldom universally representative, and because it is not stable.
[109] Charles Taylor claims that while rights-talk has its roots in Western culture, the underlying norms (against genocide, murder, torture, slavery) can be found elsewhere ('Conditions of an Unforced Consensus on Human Rights', p. 125). I go further: I think that some rights-talk can also be found elsewhere.

societies deserve, for example, not to have their lives taken wantonly. So it seems that we cannot say that human rights possessed by all members of the human species have been universally recognised. Indeed, they are not recognised even today in many liberal Western countries, where embryonic human beings have no legal right against being killed at will or upon demand by their mothers. That said, there is evidence at least that *some* traditional, non-Western societies have acknowledged the common humanity of all members of the human species and, presumably, that they all deserve at least some kinds of equal treatment.

Be that as it may, it is an empirical fact that the standard post-war lists of post-war human rights are not universally recognised, since not every state has signed up to them.[110] Indeed, we may not even take subscription as a sign of consensus: because while signing the international covenants and similar treaties 'can be seen as a route toward becoming a fully-fledged participant in the developed world's trading regimes, . . . the consensus these documents represent may be more apparent than real'.[111] This lack of universal agreement could mean that the conventional set of human rights fits modern Western polities, but not non-Western ones. Insofar as the latter are less stable, being more vulnerable to destabilising inter-ethnic or inter-religious conflict, or insofar as they lack the financial and other resources to maintain certain rights (e.g. to legal counsel), that will indeed be so. In such cases, to browbeat governments for not meeting international standards is intellectually dishonest, insensitively moralistic, and politically irritating. Instead, those who are concerned about justice should display the virtue of prudence and recognise that some circumstances really do provide moral justification for compromise. Nevertheless, international human rights standards could still be upheld as ideals of maximal security against risks to important freedoms, to which fragile governments, with aid from international partners, should approximate as circumstances allow.[112]

However, when strong and well-resourced non-Western states dispense themselves from having to uphold certain rights—say, against arbitrary detention, or to due process in criminal trial—on the ground that the latter are 'Western', we should be sceptical. It is not only Westerners who can recognise the dangers to individuals and civil society of an overweening state or political authority. But whether or not the denial or suspension of certain rights is in fact justified by political circumstance can only be determined by careful empirical assessment.

---

[110] As of the date of writing (February 2019) there are nineteen states that have neither signed nor ratified the ICCPR, and a further six (including China) that have signed but not ratified it. Twenty-two states have neither signed nor ratified the ICESCR, and a further four (including the USA) have signed but not ratified it.

[111] Angle, *Human Rights and Chinese Thought*, p. 9.

[112] Raymond Pannikar is correct: 'To accept the fact that the concept of Human Rights *is* not universal does not yet mean that it *should* not *become* so' ('Is the Notion of Human Rights a Western Concept?', *Diogenes*, 120 (1980), p. 84). The emphasis is Pannikar's.

It cannot be determined by the indignant, unreflective assertion of the moral authority of 'human rights'.

In what sense, then, is it true to say that human rights are 'Western'? In our discussions of natural and subjective rights in Chapters 2 and 6, respectively, we have seen how the concept of rights as the (legal) property of individuals began to flourish in Western Europe as early as the thirteenth century, and that there is reason to suppose that this was in part the fruit of the high status of the individual in Christian thinking. Short of conducting a comparative survey of legal thought across the globe and throughout the ages, I cannot claim with confidence that the development of the discourse of individual rights in the late medieval Christian West was unique. But I can say, given my limited reading about Confucian, Islamic, and traditional African cultures, that it seems to have been extraordinary.[113] If that is so, then I am claiming that, with regard to the importance of the protection of the freedom of individuals (and civil social bodies) from unwarranted interference by ruling authorities, be they secular or ecclesiastical, Christian Western tradition displays a superior grasp. I do not claim that Christian Western tradition displays a superior grasp in every respect, but only in this one. Whether or not this particular claim is true, the idea that one tradition might be intellectually or morally superior in particular respects over others seems to me perfectly obvious and incontrovertible. While the hackles of multiculturalists will instinctively rise up against this assertion, it is probably not as alien to them as they think; for insofar as they are *liberal* multiculturalists, they, too, will assume that liberal tradition is morally superior to illiberal traditions.

However, even if explicit talk about the rights of individuals has been delivered by one tradition to another, that does not mean that rights-talk is simply alien to the latter. Rather, it might be that the articulated insight of one tradition resonates with more or less inarticulate elements already present in the other, giving them voice and power. As a consequence, it becomes possible to reconfigure the receiving tradition so that it can own the imported ideas in an authentic fashion.[114]

---

[113] In this sense—which is not quite his own, secular one—Jack Donnelly's claim is true: the Western origins of human rights ideas 'is a simple historical fact' ('Human Rights and Asian Values', p. 69). But Paulin Hountondji is closer to the truth, when he writes that Western philosophers produced 'not the thing but discourse about the thing, not the idea of natural law or human dignity but the work of expression concerning the idea' ('The Master's Voice—Remarks on the Problem of Human Rights in Africa', in *Philosophical Foundations of Human Rights* (Paris: UNESCO, 1986); reprinted by the National University of Benin, Nigeria, p. 320; cited by Mahmood Mamdani in 'The Social Basis of Constitutionalism in Africa', *The Journal of Modern African Studies*, 28/3 (1990), p. 360).

[114] Regarding this point, I note James Silk's suggestion that the religious myth that gives rise to the recognition of universal human dignity among the Dinka people, who are native to south Sudan, might owe something to contact with the monotheisms 'just down the Nile'—Judaism, Christianity, and Islam ('Traditional Culture and the Prospect for Human Rights in Africa', in An-Naim and Deng, *Human Rights in Africa*, pp. 327–8). I note, too, that, while the Iraqi Bedia Afnan argued that women's rights could find an authentic place in Muslim culture, the necessary reconfiguration would involve borrowing from the West (Burke, *Decolonisation*, p. 124). And I also note Stephen Angle's argument that while the explicit rights-talk of Liang Qichao (1873–1929) and Liu Shipei (1884–1919) in early twentieth-

And in so doing it might well contribute something important of its own, so that the process actually becomes a dialogue between two traditions, and develops beyond a simple monologue from one to the other. As we have seen, Confucian reflection on rights points out that rights-talk is not enough—that we also need to talk about the virtues that will enable citizens to respect the rights of others, and perhaps avoid the social conflict that arises when they are asserted. In this way, Confucians remind Western rights advocates of something that lies in the Christian and Aristotelian roots of their own tradition, and about which they have become largely oblivious.

In sum, my conclusion is this. The human goods that rights seek to protect are universal: they are elements of the universal nature of human flourishing. It is unlikely that any human society has ever come into existence which failed to recognise some human goods and neglected to protect them by threatening to punish members who damage them for no good reason. It follows that it is unlikely that any society has ever existed without establishing customary or legal rights that enjoy some measure of security. Reasonable speculation, therefore, suggests that the phenomenon of rights is universal. At least what we can say with certainty is that the phenomenon is not simply or originally Western, since there is empirical evidence that some non-Western societies have in fact established rights, many of them familiar to Westerners. There are, however, many different ways in which a good can be protected by a legal right, and the way chosen by a particular society will be shaped by its historical, cultural, and other circumstances. Therefore, while the good to be protected is universal, and while the means of protecting it by establishing a right is very probably universal, the specific form of the protective right will not be universal. Circumstances might dictate (through the virtue of prudence) that certain rights should not be granted at all, or that they should be suspended; and circumstances always dictate what level of security it is prudent to accord any right. It follows that the full panoply of rights—and their forms—that are standard in modern Western societies are not universally appropriate. And insofar as post-1945 'human rights' declarations, covenants, and conventions express Western standards, they are not universally appropriate either. What is not appropriate is imprudent, and imprudence is a moral vice.

century China drew from the neo-Confucian discussion of legitimate interests, it did so in the light of the thought of the German legal philosopher Rudolf von Jhering (1818–92), and the French philosopher Jean-Jacques Rousseau (*Human Rights and Chinese Thought*, p. 23).

9
What's Wrong with Rights in Ethics?

I

In Chapter 6 we observed the tendency of contemporary rights-talk to push all other moral considerations off the table: 'rights' tend to exclude 'right'. This observation had been adumbrated in Chapter 5, where contemporary philosophical defences of natural, moral rights were seen to lack any awareness that the exercise of such rights might be subject to moral obligations and even contingent upon the performance of duties of virtue.[1] In Chapter 1 we observed the complaint of sceptics that natural, moral rights are too often not distinguished from positively legal ones, with the consequence that the qualities of the latter are imported—or, rather, smuggled—into natural morality or ethics. Thereby, what makes sense as a civil institution is assumed to make equal sense in uncivil circumstances. How conscious such smuggling is, I cannot say, but it seems to me not accidental. It seems to be part of a current cultural inclination to assimilate morality to law and replace conscience with procedures. The intention of the project is to abolish the possibility of a failure of conscience. While this might appear commendable at first sight, it becomes less commendable when seen as an expression of the general aversion to risk and denial of tragedy that characterises much contemporary culture, certainly in Britain, if not more broadly in the West. The cost of this aversion is a practical, moral rigidity that ranges from the imprudent to the absurd.

II

An instance of this general problem is visible in one of the very best recent contributions to military ethics: David Rodin's *War and Self-Defense*.[2] In this book, Rodin argues for an understanding of the justification of killing that implies

---

[1] Costas Douzinas detects a 'growing tendency of philosophers to present rights as the main component of morality *tout court*' ('The poverty of (rights) jurisprudence', in Gearty and Douzinas, *Cambridge Companion to Human Rights Law*, p. 58). If there is a trend, its roots go back at least to the 1970s, when J. L. Mackie made an explicit proposal to make rights *the* foundation of a theory of morality ('Can there be a Right-based Moral Theory?', *Midwest Studies in Philosophy*, 3 (1978)). For an early rebuttal of such a proposal in favour of a 'pluralistic' understanding of morality's foundations, see Raz, *The Morality of Freedom*, chapter 8.

[2] David Rodin, *War and Self-Defense* (Oxford: Clarendon Press, 2002).

the near-impossibility of waging just war. At the base of the argument stands the assertion of a 'right to life'. This right is not just positively legal; it is not just the property of members of societies whose legal systems grant it. Rather, it is naturally moral, being held by all morally responsible human beings. And it is fundamental, setting the terms of subsequent ethical deliberation, rather than being its conclusion.

Rodin acknowledges that this right is not 'inalienable' and possessed 'unconditionally'.[3] Indeed, he explicitly dissents from Ronald Dworkin's view of rights as trumps—that is to say, 'absolute ethical considerations which always override competing considerations'.[4] He concedes—in principle—that rights are not the whole of morality: having a right and being in the right are not logical equivalents.[5] Instead he holds it as 'absolutely certain that consequentialist considerations sometimes override rights and duties'—for example, that one should deceive a murderer about the location of his would-be victim[6]—and that 'rights may be violated and a right-bearer wronged by an action which, all things considered, is the right thing to do'.[7] Nevertheless, rights do have 'a distinctive stringency' such that they generally override competing moral considerations, especially consequential ones that appeal to the interests of society as a whole over and against those of individual agents.[8] If rights are not trumps, Rodin tells us, they are still 'a strong "breakwater"'.[9]

But even a strong breakwater can be overwhelmed. So when can that be? When can the right to life be lost? According to Rodin, it can be lost *only* when the bearer of the right forfeits it through voluntary and culpable wrongdoing. Thus the use of violent force can be justified, only when it is 'an appropriate response, not just to the situation at large, but to *them* [the culpably aggressive agents]'[10] 'as moral subjects'.[11] One may take another's life only on the basis of wrong that *he has freely chosen* to do. Therefore someone threatened by the familiar philosophical fat man, who is falling involuntarily from a great height, may not defend himself by killing the innocent threat, for '[t]o say that the falling fat man has the right to life is to say that he has an interest in his living which cannot be overridden except on the basis of his *own choosing, willing, or acting*'.[12]

Rodin's understanding of the justification of killing in terms of a right to life that can only be forfeited through culpable wrongdoing renders the waging of just war near-impossible for two reasons. First, it makes the killing of the morally innocent unjust. Note: it prohibits not merely the *intentional* killing of innocents, but any killing of them at all. It implies that soldiers may not take any deliberate action that foreseeably risks their deaths. Under such a stringent condition, very few wars could be fought victoriously. As the sixteenth-century scholastic theologian

---

[3] Ibid., p. 71.   [4] Ibid., p. 24.   [5] Ibid.   [6] Ibid., p. 9.   [7] Ibid., p. 24.
[8] Ibid., pp. 25, 9.   [9] Ibid., p. 25.   [10] Ibid., p. 92. The emphasis is Rodin's.
[11] Ibid., p. 89; see also p. 94.   [12] Ibid., p. 89. The emphasis is mine.

Francisco de Vitoria put: 'it is occasionally lawful to kill the innocent not by mistake, but with full knowledge of what one is doing, if this is an accidental effect... This is proven, *since it would otherwise be impossible to wage war against the guilty.*'[13] Certainly, it would have been impossible for the Allies to wage successful war against Hitler in 1939–45: Allied bombing during the Normandy campaign entailed the foreseeable deaths of 35,000 French civilians.[14] And if a war cannot be fought successfully, then, arguably, it should not be fought at all.

Second, if it is only ever justifiable to kill someone who has forfeited their right to life through culpable wrongdoing, then warriors in a just cause will usually be unable to fight the enemy justly. This is because, while a warrior in a just cause might correctly judge that his enemy counterpart is fighting in an unjust one, he seldom has the power to discern the unjust warrior's subjective culpability. The latter's cause may be objectively unjust, but perhaps he has been deluded into serving it and cannot reasonably be expected to have seen through the delusion. Or perhaps he has been forced into fighting, where the cost of resisting (say, execution and the persecution of his family) is unreasonably high. According to Rodin, unless just warriors *know* that the enemy is subjectively culpable for the wrong they do, they may not kill them. Since on the battlefield it is usually impossible for just warriors to assess the enemy's moral culpability, they cannot justly kill them. Therefore, usually, war in a just cause cannot be justly waged.

For pacifists, of course, this will be a happy conclusion. Since they think that less war is always better, they will have no objection to this practical implication of Rodin's moral reasoning in terms of the natural 'right to life'. War is not simply bad, however, nor peace simply good. My staying at peace might leave others at peace to perpetrate your unjust slaughter; my going to war might stop others perpetrating unjust slaughter and so restore your just peace. Very grave evil cannot always be warded off by peaceful means, and those who think that warding it off can sometimes justify the risks and tragedies of waging war will find the highly restrictive practical implication of Rodin's rights-reasoning unsatisfactory.

III

In fact, it turns out that Rodin eventually finds it unsatisfactory, too. In an extended endnote, he conducts an honest and revealing analysis of an agonising historical case. During the Rwandan genocide of 1994, Vénuste Hakizamungu, a Tutsi, was ordered by the Hutu Interahamwe to kill his older brother, Théoneste,

---

[13] Francisco de Vitoria, 'On the Law of War', in Vitoria, *Political Writings*, q. 3, a. 1.2, p. 315. The emphasis is mine.

[14] Fifteen thousand were killed by bombing in preparation for the landings and almost 20,000 during and after them (Antony Beevor, *D-Day: The Battle for Normandy* (London: Penguin, 2009), p. 519).

in order to save his family from slaughter. This he eventually did.[15] Rodin reasons that, notwithstanding the duress to which he was subject, Vénuste remained a responsible agent. However, since Théoneste eventually consented to his own death for the sake of his family, he spared Vénuste from committing murder. Note that Théoneste was an innocent, guilty of nothing. The clear implication, therefore, is that culpable wrongdoing is *not* the only condition under which the right to life may be lost. It may also be lost simply through the innocent's consent.

But Rodin searches further. Supposing that Théoneste had not consented, could he be blamed? Rodin equivocates. First, he entertains the possibility that Théoneste could be faulted (because he was morally obliged to consent), and he does not dismiss it. Does it follow from this that Vénuste would have been morally permitted or obliged to kill his brother *without his consent*? 'That Théoneste has a right to life militates against such a thought', Rodin correctly muses. 'For surely if there are moral reasons directing him to sacrifice himself, then they are operative only at the internal level. He may feel compelled to do so, but we can never say to him that he is obliged to sacrifice himself and would be at fault for not doing so.'[16] But then he actually rejects this line of thinking on the ground that the internal feeling of moral compulsion 'can be accessed in the objective sphere when we ask ourselves the question: what would we (feel ourselves compelled to) do in the circumstances?'[17] While he confesses himself unsure, he nevertheless concludes by affirming that 'internally derived obligations of sacrifice' should enter into an account of right action in such a terrible case.[18]

In the end, then, Rodin gingerly concedes that an individual's right to life can be forfeited and his killing justified on grounds other than his free choice to do wrong or his free choice to surrender his life. It can also be forfeited on the ground of an objective moral obligation to sacrifice himself for the sake of others, even if he refuses to recognise it—*that is, even without his consent.*

IV

This off-stage, end-note concession—that there are objective moral norms, to which external circumstances might subject the individual, and which might summarily remove his right to life—undermines the morally subjectivist understanding of human dignity that lies at the heart of Rodin's centre-stage thinking.

Central to his understanding of the stringency of the right to life is the notion that it obliges other people to show a certain kind of respect to the right-bearer. Thus he writes that, to be justified, the use of force against culpable aggressors should comprise 'an appropriate response, not just to the situation at large, but to

---

[15] Rodin, *War and Self-Defense*, pp. 59–60, 67–9.   [16] Ibid.   [17] Ibid.   [18] Ibid.

them[19] 'as moral subjects'.[20] But what exactly is it about the aggressor to which we should respond? The answer: his free choice. For Rodin, one may take another's life only on the basis of wrong that *he has freely chosen* to do. Remember the fat man: we may not defend ourselves by killing him, for '[t]o say that the falling fat man has the right to life is to say that he has an interest in his living which cannot be overridden except on the basis of his *own choosing, willing, or acting*'.[21] What this implies is that his right to life lies securely in the individual's own hands. It can never be taken from him; he can only ever lose it by an act of free choice. This inference is confirmed, when we read that '[t]he most basic function of a morality of rights is to locate certain extremely important normative considerations [namely, innocence and guilt] *wholly within the sphere of the subject itself so as to make them unassailable by external contingencies* such as are appealed to by consequentialism'.[22] Rodin's centre-stage conception of what it is about an individual that obliges others' respect—let us call this his 'human dignity'—is his freedom of choice.

In his Rwandan end-note, however, this radically subjectivist conception of human dignity is quietly surrendered. For there Rodin concedes that Vénuste would have been justified in killing Théoneste, *even if his consent had not been forthcoming*.[23] This implies that killing on a ground other than one created by the victim's own free choice need not offend against his dignity, provided it is done on the authority of an objective moral obligation that binds *him*. Here, therefore, human dignity consists, not in the sheer exercise of free will, but in being the responsible subject of a claim by what is objectively right. Such dignity is morally realist: it consists in responsibility before a given moral order—before an order of moral *right*.[24] Therefore I can show due respect in killing you, when I do so on the authority of an objective moral obligation, to which you are subject and responsible, *even if you fail to recognise it and withhold your consent*.

V

David Rodin intends to offer a rights-based justification of killing, one centred on the individual's supposed 'right to life'. He does not claim that this right is

---

[19] Ibid., p. 92. The emphasis is Rodin's.   [20] Ibid., p. 89; see also, p. 94.
[21] Ibid., p. 89. The emphasis is mine.   [22] Ibid., p. 88. The emphasis is mine.
[23] Ibid., pp. 67–8.
[24] Rodin muddies the waters by describing Théoneste's obligation to sacrifice himself as 'internally derived'. The meaning is ambiguous. It could be either that the obligation is Théoneste's own individual, arbitrary invention or that only he is in a position to recognise it as objectively existing. Neither meaning, however, coheres with the claim that Théoneste's internal feeling of moral compulsion 'can be accessed in the objective sphere when we ask ourselves the question: what would we (feel ourselves compelled to) do in the circumstances?' (ibid., p. 68). Rodin's ambiguity here expresses a liberal's reluctance to own moral realism and therefore the possibility that an individual can in fact be subject to a moral obligation that he himself refuses to acknowledge. That is, it signals a reluctance to own the possibility that a moral subject might be sinfully alienated from his obligation.

absolute, but he does make a high breakwater of it. One of the effects of bringing his marginal discussion of the Rwandan case out of the shadows is to lower the breakwater significantly. According to Rodin's centre-stage account, the just warrior may kill, only if he knows that the enemy is culpable of wrong he has freely chosen to do. The implication of his Rwandan endnote, however, is that the just warrior may also kill, if he knows that the enemy refuses to meet a grave social obligation that circumstances have thrust upon him.

It also shows, second, that the right to life is contingent on circumstances outside of the owner's control. Killing is not only justified, when the victim deserves it through culpable wrongdoing. Théoneste had done nothing wrong to merit death. He did not deserve to die. Nevertheless, his unfortunate situation conspired to make it right that he should die, whether willingly or not. That is to say, tragic circumstances, entirely outside his control, summarily withdrew his right to life. The right to life, therefore, is not securely in the hands of a morally responsible right-bearer. It is more contingent than that.

Third, our analysis of the Rwandan case reveals that due respect for human dignity does not always require one's action to be constrained by another's moral innocence or by his free will: Théoneste had done nothing wrong and it would have been right for Vénuste to kill him, even if he had not consented.

Fourth, the justification of Vénuste's killing Théoneste involves a judgement of proportionality. Surely it is relevant that, if his brother had not killed Théoneste, most probably the Interahamwe would have done so instead. One way or another, Théoneste was moribund. The only choice facing him in those truly dreadful circumstances was whether or not the manner of his death would—or even just *might*—save the rest of his family. All other moral considerations being equal, it is better that some should survive than none. In its simplest, quantitative sense, therefore, Vénuste's killing Théoneste was proportionate.

Fifth, it is also surely relevant to the justification of Vénuste's killing that he did it without any malice and with proper reluctance. Had Vénuste loathed his brother, killing him would still have been the objectively right thing to do, but Vénuste would have been subjectively culpable for the malicious manner of his doing it. Why does the subjective dimension matter? Why do motive and intention matter? Why are not consequences, ethically speaking, all? Motive and intention matter for two reasons. They matter *to Théoneste* because a meaningful death is easier to bear than a meaningless one, and because death by loving hands is more meaningful than death by hateful ones. They would matter *for Vénuste and for everyone else with whom he interacts*, because his investment of himself in malice to the extent of fratricide would so corrupt his character as to dispose him to further and greater wrongdoing in the future.

Therefore, sixth, our immanent criticism of Rodin has revealed that his attempt to construct a moral justification of killing solely and fundamentally in terms of a stringent right to life that can be forfeited on one condition only (culpable wrongdoing) fails. In the light of his Rwandan end-note, it turns out that the right to life is more contingent on circumstances external to the right-bearer than Rodin wants to suppose, and that therefore the justification of killing involves reference to a wider range of moral considerations than the right of the victim—namely, the obligation or duty of the victim, the motive and intention of the killer, and the proportionality of his killing. Rights-talk is not enough.[25]

VI

What, then, is the alternative? My analysis of the Rwandan case in terms of motive, intention, and proportion has already signalled it: namely, the double-effect reasoning that characterises Christian thinking about the ethics of killing from Thomas Aquinas to the present day. This intellectual tradition has been imported into the international Law of Armed Conflict and into some moral philosophy, and it operates entirely without a concept of individuals' rights. Curiously, Rodin acknowledges it, without repudiating it, but he passes it by nonetheless.[26] There are various versions of double-effect reasoning. According

[25] Rodin's reasoning runs along the same lines as the jurisprudence of the German Constitutional Court. In 2006 the court judged that the lives of innocent passengers and crew of an airliner, which had been hijacked by terrorists and targeted at a building, could not be taken simply to save the lives of a greater number of other innocent people in the building. Its reasoning was based on a concept of a 'right to life', which incorporated the Basic Law's strongly Kantian notion of human dignity as self-determination: 'By their killing being used as a means to save others, they are treated as objects and at the same time deprived of their rights; with their lives being disposed of unilaterally by the state, the persons on board the aircraft, who, as victims, are themselves in need of protection, are denied the value which is due to a human being for his or her own sake' (Bundesverfassungsgericht, Judgment of the First Senate of 15 February 2006—1BVR 357/05, section 124: <https://www.bundesverfassungsgericht. de/SharedDocs/Entscheidungen/EN/2006/02/rs20060215_1bvr035705en.html>). According to my alternative, non-Kantian, non-rights-based reasoning, the fact that the state would intend to save the innocents on the ground, and only reluctantly accept the deaths of the innocents in the air as a last resort, tends toward permitting the shooting down of the hijacked plane; and the fact that the innocents in the air were bound to die anyway and completely beyond the state's protection, secures permission by making the act proportionate.
[26] Rodin, War and Self-Defense, p. 4 and 4 n. 1; 'I do not intend to deal directly with the double-effect account of self-defense.' Rodin does briefly echo the doctrine's crucial concern about the morally transformative effects of action on the character of the agent, but he mistakenly attributes the power of transformation to the choice of a certain way of acting rather than the choice of a certain intention in acting (ibid., p. 65). In contrast, Jeff McMahan's analysis of the ethics of killing in war makes liberal use of the distinction between intended and unintended effects, even if he dissents from certain of the doctrine's traditional analyses (Killing in War (Oxford: Clarendon Press, 2009), passim and pp. 171–2). As a consequence McMahan is willing to entertain the possibility that the deliberate harming of the innocent could be morally justified: '…if causing…harm to the innocent could be the means of achieving much greater good effects, it might be permissible to cause it—though only if the agent acts with an acceptable intention, such as the intention to achieve the greater good…According to common sense intuition, intention can have a role not only in making the killing of the innocent impermissible, but also in making it permissible.' To this he adds, however, 'I am not entirely confident that these views are defensible…' (ibid., p. 29). I observe that Rodin's more recent thinking about the justification of killing has been re-shaped by his engagement with McMahan. While he continues to base his theory on the concept of a forfeitable natural right to life, he now avails himself of the wider set

to my own version, the justification of killing goes like this. I may deliberately choose to perform an act that will probably or certainly kill you, and whose probable or certain effect I foresee, provided that it is not the effect of your death that I intend, that I have therefore striven to avoid it, but that I nevertheless have proportionate reason to cause it. By 'intend' I mean 'want above all else'. In that sense, if I do not intend your death, then I will only cause it when necessary, with due reluctance, and so as a last resort.

VII

Before I proceed to explain some significant features of this double-effect justification of killing, let me first address some questions that my version of it raises: How can it be at all plausible to hold that soldiers may not intend to kill their enemy? How can this requirement avoid being quite as subversive of the practical possibility of just war as Rodin's right-to-life-based understanding of the justification of killing?

Let me answer in terms of an actual case, which is narrated in *Callsign Hades*, Patrick Bury's extraordinary account of his experience as a lieutenant in the Royal Irish Rangers in Helmand Province in 2008. His platoon is in combat with the Taliban. A small Afghan boy is spotted repeatedly popping his head over the lip of a roof in the enemy's vicinity. He is presumed to be scouting for them. Bury takes his rifle and the next time the little head pops up, he fires at a spot just below and in front of it as a warning. Then he turns to the squaddie next to him and says, 'If he does that again, kill him.'[27]

That seems unequivocal: Bury intended that the boy should be killed. But did he? I think not. Suppose that after the fire-fight was over Bury had come across the boy's still breathing body. If he had really intended the boy's death, then he would have shot him again. But that is highly unlikely for a professional, disciplined soldier such as he. It follows, therefore, that his conditional order to kill was efficient shorthand for something more complicated: namely, 'Shoot him, so as to be sure that he doesn't raise his head over that wall again. Since only his head is visible, that is where you should shoot him. It is possible, even probable, that you'll kill him. Do it anyway.' Strictly speaking, what Bury wanted or intended was absolutely assured incapacitation. Under the circumstances, that *might* have amounted to death: given the weapon and calibre of ammunition involved—the SA80 A2 with a 5.56 mm round—and given the distance from the target,

of moral considerations familiar to Christian 'just war' reasoning in general, and double-effect reasoning in particular—duty, intention, and proportionality ('Justifying Harm', *Ethics*, 122/1, Symposium on Jeff McMahan's *Killing in War* (October 2011), pp. 74–110).

[27] Patrick Bury, *Callsign Hades* (London: Simon & Schuster, 2011), pp. 263–4.

the squaddie could not have been sure of killing. Nevertheless, if his shot had killed, the boy's death would have been accepted rather than strictly intended.[28]

However, Thomas Simpson, who served in Iraq and Afghanistan as an officer in the Royal Marines, and who now lectures in philosophy and public policy at Oxford, disagrees.[29] He does think it implausible to claim that a soldier should not intend to kill the enemy. Instead, he prefers to justify killing by likening the just soldier to a public executioner, who intends to kill, not out of malice, but for the sake of the public good. I resist this analogy. As I understand it, justified war is an appropriately hostile reaction to an enemy's wrongful harms. However, the hostility should be proportioned to the ends at which it aims, and among these should *not* be the annihilation of enemy combatants as such. A just warrior is justified in using such force as is necessary to disable his unjust enemy, *even* if that force is lethal. And the unjust enemy is liable to suffer necessarily lethal force on account of the wrong he does. Nevertheless, the just warrior is not justified in making the enemy's death (as distinct from his disablement) his aim. That is, he is not justified in intending his enemy's death, although he will very probably have to accept an awful lot more of it than a police marksman.

If this were not so—if soldiers should indeed aim to kill the enemy—then Royal Marine Sergeant Alexander Blackman did nothing wrong, when in September 2011 he shot a severely wounded Taliban in the chest, saying, 'Shuffle off this mortal coil, you ***. It's nothing you wouldn't do to us.' Then he added, 'I just broke the Geneva Convention.' He had indeed, as the subsequent court-martial confirmed, when it judged him guilty of murder and sentenced him to life imprisonment and dismissal with disgrace from the British armed forces.[30]

VIII

My pre-emptive apologia completed, let me proceed to explain some notable features of the justification of killing in terms of double-effect reasoning. First of all, to say that I do not intend something is not to say that I am not responsible for it. I can choose to do something that I foresee will cause your death, without intending it. Since I both choose and foresee it, I am indeed responsible for it and am liable to give a justificatory account of my action. However, if I deliberately cause death without malice and with proportionate reason, I have done no wrong and cannot be blamed for it. I am responsible, but not culpable. So to claim that

---

[28] As it happens, I ran this reading past Patrick Bury himself, and he did not demur.

[29] Thomas Simpson, 'Did "Marine A" Do Wrong? Biggar's Lethal Intentions', *Studies in Christian Ethics*, 28/3 (August 2015). For my full response, see Nigel Biggar, 'In Response', *Studies in Christian Ethics*, 28/3 (August 2015).

[30] Sergeant Blackman was convicted of murder in 2013. However, his conviction was quashed on appeal in March 2017 and reduced to manslaughter on the ground that he was suffering mental illness at the time of the killing.

soldiers should not intend to kill the enemy is not to say that they are not responsible for deliberate acts that cause the enemy's death. But it is to say that, while responsible, they need not be culpable.

Second, this double-effect reasoning requires me, the killer, to respect you, the victim. I do that, however, not by staying my hand until, through the autonomous exercise of your own free will in an act of culpable wrongdoing, you forfeit the right to life. Rather, I respect you by not wanting to kill you, by therefore searching earnestly for alternative means of achieving the goal that I do want, and by only killing you if I have a sufficiently proportionate reason to do so—such as an overriding moral obligation to rescue the victims of grave injustice.

Third, double-effect reasoning brings into play important considerations of motive, intention, last resort, and proportion, upon which Rodin's right-to-life-based reasoning in *War and Self-Defense* is completely silent. Why are they important? Because even if you had perpetrated culpable injustice, it would still be wrong for me to kill you with malicious intent, when it was not necessary, and without proportionate reason. Indeed, were I to do this, I would be guilty of an immoral act of grave *dis*respect.

Fourth, proportionate reason can mean several things. It can mean that I have reason to take your life, because you are unjustly threatening grave harm to the innocent, and because as a police officer or soldier I am publicly authorised to use such lethal force as is necessary to stop grave injustice. Note that as a public officer I can be justified in killing you, even if you were not morally culpable for the grave injustice you are perpetrating. It might be that, when you arm yourself to the hilt, walk into a kindergarten, and start firing at anything that moves, you are clinically insane, incapable of moral responsibility, and so undeserving of blame. Nonetheless, the gravity of the objective injustice you are doing to innocents and to public peace and trust justifies my shooting you dead. That it should be right to kill you is tragic, but it is right nonetheless.

Similarly, suppose you are a Wehrmacht soldier, advancing into Poland on 1 September 1939. You have been told that you are invading to punish an outrageous and unprovoked attack by Polish troops on the German village of Gleiwitz. In fact, the troops guilty of this heinous crime were German, dressed up in Polish uniform; and the unprovoked attack was a deliberately staged pretext for Adolf Hitler's unjustified invasion of Poland. However, you, the Wehrmacht soldier, know nothing of that. Objectively, you are perpetrating a grave injustice, but you are not subjectively culpable for it (at least not yet). Nonetheless, it would be quite justifiable for a Polish soldier to shoot you dead, simply on the ground of the grave objective injustice that you are doing, not only to individual innocents but also to common goods such as international order, national sovereignty, and domestic political order and peace. That you happen to be subjectively innocent—like Théoneste—adds an element of undoubted tragedy to the situation. But it does not prevent the justification of your being killed.

So the claims of social good can justify the killing of those who are doing objective injustice, but who are not morally culpable for it. It can also justify the killing—unintentional, of course—of those who are innocent both of objective injustice and of subjective guilt (like Théoneste). I dare to suppose that the vast majority of readers of this chapter—at least the Anglo-Saxon ones—would agree with me that the Allied invasion of Normandy in 1944 was justified. If so, then they do so in spite of the fact that Allied efforts were directly responsible for the deaths of 35,000 French civilians.[31] These deaths were not intended: the Allies did not want to kill French civilians. But technology did not permit greater accuracy, and with the British struggling to make headway against the strongest concentration of German forces east of Caen, and with British reserves of manpower already scraping the national barrel, recourse to massive and unavoidably indiscriminate aerial bombardment was considered militarily necessary.

A predictable riposte would be: 'Well, tell that to the slaughtered innocents. It doesn't matter why the Allies killed them: Allied motive and intention and proportionate reason are all beside the point. All that matters is that the innocent did not deserve to die.' That would be Rodin's main-text, centre-stage view. My response is that, no, what the victim deserves is not all that matters, and in support I can invoke the testimony of at least one of the slaughtered innocents. During the Allied bombing a civilian was trapped in the cellar of a house in Caen. As he suffocated to death, he took the trouble to scratch on the wall, 'I will never see this liberation for which I have waited for so long, but I know that through my death others will be set free. Long live France! Long live the Allies!'[32] So here was someone, who stood at the dreadfully sharp end of my kind of reasoning, but who nevertheless nodded his drooping head in assent to it. He did not deserve to die, but, tragically, his death was necessary to defend very great political goods against very great political evils. So while undeserved, his death was nonetheless morally justified—as he himself acknowledged.

IX

The idea that the moral claims of the common good sometimes override legal ones is familiar to Christian ethics. As we have seen, in the thirteenth century Thomas Aquinas argued that in a case of dire necessity—say, famine—natural or divine law or right overrides property rights, so that those who have too little may take whatever they need from those who have too much. Notice that he does not describe what they do as 'rightful theft', implying that the property rights of the

---

[31] See p. 221n.14.
[32] Reported in *Les Larmes de la liberté*, a film-documentary directed by Marc Saïkhali and broadcast on France 3 Normandie in June 1994.

superabundant were rightly violated. Rather, he says that what the indigent do 'is strictly speaking no theft or robbery' at all. What he means is that in those circumstances the legal right of the superabundant *no longer commands the support of natural morality*.[33] In fact, of course, the law still stands. In the context of a legally ordered society, the superabundant do have a legal right to their property, and unless that right is formally suspended by the constitutionally authorised body, when the indigent take from the superabundant, they undoubtedly do violate a legal right and commit theft, albeit with overriding moral reason. So the indigent do commit (morally) rightful (legal) theft.[34] (Observe, again, that Aquinas' moral analysis here avoids any talk of the indigent possessing a natural right to take what is necessary from the superabundant's surplus.)

Four centuries later, the Dutch Calvinist theologian, jurist, and father of international law Hugo Grotius argued along the same lines. '[I]n a case of absolute necessity,' he tells us, 'that antient [sic] right of using things, as if they still remained common, must revive, and be in full force.'[35] That is to say, according to natural moral law, there should be an equitable distribution of material goods, such that everyone has what they need—or at least that no one has more than they need, while others have less. In extreme circumstances, therefore, this natural right to equity can override legal rights to sovereign territory or property. Accordingly, someone engaged in a just war may unilaterally occupy part of a neutral country, to prevent 'a certain danger' of the enemy's occupation and being 'capable of doing irreparable injuries', provided that he takes nothing but what is necessary for his security and that he withdraws as soon as the danger passes: 'The first right therefore that remains of the antient [sic] community, since property was introduced, is this of necessity.'[36] Similarly, in case of great scarcity (or famine), rulers may force private owners of stocks of corn to make them available for public use.[37] What applies to sovereign territory or private property also applies to freedom from harm. Commenting on a case similar to that of Théoneste and Vénuste, Grotius writes: '[I]f one subject, tho' altogether innocent, be demanded by the enemy to be put to death, he may, *no doubt of it*, be abandoned, and left to their discretion, if it is manifest, that the state is not able to stand the shock of that enemy'.[38]

---

[33] Aquinas, *Summa Theologiae*, 2a2ae, q. 66, a. 7, resp. & ad 2., p. 83.

[34] Brian Tierney observes that after 1200 several canonists argued that a poor person in extreme need, who could not assert his (legal) right in a secular court, could assert a rightful (moral) claim to a bishop in his office as a judge, who could then compel the intransigent rich man to give alms from his superfluities by 'evangelical denunciation' or, if necessary, by excommunication (*Idea of Natural Rights*, p. 74).

[35] Grotius, *The Rights of War and Peace*, II.II.VI.1, 2, 4, pp. 434–5.   [36] Ibid., II.II.X, p. 437.

[37] Ibid., II.XXV.III.4, pp. 1154–5. Had the British government in the 1840s thought like Grotius, it might have suspended the property rights of Irish landowners and grain merchants, so as to compel them to make their stocks of grain available for public use during the emergency of the Irish Famine. Sadly, it did not.

[38] Ibid., II.XXV.III.1, p. 1152. The emphasis is mine.

This contention that the claims of natural equity in a community, or of a national community's survival against an unjust enemy, can override legal rights in extremis is certainly familiar to pre-modern Christian ethics. Moreover, it is not unfamiliar to modern moral philosophy, even of a liberal temper. Remember that Rodin himself admits that it is 'absolutely certain that consequentialist considerations sometimes override rights and duties'[39]—and that 'rights may be violated and a right-bearer wronged by an action which, *all-things-considered*, is the right thing to do'.[40]

X

The idea that the moral claims of the common good may sometimes trump the legal rights of individuals is not only a familiar one, but to some pre-modern Christian and modern Roman Catholic and liberal moralists, it seems a correct one. Nevertheless, it remains a dangerous idea, as a moment's reflection on the horrors of twentieth-century state totalitarianisms would remind us. That is why it is permitted only in extreme situations of dire necessity. In normal situations within a well-ordered political society—in civil conditions—the rights of individuals will rightly constrain what the state may do. Legal rights will be a strong breakwater. A citizen's right to freedom from interference or harm will trump most other considerations, and the circumstances will be rare where another private citizen, or even a public officer, can legally override that right. The good reason for this stringency lies in the presence of effective police enforcement, which secures peace most of the time in most places, and which means that society can afford to give the accused benefit of doubt until he is proven guilty at the conclusion of elaborate (and expensive) judicial procedures.

However, the *un*civil situation of justified war is significantly different. There grave wrongdoing on a widespread scale has overwhelmed civil peace and can only be stopped by the extreme means of belligerent retribution. In order to make it possible to wage justified war successfully, the breakwater is very considerably lowered. The putative natural, moral 'right to life' of both combatants and non-combatants is made much more contingent on circumstances, and so much less secure. Non-combatants do not have a right to immunity from lethal harm, only a right not to be harmed *intentionally and disproportionately*. Combatants in an unjust cause do not have a right to life that is forfeited only through culpable wrongdoing. They only have a right to life, *when they are manifestly disabled or have manifestly surrendered, and so cannot perpetrate further wrong*. Tragically, some morally innocent people, both in uniform and out, suffer harm they did not deserve. The justice meted out is undoubtedly very rough. But even peacetime justice can be seriously imperfect. And rough justice is still justice.

---

[39] Rodin, *War and Self-Defense*, p. 9.   [40] Ibid., p. 24. The emphasis is mine.

That said, the waging of war is usually somewhat regulated, at very least by custom. Nowadays, it is regulated by the Law of Armed Conflict (and increasingly and confusingly, also by International Human Rights Law), which have been established by international treaties and are backed by the threat of trial and punishment. Thus, according to the Geneva Convention, the enemy—even the Taliban—have a legal right not to be killed when wounded and disabled; and any soldier who breaks the Convention—like Sergeant Blackman—is liable to punishment.

In recent years it seems that the British and US militaries have been tightening the interpretation of the Law of Armed Conflict under which their troops are required to operate—thereby hardening the rights of enemy combatants and non-combatants. In both cases, this has been caused partly by the political need for successful counterinsurgency to minimise civilian casualties. In the British case at least, it has also been caused by the direction of recent human rights jurisprudence, as the 2013 report *The Fog of Law* details.[41] (We shall discuss this report and the relevant jurisprudence in Chapter 10.)

Take this example. A British Army reservist, whom I shall call 'Sam', told me of his recent experience on exercise with US troops. He and two of his American colleagues were being trained in clearing buildings. At one point, they were told to enter an enemy building. This they did. Upon entering, they stumbled across a 'wounded insurgent'. He made to surrender, but then picked up his rifle, 'shot dead' the two Americans, and put his rifle down again. Sam then 'shot' him. At that point, his trainer took him aside and warned him that such behaviour could 'get him in trouble'. The trainer's warning implies that US military regulations now forbid soldiers to harm anyone who is not actually holding a weapon, regardless of what they have just done with it or what they might reasonably be supposed to do with it again. In the past, an enemy who abused the convention of surrender to perpetrate an act of treachery would have lost his right to have his surrender accepted. Now, it seems, the right accorded him has been made more absolute. While it is within our power to make the legal rights we accord more or less contingent, whether the hardening in this case is wise, and whether the burden it places on US troops is reasonable, I doubt. While it might be politically prudent, it is not morally requisite. What is more, the burden it places on law-abiding combat troops is unfair, and the unfairness will corrode their morale, render them less effective, and so diminish the chances of military success.

XI

David Rodin attempts to offer a justification of killing in terms of a fundamental, moral 'right to life', which is not absolute in the sense that it cannot be forfeited,

---

[41] Thomas Tugendhat and Laura Croft, *The Fog of Law: An Introduction to the Legal Erosion of British Fighting Power* (London: Policy Exchange, 2013).

but is absolute in the sense that its keeping or losing is entirely within the control of the individual subject. The right is an individual's property, which is entirely within his sovereign control, and which he can only lose by a responsible, culpable act. The justification operates entirely in terms of a subjective right, its grounding in respect for the individual's free choice, and the conditions of its forfeit. This centre-stage proposal, however, is shown to be inadequate by Rodin's own end-note discussion of the Rwandan case, where he concedes that an objective social obligation (of self-sacrifice) can override the right to life.

To Rodin's own inadvertent demonstration of the ethical insufficiency of his rights-talk I have added the observation that his proposal implies the practical absurdity of forbidding the police to stop an insane, morally non-responsible gunman from slaughtering schoolchildren by killing him. I have also suggested that other moral considerations are needed to make full sense of Rodin's conclusion about the Rwandan case—that it needs articulation, not just in terms of the victim's social obligation, but also in terms of the intention of the killer and the necessity and proportionality of the killing.

All of these factors are circumstantial. They belong to the circumstances in which the individual is fated to find himself. They are not under his control. His 'right to life', therefore, turns out to be much more widely contingent than was originally proposed—not only on the individual's free, responsible choices, but also on morally significant factors quite external to him.

This substantiates further what I have claimed to be a major problem with some rights-talk: namely, the danger of transferring it from the positively legal sphere to the naturally moral one. A 'natural right', as we have just seen, is contingent on moral factors external to the individual subject. It comes and goes, fades in and fades out, according to the circumstances, many of them external. Whether it exists at all, depends on the situation as a whole and can only be determined at the end of a process of moral deliberation, not posited at the beginning as *fundamental*. However, the very language of 'a right' connotes something much more substantial and stable. It connotes an 'it', a thing. This suggests that its paradigm is property or, to be more exact, property that is defined, recognised, and protected by law and so by public authority. We *could* talk of an individual 'having' a right one moment, losing it the next, and recovering it shortly after, but that would sound odd and mislead us into overestimating its security and underestimating its ephemerality. It would be better, therefore, if we were to stop talking of a natural moral 'right to life' altogether, and spoke instead of it 'being right' to kill an individual in these circumstances, but not in those ones. It would be better, not only because it would spare us the rasping sound of a word grating against its connotations, but also because it would save us from the practical absurdities to which Rodin's thinking tends.

10

What's Wrong with (Some) Judges?

1: *Al-Skeini, Al-Jedda, Smith*, and the Fog of War

I

What is wrong with rights might lie in several places. Some accuse the very concept of a right belonging to an individual as a kind of property. I have considered this charge and found it wanting. Instead, I have identified problems in misleading connotations of talk about 'natural rights', the failure to reckon with the contingency of rights upon economic and political conditions, and the importation of what is paradigmatically a legal idea into ethical deliberation.

An additional possibility is that problems lie not only in concepts of rights, but also in the way in which judges treat them. This is the topic of this chapter and Chapter 11, and we shall consider it through an examination of two sets of cases: first, recent decisions of the European Court of Human Rights and the Supreme Court of the United Kingdom, which threaten the UK's military power; and second, the 2015 decision of the Supreme Court of Canada that the Canadian Parliament should grant a right to assisted suicide and voluntary euthanasia. In this chapter, we shall focus on the military cases, where, I will argue, rights-fundamentalism has produced an imprudent jurisprudence.

II

In 2013 the London think-tank Policy Exchange published a report entitled *The Fog of Law: An Introduction to the Legal Erosion of British Fighting Power*.[1] In it Tom Tugendhat, a lieutenant colonel in the UK's Territorial Army,[2] and Laura Croft, a retired lieutenant colonel in the US Army, fully accepted that military operations should be governed by the Law of Armed Conflict (LOAC, otherwise known as 'International Humanitarian Law' (IHL)),[3] but they resisted the

---

[1] Thomas Tugendhat and Laura Croft, *The Fog of Law: An Introduction to the Legal Erosion of British Fighting Power* (London: Policy Exchange, 2013).

[2] Tom Tugendhat is now the Conservative Member of Parliament for Tonbridge and Malling and Chairman of the House of Commons Foreign Affairs Select Committee.

[3] International law governing war has traditionally been known as 'The Law of Armed Conflict'. More recently, and especially in European circles, it has been renamed 'International Humanitarian

intrusion of law apt for civil circumstances into the theatre of war.[4] Their immediate concern was 'that commanders from the most junior upwards understand that decisions made in the confusion of battle will not be held to a standard designed for those who have never known such pressures'.[5] This is especially important for small military bodies like the British Army, which, in order to succeed, need to be agile and innovative, and thus give even junior officers ample scope for the use of discretion.[6] However, growing out of this immediate concern was also a long-term one:

> If there were a grave international crisis with the threat of a major war, it would be possible to expand the armed forces rapidly, as happened in 1914 and 1939 on one condition: that the culture and the ethos survive. You can buy kit. You can recruit men. But once the military ethos is lost—that subtle yet powerful reinforcement of service and discipline and duty—everything may be lost.[7]

Most of the complaint of *The Fog of Law* was focused on the novel extension of rights under the European Convention of Human Rights (ECHR) into military operations overseas. The ECHR, the report claims, was

> intended for application within the territories of stable contracting European states. The novel reach it is now being accorded stretches into domains and into countries far beyond its original design.... The damage is done when legal norms such as the ECHR created for the relatively predictable governance mechanisms of post-war Europe are imposed on chaotic and inherently uncertain conflict zones.[8]

Law'. Comprising the Geneva Conventions of 1949, together with the Hague Conventions of 1899 and 1907 and the Additional Protocols of 1977, this should not be confused with International Human Rights Law.

[4] Tugendhat and Croft, *Fog of Law*, p. 11.   [5] Ibid.   [6] Ibid., p. 16.

[7] Ibid., p. 61. Writing in 2013, Lieutenant Colonel C. P. Heron agreed that recent jurisprudence had given rise to a perception of legal risk that had affected operational decision-making in the British armed forces. So far, the impact of juridification had been least on deployed operations and most on detention ('The Juridification of the British Armed Forces', Defence Research Paper, Advanced Command and Staff Course 16 (2013), pp. 12, 30–1, 32). For example, it had been reported that the Royal Navy's efforts to tackle piracy around the Horn of Africa had been constrained by a reluctance to detain suspected pirates, lest the Human Rights Act compel their release (ibid., p. 30; see also Nick Herbert, 'Human Rights Act: The Law that has Devalued your Human Rights', *Daily Telegraph*, 9 November 2008). Two years later five former Chiefs of the Defence Staff wrote in less cautious terms to *The Times* newspaper, lamenting how 'creeping legal expansion onto the battlefield is putting [the military] ethos at risk with potentially disastrous consequences' (Field Marshal, the Lord Guthrie et al.,'Combat Zones', *The Times*, 7 April 2015).

[8] Tugendhat and Croft, *Fog of Law*, pp. 21, 54.

•

The immediate cause of this inapt legal extension was identified as a series of judgements, first of all by the European Court of Human Rights (ECtHR)[9] and subsequently by the UK's Supreme Court. It was the latter's June 2013 judgement in *Smith and Others v. the Ministry of Defence*[10] that appears to have provoked *The Fog of Law*, which described it as 'the apogee of judicial encroachment'.[11]

According to Tugendhat and Croft, in *Smith* (2013) the UK's Supreme Court had ruled that military personnel are protected (and bound) by the UK's Human Rights Acts 1998 (HRA) even in a theatre of war, and that the Ministry of Defence's duty of care may extend as far as procurement decisions.[12] This ruling was the conclusion to almost a decade of inquests into three incidents in Iraq after the invasion of 2003 and during its occupation by, among others, British troops. In *Smith* several sets of British claimants had accused the Ministry of Defence of failing to provide equipment that could have saved the lives of their military relatives, thereby allegedly breaching their right to life as guaranteed by Article 2 of the European Convention.[13] First the High Court in 2011, and then the Court of Appeal in 2012, rejected the claimants' assertion of a breach of Article 2 on the ground that the Convention did not apply to members of the armed services, when outside of military bases in territory other than that of the Council of Europe. In *Smith* (2013), however, the Supreme Court reversed the Court of Appeal's decision, ruling that the ECHR does extend to troops outside of military bases in a theatre of war.[14]

In reaching this judgement, the Supreme Court deferred to the authority of the ruling of the European Court of Human Rights in *Al-Skeini* (2011)[15] that the rights guaranteed in the European Convention can be 'divided and tailored'.[16] Writing for the majority in *Smith*, Lord Hope argued that members of the armed forces cannot be expected to respect humanitarian law and human rights in their operations unless respect for human rights is guaranteed within their own ranks. In response, Tugendhat and Croft commented that

[t]his leads to the conclusion that it is not only impossible to surrender ECHR rights, even voluntarily, but that to do so would affect the ability of the armed forces to uphold the rights of others ... But rights that apply to all can be, and often are, set aside in order to achieve an effect ... Even Lord Hope surrendered

---

[9] The European Court of Human Rights sits in Strasbourg and is often referred to as 'the Strasbourg court' or simply as 'Strasbourg'.

[10] UK Supreme Court, *Smith and others (FC) (Appellants) v. The Ministry of Defence (Respondent); Ellis (FC) (Respondent) v. The Ministry of Defence (Appellant); Allbutt and others (FC) (Respondents) v. The Ministry of Defence (Appellant)*, (2013) UKSC 41, 19 June 2013.

[11] Tugendhat and Croft, *Fog of Law*, p. 28.   [12] Ibid., p. 28.   [13] Ibid., p. 29.

[14] Ibid., p. 30.

[15] European Court of Human Rights, Grand Chamber, *Case of Al-Skeini and Others v. The United Kingdom* (Application no. 55721/07), 7 July 2011.

[16] Tugendhat and Croft, *Fog of Law*, p. 30.

his right to vote in General Elections when he was elevated to the House of Lords. But one assumes that he still respected the democracy over which he sat in judgment.[17]

On the central issue of whether or not the Ministry of Defence should be held liable for UK soldiers' deaths, when they are attributable to inadequate equipment, *The Fog of Law* makes two observations about military tactics. First, the reasons why troops are not supplied with optimally protective equipment can be ones of tactical prudence, rather than administrative negligence. So, for example, soldiers in Iraq and Afghanistan were not issued with body armour, because it could be seen by the local population as aggressive and intimidating and because it could hinder mobility and increase the enemy's opportunity to target those wearing it:

> Both situations make [encumbered] troops less, rather than more, safe...By 2009 it was claimed that British soldiers were routinely carrying more than twice the load carried by Royal Marines and the Parachute Regiment on their march across the Falklands in 1982: observing this the Taliban nicknamed them 'donkeys'.[18]

Similarly, the Army's use of the thin-skinned 'Snatch Land Rover' could be justified in tactical terms, since more heavily protected patrol vehicles were viewed by local people as intimidating and because they caused more damage to civilian infrastructure.[19]

Second, a major increase in the number of fatal military casualties, and of corresponding legal claims, would rapidly overwhelm the capacity of both the courts and the Ministry of Defence to process them. Indeed, the need to respond to inquiries had already diverted military resources from equipment and training. It had also raised the Theatre Entry Standard—the level of equipment and training required for an individual or unit to be ready to enter a theatre of operations—so that the baseline was generally assumed to be the complexity of threats faced in Afghanistan. As a consequence, any move away from the highest standard will henceforth see a commander's judgement called into question, even if the taking of greater risks is urgently required for military success.[20]

Notwithstanding Lord Hope's disclaimer that '[i]t is of paramount importance that the work that the armed services do in the national interest should not be impeded by having to prepare for or conduct active operations against the enemy under the threat of litigation if things should go wrong',[21] and notwithstanding his stated doubt that the *Smith* claimants will be ultimately successful, the very fact that he had allowed such a case to be brought 'hangs a Sword of Damocles over the

---

[17] Ibid., p. 31.   [18] Ibid., p. 26.   [19] Ibid., p. 27.   [20] Ibid., pp. 24–5.
[21] *Smith* (2013), para. 100.

heads of commanders'. The mere possibility of the threat of litigation has created a need to preserve evidence, and the consequent 'burden of record keeping places increasing demands, and stresses, on those serving in difficult, chaotic and dangerous circumstances overseas'.[22]

Although the UK Supreme Court's ruling in *Smith* (2013) was the presenting symptom of the jurisprudential problem, in the eyes of *The Fog of Law*, its causes lay further back in earlier decisions by the European Court of Human Rights. One of the most important of these was *Al-Skeini* (2011), where the Strasbourg court found that European Convention rights can be divided and tailored to individual circumstances, and some rights made to apply overseas.[23] A major problem with this, according to Tugendhat and Croft, is that Article 5 of the Convention (guaranteeing the Right to Liberty and Security) does not allow for preventive security detention in the absence of judicial oversight: 'Under the ECHR prisoners can only be taken as part of a judicial process; they must then be processed toward trial, or released.'[24] In political environments that are highly unstable, however, the detention of those deemed to be security risks until the end of hostilities may be 'the least bad choice', in order to protect British troops, the local authorities, and the civilian population, and in 2007 it achieved a massive reduction in civilian casualties in Baghdad. At this point the report cited Marco Sassoli, an expert in international law, who, in an article published in 2008, had observed that, in the past, the Strasbourg court had accepted that states could avoid censure for some violations of the right to a judicial remedy under Article 5, by exercising their right to derogate under Article 15. However, Sassoli doubted that it would do so any longer, 'as international practice has since developed toward recognising the non-derogable nature of habeas corpus'.[25] The basic issue here is which body of law should apply to conditions of grave and violent political instability—the Law of Armed Conflict or International Human Rights Law (IHRL)? Under LOAC enemy combatants who have not surrendered or are not otherwise *hors de combat* can be killed without warning; and when they have surrendered, they can be detained until such time as hostilities have ended and their liberty presents no public threat. Under IHRL, however, 'the policing model for restraint and use of force as a last resort prevails', and detention without due legal process is forbidden.[26]

A second problematic ruling by the European Court of Human Rights, according to *The Fog of Law*, was *Al-Jedda* (2011).[27] In this case, the UK's House of Lords

---

[22] Tugendhat and Croft, *Fog of Law*, pp. 32–3.   [23] Ibid., p. 15.   [24] Ibid., p. 37.

[25] Ibid., p. 37, citing Marco Sassoli, 'The International Legal Framework for Stability Operations: When May International Forces Attack or Detain Someone in Afghanistan?', *International Law Studies*, 35 (2008): 'The War in Afghanistan: A Legal Analysis', p. 449.

[26] Tugendhat and Croft, *Fog of Law*, p. 38.

[27] European Court of Human Rights, Grand Chamber, *Case of Al-Jedda v. The United Kingdom* (Application no. 27021/08), 7 July 2011.

had held in its 2007 ruling that the United Nations Security Council Resolution (UNSCR) 1546, together with successive resolutions, had authorised British forces in Iraq to use internment where necessary for imperative reasons of security, and that, according to Article 103 of the United Nations Charter, such a binding Security Council decision superseded all other treaty commitments, including Article 5 of the ECHR.[28] In 2011 the Strasbourg court disagreed, arguing that, since Resolution 1546 merely 'authorised' rather than 'obligated' the UK to use internment, Article 103 of the UN Charter was not engaged and therefore the ECHR still applied.[29] Commenting on the effect of these judicial decisions by the Strasbourg court, Tugendhat and Croft make the alarmingly ironic observation that, given the high risks involved in detaining people suspected of being a threat to public security, together with the possibility of being forced to release them under Article 5 of the European Convention, an operational commander might well conclude

> that, in order to avoid infringing a detainee's human rights through captivity, an enemy combatant deemed a sufficient threat and a legitimate military target should be killed... There is no obligation on British forces to try and arrest a combatant, unlike police forces would have to do.[30]

The authors of the report then comment wryly: 'the legal position does not make it any easier to see that the choice to kill rather than capture an enemy combatant improves the human rights of either party.'[31]

In the course of its critique of recent jurisprudence, *The Fog of Law* makes two further, notable comments on the intrusion of rights-claims and civil courts into military affairs. First, it claims that the 'constant spotlight of scrutiny' is damaging the network of relationships through which military service operates: 'By reducing this bond into one based often on "rights", including the Right to Life, the inquiries [into the conduct of soldiers in the field] are playing their part in unpicking the web of interlocking obligations that hold the military together.'[32] Second, the report connects the expansion of the jurisdiction of rights-law with the growth of a general culture of aversion to risk:

> the unintended consequence of overregulation and the creation of a culture of risk aversion is inactivity... As Simon Wessely, Vice Dean of the Institute for Psychiatry, King's College London asserted: '... Safety first is not

---

[28] Tugendhat and Croft, *Fog of Law*, p. 40.   [29] Ibid., p. 42.   [30] Ibid.   [31] Ibid., p. 42.
[32] Ibid., p. 24. Anthony Forster reports an increasing tendency among military personnel to see themselves as possessors of rights, which sits ill with the institutional importance in the armed services of the individual's subordination to the corporate body, and also with the military virtue of 'selfless commitment' ('British Judicial Engagement and the Juridification of the Armed Forces', *International Affairs*, 88/2 (2013), p. 299).

enough...people need to know that there is a wider purpose to accepting risk...the goal of a risk-free society, let alone a risk-free armed forces is unachievable and probably unpalatable; but at present that seems to be the only purpose of policy, which lacks any vision other than precaution. "Better safe than sorry" may seem sensible, but the danger is that we will end up no safer, and a lot sorrier.'[33]

III

Two years after publishing *The Fog of Law*, Policy Exchange produced a follow-up report.[34] Written by two academic lawyers, Richard Ekins and Jonathan Morgan, in collaboration with Tom Tugendhat, *Clearing the Fog of Law* inveighed against the 'new form of judicial imperialism'[35] whose

> folly reaches its apogee on the question of the detention of insurgents. It is surely absurd that European and British courts now expect our forces to operate in violent combat conditions according to a system more suited to the regulation of police powers on a Saturday night in the West End of London.[36]

Their most fundamental objection was that recent jurisprudence had misapplied the law of the European Convention to unsuitable circumstances. Originally designed for the conditions of peace in post-war Europe, it remains suitable 'to regulate stable peacetime polities', where it makes prudent sense to forbid imprisonment without trial, and to permit lethal force only in exceptional cases as a last resort and as strictly necessary. Accordingly, the Convention and the Human Rights Act, which brings it into force in the UK, treat all types of conflict in the same way, subjecting them indiscriminately to a single legal regimen of rights-based rules. The overriding aim of this regimen is to protect the individual from abuse by the state, which, echoing its birth in the shadow of the fascist dictatorships of the 1930s and early 1940s, it assumes to be the main source of threat.[37]

However, in a condition of war or quasi-war—such as a major insurgency in a fragile polity—the main threat of abuse might not emanate from one's own state. Instead, it might come from a ruthless foreign enemy or from terroristic domestic insurgents. Accordingly, the Law of Armed Conflict claims not to apply always and everywhere, but only to times and places of armed conflict. It subjects different kinds of conflict to different regimens, which combine a few general

---

[33] Simon Wessely, 'Risk, Psychiatry and the Military', *The British Journal of Psychiatry*, 186 (2005), pp. 459–66; quoted by Tugendhat and Croft, *Fog of Law*, pp. 52–3.

[34] Richard Ekins, Jonathan Morgan, and Tom Tugendhat, *Clearing the Fog of Law: Saving our Armed Forces from Defeat by Judicial Diktat* (London: Policy Exchange, 2015).

[35] Ibid., p. 7.   [36] Ibid., p. 8.   [37] Ibid., pp. 8, 10, 26.

principles (discrimination, military necessity, humanity, proportionality) with an array of specific rules:

> The Geneva Conventions [one of the main parts of LOAC] were negotiated by those with experience of armed conflict—including military personnel, military lawyers, and the Red Cross. Their purpose was precisely to strike a balance between humanity and military necessity in the unique circumstances of war. Knowing that the Geneva Conventions would be applicable primarily to soldiers and commanders in the field, they were drafted in detailed practical form. This contrasts notably with the abstract language of human rights instruments, designed for peacetime conditions.[38]

LOAC is also more permissive than domestic law. It does not require that military force used against enemy combatants be no greater than strictly necessary, since the aim of combat is to bring the enemy to submission, and the application of 'overwhelming' force may be morally the most appropriate way to do that. It also tolerates the incidental killing of civilians on certain conditions. And it permits detention without trial on security grounds: 'Repugnant though such measures would be in peacetime civil society, in a war zone imprisonment without trial is frequently necessary, proportionate, and reasonable.'[39]

The basic problem with recent jurisprudence of the Strasbourg court is that it 'has improperly extended the reach of the ECHR and imposed inappropriate peacetime human rights notions onto the battlefield—and thus sidelined the Geneva Conventions'.[40] In addition to infecting troops with a paralysing risk-aversion, it also has the deleterious effect of burdening the military forces of states that subscribe to the European Convention with an unfair disadvantage, for, while the Law of Armed Conflict binds both sides in a non-international armed conflict, the Convention binds only the European side.[41] What is more, the judicial extension of the Convention's jurisdiction to territory beyond that of the signatory states runs roughshod over the intentions of those who originally drafted and signed the treaty, and who never envisaged such a thing.[42] It therefore jeopardises international trust both in the Strasbourg court and in any treaty subject to its interpretation.

---

[38] Ibid., p. 47.

[39] Ibid., pp. 10, 26, 27. *Clearing the Fog of Law* acknowledges that the Law of Armed Conflict is less well developed than it needs to be in respect of non-international conflict, especially as regards the detention of persons considered to pose a security risk (pp. 30, 32).

[40] Ekins et al., *Clearing the Fog of Law*, p. 28. Ekins et al. suggest that the problem applies to International Human Rights Law in general: 'According legal priority to the Geneva Conventions has, sadly, long been out of fashion at the level of general international law. In *Serdar Mohammed*, Mr Justice Leggatt firmly and expressly rejected the argument that IHL supersedes IHRL when there is a disagreement between them during armed conflict. He stated that this opinion was "impossible to maintain" in light of decisions by the International Court of Justice holding that IHRL obligations remain in force (concurrently with IHL) during armed conflict' (p. 30).

[41] Ibid., p. 33.   [42] Ibid., pp. 14, 27, 48.

242 WHAT'S WRONG WITH RIGHTS?

Such are the unhappy effects of recent developments in jurisprudence. But what do Ekins et al. have to tell us about their causes? Why has the jurisprudence developed in this way? In part there is the not uncommon conviction that human rights are fundamental and universal.[43] Then there is the Strasbourg court's view of the European Convention as a 'living instrument', fit to be made to grow way beyond its origins.[44] In addition, there is a feature of the contemporary fashion of structuring legal rights, which we will meet again in Chapter 11's discussion of recent Canadian jurisprudence:

> a bias towards expansion . . . is built into the modern law of human rights. The structure of rights affirmations is, typically, a vaguely worded reference to some valuable state of affairs or individual interest, coupled with a vague provision permitting limitation in some types of case, to secure important public interests or the rights of others. With the encouragement of many scholars, judges very often take an expansive view of the scope of the initial right—reasoning that a broad understanding puts the burden on the state to justify interferences with individual rights. The true work of determining what is permitted takes place in the course of proportionality analysis, in which the court considers the merits of some particular state action, weighed against the (expansively understood) individual right. This phenomenon, which has been termed 'rights inflation', tends to dispose the courts to expanding the reach of human rights law.[45]

Finally, there is the fact that judges are human, and being human, are sometimes insecure or vain enough to want to be well thought of at a time when the championing of human rights is highly fashionable and widely regarded as 'progressive', even heroic. Consequently,

> some judges are eager to be at the vanguard of extending human rights law. There is a transnational conversation amongst judges, in which the interpretation and development of human rights law is often assumed to be the central part of the judicial role. There is also at times competition amongst judges and courts—with judges who are seen to be in the vanguard of the development of human rights law enjoying considerable acclaim from other judges, scholars, and the media.[46]

IV

The two Policy Exchange reports object to recent jurisprudence in Strasbourg and London, because it intrudes an inappropriate legal regimen into theatres of

---

[43] Ibid., p. 31.   [44] Ibid., p. 21.   [45] Ibid., p. 49.   [46] Ibid., p. 49.

war—or at least quasi-war. The European Convention of Human Rights is apt for the largely peaceful, stable political circumstances that Europe has enjoyed since 1945; and given its birth in the shadow of the fascist dictatorships of the 1930s and early 1940s, it naturally tends to assume that the primary threat to the well-being of individuals comes from the state. However, the well-being of individuals can be threatened quite as much by a state that is too weak as by one that is too strong. In circumstances of near anarchy, where a state struggles to uphold law and order against a ruthless and unscrupulous insurgency—whose agents, for example, strap suicide vests onto teenagers and propel them into crowded market-places—the main threat to the well-being of individuals comes from the violent chaos in which the lawless strong are at liberty to terrorise the weak. In such circumstances, to subject troops acting in support of the civil authorities to the constraints of a European peacetime human rights regimen disadvantages them in relation to an enemy who suffers no such constraints, burdens them with precautionary bur- eaucracy, undermines their 'selfless commitment', and paralyses them with risk- aversion. Consequently, it makes such troops altogether militarily weaker and less likely to prevail against an enemy, who, should he triumph, would happily tear down whatever legal protection of individual rights remains standing. And why have the judges brought us to this place? The several causes include the conviction that the moral authority of rights is universal and their legal authority should become so, the view of the European Convention as a 'living instrument' in judicial hands, the abstraction of chartered rights and the correspondingly broad scope for judicial discretion, the ambition of judges, and the wider cultural context of risk-aversion.

That is the complaint. Using it to consider what might be wrong with certain judicial interpretations of human rights, we now proceed to scrutinise the three main legal judgements against which it is directed: the Strasbourg's court's rulings in *Al-Skeini* (2011) and *Al-Jedda* (2011), and the UK Supreme Court's ruling in *Smith* (2013). We begin with *Al-Skeini*.

Al-Skeini concerns the deaths of six Iraqi civilians between May and November 2003. Five were shot by British soldiers; the sixth (Baha Mousa) died in their custody. In March 2004 the UK's Secretary of State for Defence decided not to conduct independent inquiries into the deaths, nor to accept liability for them, nor to pay 'just satisfaction'. As a consequence the claimants applied to the Divisional Court in London for judicial review of these decisions, arguing that their relatives fell within the jurisdiction of the UK, and therefore under the European Convention, and that there had been no effective investigation into the deaths, in breach of Articles 2 and 3.[47]

---

[47] *Al-Skeini*, paras 1–3, 72–3. For a detailed reference to the case, see p. 236n.15.

The 2011 judgement of the European Court of Human Rights began by reviewing the December 2004 judgement of the Divisional Court. The British court, following Strasbourg's ruling in *Banković* (2001), accepted that jurisdiction under Article 1 of the Convention was limited to the territory of the contracting state, except where that state had 'effective control' of an area outside its own territory. Yet, even this exceptional basis of jurisdiction applied only within the ECHR's 'regional sphere', where the territory of one Party was controlled by another Party, and so it could not apply to Iraq.[48] However, there was a further exception, according to which jurisdiction could apply to a British military prison operating in Iraq with the consent of the Iraqi sovereign authorities and containing arrested suspects. So while deaths as a result of military operations 'in the field' fell outside of the UK's jurisdiction under Article 1, the death of Baha Mousa in a British military prison did not. The court found that there had been a breach of investigative duty under Articles 2 and 3 in respect of the sixth applicant's son.[49]

The first four applicants then proceeded to appeal against the Divisional Court's finding that their relatives did not fall within the UK's jurisdiction. The Court of Appeal of England and Wales dismissed their appeals in December 2005. Giving the leading judgement, Lord Justice Brooke argued that the British commander in Basrah

> was not provided with nearly enough troops and other resources to enable his brigade to exercise effective control of Basrah City ... [Therefore] it is quite impossible to hold that the UK, although an occupying power for the purposes of the Hague Regulations and Geneva IV, was in effective control of Basrah City for the purposes of ECHR jurisprudence at the material time.

On this point Lord Justice Sedley concurred:

> On the one hand, it sits ill in the mouth of a state which has helped to displace and dismantle by force another nation's civil authority to plead that, as an occupying power, it had so little control that it cannot be responsible for securing the population's basic rights ... [However] the fact is that it cannot: the invasion brought in its wake a vacuum of civil authority which British forces are still unable to fill. On the evidence before the Court they were, at least between mid-2003 and mid-2004, holding a fragile line against anarchy.[50]

The Court of Appeal unanimously concluded that the UK did not have jurisdiction under Article 1, except with regard to the sixth applicant's son, who from the moment he was arrested by British troops, was subject to ' State agent authority'.[51]

[48] Ibid., para. 74.   [49] Ibid., paras 75–7.   [50] Ibid., para. 80.   [51] Ibid., paras 79, 81.

Regarding his death, court-martial proceedings were pending against a number of soldiers. Therefore the court remitted the question of the adequacy of investigation to the Divisional Court for reconsideration after the courts martial had completed their work.

The first four applicants then appealed to the House of Lords.[52] There the majority found that the UK did not have jurisdiction over the deaths. They agreed with Lord Brown, who deemed *Banković* to be 'a watershed authority' in establishing that the European Convention applies wherever a State Party has 'effective control' of an area. Given this, however,

> except where a state really does have effective control of territory, it cannot hope to secure Convention rights within that territory and, unless it is within the area of the Council of Europe, it is unlikely in any event to find certain of the Convention rights it is bound to secure reconcilable with the customs of the resident population . . . During the period in question here it is common ground that the UK was an occupying power in southern Iraq and bound as such by Geneva IV and by the Hague Regulations. Article 43 of the Hague Regulations provides that the occupant 'shall take all the measures in his power to restore and ensure, as far as possible, public order and safety, while respecting, unless absolutely prevented, the laws in force in the country'. The appellants argue that occupation within the meaning of the Hague Regulations necessarily involves the occupant having effective control of the area and so being responsible for securing there all Convention rights and freedoms. So far as this being the case, however, the occupants' obligation is to respect 'the laws in force', not to introduce laws and the means to enforce them (for example courts and a justice system) such as to satisfy the requirements of the Convention. Often (for example where Sharia law is in force) Convention rights would clearly be incompatible with the laws of the territory occupied.[53]

Upon completing its review of the relevant British jurisprudence, the Strasbourg court proceeded to call to mind relevant international law. This included the 2004 Advisory Opinion of the International Court of Justice (ICJ) on the *Legal Consequences of the Construction of a Wall in the Occupied Palestinian Territory* (9 July 2004), where the ICJ considered 'that the protection offered by human rights conventions does not cease in case of armed conflict'.[54] The Advisory Opinion also observed that the Human Rights Committee (HRC) of the United Nations had 'found the Covenant [i.e. the International Covenant on

---

[52] Until the creation of the Supreme Court in October 2009, the highest court of appeal for civil cases in the UK comprised members of the judiciary sitting in the House of Lords.

[53] Ibid., para. 86.

[54] International Court of Justice, Advisory Opinion on the *Legal Consequences of the Construction of a Wall in the Occupied Palestinian Territory* (9 July 2004), para. 106; cited in *Al-Skeini*, para. 90.

Civil and Political Rights or "ICCPR"] applicable where the State exercises its jurisdiction on foreign territory' and that the HRC pointed 'to the long-standing presence of Israel in [the occupied] territories ... as well as the exercise of effective jurisdiction by Israeli security forces therein'.[55] The ICJ appeared to assume that, even in respect of extra-territorial acts, it would in principle be possible for a state to derogate from its obligations under the ICCPR, Article 4.1, 'in time of public emergency which threatens the life of the nation'.[56] In addition, Strasbourg cited a report where, regarding the right to life under Article 6 of the ICCPR, the UN Special Rapporteur, Philip Alston, opined that '[a]rmed conflict and occupation do not discharge the State's duty to investigate and prosecute human rights abuses. The right to life is non-derogable regardless of circumstances. This prohibits any practice of not investigating alleged violations during armed conflict or occupation.'[57]

Having described the relevant legal hinterland, the European Court articulated its own judgement. Regarding the issue of jurisdiction, the court noted that in *Al-Saadoon and Mufdhi v. the United Kingdom* (2009) it had held, according to the principle of 'State agent authority and control', that two Iraqi nationals detained in British-controlled military prisons in Iraq fell within the UK's jurisdiction; and in *Medvedyev and Others v. France* (2010), that the applicants fell within French jurisdiction by virtue of the exercise by French agents of 'full and exclusive control'.[58] On this the court commented, 'What is decisive in such cases is the exercise of physical power and control over the person in question.'[59] It then concluded that '[i]t is clear that, whenever the State through its agents exercises "control and authority" over an individual, and thus jurisdiction,' it is under an obligation under Article 1 to secure to that individual the rights and freedoms under Section 1 of the Convention.[60] Applied to the case before the court, this principle produced the judgement that 'the United Kingdom, through its soldiers engaged in security operations in Basrah during the period in question, exercised authority and control over individuals killed in the course of such security operations, so as to establish a jurisdictional link between the deceased and the United Kingdom for the purposes of Article 1 of the Convention'.[61]

Thus the Strasbourg court tacitly took leave of its own ruling ten years earlier in *Banković*, where it had declared boldly that '[t]he Convention was not designed to be applied throughout the world, even in respect of the conduct of Contracting States'.[62] Given the importance of the change, the reasoning that led to it deserves

---

[55] ICJ, Advisory Opinion, paras 109, 110; cited in *Al-Skeini*, para. 90.   [56] *Al-Skeini*, para. 111.

[57] United Nations Economic and Social Council, Commission on Human Rights, Report of the Special Rapporteur, Philip Alston, on Extrajudicial, Summary or Arbitrary Executions, E/CN.4/2006/53 (8 March 2006), para. 36; cited in *Al-Skeini*, para. 93.

[58] *Al-Skeini*, para. 136.   [59] Ibid., para. 136.   [60] Ibid., para. 137.

[61] Ibid., para. 149.

[62] European Court of Human Rights, Grand Chamber, *Banković and Others v. Belgium and 16 Other Contracting States* (Application no. 52207/99), 12 December 2001), para. 80.

close attention, which we shall now give it. Consider, first, the unexplored ambiguity that attends the idea of 'State agent control'. In one sense, anyone who stands within range of a soldier's firearm may be said to be in his 'control'. Context, however, makes an important moral difference—and it should make a legal one. Prisoners secured within the walls of a military detention facility are subject to a degree of control that reduces the risk to the soldiers guarding them, gives the latter more opportunity to deliberate safely, and so tightens the conditions under which their use of firearms could reasonably be considered necessary. In contrast, civilians acting suspiciously on lawless streets thick with the threat of sudden violence are subject to a much lower degree of control, since an armed soldier necessarily has to make an instant decision (for the sake of the lives of his comrades and other civilians, if not his own), with the consequence that his taking greater risks of fatal error is reasonable.

Observe, next, how the criterion established in *Al-Saadoon* and *Medvedyev* was control that is '*total*' (or '*full*') and '*exclusive*', but when applied in *Al-Skeini* it was relaxed—without explanation—to become merely 'control and authority'. Observe, too, that this relaxation occurred in spite of the court's awareness that during the relevant period, the UK had been given responsibility for a territory with a population of 4,600,000, but had only 14,500 Coalition troops to discharge it; and that the main theatre of operations within this area contained 2,750,000 people, but just over 8,000 troops.[63] Indeed, the court itself quoted without demur the Aitken Report (of 22 January 2008) on the post-conflict situation in Iraq, which reported of May 2003—the month of the first killing brought before the court—that '[l]aw and order had completely collapsed'.[64]

On the issue of the alleged breach of the investigative duty under Article 2, the court held that that article, protecting the right to life and setting out the circumstances when deprivation may be justified, 'ranks as one of the most fundamental provisions in the Convention', and that no derogation from it was permitted by Article 15, 'except in respect of deaths resulting from lawful acts of war'.[65] Since the general prohibition of arbitrary killing by agents of the state would be ineffective in practice without a procedure for reviewing the lawfulness of the use of lethal force by state authorities, and since in previous rulings the court had held that the procedural obligation under Article 2 continues to apply in difficult security conditions, including those of armed conflict, 'the obligation under Article 2 to safeguard life *entails* that, even in difficult security conditions, all reasonable steps must be taken to ensure that an effective, independent,

---

[63] *Al-Skeini*, para. 20.
[64] Ibid., para. 22. Commenting on the Strasbourg court's jurisprudence up to 2018, Ian Park observes that 'the Court has not been consistent in elucidating criteria that indicate a sufficient military presence to establish the requisite level of control' (*The Right to Life in Armed Conflict* (Oxford: Oxford University Press, 2018), p. 76).
[65] *Al-Skeini*, para. 162.

investigation is conducted into alleged breaches of the right to life'.[66] In order to be effective, the persons responsible for and carrying out the investigation must be independent from those implicated in the events.[67] Therefore the investigating authority should have been operationally independent of the military chain of command, whereas in fact it was not and was therefore 'flawed'.[68] The delay in having a fully independent investigator interview military witnesses 'entailed a high risk that the evidence was contaminated and unreliable' by the time that the Army Prosecuting Authority came to consider it.[69] Therefore the court found a violation of the procedural duty under Article 2 of the Convention.[70]

The court's reasoning here also bears critical reflection. Note, first of all, its exclusive focus, following the Convention, on killing *by agents of the state*. The threat posed to the lives of myriad innocents by ruthless insurgents and warlords, exploiting the complete collapse of law and order, was, it seems, regarded as someone else's problem. Second, Article 2 itself makes no mention of an obligation to hold an independent investigation, and whether its relationship to such a thing is as strong as one of *entailment* is may be doubted. The prohibition of arbitrary killing does not draw *all* its force from the threat of investigation, for it is also sustained by the consciences of soldiers and the moral training of their officers. So while the lack of an investigative procedure would certainly weaken the prohibition, it need not render it 'ineffective'. Third, there was in fact an investigative procedure, which was activated and presumably gave greater effect to the prohibition. But the court decided to raise the bar higher: for it to be effective, it asserted, the investigation had to be independent. This implies that the personal and professional independence of the investigator from those subject to investigation is necessary for impartiality. That is not true, however, for it is possible for investigators to possess such high moral integrity that they will not allow personal and other ties to sway their judgement. Independence merely makes impartiality more likely—and more publicly demonstrable—but it is not strictly required for it. Besides, the investigative procedure that was implemented did involve a considerable degree of independence: it was not conducted by the troops immediately involved. From June 2003 all shooting incidents involving British armed forces were investigated by non-commissioned officers of the Royal Military Police (RMP) and, if thought to fall outside the Rules of Engagement, handed over to the RMP's Special Investigation Branch (SIB). Then from April 2004 a new, more rigorous policy was adopted, whereby all shooting incidents that resulted in civilian injury or death were to be investigated directly by the SIB.[71] For sure, the greater the procedural independence, the less likely that an investigation will be contaminated by undue partiality. But the procedure merely reduces the risk of

---

[66] Ibid., paras 163–4. The emphasis is mine.   [67] Ibid., paras 166–7.
[68] Ibid., paras 168, 173.   [69] Ibid., para. 173.   [70] Ibid., para. 177.
[71] Ibid., paras 25, 27.

corruption; it is not strictly necessary for integrity. This, then, raises the unanswered question: Why did the Strasbourg court decide to make the 'absolutist' demand of minimal possible risk, even after it had admitted that in this case there was 'no evidence that the military chain of command attempted to intervene in the investigation'?[72]

The judgement of the court was unanimous, which, given that its seventeen judges were drawn from seventeen different nations, ranging from Cyprus to Iceland, is astonishing. Of the seventeen different nations represented, only two— the UK and France—have serious military capabilities, including the capacity to project military power overseas, together with experience of using that capacity. To the judgement of the court were appended two 'Concurring Opinions'. In one of these, Judge Giovanni Bonello of Malta indulged in an extraordinarily unfettered declaration of human rights idealism and associated political moralism. The judge exhorted the court to 'stop fashioning doctrines which somehow seem to accommodate the facts, but rather, to appraise the facts against the immutable principles which underlie the fundamental functions of the Convention'.[73] Appealing to the Preamble of the European Convention, with its agenda of 'the *universal* and effective recognition and observance' of fundamental human rights, he reminded his colleagues that the founding members of the ECHR, and the subsequently Contracting Parties, 'strove to achieve...the supremacy of the rule of human rights law'.[74] On the issue of jurisdiction, he commented with sarcastic gusto,

I resist any helpful schizophrenia by which a nervous sniper is within the jurisdiction, his act of shooting is within the jurisdiction, but then the victims of that nervous sniper happily choke in blood outside it...If two civilian Iraqis are together in a street in Basrah, and a United Kingdom soldier kills the first before arrest and the second after arrest, the first dies desolate, deprived of the comforts of United Kingdom jurisdiction, the second delighted that his life was evicted from his body within the jurisdiction of the United Kingdom. Same United Kingdom soldier, same gun, same ammunition, same patch of street— same inept distinctions...Did the Contracting Party ratify the Convention with the deliberate intent of discriminating between the sanctity of human rights within its own territory and their paltry insignificance everywhere else? I am unwilling to endorse *á la carte* respect for human rights. I think poorly of an

---

[72] Ibid., para. 174. Jaka Kukavica and Veronika Fikfak observe that in its 14 April 2015 ruling in *Mustafa Tunç and Fecire Tunç* (Application no. 24014/05), the Strasbourg court abandoned the 'absolutist approach' it had adopted in *Al-Skeini* ('Strasbourg's U-Turn on Independence as Part of an Effective Investigation under Article 2', Cambridge Faculty of Law Legal Studies Research Paper no. 60/2105 (Cambridge: University of Cambridge Faculty of Law, 2015), pp. 1, 3).

[73] *Al-Skeini*, 'Concurring Opinion of Judge Bonello', para. 8.

[74] Ibid., para. 9. The emphasis is Bonello's.

esteem for human rights that turns casual and approximate depending on geographical coordinates.[75]

So far Judge Bonello appeared to think that the rights guaranteed by the European Convention should apply everywhere—regardless of 'geographical coordinates'. But then he admitted that jurisdiction should be subject to a 'functional' test, namely, whether or not it was 'within the State's authority and control' to see its positive obligations under the Convention respected.[76] Applying this test to the cases before the court, he declares—four times over—that it was 'uncontested' that the UK had 'authority and control'. That is true, of course, but, being uncontested, it hardly needed labouring. Moreover, it was beside the point. However, what Judge Bonello, concurring with the court as a whole, went on to assert was contestable, because it was entirely undemonstrated: namely, that the United Kingdom had *'full* authority and control'.[77] Instead of empirical argument he supplied only political rhetoric intoxicated by its own moral indignation:

> it is well beyond surreal to claim that a military colossus which waltzed into Iraq when it chose, settled there for as long as it cared to and only left when it no longer suited its interests to remain, can persuasively claim not to have exercised authority and control over an area specifically assigned to it in the geography of the war games played by the victorious.[78]

One might have thought that the toppling of a regime responsible for the atrocious killing of at least 400,000 of its own citizens, and whose Special Treatment Department had been in the habit of putting the heads of political prisoners between steel vices and then tightening them until their brains oozed through their noses, would have attracted a modicum of sympathy from such an ardent champion of human rights.[79] But Judge Bonello was far too busy giving vent to his rights-idealism to let awkward empirical facts muddy his simple ideological waters.

V

The second main jurisprudential target at which the two Policy Exchange reports direct their complaints is the Strasbourg court's ruling in *Al-Jedda* (2011).[80] This case concerned the internment of an Iraqi-born UK citizen from 4 October 2004

---

[75] Ibid., paras 14,15, 17, 18.   [76] Ibid., para. 19.   [77] Ibid., para. 22. The emphasis is mine.
[78] Ibid., para. 27.
[79] See Nigel Biggar, *In Defence of War* (Oxford: Oxford University Press, 2013), pp. 254–8; Justin Marozzi, *Baghdad: City of Peace, City of Blood* (London: Allen Lane, 2014), pp. 351–2.
[80] For a detailed reference to the case, see p. 238n.27.

until 30 December 2007 'for imperative reasons of security', since he was believed to be responsible for recruiting terrorists outside Iraq in order to commit atrocities there, and for conspiring with an imported terrorist explosives expert to conduct attacks against Coalition Forces in Iraq.[81] His internment had been initially authorised by the senior officer in the detention facility. It was then reviewed both one week and four weeks later by the Divisional Internment Review Committee (DIRC), whose recommendations were passed to the Commander of the Coalition's Multinational Division (South-East), who examined the intelligence file on the detainee and decided to continue the internment. Between January and July 2005 a monthly review was carried out by the Commander, on the basis of the DIRC's recommendations. Between July 2005 and December 2007 the decision to continue the internment was taken by the DIRC itself, which, during this period, included the Commander, together with members of the legal and intelligence staffs.[82] When the detainee had been interned for eighteen months, his case was reviewed by the Joint Detention Committee, which included senior representatives of the Multinational Force, the Iraqi interim government, and the ambassador for the UK. After meeting once, this committee thereafter delegated powers to a Joint Detention Review Committee, which comprised Iraqi representatives and officers from the Multinational Force.[83]

In June 2005 the applicant brought a judicial review claim in the UK, challenging the lawfulness of his continued detention. The Secretary of State for Defence accepted that the applicant's detention within a British military facility brought him within the jurisdiction of the UK under Article 1 of the European Convention and that his detention did not fall within any of the permitted cases set out in Article 5.1. Nevertheless, he argued that United Nations Security Council Resolution (UNSCR) 1546 authorised the detention, and that the Resolution displaced Article 5.1.[84] Both the Divisional Court in August 2005 and the Appeal Court in March 2006 unanimously held that the Resolution explicitly authorised the Multinational Force to take all necessary measures to contribute to the maintenance of security and stability in Iraq, and that the UK's obligation under the Resolution took precedence over its obligations under the Convention.[85] The applicant then appealed to the House of Lords, arguing that the Resolution only authorised the UK to detain him, but did not oblige it, with the result that Article 103 of the UN Charter was not engaged. As reported by the European Court in its 2011 judgement, Lord Bingham, with whom the four other Law Lords agreed, commented in his ruling of December 2007 as follows:

it appears to me that during the period when the UK was an Occupying Power ... it was obliged in the area in which it effectively occupied, to take

[81] *Al-Jedda*, para. 11.   [82] Ibid., para. 12.   [83] Ibid., para. 13.   [84] Ibid., para. 16.
[85] Ibid., para. 17.

necessary measures to protect the safety of the public and its own safety... [I]f the Occupying Power considers it necessary to detain a person who is judged to be a serious threat to the safety of the public or the Occupying Power there must be an obligation to detain such a person...[86]

Further, Lord Bingham argued that the UN Security Council cannot use mandatory language in framing a Resolution concerning military or security operations overseas, since the UN has no standing forces at its disposal and is not entitled to call upon member states to provide them: 'Thus in practice the Security Council can do little more than give its authorisation to member States which are willing to conduct such tasks, and this is what... it has done for some years past.' That said, it was true that, according to Article 103, Security Council Resolutions only override existing international law when they create 'obligations'; and that therefore one could conclude that, where a state is not obliged, but merely authorised, to take action, it remains bound by its conventional obligations:

Such a result, however, would not seem to correspond with State practice at least as regards authorisations of military action. These authorisations have not been opposed on the ground of conflicting treaty obligations, and if they could be opposed on this basis, the very idea of authorisations as a necessary substitute for direct action by the SC [Security Council] would be compromised. Thus... the prevalence over treaty obligations should be recognised for the authorisation of military action as well...[87]

Further still, since '[t]he importance of maintaining peace and security in the world can scarcely be exaggerated', in a situation like the present, Article 103 should not be given 'a narrow, contract-based meaning'. The UK was 'bound to exercise its power of detention where this was necessary for imperative reasons of security. It could not be said to be giving effect to the decisions of the Security Council if, in such a situation, it neglected to take steps which were open to it.'[88] In conclusion, Lord Bingham acknowledged 'a clash' between 'a duty to detain exercisable on the express authority of the Security Council' and 'a fundamental human right' which the UK has undertaken to secure. He judged that the only way to reconcile the opposing duties is by ruling that the UK may, where it is 'necessary for imperative reasons of security', lawfully exercise the power to detain authorised by UNSCR 1546, but must ensure that the detainee's rights under

---

[86] Ibid., para. 20, pp. 9–10.

[87] Ibid., para. 20, pp. 10–11. Lord Bingham is in fact quoting here from J. Frowein and V. Krisch, 'Introduction to Chapter VII', in B. Simma, ed., *The Charter of the United Nations: A Commentary*, 2nd edn (Oxford: Oxford University Press, 2002), p. 729.

[88] *Al-Jedda*, para. 20, p. 11.

ECHR Article 5 are not infringed 'to any greater extent that is inherent in such detention'.[89]

Concurring, Lord Carswell commented that while, on the one hand, internment without trial is antithetical to the rule of law, on the other hand, '[t]here are, regrettably, circumstances in which the threat to the necessary stability of the State is so great that in order to maintain that stability the use of internment is unavoidable'. Nevertheless, in such circumstances, there must be regular reviews of the continuing need for detention and a system whereby that need and the supporting evidence can be challenged by representatives of the detainees, insofar as that is practicable.[90]

In its review of relevant case-law of the European Court of Justice (ECJ),[91] the Strasbourg court observed that in *Kadi* (2008) the ECJ had ruled that, while it was not competent to review the lawfulness of Security Council Resolutions, it could review a member state's giving effect to them. The ECJ recalled that

> the European Community was based on the rule of law, that fundamental rights formed an integral part of the general principles of law and that respect for human rights was a condition of the lawfulness of Community acts. The obligations imposed by an international agreement could not have the effect of prejudicing the 'constitutional principles of the European Community Treaty', which included the principle that all Community acts had to respect fundamental rights.[92]

Proceeding to make its own judgement, the Strasbourg court identified as the 'key question' that of whether UNSCR 1546 placed the UK under an obligation to hold the applicant in internment.[93] It held that there must be a presumption that the UNSC 'does not intend to impose any obligation on member States to breach fundamental principles of human rights'.[94] The court then declared that it

> does not consider that that the language used in this Resolution [1546] indicates unambiguously that the Security Council intended to place member States within the Multinational Force under an obligation to use measures of indefinite internment without charge and without judicial guarantees, in breach of their undertakings under international human rights instruments including the Convention. Internment is not explicitly referred to in the Resolution... [Its] terminology ... appears to leave the choice of the means to achieve this

---

[89] Ibid., para. 20, pp. 11–12.   [90] Ibid., para. 22.

[91] The European Court of Justice is one of three courts of the Court of Justice of the European Union, and is located in Luxembourg. It should not be confused with the European Court of Human Rights, which is charged with enforcing the European Convention on Human Rights in the member states of the Council of Europe, and is located in Strasbourg.

[92] *Al-Jedda*, para. 53.   [93] Ibid., para. 101.   [94] Ibid., para. 102.

end [of maintaining security and stability in Iraq] to the member States within
the Multinational Force...In the absence of clear provision to the contrary, the
presumption must be that the Security Council intended States within the
Multinational Force to contribute towards the maintenance of security in Iraq
while complying with their obligations under international human rights law.[95]

The court then considered whether a further legal basis for internment might be
supplied, not by the Resolution itself, but by the annexe to it, which comprised the
international agreement between the Iraqi government and the US government
(on behalf of the other states contributing troops to the Multinational Force,
including the UK), that the Force would continue to carry out internment in Iraq
where 'necessary for imperative reasons of security'. On this the court ruled that
'such an agreement could not override the binding obligations under the
Convention'. In conclusion, the Strasbourg court judged that UNSCR1546
authorised, but did not 'explicitly or implicitly' require the UK to take an individual considered to be a security-risk into indefinite detention without charge;
that there was no conflict between the UK's obligations under the UN Charter and
those under Article 5.1 of the ECHR; and that therefore the applicant's detention
was indeed a violation of the Convention.[96]

As in *Al-Skeini*, this judgement commanded a remarkable degree of agreement
from the seventeen members of the court drawn from seventeen different countries. Unlike *Al-Skeini*, however, it did provoke one Partly Dissenting Opinion
from Judge Poalelungi (of the Republic of Moldova), who, picking up a line of
argument pursued by Lord Bingham, held that the UNSC was not able to use the
language of obligation. To this he added that it was 'unrealistic to expect the
Security Council to spell out in advance, in detail, every measure which a military
force might be required to use to contribute to peace and security under its
mandate'. Therefore, in his view, there had been no violation of Article 5.1.[97]

The near unanimity commanded by the European Court's judgement in *Al-
Jedda* is not its only remarkable feature. Also notable is its complete failure, to
which Judge Poalelungi alluded, to address Lord Bingham's point that the Security
Council *could* not have used obligatory language in framing Resolution 1546,
since it had no standing military forces at its disposal. It is possible that the court
ignored this, because Lord Bingham himself had conceded that Article 103 of the
UN Charter only permits UNSC Resolutions to override existing international law
when they create 'obligations', and that therefore one 'could' conclude that a State
that is merely authorised, but not obliged, to take action remains bound by its
conventional obligations. However, even if that charitable reading were correct,
the court also failed to address Lord Bingham's response to it, namely, that such a

conclusion does not correspond to state practice, and that it undermines the very idea of authorizations as a necessary substitute for direct action by the Security Council.

Lord Bingham's reasoning was decisively shaped by an acute awareness of the importance of the need to maintain some measure of political order: '[t]he importance of maintaining peace and security in the world', he wrote, 'can scarcely be exaggerated.' (This concern was echoed by Lord Carswell: '[t]here are, regrettably, circumstances in which the threat to the necessary stability of the State is so great that in order to maintain that stability the use of internment is unavoidable.') It was for this reason that Lord Bingham held that the UNSCR 1546's authorisation of the Multinational Force 'to take all necessary measures to contribute to the maintenance of security and stability in Iraq' amounted to an obligation to detain, where necessary; that this 'duty to detain' did clash with the UK's obligation to secure the 'fundamental human right' asserted in Article 5 of the European Convention; and that Article 103 should not be given 'a narrow, contract-based meaning'. Accordingly, he ruled that the two opposing duties should be 'reconciled' by giving the Resolution priority over the Convention.

It is most striking that, except in its report of the deliberations of the British Law Lords, the recognition of the vital importance of the maintenance of political stability finds no expression whatsoever in the judgement of the European Court. Consequently, the court's presumption that the UNSC 'does not intend to impose any obligation on member States to breach fundamental principles of human rights' remains entirely undisturbed, and its reasoning proceeds on narrowly, even pedantically, textual grounds. Accordingly, since the UNSC Resolution did not 'unambiguously' *oblige* states party to the Multinational Force to use internment to maintain security and stability, but left the choice of means to their discretion;[98] and since Article 103 of the UN Charter permits Security Council Resolutions to override existing international law only when they create 'obligations'; therefore, UNSCR 1546 did not override the UK's treaty obligation to uphold the European Convention, and its use of indefinite detention in Iraq was in violation of Article 5. True to its consistent neglect of political realities, the Strasbourg court did not pause to think how practically absurd it would have been, had the Security Council expressly *obliged* the use of detention (in all circumstances?), rather than leave it to the Multinational Force to deploy it according to its judgement of conditions on the ground. Besides, what exactly is the difference between authorising internment *when necessary*, and obliging it? For if one is obliged to maintain security and stability, if internment really is necessary

---

[98] Ibid., para. 105. In the conclusion to its judgement (para. 109), however, the Strasbourg court went further: not only did UNSCR 1546 not oblige the Multinational Force 'unambiguously'; it did not oblige it 'explicitly or implicitly' (para. 109). Lord Bingham, of course, had argued that the Resolution did oblige implicitly. Evidently, the court disagreed, but as to why, it did not care to explain.

to achieve that, and if authorisation permits internment, then surely one is obliged to use it. The European Court did not trouble itself with these or any other practical thoughts, so determined was it to ensure that 'fundamental human rights' remained *fundamental*—and that therefore nothing should be allowed to override them.

VI

The most recent judgement that attracted the fire of *The Fog of Law* and its successor was the UK Supreme Court's 2013 ruling in *Smith*.[99] This case concerned the deaths and serious injury of British soldiers in three separate incidents in Iraq. First, on the night of 25 March 2005 British Challenger tanks mistakenly fired at, and hit, another British tank, killing two members of the crew and seriously wounding two others. Then in the early hours of 16 July 2005 a British patrol, comprising three lightly armoured Snatch Land Rovers, detonated an improvised explosive device (IED), killing three soldiers in the vehicle and seriously wounding two others. Finally, on 28 February 2006 another Snatch Land Rover on patrol detonated an IED, killing two soldiers and seriously injuring another.[100]

These three incidents gave rise to two sets of claims in *Smith*. First, under common law tort only, the 'Challenger claims' alleged a failure to ensure that the claimants' tank, which was hit, and the tanks that fired upon it, were properly equipped with the technology and equipment that would have prevented the tragic mistake; and that the Ministry of Defence had been negligent in failing to provide the tank crews with adequate recognition-training before deployment and in theatre.[101] Second, under Article 2 of the European Convention and at common law, the 'Snatch Land Rover claims' alleged that the Ministry of Defence breached Article 2 of the ECHR 'by failing to take measures within the scope of its powers which, judged reasonably, it might have been expected to take in the light of the real and immediate risk to life of soldiers who were required to patrol in Snatch Land Rovers'.[102] The process of litigation was at its earliest stage, and the Supreme Court's responsibility was to decide whether the claims should be struck out as lacking grounds in law, or whether they should proceed to trial as to the facts. The two sets of claims raised three main issues: that of jurisdiction under Article 1 of the European Convention; that of claims under Article 2; and that of combat immunity.

On the issue of jurisdiction Lord Hope, writing for the majority of the Supreme Court, recalled that in *Al-Skeini* (2007) the House of Lords had held that an

---

[99] For a detailed reference to the case, see p. 236n.10.   [100] *Smith*, paras 2–8.
[101] Ibid., para. 9.   [102] Ibid., para. 10.

obligation to secure Convention rights would arise only where a contracting state had such effective control over an area as to be able to provide the complete package of rights and freedoms guaranteed by Article 1 to everyone within that area; and that since the United Kingdom's presence in Iraq fell far short of such control, the idea that the UK was obliged to secure 'the observance of all the rights and freedoms as interpreted by the European court in the utterly different society of southern Iraq was manifestly absurd'.[103] Lord Hope also recalled that, in its judgement in *Catherine Smith* (2011), the Supreme Court had held, by a majority of six to three, that the contracting states would not have intended the European Convention to apply to their armed forces when operating outside their territories, and that to extend the Convention to armed forces abroad 'would ultimately involve the courts in issues relating to the conduct of armed hostilities which was essentially non-justiciable'.[104] Against this prevailing judgement, however, Lord Mance had taken the view that the UK could be expected to take steps to provide 'proper facilities and proper protection against risks falling within its responsibility or its ability to control or influence when despatching and deploying armed forces overseas'.[105]

Lord Hope then moved on to review the European Court of Human Rights' decision in *Al-Skeini* (2011). While agreeing with Strasbourg's affirmation of the UK's 'authority and control' over its armed forces when serving abroad, he introduced a subtle, but crucial distinction. On the one hand, 'the legal and administrative structure of the control is, necessarily, non-territorial in character'; but '[t]he extent of the day to day control will, of course, vary from time to time when the forces are deployed in active service overseas, especially when troops are in face to face combat with the enemy'.[106] Lord Hope acknowledged Strasbourg's view that '[w]hat is decisive . . . is the exercise of physical power and control over the person in question'.[107] He cited Lord Bingham's word of caution, when he had written in *Ullah* (2004) that, while the Convention was to be seen as a 'living tree capable of growth and expansion within natural limits', those limits will often call for very careful consideration.[108] Nevertheless, he went on to concede that Strasbourg's judgement that the European Convention can be 'divided and tailored', resulting in a state being obliged under Article 1 to secure the rights relevant to the situation of an individual under its authority and control, implied that the view of the Law Lords in *Al-Skeini* (2007) and the majority in *Catherine Smith* (2011) that the rights of Section 1 are indivisible 'can no longer be

---

[103] Ibid., para. 20, referring to *R (Al-Skeini) v. Secretary of State for Defence* [2007] UKHL 26, [2008], AC 153, para. 78.
[104] *Smith*, para. 25, referring to *R (Catherine Smith) v. Oxfordshire Assistant Deputy Coroner (Equality and Human Rights Commission intervening)* [2010] UKSC 29, [2011] 1 AC 1, para. 308.
[105] *Smith*, para. 26, referring to *Catherine Smith*, para. 194.   [106] Ibid., para. 28.
[107] Ibid., para. 36.
[108] *R (Ullah) v. Special Adjudicator* [2004] UKHL 26, [2004] 2 AC 323, para. 20; referred to in *Smith*, para. 43.

maintained'.[109] In conclusion, Lord Hope ruled that the jurisdiction of the UK under Article 1 does extend to securing the protection of Article 2 to members of the armed services when they are serving outside its territory.[110]

With regard to the second issue of the claims under Article 2 of the Convention, which guarantees the 'right to life'—that is, the right not to be 'deprived of [one's] life intentionally save in the execution of a sentence of a court'—Lord Hope observed that Article 15 permits a contracting state to derogate from its conventional obligations as necessary in time of war or other public emergency 'threatening the life of the nation'. However, this implied 'an exceptional situation of crisis or emergency which affects the whole population and constitutes a threat to the organised life of the community of which the state is composed'. Since such a situation could hardly be said to obtain where a state had chosen to conduct an overseas peacekeeping operation from which it could withdraw, such a right did not apply to the *Smith* case.[111]

In his review of domestic jurisprudence, Lord Hope recalled that in *Catherine Smith* both he and Lord Mance had judged that the European Convention was applicable to the relationship between a state and its armed forces on active service overseas in matters of the adequacy of equipment, planning, or training. After all, there had been many cases where the death of service personnel indicated a systemic or operational failure on the part of the state, 'ranging from a failure to provide them with the equipment that was needed to protect life on the one hand to mistakes in the way they are deployed due to bad planning or inadequate appreciation of the risks that had to be faced on the other'.[112] Nevertheless, Lord Hope reckoned that there was 'a fundamental difference' between manoeuvres conducted under controlled conditions in a training area which can be accurately planned for, and what happens when troops are deployed on active service in situations over which they do not have 'complete control'. Given the fact that '[m]ilitary operations conducted in the face of the enemy are inherently unpredictable', as Lord Rodger had written in *Catherine Smith*, '[a] court should be very slow indeed to question operational decisions made on the ground by commanders'.[113] To this Lord Hope added:

> subjecting the operations of the military while on active service to the close scrutiny that may be practicable and appropriate in the interests of safety in the barrack block or in the training area is an entirely different matter. It risks undermining the ability of a state to defend itself, or its interests, at home or abroad. The world is a dangerous place, and states cannot disable themselves from meeting its challenges. Ultimately democracy itself may be at risk.[114]

---

[109] *Smith*, paras 37, 45.   [110] Ibid., para. 55.   [111] Ibid., paras 56, 59, 60.
[112] Ibid., para. 63.   [113] Ibid., para. 64.   [114] Ibid., para. 66.

Notwithstanding the 'fundamental difference' between training and active operations, Lord Hope paraphrased Lord Bingham's view in *A v. Secretary of State for
the Home Department* (2005) that '[t]he allocation of resources to the armed
services and as between the different branches of the services, is also a question
which is more appropriate for political resolution than it is by a court'.[115] Thereby
he implicitly acknowledged the possibility that the lack of provision of life-saving
equipment could be the consequence of a politically justified allocation of scarce
resources rather than a morally or legally culpable 'failure'.

Turning to Strasbourg, Lord Hope reported that its jurisprudence had interpreted Article 2 as generating two general obligations:

> [t]he first is a systemic duty, to put in place a legislative and administrative
> framework which will make for the effective prevention of the risk to ... health
> and well-being or ... effective deterrence against threats to the right to life.
> Depending on the facts, this duty could extend to issues about training and the
> procurement of equipment before the forces are deployed on operations that will
> bring them into contact with the enemy. The second ... is to ensure that, where
> there is a real and immediate risk to life, preventative operational measures of
> whatever kind are adopted to safeguard the lives of those involved so far as this is
> practicable.[116]

Appealing to the European Court's judgement in *Engel v. the Netherlands* (1976),
Lord Hope inferred that 'it would not be compatible with military life to expect the
same standard of protection as would be afforded by article 2(1) to civilians who
had not undertaken the obligations and risks associated with life in the military'.
To this he added the comment: 'it is different when the serviceman or woman
moves from recruitment and training to operations on active service, whether at
home or overseas. It is here that the national interest requires that the law should
accord the widest measure of appreciation to commanders on the ground who
have the responsibility of planning for and conducting operations there.'[117] In
sum, he concluded from the Strasbourg jurisprudence that 'the court must avoid
imposing positive obligations on the state in connection with the planning for and
conduct of military operations in situations of armed conflict which are unrealistic
and disproportionate'. This meant that the allegations of the claimants would be
beyond the reach of Article 2, if the decisions that ought to have been taken about
training, procurement, or the conduct of operations were 'at a high level of
command and closely linked to the exercise of political judgment and issues of
policy' or if those thought to be responsible 'were actively engaged in direct
contact with the enemy'. However, whether the decisions belonged to either of

---

[115] Ibid., para. 65.   [116] Ibid., para. 68.   [117] Ibid., paras. 70, 71.

those kinds, or fell somewhere in between, could only be determined by examining the facts of the case.[118] Therefore the claims should not be struck out. Nevertheless, he warned that

> [t]he claimants are, however, on notice that the trial judge will be expected to follow the guidance set out in this judgment as to the very wide measure of discretion which must be accorded to those who were responsible on the ground for the planning and conduct of operations during which these soldiers lost their lives and also to the way issues as to procurement too should be approached. It is far from clear that they will be able to show that the implied positive obligation under article 2(1) of the Convention to take preventative operational measures was breached in either case.[119]

On the third issue of combat immunity in tort law and whether it could be successfully invoked by the Ministry of Defence to deflect the Challenger claims, Lord Hope argued that the scope of immunity should be narrowly construed.[120] As Justice Stark had observed in *Shaw Savill* (1940), 'not every warlike operation done in time of war is an operation or an act of war'.[121] Decisions about training or the fitting of equipment 'are sufficiently far removed from the pressures and risks of active operations against the enemy for it to not be unreasonable to expect a duty of care to be exercised, so long as the standard of care that is imposed has regard to the nature of these activities and their circumstances'.[122] For that reason, Lord Hope judged it premature to strike out the Challenger claims on the ground of combat immunity.[123] Nevertheless, he went on to stress the need to avoid the risk of 'judicialising warfare'.[124] The more constrained a decision-maker in theatre was by decisions taken for reasons of policy at a high level of command beforehand or by the effects of contact with the enemy, the more difficult it will be to find that he was at fault: 'Great care needs to be taken not to subject those responsible for decisions at any level that affect what takes place on the battlefield, or in operations of the kind that were being conducted in Iraq after the end of hostilities, to duties that are unrealistic or excessively burdensome'[125]

> it is of paramount importance that the work that the armed forces do in the national interest should not be impeded by having to prepare for or conduct active operations against the enemy under the threat of litigation if things should

---

[118] Ibid., paras 76, 80.

[119] Ibid., para. 81. In referring to 'the trial judge', Lord Hope was anticipating that the case would return to the High Court in London.

[120] Ibid., paras 90, 92.

[121] *Shaw Savill & Albion Co. Ltd v. Commonwealth* (1940) 66 CLR 344, p. 354; quoted in *Smith*, para. 94.

[122] *Smith*, para. 95.   [123] Ibid., para. 96.   [124] Ibid., para. 98.   [125] Ibid., para. 99.

go wrong. The court must be especially careful, in their case, to have regard to the public interest, to the unpredictable nature of armed conflict and to the inevitable risks that it gives rise to when it is striking the balance as to what is fair, just and reasonable.[126]

Lord Hope's judgement was supported by three out of his seven fellow judges and so commanded a majority, constituting the judgement of the court as a whole. Among the dissenting minority of three was Lord Mance, who wrote an extensive opinion, running to fifty paragraphs. Given that a state has no general duty of care to avoid injury or death 'in the conduct of an active military operation or act of war', Lord Mance identified the key question as that of whether the state can be held to have failed in its duty of care if a combat death can be attributed to its procurement and training decisions.[127] In his view there was an 'inevitable inter-linking' of issues about the supply of equipment and training with decisions taken on the ground during active service: 'it is not possible to consider the Challenger claims without considering the conduct of those on the ground'.[128] The complaint about a failure to supply better equipment was really, he suggested, 'a complaint about tactics'.[129] Besides, '[p]olicy decisions concerning military procurement and training involve predictions as to uncertain future needs, the assessment and balancing of multiple risks and the setting of difficult priorities for the often enormous expenditure required, to be made out of limited resources. They are often highly controversial and not infrequently political in their nature'.[130] Referring to the Anglo-Zulu War of 1879, and to the two world wars, he commented:

It will often not be difficult with hindsight to point to different decisions that might have been made or preparations made. Would the disaster of Isandlwana have been avoided had the army command equipped Lord Chelmsford's forces with the heliograph? Or was the cause the failure to form a laager? Or the deployment of troops over too wide a perimeter? Or the lack of screwdrivers to open the ammunition boxes quickly enough? And would many disastrous casualties of the First World War have been avoided if the War Office had recognised the significance of the proposal for a tank put to it in 1912, 1914, and 1916 by the Australian engineer Lancelot de Mole...[?] Was the fall of Singapore [in 1941] to numerically inferior forces, with the ensuing slaughter and torture, due to culpable failures to fortify the Malay peninsular or landward side of Singapore or to provide armoured vehicles or aircraft to protect both?

---

[126] Ibid., para. 100.   [127] Ibid., paras 114, 117.   [128] Ibid., para. 125.

[129] Ibid., para. 126. Lord Mance's suggestion is substantiated by the *Fog of Law*'s explanation of the tactical choices not to wear body-armour and to use lightly armoured vehicles, in order to enhance mobility and avoid intimidating the civilian population. See above, p. 237.

[130] Ibid., para. 128.

Or was it inevitable in the context of what Churchill described as 'our bitter needs elsewhere'?[131]

To do as Lord Hope had done, and 'offer as a panacea' the injunction that courts should be very cautious before finding in favour of Challenger claims 'is to acknowledge the problem, but to offer no real solution'.[132] The inter-twining of the issues of procurement and training with issues to do with the causation of battlefield injury or death seemed highly likely to lead to a court attempting to try '"unimaginable" issues as to whether a soldier on the field of battle or a sailor on his ship might reasonably have been more careful'.[133] Therefore the court should 'not invade a field which would involve, in the context of claims for civil compensation, extensive and highly sensitive review with the benefit of hindsight [of] the United Kingdom's . . . policies, strategy and tactics relating to the deployment and use of its armed forces in combat'.[134] Instead, the court should proceed on the assumption that the outcome in Strasbourg would not differ from that at common law, and strike out the Challenger claims, because 'the state owes no . . . duty of care as alleged with regard to the provision of technology, equipment or training to avoid death or injury in the course of an active military operation'.[135]

It would be beside our purpose to consider the main issues raised by *Smith* (2013)—the propriety of derogation, the 'intertwining' of supply and training with military tactics, and the wisdom of permitting the Challenger and Snatch Land Rover claims to proceed. One point that is germane, however, is the reference to *Catherine Smith* (2011), where the Supreme Court held that the states subscribing to the European Convention never intended it to apply to their armed forces on active service overseas. This adds weight to Lord Bingham's word of caution about the European Court of Human Rights' view of the Convention as a 'living tree capable of growth and expansion'. For in deciding to expand the jurisdiction of Convention rights to circumstances that contracting states not only never intended, but would never have accepted, the court undermines states' confidence in international treaties generally. It gives them good reason to feel cheated and so makes them much more cautious in subscribing to anything similar in the future. Thus the presumptuousness of the court's rights-enthusiasm risks hindering its own mission.

Most relevant to our purpose is a striking contrast between the reasoning of the UK's Supreme Court in *Smith* (2013) and that of the European Court in *Al-Skeini* (2011) and *Al-Jedda* (2011). The British judges displayed a concern, repeatedly expressed, that the law should be very careful not to make unreasonable demands

---

[131] Ibid., para. 133.   [132] Ibid., para. 134.   [133] Ibid., para. 148.   [134] Ibid., para. 146.
[135] Ibid., paras 136, 151. In another dissenting opinion Lord Carnwath, agreeing with Lord Mance, opined that the UK Supreme Court's primary responsibility should be for 'the coherent and principled development of the common law, which is within our own control. We cannot determine the limits of article 2' (ibid., para. 156).

of troops operating in the dangerous and unpredictable circumstances of active service. Hence Lord Hope's distinction between formal ('legal and administrative') control and actual ('day to day') control on the ground, and between training situations where there is 'complete control' and active operations where there is not. Hence, too, Lord Mance's impressive rhetorical deployment of his detailed reading in military history. In contrast, the European court showed little such concern, admitting the distinction between 'control' and 'full control', only to slide quietly past it. And it showed no imaginative empathy at all for those struggling against the odds to keep a society from sliding into rights-trampling anarchy. So while Judge Bonello's intemperate rhetoric was out of keeping with the court's sober judgement, the substance of his refusal to accommodate 'immutable', 'fundamental', and 'universal' rights to facts on the ground was consonant.

VII

Our critical analysis of the jurisprudence targeted by *The Fog of Law* and *Clearing the Fog of Law* has vindicated the two reports. In the course of it, we have observed a marked resistance on the part of the European Court of Human Rights to taking into account the importance of maintaining political security and stability, from which stemmed its lack of interest in telling the crucial difference between the 'authority and control' possible in Strasbourg and that possible in Basra. This was highlighted when set against the reasoning of the British courts. Thus in *Al-Jedda* Strasbourg chose to report Lord Bingham's conviction that '[t]he importance of maintaining peace and security in the world can scarcely be exaggerated',[136] and his associated interpretation of UNSC Resolution 1546 (that it *could* not have used obligatory language), but then omitted any mention of them in its own ruling. Thus, too, where the British judges in *Smith* took seriously the distinction between formal control by an occupying power and actual, 'complete' control, Strasbourg in *Al-Skeini* acknowledged the distinction but, without any explanation, denied it a role in its judgement.[137]

---

[136] *Al-Jedda*, para. 20, p. 11.

[137] The arbitrary gaps in the Strasbourg court's reasoning that I have detected in the two cases of *Al-Skeini* and *Al-Jedda* are not, it seems, unusual. Commenting on the court's record up to 2005, the generally approving Alastair Mowbray wrote that '[a] weakness in the Court's resort to the "living instrument" doctrine is the sparseness of the justifications for its application in some cases ... A greater judicial willingness to elaborate upon the application of the doctrine in specific cases would help alleviate potential fears that it is simply a cover for subjective ad-hockery' ('The Creativity of the European Court of Human Rights', *Human Rights Law Review*, 5/1 (January 2005), p. 71). Twelve years later, according to Sir Noel Malcolm, nothing had changed for the better. Writing in 2017, he concluded his own painstaking and searching analysis of Strasbourg's jurisprudence thus: 'Any careful study of the ways in which the Court's jurisprudence has developed, and is still developing, exposes a mass of uncertainties, unpredictabilities, inscrutable "balancing acts", and applications of arbitrary or subjective criteria ... Academic lawyers who have studied these matters have issued damning

One reason for this resistance appears to lie in rights-fundamentalism. This found overt expression in Judge Bonello's rhetorical outburst at the end of *Al-Skeini*, where he exhorted the European Court *not* to accommodate doctrine to the facts, but instead to judge the facts against 'the immutable principles' underlying 'the fundamental functions' of the Convention. He then invoked 'the one aim' of every party to the Convention, that of achieving 'the supremacy of human rights law'. It is true that he acknowledged that this supremacy is to be achieved within the jurisdiction of the contracting states. But it is also true that, jibbing against this limitation, he appealed to the agenda laid down in the Convention's Preamble, namely, 'the *universal* and effective recognition and observance' of 'fundamental human rights', commenting, '"Universal" hardly suggests an observance parcelled off by territory on the checkerboard of geography'.[138] It is possible, of course, that the Maltese judge's views were entirely eccentric among those of his fellow judges. However, there is some evidence of a similar fundamentalism elsewhere in the judgement of the court, for example, where it chose to invoke the authority of the UN Special Rapporteur, Philip Alston, on the right to life under Article 6 of the ICCPR. Implicitly dismissing the jurisdiction of the Law of Armed Conflict, Alston asserted that '[a]rmed conflict and occupation do not discharge the State's duty to investigate and prosecute human rights abuses. The right to life is non-derogable regardless of circumstances.'[139] Further evidence can be found in *Al-Jedda*, where Strasbourg, invoking the European Court of Justice, recalled that the European Community was based on the rule of law, that fundamental rights formed an integral part of the general principles of law, and that therefore no obligation generated by an international agreement could prejudice the constitutional principle that all Community acts had to respect fundamental rights.[140] The Strasbourg court's commitment to the *literally* fundamental character of conventional rights is thrown into sharp relief, when contrasted with Lord Bingham's view that the UK's obligation under UNSCR 1546 trumped its obligation under the European Convention to secure a 'fundamental human right'.[141] For Lord Bingham, it seems, the right was only relatively fundamental—most clearly, within the territory of the states party to the Convention (but even there, subject to a right to derogate), and by implication also in foreign territory where the troops of a contracting state have 'complete' control and are not subject to a contradictory obligation under a Security Council Resolution. Beholding all of these qualifications, one might be forgiven for

---

judgments on one point after another, using terms such as "vague and unsatisfactory", "radical indeterminacy", "disturbingly elusive" and "massive doses of speculation"... This unclear, indeterminate, subjective and unpredictable system of human rights adjudication can barely meet some of the most basic requirements of the rule of law' (Malcolm, *Human Rights and Political Wrongs*, pp. 137–8; for Malcolm's quotations of two academic lawyers, Aileen McHarg and Marie-Bénédicte Dembour, see Chapter 11, n. 70).

[138] *Al-Skeini*, 'Concurring Opinion of Judge Bonello', paras 8, 9. The emphasis is Bonello's.
[139] Ibid., para. 93.   [140] *Al-Jedda*, para. 53.   [141] Ibid., para. 20, pp. 11–12.

wondering how the right is supposed to remain 'fundamental' at all. No such doubt arises, however, in relation to the view of the Strasbourg court, which at every turn manoeuvred to preserve conventional rights from limitation.[142]

Such rights-fundamentalism is a symptom of a signal lack of historical and political imagination. The European Convention was born in post-war reaction against the fascist dictatorships of the 1930s and early 1940s, when the totalitarian state was the overwhelming threat to human well-being. Accordingly, the rights guaranteed by the Convention were designed to keep such a state at bay. Judging by its reasoning in *Al-Skeini* and *Al-Jedda*, the European Court of Human Rights remains imaginatively captive to the Convention's original, parochial assumptions. That is why, notwithstanding evidence that it itself cited, the court proved consistently incapable of taking into account the circumstances of near-anarchy in Iraq, where the main threat to human well-being—and to any protective human rights regimen—was the imminent collapse of state authority.

Discernible here, too, is a culture of risk-aversion, to which *The Fog of Law* drew our attention. Positive rights, with their attendant legal apparatus of enforcement, are a means of reducing the risk of harm to human goods. They cannot guarantee security from harm, since rights can always be violated, but they can discourage violation by threatening legal sanction. Where there is a strong and stable state, the costs of reducing risks via rights—for example the limitations and burdens imposed on the police—can be afforded. But where the state is fragile, the costs to the police (and their military support) can become too high, hampering their ability to uphold any political and legal order at all. In such circumstances, it can be reasonable to suspend rights (or not to apply them), to trust instead to the security forces' consciences, moral training, and respect for the more permissive Law of Armed Conflict, and to suffer a temporary increase in the risk of harm to goods. In this light, the error in the reasoning of the European court could be described as one, first, of mistaking rights for ends rather than means, and then of refusing to consider the possibility that, sometimes, an insistence on minimising risk in the short term by means of rights can have the effect of exposing goods (and any rights-apparatus for protecting them) to greater risk in the long term.

Blinkered by a post-1945, Eurocentric political imagination, and fuelled by the utopian assumption that risk is eliminable, Strasbourg's rights-fundamentalism

---

[142] Ian Park provides broader jurisprudential substantiation of the claim that the roots of Strasbourg's resistance to the geographical limitation of Convention rights lie in its view that their moral authority is in fact universal and that their legal authority should become so. Commenting on the development of the court's jurisprudence about jurisdiction since *Banković*, he writes that *Banković*'s 'narrow focus is gradually broadened in subsequent judgments to reflect the universal nature of human rights'; and that such broadening accords with the view 'that the notion of jurisdiction contains an element of "normative guidance" in addition to "effective power" and "overall control", the normative dimension being vested in the universal nature of human rights as opposed to any narrow regional conception' (*The Right to Life in Armed Conflict*, pp, 77, 78).

has also been propelled by a measure of universal missionary zeal. In 2013 Jean-Paul Costa, a former President of the European Court of Human Rights, wrote that

> the Preamble of the Convention shows that the aim of the Council of Europe and therefore of the Court, is not only the protection of rights and freedoms, but also their *development*. That implies an evolutive and progressive conception of the rights that are recognised, and the Court would be failing in part of its duties if it attended only to the protection of the rights, and ignored the imperative to develop them.[143]

Of this progressive, expansionary gospel Judge Bonello was evidently a zealous evangelist. Far from being embarrassed at the thought 'of being branded in perpetuity a human rights imperialist', he reminded his colleagues in *Al-Skeini* that all the states party to the Convention strove to achieve 'one aim, at once infinitesimal and infinite: the supremacy of human rights law'.[144] If there were any dissenters among them, they did not reveal themselves. For neither in *Al-Skeini* nor in *Al-Jedda* did the Strasbourg court show any compunction about extending the reach of the Convention into territory and circumstances that, as the UK's Supreme Court observed in *Catherine Smith* (2011) and again in *Smith* (2013), the contracting states had never intended and would never have agreed to.[145]

---

[143] J.-P. Costa, *La Cour européenne des droits de l'homme: des juges pour la liberté* (Paris: Dalloz-Sirey, 2013), p. 43; quoted and translated by Malcolm in *Human Rights and Political Wrongs*, p. 72. Malcolm argues that Costa misinterprets the Preamble—that the task of 'development' was supposed to belong to the Council of Europe, not the court; and that this development would occur by the addition of internationally agreed protocols, not by innovative judicial rulings (*Human Rights and Political Wrongs*, pp. 73–5).

[144] *Al-Skeini*, paras 39, 9. The kind of zealous moral certainty evident in Judge Bonello's behaviour seems not to be unique. Writing of the conduct of the judiciary in New Zealand in the wake of the 1990 Bill of Rights Acts, James Allan, former law professor at the University of Otago, has observed an 'underlying assumption that rights and justice are uncontentious, and only questioned by those beyond the moral pale... This is what gives such force to the desire to make rights justiciable. The forces of good and evil are seen to be clearly demarcated and the job of the judge [is] to ensure the triumph of the former' ('The Effect of a Statutory Bill of Rights where Parliament is Sovereign: The Lesson from New Zealand', in Campbell et al., *Sceptical Essays*, p. 388).

[145] *Smith*, para. 25. In *Catherine Smith* Lord Collins had stated that extra-territorial application was 'plainly not contemplated in the drafting process [of the ECHR]' and that 'it was hardly conceivable that in 1950 the framers of the Convention would have intended the Convention to apply to the armed forces of Council of Europe states engaged in operations in or elsewhere outside the contracting states' (para. 303). This is true, but not exactly. As A. W. Brian Simpson shows in his magisterial history of the European Convention, Britain did agree to the extension of the Convention to its overseas colonial dependencies in late 1953 (*Human Rights and the End of Empire: Britain and the Genesis of the European Convention* (Oxford: Oxford University Press, 2001), p. 6). However, it did so with 'a lively understanding that what may be a reasonable provision in Europe does not necessarily make sense here and now for Africa [and the like]' (ibid., p. 825, quoting a Colonial Office minute of 18 January 1951), and fully intending to fend off inappropriate interference by appeal to Article 63 on 'Territorial application', whose clause 3 reads: 'The provisions of this Convention shall be applied in such [colonial] territories with due regard, however, to local requirements' (ibid., p. 827. With the entry into force of Protocol No. 11, Article 63 became Article 56.) I note that Simpson explains the concerns

That such an innovative deployment of the 'living instrument' might undermine national confidence in the Convention and in the European Court seems not have disturbed the Strasbourg judges' minds.[146]

Whatever its several causes, the failure of the Strasbourg judges in *Al-Skeini* and *Al-Jedda* to let the jurisdiction of Convention rights vary according to morally significant facts on the ground has had several unhappy effects. For it has produced an imprudent jurisprudence that serves to weaken the military effectiveness of European States Party and their ability to support politically fragile states, to undermine states' confidence in international treaties, and to provoke calls for states' withdrawal from the Convention altogether.[147]

---

of the colonial authorities in sympathetic tones: 'The principal trouble, so far as the protection of individual rights was concerned, was that times in the colonies were sometimes not normal, either because of inter-tribal fighting... or because of violent conflict between ethnic or religious communities... or because political activity and nationalism became channelled into riots or more general insurrections, guerrilla warfare, or insurrectionary movements...' (ibid., p. 53); 'Where control is seriously threatened it is the direct use of coercive violence, rather than the later criminal trials, and punishment of offenders, which is critical to the restoration of state control' (ibid., p. 54); 'Regular criminal law, with its requirement of trial, proof of guilt, and presumption of innocence, does not operate effectively in conditions of insurrection... Regular law also largely excludes preventive action, being based upon the principle of punishing the groom for not shutting the stable door only after the horse has escaped. *This is a luxury which cannot be indulged in conditions which border on war*' (ibid., p. 55. The emphasis is mine.). No doubt Simpson's National Service from 1949 to 1951 in the Nigeria Regiment, where he commanded a company, heightened his appreciation of the importance and difficulty of maintaining law and order in fragile states. And perhaps the fact that his father had witnessed the Easter Rising in Dublin in 1916 heightened it further.

[146] The European Court had been warned of this danger thirty years before *Al-Skeini* and *Al-Jedda*. According to Jonathan Fisher, QC, the jurisprudential fork in the road, where the court abandoned a conservative textual approach to treaty-interpretation for 'the principle of judicial activism', was *Golder v. United Kingdom* (1979–80), 1 EHRR. There the court had determined the issue 'by reference to the broad aspirations articulated in the Convention's preamble instead of conducting a textual analysis of the words used by the Convention's drafters at the time when the Convention was concluded' (*Rescuing Human Rights* (London: Henry Jackson Society, 2012), p. 20). The UK member of the court, Sir Gerald Fitzmaurice, profoundly disagreed: 'In my view, the correct approach to the interpretation of Article 6 (1) is to bear in mind... that it is a provision embodied in an instrument depending for its force upon the agreement—and indeed the *continuing* support—of governments... Speaking generally, the various conventions and covenants on Human Rights, but more particularly the European Convention, have broken entirely new ground internationally, making heavy inroads on some of the most cherished preserves of governments in the sphere of their domestic jurisdiction or *domaine réservé*... For these reasons governments have been hesitant to become parties to instruments most of which, apart the European Convention, have apparently not so far attracted a sufficient number of ratifications to bring them into force...' (*Golder*, para. 38; quoted in Fisher, *Rescuing Human Rights*, pp. 20–1). Thirteen years after *Golder*, Franz Matscher, a Strasbourg judge for more than twenty years, confirmed Fitzmaurice's reading of the court's behaviour, albeit with less alarm: 'the Convention organs have... [a]t times... perhaps... entered territory which is no longer that of treaty interpretation but is actually legal policy-making' ('Methods of Interpretation of the Convention', in R. St J. Macdonald, F. Matscher, and H. Petzold, eds, *The European System for the Protection of Human Rights* (Dordrecht: Martinus Nijhoff, 1993), pp. 69–70).

[147] For example, in the conclusion of his damning analysis of the Strasbourg court's jurisprudence, Sir Noel Malcolm declares, '[w]ith regret, I see no alternative to leaving the Convention' (*Human Rights and Political Wrongs*, p. 139).

11

What's Wrong with (Some) Judges?

2: *Carter* and the Invention of a Right to 'Physician-Assisted Dying'

I

In the last chapter I argued that one problem sometimes attending the judicial treatment of rights is a fundamentalism that refuses to reckon with empirical contingencies, and which thereby produces an imprudent jurisprudence. In this chapter I shall argue that another problem lies in the 'progressive' zeal of some judges, which moves them to exploit the room for creativity granted by abstract concepts, in order to invent novel rights. This is also imprudent, not in refusing to acknowledge contingencies, but in having a court decide an ethical issue that is politically controversial.

On 6 February 2015, in *Carter v. Canada (Attorney General)*, the nine justices of the Supreme Court of Canada made a unanimous decision that an absolute prohibition of 'physician-assisted dying' constituted a violation of Section 7 of the *Canadian Charter of Rights and Freedoms*. As a consequence, the *Criminal Code of Canada* provisions (Sections 241 [b] and 14) prohibiting assisted suicide and killing upon consent were struck down as void in relation to any competent adult who (1) clearly consents to the termination of life and (2) has a grievous and irremediable medical condition (including an illness, disease, or disability) that causes enduring suffering that is intolerable to the individual in the circumstances.[1] The government of Canada was given twelve months from the date of the judgement to enact legislation permitting 'physician-assisted dying' under the stipulated conditions.[2]

The road that had led to this decision was as follows.[3] In 2011 Gloria Taylor, a resident of British Columbia diagnosed with amyotrophic lateral sclerosis, challenged the constitutionality of the prohibition of 'physician-assisted dying' in the *Criminal Code*. In her challenge she was subsequently joined by Lee Carter and her husband, Hollis Johnson, who had arranged for the former's mother, at her

---

[1] *Carter v. Canada (Attorney General) 2015 SCC 5*, para. 127.   [2] *Carter SCC*, paras 125, 128.
[3] My account here draws heavily on Benny Chan and Margaret Somerville, 'Converting the 'Right to Life' to the 'Right to Physician-Assisted Suicide and Euthanasia: An Analysis of *Carter v. Canada (Attorney General)*, Supreme Court of Canada', *Medical Law Review*, 24/2 (Spring 2016).

own request, to obtain assistance in suicide at a Dignitas clinic in Switzerland. The British Columbia Civil Liberties Association also joined the challenge.

The trial judge at the British Columbia Supreme Court, Madam Justice Lynn Smith, identified the core of the challenge as the claim that Section 241 (b) of the *Criminal Code* violated Section 7 of the *Canadian Charter of Rights and Freedoms*, which asserts that '[e]veryone has the right to life, liberty, and security of the person and the right not to be deprived thereof except in accordance with the principles of fundamental justice', as well as Section 15 rights against discrimination, and that these violations could not be justified under the saving provisions of Section 1 of the *Charter*, which subjects the asserted rights 'only to such reasonable limits prescribed by law as can be demonstrably justified in a free and democratic society'.

In her 2012 judgement, Justice Smith argued that the 'preponderance of the evidence from ethicists is that there is no ethical difference between physician-assisted death and other end-of-life practices whose outcome is highly likely to be death', and that the safeguards in place in permissive jurisdictions were sufficiently effective in preventing vulnerable people from being pressured into choosing assisted death and in preventing legalised euthanasia from being abused.[4] She also reasoned that she was not bound by the Supreme Court of Canada's 1993 judgement in *Rodriguez v. British Columbia (Attorney General)*, the then precedent governing 'physician-assisted dying' in which the court had upheld the constitutional validity of the *Criminal Code*'s prohibition, on the ground of subsequent social and legal developments.[5] Justice Smith concluded in favour of the claimants, deciding that the absolute prohibition of assisted suicide and of inflicting death in cases of competent adults suffering intolerably as a result of a grievous and irremediable medical condition violated the *Charter*'s rights both against discrimination and to 'life, liberty, and security of the person'; that these violations did not comply with the principles of fundamental justice; and that they could not be saved by Section 1's restrictions. As a result she declared the *Criminal Code*'s absolute prohibition of 'physician-assisted dying' unconstitutional and granted a one-year suspension of invalidity to give the federal government time to draft legislation allowing for assisted suicide or voluntary euthanasia under certain circumstances.

The Attorney General appealed against this decision, and the British Columbia Court of Appeal overruled the British Columbia Supreme Court by a two to one majority on the basis that the Supreme Court of Canada decision in *Rodriguez* was the governing law. It was this decision that the Supreme Court of Canada, upon further appeal, overruled in 2015, when it upheld Justice Smith's judgement in *Carter v. Canada (Attorney General)*.

---

[4] *Carter v. Canada (Attorney General)* 2012 BCSC 886, paras 335, 682–5, 815, 843, 1243.
[5] *Carter BCSC*, para. 942.

The Supreme Court argued that Justice Smith had been entitled to revisit *Rodriguez* because the law relating to the principles of 'over-breadth' and proportionality had since advanced, with the law on over-breadth now explicitly recognised 'as a principle of fundamental justice', and because 'the matrix of legislative and social facts' in the case before her differed from the evidence considered by the Supreme Court in 1993.[6] In particular, by 2010 eight jurisdictions around the world had come to permit some form of 'physician-assisted dying', and together they furnished a new body of evidence about the practical and legal workings of physician-assisted death and the efficacy of safeguards for the vulnerable.[7] The Supreme Court noted, without demurring, that Justice Smith had concluded that 'expert evidence' had established that the predicted abuse and disproportionate impact on vulnerable populations had not materialised in Belgium, the Netherlands, and Oregon;[8] that physicians are capable of reliably assessing patient competence; that it is possible to detect coercion, undue influence, and ambivalence as part of this assessment process; and that the risks of physician-assisted death 'can be identified and very substantially minimized through a carefully designed system'.[9] The court also endorsed Justice Smith's judgement that the 'preponderance of the evidence from ethicists is that there is no ethical distinction between physician-assisted death and other end-of-life practices whose outcome is highly likely to be death'—such as palliative sedation and withholding or withdrawing of life-saving or -sustaining treatment.[10]

The Supreme Court argued that the right to life under Section 7 of the *Canadian Charter* is engaged where either the law or state action 'imposes' death or an increased risk of death, either directly or indirectly;[11] that the right to liberty is engaged where the law or state action limits an individual's response to a grievous and irremediable medical condition, which is 'a matter critical to their dignity and autonomy';[12] and that the right to security is engaged by state interference with an individual's physical or psychological integrity, 'including any state action that causes physical or serious psychological suffering'.[13] The court then judged that Sections 241(b) and 14 of the *Criminal Code* deprive competent adults, who seek 'assisted dying' 'because of a grievous and irremediable medical condition that causes enduring and intolerable suffering', of their right to life, since the prohibition has the effect of forcing some individuals to take their own lives prematurely for fear they would be incapable to doing so when their suffering became intolerable; of their right to liberty, because it denies people in a grievous and irremediable medical condition the right to make decisions about their bodily integrity and medical care, which is 'a matter critical to their

---

[6] *Carter SCC*, p. 334 and paras 44, 46, 47. [7] Ibid., para. 8. [8] Ibid., para. 25.
[9] Ibid., para. 27. [10] Ibid., para. 23. [11] Ibid., para. 62. [12] Ibid., para. 66.
[13] Ibid., para. 64.

dignity and autonomy'; and of their right to security, because it leaves them to endure intolerable suffering.[14]

The court observed that Section 7 recognises that state interference with the rights to life, liberty, and security can be justified, but not if it violates 'the principles of fundamental justice'.[15] Among these, three principles had emerged as central in recent jurisprudence: laws impinging on life, liberty, and security 'must not be arbitrary, overbroad, or have consequences that are grossly disproportionate to their object'.[16] In order to determine whether a legal prohibition on 'assisted dying' violates these principles, the law's object must first be identified.[17] This should be understood as the protection 'of vulnerable persons from being induced to commit suicide in a time of weakness', rather than, more broadly, 'the preservation of life'.[18] The latter should be understood as 'an animating social value rather than ... a description of the specific object of the prohibition', since if it were the object, it would become difficult to say whether or not the means used to further it are overbroad or grossly disproportionate—and the law would be immunised against challenge under the Charter.[19] Besides, consideration of 'competing social interests or public benefits conferred by the impugned law' are more appropriately considered at the stage of justification under Section 1 than while determining whether the deprivation of life, liberty, security accords with the principles of fundamental justice under Section 7.[20]

Given that the object of the law prohibiting 'physician-assisted dying' is to protect vulnerable persons from being induced to commit suicide in a time of weakness, a total ban does help achieve it. Therefore, the deprivation of certain individuals' rights cannot be said to be arbitrary.[21] Nevertheless, since '[t]he blanket prohibition sweeps conduct [i.e. not of the vulnerable in moments of weakness] into its ambit that is unrelated to the law's objective', and so limits the

---

[14] Ibid., p. 335 and paras 57–8.   [15] Ibid., para. 71.   [16] Ibid., para. 72.

[17] Ibid., para. 73.

[18] Ibid., paras 74–8. This narrow interpretation of the law's object, first made by Justice Smith and then confirmed by the Supreme Court, was a major determinant of the subsequent ruling. Had the courts followed the precedent of Justice Sopinka's judgement in *Rodriguez*, it would have recognised that the law had more than one object: not only to protect the vulnerable from undue pressure to choose assisted suicide or voluntary euthanasia, but also more generally to 'discourage the terminally ill from choosing death over life' (*Rodriguez v. British Columbia (Attorney General) [1993] 3 SCR 519*, p. 614). Recognition of this second object would have made it much more difficult for the trial judge, and then the Supreme Court, to argue in *Carter* that the law's blanket prohibition was 'overbroad'. As Chan and Somerville have observed, '[w]hether a law survives an overbreadth analysis will depend on how a reviewing judge construes its objective' (Chan and Somerville, 'Converting the 'Right to Life' to the 'Right to Physician-Assisted Suicide and Euthanasia', p. 165).

[19] *Carter SCC*, paras 76–7.

[20] Ibid., para. 78. In para. 80, the court argues that a claimant under Section 7 should not be tasked with showing that the principles of fundamental justice are 'not overridden by a valid state or communal interest in these circumstances', invoking the authority of T. J. Singleton, 'The Principles of Fundamental Justice: Societal Interests and Section 1 of the Charter', *Canadian Bar Review*, 74 (1995), p. 449.

[21] *Carter SCC*, paras 83–4.

rights of people outside the class of intentionally protected persons, that limitation is not connected to the objective and the prohibition may be overbroad.[22] Further, since is not difficult to 'conclusively identify the "vulnerable"', it is in fact overbroad.[23]

The question then arises as to whether the blanket prohibition can nevertheless be 'saved' by Section 1 of the *Canadian Charter*, which makes the asserted rights subject 'to such reasonable limits prescribed by law as can be demonstrably justified in a free and democratic society'. The Supreme Court reasoned that such 'saving' would require that the law have 'a pressing and substantial object' and that the means chosen are proportionate to that object. A law is proportionate if (1) the means adopted are rationally connected to that objective; (2) the law is minimally impairing of the right; and (3) there is proportionality between the deleterious and salutary effects of the law.[24] The court conceded that there is a rational connection between the blanket prohibition and its objective,[25] but was not persuaded that 'less drastic' means were unavailable.[26] 'This question', it said, 'lies at the heart of this case.'[27] The trial judge had heard 'evidence from scientists, medical practitioners, and others who were familiar with end-of-life decision-making in Canada and abroad', and had concluded that 'a permissive regime with properly designed and administered safeguards' is capable of protecting vulnerable people from abuse and error.[28] She had found 'no evidence' from permissive jurisdictions that people with disabilities are at heightened risk of accessing 'physician-assisted dying'; 'no evidence' of inordinate impact on socially vulnerable populations in the permissive jurisdictions; and 'no compelling evidence that a permissive regime in Canada would result in a "practical slippery slope"'.[29] The existence of conflicting evidence, the court added, is not sufficient to establish 'a palpable and overriding error'.[30] In particular, the court referred to evidence presented directly to it at the appellate stage by Professor Étienne Montero, a professor of bioethics and an expert on the practice of euthanasia in Belgium.[31] Professor Montero had argued that issues with compliance and the expansion of criteria of eligibility 'inevitably arise, even in a system of ostensibly strict limits and safeguards', and that '[o]nce euthanasia is allowed, it becomes very difficult to maintain a strict interpretation of the statutory conditions'.[32] Against this, the Supreme Court supported Justice Smith's argument that it was 'problematic' to draw inferences for Canada from the permissive regime in Belgium, which 'is the product of a very different medico-legal culture', where the practice of assisted death was 'already prevalent and embedded'.[33] Further, against the argument that

---

[22] Ibid., pp. 335–6 and paras 85–6.   [23] Ibid., paras 87–8.   [24] Ibid., para. 94.
[25] Ibid., para. 100.   [26] Ibid., paras 102–3.   [27] Ibid., para. 104.
[28] Ibid., paras 104–5.   [29] Ibid., para. 107.   [30] Ibid., para. 109.
[31] Chan and Somerville, 'Converting the 'Right to Life' to the 'Right to Physician-Assisted Suicide and Euthanasia', p. 145 n. 7.
[32] *Carter SCC*, paras 110–11.   [33] Ibid., para. 112.

a blanket prohibition is necessary because 'there is no reliable way to identify those who are vulnerable and those who are not',[34] the court held that vulnerability can be assessed on an individual basis, using the procedures that physicians apply in their assessment of informed consent and decisional capacity in the context of medical decision-making more generally:

> Logically speaking, there is no reason to think that the injured, ill, and disabled who have the option to refuse or to request withdrawal of life-saving or life-sustaining treatment, or who seek palliative sedation, are less vulnerable or less susceptible to biased decision-making than those who might seek more active assistance in dying. The risks...are already part and parcel of our medical system.[35]

Therefore, the court judged, 'it is possible for physicians, with due care and attention to the seriousness of the decision involved, to adequately assess decisional capacity', and the risks can be limited through 'a carefully designed and monitored system of safeguards'.[36] Accordingly, it confirmed the trial judge's finding that 'a properly administered regulatory regime is capable of protecting the vulnerable from abuse or error',[37] and that the Criminal Code's blanket prohibition was not proportionate to its objective. In effect, the court concluded by instructing the Canadian Parliament to legislate for a suitably permissive regime.

II

Thus the jurisprudence of Canada's Supreme Court gave birth to a new legal right to physician-assisted suicide and voluntary euthanasia. This is not the place to offer a comprehensive ethical critique of the court's judgement, for that would be beside our focal concern, which is the manner in which novel legal rights come into being. However, a presentation of some of the ethical issues raised by the judgement will serve our purpose, insofar as it shows how morally complex and controversial is the question of legalising physician-assisted suicide and voluntary euthanasia, and thereby highlights the fact that a judge qua judge, expert in the law, has no special, professional authority to pronounce upon ethical matters.

One basic feature of the court's reasoning that is controversial is its prevailing use of the phrase 'physician-assisted dying' and its correlative avoidance of the

---

[34] Ibid., para. 115.   [35] Ibid., para. 115.   [36] Ibid., paras 116–17.
[37] Ibid., paras 3, 29, 31.

phrase 'physician-assisted suicide' or the word 'killing'.[38] Nowhere does the court reflect upon and justify this verbal choice, even though it prejudices its reasoning from the beginning. The phrase 'physician-assisted dying' obscures the fact that what is under discussion is the legal permissibility of medical patients being given assistance to bring an end to their suffering *by intentionally killing themselves* or by having *someone else kill them upon request*. Intentional self-killing is what we call 'suicide', and intentional killing, 'homicide', because that is what the words literally mean. Whether or not assistance in killing oneself and killing someone else upon request are morally right, they are distinct from assistance in passive dying. Otherwise known as palliative care, that is where a patient is given comfort and pain-relief in the process of dying. It is true that there are cases where palliative treatment can increase the probability of dying, and so has the effect of hastening death. Nevertheless, it is a commonplace of human experience that we cause things we do not intend. And sometimes at least there is an important moral and legal distinction between effects that we cause intentionally, effects we risk but do not intend, and effects we cause accidentally. It matters whether I intended to kill you, or merely risked your life, or killed you by accident. The presence or absence of intention alone might not finally decide the moral or legal status of my action, but it is nevertheless an important factor.[39] This is obscured by the choice to describe assistance in intentionally killing oneself and being killing upon request as 'assistance in dying'. The question before the court was not simply about the legal permissibility of giving help to the dying, but rather about whether or not to enshrine in law the obligation of healthcare professionals to assist patients to commit suicide or to kill them at their request.

In addition to being conceptually obfuscating, the court's verbal choice had the effect of siding with campaigners for the liberalisation of the law, who studiously eschew talk about 'assisted suicide' or 'killing upon request' for political reasons. This is because, when members of the public are asked if they support 'assistance in dying', they (naturally) tend to respond affirmatively. However, there is evidence that when the phrasing of the question is changed to 'assistance in suicide', popular support plummets.[40]

As to why the Supreme Court should have made this obfuscating and politically biased choice, we can only speculate, since it does not tell us. One reason that finds

---

[38] The only places where *Carter v. Canada* uses the phrase 'assisted suicide' is when it refers back to the *Criminal Code*—for example, in paragraphs 5 and 93.

[39] See John Keown's extended discussion of intention in relation to *Carter v. Canada 2012 BCSC 886* in 'A Right to Voluntary Euthanasia? Confusion in Canada in Carter', *Notre Dame Journal of Law, Ethics, and Public Policy*, 28/1 (2014), pp. 5–17.

[40] See the US Gallup poll of May 2013 that found that 70 per cent of those surveyed favoured doctors being allowed to 'end the patient's life by some painless means'. However, when the question was rephrased as allowing doctors to help patients 'commit suicide', support dropped to 51 per cent: <https://news.gallup.com/poll/162815/support-euthanasia-hinges-described.aspx> (as at 11 September 2018).

textual support appears where the court reports Justice Smith's judgement that the 'preponderance of the evidence from ethicists is that there is no ethical distinction between physician-assisted death and other end-of-life practices whose outcome is highly likely to be death'—such as palliative sedation and withholding or withdrawing of life-saving or -sustaining treatment.[41] The court makes no comment on this, but, since it does not demur, we can reasonably infer endorsement. This is unfortunate, since Justice Smith's reasoning here is weak. While the distinction between 'physician-assisted death' and palliative treatment that risks death is indeed not logically clear, the distinction between assistance in intentional suicide and killing upon request on the one hand, and death-risking treatment on the other, is much clearer. The prejudicial description, 'physician-assisted death', serves to muddy the waters. It is, therefore, perhaps not surprising that a preponderance of ethicists could not tell the difference. It is even less surprising when we realise which preponderance she was referring to. She was not making a global, comprehensive reference, but a local, random one. What she actually wrote was this: 'The preponderance of the evidence from ethicists is that there is no ethical distinction between physician-assisted death and other end-of-life practices whose outcome is highly likely to be death. I find the arguments put forward by those ethicists, such as Professor Battin, Dr Angell and Professor Sumner, to be persuasive.'[42] The ethicists to whom Justice Smith was referring were three of the seven that the plaintiffs happened to have furnished as witnesses. Since the defendants put forward only two, the plaintiffs' ethicists were preponderant. To be fair, the judge did not merely appeal to the doubtful authority of a superior number; she did say that she found their arguments persuasive. But she did not pause to tell us why.

III

Three further doubtful features of the Supreme Court's judgement in *Carter v. Canada (Attorney General)*, directly germane to our main concern, are these: the abstraction and indeterminacy of some of the rights guaranteed the individual by the *Canadian Charter*; the licence this gives judges to stray beyond their professional, legal expertise; and the conceptual independence of these rights from any consideration of the common good.

The rights engaged by the claimants' challenge, according to the court, were those guaranteed by Section 7, namely, 'the right to life, liberty, and security of the

---

[41] *Carter SCC*, para. 23.
[42] *Carter BCSC*, para. 335. By my reckoning the following were ethicists presented as witnesses by the plaintiffs: Marcia Angell, Margaret Pabst Battin, Georg Bossard, Gerrit Kimsma, Sheila McLean, Wayne Sumner, and Johannes J. M. Van Delden. I count only two ethicists presented by the defendants: Eugene Bereza and John Keown (ibid., para. 160).

person'. Our critique of natural rights-talk in Chapters 1 to 5 should make us immediately alert to the striking abstraction of these rights; and, indeed, when we compare them to all of the other rights guaranteed by the *Canadian Charter*, we see that they are uniquely abstract.[43] If we were minded to be pedantic, we might complain that the 'right to life', as it stands literally and without qualification, could ground a suit against the Almighty for lumbering human creatures with mortality. However, if we were more charitable, we could speculate that 'the right to life' is shorthand, paradigmatically, for something like 'the right not to have one's life damaged or taken away except as an unintended side-effect of proportionate self-defence by a private citizen or proportionate defence of others by a public officer'. Even so, the paradigm does not exhaust the possible meaning, and, unspecified, 'the right to life' leaves plenty of room for creative—indeed ingenious—jurisprudential interpretation that strays from the obvious, common sense cases.

The same applies even more to the rights to 'liberty' and 'security'. We could speculate that 'the right to liberty' means, paradigmatically, such things as 'the right not to be subject to arbitrary arrest and imprisonment' and 'the right to freedom of expression'. Yet the former is explicitly guaranteed in Section 9 and the latter as a 'fundamental freedom' in Section 2. So the distinct meaning of the unspecified 'liberty' in Section 7 remains obscure. So, too, does the meaning of the unspecified 'security', insofar as that is distinct from 'life' and 'liberty'.

In *Carter* the Canadian Supreme Court, following Justice Smith, exploited the room given it by the *Charter* for jurisprudential creativity. Thus it argued that the right to life is engaged where either the law or state action 'imposes' death or an increased risk of death, either directly or indirectly,[44] and argued that the *Criminal Code*'s prohibition of 'physician-assisted dying' infringes 'the right to life' by 'forcing' individuals to take their own lives prematurely for fear they would be

---

[43] The *Charter* affirms 'Democratic Rights' such as the right to vote (S. 3); 'Mobility Rights' such as the right to enter and leave Canada (S. 6.1); 'Equality Rights' such as equal standing before the law (S. 15); the 'Official Languages of Canada', and the right to use either English or French in the proceedings of Parliament (S. 17.1); and 'Minority Educational Rights', such as the right of native English- and French-speakers to have their children receive school education in their parents' language. The 'right to life, liberty, and security' (S. 7) comes first in the list of 'Legal Rights'. All the other subsequent rights listed are specific—e.g. to be secure against unreasonable search or seizure (S. 8) or not to be arbitrarily detained or imprisoned (S. 9).

The extraordinary abstraction of the 'right to life etc.' in the *Canadian Charter* also becomes clear when it is contrasted with the right to life (Art. 2), and the right to liberty and security (Art. 5), in the European Convention of Human Rights (ECHR). In the ECHR the right to life is immediately defined as a right not to 'be deprived of [one's] life intentionally save in the execution of a sentence of a court following his conviction of a crime for which the penalty is provided by law' (Art. 2.1); and the right to liberty and security is immediately defined as a right not to be deprived of one's liberty except through various kinds of 'lawful detention' or 'lawful arrest' (Art. 5, [a]–[f]). It is no coincidence that in *Pretty v. United Kingdom* (Application no. 2346/02) (2002) 35 EHHR 1, the European Court of Human Rights found that that 'no right to die, whether at the hands of a third person or with the assistance of a public authority, can be derived from Article 2 of the Convention' (para. 40).

[44] *Carter SCC*, para. 62.

incapable of doing so when they reached the point where their suffering became intolerable.[45] Here the court's creativity produced logic that is strained, if not tortured. For, of course, the code's prohibition of 'physician-assisted dying' does not force individuals to do anything. Nor does it impose death on them. Rather, it leaves them free to choose how to react to the prospect of a distressing death— either by trusting palliative medicine and care or by committing suicide. Most people choose the first; the minority who choose the second cannot be said to have been 'forced'—except by an inner, personal compulsion combining fear of distress with horror at dependence. If they choose suicide, it is they who deprive themselves of life, not the law. One could argue, as the court does, that 'the right to life' should be taken to mean that citizens have 'the right not to be exposed to the risk that they might choose to commit suicide earlier, for fear that they might lack the ability to do so later', and that the legal guarantee of 'physician-assisted dying' would serve to relieve that fear. One could argue that. But such an argument strays a very long way from the obvious, common sense, paradigmatic meaning of 'the right to life', and it raises a host of controversial questions that are not easily answered. For one, what should be the criteria of eligibility? The Supreme Court, following Justice Smith, decided that, to be eligible, someone must suffer from 'a grievous and irremediable medical condition (including an illness, disease, or disability) that causes enduring suffering that is intolerable to the individual in the circumstances'.[46] However, if the purpose of legalising physician-assisted suicide and voluntary euthanasia is to relieve individuals of the felt need to kill themselves prematurely, in order to avoid 'enduring suffering' that they find intolerable, why restrict eligibility to those subject to 'an irremediable medical condition'? What about psychological suffering? Surely there are individuals who find that quite as intolerable as physical pain? Why should they not enjoy the reassurance that a legal right to physician-assisted suicide and voluntary euthanasia would provide? If a paraplegic, intolerably frustrated at his confinement and dependence, why not also a convicted criminal sentenced to life imprisonment? If a patient suffering from cancer, whose pain cannot be palliated short of sedation, why not also a middle-aged woman who feels she cannot face the prospect of life bereaved of her children? That is one set of questions raised by the court's creative interpretation of 'the right to life', which are not easily answered. There are others, too, as we shall see. However, because of the court's choice of a particular jurisprudential method, none of these considerations was permitted to enter into deliberation about whether or not a right to 'assisted death' exists in the first place. We will return to this methodological issue shortly.

The Supreme Court's interpretation of 'the right to liberty' is not so much creative as it is revealing. It tells us that this right is engaged where the law limits

---

[45] Ibid., p. 335 and paras 57–8.   [46] Ibid., para. 127.

an individual's response to a grievous and irremediable medical condition, which is 'a matter critical to their dignity and autonomy'.[47] Quite what 'dignity' means here is not clear. Generally, 'dignity' means 'a status of worth', and here it would be reasonable to take it to mean the status proper to a human being. In the context, it would also be reasonable to take 'dignity' and 'autonomy' as a pair of words that qualify each other, and to infer that what endows the human being with 'dignity' is his 'autonomy'. Certainly, for the many influenced by contemporary liberal political philosophy—not least that of Ronald Dworkin—such an equation would be perfectly natural. It follows, therefore, that what the court is saying is that the law's constraint conflicts with the individual's 'autonomy'. This is revealing, because what is at issue is precisely what the individual's legal autonomy, all things considered, *should be*—how far, all things considered, the individual's freedom of choice *should be* constrained by the law. Yet here, the court assumes from the beginning that there is some 'autonomy' that the law is already infringing. So what its reasoning implies is that the unspecified 'liberty' to which the *Canadian Charter* grants a right is deliberately unspecified, because it is originally absolute. Any constraint whatsoever is therefore prima facie suspect as an infringement of it, and required to give a strong, demonstrable self-justification. However, such a concept of original liberty or autonomy is incoherent, since one individual's right to liberty implies other individuals' duty to respect that right— since we are evidently talking of 'right' in a non-Hobbesian, normative, moral sense. In other words, the right and the duty are co-original, and all rights-holders are at one and the same time duty-bearers, their liberties qualified by their obligations. So whatever liberty was original was never absolute; the question of its moral limitations arose from the very beginning. Therefore the appropriate question is not, How can this proposed moral or legal constraint possibly justify its infringement of originally absolute liberty or autonomy? Rather, it is, What should be the extent of liberty or the limits of autonomy in the light of social obligations? But, again, because of its choice of jurisprudential method, the court excluded consideration of such obligations from deliberation about the proper nature of 'the right to liberty'.

The ample, even anarchic room for philosophical discretion accorded courts by the *Canadian Charter's* abstract rights is evident again in the Supreme Court's interpretation of 'the right to security' as the right to be free from 'physical or serious psychological suffering'.[48] In effect, the court follows the view of the philosopher Margaret Pabst Battin, one of the expert witnesses in the original *Carter* trial. According to Battin, one of the principles central to the debate is 'compassion, or the right to be free from pain and suffering'.[49] This is confused. Compassion is a virtue, which we ought always to show those who suffer, and

---

[47] Ibid., para. 66.   [48] Ibid., para. 64.   [49] *Carter BCSC*, para. 239.

which can take a variety of forms. *If* we have the power to liberate from suffering, and *if* no other moral obligation prevents us from exercising that power, then, of course, we are obliged to liberate. But if we lack either the power or the moral permission, then, far from being obliged, we are either incapable or forbidden. From this it follows that, if we are not always and everywhere obliged to liberate from suffering, then those who suffer cannot possess an unconditional right to liberation, which they can assert against us. There is no general, natural right to be free from suffering. Elsewhere Battin qualifies her assertion when she writes, 'No one should be... forced to suffer, *without adequate cause.*'[50] Of course, that is so. But in order to determine whether one has a 'right' to be freed from suffering, we first have to determine whether 'adequate cause' (such as impotence or counter-vailing moral obligation) obtains. So, the appropriate question is not, Does this law infringe the assumed, natural, indefinite right to be free from suffering? Rather, the appropriate question is, Is the suffering (indirectly) caused by this law justified, all things considered? Instead of assuming an absolute right at the beginning, the latter question appreciates that it is precisely the scope of the putative right that is up for discussion in the light of other considerations of morality and public policy. Again, however, these considerations were methodically excluded from the definition of the right.

IV

The *Canadian Charter* allows courts ample room to invent new positive individual rights out of the abstract ones it guarantees. In *Carter* the Supreme Court's jurisprudential method clearly separated consideration of the substance of the rights to life, liberty, and security, and whether their deprivation accords with 'the principles of fundamental justice' (under S. 7), from any consideration of 'competing social interests or public benefits' conferred by the impugned law (under S. 1); and it turned to the latter only after having already decided the former.[51] In support, it invoked its own ruling in *R. v. Swain* (1991): 'It is not appropriate for the state to thwart the exercise of the accused's right by attempting to bring societal interests into the principles of fundamental justice and to thereby limit an accused's s. 7 rights. Societal interests are to be dealt with under s. 1 of the *Charter*...'[52]

---

[50] Ibid., para. 239. The italics are mine.
[51] *Carter SCC*, para. 79. The court considers S. 7 of the *Charter* first in chapter VIII, and S. 1 only subsequently in chapter X.
[52] Ibid., para. 80. There appears to be a measure of discrepancy on this point between the Supreme Court's judgement and the trial judge's, albeit not one on which the higher court chose to comment. In her ruling Justice Smith noted that in *Rodriguez* (1993) the majority had 'incorporated consideration of societal interests in its assessment of whether Ms. Rodriguez's s. 7 right had been infringed, as opposed to leaving such consideration to the justification stage under s. 1' (*Carter BCSC*, para. 949). Against the

Shortly afterwards, however, the court inadvertently blurred the clear distinction it had so firmly asserted, when it came to discuss the principles of fundamental justice. One of these is that a law should not infringe a person's rights in a 'grossly disproportionate' manner. While the court agreed with the trial judge that the rights-infringement of the *Criminal Code*'s blanket prohibition of 'assisted dying' was 'very severe', it demurred in pronouncing it 'grossly disproportionate to its objective'. That could only be determined, it implied, by (somehow) weighing the severity of the infringement against the 'high importance' of the law's object.[53] In this case, the law's object was to protect vulnerable citizens in general from abuse. Such protection is surely a 'societal interest'. Therefore the court itself unwittingly acknowledged that the determination of what fundamental justice requires cannot be isolated from societal or public considerations.

An important effect of the court's artificial separation of the consideration of rights from the consideration of societal interests is to shift the burden of proof away from the individual, who is claiming a right, and onto the state, which is defending the interests of society as a whole. Thus Justice Smith asserted that the burden lies on the defendants (Canada) 'to prove on the balance of probabilities' that the limit on the plaintiff's Charter right is justified. In support she cited Chief Justice Dickson in *R. v. Oakes* (1986), who opined that '[t]he presumption is that the rights and freedoms are guaranteed unless the party invoking s. 1 can bring itself within the exceptional criteria which justify their being limited.'[54] The Canadian Supreme Court followed suit, arguing that it is not for the claimants 'whose rights are [*already known to be*] infringed' by the law prohibiting 'physician-assisted dying' to prove less invasive ways of achieving the prohibition's object. Rather, the burden of establishing minimal impairment is on the government.[55]

As for the stringency of the proof that the state must furnish, Justice Smith oscillated. On the one hand, she cited the majority *Sauvé v. Canada* (2002): 'While some matters can be proved with empirical or mathematical precision, others, involving philosophical, political and social considerations cannot. In this case, it is enough that the justification be convincing, in the sense that it is sufficient to satisfy the reasonable person looking at all the evidence and relevant considerations, that the state is justified in infringing the right at stake to the degree it has.'[56] But on the other hand, she could be thought to raise the bar in asserting that, to meet its burden under Section 1, the state must show that the violating law

plaintiffs, she held that subsequent Supreme Court jurisprudence had consistently supported this approach (ibid., paras 970–2). However, I have not been able to identify any point in her determination of the meaning of the rights to life, liberty, and security, where she actually brought consideration of societal interests to bear.

[53] *Carter SCC*, para. 90.   [54] *Carter BCSC*, para. 1172.   [55] *Carter SCC*, para. 118.
[56] *Carter BCSC*, para. 1178.

is 'demonstrably justified'.[57] Of course, what appears 'convincing', 'reasonable', and 'demonstrable' will depend heavily on the moral, political, and cultural assumptions and convictions of the judge.

Then, in reviewing Justice Smith's findings under a standard that required the state-defendant to show that the court's conclusion was 'unsupported, arbitrary, insufficiently precise or otherwise in error', amounting to a 'palpable and over-riding error',[58] the Supreme Court entrusted 'an extraordinary amount of power in the hands of a single trial court judge'.[59]

V

The Canadian Supreme Court's jurisprudential method in *Carter* is typical of judicial review by courts in other jurisdictions—not least, the European Court of Human Rights.[60] This follows a two-stage adjudicative model: first, the determination of whether a right has been limited; and second, the determination of whether that limitation is justified in terms of the principle of proportionality, which weighs the publicly interested aims and effects of the measure against the burdens imposed on the rights claimant.[61] Legal philosophical critics have made the same complaint of judicial review in general as I have just made of *Carter* in particular: namely, that it starts by immunising the (already assumed) rights of individuals against any infection by social claims. Thus Bradley Miller writes that, while the first stage of adjudication frames the question for resolution, in it 'there is scarcely any consideration of the needs of other persons living in community with the rights-holder. The requirements of justice are to be considered only from one point of view. All other points of view are to be postponed to the justification stage.'[62]

From the same critical perspective Grégoire Webber and Paul Yowell take issue with the reasoning of the UK's Supreme Court in *R. (Nicklinson) v. Ministry of Justice* (2014). Following the two-stage model, *Nicklinson* interprets the 1961 decision of the Westminster Parliament to make anyone assisting in suicide criminally liable as intending to infringe a person's 'right to decide how and when to die, and in particular the right to avoid a distressing and undignified

---

[57] Ibid., para. 1175.   [58] *Carter SCC*, para. 109.

[59] Paul Yowell, *Constitutional Rights and Constitutional Design: Moral and Empirical Reasoning in Judicial Review* (London: Hart, 2018), p. 87.

[60] The two-stage process exemplified in the jurisprudence of the European Court of Human Rights is 'a paradigm widely followed by national constitutional courts' (Yowell, *Constitutional Rights*, p. 15).

[61] Bradley W. Miller, 'Majoritarianism and Pathologies of Judicial Review', in Grégoire Webber, Paul Yowell, Richard Ekins, Maris Köpcke, Bradley W. Miller, and Francisco J. Urbina, *Legislated Rights: Securing Human Rights through Legislation* (Cambridge: Cambridge University Press, 2018), p. 198.

[62] Miller, 'Majoritarianism and Pathologies of Judicial Review', p. 198.

end to life', albeit justifiably. Webber and Yowell argue that this is an inaccurate and misleading description. Rather,

> Parliament is better understood to have reasoned about how to affirm and protect human life in the special context of the criminal law, with a view that the intentional taking of life is to be avoided, and to have considered (alongside compassion for the would-be suicide-seeker and his or her family) the rights of other persons, who, but for the criminal prohibition of this and other forms of participation in intentional killing, would be at increased risk of oppression and death.[63]

I have observed how the *Canadian Charter*, with its affirmation of the abstract and indeterminate rights to life, liberty, and security, gives courts ample room for philosophical creativity and discretion. Francisco Urbina echoes this point when he distinguishes rights-as-values from rights as particular legal relationships between persons,[64] and observes that, in determining whether a right-as-value is engaged and whether this engagement is justified, courts are involved in moral and political reasoning largely unconstrained by law. The question before them is not the legal one, Which are the legal relations that govern this case? Rather, it is the philosophical one, Can those legal relations be justified against the higher values embodied in 'human rights'? An answer to this question requires a determination of the higher values, their reach, and their force, which is 'largely an exercise in general practical reasoning' (Matthias Kumm) unbounded by positive law.[65] The problem with this is that while judges can claim expert authority in the interpretation of positive law, they cannot claim the same authority in moral reasoning.

---

[63] Webber and Yowell, 'Introduction', p. 20. Richard Ekins makes a similar point. In the Suicide Act 1961, he argues, the Westminster Parliament cancelled the duty in criminal law not to commit suicide, created a liberty to attempt to commit suicide, and introduced a new rule prohibiting assistance in suicide. In so doing, it rejected 'a broad understanding of autonomy as a justification for freedom to be assisted in one's suicide' ('Legislation as Reasoned Action', in Webber et al., *Legislated Rights*, 92, 102–3). He comments: 'This series of legal relationships cannot be simply read off from the right to life or from a principle of autonomy. They are particular choices about how the law should be framed to protect the lives of members of the community...' (ibid., p. 103).

[64] Francisco J. Urbina, 'How Legislation Aids Human rights Adjudication', in Webber et al., *Legislated Rights*, p. 157.

[65] Urbina, 'How Legislation Aids Human rights Adjudication', pp. 158–9. Noel Malcolm makes the same observation about the jurisprudence of the European Court of Human Rights, where 'rights' often amount to individuals' 'interests', and where conflict between rights-claims cannot be resolved by appeal to rights themselves: 'Judgments in such cases are less like technical applications of settled law, and more like political decisions: they are infused with values, and depend in the end on particular assumptions about what is a good life, and what is good for society at large. Such assumptions are not arrived at by making deductions from statements about objective rights; on the contrary, the real nature of what is going on may be obscured by conducting it in rights-language' (*Human Rights and Political Wrongs*, pp. 25, 26, 27).

VI

So far I have identified and explained five ethically problematic and controversial features of the judgement of Canada's Supreme Court in *Carter:* first, the uncritical adoption of the loaded phrase 'physician-assisted dying'; second, the abstraction and indeterminacy of some of the rights enshrined in the *Canadian Charter*; third, the licence this gives judges to stray beyond their professional, legal expertise; fourth, the conceptual independence of these rights of individuals from any consideration of the common good; and fifth, the priority accorded them in jurisprudential method. A sixth problematic feature, albeit an ineffectual one, lies in the court's understanding of proportionality.

The Supreme Court endorsed Justice Smith's decision that *Rodriguez* should be revisited, since it had since been overtaken by advances in the law relating to 'fundamental principles of justice'.[66] The principles that the trial judge had in mind were those of 'overbreadth' and 'gross disproportionality'.[67] With regard to the latter, she appealed to the Supreme Court's ruling in *Alberta v. Hutterian Brethren of Wilson Colony* (2009), where the majority had distinguished two stages of proportionality analysis. The first stage focuses on the relationship between the law's end and its means, considering whether the effects of a law are necessary, in terms of the 'pressing' nature of the end, the rational connection between end and means, and the minimum impairment of rights. The second stage focuses on the relationship between legal measures and the Charter right, weighing good against bad effects, and alone taking 'full account of the "severity of the deleterious effects of a measure on individuals or groups"'. As Aharon Barak puts it, this second 'test of proportionality (stricto sensu) examines whether the realization of this proper objective is commensurate with the deleterious effect upon the human right... It requires placing colliding values and interests side-by-side and balancing them according to their weight.' According to the court in *Hutterian Brethren*, this second stage is 'decisive', 'where the demand is that the right be fully respected without compromise'.[68] Justice Smith concluded from this that *Hutterian Brethren* marks 'a substantive change' in the court's jurisprudence:

> Courts are to widen their perspective at the final stage to take full account of the deleterious effects of the infringement on individuals or groups, and determine whether the benefits of the legislation are worth the cost. That is a different question than whether the legislation is rationally connected to the government's objective or impairs the rights as little as possible.[69]

[66] *Carter SCC*, para. 46; *Carter BCSC*, para. 973.   [67] *Carter BCSC*, paras 977–85.
[68] Ibid., para. 993.   [69] Ibid., para. 994.

The decision in *Hutterian Brethren* to place decisive weight on the second stage of proportionality analysis was most unfortunate, because it is the least susceptible of rational control. The first stage can be rational, for it is often possible to offer decent reasons for supposing that a law's object or end is or is not sufficiently 'pressing' or important to warrant non-trivial costs, that its chosen means do or do not serve its object, and that the costs incurred are or are not the minimum necessary. But the second stage, requiring as it does the metaphorical 'weighing' against each other of widely disparate, incommensurable, and imponderable goods and evils, is often reduced to intuitive assertions whose confidence far outstrips their rational authority.[70] For example, how, exactly, can one 'weigh' against each other, on the one hand, the evil of the intense frustration felt by a few thousand ill or disabled people at their lack of access to assisted suicide or voluntary euthanasia, and, on the other hand, the good of heightened protection from abuse of hundreds of thousands of vulnerable and dependent fellow citizens, which is provided by a clear, legal bright-line against medical involvement in deliberate killing? Whatever process of decision-making might be involved here, it is certainly not the actual weighing of quantities, to see which one tips the scales. But if it is not that, what it actually is remains a mystery. It should not surprise, therefore, that judges 'rarely provide a robust, comprehensive discussion of the values at stake and the moral reasons for favouring the conclusion'.[71] They do not, because they cannot. Usually, what is presented as the proportionate weighing of goods and evils is little more than opinion masquerading as arithmetic.[72]

---

[70] Noel Malcolm reports that '[a]fter an exhaustive study of the [European Court of Human Rights'] case-law, [the standard modern work on proportionality] concludes that while the doctrine of proportionality has an outward appearance of objectivity and universality, its use in practice turns out to be "fluid . . . or even, to be honest, gaseous"'(*Human Rights and Political Wrongs*, p. 28, quoting S. van Drooghenbroeck, *La Proportionnalité dans le droit de la Convention Européenne des Droits de l'Homme: prendre l'idée simple au sérieux* (Brussels: Publications des Facultés universitaires Saint-Louis, 2001), p. 15). Aileen McHarg concurs: 'Frequently . . . decisions as to proportionality are stated baldly without elaborating the weight to be ascribed to the various factors involved. Equally, the rhetoric used is often at variance with the practice' ('Reconciling Human Rights and the Public Interest: Conceptual Problems and Doctrinal Uncertainty in the Jurisprudence of the European Court of Human Rights', *The Modern Law Review*, 62 (1999), p. 687; quoted in *Human Rights and Political Wrongs*, p. 35). Marie-Bénédicte Dembour agrees: 'The Court does not necessarily refer to the same factors across apparently similar cases. When it does, it does not always attribute to a given factor the weight it seems to have been given in previous cases. The Court never explains which factor is important and why. It obviously, and regrettably, does not feel that it needs to explain the way it achieves its balancing exercise—its calculus . . . The Court's method is vague and unsatisfactory' (*Who Believes in Human Rights? Reflections on the European Convention* (Cambridge: Cambridge University Press, 2006), pp. 89–90; quoted in *Human Rights and Political Wrongs*, pp. 35–6).

[71] Yowell, *Constitutional Rights*, p. 114.

[72] John Finnis analyses the proportionality test into four criteria. The first three comprise my 'first stage', the fourth criterion my 'second stage', that is, proportionality *stricto sensu*. He comments: 'All these criteria, and most obviously the suddenly popular fourth one, involve matters of fact (including counter-factuals) and evaluative opinion in which legal learning is of little assistance and forensically ascertainable evidence is unavailable' ('Judicial Power: Past, Present, and Future', Policy Exchange Judicial Power Project lecture, Gray's Inn Hall, 20 October 2015, p. 20 <https://judicialpowerproject.org.uk/john-finnis-judicial-power-past-present-and-future>, as at 18 September 2018). What is more,

It is true that, in *Carter*, the Supreme Court does not explicitly endorse Justice Smith's appeal to *Hutterian Brethren* on the matter of proportionality. While it agrees that the law has developed since *Rodriguez* in its conception of the 'fundamental principles of justice', it explains its agreement only in terms of 'overbreadth'.[73] Accordingly, it argues later that, since it has already decided that the law was 'overbroad' in 'denying the rights of some individuals in a way that bears no relation to the [law's] object',[74] it has no need to decide the issue of 'gross disproportionality' by weighing the 'very severe' bad impact on life, liberty, and security of the person against the 'high importance' of the good end of the protection of vulnerable persons from hostile pressure.[75] If the court avoided the second stage of proportionality analysis with a sigh of relief, because it recognised its problematic nature, it did not actually say so. Nor did it anywhere contradict the ruling in *Hutterian Brethren*.

VII

A seventh problematic feature of *Carter* lies in the court's treatment of the empirical evidence. The Supreme Court endorsed Justice Smith's finding that there was 'no evidence' from permissive jurisdictions that people with disabilities are at heightened risk of accessing 'physician-assisted dying', 'no evidence' that socially vulnerable populations had suffered 'inordinate impact', and 'no compelling evidence that a permissive regime in Canada would result in a "practical slippery slope"'.[76] With regard to the latter the court commented, acerbically, that '[t]he resolution of the issue before us falls to be resolved not by competing anecdotes, but by the evidence'.[77] The court then referred to Professor Montero's evidence. Montero had argued that issues with compliance and the expansion of criteria of eligibility 'inevitably arise, even in a system of ostensibly strict limits and safeguards', and that '[o]nce euthanasia is allowed, it becomes very difficult to maintain a strict interpretation of the statutory conditions'.[78] Brushing this aside, the court supported Justice Smith's claim that it was 'problematic' to draw inferences for Canada from the permissive regime in Belgium, which 'is the product of a very different medico-legal culture', where the practice of assisted death was 'already prevalent and embedded' before legalisation.[79]

since proportionality analysis's goal of 'striking a fair balance' between the rights of individuals affected by a measure's adoption or non-adoption and other pressing social needs is 'essentially non-judicial, non-juristic, non-juridical', judges should give 'considerable weight' to legislators' assessment of the available evidence and the choices to be made in its light (John Finnis, 'Case Comment: A British "Convention Right" to Assistance in Suicide?', *Law Quarterly Review*, 131 (January 2015), p. 3).

[73] *Carter CSC*, para. 46.   [74] Ibid., para. 85,   [75] Ibid., para. 90.   [76] Ibid., para. 107.
[77] Ibid., para. 120.   [78] Ibid., paras 110–11.   [79] Ibid., para. 112.

The problems with the court's handling of the empirical data are several. First of all, it is not true that there is 'no evidence' from permissive jurisdictions that people with disabilities are at heightened risk of accessing 'physician-assisted dying', that socially vulnerable populations had suffered 'impact', and that a permissive regime in Canada would result in a 'practical slippery slope'. Indeed, the court itself admitted this when it acknowledged that the Attorney General of Canada had pointed out 'conflicting evidence'.[80]

In the debate about legalising assisted suicide and voluntary euthanasia, the main concern about disabled people is that over time legalisation will precipitate a change in cultural attitudes such that persevering with a disabled life is no longer generally considered the rational thing to do, and social support of disabled people diminishes accordingly. The a priori argument runs as follows. The basic motive for legalisation is to allow individuals a professionally managed way out of intolerable suffering. If eligibility for assisted suicide and voluntary euthanasia is initially subject to the condition of terminal illness, political pressure to abandon that will quickly build, since it is quite possible for people who are not terminally ill to suffer as intolerably as those who are. When that condition is abandoned—or if it was never adopted in the first place—then assisted suicide and voluntary euthanasia will become available to an increasing number of classes of people who can be said to suffer intolerably—or rather, who declare themselves to suffer intolerably, since no one else will be in a authoritative position to contradict them. Over time society will become accustomed to the idea that assisted suicide and voluntary euthanasia are normal ways of responding to suffering that is subjectively felt to be intolerable—and what is socially normal (usual) gradually comes to be seen as normative (rational, right). Correlatively, society will first become unaccustomed to bearing the costs of supporting disabled or hindered human life, and then resentful of having to do so. Social pressure, some subtle, some not so subtle, will then be brought to bear on people with various disabilities to 'do the right thing' and exit efficiently.

That is how the a priori argument goes. Do the permissive jurisdictions yield any a posteriori evidence that the argument tracks reality? Yes, they do. Guenter Lewy is himself inclined to conclude from his study of the experience of permissive jurisdictions in the Netherlands, Belgium, Switzerland, and Oregon that it is possible 'to satisfy the need for dignity in dying, assure accountability, and provide adequate safeguards against abuse'. Nevertheless, he acknowledges that in Switzerland 'there prevails a right-to-die mentality that has been shown to exert psychological pressure upon vulnerable persons with serious psychological problems'.[81] Montero's account of the Belgian experience echoes this, insofar as he

[80] Ibid., para. 109.
[81] Guenter Lewy, *Assisted Death in Europe and America: Four Regimes and their Lessons* (New York: Oxford University Press, 2011), pp. 97–8, 153, 160.

observes a correlation between the growth of a right-to-die attitude and the gradual extension of eligibility to psychiatric patients. 'Initially,' he writes, 'euthanasia was presented as an ethical transgression, an exceptional act. Rapidly, by blurring the standards, euthanasia became a norm: it became one medical procedure among many, and then a right to be claimed.'[82] During the debate leading up to the passing of the Act on Euthanasia in 2002, reassurances were repeatedly given that patients with psychiatric disorders, dementia, or depression would not be eligible. Now, however, the Federal Control and Evaluation Commission is approving an increasing number of such cases.[83]

Theo Boer, originally a supporter of Dutch liberalisation and from 2005 to 2014 a member of a Regional Euthanasia Review Committee who reviewed 4,000 cases, tells the same tale and expresses the same concern about the Netherlands. In the absence of a criterion restricting euthanasia to end-of-life situations, eligibility has been progressively extended to psychiatric patients and those suffering from dementia, autism, and blindness.[84] Boer suspects that this development 'may have contributed to a change in how chronic illnesses, psychiatric illnesses, care-dependence, and ageing are experienced, perceived, and handled',[85] by weakening the capacity of society as a whole and individuals in particular to cope with human dependence and limitations, and leading to a widely shared conviction that death is the best solution to any form of lasting suffering.[86] In support he quotes an unlikely witness, the euthanasia pioneer and psychiatrist, Boudewijn Chabot: 'What happens to doctors for whom a deadly injection becomes a monthly routine? There is no doubt about their good intentions, but do they realize that the fire they cause can become a blaze because they stir death wishes in vulnerable people who try their best to live with their handicap?'[87] Boer concludes that '[d]ata from the Netherlands in the period 2007–2017 speak an unambiguous language: when the main criterion is no longer a foreseeable death but rather irremediable and unacceptable suffering, a society sends the signal to a whole category of patients that if they think they are better off dead, they may in fact be right'.[88] Given all this, we may say that there is both a priori reason to expect, and

---

[82] Étienne Montero, 'The Belgian Experience of Euthanasia Since its Legal Implementation in 2002', in D. A. Jones, C. Gastmans, and C. MacKellar, eds, *Euthanasia and Assisted Suicide: Lessons from Belgium* (Cambridge: Cambridge University Press, 2017), p. 44.

[83] Montero, 'The Belgian Experience of Euthanasia', p. 33.

[84] Theo A. Boer, *Euthanasia in the Netherlands in the Absence of a Foreseeable Death Criterion*, Expert Report for the Department for the Department of Justice, Government of Canada, Quebec Regional Office (February 2018), para. 82.

[85] Ibid., para. 86.

[86] Theo Boer, covering letter to David Lucas, Quebec Regional Office, Department of Justice, Canada, 13 August 2018. In this letter, Boer also reports that in 8.9 per cent of the 2,260 cases that he reviewed in 2010–14 there was evidence of family pressure being applied.

[87] Boer, *Euthanasia in the Netherlands*, para. 36, quoting (in English translation) Boudewijn Chabot, 'Verontrustende cultuuromslag rond de zelfgekozen dood', *NRC Handelsblad*, 16 June 2017: <https://www.nrc.nl/nieuws/2017/06/16/de-euthanasiegeestis-uit-de-fles-11123806-a1563406>.

[88] Boer, *Euthanasia in the Netherlands*, para. 99.

authoritative a posteriori testimony to substantiate the view, that support for disabled and other hindered people to persevere with living in spite of adversity is being weakened in permissive jurisdictions. In that sense, therefore, there is evidence that people with disabilities are at heightened risk of accessing 'physician-assisted dying' and that socially vulnerable populations have suffered 'impact'.

In addition, we may say that in some of these permissive regimes a 'slippery slope' is also visible. In the Netherlands and Belgium eligibility for assisted suicide and voluntary euthanasia has not been restricted to the terminally ill. Instead, the Dutch patient need only be subject to 'lasting and unbearable' suffering,[89] and the Belgian patient need only be 'in a medically futile condition of constant and unbearable physical or mental suffering that cannot be alleviated, resulting from a serious and incurable disorder caused by illness or accident'.[90] As a consequence of the subjectivity of 'lasting (constant) and unbearable' suffering, assisted suicide and voluntary euthanasia have been extended ever more widely to groups of people who, at least in the minds of many, were never intended to be eligible at all. In the Netherlands, voluntary euthanasia has been administered to a physically healthy 50-year-old woman, who was in chronic grief over the death of her two sons;[91] an elderly man suffering no ailment other than feeling his life to be pointless;[92] and a 29-year-old woman with a severe psychiatric illness. In 2016 the Dutch government announced plans to make euthanasia available to anyone over 70 or 75 who considers their life to be 'completed'.[93] Meanwhile in Belgium, euthanasia has been administered to a 48-year-old prisoner with psychiatric problems, a transgender 44-year-old whose sex-change operation had been botched, and a 24-year-old woman suffering from chronic depression;[94] and it has been made legally available to minors, regardless of age, albeit (so far) only to those suffering a physical, terminal illness.[95] The a posteriori record of the Netherlands and Belgium, then, confirms the a priori argument that the logic of the unqualified criterion of 'unbearable suffering', combined with the culturally dominant values of autonomy and equality, will lead step by step to assisted suicide or voluntary euthanasia on demand by mentally competent persons. 'Progressive', libertarian advocates of 'the right to die' will rejoice at this, of course.

---

[89] The Dutch Termination of Life on Request and Assisted Suicide (Review Procedures) Act (2000), Chapter II, Article 2.1.b, in Lewy, *Assisted Death in Europe and America*, Appendix 1, p. 162.

[90] The Belgian Act on Euthanasia (2002), Chapter II, Section 3.1, ibid. Appendix 2, p. 173.

[91] John Keown, *Euthanasia, Ethics, and Public Policy: An Argument against Legalisation* (Cambridge: Cambridge University Press, 2002), p. 87.

[92] Ibid., p. 87.

[93] Boer, *Euthanasia in the Netherlands*, para. 82. At the time of writing (September 2018), the governing coalition of Christian Democrats and Liberals had decided that the Liberals would be at liberty to propose a parliamentary bill that would extend eligibility to those considering their lives to be 'complete', once the results of research into the need for such an extension had become available. The process for bidding to conduct this research had only just opened.

[94] Montero, 'The Belgian Experience of Euthanasia', pp. 33, 34.   [95] Ibid., p. 41.

Others, however, who do not take a humane social ethos for granted, will be alarmed. For, as I have written elsewhere,

> if we were to regard the individual as the sole arbiter of the worth of his or her life, then how could it continue to oblige the care and commitment of other people? If the worth of your life is entirely contingent upon your judgement, and if I view your judgement as wrong-headed, why should I expend my time and energy in supporting your life? Suppose that you value your life rather more than I value it. Why should I prefer your judgement to my own? Perhaps indifference or self-interest would move me to 'respect' your judgement in the thin, negative sense of not interfering with it; but such arm's-length respect falls a long way short of positive care. One problem with dissolving human worth into individual freedom, instead of making individual freedom serve objective human worth, is that it becomes very hard to see why that worth should command our neighbour's love. Another problem is that when arbitrary autonomy severs itself from responsibility, it haemorrhages its own value... [T]he relaxation of the law prohibiting intentional killing would give us a radically libertarian society at the cost of a socially humane one.[96]

One slippery slope for which there is evidence descends from strictly limited to progressively relaxed eligibility. But, *pace* the Supreme Court's ruling in *Carter*, there is more than one slope. Another descends from voluntary to non-voluntary euthanasia. There are a priori reasons to expect this, too, as David Albert Jones has argued. Where voluntary euthanasia becomes integrated with palliative care, the intention to hasten death will tend to become an ordinary part of end-of-life practice. Since other kinds of that practice (e.g. the use of analgesia or terminal sedation, or the withdrawal of treatment) can be instituted without consent where the patient lacks capacity, it will come to seem reasonable to perform euthanasia without consent, too.[97] Again, the a priori prediction finds some substantiation in the empirical records of the Netherlands and Belgium. John Keown's analysis of the Dutch data furnished by the P. J. van der Maas survey of 1990 discovered a significant slide from official insistence in the 1980s of the necessity of an explicit request for euthanasia, and on the impermissibility of the termination of the lives of incompetents, to substantial official condonation of non-voluntary euthanasia in the 1990s.[98] More recent work by B. D. Onwuteaka-Philipsen and colleagues

---

[96] Nigel Biggar, 'Autonomy's Suicide', *Newman Rambler*, 12 (Winter 2016), pp. 29, 31. The original version of this article appeared in *Standpoint* (March 2010) under the title, 'The Road to Death on Demand': <http://www.standpoint.co.uk/node/2726/full>.

[97] David Albert Jones, 'A Submission to the External Panel on Options for a Legislative Response to Carter v. Canada' (30 October 2015), pp. 11–12.

[98] Keown, *Euthanasia, Ethics, and Public Policy*. I discuss Keown's analysis in Nigel Biggar, *Aiming to Kill: The Ethics of Suicide and Euthanasia* (London: Darton, Longman, and Todd, 2004), pp. 126–41.

has evidenced cases of the 'ending of life without an explicit patient request' in 2010, albeit on a smaller scale than in 2005, 2001, 1995, and 1990.[99] Research on the situation in Belgium by K. Chambaere and colleagues has revealed that cases of hastening death without an explicit request from the patient continue to occur, albeit at a reduced rate compared to 1998';[100] and Benoit Beuselinck reports that continuous deep sedation until death was initiated without the consent or request, either of the patient or of the family, in about 28 per cent of the cases reported by medical specialists in Belgium.[101] In its careful consideration of the empirical evidence from Belgium, the Netherlands, and Switzerland, as presented by Justice Smith in her 2012 ruling, the High Court of Ireland found the number of lives being ended without explicit request to be 'strikingly high'.[102]

One obvious response to these two slippery slopes is to argue that, insofar as they are undesirable, they can be prevented by more effective regulation. Given the experience of the Netherlands and Belgium over the past thirty years, however, this seems excessively optimistic. In 2002 John Keown's analysis of the 1990 van der Maas and 1995 G. van der Wal surveys revealed significant non-reporting of physician-assisted suicide and voluntary euthanasia by physicians, some of which was because of non-compliance.[103] Four years earlier John Griffiths, a vigorous defender of Dutch legalisation, had not only conceded that the Dutch regulatory regime was ineffective, but argued that a regime depending on self-reporting could not be made effective and that an effective regime could not be managed by the criminal law system.[104] Since Belgium had almost two decades of Dutch experience from which to learn before it legalised voluntary euthanasia in 2002, we could reasonably expect it to have found and instituted better means of regulation. If so, we would be disappointed. Research published by Tinne Smets and colleagues in 2010 exposed widespread under-reporting in Belgium, most probably because of

---

[99] B. D. Onwuteaka-Philipsen, A. Brinkman-Stoppelenburg, C. Penning, G. J. de Jong-Krul, J. J. van Delden, and A. van der Heide, 'Trends in End-of-Life Practices before and after the Enactment of the Euthanasia Law in the Netherlands from 1990–2010: A Repeated Cross-Sectional Survey', *The Lancet*, 380/9845 (8 September 2012), pp. 908–15.

[100] K. Chambaere, Stichele R. Vander, F. Mortier, J. Cohen, and L. Deliens, 'Recent Trends in Euthanasia and Other End-of-Life Practices in Belgium', *New England Journal of Medicine*, 372/12 (19 March 2015), pp. 1179–81.

[101] Benoit Beuselinck, '2002–2016: Fourteen Years of Euthanasia in Belgium: First-Line Observations by an Oncologist', in Jones et al., *Euthanasia and Assisted Suicide*, p. 113.

[102] *Fleming v. Ireland & Ors* [2013] IEHC 2, paras 102, 104.

[103] Keown, *Euthanasia, Ethics, and Public Policy*, pp. 132, 134–5. For my discussion of Keown's analysis, see Biggar, *Aiming to Kill*, pp. 131–2.

[104] John Griffiths, 'The Slippery Slope: Are the Dutch Sliding Down or Are They Clambering Up?', in David Thomasma, Thomasine Kimbrough-Kushner, Gerrit Kimsma, and Chris Ciesielski-Carlucci, eds, *Asking to Die: Inside the Dutch Debate about Euthanasia* (Dordrecht: Kluwer, 1998), p. 102; John Griffiths, Alex Bood, and Helen Weyers, *Euthanasia and the Law in the Netherlands* (Amsterdam: Amsterdam University Press, 1998), pp. 29, 236, 238, 245–6, 253, 254–5, 264, 268–9, 274. For my discussion of Griffiths's views, see Biggar, *Aiming to Kill*, pp. 132–40.

significant deviations from the legal requirements.[105] Étienne Montero's comments on the Belgian model echo John Griffith's comments on the self-reporting Dutch one:

> it is obvious that a control system, which operates after the fact ... is not capable of protecting patients against euthanasia procedures that violate the statutory conditions. The monitoring is based on self-reporting; it depends completely on trusting information supplied by the physician who has carried out the euthanasia. It is at best naïve to assert that physicians will report their own failure to comply with the fundamental conditions or procedures prescribed by law ... [I]ndependent research carried out in Flanders presents evidence of around 50 per cent underreporting ... [106]

Montero continues, arguing that it is practically impossible for the Belgian Federal Control and Evaluation Commission on Euthanasia to verify whether most of the 'strict legal conditions' for euthanasia have been met. How can it verify, after the fact, that a request was fully voluntary, well thought out, and not due to external pressure; or that the physician who agreed and the second physician who was consulted were able to take the full measure of the constraints and pressures, including subconscious ones, to which the patient was subject; and that the compulsory consultation of a second physician had not become a routine performed for form's sake?[107]

But perhaps all this is irrelevant to Canada and can be put aside, since, if Justice Smith was correct, Canada's medico-legal culture is significantly different from Belgium's—and, presumably, from the Netherlands' and Switzerland's, too. The main point of difference she supposed to be the fact that the practice of 'assisted death' was 'already prevalent and embedded' before Belgian legalisation. Yet her own ruling recorded, without demur, the plaintiffs' claim that the blanket prohibition of assisted dying in Canada had created a 'maze of back alleys' that put vulnerable patients at greater risk than a regulated scheme, which was based on evidence 'that [Canadian] physicians have ignored the prohibition of assisted death' and broken the law.[108] Shortly afterwards, she herself admitted that 'the evidence supports the conclusion that, from time to time, assisted death occurs in Canada, contrary to the law'.[109] Nevertheless, she confidently asserted that '[t]here is no evidence suggesting a ... history in Canada [comparable to that in the Netherlands and Belgium]. Indeed, it appears that, with very few exceptions, Canadian medical practitioners are compliant with the current absolute legal

---

[105] Tinne Smets, Johan Bilsen, Joachim Cohen, Mette L. Rurup, Freddy Mortier, and Luc Delien, 'Reporting of Euthanasia in Medical Practice in Flanders, Belgium: Cross-Sectional Analysis of Reported and Unreported Cases', *British Medical Journal*, 341 (2010).
[106] Montero, 'The Belgian Experience of Euthanasia', p. 28.   [107] Ibid., pp. 29–30.
[108] *Carter BCSC*, para. 1260.   [109] Ibid., para. 1282.

prohibition of assisted death',[110] and 'the evidence suggests that it is extremely unlikely that physicians in Canada would be other than rigorously compliant with legislation'.[111] Quite how Justice Smith could have been so sure about the very low incidence of illegal conduct by Canadian physicians is a bit of a puzzle. After all, it does tend to be a feature of illegal activity that those who perform it, hide it. And, as John Keown tersely puts it, the 'absence of evidence of abuse is not evidence of absence of abuse'.[112] Besides, even if physicians in Canada had been as law-abiding as the trial judge liked to think, what could be the effect of her own judgement, over time, other than to make the practice of assisted death prevalent and embedded in Canada? Even if Canada's medico-legal culture had been very different from Belgium's, it will not remain so in the wake of *Carter v. Canada*. What is more, David Albert Jones is surely correct to observe that the list of jurisdictions that had legalised some form of physician-assisted suicide or voluntary euthanasia by 2012

> is almost entirely comprised of liberal Western democracies with a cultural inheritance from Christianity and indeed most are either Anglophone (Oregon and Washington) or include sizeable Francophone communities (Belgium, Luxembourg and Switzerland). This list does not include any country from Africa, Asia, Latin America... no communist states or former communist states, no country of predominant Islamic, Buddhist or Hindu population. The list is as culturally homogeneous as any list of different countries from different continents could be, and the prevalent culture is one that is shared by Canada.[113]

To this should be added two further observations. First, Justice Smith appears to have accepted that between 4 and 10 per cent of elderly Canadians suffer abuse from someone they rely on, that this could influence a patient's medical decision-making and escape detection by a physician, and that assessing cognitive impairment and accurately diagnosing depression in elderly people is 'challenging'.[114] She also accepted that depression (including that caused by abuse) could be detected 'so long as a relationship was established and a thorough assessment conducted'. Yet she acknowledged that there is 'a much greater likelihood' in the Netherlands and Belgium than in Canada that a patient will have a long-term relationship with a family physician.[115] The clear implication, which she fails to draw, is that the abuse of elderly people is *more* likely to escape detection in Canada, and depression *more* likely to escape diagnosis, than in the Netherlands and Belgium. The second observation is that Justice Smith's original ruling, and

---

[110] Ibid., para. 680.   [111] Ibid., para. 1284.
[112] Keown, 'A Right to Voluntary Euthanasia?', p. 31.
[113] Jones, 'A Submission to the External Panel', p. 7.   [114] *Carter BCSC*, paras 844–5.
[115] Ibid., para. 678.

the Supreme Court's subsequent confirmation of it, declare that that the blanket prohibition of 'assisted dying' is void where it concerns a person who 'has a grievous and irremediable medical condition (including an illness, disease, or disability) that causes enduring suffering that is intolerable to the individual in the circumstances of his or her condition'.[116] Neither ruling makes any distinction between physician-assisted suicide and voluntary euthanasia What this implies, therefore, is that the Canadian courts expect Parliament to legislate to permit voluntary euthanasia and to extend eligibility beyond the terminally ill—*just like Belgium.*

On the whole, neither Justice Smith nor the Supreme Court of Canada argued that there is simply no evidence at all from permissive jurisdictions of troubling developments. Rather, Justice Smith judged that the evidence is not 'compelling', and the Supreme Court judged that it fails to establish any 'palpable and overriding error' in the trial judge's argument.[117] The rigour of these judgements stands in some tension with the general concession made in *Carter* that proportionality need only be 'reasonable', not 'perfect'.[118] But, more important, its rationality is obscure, for 'compulsion' and 'palpability' lie largely in the eye of the (judicial) beholder—or rather, hidden behind it in a process of deliberation that mysteriously decides when evidence is 'compelling' and error 'palpable', and when they are not. Nonetheless, we may reasonably infer that both courts reckoned that the scale of risk and abuse in permissive jurisdictions was small, that it was declining, and that increasingly effective procedures would reduce it further, if not abolish it altogether.[119]

We have seen, however, that there is expert evidence, even from supporters of legalisation, that regulation still fails to achieve the strictness originally promised *after more than three decades of experimentation.* What is more, other judicial eyes can view the same evidence as their Canadian counterparts and come to a diametrically opposite conclusion. Thus in its ruling on *Fleming v. Ireland & Ors* (2013), the High Court of Ireland, while impressed by Justice Smith's 'enormously comprehensive judgment',[120] said that it 'simply cannot agree that the accumulated evidence from other jurisdictions to which the judge referred "shows that the risks inherent in legally permitted death have not materialized in the manner that may have been predicted"'.[121] After all, they continue, 'it was not in dispute but that in 2005—the year for which the latest data is available for the

---

[116] *Carter SCC*, p. 333, para. 127.   [117] Ibid., para. 109.   [118] Ibid., para. 97.

[119] This inference is reasonable, because *Carter BCSC* reported that Dutch surveys from 1990 to 2005 of the incidence of life-terminating acts without the explicit request of the patient had shown a steady decline from 0.8 per cent (1031 deaths) in 1990 to 0.4 per cent (546 deaths) in 2005, and that the rate of reporting had increased steadily from 18 per cent in 1990 to 80 per cent in 2005 (paras 471, 475, 481). On this basis, the ruling asserted that '[t]he evidence supports the conclusion that the compliance with the safeguards in the Netherlands is continually improving, but that it is not yet at an ideal level' (para. 656).

[120] *Fleming v. Ireland & Ors* (2013) IEHC 2, para. 92.   [121] Ibid., para. 94.

Netherlands—560 patients (some 0.4% of *all* deaths) were euthanized without having given their explicit consent'.[122] (The significance of this number becomes clear in the light of the fact that the total number of intentional homicides in the Netherlands in 2005 was 174.)[123] Moreover, the corresponding figure for Belgium appeared to be higher, 'as 1.9% of *all* deaths which took place in the entirety of Flanders between June and November 2007 were without explicit request'.[124] According to the very evidence summarised by Justice Smith, the Irish court judged that 'the incidence of legally assisted death without explicit request in the Netherlands, Belgium and Switzerland is strikingly high'.[125] In addition, while the Irish judges fully agreed with their Canadian colleague that the 'scrutiny regarding physician-assisted death decisions would have to be at the highest level", they dryly observed that she herself had acknowledged 'that compliance with essential safeguards in the Netherlands—more than thirty years after liberalisation—was "not yet at an ideal level"'.[126]

As to why the Canadian judges interpreted—and in my view, misinterpreted—the empirical evidence they way they did, we can only speculate, but our speculation can still command reasons. One factor might have been the prevalence of the kind of sunny cultural optimism evident in the report of the Québec National Assembly's Select Committee on Dying with Dignity, when it wrote that 'the argument of abuse presupposes the complicity of physicians, nurses, health system administrators and patients' families. We feel this is highly improbable. We have full confidence in our health professionals and cannot imagine they would become agents of death overnight.'[127] The same cultural self-assurance—or complacency—is evident in Justice Smith's confident distinction between Belgium's suspect 'medico-legal culture' and Canada's. The idea that Canada's culture might *degenerate* appears to have been inconceivable. Hence the complete lack in either the 2012 or the 2015 rulings in *Carter* of any concern that the legalisation of 'assisted dying' might, over time, change and malform physicians' attitudes to killing and society's attitudes to those in need of chronic and costly care. The contrast with the Irish High Court's ruling in *Fleming* is stark. There the judges write that they find 'compelling and deeply worrying' the possibility that relaxing the ban on assisted suicide would bring about 'a paradigm shift with unforeseeable (and perhaps uncontrollable) changes in attitude and behaviour'.[128] In particular, they think that relaxation of the law 'might well send out a subliminal message to particular

---

[122] Ibid., para. 96. The emphasis is original to the text. *Carter BCSC* acknowledges this piece of data, but puts the number of deaths slightly lower at 546 (para. 471).

[123] United Nations Office on Drugs and Crime, 'Intentional homicide count and rate per 100,000 population, by country/territory (2000–2012)': <http://www.unodc.org/gsh/en/data.html>.

[124] *Fleming v. Ireland*, para. 99. The emphasis is original to the text.   [125] Ibid., para. 102.

[126] Ibid., para. 104.

[127] Select Committee on Dying with Dignity, Québec National Assembly, *Dying with Dignity Report*, March 2012, p. 74.

[128] *Fleming v. Ireland*, para. 67.

vulnerable groups—such as the disabled and the elderly—that in order to avoid consuming scarce resources in an era of shrinking public funds for health care, physician-assisted suicide is a "normal" option which any rational patient face with terminal or degenerative illness should seriously consider'.[129] They also reckon that where the new paradigm comes to prevail, participating physicians would become accustomed to it, and in that context 'the risk of complacency with regard to the maintenance of statutory safeguards—which all are agreed would be absolutely essential—could not be discounted as negligible'.[130] My own view is that the Irish judges were not being unduly pessimistic, but only realistic—for, to quote the German moral philosopher Dieter Birnbacher, '[t]he veneer of civilisation is perhaps thinner than we allow ourselves to imagine'.[131]

However, my main purpose here has not been to prove that the Canadian courts' rulings were seriously unwise—although I believe that they were. Rather, my main purpose has been to show that the rulings' interpretation of the empirical data is at least subject to reasonable doubt and so controversial. This then raises the question of whether the courts should have taken upon themselves the task of deciding whether or not to grant a right to physician-assisted suicide and voluntary euthanasia in the first place. More specifically, it raises the question of whether the courts should have assumed that task, in spite of the fact that no less than nine bills proposing legalisation had been proposed to the Canadian Parliament between 1991 and 2012, that most of them had been subject to parliamentary discussion, and that the last one had been overwhelmingly rejected in the House of Commons by 228 votes to 59 as late as April 2010.[132]

VIII

On the one hand, in *Carter* the trial judge accepted that 'considerable deference is due to Parliament', since the choice to be made 'implicates fundamental social values' and involves 'complex and difficult predictions about human behaviour'.[133] She identified several particular factors in the case that favour deference to Parliament: the question of physician-assisted dying 'involves a fundamental and complex social policy choice about which there are conflicting views in Canada'; making that choice 'involves weighing the suffering of known individuals against the potential harm to

---

[129] *Fleming v. Ireland*, para. 68.   [130] *Fleming v. Ireland*, para. 69.

[131] Dieter Birnbacher, 'Das Tötungsverbot aus der Sicht des klassischen Utilitarismus', in Rainer Hegselman and Reinhard Merkel, eds, *Zur Debatte über Euthanasie* (Frankfurt am Main: Suhrkamp Verlag, 1991), p. 42: 'Die zivilisatorische Decke ist vielleicht dünner also wir es uns träumen lassen...' My translation. For further discussion of the possibility of cultural degeneration with regard to euthanasia, see Biggar, *Aiming to Kill*, pp. 157–60.

[132] See Chan and Somerville, 'Converting the "Right to Life" to the "Right to Physician-Assisted Suicide and Euthanasia"', table 1, pp. 152–4.

[133] *Carter BCSC*, para. 1227.

other unknown individuals and to societal values'; and the potential harms and benefits to society are 'not amenable to scientific proof'.[134] The Supreme Court endorsed the British Columbia court's view, writing that, in analysing whether the law's blanket prohibition of assisted suicide and voluntary euthanasia comprises means proportionate to its object, courts must accord the legislature 'a measure of deference', because physician-assisted death 'involves complex issues of social policy and a number of competing societal values',[135] because more than one solution is possible, and because '[p]roportionality does not require perfection' but need only be 'reasonable'.[136] Nevertheless, the Supreme Court followed the lower court in arguing that deference is only due where the legislature's regulatory response to the complex problem is itself aptly complex; and it judged that the *Criminal Code*'s blanket prohibition cannot be described as such.[137]

It is true that a blanket prohibition is indiscriminate, applying to everyone without exception, and in that sense it is not 'complex'. However, whether or not the law should become more discriminate and complex hangs upon fine judgements about the logical and practical effects of more discriminate legislation. As we have seen, the Canadian courts have been very sanguine about those; and, as I have argued, they have been far too sanguine. It is noteworthy that at no point did either the provincial or federal supreme courts pause to consider why the Canadian Parliament had not shared their optimism.

IX

So, should the Canadian courts have assumed the task of deciding an ethico-legal issue as difficult and controversial as the legalisation of physician-assisted suicide and voluntary euthanasia, and one which deeply implicates the ethos of the health-care professions and society in general and which had been frequently discussed in Parliament? I think not, for several reasons. First of all, the issue of whether to grant a right to assisted suicide or voluntary euthanasia has been the subject of decades of academic and public controversy in Western jurisdictions around the world, the vast majority of which have decided against it, often repeatedly. It is true that opinion polls regularly show predominant support among the general public for legalising 'assisted dying'. However, as already indicated above, there is reason to suppose that that level of support hangs upon the ambiguity of the meaning of 'assisted dying' (which bundles together palliative medicine and care on the one hand, with assistance in committing suicide on the other), and that when the polls use the phrase 'assisted suicide' instead, support

---

[134] Ibid., para. 1179.   [135] *Carter SCC*, para. 98.   [136] Ibid., para. 97.
[137] *Carter BCSC*, para. 1180; *Carter SCC*, paras 97–8.

drops dramatically.[138] Whatever the state of public opinion, associations of health-care professionals and parliamentarians often remain doggedly opposed to legal-isation.[139] This could be, as critics sometimes claim, because the professionals and the politicians are simply 'out of touch' or because (in England) they let the twenty-six Anglican bishops in the House of Lords lead them by the nose.[140] Much more plausible, however, is the surmise that doctors, nurses, and members of Parliament are able to see the professional, institutional, and social ramifications of adding assisted suicide and voluntary euthanasia to the panoply of health care—and the risks they pose—much more clearly than the proverbial man-in-the-street. Given how persistently controversial has been the issue of granting a right to assisted suicide and voluntary euthanasia; given how often, how widely, and how exhaustively it has been debated by academics, professionals, and legislators; and given how, as Justice Smith herself admitted, 'thoughtful and well-motivated people can and have come to different conclusions about whether physician-assisted death can be ethically justifiable':[141] it seems both ethically and politically presumptuous for a court comprising either a single unelected judge, or at most a handful of them, to assume the authority to decide the matter. It also puts public respect for the law at risk. When decisions are made about law and public policy, it is invariably the case that some citizens will be aggrieved by them. However, insofar as they are assured that their parliamentary representatives have given voice to their views, and since they know that they have the liberty to work for the democratic reversal of the adverse decision, they will be able to swallow their grievance and accept the law or policy, provisionally. But when that decision is made by unelected judges, the ordinary citizen lacks both the assurance and the liberty, and will therefore be tempted to regard the court's judgement as an expression of judicial tyranny.

A second reason for thinking Canada's Supreme Court unwise in presuming to grant a right to physician-assisted suicide and voluntary euthanasia is that, by its very nature, a court focuses on the particular case brought before it. There are several points in the trial judgement, which the Supreme Court confirmed, where this natural myopia finds expression. For example, Justice Smith writes that the question of a 'logical slippery slope', 'requires speculation and arises only tangentially in connection with the issues in this case. Accordingly, I will not address

[138] See p. 274n.40.
[139] As already stated, between 1991 and 2012 no less than nine bills proposing legalisation were proposed to the Canadian Parliament, the last one being overwhelmingly rejected in the House of Commons by 228 votes to 59 as late as April 2010.
[140] Proponents of the legalisation of physician-assisted suicide in England and Wales, who have been frustrated in recent years by the lack of sufficient support in the House of Lords, have frequently blamed the regressive, 'religious' influence of the Church of England's bishops who sit there. However, since the total number of Lords eligible to take part in the work of the House is currently about 800, and since the bishops never number more than twenty-six, it is quite implausible to suppose that the latter somehow manage to dominate the views of the former.
[141] *Carter BCSC*, para. 343.

it...'[142] Thus she passes entirely by one of the major objections to liberalisation, namely, that once the 'bright line' of an absolute prohibition is transgressed, and the intentional killing of some people is sanctioned by the law, the force of logic will tend to extend eligibility from the terminally ill to the chronically suffering to the existentially miserable, and to broaden the array of 'treatments' from assisted suicide to voluntary euthanasia and even to non-voluntary euthanasia.[143] Moreover, a court operating with reference to a charter of rights focuses on the rights of the individual plaintiff(s) standing before it. Its primary concern is not with the systemic effects of its judgements, whether on a profession, an institution, or a society. Accordingly, Justice Smith opined that '[t]he benefits [of the absolute prohibition] are experienced by unknown persons', whereas '[t]he costs are experienced by persons who are in the position of Sue Rodriguez or Gloria Taylor, and are considerable'.[144]

More specifically, third, a court can only consider the evidence presented to it. Unlike a legislature, it cannot create a commission of enquiry to gather a broad range of evidence and reach comprehensive conclusions about it. Its view is necessarily non-comprehensive. This was certainly so in the case of Justice Smith's treatment of the empirical evidence, which the Supreme Court endorsed. Her own admission that 'independent analysis of the data beyond that which the expert witnesses have undertaken is not possible'[145] serves to undermine the authority of the categorical confidence with which she claimed that there was 'no evidence' from permissive jurisdictions that people with disabilities are at heightened risk of accessing 'physician-assisted dying'.[146]

I believe that Canada's Supreme Court was unwise to declare that the *Criminal Code* infringes the *Charter* in its blanket prohibition of 'physician-assisted dying', and in urging the national Parliament and provincial legislatures to enact permissive legislation. As to why it did so I can only speculate. It is certainly possible, and not unlikely, that the court's understanding of its role was shaped by the influential school of legal philosophy that supposes elected legislatures to be incapable of protecting the rights of minorities, and that such protection is therefore the special responsibility of the judiciary.[147] The pre-eminent exponent of this view was Ronald Dworkin. As he saw it, the court is the forum of principle and right,

---

[142] Ibid., para. 365.
[143] Keown, 'A Right to Voluntary Euthanasia?', pp. 22, 26: 'once the law abandons the bright line prohibition on any intentional ending of patients' lives, it enters a fuzzy world of arbitrary judgments about whose lives are, or are not, "worth living". It is not surprising that disability groups in general strongly oppose legalization.'. See also Biggar, 'Autonomy's Suicide'.
[144] *Carter BCSC*, paras 1275–6.   [145] Ibid., para. 647.   [146] See above pp. 272, 285.
[147] Jonathan (Lord) Sumption, formerly a Justice of the Supreme Court of the United Kingdom, has written: 'In many countries...there is widespread disdain for the political process and some articulate support for an approach to lawmaking that takes the politics out of it. This reflects the contempt felt by many intelligent commentators for what they regard as the illogicality, intellectual dishonesty and the irrational prejudice characteristic of party politics. The American philosophers John Rawls and Ronald Dworkin have been perhaps the most articulate modern spokesmen for this point of view... [T]heir

whereas the legislature is the forum of policy and general interest; and that whereas a court engages in reasoned deliberation, a legislature merely aggregates preferences. 'The political process', he once wrote, 'is a machine which is calculated...to reach decisions such that...the *overall* preferences of all the people, considered neutrally with the same consideration for the preferences of each, is improved'.[148] 'Ordinary politics generally aims...at a political compromise that gives all powerful groups enough of what they want to prevent their disaffection, and reasoned argument elaborating underlying moral principles is rarely part or even congenial to such compromises.'[149] It follows that '[a] judge who is insulated from the demands of the political majority whose interests the rights would trump is therefore in a better position to evaluate the argument'.[150] It is the special responsibility of courts, therefore, to protect the rights of minorities against the predominant political power of democratic majorities.

It is difficult to believe that anyone but a philosopher could have mistaken such a caricature of parliamentary politics for a description. Given the plurality and diversity of interests and points of view among several hundred legislators, and given that strict utilitarianism is not usually their common faith, likening the legislature to a preference-aggregating 'machine' could hardly be less appropriate. What is more, elected legislators are not usually the passive mouthpieces of their electors' preferences, partly because the electors are seldom of a common mind, partly because there are many issues on which electors themselves do not know what to think, and partly because both they and those they elect often taken the Burkean view that elected representatives are expected and trusted to serve the interests of their constituents as *they*, in their wisdom, think best.

Dworkin not only caricatures the role of elected legislators, but also misunderstands the nature of political majorities and compromises. As he tells it, political majorities have interests and make demands, and political compromises are made to retain their support. Principle and reason, apparently, have nothing to do with any of this. By implication, therefore, the interests and demands of majorities are unprincipled, simply selfish, and compromises are merely, grubbily political. Generally speaking, however, this is not true. Interests need not be selfish; they can be public. Further, legislative majorities are never simply intellectually homogeneous blocs; their members may vote the same way, but their reasons for doing

---

attitude...is shared by some judges...' ('The Limits of Law', in N. W. Barber, Richard Ekins, and Paul Yowell, eds, *Lord Sumption and the Limits of Law* (Oxford and Portland, Ore.: Hart, 2016), pp. 23–4).

[148] Ronald Dworkin, 'Social Sciences and Constitutional Rights—the Consequences of Uncertainty', *Journal of Law and Education*, 6/1 (1977), p. 10. The emphasis is Dworkin's.

[149] Ronald Dworkin, *Freedom's Law: The Moral Reading of the American Constitution* (Oxford: Oxford University Press, 1996), pp. 344–5.

[150] Ronald Dworkin, *Taking Rights Seriously*, new edn (London: Bloomsbury, 1997), p. 110.

so will vary.[151] Usually those members will have consciences, possess moral reasons, be susceptible to rational persuasion, and vote in favour of what they believe to be right. Legislators who turn out to be part of a majority will often have voted in good faith and in a public spirit. Here Jeremy Waldron shines a sharp, critical light back onto a basic assumption of Dworkin's and exposes its inconsistency: 'It simply will not do for the theorists of rights to talk about us as upright and responsible autonomous individuals when they are characterising our need for protection against majorities, while describing the members of majorities against whose tyranny such protection is necessary as irresponsible Hobbesian predators. They cannot have it both ways.'[152] Dworkin's cynicism extended from majorities to compromise, too. For, in a plural society, whose members not only have rival material interests but also conflicting views of what right is, political compromise, far from being merely grubby, is often morally justified as a prudent alternative to deadlock, even bloodshed.[153]

The view that elected legislatures are incapable of protecting the rights of minorities, because they only aggregate preferences and rarely deliberate in terms of moral principles or right, depends on a caricature of the conduct of legislators and a misunderstanding of the nature of voting majorities. The correlative view that courts are better placed to protect the rights of minorities, because judges are better equipped to deliberate about them, is also doubtful. First of all, as we have seen, the scope of a court's deliberation suffers from a natural myopia, being focused on the concrete case brought before it and limited to the evidence presented:[154]

while the putative rights infringements placed before them [the judges] are actual and concrete, attaching to persons represented before the court with specific

---

[151] Grégoire Webber and Paul Yowell: 'In any given vote, the majority of ayes or nays will win, but it is a conceptual mistake to think that this entails the existence of a "majority" as a stable, unified, collective group that acts through time and transmits its preferences through the political process' ('Introduction', p. 8); Richard Bellamy: 'Most legislation is not the product of a homogeneous majority imposing its will upon a constitutional minority, but of a series of compromises brokered by winning coalitions of different minorities' (*Political Constitutionalism* (Cambridge: Cambridge University Press, 2007), p. 241); Richard Ekins: 'The use of a rule of majority vote tells one little about how members of the group decide' ('Legislation as Reasoned Action', p. 98); and John Finnis: '[W]hat the majority is believed to think does not, characteristically, figure much (let alone exclusively) in the grounds by which a voter justifies his vote, a vote which will help to enact law only if more than a minority of voters happens to vote likewise' ('Human Rights and their Enforcement' (1985) in John Finnis, *Human Rights and Common Good*, Collected Essays: Volume III (Oxford: Oxford University Press, 2011), pp. 25–6).

[152] Jeremy Waldron, *Law and Disagreement* (Oxford: Oxford University Press, 1999), p. 14.

[153] See Biggar, 'Compromise: What Makes it Bad?'. Ekins: 'legislators often have good reason to try to compromise, to secure widespread support for changes in the law . . . Importantly, that legislating often involves compromise does *not* entail that it does not involve a principle, or that it is somehow divorced from reason. The legislature often—and rightly—chooses a principled, reasoned compromise' ('Legislation as Reasoned Action', p. 101).

[154] Ekins, 'Legislation as Reasoned Action', p. 93.

names, histories, and aspirations, the persons who are intended to benefit from
the law and its protection are present only as an abstraction...

For example,

> it is no straightforward task... to explain how decriminalising euthanasia may
> change a medico-legal culture in evaluating the merits of preserving some lives;
> how these changes may result in the devaluation of the lives of the disabled and
> may increase pressure on some of them to submit to euthanasia; and how
> attitudes may shift towards accepting the proposition that an increasing set of
> lives are not worth the expenditures and attentions that are required to maintain
> them. What is much more difficult is to produce in court the individuals to make
> these concerns concrete: the vulnerable elderly, for example...[155]

In contrast, a legislature is at liberty to broaden its scope and deliberate more
comprehensively.[156] Moroever,

> [w]hen it comes to addressing diverse interests and claims, the legislature has
> specific strengths. Its larger and more diverse composition, its more direct
> relationship with people affected by its decisions, its ability to gather information
> through hearings and written evidence, and its professional staff devoted to
> conducting research, all provide it with a capacity to perceive and process the
> different interests and claims involved and to understand complex schemes of
> social coordination. Furthermore, there are countless cases in which resolving the
> issue requires assessment of possible or likely consequences of a given measure so
> as to evaluate the way in which that measure will affect interests, claims, and
> schemes of co-ordination. Here, legislatures also have an advantage, in that they
> have the required institutional capacity to assess empirical evidence and to
> understand likely consequences.[157]

---

[155] Miller, 'Majoritarianism and Pathologies of Judicial Review', p. 197.
[156] Ekins, 'The legislature responds directly to the complexity of the common good in that its
deliberation is open to whatever is relevant to the good of the community' ('Legislation as Reasoned
Action', p. 94); Francisco J. Urbina: 'legislation takes a more abstract and general perspective... It
assumes a more architectonic point of view, legislating for the whole of a community and its members
instead of deciding a particular case involving particular parties' ('How Legislation Aids Human Rights
Adjudication', in Webber, *Legislated Rights*, p. 173).
[157] Urbina, 'How Legislation Aids Human Rights Adjudication', pp. 173–4. David Faigman, who is
generally a supporter of rights-based judicial review of legislation, agrees: 'They [legislatures] have
greater resources than courts, for instance, to sponsor research, hold hearings, and call expert witnesses.
They have the power to define research questions and the flexibility to follow them up by redefining the
scope, direction, and size of any inquiries' (*Constitutional Fictions: A Unified Theory of Constitutional
Facts* (New York: Oxford University Press, 2008), p. 176); quoted by Yowell in *Constitutional Rights*,
p. 89. In judging a case similar to *Carter*, Lord Sumption agrees, too: 'the parliamentary process is a
better way of resolving issues involving particular and complex questions of fact arising out of moral
and social dilemmas. The legislature has access to a fuller range of expert judgment and experience than

Further, because a legislature is composed of a wide variety of people belonging to opposing political groups, it comprises an agonistic forum in which ideas are presented, challenged, and tested, and in which opposing minds serve to refine each other. In a court, however, judges face no opposition,[158] and, according to the US jurist Richard Posner, they 'do not deliberate... *collectively*... very much' at all. He cites the experience of a US federal court of appeal judge, who had fondly 'imagined that conferences [on cases] would be reflective, refining, analytical, dynamic', only to discover that they usually consist of brief discussions that change few minds.'[159]

Further still, legislatures have an important advantage in their power to command greater democratic legitimacy. For something to be democratically legitimate is for it to be regarded as authoritative, even by those who disagree with it, because it was achieved by a fair process. Fairness here will include openness to diverse points of view, such that dissenters can be confident that their voices have been heard and considered, and thus that they have been treated with a measure of respect. It will also include the possibility of reversal, such that dissenters know that they have the opportunity to persuade the majority to change their minds. In this way democratic legitimacy possesses the authority to command the compliance of those who find themselves on the losing side in a decisive vote. It is obviously important that law should possess democratic legitimacy, lest it lack authority in the eyes of dissenters and they be tempted to give expression to their dissent outside of the law. The need for legitimacy is heightened in the case of decisions about rights, for '[r]ights are claims against the claimant's own community. In a democracy, they depend for their legitimacy on a measure of recognition by that community. To be effective, they require a large measure of public acceptance through an active civil society.' However, in the opinion of Lord Sumption, formerly a Justice of the Supreme Court of the United Kingdom, '[t]his is something which no purely judicial decision-making process can deliver'.[160] The reasons for this are several. One is that, because judges are not democratically elected, citizens cannot perceive themselves to be indirect participants in the deliberation of a court as they can in that of a legislature.[161] The second reason is the limited vision of a court, given its naturally myopic focus on the case

---

forensic litigation can possibly provide. It is better able to take account of the interests of groups not represented or not sufficiently represented before the court in resolving what is surely a classic "polycentric problem"' (*R (on the Application of Nicklinson) (AP) v. Ministry of Justice* [2014] UKSC 38, para. 232).

[158] J. Kenny, 'The Advantages of a Written Constitution Incorporating a Bill of Rights', *Northern Ireland Legal Quarterly*, 30 (1979), pp. 189, 196; quoted by Yowell in *Constitutional Rights*, p. 112.

[159] Richard A. Posner, *How Judges Think* (Cambridge, Mass.: Harvard University Press, 2008), p. 2. The emphasis is Posner's.

[160] Sumption, 'The Limits of Law', p. 25. Urbina agrees: 'Judicial decisions need to be legitimate and seen to be so, and because many human rights cases coincide with politically contested issues, this need for legitimacy is perhaps more pronounced in human rights adjudication than in many other areas of law' ('How Legislation Aids Human Rights Adjudication', p. 167).

[161] Richard Ekins, 'Legislation as Reasoned Action', p. 110.

set before it. A court cannot be as open to a diversity of viewpoints, arguments, and evidence as a legislature. Therefore, citizens who disagree with a court's decision cannot be so confident that their views have been heard and considered, and so that they have been treated with a modicum of respect. Nor do they have the consolation that they could have the court's decision reversed by democratic persuasion. Finally, the special authority of a court lies in its legal expertise, whereby it interprets the law of the community according to established, common, constant legal principles and rules. To some extent the legitimacy of its judgements rests on its claim to expert legal authority. However, where a court must judge a claim with reference to a charter of rights, vaguely and abstractly formulated, its room for discretion expands considerably, and its discretion strays, as it must, from the territory of law into that of moral principle and social policy. But the further it strays from the territory where it exercises special expertise, the weaker its claim to special authority:

> in circumstances where questions of law draw close to unbounded moral reasoning or evaluations of competing policy options, that comparative expertise [in resolving technical questions of law] disappears. Where the moral evaluation in question will be particularly controversial, courts risk push-back from dissatisfied legislators and members of the community who understand themselves to have been second-guessed on matters not solidly within the expertise of judges or lawyers.[162]

And since 'the judges disagree among themselves along exactly the same lines as the citizens and representatives do, and ... the judges make their decisions, too, in the courtroom by majority-voting', 'citizens may well feel that if disagreements on these matters are to be settled by counting heads, then it is their heads or those of their accountable representatives that should be counted'.[163]

X

One of the most common arguments in favour of relying on courts to protect the rights of minorities is that, historically, that is what they have done, where legislatures have failed. The most celebrated instance of this is the case of *Brown v. Board of Education* (1954), where the US Supreme Court struck down legislation that sanctioned racial segregation. However, as Paul Yowell reports, there is now a considerable body of historical study that shows that the *Brown* judgement

---

[162] Bradley W. Miller, 'Majoritarianism and Pathologies of Judicial Review', p. 195.
[163] Waldron, *Law and Disagreement*, p. 15.

itself actually made little difference. It was only a decade later, when the US Congress enacted the 1964 Civil Rights Act, the 1965 Voting Rights Act, and the 1965 Elementary and Secondary Education Act, that schools become substantially integrated.[164] As Gerald Rosenberg has written, 'before Congress and the executive branch acted, courts had virtually no direct effect on ending discrimination in the key fields of education, voting, transportation, accommodations and public places, and housing'.[165]

At least in 1954 the Supreme Court in *Brown* intended reform in favour of social justice; before that date, it was more often than not a force of resistance to change. As Cass Sunstein has written: 'Before the Warren Court [in *Brown*], the justices [of the Supreme Court] were almost never a force for social reform, and they have rarely assumed that role in the past two decades. Most of the time, the judiciary has been an obstacle to racial equality.'[166] Thus, in *Dred Scott v. Sandford* (1857) the court entrenched slavery; in *Civil Rights Cases* (1883) it struck down the 1875 Civil Rights Act, which prohibited racial discrimination in public places;[167] and in *Lochner v. New York* (1905) it struck down legislation that limited the working hours of bakery employees to ten hours a day and sixty hours a week.[168] In 1949, Robert Jackson, justice of the US Supreme Court and the Chief US Prosecutor at the Nuremberg Trials, reckoned that

> time has proved that [the court's] judgment was wrong on the most outstanding issues upon which it has chosen to challenge the popular branches. Its judgment in the *Dred Scott* case was overruled by war ... Its judgments repressing labor and social legislation are now abandoned. Many of its judgments against New Deal legislation are rectified by confession of error. In no major conflict with the representative branches on any question of social or economic policy has time vindicated the court.[169]

As courts have not always been engines of change, so legislatures have not always been bastions of conservative reaction. Yes, many legislatures in the southern USA were for a long time captured by a majoritarian bias in favour of

---

[164] Paul Yowell, 'From Universal to Legislated Rights', in Webber et al., *Legislated Rights*, p. 143.

[165] Gerald N. Rosenberg, *The Hollow Hope: Can Courts Bring About Social Change?* 2nd edn (Chicago: University of Chicago Press, 2008), p. 70; quoted by Yowell in 'From Universal to Legislated Rights', pp. 143–4. Rosenberg's argument is controversial, but the view that *Brown*'s effect was limited 'is now approaching scholarly consensus' (T. M. Keck, 'Does the Court Follow the Election Returns?', *Reviews in American History*, 32 (2004), pp. 602, 608; quoted by Yowell in *Constitutional Rights*, p. 122 n. 114).

[166] Cass Sunstein, 'Did Brown Matter?', *The New Yorker* (3 May 2004): <https://www.newyorker.com/magazine/2004/05/03/did-brown-matter> (as at 10 September 2018).

[167] Paul Yowell, 'From Universal to Legislated Rights', p. 148.

[168] Waldron, *Law and Disagreement*, pp. 247 n. 40, 288.

[169] Robert Jackson, *The Struggle for Judicial Supremacy: A Study of a Crisis in American Power Politics* (New York: Alfred Knopf, 1941), p. x.

racial segregation, but one cannot fairly make the inference that legislatures are necessarily or usually dominated by social conservatism. As early as 1807 the British Parliament voted to abolish the slave trade, and twenty-six years later it abolished slavery throughout the British Empire. In 1853 the newly established Parliament of Cape Colony in South Africa granted the vote on equal terms to whites and blacks. After the American Civil War, the US Congress proposed the Thirteenth Amendment (which abolished slavery and was ratified in 1865), the Fourteenth Amendment (which guarantees all citizens, regardless of race, equal protection under the law and equal civil and political privileges, and was ratified in 1868), and the Fifteenth Amendment (which guarantees the right to vote, regardless of race, and was ratified in 1870). It also passed a series of Civil Rights Acts 1866–77 and 1964–5.

Neither their record nor their nature gives us reason to suppose that courts are generally better disposed and equipped than legislatures to protect the rights of minorities against majority tyranny. Or to put the point more exactly and in a fashion less burdened by questionable assumptions: courts are generally less well fitted than legislatures to deliberate about, and decide, what politically controversial rights should be accorded which groups of citizens, in the light of the consequent risks and costs to the common good. Lord Sumption sums up the point thus:

> politics is quite simply a better way of resolving questions of social policy than judge-made law . . . The essential function of politics in a democracy is to reconcile inconsistent interest and opinions by producing a result which it may be that few people would have chosen as their preferred option, but which the majority can live with. Political parties are rarely monolithic. Although generally sharing a common outlook, they are unruly coalitions between shifting factions, united only by a common desire to win elections. They therefore mutate in response to changes in public sentiment in the interests of winning or retaining power. In this way, they can often be a highly effective means of mediating between those in power and the public from which they derive their legitimacy . . . It is true that the political process is often characterised by opacity, fudge or irrationality . . . [But these] are the tools of compromise, enabling divergent views and interests to be accommodated. The result may be intellectually impure, but it is frequently in the public interest . . . The judicial resolution of major policy issues undermines our ability to live together in harmony by depriving us of a method of mediating compromises among ourselves. Politics is a method of mediating compromises in which we can all participate, albeit indirectly, and which we are therefore more likely to recognise as legitimate.[170]

---

[170] Sumption, 'The Limits of Law', pp. 24–5.

Therefore, insofar as the conduct of Canada's Supreme Court in *Carter* owed something to the cynical view of parliamentary politics and the correlatively idealised view of judicial deliberation, which have been promoted by the likes of Ronald Dworkin, I think it mistaken.

XI

What, then, has our analysis of the judicial reasoning in *Carter v. Canada* revealed to us about what's wrong with rights? First of all, there is the problem of charters (or bills or conventions) of rights, which include vague, unspecified items—rights, as Dworkin himself puts it, of 'near limitless abstraction'.[171] This problem has several parts. First, in contrast to the specified rights created by ordinary law, which 'express firm, relatively precise requirements regarding relationships between persons, specifying the acts and forbearances required by law in particular situations',[172] these rights give judges no determinate guidance in deciding cases and hardly amount to law at all.[173]

Second, they purport to exist *before* their limits have been set in relation to competing rights or the rightful claims of the common good. This prior, original existence accords them a presumption in favour of their authority and displaces the burden of proof onto anyone who would limit them. In fact, however, we cannot know whether or not a right exists until we have first considered the competing claims.[174] As we saw in our discussion of the right against torture in Chapter 7, the rationale for granting a positive, legal right *contains* deliberation

---

[171] Dworkin, *Freedom's Law*, p. 73.   [172] Yowell, *Constitutional Rights*, pp. 14–15.

[173] Ibid., pp. 4–5.

[174] With reference to Article 8 of the European Convention on Human Rights, which guarantees the right to 'a private life', John Finnis makes the same point: 'So the subject matter and content of the Article 8 right are not even definable, or juridically identifiable, until one has taken into account, at least in outline, all those kinds of state action that are justifiable under Article 8(2), including all those countless kinds of law that do justifiably restrict what one can legitimately do in private—and the outlines of all those many kinds that *might*' ('Judicial Law-Making and the "Living" Instrumentalisation of the ECHR', in Barber et al., *Lord Sumption*, p. 81. The emphasis is Finnis's). In support he cites Lords Mance and Hughes in *Nicklinson*: Article 8 does not create 'a prima facie right to obtain voluntary assistance [in suicide] . . . A right only exists (at least in any coherent sense) if and when it is concluded under art. 8.2 that there is no justification for a ban or restriction' (Mance, para. 159); 'Whether there is a right to do the particular thing under consideration depends on whether the State is or is not justified in prohibiting it, or placing conditions upon it, and that in turn depends on whether the State's rules meet the requirements of article 8.2' (Hughes, para. 263; Finnis, 'A British "Convention Right" to Assistance in Suicide?'). Elsewhere, Finnis puts it thus: 'in truth, one's *interest* in such a good (or domain) as private life is *only properly a right* in those areas, matters, and actions left free from the proper measures for preventing crime, protecting health and so on. One has no *right* of speaking incitement to murder or of private car-bomb construction' ('Judicial Power: Past, Present, and Future', p. 19. The emphasis is Finnis's). Noel Malcolm thinks along similar lines. Observing that some items in the European Convention comprise two distinct elements, he asks: 'What exactly is the statement of the human right: is it the "pure" description of the right in the first part of the article, or the whole article, including the limitations?' (*Human Rights and Political Wrongs*, pp. 22–3).

WHAT'S WRONG WITH (SOME) JUDGES? (2) 307

about the risks and costs to society. Therefore, what the *Canadian Charter* affirms as the 'right to life, liberty, and security of the person' is really no right at all. It does not exist.

The third part of the problem with abstract rights is that they afford judges vast room for the exercise of philosophical and political discretion, in which they have no professional expertise or authority. Writing of the US Bill of Rights, Dworkin comments that it 'seems to give judges almost incredible power ... judges must answer intractable, controversial, and profound questions of political morality that philosophers, statesmen, and citizens have debated for many centuries, with no prospect of agreement'.[175]

In addition to the problems attending the abstractness of some of the rights guaranteed by charters, bills, and conventions, there are also problems with the attitudes of judges in interpreting them. There is certainly abroad among legal philosophers the view that judges are possessed of superior discernment into what 'real rights' are. Thus Dworkin says that he 'cannot imagine what argument might be thought to show that legislative decisions about rights are inherently more likely to be right than judicial decisions';[176] and George Letsas urges that the European Court of Human Rights should protect 'whatever human rights people *in fact* have, and not what human rights domestic authorities or public opinion *think* people have'.[177] Lord Sumption comments dryly on Dworkin that he 'assumes a definition of "rightness" that is hard to justify in a political community';[178] and Finnis on Letsas that 'judges do not occupy an Archimedean position outside the possibility of error which afflicts "domestic authorities or public opinion"'.[179] How far the view of Dworkin and Letsas influences the way in which judges view their role, we cannot be sure; but since it flatters judges, and since judges are human, we can be sure that it influences some. Certainly, there is evidence that some judges view themselves, not simply as interpreters of the law, but as developers of it, responsible for keeping it abreast of 'modern' social mores. This view is incarnated in the idea of the Canadian Constitution as 'a living tree' (equivalent to the idea of the European Convention of Human Rights as a 'living instrument'), which the Supreme Court of Canada has wholeheartedly embraced. Thus, in 2004 the Court referred to 'one of the most fundamental principles of Canadian constitutional interpretation: that our Constitution is a living tree which, by way of progressive interpretation, accommodates and addresses the realities of modern life'.[180] The word 'progressive' is telling, for 'progress' is more

---

[175] Dworkin, *Freedom's Law*, p. 74.   [176] Quoted by Sumption in 'The Limits of Law', p. 25.
[177] George Letsas, 'The ECHR as a Living Instrument: Its Meaning and its Legitimacy' (March 2012): <http://ssrn.com/abstract=2021836>, p. 23; quoted by Finnis in 'Judicial Law-Making', p. 90. The emphases are Letsas'.
[178] Sumption, 'The Limits of Law', p. 25.   [179] Finnis, 'Judicial Law-Making', p. 90.
[180] *Reference re Same-Sex Marriage* (2004) SCC 79, para. 22; quoted by Sandra Fredman in 'Living Trees or Deadwood: The Interpretive Challenge of the European Convention on Human Rights', in

than 'change'. Change merely happens; progress is the direction in which, it is thought, change *ought* to happen. So what the adoption of 'progressive interpretation' implies is that the judiciary sees its role, not merely as that of causing the law to respond to changing social mores, but also as that of using the law to cause mores to change *in the right direction*.

But whether or not such a flattering self-understanding is the reason, it is clear from *Carter* that some judges are too little aware of the natural and distorting myopia of their case-focused attention, of the limitations of courts in achieving a comprehensive view of relevant social facts, of judges' lack of responsibility and accountability for the policy and social effects of their decisions, and of their relative immunity from direct challenge by diverse and opposing points of view. That they are so little aware of these things that that they presume to stray far beyond their own professional, legal expertise to create novel and controversial rights by judicial fiat, which cannot be undone by normal democratic processes and so strains democratic legitimacy, is a problem. And if Paul Yowell is correct to observe that '[t]he decision in *Carter* represents the overwhelming trend of cases globally',[181] then it is an alarmingly widespread problem.

Barber et al., *Lord Sumption*, p. 57. Fredman comments that 'Canada has been at the forefront of the development of the organic metaphor of the living tree' (ibid., p. 56).
[181] Yowell, *Constitutional Rights*, pp. 29–30.

12

What's Wrong with (Some)
Human Rights Lawyers?

I

Our critical analysis of some recent jurisprudence of the European Court of Human Rights, and of the Supreme Courts of Canada and the United Kingdom, has uncovered a variety of problems. First of all, there are charters of rights that include absurdly ill-defined items, which place the burden of rigorous proof onto anyone wishing to limit them, and afford judges vast freedom to exercise philosophical and political discretion that far exceeds their professional expertise and authority. Second, there is the flattering self-understanding of judges as best able to discern what 'real rights' are and as responsible for the 'progressive' interpretation of the law. Third, is some judges' lack of awareness of their natural, case-focused myopia. Fourth, is their lack of self-restraint in the light of their relative immunity from democratic accountability. Fifth, we have observed signs of a rights-fundamentalism and a deficiency in historical imagination, which express themselves in a practically absolute resistance to accommodating rights to political realities. Sixth, we have also found evidence of a culture of risk-aversion. Finally, a universal missionary zeal has produced an innovative expansion of jurisdiction that threatens to jeopardise national confidence in international law.

We turn now from judges to human rights lawyers. Judges are normally constrained by their role—Giovanni Bonello notwithstanding—which requires them to take into careful account arguments on both sides of a dispute and to assess them in the light of law and precedent, before reaching an all-things-considered judgement. Human rights lawyers are not judges, but advocates. Their role gives rise to different problems or at least to some of the same problems in more overt form. In what follows, I will analyse and reflect upon the writings of several prominent British lawyers, especially Shami Chakrabarti, Conor Gearty, and Anthony Lester. As Director of Liberty 2003–16, Shami Chakrabarti rose to public prominence through her opposition to 'excessive' anti-terrorist legislation.[1] She now sits in the House of Lords. Conor Gearty is Professor of Human Rights Law at the London School of Economics, where he directed the Centre for the

---

[1] Liberty is a London-based body that campaigns in favour of civil liberties and human rights.

Study of Human Rights 2002–9. He is also a practising barrister and a Fellow of the British Academy. Anthony Lester, QC, has been described as 'the founding father of modern human rights in the UK'[2] and 'Britain's greatest human rights lawyer',[3] and has been a peer in the House of Lords for over two decades. I make no pretence to comprehensiveness in my scrutiny of their work, and will only refer to a handful of publications that they have addressed to the general public, since it is the quality of their public advocacy, rather than their courtroom skills, that is of interest here. Nor do I argue that these three are representative of all human rights lawyers in the UK. Yet, while it is possible that they are eccentric, it is doubtful. After all, they have been propelled into public and professional prominence by the esteem of influential others. Again, it is possible that, since they are all British, their views and attitudes are peculiar to the UK and have no wider significance. But that, too, is doubtful, since, as we shall see, their views echo and amplify what we have already heard from judges in Strasbourg and Ottawa, and from Human Rights Watch in New York.

II

To begin with, let credit be given where credit is due. Another high-profile human rights lawyer, Baroness Helena Kennedy, has written of herself: 'my life has been the law and I believe in the law's role in safeguarding those who are vulnerable and marginalised. These are the people to whom my loyalty lies.'[4] What she writes, each of the three rights lawyers under our consideration could probably write, too. At the heart of their work is an admirable concern to protect individuals, especially members of unpopular or vulnerable groups, from harm at the hands of the state. Even when states are not intentionally malicious, they can often be negligent of the welfare of politically weak classes of citizen, or impatient with the liberty of individuals. At the beginning of his chapter on human rights in *Five Ideas to Fight For*, Anthony Lester quotes this notice once observed adorning the desk of an immigration official in the UK Government's Home Office: 'Power is delightful and absolute power is absolutely delightful.'[5] No doubt the official found the saying amusing and understood it ironically, in which case it expresses a reassuring self-awareness. Nevertheless, it also expresses a real temptation: hard-pressed civil servants charged with developing and implementing generally applicable

---

[2] Helena Kennedy, QC, commendation on the back cover of Anthony Lester, *Five Ideas to Fight For: How our Freedom is under Threat and why it Matters* (London: Oneworld, 2016).
[3] Harold Hongju Koh, Sterling Professor of International Law at Yale Law School and former Legal Adviser to the US Department of State under President Obama, commendation on the back cover of Lester, *Five Ideas*.
[4] Helena Kennedy, *Just Law: The Changing Face of Justice and Why It Matters to Us All* (London: Vintage, 2004), p. xi.
[5] Lester, *Five Ideas*, p. 13.

policy would much prefer not to suffer hindrance by awkward individual cases, whatever their merits. For that reason alone a healthy polity needs advocates who will bend the ear of those with their hands on the levers of power, whose haste to complete their agenda makes them deaf or distracted, and give effective voice to the vulnerable voiceless.

What is more, if we are to be fair, we should not expect judicial impartiality from a public advocate. A public advocate needs to attract attention, muster political support, push back against political opponents, and make a compelling case. Accordingly, her manner of discourse is bound to be more rhetorical, more partisan, more selective, and more forceful than that of a judge.

III

All that said, busy civil servants are not the only ones subject to temptation. Human rights lawyers, who understand themselves as champions of the weak, sometimes succumb to an excessive self-regard that makes it harder for them to achieve a fair understanding of their opponents—and so to do justice to them. The mirror of self-inflation is the caricature of others. Thus Shami Chakrabarti tells us that, before working for Liberty, she was a government lawyer in the Home Office, and she comments: 'You might say that I am a Jedi Knight who began on the dark side of the force.'[6] One hopes that her tongue was firmly in her cheek when she wrote that, but her persistent attachment to metaphors of the same kind gives rise to doubt. A few pages on, shifting from *Star Wars* to *The Lord of the Rings*, she describes a new Foreign Secretary as a 'previous occupant of the Dark Tower'.[7] And a little later, she tells us that 'Mordor...[is] yet another nickname for the Home Office'.[8]

Conor Gearty is much more careful to steer clear of self-flattering metaphors, but even he instinctively numbers himself among the Children of Light—or, to use his preferred label, the 'progressives'.[9] This is now a very common self-appellation among those Britons—usually middle-class, university educated, professional, and salaried—who subscribe to causes such as 'inclusivity', 'diversity', liberal immigration policy, membership of the European Union, global justice, and, of course,

---

[6] Shami Chakrabarti, *On Liberty* (London: Allen Lane, 2014), p. xi.   [7] Ibid., p. 5.
[8] Ibid., p. 12.
[9] To be fair, Gearty never directly describes himself as 'progressive'. Yet he manifestly approves of those who do and he implicitly aligns himself with them: 'progressives (and human rights advocates) do not care very much for the ethics they find so sharply defined and deeply embedded [in the common law]' (Conor Gearty, *On Fantasy Island: Britain, Europe, and Human Rights* (Oxford: Oxford University Press, 2016), p. 29); 'the Human Rights Act is one of a number of innovative laws enacted in the first years of a progressive Labour administration at the end of the last millennium' (ibid., p. 215); and 'the language of fairness, justice, inclusivity runs with the grain of *our* progressive instincts' (ibid., p. 217. The emphasis is mine).

312 WHAT'S WRONG WITH RIGHTS?

human rights. The problem with the label is that it divides the world into two Manichaean camps—the 'progressives' (or the Children of Light) on the one hand, and, by implication, the 'regressives' (or the Children of Darkness) on the other hand. If, as Gearty tells us, 'the language of fairness, justice, inclusivity runs with the grain of our progressive instincts',[10] then presumably the regressives instinctively speak the language of unfairness, injustice, and exclusivity. But where does that leave those of us whose views of fairness, justice, inclusivity, and, indeed, human rights *differ* from those of Professor Gearty and his *soi-disant* 'progressive' allies? The danger of identifying oneself as 'progressive' is that it gives one permission simply to dismiss views that differ. After all, what is not progressive must be regressive, what is not Light must be Darkness, and Darkness is only to be dispelled, not parlayed with.

Self-flattery is the mother of contempt, and contempt for political opponents is spread quite thickly over the pages of Baroness Chakrabarti's *On Liberty* and Professor Gearty's *On Fantasy Island*. For one example, Chakrabarti cannot contain her irritable disdain for David Blunkett, Home Secretary under Tony Blair 2001–4, describing him dismissively as 'drinking the Home Office Kool-Aid'.[11] For another example, she has this to say of concern about the authority of the courts vis-á-vis Parliament: 'Over the years I have talked to many highly educated and senior UK politicians who espouse a belief that an independent or "unelected" judiciary is somehow "undemocratic" and that the only legitimate power is their own. These increasingly shrill voices lack both intellectual humility and constitutional literacy...'[12] With all due respect, however, Chapter 11 of this book has shown that there are plenty of intelligent and thoughtful people, some of them academic experts in constitutional law and at least one of them a UK Supreme Court judge, who have long been concerned about judicial presumptuousness in deciding to grant rights that the legislature has deliberately refused to grant, and I have argued—unshrilly, I trust—that their concern commands some very good reasons.

Conor Gearty fully shares Shami Chakrabarti's tendency toward contempt for politicians—and he expresses a Dworkinesque idealisation of courts and correlative caricature of democratic politics of the kind that we criticised in the previous chapter:

> Courts deal in fact and data. Their weapon is reason, their audience their own community of the legally informed. They do not need to get elected and have no obligation to court much less cave into the populist passions of the mass media. Real people appear before them, people on whom by definition the law has impacted in a severe, often devastating way... Politicians in contrast deal with

---

[10] Ibid., p. 217.   [11] Chakrabarti, *On Liberty*, p. 40.   [12] Ibid., p. xii.

WHAT'S WRONG WITH (SOME) HUMAN RIGHTS LAWYERS?

the carelessly thrown together passing truths of the moment. Their careers
depend on the sum of these producing a positive reaction in a polling booth
every five years or so, and in opinion polls on an almost weekly basis apart from
that. Solid argument is their enemy, worthiness and a devotion to accuracy two
guarantors of failure. There are not criticisms necessarily, merely statements as
obvious in their accuracy as the description a moment ago of the space the judges
inhabit ... [13]

Carelessness with the truth, hostility to solid argument, careerist captivity to
popular opinion: are we *really* supposed to believe that these are not intended as
criticisms? I think not. And if they are criticisms, then it is fair to ask them to give an
account of themselves. Is it really true that most politicians do not struggle to
maintain their rationality and integrity in the face of relentless media and political
pressures? Do they never succeed? Did the UK Parliament not defy (rightly) for
decades the constant support of an overwhelming popular majority for the
reinstatement of capital punishment? And is it even now not defying (rightly, in
my opinion) majority support for the invention of a right to assisted suicide? In
their struggle to do what they believe to be right, at some considerable risk to their
own political careers, it seems to me that democratic politicians deserve far more
sympathy and appreciation than safely academic lawyers like Professor Gearty are
willing to extend to them. At the very least they should be spared his condescension.

IV

As I have already said, one of the benefits of identifying oneself as 'progressive' is
that one's own self-righteous identity authorises an exemption from having to
listen carefully to what 'regressives' say. After all, what could Darkness possibly
have to say to Light, which would be worth heeding? Thus Professor Gearty writes:

> For years human rights law has been the object of scorn among a wide range of
> Right-leaning politicians, and their supporters in the traditional print
> media ... Now that the larger European entanglement has been seen off, the
> time has come for finishing the unfinished business of human rights destruction.[14]

In many respects I am a rights-sceptic, who for decades has been a daily reader of
the 'traditional print media', yet I have never come across a politician of any stripe
who was intent on 'human rights destruction'. Caricature is a sure symptom of

---

[13] Gearty, *On Fantasy Island*, p. 72. The lack of punctuation in some of the more breathless
sentences is Gearty's.
[14] Ibid., p. xiii.

stopped ears. Later, discussing criticism of the European Court of Human Rights, Gearty observes acerbically that '[e]ven a serving Supreme Court judge, Lord Sumption, could not resist using a speech in Malaysia to knock the Court'.[15] Jonathan Sumption was (until December 2018) one of the most highly respected members of the UK's Supreme Court, and has articulated principled objections to aspects of Strasbourg's jurisprudence—as we have seen. To suggest, as Conor Gearty does here, that he criticised the court on cavalier impulse ('could not resist') or just for fun ('knock') is completely without foundation and unfairly, even insultingly dismissive.

To his credit, Lord Lester does not indulge in caricature. Instead, however, having stated the critics' objections to human rights, he tends to leave them completely unanswered, apparently assuming that their wrong-headedness will be patently obvious to the reader. Thus at one point he writes:

> The way we protect human rights is under sustained attack. Politicians and sections of the press...complain that it hampers governments in tackling terrorism and serious crime. They decry rulings preventing deportation to a country where there is a risk of torture or the death penalty. They object when a court rules that bed and breakfast owners must not refuse to accommodate a gay couple. They blame the Human Rights Act when our soldiers are made to account for complicity in torture. They accuse the Strasbourg Court of undermining democracy by being too activist and overriding our sovereign Parliament.[16]

For almost all of the complaints listed here I have some sympathy, and to me their wrong-headedness is not immediately obvious. Indeed, with regard to the last one I have given an extensive explanation of why I think it justified in Chapter 10. The only complaint with which I do not align myself is the one against British soldiers being made to account for their complicity in torture. How could I possibly object to that? How could anyone object? Certainly, as Chapter 10 showed, neither of the two Policy Exchange reports on the military impact of recent Strasbourg and UK jurisprudence—both of which were published before Lord Lester's book[17]—complained about British troops being held to account, prosecuted, and convicted of complicity in torture. Their concerns were quite different, but of those Lester makes no mention. As for the other complaints he lists, he does not dignify them with a response.

The same pattern is repeated twenty-five pages later, when Lester claims that '[o]ur system has come under increasing onslaught...from political opportunists

---

[15] Ibid., p. 102.   [16] Lester, *Five Ideas*, p. 14.
[17] *The Fog of Law* appeared in 2013, *Clearing the Fog of Law* in 2015, and Lord Lester's *Five Ideas* in 2016.

supported by right-wing newspapers that have made "human rights" dirty words'.[18] (Observe how describing the critics as 'political opportunists' absolves the author from having to take why they say what they say with any rational seriousness.) What the critics complain of is the Strasbourg court's judicial 'activism', one publicly controversial example of which is its ruling in *Hirst v. United Kingdom* (2005). In this case John Hirst, a convicted murderer, appealed to the European Convention to challenge English law's ban on all convicted prisoners from voting in parliamentary and local elections while in custody. Strasbourg found the ban 'arbitrary and disproportionate', but permitted the UK the 'margin of appreciation'—that is, room for discretion—in choosing how to comply with its ruling.[19] Nevertheless, Lester reports, Hirst's victory 'aroused fury among opponents of the Court, on the left and right of British politics'.[20] My own view of this case is that there are decent arguments to be made on both sides and that there is, accordingly, room for reasonable people to take opposing views. Therefore, I think that the Strasbourg court was presumptuous and unwise to decide to override the British legislature, and deserved the irritation it attracted. However, the relevant point here is not the rights or wrongs of the court's judgement, but rather Lord Lester's complete lack of curiosity as to why its critics reacted as they did, not only on the political right, but also, by his own admission, *on the political left*. Maybe he knew why; but if he did, he kept it entirely to himself.

The kind of public defence of human rights offered by Conor Gearty, Anthony Lester, and Shami Chakrabarti involves several problems: its general contempt for politicians and civil servants is arrogant and unjustified; where it is not deaf to the critics, or dismissive of them, it is unfair to them; and it does nothing to augment the rationality of public debate, instead eroding civility and exacerbating political polarisation. As a result, their defence of rights is a poor one, since, instead of wooing the critics, they alienate them—instead of paying them the respect of taking their views seriously and trying to persuade them, they indulge in caricature, insult, and neglect. No doubt this delights the already converted, but it does nothing to rescue rights from the doubt of sceptics. A strong defence is always a just one, and the strongest is charitable to boot. It takes what the critics say seriously, treats it accurately, and seeks to understand why they say it. Where the critics are unclear or ambiguous, the defence makes the strongest construction of their position, not the weakest. Then it sets about crafting a response that, through its respect, justice, and charity, wins trust and keeps hostile ears open, and then through its careful argument persuades. It has been said of Barack Obama that, when he used to practise as an attorney, he would always open his argument by summarising the opposition's case with scrupulous accuracy, fairness, and generosity, and *only then* set about dismantling it to devastating effect. The

[18] Lester, *Five Ideas*, p. 39.   [19] Ibid., p. 43.   [20] Ibid., p. 44.

human rights lawyers under review here would have done better, had they taken Obama's courtroom practice as the model for their public promotion of rights. They would have been well advised to listen more carefully, give credit where credit is due, and offer genuinely thoughtful answers, had they really wanted to convert the sceptics rather than just excite the prejudices of their own tribe.[21]

V

Given their role as advocates, their single-minded focus on the plight of vulnerable individuals, their tendency toward contempt for and caricature of politicians and civil servants, and their consequent disinclination to give the views of their opponents serious attention, it will come as no surprise that our human rights lawyers show no sympathy for those burdened with the responsibilities of government. In particular, they express no appreciation of the fragility of national or public security or of the difficulty of maintaining it. It seems that either they consider it unimportant, or they take it entirely for granted, or they assume that responsibility for it lies elsewhere.

For example, in her discussion of the Prevention of Terrorism (Control Order) Bill, which was introduced to Parliament in February 2005 by the government of Tony Blair, Shami Chakrabarti shows herself incapable of sympathetic grasp of the motives and reasons of those supporting it. The history of the bill is as follows. Two months after the terrorist attacks in the USA on 11 September 2001, the UK Parliament had passed the Anti-terrorism, Crime and Security Act 2001. Under this law foreigners suspected of terrorism could be interned without trial, if they could not be deported to their native country for fear of being subject to torture or

---

[21] It might be thought that the rights-rhetoric of the three lawyers under scrutiny in this chapter is eccentric, or that my criticism is born of ignorance of the legal profession. If so, let me point out that many of my complaints were anticipated over quarter of a century ago by an eminent academic member of the profession, Mary Ann Glendon, Learned Hand Professor of Law at Harvard University. In *Rights Talk* (1991), Glendon wrote as follows: 'A large legal profession whose most visible members habitually engage in strategic exaggeration and overstatement already was having a substantial effect on popular discourse in Tocqueville's day'; 'Courtroom law talk ... rests on an assumption that is not generally to be commended for civil conversation' (ibid., p. 44); 'In the common enterprise of ordering our lives together, much depends on communication, reason-giving, and mutual understanding. Even the legal profession is beginning to question the utility and legitimacy of the traditional strategic adoption of extreme positions by lawyers' (ibid., p. 45); 'Our stark, simple rights dialect puts a damper on the processes of public justification, communication, and deliberation upon which the continuing vitality of a democratic regime depends. It contributes to the erosion of the habits, practices, and attitudes of respect for others that are the ultimate and surest guarantors of human rights. It impedes creative long-range thinking about our most pressing social problems. Our rights-laden public discourse easily accommodates the economic, the immediate, and the personal dimensions of a problem, while it regularly neglects the moral, the long-term, and the social implications' (ibid., p. 171); 'The predilection for exaggeration and absoluteness that all of us often indulge when speaking of rights seems recognisably related to the strategic use of language by courtroom performers, hardball negotiators, takeover artists, and other zealous advocates ready to go to almost any lengths on behalf of a client or a cause' (ibid., p. 175).

WHAT'S WRONG WITH (SOME) HUMAN RIGHTS LAWYERS?   317

the death penalty, and so without violating their rights under the Human Rights Act 1998. Several individuals were interned on the ground of evidence that was either inadmissible in court or unusable in open court, lest secret intelligence operations be compromised. The internees were nevertheless free to leave, on condition that they departed the country altogether, which some did. In late 2004 the Appellate Committee of the House of Lords, then the court of last resort, ruled that the 2001 Act was contrary to the Human Rights Act, because it was unlaw-fully discriminatory in applying to foreign nationals only. This meant that the government's power of internment would expire in March 2005. In response, the Blair government introduced the Prevention of Terrorism (Control Order) Bill, which would allow 'control orders' to be issued against British citizens as well as foreign nationals, thus restoring the legality of internment.

I make no comment on the rights or wrongs of the legislation as such. My interest is only in the way that Shami Chakrabarti treated it. Those who opposed the bill she writes of with respect, and often quotes, sometimes at length. Those who supported the bill, however, receive nothing but disdainful short shrift. During the parliamentary process the government conceded a number of amend-ments, including one that required each control order to be authorised by a judge. This Chakrabarti describes, with supercilious world-weariness, as 'the now entirely predictable presentational trick of co-opting the judiciary into a one-sided secret process'.[22] The implication is that judges cannot be expected to maintain their integrity, impartiality, and independence of judgement: that is why the concession was a mere 'presentational trick'. This unflattering view is confirmed by her comment elsewhere on the case of Karamjit Singh Chahal, an Indian national who was detained in 1990, pending deportation, on suspicion of involvement in Sikh separatist terrorism. In such 'national security' cases, Chakrabarti tells us, 'proper appeals were replaced by a paper review by retired judges (often referred to as "three wise men") over lunch in the House of Lords'.[23] Observe the disparaging picture drawn: old, conservative members of the estab-lishment ('retired...."wise men"...Lords') treating appeals against detention without trial with a nonchalant lack of seriousness ('over lunch'). A similar picture is implied a few pages later in a discussion of the Special Immigration Appeals Commission Act of 1997, which sought to implement the greater legal scrutiny in 'national security' cases required by the Strasbourg court's judgement in *Chahal v. UK* (1996).[24] According to the Act, the appellant and his lawyer would appear at a tribunal, opposite a lawyer from the Home Office, and before a senior judge and two other commission members. Should the Home Office wish to present secret intelligence as evidence, however, the Commission could withhold 'full

---

[22] Chakrabarti, *On Liberty*, p. 50.   [23] Ibid., p. 12.
[24] European Court of Human Rights, Grand Chamber, *Chahal v. United Kingdom* (Application 70/ 1995/576/662), 11 November 1996.

particulars' of the reasons for the detention and exclude the appellant and his lawyers, as well as the press and public, from some of its proceedings, in order to preserve the secrecy of intelligence operations. In such circumstances, a Special Advocate would be appointed to represent the appellant and test the government's case. This arrangement, which represents a compromise between the need to protect agents of the security services and the need for appellants to test the case against them, and which satisfies Strasbourg's requirements, Chakrabarti chooses to dismiss as 'a secret chat with a judge'.[25]

So far readers could be forgiven for concluding that Shami Chakrabarti has a generally dim view of the judiciary and its integrity. But, in fact, such a conclusion would be mistaken, for when judges agree with her, her view suddenly brightens. Thus when a majority of the judicial committee of the House of Lords found against the government in *A and Others v. Secretary of State for the Home Department* (2004),[26] she becomes almost generous in praising them for relying on 'the cold forensic, legal logic that senior judges do so much better than politicians and campaigners'.[27] And when she wants to counter the complaint of politicians that the Human Rights Act 1998 surrendered too much parliamentary sovereignty to 'unelected judges', she rediscovers the virtues of the judiciary and leaps to their defence: 'But haven't we seen case after case of independent judges doing vital work in holding our politicians to account?'[28] It seems, then, that when judges oppose government, they are paragons of relentless reason and independent judgement; but when they cooperate in a judicial arrangement designed to protect the work of the secret intelligence agencies, even the lives of their agents, they automatically degenerate into lackeys of the political establishment.

To be fair, at one point Chakrabarti does appear to accept that the 1997 Act that created the Special Immigration Appeals Commission was '[i]nevitably an imperfect compromise'. She even acknowledges that '[n]o doubt the [intelligence] agencies would argue that to reveal this detail [i.e. secret intelligence] would somehow risk identifying the undercover agent or informant who ran the café or also attended breakfast as a mole with the terrorist cell'.[29] But then she proceeds to point out 'the obvious flaw in this fudge', namely, that once the Special Advocate has seen the secret intelligence, he is not allowed to communicate with the appellant, who therefore cannot 'demonstrate that she was on the other side of the world... at just the time of the alleged sighting'.[30] So what she seemed to accept as an inevitably imperfect compromise has now become just 'a creative wheeze... to replace centuries-old fair criminal traditions—where you know the case against you and face a public trial in front of your peers—with administrative

---

[25] Chakrabarti, *On Liberty*, p. 15.
[26] *A and Others v. Secretary of State for the Home Department* (2004) UKHL 56. This is commonly referred to as the 'Belmarsh 9 case'.
[27] Chakrabarti, *On Liberty*, p. 45.   [28] Ibid., p. 143.   [29] Ibid., pp. 13–14.
[30] Ibid., p. 14.

law "immigration style" as a means of locking people up indefinitely without trial, charges or even a police interview'.[31] How did she argue that the inevitable imperfection of the compromise was unacceptably imperfect? She did not argue at all. She merely raised the supercilious eyebrow of habitual doubt at the intelligence agencies' claim about risk to their agents—the claim that the revelation of secret intelligence would 'somehow' risk identifying the undercover agent. For her doubt, she did not pause to offer reasons.

Conor Gearty shares Shami Chakrabarti's politically partisan ambivalence toward judges. Defending the courts and their treatment of rights against their conservative critics, he writes:

> Viewed in the round, what these various cases on social and economic as well as political rights show are benches of judges—both here and in Strasbourg—seeking on a case-by-case basis to make the correct call, often asserting the rights of the individual against the state it is true, but also (especially in the former field) coming down on the other side, in the process of doing so fortifying a controversial state action with a veneer of human rights protection.[32]

The word 'veneer' suggests that Gearty does not approve of those occasions when the courts have found in favour of the state. That impression deepens when he goes on to speak of the judicial 'legitimization' of 'what might otherwise have been thought to have been anti-libertarian action by government: "kettling", detaining, expelling, and so on', and when, in the next sentence, he describes such state action as '(broadly speaking) "illiberal"'.[33]

Gearty takes his habitual hostility toward the state up onto the global stage when he turns to 'military aggression', which, he tells us, has been 'legitimized' in international law in two ways. The first is through Article 51 of the UN Charter, which

> has been turned into a vehicle for the justification of international aggression...and...has received lip-service so increasingly perfunctory that the disguise of legality was hard to maintain with a straight legal face, even for international lawyers gloomily familiar (as they all must be) with the need to accommodate legal norms to the situation on the unforgiving ground of national

---

[31] Ibid., p. 15.   [32] Gearty, *On Fantasy Island*, pp. 121–2.

[33] Ibid., p. 122. It is true that Gearty is ambiguous here. The qualification of 'anti-libertarian' by the clause 'what might otherwise have been thought to have been', and the adornment of 'illiberal' with inverted commas, could be read as meaning that, in the light of the courts' judgements, he accepts that the state's conduct was not *really* anti-libertarian or illiberal. This charitable interpretation is undermined, however, by his critical description of the judgement of the Strasbourg court in *Austin v. United Kingdom* (2012) 55 EHRR 359, which sanctioned the 'kettling' of protesters. It was, he writes, 'a rather contrived analysis' (Gearty, *On Fantasy Island*, pp. 120–1). 'Kettling' is a method of crowd control used by the police, which involves confining demonstrators to a small area, sometimes for long periods.

interest that is their main field of work. Where there is power, there will always be a lawyer tasked with delivering a legal justification, and this can usually be achieved with enough plausibility to provide some diversionary noise while force does its work.[34]

The second means of legitimising military aggression has been 'by the spirit of human rights itself, lurking with the U.N. and selectively available to be picked from and used whenever sovereign power demands', whose moral force has been deployed 'as a cover to justify military aggression abroad and even a little bit of "necessary evil" towards one's enemies wherever one finds them'.[35] Once again we observe the thoughtless cynicism about states, which are basically all about 'national interest' and 'power', and only use the law 'selectively' as 'cover' for their 'aggression'. I describe this cynicism as thoughtless, because it assumes that national interest, power, force, aggression, and selectivity are all necessarily morally wrong. But is it really wrong for a state to act in the national interest of the physical security of millions of its own citizens? Does the national interest never take the form of maintaining moral self-respect and international reputation by suffering the costs of military intervention to rescue foreign innocents from atrocious oppression? Is it immoral for a state to use its power in such a way? Is the 'necessary evil' of force never really necessary? When military power is deployed to defend the innocent abroad, is it not simplistic, misleading, and perhaps even disingenuous to describe it merely as 'aggression'? And since no state has the power to save the innocent everywhere, since democratic states cannot always muster popular support for faraway military operations, and since sometimes the risks would be imprudently high, surely states must be— *and should be*—selective in their overseas interventions?[36] It does not seem to have occurred to Gearty that sometimes the strict, black letter of international law, combined with the threat of veto by one of the Permanent Five members of the UN Security Council, serves to shield states engaged in perpetrating atrocious injustice against their own people on a massive scale, by forbidding any other states to intervene. That is why government lawyers sometimes have to be creative in appealing to other sources of international law—and indeed to natural morality—to justify humanitarian intervention, that is to say, military intervention to uphold what we might call the rights of the innocent. Even if, having contemplated the tension between the constraints of strict legality and the duties of morality, one were to conclude that it is always best to abide by the law, some appreciation of the moral dilemma facing government ministers and their lawyers,

---

[34] Gearty, *On Fantasy Island*, p. 57.   [35] Ibid., pp. 56–7.
[36] I have discussed the ethics of military intervention and the morality of national interest elsewhere, most notably in *In Defence of War* (Oxford: Oxford University Press, 2013), chapter 6, and 'After Iraq: When to Go to War?' (London: Policy Exchange, 2016).

and of the disturbing impossibility of any perfect resolution, would be appropriate. But all that Professor Gearty can muster is yet another expression of self-righteous disdain for those burdened with the responsibilities of government.

On other occasions, the problem is not disdain, just a complete indifference to the concerns of public servants. Again on the topic of military intervention overseas, Gearty turns to the European Court of Human Rights' judgement in *Al-Skeini*, which was the subject of our analysis in Chapter 10. He quotes approvingly from Judge Bonello's blistering concurring opinion, and summarises the significance of the ruling as clarifying that, 'if a country decides to engage militarily outside the jurisdiction [of the Convention] then it must do so in the knowledge that it has taken its human rights obligations as well its weapons along for the ride'.[37] He reports that, in this case and others, 'the reach of the Convention into military conduct abroad has drawn the ire of the generals and their supporters in government and the press'.[38] He even shows some grasp of why their ire was drawn by quoting the British Army's Chief of Staff, Sir Nicholas Carter, as warning in 2016 that legal actions against soldiers 'could undermine Britain on the battlefield' by creating a risk-averse military culture.[39] Beyond this point, however, Gearty shows no interest at all in the generals' concerns.[40] He describes their alarm merely as an instance of the controversy that the Convention can generate 'when it reaches out to those vulnerable to state power wherever they happen to be';[41] and in what follows his attention is fixed completely upon the benefits that accrue to individuals, when the courts breach the legal immunity traditionally accorded public authorities such as the armed forces, and make them liable for negligence—as they did in *Catherine Smith* (2010) and *Smith* (2013).[42] He does not challenge the grounds of anxiety about the damage to military culture and success; nor does he argue that, while the worry is well founded, the damage is of no importance. It seems, therefore, that Gearty accepts that the expansion of the rights of individuals does damage the efficacy of public bodies such as the armed forces, but regards that as entirely someone else's problem. The idea that the social good might sometimes justify letting individuals be exposed to greater risks is never entertained.

VI

This is because Conor Gearty is, in practice, a rights-fundamentalist—like Shami Chakrabarti. In theory they acknowledge that only a few rights—such as those

---

[37] Gearty, *On Fantasy Island*, p. 159.   [38] Ibid., p. 160.   [39] Ibid., pp. 161–2.

[40] Gearty gives no sign that he has read either *The Fog of Law* or *Clearing the Fog of Law*, even though both were published (2013 and 2015, respectively) before his book (2016). This is despite the fact that he is aware of 'the right-leaning think tank' that produced them, Policy Exchange (*On Fantasy Island*, pp. 17 n. 1, 18–19), and of one of *Clearing*'s authors, Richard Ekins (ibid., p. 211 n. 33).

[41] Ibid., p. 161.   [42] Ibid., pp. 162, 169–70.

against torture and slavery—are absolute. Most are not. Thus Chakrabarti writes that

> [w]hile we cherish our privacy, liberty, free expression and association rights among so many others, few of us would suggest that they can ever be completely absolute or unqualified. So we argue for any interference with these rights to be proportionate rather than counterproductive to the threats we seek to address.[43]

Similarly, Gearty recognises that there may be departures from 'mainstream' rights, but that these must be proportionate to the deleterious impact of the right affected.[44] Indeed, he goes so far as to say that proportionality 'is the engine at the heart of the whole human rights project'. However, rather than thinking of proportionality in terms of the rational justification of the limitation of a right or its suspension *in terms of the claims of the social good*, he tells us that 'a major factor in assessing the proportionality of an intrusion into a right will often be whether or not the individual affected has been treated properly as an individual, his or her situation properly understood'.[45] This is part of the truth, of course. As we saw in Chapter 11, the issue in *Carter* was whether or not the law should be refined so as to allow individuals in highly distressing conditions the freedom— the right—to choose (or rather, demand) physician-assisted suicide or voluntary euthanasia. But in order to decide that issue a way must be found to deliberate rationally about the interests of the individual *in relation to the competing interests of society*, and to adjudicate between them. This adjudication between *both* sets of interests is the crux of the matter, and yet Gearty's eyes never really manage to focus on the social good at all. And, as we have seen, whenever the courts have ruled in favour of the state, rather than the individual, he never fully accepts the judgement as proportionate and therefore justified, but always insinuates that it is somehow wrong ('illiberal'). We find in him the same fundamental resistance to having rights accommodate themselves to circumstances—or, to be more precise, the moral counter-claims that circumstances sometimes occasion—that we have already witnessed in Judge Bonello and Human Rights Watch. Notwithstanding his acknowledgement of the possibility of the proportionate (and therefore justified) limitation of rights, Gearty tells us that 'the need to accommodate legal norms to the situation on the unforgiving ground of national interest' produces a mere 'disguise of legality' and is reason for lawyerly gloom;[46] and that adhering to 'the ethical position' is the opposite of being 'pragmatic (hypocritical)'.[47] Shami Chakrabarti is no different. At one moment, as we have seen, she admits that our privacy, liberty, free expression, and association rights are not absolute, but at the

---

[43] Chakrabarti, *On Liberty*, p. 95. [44] Gearty, *On Fantasy Island*, p. 138. [45] Ibid., p. 141.
[46] Ibid., p. 57. [47] Ibid., p. 95.

next she asserts that our freedoms, not only from torture, but also 'of conscience, speech, and association', are 'non-negotiable'.[48]

VII

Human rights lawyers have a vitally important role to play in standing up for vulnerable individuals against the negligence or impatience, if not exactly the malice, of the state. Given their courtroom role as advocates, their professional stance will necessarily tend to be assertive of the rights of individuals and critical of government constraints of freedom or lack of care. Nonetheless, it remains true that the strongest case is always one that strains to be just and charitable toward the opposition, and whose criticism therefore tells forcefully against the real target, not a straw man. So when public advocacy for the individual involves habitual cynicism toward government, and a constantly deaf ear to its genuine concerns, it is poor advocacy. It is poor, because it can only succeed in delighting the already converted; it cannot persuade the sceptical.

Moreover, it is widely acknowledged, even by human rights lawyers, that very few rights are absolute and unconditional. If that is so, then it follows that there are circumstances when it would be proportionate for rights to be limited or suspended, or not to be extended. In those circumstances, an injustice would be done, if rights were *not* limited or suspended, or if they *were* extended. Therefore, human rights lawyers should be willing to put their minds to thinking about what those circumstances would be, and actually to recognise them when they obtain, instead of treating every concession to circumstance as if it were a grubby betrayal of principle. A defence of rights that fully accepted that 'inevitably imperfect compromise' sometimes really is inevitable, that acknowledged that sometimes the claims of the social good really do justify exposing individuals to greater risk, would be a more honest defence, and so much the stronger for it.

---

[48] Chakrabarti, *On Liberty*, p. x.

Conclusion

I

There is much that is right with rights. Paradigmatically, a right is a social institution designed to secure an important element of human flourishing—that is, a good. It achieves this through a combination of the assertion of authority and the threat of punishment.[1] The authority is that of 'law', which comes in the form either of a treaty, a statute, a custom, or a social norm.[2] Punishment ranges from the deprivation of life or liberty to social opprobrium. A right gives an individual or a social body the power to appeal through law to international, national, or social authorities, in order to defend their possession of a good against a threat. The security offered by law can be more or less strong—strongest in the form of treaty or statute, weakest in the form of custom or social norms.

Since the goal of human flourishing is common to all who share in the constant nature of human being, its basic elements or goods are universal. If we make the reasonable assumption that no society has ever existed that did not try to secure at least some basic goods, then we may say that the phenomenon of a right is universal. Certainly, there is historical and empirical evidence that it has not been confined to modernity or to the West. It has appeared throughout history and around the world in substance, if not in name. However, while the general phenomenon is universal, the specific forms it takes are not. Not every society recognises the full range of goods. All societies value some goods more highly than others, and chosen priorities differ across them. In some cases, resources are available to provide maximal security to a wide range of basic and derivative rights; in other cases, available resources can only secure some rights, and sometimes only at the weakest level, through an appeal to the authority of social norms and the threat of social opprobrium. Since no society commands infinite resources, each must decide which rights to secure and how far. And since none can secure any right absolutely, the taking of risks cannot be avoided.

Pace culturally conservative or declinist critics, rights need not be conceived in egoistic, individualist terms. Indeed, since any right implies a corresponding duty, and since every right-holder will be a duty-bearer to other people, rights create a social nexus. And since a society will be happier if every member does his duty to

---

[1] I use the word 'punishment' broadly to mean any penalising sanction.

[2] As I explained in Chapter 5, note 2, I think that prevalent public opinion alone is too patchy and unstable to provide the minimum of security requisite for a right.

others, then rights, which remind and press us all to do our duty, promote social flourishing. Further, rights can be held by social bodies as well as individuals. Further still, as we have seen in the case of the right against torture, a right's rationale can incorporate considerations of the social good and the risks posed to it.

Finally, of course, human rights, which enjoy a measure of international legal status, are powerful means of holding states to account—although the ways of invoking them can be more or less prudent.

II

All of that is right with rights. What is wrong with them? One basic mistake is to conceive of rights as fundamental to ethical deliberation. Of course, once natural morality has determined that a legal right should be granted, that right will be a fundamental element of subsequent legal deliberation or jurisprudence. It will be taken as given. Law, however, is not the same as natural morality. Indeed, natural morality is prior to law, since, if that were not so, there could be no such thing as an unjust law and no justification for breaking it. And natural morality operates with a variety of concepts—human flourishing and its component goods, duty, virtue, motive, intention, culpable negligence, proportionality, consequences, and the principle that duty presupposes feasibility. At the end of a process of deliberation, natural morality might authorise the granting of a legal right in a particular set of political, social, cultural, and economic circumstances. Such a right will be the conclusion, not the premise, of ethical deliberation. The problem with 'rights-fundamentalism', therefore, is that it conflates morality with legality, reducing the former to the latter. It then proceeds to take rights as given, and by asserting at the beginning what is properly a conclusion, pre-empts and shuts down ethical deliberation. That is why rights-talk has the tendency to push all other moral considerations off the table.[3]

What is more, by substituting what is paradigmatically a legal concept for the whole of ethics, rights-talk makes it very difficult to recognise that what may be rightly claimed *morally* is usually subject to a greater number of qualifying conditions, which might or might not obtain. For example, the legal rights to freedom of speech and expression often permit all manner of immoral behaviour—gratuitous insult, wilful provocation, malicious misrepresentation,

---

[3] Therefore, while I applaud Michael Ignatieff for wanting to puncture '[t]he...illusion...that human rights is above politics, a set of moral trump cards whose function is to bring political disputes to closure and conclusion', I cannot agree with him that 'the fundamental moral commitment entailed by rights' is to deliberation (*Human Rights as Politics and Idolatry*, p. 84), and that therefore human rights-talk can help to reconcile political partisans (ibid., p. 21). Rights-talk can only do this if it ceases to be only rights-talk. Rights-talk alone shuts down the necessary ethical deliberation.

and gross unfairness. The legal rights are permissive, partly because some kinds of wrongdoing are not easily justiciable, partly because they are too trivial to warrant the expense of judicial proceedings, and partly to limit excessive state intrusion. Morally, however, gratuitous insult, etc. are forbidden. So, whether or not *it is morally right* that I speak or express myself is conditional upon my exercising the virtues of self-restraint, charity, justice, and fairness. *Whether or how* I should exercise my legal rights is conditional upon these moral considerations. Mistaking law for ethics obscures all this.

That is the main reason why I have concluded that it is misleading to talk of natural, moral rights. The paradigmatically legal concept of a right implies that what I have a right to—say, a liberty—lies securely in my possession, thanks to the support of social institutions, provided I do not transgress permissive boundaries, and except in rare political circumstances that might justify suspension. Morally, however, my possession is far more insecure, since it depends on contingencies such as my meeting obligations of virtue. It also depends on other, empirical contingencies such as the feasibility of the corresponding duties, economic circumstances, and political stability. For these reasons, therefore, it is less misleading to talk in terms of 'all-things-considered rightness' than of 'natural rights'—to say that, 'here and now, it is morally right' that I should speak freely and others are obliged not to hinder me, rather than to say, baldly, that I 'have a natural right to freedom of speech'. The position I have arrived at here is very close to that already occupied by Edmund Burke.

III

The post-war international declarations, covenants, and conventions sometimes acknowledge that most human rights may be suspended in case of grave threats to public order or national security. In so doing they implicitly recognise the legal paradigm of rights, which assumes claims that are more or less secured by stable, powerful social institutions. However, the fundamentalist view that regards rights as ethically fundamental, and forgets their legal paradigm, cannot recognise this political and economic contingency. That was why human rights bodies kept on scolding the post-genocide government of Rwanda for not complying with Western standards of a fair trial, even though they themselves virtually admitted that such compliance was not possible in the circumstances.

That was also why the European Court of Human Rights saw fit to extend Convention rights to a territory occupied by British troops, even though their judgement implicitly admitted that the situation was one of near-anarchy and that the 'effective control' of the military was almost non-existent. Without any demurral, the court even quoted Lord Justice Sedley, when he wrote that, while 'it sits ill in the mouth of a state which has helped to displace and dismantle by force another nation's civil authority to plead that, as an occupying power, it had so little control that it cannot be responsible for securing the population's basic rights... *the fact is that it cannot*'.[4] David Ritchie's Burkean judgement damns the Strasbourg court's: 'whoever appeals to an abstract justice that is incompatible with the continuance of orderly social organisation is... talking nonsense—and mischievous nonsense too.'[5]

IV

Because legal rights are properly the conclusion of an all-things-considered process of ethical deliberation, their rationale will often incorporate consideration of a range of morally relevant factors, including that of social costs and risks. Judgements about what costs are worth shouldering and what risks are worth taking cannot be technical or scientific, will be controversial, and should therefore be open to revision. Reasonable views will often be found on both sides of the argument, and whatever decision is made, it will not be beyond rational challenge. Therefore, it is very important that the body which makes the controversial decision is politically accountable, if its decision is to be tolerated by those on the losing side of the argument at any one time.

That is the most important reason why elected legislatures are better placed than courts to decide whether or not certain rights—such as those to assisted suicide and voluntary euthanasia—should be granted. For then those on the losing side of the decisive vote will be able to console themselves that at least their views have been heard, and that the opportunity to reverse the decision still lies open to them. The bitterness of defeat will be easier to swallow, trust in the fairness of the process will be maintained, and confidence in democratic politics will survive.[6] By contrast, if a court should take it upon itself to decide the matter, citizens will have reason to feel subjected to the tyranny of a judicial oligarchy, whose fundamentalist conviction and 'progressive' zeal has presumed to propel them to overlook their professional myopia and run far ahead of their professional expertise.

V

Fundamentalism not only makes for imprudent jurisprudence, but also infects rights advocacy and undermines its plausibility. As Lord Sumption has observed, '[s]ingle-interest pressure groups, which stand behind a great deal of public law

---

[4] *Al-Skeini*, para. 80.   [5] Ritchie, *Natural Rights*, p. 106.
[6] I was first alerted to this important point by Christopher Eberle in *Religious Conviction in Liberal Politics* (Cambridge: Cambridge University Press, 2002), pp. 104–8.

litigation in the UK and the US, have no interest in policy areas other than their own'.[7] The reason for this is that they assume that the particular rights for which they contend are absolute, impervious to conditions. Accordingly, they do not think that their assertion of such rights needs reference to anything else, since they should be established, *regardless*.

Such a view is not confined to groups. For example, at the June 2018 meeting of the Pontifical Academy for Life, the Roman Catholic moral theologian Lisa Sowle Cahill lamented the fact that 'the world has fallen short in its responsibility for the health and well-being of children, especially girl children, and their mothers', mainly because 'most of the world's societies' suffer from a 'lack of political will'.[8] In response, she urged that the welfare of children and mothers be made 'a practical priority, as well as a legally and politically recognized obligation'.[9] While she herself did not speak explicitly of the 'rights' of children and mothers, she did appeal to Catholic social teaching's recognition of such rights, and she did not demur when her respondent, Laura Palazzani, interpreted her to be asserting 'the fundamental human rights to life and health, the rights of children, and the rights of women'.[10]

There is no doubt that that health and welfare of children and mothers across the globe are very important goods that deserve protection and promotion. However, there are many other goods—some of them equally or perhaps even more important—that deserve protection and promotion. Moreover, some very important goods cannot sensibly be made the subject of a right—for example, national security. Unlike single-interest lobbyists and bodies, however, governments bear the unenviable responsibility of having to decide how to allocate finite resources to secure which rights and goods, and to what degree. They have to work within the unyielding limits of material, financial, and political feasibility. No government can give all rights equal priority; every government has to make compromises.[11] But Professors Cahill and Palazzani, riding high on rights-fundamentalism and professionally unburdened by the responsibility to make any political compromises, saw no need to rein in their moralistic lamentation and exhortation.

Behind rights-fundamentalism appears to lie a secularised version of biblical religion. On the one hand, shining with hope for the ultimate and universal

---

[7] Sumption, 'The Limits of Law', p. 26.

[8] Lisa Sowle Cahill, 'Ethics of "Coming into the World"', in Vincenzo Paglia and Renzo Pegoraro, eds, *Equal Beginnings. But Then? A Global Responsibility*, Proceedings of the XXIV General Assembly of Members of the Pontifical Academy for Life (Rome: Pontifical Academy for Life, 2018), p. 83.

[9] Cahill, 'Ethics of "Coming into the World"', p. 88.

[10] Ibid., pp. 85–7; Laura Pallazani, 'Commentary on the Paper, "The Ethics of Coming into the World" by Lisa S. Cahill', in Paglia and Pegoraro, *Equal Beginnings*, p. 96.

[11] Referring to the rights created by the ICESCR, Eric Posner comments: 'States that seek to satisfy these rights [to work, health care, education, and social welfare] must make tradeoffs. Because states have limited resources, money used to provide health care comes from education, or vice-versa' (*The Twilight of Human Rights Law*, p. 87).

triumph of justice, there is the admirable commitment to the cause of the disadvantaged and the injured, which was so pronounced in the tradition of the Hebrew prophets, to which Jesus belonged. On the other hand, believing neither in God, nor the world-to-come, nor the sin that lies *in here* rather than *over there*, it displays an impatient, utopian rigidity that refuses to compromise with facts, acknowledge the inevitability of risk, and reckon with tragedy. So, when it meets those who do take on the public burden of managing such things honestly, it treats them with a self-righteous, uncharitable, finger-wagging condescension.

VI

The unhappy consequences of this rights-fundamentalism are several. First, by pushing a wider range of moral considerations off the table at the beginning, it makes it difficult to voice the vital importance of the duties of virtue and the need of deliberate virtue-formation. Of course, legal rights imply duties: my right is your duty, as yours is mine. But if my claim-right is to be effective, apart from socially expensive recourse to the courts, you have to be *capable* of respecting it. No doubt, the fear of punishment will go some way to generating such respect, but, being externally compelled, that will be at most grudging and weak. And even then, your natural interest in self-preservation could easily be overwhelmed by your hurt pride, political contempt, or racial hatred. Your irritable passions could so overwhelm your prudence as to goad you into taking the risk of violating my right. So how will you become the kind of person who is capable of fulfilling your duty to respect my right? How will you acquire the necessary virtues of self-restraint? Further, as a legal right-bearer, I have a moral responsibility to assert my right against you well rather than badly. It might be that you have a legal duty to respect my right to express myself, even when I insult, misrepresent, and provoke you—but I have a moral duty not to abuse my legal right by abusing you. Indeed, whatever the law permits me, I have no *moral* right to abuse you at all. How, then, will I become the kind of person capable of exercising my legal rights virtuously, that is, in accordance with larger, moral right?[12] Further still, sometimes the question of duties of virtue arises outside the terms of rights altogether. Sometimes, I have a duty to show and give you what you do not deserve and have no right to at all—say, compassion and forgiveness. In all these ways,

---

[12] The Orthodox moral theologian Vigen Guroian puts the point thus: 'If repentance and forgiveness do not fill the brittle shell of this ethical and legal formalism, how can sinful human beings resist turning their claims to human rights into swords of vengeance or into injurious pretexts for self-aggrandizement? What is to prevent even the championing of the rights of the oppressed from becoming an exercise in self-righteous self-magnification?' ('Human Rights and Modern Western Faith: An Orthodox Christian Assessment', in Elizabeth Bucar and Barbra Barnett, eds, *Does Human Rights Need God?* (Grand Rapids, Mich.: Eerdmans, 2005), p. 47).

therefore, the issues of virtue and of its formation arise alongside that of rights, and sometimes quite apart from it. Liberal society cannot live on rights alone; indeed, rights cannot survive on rights alone. That rights-fundamentalism obscures this is one of its most corrosive ill-effects.

Another unhappy effect is that rigidly imprudent, dogmatically unrealistic rhetoric undermines the authority and credibility of rights. If the best that advocates can do is stridently insist that rights be upheld in bone-headed defiance of infeasibility, the need to take higher or lower risks, and the inevitability of tragic choices, then it should not surprise them when those burdened with the responsibility to decide to do what *can* be done grow deaf to their criticism and display a 'lack of political will'. And if international judges insist on asserting universal, fundamental rights in proud disregard for political realities, and at risk of precipitating an anarchical state of nature where rights of any kind are maximally insecure, it should not surprise them that national clamour grows to reject the court's authority altogether. A secure civil society can afford to wait and punish the groom for not shutting the stable-door after the horse has escaped. But in an insecure society, whose stability depends on the horse's escape being prevented in the first place, '[t]his is a luxury which cannot be indulged in'.[13]

A third ill-effect of rights-fundamentalism, whether judicial or philosophical, is that, when applied to military affairs, it places unreasonable and demoralising burdens on troops, and undermines their military effectiveness. And since it is only liberal governments that pay attention to rights-rhetoric, partly because they half-believe it and partly for electoral reasons, it is only *their* militaries that are weakened. Thus, rights-fundamentalism increases the prospect of the military victory of the enemies of liberal rights. Not for the first time, David Ritchie spoke wisely, when he wrote: '[t]he principle that there is an inalienable and imprescriptible right in all men to preserve their lives, however much social utility may demand the sacrifice of some lives ... would lead to a rapid disappearance of the civilised men who adopted such a principle before barbarians who did not...'[14]

Fourth, the presumptuousness of 'progressive' judges in deducing novel, debatable, and controversial rights from highly abstract, 'fundamental' charter rights— or in dogmatically extending normal, civil rights to abnormal, uncivil places—will tend to undermine the democratic legitimacy of the law and thus its effective social authority. It will make national courts the target of political scepticism and animosity, and foster the kind of bitter, polarised 'culture wars' that are now so visible in the United States.[15] And it will corrode fragile national confidence in international courts.

---

[13] Simpson, *Human Rights and the End of Empire*, p. 55. See further, Chapter 10, note 145.

[14] Ritchie, *Natural Rights*, p. 120.

[15] It seems that similar unhappy political effects have been manifest in Canada, too, for several decades. According to Judy Fudge, Professor of Law at the University of Kent and Adjunct Professor at the University of Victoria, British Columbia, since the entrenchment of the Canadian Charter of Rights

Finally, several factors combine to cause rights to proliferate. One is the assumption that rights are fundamental and so impervious to variation in morally significant circumstances—with the result that some rights are granted, or maintained at a level of security, which should not be. Another is the fundamentalist zeal of 'progressive' rights advocates and judges, for whom the multiplication and extension of rights is always reason for celebration. Yet another cause of proliferation is the excessively abstract and indeterminate nature of some charter rights that afford adventurous judges ample room for prolific creativity. A fourth cause is that rights have been let loose from their primary, political purpose. This is Noel Malcolm's thesis, and I find it persuasive.[16] Historically, resort to rights-talk has usually been provoked by the need to fend off unjust political interference, whether by popes, kings, emperors, or invading foreigners. English history attests this, of course, in Magna Carta, the Petition of Right, and the 1688 Bill of Rights. So does the history of the United States, where the rhetorical appeal to fundamental, universal, natural rights in the 1774 Declaration of Rights by the First Continental Congress really functioned to endow with moral authority the rebels' particular demands for protection against King George III's taxing, billeting of troops, and suspension of trial by jury.[17] It is true, too, of the assertion of human rights after 1945, which was initially provoked by the manifest need to invoke supra-positive moral authority against the murderous, racist laws of a totalitarian state like the Nazi one. And it is true of the European Convention of Human Rights, whose original purpose was to protect democracy against totalitarian tyranny.[18] Since the adoption by the UN of the International Covenant on Economic, Social, and Cultural Rights in 1966, however, human rights have been made to expand well beyond their original, political territory to become a proliferating vehicle of the ambition to liberate the world from poverty and suffering and to advance global equality.

But why is all this a problem? Proliferation as such is a problem, insofar as rights are often burdensome to uphold. This means that the more finite resources are spent on securing rights, the less are available for other important public purposes. But because rights are thought to be fundamental, the costs and risks of

---

and Freedoms in 1982, and over two decades during which judges have given concrete meaning to abstract rights, 'celebration of constitutional rights has turned to scepticism and the institutional legitimacy of the courts has been questioned', because of growing controversy about the relationship between judicially enforced rights and democracy ('The Canadian Charter of Rights: Recognition, Redistribution, and the Imperialism of the Courts', in Tom Campbell, K. D. Ewing, and Adam Tomkins, *Sceptical Essays on Human Rights* (Oxford: Oxford University Press, 2001), p. 335). In 1999 a poll showed that those Canadians questioned were evenly divided on the proposition that 'the right of the Supreme Court to decide certain controversial issues should be reduced' (ibid., p. 336), and right-wing 'populists' now criticise the Charter for shifting power to unaccountable judges, especially to decide moral matters involving family or sexuality (ibid., p. 337).

[16] Malcolm, *Human Rights and Political Wrongs*, p. 109.   [17] Ibid., p. 132.
[18] Ibid., pp. 134–5.

implementing them, and the necessary compromises involved, are imprudently overlooked and downplayed.[19] Next, and consequently, states are held to impossible standards, with the result that weary governments become increasingly deaf to utopian criticism, and the currency of rights-rhetoric declines in value through nagging overuse. Further, rights are multiplied in a vain attempt to abolish risk, the impossibility of which is an ever-fruitful source of thoughtless frustration that clamours for yet more multiplication. As a result, the room for the exercise of personal judgement, which has been one of the main satisfactions of professional life—and in soldiering remains vital for tactical success—has become increasingly constrained, the need to demonstrate compliance has become ever more oppressive and demoralising, and the power of the surveillance state has increased. Finally, there is the ironic undermining of rights' primary *raison d'être*: the protection of democracy itself. As Malcolm has written of the European Convention, its real purpose was 'not to enter the nooks and crannies of local life, not to serve as an all-purpose device to correct minor injustices, not to develop questionable doctrines to enable the generation of rights at an ever greater level of detail, and above all not to undermine democracy by taking more and more areas of policy-making out of the hands of democratic legislatures'.[20] But this is what the Strasbourg court is now doing. And, as we saw in Chapter 11, it is not alone.

VII

That is what is wrong with rights—with certain ways of thinking and talking about them. What is it, then, that needs to change? In brief, we all need to abandon rights-fundamentalism.

Judges need to recognise that rights come at the end of a process of moral deliberation, if at all, not at the beginning. The question of whether a legal right should be granted at all, and with what level of security, cannot be answered without reference to such considerations as feasibility, cost, and risk. Our scrutiny of jurisprudence in relation to military cases in Chapter 10 revealed that it is possible for courts to recognise this, for we found there that the UK Supreme Court displayed a practical wisdom that the Strasbourg court saw fit to quote, but then, inexplicably, chose to ignore. Were it more fully understood that the moral rationale for rights

---

[19] Paul Collier suggests another reason for the oversight: that, since the 1970s, politicians have found it politically expedient to champion novel rights, while keeping quiet about the burdensome obligations needed to meet them. '[P]oliticians struggling to win elections began to find proclamations of new rights convenient... rights kept the obligations needed to meet them discretely offstage... rights may well be appropriate, but this can only be determined by a public discussion of the corresponding obligations. Detached from such an assessment, the process of teasing new rights from old texts is like printing money: individual rights shower down like banknotes' (*The Future of Capitalism* (London: Penguin, 2019), pp. 12–13, 45).

[20] Malcolm, *Human Rights and Political Wrongs*, p. 135.

requires politically controversial decisions about social costs and risks, international courts such as the one in Strasbourg would become much more sensitive to the fragility of its legitimacy in the eyes of national populations and accordingly more inclined to give national courts generous room for discretion (or 'margins of *appréciation*', as the Strasbourg court puts it).[21] And national courts would become much more cautious in exploiting the room for creative manoeuvre given them by charters of more or less abstract rights, and would restrain themselves from creating novel rights about which the legislature is better placed to decide.

However, should courts fail to be duly cautious, legislatures that have the constitutional right to ignore their judgements should have the courage to exercise it. Unlike the USA, where the Supreme Court's authority to 'strike down' unconstitutional legislation is final, the Canadian Charter of Rights and Freedoms contains a 'Notwithstanding' clause (Section 33), which permits the government to defy a court's ruling by declaring that legislation will operate in spite of certain Charter rights.[22] The UK's Human Rights Act altogether eschews the power to 'strike down' legislation. Instead, it gives judges only the authority of make a 'declaration of [legislative] incompatibility' with the Act, which empowers government ministers to change the incompatible law without parliamentary authorisation. A power is not a duty, however, and ministers are not obliged to use it: they may reject the court's 'ethical guidance'.[23] In practice, governments have naturally been reluctant to be seen to defy what has been sold as the ultimate moral authority of 'fundamental rights', and, indeed, they have sometimes been relieved to hand over to the courts the responsibility for imposing controversial laws.[24] However, in the light of the fact that so-called 'fundamental rights' are not

---

[21] Of the fragility of the legitimacy of an international court, Eric Posner writes: 'the difference between the Supreme Court [of the USA] and the ECHR [that is, the ECtHR] is that the Supreme Court is an American institution, staffed by American justices, who are appointed by American politicians. From the perspective of the UK or any of its other members, the ECHR is a foreign institution, staffed mostly by foreigners, who are appointed mainly by foreign politicians. While Americans feel that they can trust the Supreme Court to rule in the public interest, it is harder for the British to know whether the ECHR will rule in the UK's interest. The Supreme Court justices understand American cultural and political norms and live in the country to which their rulings apply. For the non-British members of the ECHR, the UK is a foreign country where people do things differently. Thus, American Supreme Court justices have more legitimacy for Americans than the ECHR judges have for the British' (*The Twilight of Human Rights Law*, p. 97). Posner also identifies a practical reason why the Strasbourg court should rein itself in: in 2012 the backlog of cases brought to it was more than 113,000 (ibid., p. 48).

[22] Such Section 33 overrides can only last five years, but they may be renewed.

[23] Conor Gearty, 'Spoils for which Victor? Human Rights within the Democratic State', in Gearty and Douzinas, *Cambridge Companion to Human Rights Law*, p. 224.

[24] Ibid., p. 222; Tom Campbell, 'Incorporation through Interpretation', in Campbell et al., *Sceptical Essays*, p. 81: 'At a time when judicially enforced "human rights" have, in the eyes of the public and the media, greater political legitimacy than the outcome of partisan electoral political processes, governments may not wish to subject themselves to the politically damaging opprobrium which would arise from their ignoring a declaration of incompatibility or legislating to negate a development in the common law that has been presented as necessary to bring existing law into line with the ECHR. Being mindful of the prospect of an appeal to the European Court of Human Rights, and relieved to hand over responsibility for imposing morally controversial laws to the courts, government are

ethically fundamental at all, and that courts have no special claim to ethical authority in deciding to invent new rights, governments should become much more confident in exercising their right to ignore a presumptuous court, and to regard their determinations as provisional rather than final.[25]

Rights advocates need to grasp the nettle of the conditionality of rights and the need for principled compromise. And instead of thoughtlessly banging the indignant, rhetorical drum of 'universal and fundamental rights', they should get down to the difficult business of demonstrating why *empirically, in these circumstances*, a certain right *can* be granted and secured, all things considered, and therefore should be. If they were to do that, their criticism would be responsible and charitable, and their exposure of a government's malevolent intransigence all the more cogent for it. Alternatively, if they cannot demonstrate that it would be possible or prudent to grant a right or a highly secure form of it, then they should have the honesty to say so.

Most of all, however, the rest of us in the rights-saturated West need to get beyond whatever it is that is tying our tongues over duty and virtue. Rights-talk is just not enough. It implies as much, of course, since legal rights must have correspondent legal duties. But legal right-holders are also subject to moral duties that determine how they should exercise their rights, and whether they should exercise them at all; and all legal duty-bearers need moral virtues that enable them to carry out their duties. These ideas are not unfamiliar to us, and it does not take very much reflection to bring them to the surface of consciousness. Nevertheless, for too long we have suppressed them, acquiescing in the lazy notion that law suffices to structure our public relations and that morality can and should be left at home. But this is not true. We cannot out-source all responsibility for governing relations between citizens to the police, the courts, and penal institutions. They lack sufficient resources, and even if they possessed them, the result would be an illiberal degree of state intrusion. So, in addition to law and legal rights, we need common moral norms that civil social bodies own, promote, and enforce. For the sake of the plausibility of rights-talk, the prudence of rights, and the possibility of respecting them, we need to muster the courage to own and affirm duty and virtue in public, as the history of pre-modern ethics shows we used to. And, if the whole truth be told, those ethics are actually not just pre-modern, for they continue to live among us today, contending for a sustainable, morally realist form of modernity—one that recognises *right* before it asserts and multiplies *rights*.

---

not . . . likely to challenge changes to the common law or interpretations of Acts of Parliament which are said to derive from the provisions of the ECHR'.

[25] Campbell, 'Incorporation through Interpretation', p. 99: 'courts should be regarded as having the right to make only provisional determinations of what it is that human rights asserted in the ECHR require us to do. These determinations may, with perfect propriety, be challenged and overturned by elected governments after public debate.'

Bibliography

Allan, James. 'The Effect of a Statutory Bill of Rights where Parliament is Sovereign: The Lesson from New Zealand'. In Tom Campbell, K. D. Ewing, and Adam Tomkins, eds, *Sceptical Essays on Human Rights*. Oxford: Oxford University Press, 2001.

Althusius, Johannes. *Dicaeologicae libri tres, totum et universum ius, quo utimur, methodice complectentes*. Herborn, 1617.

Ames, Roger T. 'Continuing the Conversation on Chinese Human Rights'. *Ethics and International Affairs*, 11 (1997).

Amnesty International. *Rwanda: Gacaca—A Question of Justice*. AI Index: AFR 47/007/ 2002. Amnesty International, 2002.

Angle, Stephen. *Human Rights and Chinese Thought: A Cross-Cultural Inquiry*. Cambridge: Cambridge University Press, 2002.

An-Naim, Abdullahi Ahmed and Francis M. Deng, eds. *Human Rights in Africa: Cross-Cultural Perspectives*. Washington, DC: Brookings Institution, 1990.

Aquinas, Thomas. *Summa Theologiae*. Blackfriars edn Vol. 38, 'Injustice' (2a2ae, 63–79). Ed., trans., and introd. Marcus Lefébre, OP. London: Eyre & Spottiswoode, 1975.

Ashford, Elizabeth. 'The Alleged Dichotomy between Positive and Negative Rights and Duties'. In Charles R. Beitz and Robert F. Goodin, eds, *Global Basic Rights*. New York: Oxford University Press, 2011.

Ashford, Elizabeth. 'The Duties Imposed by the Human Right to Basic Necessities'. In Thomas Pogge, ed., *Freedom from Poverty as a Human Right: Who Owes What to the Very Poor?* New York: UNESCO and Oxford University Press, 2007.

Arendt, Hannah. *Origins of Totalitarianism*. New York: Harcourt, Brace, Jovanovich, 1973.

Arnold, Matthew. *Mixed Essays*. London: Smith, Elder & Co., 1880.

Barber, N. W., Richard Ekins, and Paul Yowell, eds. *Lord Sumption and the Limits of Law*. Oxford and Portland, Ore.: Hart, 2016.

Bary, William Theodore de. *The Liberal Tradition in China*. New York: Columbia University Press, 1983.

Bauer, Joanne R. and Daniel A. Bell, eds. *The East Asian Challenge for Human Rights*. Cambridge: Cambridge University Press, 1999.

Beestermöller, Gerhard and Brunkhorst Hauke, eds. *Rückkehr der Folter: Der Rechtstaat im Zwielicht?* Munich: C. H. Beck, 2006.

Beevor, Antony. *D-Day: The Battle for Normandy*. London: Penguin, 2009.

Beitz, Charles R. 'Human Rights and the Law of Peoples'. In Deen Chatterjee, ed., *The Ethics of Assistance: Morality and the Distant Needy*. Cambridge: Cambridge University Press, 2004.

Beitz, Charles R. and Robert F. Goodin, eds. *Global Basic Rights*. New York: Oxford University Press, 2011.

Bekentnis und unterricht und vermanung der pfarrhern und prediger der christlichen kirchen zu Magdeburgk. Magdeburg, 1550.

Belgian Act on Euthanasia of May 28, 2002. European Journal of Health Law, 10 (2003).

Benn, Stanley I. 'Rights'. In Paul Edwards, ed., *The Encyclopedia of Philosophy*. New York & London: MacMillan, 1967.

Bentham, Jeremy. 'Anarchical Fallacies; being an examination of the Declaration of Rights issued during the French Revolution'. In Jeremy Waldron, introd. and ed., *Nonsense on Stilts: Bentham, Burke, and Marx on the Rights of Man*. London: Methuen, 1987.

Bentham, Jeremy. *Jeremy Bentham's Economic Writings*. 3 vols. Ed. W Stark. London: Allen and Unwin, 1952.

Bentham, Jeremy. 'Supply Without Burthen or Escheat *Vice* Taxation: Being a Proposal for a Saving of Taxes by an Extension of the Law of Escheat: Including Strictures on the Taxes on Collateral Succession, Comprised in the Budget on 7th December, 1795'. In Jeremy Waldron, introd. and ed., *Nonsense on Stilts: Bentham, Burke, and Marx on the Rights of Man*. London: Methuen, 1987.

Beuselinck, Benoit. '2002–2016: Fourteen Years of Euthanasia in Belgium: First-Line Observations by an Oncologist'. In D. A. Jones, C. Gastmans, and C. MacKellar, eds, *Euthanasia and Assisted Suicide: Lessons from Belgium*. Cambridge: Cambridge University Press, 2017.

Bew, John. 'The Real Origins of Realpolitik'. *The National Interest*, 130 (March/April 2014).

Bew, John. *Realpolitik: A History*. New York: Oxford University Press, 2016.

Beza, Theodore. *De Iure Magistratum* (1580). Ed. Klaus Sturm. Texte zur Geschichte der Evangelischen Theologie. Neukirchen-Vluyn: Neukirchener Verlag des Erziehungsvereins, 1965.

Beza, Theodore. (Bèze, Théodore de). *Du droit des Magistrats*. Ed. and introd. Robert M. Kingdon. Les Classiques de la Pensée Politique 7. Geneva: Librairie Droz, 1971.

Biggar, Nigel. 'Not Translation, but Conversation: Theology in Public Debate about Euthanasia'. In Nigel Biggar and Linda Hogan, eds, *Religious Voices in Public Places*. Oxford: Oxford University Press, 2000.

Biggar, Nigel. *Aiming to Kill: The Ethics of Suicide and Euthanasia*. London: Darton, Longman, and Todd, 2004.

Biggar, Nigel. *Behaving in Public: How to do Christian Ethics*. Grand Rapids, Mich.: Eerdmans, 2011.

Biggar, Nigel. 'Evolutionary Biology, "Enlightened" Anthropological Narratives, and Social Morality: A View from Christian Ethics'. *Studies in Christian Ethics*, 26/2 (2013).

Biggar, Nigel. *In Defence of War*. Oxford: Oxford University Press, 2013.

Biggar, Nigel. 'In Response'. *Soundings*, 97/2 (2014).

Biggar, Nigel. 'Individual Rights versus Common Security? Christian Moral Reasoning about Torture'. *Studies in Christian Ethics*, 27/1 (February 2014).

Biggar, Nigel. 'Imprudent Jurisprudence? Human Rights and Moral Contingency'. *Journal of Law and Religion*, 30/3 (October 2015).

Biggar, Nigel. 'In Defence of Just War: Christian Tradition, Controversies, and Cases'. *De Ethica: A Journal of Philosophical, Theological, and Applied Ethics*, 2/1 (2015).

Biggar, Nigel. 'In Response'. *Studies in Christian Ethics*, 28/3 (August 2015).

Biggar, Nigel. 'After Iraq: When to Go to War?' London: Policy Exchange, 2016.

Biggar, Nigel. 'Autonomy's Suicide'. *Newman Rambler*, 12 (Winter 2016).

Biggar, Nigel. '*Charlie Hebdo* Took Offensiveness too Far'. *The Times* (9 January 2016).

Biggar, Nigel. 'Compromise: What Makes it Bad?' *Studies in Christian Ethics*, 31/1 (February 2018).

Birnbacher, Dieter. 'Das Tötungsverbot aus der Sicht des klassischen Utilitarismus'. In Rainer Hegselman and Reinhard Merkel, eds, *Zur Debatte über Euthanasie*. Frankfurt am Main: Suhrkamp Verlag, 1991.

Black, Antony. 'Chapter 18: The Individual and Society'. In J. H. Burns, ed., *Cambridge History of Medieval Political Thought, c.350–c.1450*. Cambridge: Cambridge University Press, 1988.

Boer, Theo A. Covering letter to David Lucas, Quebec Regional Office, Department of Justice, Canada (13 August 2018).

Boer, Theo A. 'Euthanasia in the Netherlands in the Absence of a Foreseeable Death Criterion'. Expert Report for the Department of Justice, Government of Canada, Québec Regional Office (February 2018).

Bonald, Louisde. *Théorie du pouvoir politique et religieux dans la société civile, démontrée par le raisonnement et par l'histoire* (1796). In *Œuvres de M. de Bonald*. 2 vols. Paris: Librairie d'Adrien le Clere, 1854.

Brett, Annabel S. *Liberty, Right, and Nature: Individual Rights in Later Scholastic Thought.* Cambridge: Cambridge University Press, 2003.

Breuer, Clemens. 'Das Foltern von Menschen: Die Differenz zwischen dem Anspruch eines weltweiten Verbots und dessen praktischer Missachtung und die Frage der möglichen Zulassung der "Rettungsfolter"'. In Gerhard Beestermöller and Hauke Brunkhorst, eds, *Rückkehr der Folter: Der Rechtstaat im Zwielicht?* Munich: C. H. Beck, 2006.

Bromwich, David. *The Intellectual Life of Edmund Burke: From the Sublime and Beautiful to American Independence.* Cambridge, Mass.: Harvard University Press, 2014.

Browning, Don. 'The United Nations Convention on the Rights of the Child: Should it be Ratified and Why?' *Emory International Law Review*, 20 (2006).

Bucar, Elizabeth and Barbra Barnett, eds. *Does Human Rights Need God?* Grand Rapids, Mich.: Eerdmans, 2005.

Buchanan, Allen. *The Heart of Human Rights.* Oxford: Oxford University Press, 2015.

Burke, Edmund. 'Speech on Fox's East India Bill (1 December 1783)'. In Burke, *Writings and Speeches*, V: 'India: Madras and Bengal, 1774–1785'. Ed. Peter James Marshall and William B. Todd. Oxford: Clarendon Press, 1981.

Burke, Edmund. *Reflections on the Revolution in France.* Ed. Conor Cruise O'Brien. London: Penguin, 1984.

Burke, Edmund. 'Reflections on the Revolution in France (1790)'. In Burke, *The Writings and Speeches*, VIII: 'The French Revolution, 1790–1794'. Ed. L. G. Mitchell and William B. Todd. Oxford: Clarendon Press, 1989.

Burke, Edmund. 'Letter to Sir Hercules Langrishe (1782)'. In Burke, *Writings and Speeches*, IX: 'I. The Revolutionary War, 1794–1797; II. Ireland'. Ed. R. B. McDowell and William B. Todd. Oxford: Clarendon Press, 1991.

Burke, Edmund. 'Speech on Conciliation with America (22 March 1775)'. In Burke, *Writings and Speeches*, III: 'Party, Parliament, and the American War, 1774–1780'. Ed. Warren M. Elofson, John A. Woods, and William B. Todd. Oxford: Clarendon Press, 1996.

Burke, Edmund. 'Speech on Repeal of Test and Corporation Acts (2 March 1790)'. In Burke, *Writings and Speeches*, IV: 'Party, Parliament, and the Dividing of the Whigs, 1780–1794'. Ed. Peter James Marshall and Donald Bryant. Oxford: Clarendon Press, 2015.

Burke, Roland. *Decolonization and the Evolution of International Human Rights.* Philadelphia: University of Pennsylvania Press, 2010.

Bury, Patrick. *Callsign Hades.* London: Simon & Schuster, 2011.

Cahill, Lisa Sowle. 'Ethics of "Coming into the World"'. In Vincenzo Paglia and Renzo Pegoraro, eds, *Equal Beginnings. But Then? A Global Responsibility*, Proceedings of the XXIV General Assembly of Members of the Pontifical Academy for Life. Rome: Pontifical Academy for Life, 2018

Calo, Zachary. 'Catholic Social Thought, Political Liberalism and the Idea of Human Rights'. *Journal of Christian Legal Thought* (Fall 2011).

Camosy, Charles C. *Peter Singer and Christian Ethics: Beyond Polarization.* Cambridge: Cambridge University Press, 2012.

Campbell, Tom. 'Incorporation through Interpretation'. In Tom Campbell, K. D. Ewing, and Adam Tomkins, eds, *Sceptical Essays on Human Rights*. Oxford: Oxford University Press, 2001.

Campbell, Tom, K. D. Ewing, and Adam Tomkins, eds. *Sceptical Essays on Human Rights*. Oxford: Oxford University Press, 2001.

Chabot, Boudewijn. 'Verontrustende cultuuromslag rond de zelfgekozen dood'. *NRC Handelsblad* (16 June 2017): <https://www.nrc.nl/nieuws/2017/06/16/de-euthanasie-geestis-uit-de-fles-11123806-a1563406>.

Chakrabarti, Shami. *On Liberty*. London: Allen Lane, 2014.

Chakravarty, Anuradha. 'Gacaca Courts in Rwanda: Explaining Divisions within the Human Rights Community'. *Yale Journal of International Affairs* (Winter/Spring 2006).

Chambaere, K., R. Vander Stichele, F. Mortier, J. Cohen, and L. Delien. 'Recent Trends in Euthanasia and Other End-of-Life Practices in Belgium'. *New England Journal of Medicine*, 372/12 (19 March 2015).

Chan, Benny and Margaret Somerville. 'Converting the "Right to Life" to the "Right to Physician-Assisted Suicide and Euthanasia": An Analysis of *Carter v. Canada (Attorney General)*, Supreme Court of Canada'. *Medical Law Review*, 24/2 (Spring 2016).

Chan, Joseph. 'A Confucian Perspective on Human Rights for Contemporary China'. In Joanne R. Bauer and Daniel A. Bell, eds, *The East Asian Challenge for Human Rights*. Cambridge: Cambridge University Press, 1999.

Churchill, Winston. *Great Contemporaries*. London: Thornton Butterworth, 1937.

Clark, Phil. *The Gacaca Courts, Post-genocide Justice and Reconciliation in Rwanda: Justice without Lawyers*. Cambridge Studies in Law and Society. Cambridge: Cambridge University Press, 2010.

Cohen, Andrew. 'Must Rights Impose Enforceable Positive Duties?' *Journal of Social Philosophy*, 35 (2004).

Collier, Paul. *The Future of Capitalism*. London: Penguin, 2019.

Costa, J.-P. *La Cour européenne des droits de l'homme: des juges pour la liberté*. Paris: Dalloz-Sirey, 2013.

Cranston, Maurice. *What Are Human Rights?* London: Bodley Head, 1973.

Crisp, Roger, ed. *Griffin on Human Rights*. Oxford: Oxford University Press, 2014.

Crisp, Roger. 'Human Rights: Form and Substance'. In Crisp, *Griffin on Human Rights*. Oxford: Oxford University Press, 2014.

Cronin, Kieran. *Rights and Christian Ethics*. Cambridge: Cambridge University Press, 1992.

Cunningham, Cyril. 'Letter'. *The Times* (25 November 1971).

Danish Institute for Human Rights. *Legal Aid in Rwanda: A Report on the Legal Assistance Available in Rwanda*. Kigali: Danish Institute for Human Rights, April 2004.

Davis, Michael C. 'Adopting International Standards of Human Rights in Hong Kong'. In Davis, *Human Rights and Chinese Values: Legal, Philosophical, and Political Perspectives*. Hong Kong: Oxford University Press, 1995.

Davis, Michael C. 'Chinese Perspectives on Human Rights'. In Davis, *Human Rights and Chinese Values: Legal, Philosophical, and Political Perspectives*. Hong Kong: Oxford University Press, 1995.

Davis, Michael C., ed. *Human Rights and Chinese Values: Legal, Philosophical, and Political Perspectives*. Hong Kong: Oxford University Press, 1995.

Decosimo, David. 'Killing and the Wrongness of Torture'. *Journal of the Society of Christian Ethics*, 36/1 (Spring/Summer 2016).

Dembour, Marie-Bénédicte. *Who Believes in Human Rights? Reflections on the European Convention*. Cambridge: Cambridge University Press, 2006.

Dershowitz, Alan. *Why Terrorism Works*. New Haven: Yale University Press, 2002.

Dershowitz, Alan. 'The Torture Warrant: A Response to Professor Strauss'. *New York Law School Law Review*, 48 (2003).

Dershowitz, Alan. 'Tortured Reasoning'. In Sanford Levinson, ed., *Torture: A Collection*. Oxford: Oxford University Press, 2004.

De Wulf, Maurice. 'L'Individu et le groupe dans la scolastique du XIIIe siècle'. *Revue néo-scolastique de philosophie*, 22/88 (1920).

Dimbleby, Jonathan. *The Last Governor: Chris Patten and the Handover of Hong Kong*. Reprint. London: Pen & Sword, 2017.

Donnelly, Jack. 'Human Rights and Asian Values: A Defense of "Western" Universalism'. In Joanne R. Bauer and Daniel A. Bell, eds, *The East Asian Challenge for Human Rights*. Cambridge: Cambridge University Press, 1999.

Drooghenbroeck, S. van. *La Proportionnalité dans le droit de la Convention Européenne des Droits de l'Homme: prendre l'idée simple au sérieux*. Brussels: Publications des Facultés universitaires Saint-Louis, 2001.

Dutch Termination of Life on Request and Assisted Suicide (Review Procedures) Act, 28 November 2000: <http://www.ethical-perspectives.be/viewpic.php?LAN=E&TABLE=EP&ID=58> (as at 22 April 2019).

Dworkin, Ronald. 'Social Sciences and Constitutional Rights—the Consequences of Uncertainty'. *Journal of Law and Education*, 6/1 (1977).

Dworkin, Ronald. 'Do We Have a Right to Pornography?' In Dworkin, *A Matter of Principle*. Cambridge, Mass.: Harvard University Press, 1985.

Dworkin, Ronald. *Freedom's Law: The Moral Reading of the American Constitution*. Oxford: Oxford University Press, 1996.

Dworkin, Ronald. *Taking Rights Seriously*. New edition. London: Bloomsbury, 1997.

Eberle, Christopher. *Religious Conviction in Liberal Politics*. Cambridge: Cambridge University Press, 2002.

Eckel, Jan. 'The Rebirth of Politics from the Spirit of Morality: Explaining the Human Rights Revolution of the 1970s'. In Jan Eckel and Samuel Moyn, eds, *The Breakthrough: Human Rights in the 1970s*. Philadelphia: University of Pennsylvania Press, 2014.

Ekins, Richard. 'Legislation as Reasoned Action'. In Grégoire Webber, Paul Yowell, Richard Ekins, Maris Köpcke, Bradley W. Miller, and Francisco J. Urbina, *Legislated Rights: Securing Human Rights through Legislation*. Cambridge: Cambridge University Press, 2018.

Ekins, Richard, Jonathan Morgan, and Tom Tugendhat. *Clearing the Fog of Law: Saving our Armed Forces from Defeat by Judicial Diktat*. London: Policy Exchange, 2015.

El-Obaid, Ahmed El-Obaid and Kwadwo Appiagyei-Atua. 'Human Rights in Africa—a New Perspective on Linking the Past to the Present'. *McGill Law Journal*, 1 (1996).

European Court of Human Rights, Grand Chamber. *Ireland v. United Kingdom* (Application no. 5310/71), 18 January 1978.

European Court of Human Rights, Grand Chamber. *Golder v. United Kingdom* (1979–80), 1 EHRR.

European Court of Human Rights, Grand Chamber. *Chahal v. The United Kingdom* (Application no. 70/1995/576/662), 11 November 1996.

European Court of Human Rights, Grand Chamber. *Banković and Others v. Belgium and 16 Other Contracting States* (Application no. 52207/99), 12 December 2001.

European Court of Human Rights, Grand Chamber. *Pretty v. United Kingdom* (Application no. 2346/02) (2002) 35 EHHR 1, 29 July 2002.

European Court of Human Rights, Grand Chamber. *Al-Jedda v. The United Kingdom* (Application no. 27021/08), 7 July 2011.

European Court of Human Rights, Grand Chamber. *Al-Skeini and Others v. The United Kingdom* (Application no. 55721/07), 7 July 2011.

Faigman, David. *Constitutional Fictions: A Unified Theory of Constitutional Facts*. New York: Oxford University Press, 2008.

Feinberg, Joel. 'Pornography and the Criminal Law'. In D. Copp and S. Wendell, eds, *Pornography and Censorship*. Buffalo, NY: Prometheus, 1983.

Feinberg, Joel. *Offense to Others*. Oxford: Oxford University Press, 1985.

Feinberg, Joel. *Harm to Self*. Oxford: Oxford University Press, 1986.

Feinberg, Joel. *Problems at the Roots of Law: Essays in Legal and Political Theory*. New York: Oxford University Press, 2002.

Feinberg, Joel. 'In Defense of Moral Rights'. In Feinberg, *Problems at the Roots of Law: Essays in Legal and Political Theory*. New York: Oxford University Press, 2002.

Fernyhough, Timothy. 'Human Rights and Precolonial Africa'. In Ronald Cohen, Goran Hyden, and Winston P. Nagan, eds, *Human Rights and Governance in Africa*. Gainesville: University of Florida Press, 1993.

Finnis, John. *Natural Law and Natural Rights*. Clarendon Law Series. Oxford: Clarendon Press, 1980.

Finnis, John. *Moral Absolutes: Tradition, Revision, and Truth*. Washington, DC: Catholic University of America Press, 1991.

Finnis, John. 'Human Rights and their Enforcement' (1985). In *Human Rights and Common Good*, Collected Essays: Volume III. Oxford: Oxford University Press, 2011.

Finnis, John. 'A British "Convention Right" to Assistance in Suicide?'. *Law Quarterly Review*, 131 (January 2015).

Finnis, John. 'Judicial Power: Past, Present, and Future'. Policy Exchange Judicial Power Project lecture, Gray's Inn Hall (20 October 2015): <https://judicialpowerproject.org.uk/john-finnis-judicial-power-past-present-and-future>. Accessed 18 September 2018.

Finnis, John. 'Judicial Law-Making and the "Living" Instrumentalisation of the ECHR'. In N. W. Barber, Richard Ekins, and Paul Yowell, eds, *Lord Sumption and the Limits of Law*. Oxford and Portland, Ore.: Hart, 2016.

Fisher, Jonathan. *Rescuing Human Rights*. London: Henry Jackson Society, 2012.

Forster, Anthony. 'British Judicial Engagement and the Juridification of the Armed Forces'. *International Affairs*, 88/2 (2013).

Fortin, Ernest L. '"Sacred and Inviolable": *Rerum Novarum* and Natural Rights'. *Theological Studies*, 53 (1992).

Fortin, Ernest L. 'On the Presumed Medieval Origin of Individual Rights'. *Communio*, 26 (Spring 1999).

Fredman, Sandra. 'Living Trees or Deadwood: The Interpretive Challenge of the European Convention on Human Rights'. In N. W. Barber, Richard Ekins, and Paul Yowell, eds, *Lord Sumption and the Limits of Law*. Oxford and Portland, Ore.: Hart, 2016.

Freeman, Michael. *Edmund Burke and the Critique of Political Radicalism*. Oxford: Basil Blackwell, 1980.

Friedrich, Carl Joachim. 'Introductory Remarks'. In Johannes Althusius, *Politica Methodice Digesta*. Ed. Carl Joachim Friedrich. Harvard Political Classics, Vol. II. Cambridge, Mass.: Harvard University Press, 1932.

Fudge, Judy. 'The Canadian Charter of Rights: Recognition, Redistribution, and the Imperialism of the Courts'. In Tom Campbell, K. D. Ewing, and Adam Tomkins, eds, *Sceptical Essays on Human Rights*. Oxford: Oxford University Press, 2001.

Gardner, John. 'Simply in Virtue of Being Human: The Whos and Whys of Human Rights'. *Journal of Ethics and Social Philosophy*, 2/2 (February 2008).

Gearty, Conor. *On Fantasy Island: Britain, Europe, and Human Rights*. Oxford: Oxford University Press, 2016.

Gearty, Conor. 'Spoils for which Victor? Human Rights within the Democratic State'. In Gearty and Costas Douzinas, eds, *Cambridge Companion to Human Rights Law*. Cambridge: Cambridge University Press, 2012.

Gearty, Conor and Costas Douzinas, eds. *Cambridge Companion to Human Rights Law*. Cambridge: Cambridge University Press, 2012.

Gerson, Jean. 'De Potestate Ecclesiastica'. In *Œuvres complètes* VI: 'L'Œuvre ecclésiologique'. Ed. P. Glorieux. Paris: Desclée, 1965.

Gibbons, William J. *Seven Great Encyclicals*. Introd. William J. Gibbons, SJ. New York: Paulist Press, 1963.

Ginbar, Yuval. *Why Not Torture Terrorists? Moral, Practical, and Legal Aspects of the 'Ticking Bomb' Justification for Torture*. Oxford: Oxford University Press, 2008.

Glendon, Mary Ann. *Rights Talk: The Impoverishment of Political Discourse*. New York, Free Press, 1991.

Goodin, Robert. 'The Development–Rights Trade-off: Some Unwarranted Economic and Political Assumptions'. *Universal Human Rights*, 1/2 (April–June 1979).

Goodman, Christopher. *How Superior Powers Ought to be Obey'd*. Geneva: John Crispin, 1558; Amsterdam: Theatrum Orbis Terrarum, 1972.

Griffin, James. *On Human Rights*. Oxford: Oxford University Press, 2008.

Griffiths, John. 'The Slippery Slope: Are the Dutch Sliding Down or Are They Clambering Up?' In David Thomasma, Thomasine Kimbrough-Kushner, Gerrit Kimsma, and Chris Ciesielski-Carlucci, eds, *Asking to Die: Inside the Dutch Debate about Euthanasia*. Dordrecht: Kluwer, 1998.

Griffiths, John, Alex Bood, and Helen Weyers. *Euthanasia and the Law in the Netherlands*. Amsterdam: Amsterdam University Press, 1998.

Gross, Michael L. *Moral Dilemmas of Modern War: Torture, Assassination, and Blackmail in an Age of Asymmetric Conflict*. Cambridge: Cambridge University Press, 2010.

Grotius, Hugo. *The Rights of War and Peace*. 3 vols. Ed. Richard Tuck. Indianapolis: Liberty Fund, 2005.

Guess, Raymond. *History and Illusion in Politics*. Cambridge: Cambridge University Press, 2001.

Guroian, Vigen. 'Human Rights and Modern Western Faith: An Orthodox Christian Assessment'. In Elizabeth Bucar and Barbra Barnett, eds, *Does Human Rights Need God?* Grand Rapids, Mich.: Eerdmans, 2005.

Guthrie, Charles, et al. 'Combat Zones'. *The Times* (7 April 2015).

Haakonssen, Knud. *Natural Law and Moral Philosophy: From Grotius to the Scottish Enlightenment*. Cambridge: Cambridge University Press, 1996.

Haakonssen, Knud. 'The Moral Conservatism of Natural Rights'. In Ian Hunter and David Saunders, eds, *Natural Law and Civil Sovereignty: Moral Right and State Authority in Early Modern Political Thought*. Basingstoke and New York: Palgrave, 2002.

Halliday, Fred. 'Relativism and Universalism in Human Rights: The Case of the Islamic Middle East'. *Political Studies*, 43 (1995).

Hart, H. L. A. 'Are there any Natural Rights?' In Jeremy Waldron, ed., *Theories of Rights*. Oxford Readings in Philosophy. Oxford: Oxford University Press, 1984.

Hehir, J. Bryan. 'The Modern Catholic Church and Human Rights: The Impact of the Second Vatican Council'. In John Witte and Frank Alexander, eds, *Christianity and Human Rights: An Introduction*. Cambridge: Cambridge University Press, 2010.

Helmholz, R. R. 'Human Rights in the Canon Law'. In John Witte and Frank Alexander, eds, *Christianity and Human Rights: An Introduction*. Cambridge: Cambridge University Press, 2010.

Herbert, Nick. 'Human Rights Act: The Law that has Devalued your Human Rights'. *The Daily Telegraph* (9 November 2008).

Heron, C. P. 'The Juridification of the British Armed Forces'. United Kingdom Defence Academy Research Paper, Advanced Command and Staff Course 16. Unpublished, 2013.

High Court of Australia. *Shaw Savill & Albion Co. Ltd v. Commonwealth*, 66 CLR 344, 5 December 1940.

High Court of Ireland. *Fleming v. Ireland & Ors*, IEHC 2, 10 January 2013.

Hobbes, Thomas. *Leviathan*. Ed. M. Oakeshott. New York: Collier, 1962.

Hobbes, Thomas. *Leviathan*. Ed. and introd. C. B. MacPherson. Harmondsworth: Penguin, 1968.

Hollenbach, David. *Claims in Conflict: Retrieving and Renewing the Catholic Human Rights Tradition*. New York: Paulist Press, 1979.

Hountondji, Paulin. 'The Master's Voice—Remarks on the Problem of Human Rights in Africa'. In *Philosophical Foundations of Human Rights*. Paris: UNESCO, 1986.

Howard, Rhoda E. 'Group Identity versus Individual Identity in the African Debate on Human Rights'. In Abdullahi Ahmed An-Naim and Francis M. Deng, eds, *Human Rights in Africa: Cross-Cultural Perspectives*. Washington, DC: Brookings Institution, 1990.

Human Rights Watch. *Justice Compromised: The Legacy of Rwanda's Community-Based Gacaca Courts*. New York: Human Rights Watch, 2011.

Human Rights Watch/Africa. *World Report 1996: Rwanda*. New York: Human Rights Watch, 1996.

Hyde, Edward, Earl of Clarendon. *The History of the Rebellion*. Ed. and introd. Paul Seaward. Oxford World's Classics. Oxford: Oxford University Press, 2009.

Ibhawoh, Bonny. 'Cultural Relativism and Human Rights: Reconsidering the Africanist Discourse'. *Netherlands Quarterly of Human Rights*, 19/1 (2001).

Ignatieff, Michael. *Human Rights as Politics and Idolatry*. Princeton: Princeton University Press, 2001.

Insole, Christopher J. 'Burke and Natural Law'. In David Dwan and Christopher J. Insole, eds, *The Cambridge Companion to Edmund Burke*. Cambridge: Cambridge University Press, 2012.

Insoue, Tatsuo. 'Liberal Democracy and Asian Orientalism'. In Joanne R. Bauer and Daniel A. Bell, eds, *The East Asian Challenge for Human Rights*. Cambridge: Cambridge University Press, 1999.

International Court of Justice. *Advisory Opinion on the Legal Consequences of the Construction of a Wall in the Occupied Palestinian Territory* (9 July 2004).

Jackson, Robert. *The Struggle for Judicial Supremacy: A Study of a Crisis in American Power Politics*. New York: Alfred Knopf, 1941.

Jennings, Jeremy. *Revolution and the Republic: A History of Political Thought in France since the Eighteenth Century*. Oxford: Oxford University Press, 2011.

Jones, David Albert. 'A Submission to the External Panel on Options for a Legislative Response to Carter v. Canada' (30 October 2015).

Kannyo, Edward. *Human Rights in Africa: Problems and Prospects*, a report prepared for the International League for Human Rights (May 1980).

Keck, T. M. 'Does the Court Follow the Election Returns?' *Reviews in American History*, 32 (2004).

Kennedy, Helena. *Just Law: The Changing Face of Justice and Why It Matters to Us All.* London: Vintage, 2004.

Kenny, J. 'The Advantages of a Written Constitution Incorporating a Bill of Rights'. *Northern Ireland Legal Quarterly*, 30 (1979).

Keown, John. *Euthanasia, Ethics, and Public Policy: An Argument against Legalisation.* Cambridge: Cambridge University Press, 2002.

Keown, John. 'A Right to Voluntary Euthanasia? Confusion in Canada in Carter'. *Notre Dame Journal of Law, Ethics, and Public Policy*, 28/1 (2014).

Ketcham, Ralph. *James Madison: A Biography.* Charlottesville: University of Virginia, 1990.

Kirk, Russell. 'Burke and Natural Rights'. *The Review of Politics*, 13/4 (October 1951).

Koskenniemi, Martti. 'The Lady Doth Protest Too Much': Kosovo and the Turn to Ethics in International Law'. *The Modern Law Review*, 65/2 (March 2002).

Kramer, Matthew. 'How Law Protects Dignity'. *Cambridge Law Journal*, 71 (2012).

Kramer, Matthew. *Torture and Moral Integrity: A Philosophical Enquiry.* Oxford: Oxford University Press, 2014.

Kraynack, Robert P. *Christian Faith and Modern Democracy: God and Politics in a Fallen World.* Notre Dame: University of Notre Dame, 2001.

Kukavica, Jaka and Veronika Fikfak. 'Strasbourg's U-Turn on Independence as Part of an Effective Investigation under Article 2'. Cambridge Faculty of Law Legal Studies Research Paper no. 60/2105. Cambridge: University of Cambridge Faculty of Law, 2015.

Lee Kuan Yew. Interview in *International Herald Tribune* (9–10 November 1991).

Lee Kuan Yew. 'Democracy, Human Rights and the Realities'. Speech in Tokyo (10 November 1992).

Lee Seung-hwan. 'Liberal Rights or/and Confucian Virtues?' *Philosophy East and West*, 46/3 (July 1996).

Legge, Dominic. 'Do Thomists Have Rights?' *Nova et Vetera*, 17/1 (2019).

Le May, G. H. L. *British Supremacy in South Africa, 1899–1907.* Oxford: Clarendon Press, 1965.

Lester, Anthony. *Five Ideas to Fight For: How our Freedom is under Threat and why it Matters.* London: Oneworld, 2016.

Letsas, George. 'The ECHR as a Living Instrument: Its Meaning and its Legitimacy' (March 2012): <http://ssrn.com/abstract=2021836>.

Levinson, Sanford, ed. *Torture: A Collection.* Oxford: Oxford University Press, 2004.

Lewy, Guenter. *Assisted Death in Europe and America: Four Regimes and their Lessons.* New York: Oxford University Press, 2011.

Lindsnaes, Birgit, Tomas Martin, and Lisbeth Arne Pedersen. *Partners in Progress: Human Rights Reform and Implementation.* Second edition. Copenhagen: Danish Institute for Human Rights, 2007.

Little, David. *Essays on Religion and Human Rights: Ground to Stand on.* Cambridge: Cambridge University Press, 2016.

Lock, F. P. *Edmund Burke,* I: *1730–1784.* Oxford: Clarendon Press, 1998.

Lock, F. P. *Edmund Burke,* II: *1784–1797.* Oxford: Clarendon Press, 2006.

Locke, John. 'An Essay Concerning the True Original, Extent, and End of Civil Government' ('Second Treatise'). In *Two Treatises of Civil Government.* Introd. W. S. Carpenter. London: J. M. Dent, 1924.

Luban, David and Henry Shue. 'Mental Torture: A Critique of Erasures in U.S. Law'. *Georgetown Law Journal*, 100 (2012).

McDonald, Margaret. 'Natural Rights'. In Jeremy Waldron, ed., *Theories of Rights,* Oxford Readings in Philosophy. Oxford: Oxford University Press, 1984.

McHarg, Aileen. 'Reconciling Human Rights and the Public Interest: Conceptual Problems and Doctrinal Uncertainty in the Jurisprudence of the European Court of Human Rights'. *The Modern Law Review*, 62 (1999).

MacIntyre, Alasdair. *After Virtue*. Notre Dame: University of Notre Dame Press, 1981.

MacIntyre, Alasdair. 'Community, Law, and the Idiom and Rhetoric of Rights'. *Listening: Journal of Religion and Culture*, 5 (1991).

McMahan, Jeff. 'Torture in Principle and Practice'. *Public Affairs Quarterly*, 22/2 (April 2008).

McMahan, Jeff. *Killing in War*. Oxford: Clarendon Press, 2009.

Macpherson, C. B. *The Political Theory of Possessive Individualism: Hobbes to Locke*. Oxford: Clarendon Press, 1962.

Malcolm, John. *Malcolm: Soldier, Diplomat, Ideologue of British India*. Edinburgh: John Donald, 2014.

Malcolm, Noel. *Human Rights and Political Wrongs: A New Approach to Human Rights Law*. London: Policy Exchange, 2017.

Mamdani, Mahmood. 'The Social Basis of Constitutionalism in Africa'. *The Journal of Modern African Studies*, 28/3 (1990).

Maritain, Jacques. *The Rights of Man and Natural Law*. London: Geoffrey Bles, 1944.

Maritain, Jacques. 'Introduction'. In UNESCO, *Human Rights: Comments and Interpretations*. London and New York: Allan Wingate, 1949.

Maritain, Jacques. 'On the Philosophy of Human Rights'. In UNESCO, *Human Rights: Comments and Interpretations*. London and New York: Allan Wingate, 1949.

Marlowe, John. *Milner, Apostle of Empire*. London: Hamish Hamilton, 1976.

Marozzi, Justin. *Baghdad: City of Peace, City of Blood*. London: Allen Lane, 2014.

Matscher, Franz. 'Methods of Interpretation of the Convention'. In R. St J. Macdonald, F. Matscher, and H. Petzold, eds, *The European System for the Protection of Human Rights*. Dordrecht: Martinus Nijhoff, 1993.

Milbank, John. 'Against Human Rights: Liberty in the Western Tradition'. In Conor Gearty and Costas Douzinas, *The Meanings of Rights*. London and New York: Allan Wingate, 1949.

Miller, Bradley W. 'Majoritarianism and Pathologies of Judicial Review'. In Grégoire Webber, Paul Yowell, Richard Ekins, Maris Köpcke, Bradley W. Miller, and Francisco J. Urbina, *Legislated Rights: Securing Human Rights through Legislation*. Cambridge: Cambridge University Press, 2018.

Mintz, Samuel. *The Hunting of Leviathan: Seventeenth-Century Reactions to the Materialism and Moral Philosophy of Thomas Hobbes*. Cambridge: Cambridge University Press, 1962.

Montero, Etienne. 'The Belgian Experience of Euthanasia Since its Legal Implementation in 2002'. In D. A. Jones, C. Gastmans, and C. MacKellar, eds, *Euthanasia and Assisted Suicide: Lessons from Belgium*. Cambridge: Cambridge University Press, 2017.

Montlosier, Comte de. *Essai sur l'art de constituer les peuples; ou Examen des opérations constitutionnelles de l'Assemblée nationale de France*. 2nd edn. Paris: Gattey, 1791.

Mowbray, Alastair. 'The Creativity of the European Court of Human Rights'. *Human Rights Law Review*, 5/1 (January 2005).

Moyn, Samuel. *Christian Human Rights*. Philadelphia: University of Pennsylvania Press, 2015.

Mutua, Makau. 'The Banjul Charter and the African Cultural Fingerprint: An Evaluation of the Language of Rights and Duties'. *Virginia Journal of International Law*, 35/1 (1995).

Mutua, Makau. 'Limitations in Religious Rights: Problematizing Religious Freedom in the African Context'. *Buffalo Human Rights Law Review*, 5 (1999).

Mutua, Makau. *Human Rights: A Political and Cultural Critique*. Philadelphia: University of Pennsylvania Press, 2008.

Nagel, Thomas. *Mind and Cosmos: Why the Materialist Neo-Darwinian Conception of Nature is Almost Certainly False*. New York: Oxford University Press, 2012.

Ng, Margaret. 'Are Rights Culture-bound?' In Michael C. Davis,ed., *Human Rights and Chinese Values: Legal, Philosophical, and Political Perspectives*. Hong Kong: Oxford University Press, 1995.

Nowak, Manfred. 'What's in a Name? The Prohibitions on Torture and Ill Treatment Today'. In Conor Gearty and Costas Douzinas, eds, *Cambridge Companion to Human Rights Law*. Cambridge: Cambridge University Press, 2012.

Oakley, Francis. 'Locke, Natural Law, and God: Again'. *History of Political Thought*, 17 (1997).

Oakley, Francis. *Natural Rights, Laws of Nature, Natural Rights: Continuity and Discontinuity in the History of Ideas*. New York: Continuum, 2005.

Oakley, Francis and Elliot Urdang. 'Locke, Natural Law, and God'. *Natural Law Forum*, 11 (1966).

O'Brien, Terence H. *Milner: Viscount Milner of St James's and Cape Town, 1854–1925*. London: Constable, 1979.

O'Connell, Mary Ellen. *The Power and Purpose of International Law: Insights from the Theory and Practice of Enforcement*. New York: Oxford University Press, 2008.

O'Donovan, Joan Lockwood. 'Historical Prolegomena to a Theological Review of "Human Rights"'. *Studies in Christian Ethics*, 9/2 (1996).

O'Donovan, Joan Lockwood. 'Rights, Law, and Political Community: A Theological and Historical Perspective'. *Transformation*, 20/1 (January 2003).

O'Donovan, Oliver. *The Desire of the Nations: Rediscovering the Roots of Political Theology*. Cambridge: Cambridge University Press, 1996.

O'Donovan, Oliver. 'The Justice of Assignment and Subjective Rights in Grotius'. In Oliver O'Donovan and Joan Lockwood O'Donovan, eds, *Bonds of Imperfection: Christian Politics, Past and Present*. Grand Rapids, Mich.: Eerdmans, 2004.

O'Donovan, Oliver. *The Ways of Judgment*. Grand Rapids, Mich.: Eerdmans, 2005.

O'Donovan, Oliver. 'The Language of Rights and Conceptual History'. *Journal of Religious Ethics*, 37/2 (June 2009).

Omand, David. *Securing the State*. London: Hurst, 2010.

O'Neill, Onora. *Toward Justice and Virtue: A Constructive Account of Practical Reasoning*. Cambridge: Cambridge University Press, 1996.

O'Neill, Onora. 'The Dark Side of Human Rights'. *International Affairs*, 81/2 (2005).

O'Neill, Onora. *Justice Across Boundaries: Whose Obligations?* Cambridge: Cambridge University Press, 2016.

O'Neill, Onora. 'From Edmund Burke to Twenty-First Century Human Rights: Abstraction, Circumstances and Globalisation'. In O'Neill, *Justice Across Boundaries: Whose Obligations?* Cambridge: Cambridge University Press, 2016.

O'Neill, Onora. 'Global Justice: whose Obligations?' In O'Neill, *Justice Across Boundaries: Whose Obligations?* Cambridge: Cambridge University Press, 2016.

O'Neill, Onora. 'Pluralism, Positivism, and the Justification of Human Rights'. In O'Neill, *Justice Across Boundaries: Whose Obligations?* Cambridge: Cambridge University Press, 2016.

O'Neill, Onora. 'Justice without Ethics: A Twentieth Century Innovation?' In John Tasioulas, ed., *Cambridge Companion to the Philosophy of Law*. Cambridge: Cambridge University Press, 2020.

Onwuteaka-Philipsen, B. D., A. Brinkman-Stoppelenburg, C. Penning, G. J. de Jong-Krul, J. J. van Delden, and A. van der Heide. 'Trends in End-of-Life Practices before and after the Enactment of the Euthanasia Law in the Netherlands from 1990–2010: A Repeated Cross-Sectional Survey'. *The Lancet*, 380/9845 (8 September 2012).

Ortiz, Diana. 'Theology, International Law, and Torture: A Survivor's View'. *Theology Today*, 63/3 (October 2006).

Paglia, Vincenzo and Renzo Pegoraro, eds. *Equal Beginnings. But Then? A Global Responsibility.* Proceedings of the XXIV General Assembly of Members of the Pontifical Academy for Life. Rome: Pontifical Academy for Life, 2018.

Paine, Thomas. *Rights of Man, Common Sense, and Other Political Writings.* Ed. and introd. Mark Philp. Oxford: Oxford University Press, 1995.

Pallazani, Laura. 'Commentary on the Paper "The Ethics of Coming into the World" by Lisa S. Cahill'. In Vincenzo Paglia and Renzo Pegoraro, eds, *Equal Beginnings. But Then? A Global Responsibility*, proceedings of the XXIV General Assembly of Members of the Pontifical Academy for Life. Rome: Pontifical Academy for Life, 2018.

Pannikar, Raymond. 'Is the Notion of Human Rights a Western Concept?' *Diogenes*, 120 (1980).

Park, Ian. *The Right to Life in Armed Conflict.* Oxford: Oxford University Press, 2018.

Parkin, Jon. *Taming the Leviathan: The Reception of the Political and Religious Ideas of Thomas Hobbes in England 1640–1700.* Cambridge: Cambridge University Press, 2007.

Perry, Michael J. *Towards a Theory of Human Rights: Religion, Law, and Courts.* Cambridge: Cambridge University Press, 2007.

Pogge, Thomas, ed. *Freedom from Poverty as a Human Right: Who Owes What to the Very Poor?* New York: UNESCO and Oxford University Press, 2007.

Ponsonby, Lord John. Letter to Viscount Palmerston (27 December 1840). Public Records Office, FO/195/108.

Pope John XXIII. 'Pacem in Terris' (1963). In William J. Gibbons, SJ, introd., *Seven Great Encyclicals.* New York: Paulist Press, 1963.

Pope Leo XIII. *Rerum Novarum.* In William J. Gibbons, SJ, introd., *Seven Great Encyclicals.* New York: Paulist Press, 1963.

Pope Pius IX. 'The Syllabus of Errors' (1864).

Pope Pius XI. 'Mit brennender Sorge' (14 March 1937). In *The Hidden Encyclical of Pius XI.* Ed. Georges Passelecq and Bernard Suchecky. Trans. Steven Randall. New York: Harcourt Brace, 1997.

Pope Pius XII. 'The Anniversary of *Rerum Novarum*' (1 June 1941). *Logos*, 5/4 (Fall 2002).

Porter, Jean. 'Torture and the Christian Conscience: A Response to Jeremy Waldron'. *Scottish Journal of Theology*, 61/3 (2008).

Posner, Eric A. *The Twilight of Human Rights Law.* New York: Oxford University Press, 2014.

Posner, Eric and Adrian Vermeule. 'Should Coercive Interrogation be Legal?' *Michigan Law Review*, 104 (2006).

Posner, Eric and Adrian Vermeule. *Terror in the Balance.* Oxford: Oxford University Press, 2007.

Posner, Richard A. *How Judges Think.* Cambridge, Mass.: Harvard University Press, 2008.

Posner, Richard A. 'Torture, Terrorism, and Interrogation'. In Sanford Levinson, ed., *Torture: A Collection.* Oxford: Oxford University Press, 2004.

Pyrah, G. B. *Imperial Policy in South Africa, 1902–10.* Oxford: Clarendon Press, 1955.

Raz, Joseph. *The Morality of Freedom.* Oxford: Clarendon Press, 1986.

Ritchie, David G. *Natural Rights: A Criticism of Some Political and Ethical Conceptions.* London: Swan Sonnenschein, 1895.

Rodin, David. *War and Self-Defense*. Oxford: Clarendon Press, 2002.

Roper, Hugh Trevor. *Catholics, Anglicans, and Puritans: Seventeenth Century Essays*. London: Fontana, 1989.

Rosenberg, Gerald N. *The Hollow Hope: Can Courts Bring About Social Change?* Second edn. Chicago: University of Chicago Press, 2008.

Saad, Lydia. 'U.S. Support for Euthanasia Hinges on How It's Described': <https://news.gallup.com/poll/162815/support-euthanasia-hinges-described.aspx>.

Saïkhali, Marc. 'Les Larmes de la Liberté'. France 3 (1994).

Sassoli, Marco. 'The International Legal Framework for Stability Operations: When May International Forces Attack or Detain Someone in Afghanistan?' *International Law Studies*, 35 (2008): 'The War in Afghanistan: A Legal Analysis'.

Schabas, William A. 'Justice, Democracy, and Impunity in Post-Genocide Rwanda: Searching for Solutions to Impossible Problems'. *Criminal Law Forum*, 7/3 (1996).

Select Committee on Dying with Dignity, National Assembly of Québec. *Dying with Dignity Report*. Québec, Parliamentary Proceedings Directorate, 2012.

Sen, Amartya. 'Human Rights and Economic Achievements'. In Joanne R. Bauer and Daniel A. Bell, eds, *The East Asian Challenge for Human Rights*. Cambridge: Cambridge University Press, 1999.

Shue, Henry. *Basic Rights: Subsistence, Affluence, and U.S. Foreign Policy*. Second edn. Princeton: Princeton University Press, 1980, 1996.

Shue, Henry. 'Torture'. In Sanford Levinson, ed., *Torture: A Collection*. Oxford: Oxford University Press, 2004.

Shue, Henry. 'Torture in Dreamland: Disposing of the Ticking Bomb'. *Case Western Journal of International Law*, 37 (2006).

Shue, Henry, ed. *Fighting Hurt: Rule and Exception in Torture and War*. Oxford: Oxford University Press, 2016.

Shue, Henry. 'Torture (2015)'. In Henry Shue, ed., *Fighting Hurt: Rule and Exception in Torture and War*. Oxford: Oxford University Press, 2016.

Shupack, Martin. 'The Church and Human Rights: Catholic and Protestant Human Rights Views as Reflected in Church Statements'. *Harvard Human Rights Journal*, 6 (1993).

Siedentop, Larry. *Inventing the Individual: The Origins of Western Liberalism*. London: Allen Lane, 2014.

Silk, James. 'Traditional Culture and the Prospect for Human Rights in Africa'. In Abdullahi Ahmed An-Naim and Francis M. Deng, eds, *Human Rights in Africa: Cross-Cultural Perspectives*. Washington, DC: Brookings Institution, 1990.

Simma, B., ed. *The Charter of the United Nations: A Commentary*. 2nd edn. Oxford: Oxford University Press, 2002.

Simpson, A. W. Brian. *Human Rights and the End of Empire: Britain and the Genesis of the European Convention*. Oxford: Oxford University Press, 2001.

Simpson, Thomas. 'Did "Marine A" Do Wrong? Biggar's Lethal Intentions'. *Studies in Christian Ethics*, 28/3 (August 2015).

Singer, Peter. 'The Most Significant Work in Ethics since 1873'. *Times Literary Supplement* (20 May 2011).

Singleton, T. J. 'The Principles of Fundamental Justice: Societal Interests and Section 1 of the Charter'. *Canadian Bar Review*, 74 (1995).

Skinner, Quentin. *Foundations of Modern Political Thought*. 2 vols. II: *The Age of Reformation*. Cambridge: Cambridge University Press, 1978.

Smets, Tinne, Johan Bilsen, Joachim Cohen, Mette L. Rurup, Freddy Mortier, and Luc Deliens. 'Reporting of Euthanasia in Medical Practice in Flanders, Belgium: Cross-

Sectional Analysis of Reported and Unreported Cases'. *British Medical Journal*, 341 (2010).

Strauss, Leo. *Natural Right and History*. Chicago: University of Chicago, 1953.

Sumption, Jonathan. 'The Limits of Law'. In N. W. Barber, Richard Ekins, and Paul Yowell, eds, *Lord Sumption and the Limits of Law*. Oxford and Portland, Ore.: Hart, 2016.

Sunstein, Cass. 'Did Brown Matter?' *The New Yorker* (3 May 2004): <https://www.newyorker.com/magazine/2004/05/03/did-brown-matter>. Accessed 10 September 2018.

Supreme Court of British Columbia. *Carter v. Canada (Attorney General)* 2012 BCSC 886, 15 June 2012.

Supreme Court of Canada. *Rodriguez v. British Columbia (Attorney General)*, [1993] 3 SCR 519, 30 September 1993.

Supreme Court of Canada. *Reference re Same-Sex Marriage*, 2004 SCC 79, 9 December 2004.

Supreme Court of Canada. *Carter v. Canada (Attorney General)* 2015 SCC 5, 6 February 2015.

Supreme Court of the United Kingdom. *R (Catherine Smith) v. Oxfordshire Assistant Deputy Coroner (Equality and Human Rights Commission Intervening)* (2010) UKSC 29 (2011) 1AC 1.

Supreme Court of the United Kingdom. *Smith and others (FC) (Appellants) v. The Ministry of Defence (Respondent); Ellis (FC) (Respondent) v. The Ministry of Defence (Appellant); Allbutt and others (FC) (Respondents) v. The Ministry of Defence (Appellant)*, (2013) UKSC 41, 19 June 2013.

Supreme Court of the United Kingdom. *R (on the Application of Nicklinson) (AP) v. Ministry of Justice*, UKSC 38, 25 June 2014.

Sussman, David. 'What's Wrong with Torture?' *Philosophy and Public Affairs*, 33 (2005).

Tasioulas, John. 'Human Rights, Universality, and the Values of Personhood: Retracing Griffin's Steps'. *European Journal of Philosophy*, 10/1 (2002).

Tasioulas, John. 'The Moral Reality of Human Rights'. In Thomas Pogge, ed., *Freedom from Poverty as a Human Right: Who Owes What to the Very Poor?* New York: UNESCO and Oxford University Press, 2007.

Tasioulas, John. 'Taking Rights out of Human Rights'. In Roger Crisp, ed., *Griffin on Human Rights*. Oxford: Oxford University Press, 2014.

Taylor, Charles. 'Conditions of an Unforced Consensus on Human Rights'. In Joanne R. Bauer and Daniel A. Bell, eds, *The East Asian Challenge for Human Rights*. Cambridge: Cambridge University Press, 1999.

Tew, Yvonne. 'Beyond "Asian Values": Rethinking Rights'. Centre of Governance and Human Rights Working Paper 5. Cambridge: University of Cambridge, 2012.

Thielicke, Helmuth. *Theological Ethics*. 2 vols. Ed. William H. Lazareth. Vol. II: *Politics*. Grand Rapids, Mich.: Eerdmans, 1979.

Tierney, Brian. *The Idea of Natural Rights*. Grand Rapids, Mich.: Eerdmans, 1997.

Toledano, Ehud R. *Slavery and Abolition in the Ottoman Middle East*. Seattle: University of Washington, 1998.

Tuck, Richard. *Natural Rights Theories: Their Origin and Development*. Cambridge: Cambridge University Press, 1979.

Tugendhat, Thomas and Laura Croft. *The Fog of Law: An Introduction to the Legal Erosion of British Fighting Power*. London: Policy Exchange, 2013.

Tully, J. A. *Discourse on Property: John Locke and his Adversaries*. Cambridge: Cambridge University Press, 1980.

Turley, Thomas. 'John XXII and the Franciscans: A Reappraisal'. In James Ross Sweeney and Stanley Chodorow, eds, *Popes, Teachers, and Canon Law in the Middle Ages*. Ithaca, NY, and London: Cornell University Press, 1989.

United Kingdom House of Lords. *A and Others (Appellants) v. Secretary of State for the Home Department (Respondent)* [2004] UKHL 56, 16 December 2004.

United Kingdom House of Lords. *R (Ullah) v. Special Adjudicator* (2004) UKHL 26, (2004) 2 AC 323.

United Kingdom House of Lords. *R (Al-Skeini) v. Secretary of State for Defence* (2007) UKHL 26, (2008), AC 153.

United Nations Economic and Social Council. *Commission on Human Rights, Report of the Special Rapporteur, Philip Alston, on Extrajudicial, Summary or Arbitrary Executions*, E/CN.4/2006/53, 8 March 2006.

United Nations Educational, Scientific, and Cultural Organisation, ed. *Human Rights: Comments and Interpretations*. London and New York: Allan Wingate, 1949.

United Nations General Assembly. *International Covenant on Civil and Political Rights* (1966): <https://www.ohchr.org/Documents/ProfessionalInterest/ccpr.pdf>.

United Nations General Assembly. *International Covenant on Economic, Social, and Cultural Rights* (1966): <https://www.ohchr.org/documents/professionalinterest/cescr.pdf>.

United Nations Office on Drugs and Crime. 'Intentional Homicide Count and Rate per 100,000 Population, by Country/Territory (2000–2012)': <http://www.unodc.org/gsh/en/data.html>.

Urbina, Francisco J. 'How Legislation Aids Human Rights Adjudication'. In Grégoire Webber, Paul Yowell, Richard Ekins, Maris Köpcke, Bradley W. Miller, and Francisco J. Urbina, *Legislated Rights: Securing Human Rights through Legislation*. Cambridge: Cambridge University Press, 2018.

Vitoria, Francisco de. *Relectio de Indis*. Ed. L. Pereña and J. M. Perez Prendes. Corpus Hispanorum de Pace. Madrid: Consejo Superior de Investigaciones Científicas, 1967.

Vitoria, Francisco de. *Political Writings*. Ed. Anthony Pagden and Jeremy Lawrance. Cambridge Texts in the History of Political Thought. Cambridge: Cambridge University Press, 1991.

Vitoria, Francisco de. 'On the American Indians'. In Vitoria, *Political Writings*. Ed. Anthony Pagden and Jeremy Lawrance. Cambridge Texts in the History of Political Thought. Cambridge: Cambridge University Press, 1991.

Vitoria, Francisco de. 'On the Law of War'. In Vitoria, *Political Writings*. Ed. Anthony Pagden and Jeremy Lawrance. Cambridge Texts in the History of Political Thought. Cambridge: Cambridge University Press, 1991.

Vitoria, Francisco de. *On Homicide*. Trans. and introd. John P. Doyle. Milwaukee, Wis.: Marquette University Press, 1997.

Waldron, Jeremy. 'Torture'. *Philosophy and Public Affairs*, 7 (1978).

Waldron, Jeremy, ed. *Theories of Rights*. Oxford Readings in Philosophy. Oxford: Oxford University Press, 1984.

Waldron, Jeremy. 'Introduction'. In Jeremy Waldron, ed., *Theories of Rights*. Oxford Readings in Philosophy. Oxford: Oxford University Press, 1984.

Waldron, Jeremy, ed. *Nonsense on Stilts: Bentham, Burke, and Marx on the Rights of Man*. London: Methuen, 1987.

Waldron, Jeremy. *Law and Disagreement*. Oxford: Oxford University Press, 1999.

Waldron, Jeremy. *Torture, Terror, and Trade-Offs: Philosophy for the White House*. Oxford: Oxford University Press, 2010.

Webber, Grégoire, Paul Yowell, Richard Ekins, Maris Köpcke, Bradley W. Miller, and Francisco J. Urbina. *Legislated Rights: Securing Human Rights through Legislation.* Cambridge: Cambridge University Press, 2018.

Wessely, Simon. 'Risk, Psychiatry and the Military'. *The British Journal of Psychiatry,* 186 (2005).

Whitford, David Mark. *Tyranny and Resistance: The Magdeburg Confession and the Lutheran Tradition.* St Louis: Concordia, 2001.

William of Ockham. *Breviloquium,* III.7. In *Wilhelm von Ockham als politischer Denker und sein Breviloquium de principatu tyrannico,* ed. Richard Scholz. Schriften des Reichinstituts für ältere deutsche Geschichtskunde, Monumenta Germaniae historica 8. Stuttgart: Hiersemann Verlag, 1944.

William of Ockham. *Opus Nonaginta Dierum.* In *Opera politica,* ed. H. S. Offler. 4 vols. Vol. II. Manchester: Manchester University Press, 1963.

William of Ockham. *A Short Discourse on Tyrannical Government.* Cambridge Texts in the History of Political Thought. Ed. A. S. McGrade. Trans. John Kilcullen. Cambridge: Cambridge University Press, 1992.

Williams, Bernard. *Report of the Committee on Obscenity and Film Censorship.* Cmnd. 7772. London: HMSO 1979.

Wiredu, Kwasi. 'An Akan Perspective on Human Rights'. In Abdullahi Ahmed An-Naim and Francis M. Deng, eds, *Human Rights in Africa: Cross-Cultural Perspectives.* Washington, DC: Brookings Institution, 1990.

Witte, John. *God's Joust, God's Justice: Law and Religion in the Western Tradition.* Grand Rapids, Mich.: Eerdmans, 2006.

Witte, John. 'A Dickensian Era of Religious Rights'. In John Witte, *God's Joust, God's Justice: Law and Religion in the Western Tradition.* Grand Rapids, Mich.: Eerdmans, 2006.

Witte, John. *The Reformation of Rights: Law, Religion, and Human Rights in Early Modern Calvinism.* Cambridge: Cambridge University Press, 2007.

Witte, John. 'Introduction'. In John Witte and Frank Alexander, eds, *Christianity and Human Rights: An Introduction.* Cambridge: Cambridge University Press, 2010.

Witte, John. 'Christianity and Human Rights: Past Contributions and Future Challenges'. *Journal of Law and Religion,* 30/3 (October 2015).

Witte, John. 'Review of Samuel Moyn, *Christian Human Rights* (2015)'. *Books and Culture,* 22/2 (March/April 2016).

Witte, John and Frank Alexander, eds. *Christianity and Law: An Introduction.* Cambridge: Cambridge University Press, 2008.

Witte, John and Frank Alexander, eds. *Christianity and Human Rights: An Introduction.* Cambridge: Cambridge University Press, 2010.

Wollstonecraft, Mary. *A Vindication of the Rights of Woman.* Mineola, NY: Dover Publications, 1996.

Wolterstorff, Nicholas. *Justice: Rights and Wrongs.* Princeton: Princeton University Press, 2008.

Wolterstorff, Nicholas. 'Protestant Developments in Human Rights'. In John Witte and Frank Alexander, eds, *Christianity and Human Rights: An Introduction.* Cambridge: Cambridge University Press, 2010.

Yowell, Paul. 'From Universal to Legislated Rights'. In Grégoire Webber, Paul Yowell, Richard Ekins, Maris Köpcke, Bradley W. Miller, and Francisco J. Urbina, *Legislated Rights: Securing Human Rights through Legislation.* Cambridge: Cambridge University Press, 2018.

Yowell, Paul. *Constitutional Rights and Constitutional Design: Moral and Empirical Reasoning in Judicial Review*. London: Hart, 2018.

Yu, Anthony C. 'Enduring Change: Confucianism and the Prospect of Human Rights'. In Elizabeth Bucar and Barbra Barnett, eds, *Does Human Rights Need God?* Grand Rapids, Mich.: Eerdmans, 2005.

Zakaria, Fareed and Lee Kuan Yew. 'Culture is Destiny: A Conversation with Lee Kuan Yew'. *Foreign Affairs*, 73/1 (March–April 1994).

Index

For the benefit of digital users, indexed terms that span two pages (e.g., 52–53) may, on occasion, appear on only one of those pages.

proportionality 224, 226, 228, 241, 242, 270, 272, 273, 281, 283–5, 293, 322–3, 325, 334
and 'overbreadth' 271, 272
Pufendorf, Samuel (1632–94) 43n.50, 118n.111, 153, 154, 160n.192
punishment 170, 177–8

Qichao, Liang (1873–1929) 217n.114
Québec National Assembly's Select Committee on Dying with Dignity 294

R (Catherine Smith) v. Oxfordshire Assistant Deputy Coroner [Supreme Court of the UK, 2011] 257, 258, 262, 266, 321
R. (Nicklinson) v. Ministry of Justice [Supreme Court of the UK, 2014] 2, 281, 302n.157, 306n.174
R. v. Oakes [Supreme Court of Canada, 1986] 280
R. v. Swain [Supreme Court of Canada, 1991] 279
Rawls, John 162
Raz, Joseph 96–7n.15
realism, moral: see moral realism
Realpolitik 206, 206n.63
rebellion, justified 127–9, 128n.124
Rerum Novarum (1891) 75, 76, 90, 142
Réseau de Citoyens 211n.98
right, moral 7
see also moral realism
right
against lying 89–90
against severe poverty 93–105
see also right to freedom from hunger; right to subsistence
against slavery 129–31
against torture 114, 119, 129–31, Chapter 7 passim
of the family 74
to a fair trial 98, 115n.92, 120, 207–8, 211, 326
to education 96–7n.15
to equality: see rights and equality; natural rights and equality
to freedom from hunger 70
see also right against severe poverty; right to subsistence
to freedom from pain and suffering 278–9
to freedom of speech 20, 212–13
to liberty 19–20, 42–5, 115–16
to life 19, 100–11, Chapter 9, passim
and war 220–1, 231–2
to obtaining happiness, natural 21
to physician-assisted suicide Chapter 11 passim

to political participation 124, 127–8
to property 20–1, 33–6, 38–9, 50–1
to publish pornography 202–3
to regime-change 57, 63–5, 127–9
to religious freedom 198–9
to resist execution, a prisoner's 155–6, 158
to self-defence 40
to self-government 39
to subsistence 37–8, 51, 109, 120n.119, 137–8
see also right against severe poverty; right to freedom from hunger
to suicide 155–6, 160
to trade and migrate 41, 52–3, 54–5
to undertake humanitarian intervention 26, 129
to vote 20
rights
see also natural rights; subjective rights
absolute 2, 9, 11, 17, 19, 21, 31, 34, 35, 37, 39, 53, 54, 57, 58, 59, 61, 67, 68, 70, 71, 72–80, 82, 84–90, 91–2, 114–15, 117, 122, 136, 137, 138, Chapter 7 passim, 220, 223–4, 232, 233, 279, 322, 323, 328
abstract 27n.107, 29–31, 308–9
see also natural rights and abstraction
communitarian critique of 194
conclusory force of 37n.17, 82, 84, 91, 125
connotation of 123
forfeit of 220–1, 221–2, 231, 232–3
inter-cultural dialogue about 217–18
legal: see legal rights
liberty and welfare 27, 32, 69, 70, 71, 81, 94, 95–6, 97–105, 110–11, 116
proliferation of 110–11, 117–18, 331–32
stability and security of 123–4
structure of formulation of 242
Western critics of 201–2
and Christian anthropology 53, 164
and Christianity Chapter 2 passim, Chapter 4 passim, 127, Chapter 6 passim
and claimability 95, 99, 116, 117
and colonial authorities 200n.42, 204–6
and compromise: see compromise
and Confucianism 2, 193, 194, 195n.20, 195n.21, 195n.22, 205, 212, 212n.99, 213–14, 217, 218
and contingency: see natural rights and contingency
and cultural pessimism 141–2, 146
and duties 60, 72, 222, 334
and egoism 17, 132, 135–6, 154
and enforceability 93n.2
and equality 276n.43
see also natural rights and equality